"Encyclopedic in its aims, this volume is as much a lively intervention as it is a trusted companion to the field. You can safely add it to your collection of 'really useful' books."

Andrew Ross, New York University

"The book will provide a very welcome service in the classroom. Toby Miller has produced a volume of sound structure and organization. The contributors bring a rich mix of authority and experience to the book."

Tony Bennett, The Open University

"As a whole the collection beautifully captures the restlessness, the malleability, and the theoretical flexibility of cultural studies, while at the same time exposing some of its limitations and failings ... Overall this is a provocative, readable and useful collection which points as much to the future as the past of cultural studies. It is a valuable point of reference for those who teach or research in any of the disciplines and fields touched by cultural studies, and especially those who are in the process of discovering and grappling with this 'tendency across disciplines.'"

Media International Australia

"Topics and methods of the global contributors are diverse and imaginative ... readable and accessible to unitiated outsiders and curious onlookers."

Choice

"This edition has enough to be beneficial for the experienced student or teacher, and an appropriate enough introduction for the novice."

Design Issues

Blackwell Companions in Cultural Studies

Advisory editor: David Theo Goldberg, University of California, Irvine

This series aims to provide theoretically ambitious but accessible volumes devoted to the major fields and subfields within cultural studies, whether as single disciplines (film studies) inspired and reconfigured by interventionist cultural studies approaches, or from broad interdisciplinary and multidisciplinary perspectives (gender studies, race and ethnic studies, postcolonial studies). Each volume sets out to ground and orientate the student through a broad range of specially commissioned articles and also to provide the more experienced scholar and teacher with a convenient and comprehensive overview of the latest trends and critical directions. An overarching *Companion to Cultural Studies* will map the territory as a whole.

1. A Companion to Film Theory
Edited by Toby Miller and Robert Stam

2. A Companion to Postcolonial Studies
Edited by Henry Schwarz and Sangeeta Ray

3. A Companion to Cultural Studies
Edited by Toby Miller

4. A Companion to Racial and Ethnic Studies
Edited by David Theo Goldberg and John Solomos

5. A Companion to Art Theory
Edited by Paul Smith and Carolyn Wilde

6. A Companion to Media Studies
Edited by Angharad Valdivia

7. A Companion to Literature and Film
Edited by Robert Stam and Alessandra Raengo

8. A Companion to Gender Studies
Edited by Philomena Essed, David Theo Goldberg, and Audrey Kobayashi

9. A Companion to Asian American Studies
Edited by Kent A. Ono

10. A Companion to Television
Edited by Janet Wasko

11. A Companion to African American Studies
Edited by Lewis R. Gordon and Jane Anna Gordon

12. A Companion to Museum Studies
Edited by Sharon Macdonald

A Companion to Cultural Studies

Edited by

Toby Miller

Blackwell
Publishing

11/7/13

BLACKWELL PUBLISHING
350 Main Street, Malden, MA 02148-5020, USA
9600 Garsington Road, Oxofrd OX4 2DQ UK
550 Swanston Street, Carlton, Victoria 3053, Australia

First published 2001
First published in paperback 2006 by Blackwell Publishing Ltd

1   2006

Library of Congress Cataloging-in-Publication Data

A companion to cultural studies / edited by Toby Miller.
  p. cm.—(Blackwell companions in cultural studies; 3)
  ISBN 0-631-21788-6 (hb : alk. paper)
  1. Cultural—Study and teaching. I. Miller, Toby. II. Series.

HM623.B55 2001
306.071—dc21

                                                        00-069769

ISBN-13: 978-0-631-21788-6 (hb : alk. paper)
ISBN-13: 978-1-4051-4175-8 (paperback)
ISBN-10: 1-4051-4175-1 (paperback)

A catalogue record for this title is available from the British Library.

Set in 11 on 13pt Ehrhardt
by SPI Publishers Services, Pondicherry, India
Printed and bound in the United Kingdom
by TJ International Ltd, Padstow, Cornwall

The publisher's policy is to use permanent paper from mills that operate a sustainable forestry policy, and which has been manufactured from pulp processed using acid-free and elementary chlorine-free practices. Furthermore, the publisher ensures that the text paper and cover board used have met acceptable environmental accreditation standards.

For further information on
Blackwell Publishing, visit our website:
www.blackwellpublishing.com

Visit the Blackwell Cultural Studies Resources
website,
edited by Sarah Berry and Toby Miller:

www.blackwellpublishing.com/Cultural/

Contents

List of Contributors   x

Introduction to the Paperback Edition: What changed and
what didn't: Prefacing . . . Cultural Studies   xvii

1   What it is and what it isn't: Introducing . . . Cultural Studies   1
    Toby Miller

Part I: Disciplines   21

2   Interdisciplinarity   23
    Mark Gibson and Alec McHoul

3   Is there a Cultural Studies of Law?   36
    Rosemary Coombe

4   The Renewal of the Cultural in Sociology   63
    Randy Martin

5   Sociology, Cultural Studies, and Disciplinary Boundaries   79
    Frank Webster

6   Notes on the Traffic between Cultural Studies and
    Science and Technology Studies   101
    Marianne de Laet

7   Political Economy within Cultural Studies   116
    Richard Maxwell

8   Cultural Studies and Philosophy: An Intervention   139
    Douglas Kellner

Contents

9 "X" never, ever marks the spot: Archaeology and Cultural Studies   154
   Silke Morgenroth

10 The Unbalanced Reciprocity between
    Cultural Studies and Anthropology   169
    George E. Marcus

11 Media Studies and Cultural Studies: A Symbiotic Convergence   187
    John Nguyet Erni

Part II: Places   215

12 Comparative Cultural Studies Traditions:
    Latin America and the US   217
    George Yúdice

13 Can Cultural Studies Speak Spanish?   232
    Jorge Mariscal

14 Australasia   246
    Graeme Turner

15 Peripheral Vision: Chinese Cultural Studies in Hong Kong   259
    Eric Kit-wai Ma

16 Decentering the Centre: Cultural Studies in Britain and its Legacy   275
    Ben Carrington

17 European Cultural Studies   298
    Paul Moore

Part III: Issues   315

18 Let's Get Serious: Notes on Teaching Youth Culture   317
    Justin Lewis

19 Looking Backwards and Forwards at Cultural Studies   331
    Paul Smith

20 Close Encounters: Sport, Science, and Political Culture   341
    C. L. Cole

21 Intellectuals, Culture, Policy: The Practical and the Critical   357
    Tony Bennett

22 Listening to the State: Culture, Power, and
    Cultural Policy in Colombia   375
    Ana María Ochoa Gautier

23 Museum Highlights: A Gallery Talk   391
    Andrea Fraser

24 The Scandalous Fall of Feminism and the "First Black President"   407
    Melissa Deem

25 Rap and Feng Shui: On Ass Politics, Cultural Studies,
    and the Timbaland Sound   430
    Jason King

26 Fashion   454
    Sarah Berry

27 Cultural Studies and Race   471
    Robert Stam

28 Globalization and Culture   490
    Toby Miller and Georey Lawrence

29 "Cricket, with a Plot": Nationalism, Cricket,
    and Diasporic Identities   510
    Suvendrini Perera

Part IV: Sources   529

30 Bibliographical Resources for Cultural Studies   531
    Toby Miller

Index   553

Contributors

Tony Bennett is Professor of Sociology at the Open University, where he is also Director of the Pavis Centre for Social and Cultural Research. His recent publications include *The Birth of the Museum* (1995), *Culture: A Reformer's Science* (1998) and, as co-author, *Accounting for Tastes: Australian Everyday Cultures* (1999).

Sarah Berry is author of *Screen Style: Fashion and Femininity in 1930s Hollywood* and has published articles on interactive media, fashion, and film. She works as an information architect and interactive media developer.

Ben Carrington teaches sociology and cultural studies at the University of Brighton, UK.

C. L. Cole is an Associate Professor of kinesiology, sociology, and women's studies at the University of Illinois at Urbana-Champaign. Her teaching and research investigate sexuality, citizenship, and the production of deviant bodies in post-Second World War America. She is also working on two new projects: the new urban health culture, which takes San Francisco as its central case; and transsexuals and sporting bodies, which uses the Gay Games as its case study.

Rosemary Coombe occupies the Canada Research Chair in Law, Communication, and Cultural Studies at York University. She is the author of *The Cultural Life of Intellectual Properties: Authorship, Appropriation and the Law* (1998). Currently she is working on issues involving indigenous knowledge, human rights, and the politics of globalizing intellectual property laws.

Melissa Deem is an Assistant Professor in Women's Studies and Rhetoric at the University of Iowa. Her work has been published in *Public Culture* and *Critical Studies in Mass Communication*. She is currently writing a book which maps the contemporary political discourses of and about feminism in the United States, as well as establishes the contemporary relevance of various anomalous feminist rhetorical practices dating to about 1968, the period commonly referred to as second wave feminism.

Marianne de Laet is an anthropologist of science and technology, with a background in the sociology of scientific knowledge. Her research concerns technology transfer, appropriate technology, and intellectual property issues – especially as they play out in developing countries and in big science and engineering projects. She is currently a Senior Research Fellow and Lecturer in the Humanities at the California Institute of Technology.

John Nguyet Erni is an Associate Professor in the Department of Communication, University of New Hampshire, where he teaches media and cultural studies. He is the author of *Unstable Frontiers: Technomedicine and the Cultural Politics of "Curing" AIDS* (1994), *Epidemic Imaginary in a Southeast Asian City: HIV/AIDS, Empirical Worlds, Postcolonial Readings* (forthcoming), and special issue editor of "Becoming (Postcolonial) Hong Kong," *Cultural Studies* (forthcoming). In addition, he has published in various journals, among them *Cultural Studies, Critical Studies in Mass Communication, Identities: Global Studies in Culture and Power, Science as Culture, Sexualities, Praxis,* and *Hong Kong Cultural Studies Bulletin*. His research and teaching focus on the intersections of culture, media, biomedical health, cities, gender and sexual politics, and Asian modernity. In 2000–1 he is Visiting Associate Professor at the City University of Hong Kong.

Andrea Fraser is a New York-based artist whose work is identified with Institutional Critique. Since 1984 she has produced performances, videos, installations, and publications with museums and foundations throughout the United States, Europe, and Latin America. She is currently working on a collection of her essays and scripts.

Ana María Ochoa Gautier is currently Professor in the Anthropology Department of the Universidad Autónoma del Estado de Morelos in Cuernavaca, Mexico. Until last year she was researcher at the Instituto Colombiano de Antropologia in Bogotá, Colombia. Her work is on cultural policy and on the music industry in Latin America.

Mark Gibson teaches Cultural Studies at Murdoch University in Western Australia. He has published around the theme of "post-Cold War" political formations in popular culture, and is currently completing a project on the history of the concept of power in Cultural Studies.

Douglas Kellner is George Kneller Chair in the Philosophy of Education at UCLA and is author of many books on social theory, politics, history, and culture, including *Camera Politica: The Politics and Ideology of Contemporary Hollywood Film*, co-authored with Michael Ryan, *Critical Theory, Marxism, and Modernity*, *Jean Baudrillard: From Marxism to Postmodernism and Beyond*, *Postmodern Theory: Critical Interrogations* (with Steven Best), *Television and the Crisis of Democracy*, *The Persian Gulf TV War*, *Media Culture*, and the *Postmodern Turn* (with Steven Best).

Jason King is a performer, playwright, songwriter, musician, and vocal arranger. In his spare time, he is a doctoral candidate in Performance Studies at New York University and adjunct faculty in the Asian/Pacific American Studies Program, Tisch Drama and the Gallatin School of Individualized Study. Most recent essays appear in: *Callaloo*, *The Velvet Light Trap*, *Women and Performance: A Journal of Feminist Theory*. Creative work includes: *The Story of My Father* (Crossroads Theater Company); a pop soul children's musical, *Jump Up to the Future*!; and a forthcoming revue on jazz legend Abbey Lincoln.

Georey Lawrence is Foundation Professor of Sociology at Central Queensland University, Australia. He has been involved in the critical analysis of sport for several decades with co-edited titles including: *Power Play: Essays in the Sociology of Australian Sport* (1986); *Sport and Leisure: Trends in Australian Popular Culture* (1990); and *Tourism, Leisure, Sport: Critical Perspectives* (1998).

Justin Lewis has written several books about media and culture. His particular interests are media influence, cultural policy and the ideological role of media in contemporary societies. His most recent book: *Contructing Public Opinion: How Elites Do What they Like and Why We Seem to Go Along With It*, is an analysis of the media and public opinion.

Eric K. W. Ma is an Associate Professor at the School of Journalism and Communication, the Chinese University of Hong Kong. He is the author of *Culture, Politics and Television in Hong Kong* (1999).

George E. Marcus is Professor and Chair of the Department of Anthropology at Rice University. In 1986, he edited with James Clifford the volume *Writing Culture*, and co-authored with Michael Fischer, *Anthropology as Cultural Critique*. In the same period, he established the journal *Cultural Anthropology*. More recently, he founded and edited a documentary series of annuals, focused on communicating through conversations with diverse social actors the conditions of the *fin-de-siècle*. This series, known as Late Editions, has come to a close with *The Final Edition – Zeroing in on the Year 2000*. His latest work is *Ethnography Through Thick and Thin* (1998), in which he argues for changes in the research practice at the heart of anthropology.

Jorge Mariscal is Associate Professor of Chicano and Spanish literature at the University of California, San Diego. He is the editor of *Aztlán and Viet Nam: Chicano and Chicana Experiences of the War* (1999), and is currently completing a collection of essays on the Chicano Movement. He has served on the board of directors of the Centro Cultural de la Raza in San Diego and is an active member of Project YANO, a volunteer antimilitarism organization.

Randy Martin is Professor of Art and Public Policy and Associate Dean of Faculty and Interdisciplinary Programs at Tisch School of the Arts, New York University. Previously he was Chair of the Department of Social Science at the Pratt Institute, where he developed an undergraduate program in Cultural Studies. His *On Your Marx: Relinking Socialism and the Left* is forthcoming from University of Minnesota Press.

Richard Maxwell is Associate Professor of Media Studies at Queens College-City University of New York. He is the author of *The Spectacle of Democracy: Spanish Television, Nationalism, and Political Transition* (1995) and editor of the forthcoming *Culture Works: The Political Economy of Culture*. His essays on global marketing have appeared in *Media, Culture, and Society, Cultural Studies, The Journal of International Communication, Social Text*, and in the recent collections entitled, *Contemporary Spanish Cultural Studies* (2000) and *Consuming Audiences: Production and Reception in Media Research* (2000).

Alec McHoul is Professor of Communication Studies at Murdoch University, Western Australia. He is currently working on an edited collection called *How to Analyse Talk in Institutional Settings* (with Mark Rapley) and a book which analyzes the problematic concept of representation in Cultural Studies.

Toby Miller is Professor of Cultural Studies and Cultural Policy, New York University. He is editor of *Television & New Media* (1999–); co-editor of *Social Text* (1997–). Author of *The Well-Tempered Self: Citizenship, Culture, and the Postmodern Subject* (1993), *Contemporary Australian Television* (1994, with Stuart Cunningham), *The Avengers* (1997), *Technologies of Truth: Cultural Citizenship and the Popular Media* (1998), *Popular Culture and Everyday Life* (1998, with Alec McHoul), *SportCult* (1999, ed. with Randy Martin), *A Companion to Film Theory* (1999, ed. with Robert Stam), *Film and Theory: An Anthology* (2000, ed. with Robert Stam), *Globalization and Sport: Playing the World* (forthcoming, with Geoff Lawrence, Jim McKay, and David Rowe), *SportSex* (forthcoming), *Critical Cultural Policy: An Introduction* (forthcoming, ed. with Justin Lewis).

Paul Moore is a lecturer in Cultural and Media Studies at the University of Ulster, Coleraine. His Ph.D. research was an ethnographic study of an outlaw motorcycle group in Northern Ireland, a group he rode with for two years. He is involved with production work, particularly in the area of sound, and is a regular contributor on cultural matters for BBC Northern Ireland.

Silke Morgenroth studied archaeology, history, and literature in Bochum and Hamburg. She is the author of *Analysen und Interpretation: Hausreste im archäologischen Befund* (1998). She has been working as a journalist and since 1999 as an author, mainly on fictional projects.

Suvendrini Kanagasabai Perera completed her BA at the University of Sri Lanka and her Ph.D. at Columbia University, New York. She currently teaches in the School of English at La Trobe University, Melbourne, Australia. Her essays have appeared in *Cultural Studies, The Journal of Intercultural Studies, Social Identities, Discourse, Journal of Postcolonial Studies*, and *Race & Class*. She is author of *Reaches of Empire* and editor of *Asian and Pacific Inscriptions: Identities/ Ethnicities/ Nationalities*. Her current research interests are in counter-histories of multiracial societies.

Paul Smith is currently working as Professor of Media and Cultural Studies at the University of Sussex. His most recent books are: *Clint Eastwood, Boys* (ed.), and *Millennial Dreams*. He is currently working on a cultural studies manifesto and a book about the political economy of the new media.

Robert Stam teaches cinema in the Cinema Stduies Department at NYU. He is the author of many books on cinema and culture, including, most recently, *Film Theory: An Introduction, Tropical Multiculturalism, Unthinking Eurocentrism* (with Ella Shohat), and *Subversive Pleasures*. He has won Fulbright, Guggenheim, and Rockefeller awards.

Graeme Turner is Professor of Cultural Studies and Director of the Centre for Critical and Cultural Studies, University of Queensland, Brisbane, Australia. He is the author of a number of books on cultural studies, including *British Cultural Studies: An Introduction* (1990 and 1996). His most recent book is (with Frances Bonner and P. David Marshall), *Fame Games: The Production of Celebrity in Australia* (2000).

Frank Webster is Professor of Sociology and Head of Department, Cultural Studies and Sociology, University of Birmingham, UK. His books include *Theories of the Information Society* (1995), *Times of the Technoculture* (with Kevin Robins, 1999), *Information Technology: A Luddite Analysis* (with Kevin Robins, 1986), and *Culture and Politics in the Information Age: A New Politics?* (2001)

George Yúdice is Professor of American Studies and Spanish and Portuguese, and Director of the Privatization of Culture Project for Research on Cultural

Policy, at New York University. He is the author of *Vicente Huidobro y la motivación del lenguaje poetico* (1977); *Culture and Value: Essays on Latin American Literature and Culture* (forthcoming), *The Expediency of Culture* (forthcoming), and *Cultural Policy*, with Toby Miller (forthcoming). He is also co-editor (with Jean Franco and Juan Flores) of *On Edge: The Crisis of Contemporary Latin American Culture* (1992) and co-editor of the "Cultural Studies of the Americas" book series with the University of Minnesota Press.

What changed and what didn't: Prefacing . . . Cultural Studies

Toby Miller

In the five years since I wrote the Introduction to this book, and the publisher decided to release it in paperback form (where it might actually be used by students and scholars) we have seen the further institutionalization of cultural studies, via new professional associations, more conferences, and so on. It is no longer necessary for the disciplines to take account of cultural studies in quite the way that was evident through the 1980s and 1990s, with all those special issues of academic journals that declared its arrival.

I see two new trends, plus the acceleration of a third. Within universities, an organic interdisciplinarity is emerging between the arts and humanities and the sciences. It has been generated because young scholars within aesthetics and production are now familiar with code, while code-writers and technology faculty are now familiar with narrative and imagery. The industrial expression and stimulus to these developments comes from electronic gaming as well as the Internet. The social sciences seem somehow lost in this new move, with little to offer, because of their contempt for the form, style, and audiences of popular culture. What could be a valuable social-science perspective on labor, state, and corporate power, is absent from this new world of the professorial geek. Second, cultural studies has been revealed as a new administrative tool for universities in a time of scarcity. Consider this situation, confronted by an imagined college dean. The medievalist is dying, the classics professor is retiring, the graduate students are clamoring for cultural studies, minorities are concerned about the affirmative action for white men that characterises the faculty, and the state is cutting funding. How to respond? Ah, I know – in place of the two full-professor salaries in areas no-one enrolls in, let's hire a junior minority woman who does cultural studies, and require her to undertake multiple representational duty on commit-tees, as well as in her scholarship and pedagogy. This makes an impossible burden, and it can irritate other disciplinary formations.

The third tendency is really a development of some directions that were already clear within the field and are in need of remedy, even as there are signs that help is on its way. It has been a *donnée* of much US cultural studies that the mainstream media are not responsible for – well, anything. This position is a virtual *nostrum* in some research into, for instance, fans of TV drama, who are thought to construct connections with celebrities and actants in ways that mimic friendship, make sense of human interaction, and ignite cultural politics. This critique commonly attacks opponents of television for failing to allot the people's machine its due as a populist apparatus that subverts patriarchy, capitalism, and other forms of oppression. Commercial TV is held to have progressive effects, because its programs are decoded by viewers in keeping with their social situations. The active audience is said to be weak at the level of cultural production, but strong as an interpretative community. All this is supposedly evident to scholars from their perusal of audience conventions, web pages, discussion groups, quizzes, and rankings, or by watching television with their children. Very droll. But can fans be said to resist labor exploitation, patriarchy, racism, and US neo-imperialism, or in some specifiable way make a difference to politics beyond their own selves, when they interpret texts unusually, dress up in public as men from outer space, or chat about their romantic frustrations? And why have such practices become so popular in the First World at a moment when media policy fetishizes consumption, deregulation, and self-governance?

The strand of US cultural studies that I am questioning is a very specific uptake of venerable UK critiques of cultural pessimism, political economy, and current-affairs-oriented broadcasting. These critiques originated from a heavily regulated, duopolistic broadcasting system – 1950s–1970s Britain – in which the BBC represented a high-culture snobbery that many leftists associated with an oppressive class structure.[1] Hence the desire for a playful, commercial, anti-citizen address as a counter. When cultural-studies accounts of TV made their Atlantic crossing, there was no public-broadcasting behemoth in need of critique – more a tiny endangered species. And there were lots of not-very-leftist professors and students seemingly aching to hear that US audiences learning about parts of the world that their country bombs, invades, owns, misrepresents, or otherwise exploits was less important, and less political, than those audiences' interpretations of actually existing local soap operas, wrestling bouts, or science-fiction series. They even had allies amongst reactionary political scientists, who extolled the virtues of market-driven minimization of news, pared down to the essentials: the survival and entertainment of audiences (Baum 2002; Zaller 2003).

Perhaps the dominant strand of US cultural studies had lost political economy as its animator, in favor of some ghastly academic mirror of the post-welfare state. In this sense, cultural studies could be seen as a polite academic reaction to cultural reindustrialization. The substructural corollary would be the way in which gentrification guts working life for proletarians and minorities, as it creates a space of safety, entitlement, and groove for corporate gays, white liberal feminists, frat boys, and sorority girls who eschew suburbia until the children arrive, and people like my friends and me (to the extent we are not covered by any or all of the above categories).

Significantly, the idea of a "creative class" drawn to cities that cultivate "the arts, music, night life, and quaint historical districts" has been quantified in the US by two indices: the Technological Index and the Gay Index. These are said to measure technical innovation, entrepreneurship, and the *avant garde*, effortlessly blending Big Blue with Big Bohemian in a shared search for knowledge infra-structures and "lifestyle amenities". Newness meets diversity via "technology, talent, and tolerance" (Dreher 2002) – a grand middle-class melting-pot of corporate cybertarianism and multiculturalism that generates a civic gold rush (Stevenson 2004). Labor is subordinate, an "X-factor" inefficiency, and the consumer is sovereign, the creative person at the heart of the "New Economy." In Britain, the Association for the Business Sponsorship of the Arts highlights the fascination of corporations with "how they can benefit from the arts, how new experiences, values and skills can unlock 'creativity'." Other than in organizational *argot*, this is a bee's knee away from the Royal Society of the Arts opining that "creativity and innovation are the lifeblood of any organization concerned with survival and prosperity" and the Arts and Humanities Research Board announcing that the work it funds must make "the transition from creativity into productivity" (Day 2002; Curtis 2002). So the Body Shop asks its executives to practice body painting, Mars puts on a musical, *Henry V* becomes a management text, and *Sandalistas* is simultaneously an advertisement for sandals on sale at Barney's, and *Condé Nast*'s term for Yanquis buying real estate in post-revolutionary Nicaragua – a mocking reverse trope of the *Sandanistas* (Day 2002: 38; Babb 2004). Does this mean cultural studies is now the handservant of capital?

No. Many leading practitioners have always blended political economy with cultural studies.[2] Much has changed since the Simple-Simon, academic-reader-as-hegemon narcissism that plagued US cultural studies through much of the 1980s and 1990s, via professors earnestly spying on young people at the mall, or obsessively staring at them in virtual communities. Political economy has reasserted itself, as it always does. Vincent Mosco starts from the power of cultural myths then "builds a bridge to political economy" in his excoriation of neoliberal phantasies about empowerment, insisting on "the mutually constitu-tive relationship between political economy and cultural studies" as each mounts "a critique of the other" (2004: 6–7). Richard Maxwell explains that we must "identify ways to link a critique of neo-liberalism and a cultural studies approach to consumption ... not by issuing nostrums against the pleasures of shopping[,] but by paying attention to the politics of resource allocation that brings a consumption infrastructure into the built environment" (2002). This has already been achieved in cultural studies beyond Britain, the US, and their white-settler academic satellites (Israel, Australia, Canada, and Aotearoa/New Zealand). Arvind Rajagopal notes that because television, the telephone, the Internet, and the neoliberal are all new to India, "markets and media generate new kinds of rights and new kinds of imagination ... novel ways of exercising citizenship rights and conceiving politics" (2002). We see the evidence in organizations such as sarai.net. And for Rosalía Winocur, talk radio in Latin America since the fall of

US-backed dictatorships has offered a simultaneously individual and social forum for new expressions of citizenship, in the context of decentered politics, emergent identities, minority rights, and gender issues – a public space that transcends old ideas subordinating difference and privileging élite experience (2002: 15, 91–3). These are exemplary instances of work that understands the importance of material conditions in the formation and exercise of subjectivity.

We simply must address the destructive implications of the fact that "consumption is now virtually out of control in the richest countries." The wealthiest 20% of the world consume over five times more food, water, fuel, minerals, and transport than their parents did, and expenditure on advertising in the US alone is heading towards US$150 billion a year (Beck 1999: 6; Klaassen 2005). In the last two centuries, the global population has increased by a factor of five – and goods and services by a factor of fifty (Sattar 2001). In highlighting these figures, I am not arguing for an absolute choice between pleasure and politics, leisure and labor, or consumption and citizenship. It is as absurd to *ignore* markets as it is to reduce society to them (Martín-Barbero 2001: 26). I endorse the stress on freedom to choose, and the use of commodities to build culture, but I abjure the model of the consumer, audience member, or artist as the center of politics and theory, in favor of a commitment to difference understood through disability, religion, class, gender, race, and sexuality.

Clearly, cultural studies latched onto something real in its focus on consumption as politics. Examples include the eco-consumerism of Greenpeace, chronicled in *Ethical Consumer* magazine as an "economic vote" via "shareholder activism", whereby social movements purchase a financial stake in polluters and change corporate conduct (Newell 2001: 92, 99). This induces apoplexy in fossil-fuel capitalists and their political and intellectual hegemons. Similarly, because of racist hiring practices, Denny's restaurant chain has been *boy*cotted by leftists in the United States, some of whom, conversely, *buy*cott the Working Assets long-distance telephone service, which donates a portion of its proceeds to left-wing causes. The coyBOTt software package has revealed interesting correlations between boycotts, brand popularity, and corporate cultural sponsorship. Consumer activism tends to occur in struggles with the most successful companies, and their response often includes the assiduous cultivation of "corporate social responsibility" projects, notably support of major and minor cultural institutions to show they are good global, national, and local corporate citizens – appropriating *avant-garde* practices previously used against them by activists (Costanza-Chock 2002).

The turn of the twenty-first century saw the uptake of ethical principles by International Shareholder Services (ISS). ISS acts as the proxy advisor for many large institutional investors, such as mutual and pension funds. It exerts major influence on votes at over 20,000 shareholder meetings a year. Previously a stalwart of the right on issues of social responsibility, in 2002 ISS changed its position, astonishing outsiders by recommending votes in favor of renewal-fuel research and anti-sexual discrimination policies by ExxonMobil stockholders, and against child labor in Marriot hotels. The advisor did so because it had determined that "being perceived as a good corporate citizen might affect shareholder value" by appealing to socially concerned investors. Put another way, for the first time, ISS judged that being on the same side as environmentalists and unions made both sense and dollars, in keeping with studies that indicate higher stock valuations of companies with strong pro-environmental programs. Whereas growth in professionally managed assets in the US is about 15% annually, the figure is 40% for those with mandates for "social responsibility", with the total amount in the trillions of dollars (Cordasco 2002; Keeler 2002). This imperative has become an urgent one after the multiple disgraces of US big business, and Third-World issues such as child labor and pharmaceutical pricing (Maitland, 2002). When some public pension funds lost US$300 billion to the Enron scandal, they became more interventionist about their investments, leading to aggressive criticism from business front organizations as part of the Republican Party's "shadow civil society" (Greider 2005; Schell 2005). And corporations are aware that mutual funds serving academics and unionists want to see social as well as financial value flowing from their investments. For example, the California Public Employees' Retirement System controls more than US$186 billion in pension funds for nearly one and a half million people, many of whom are educators and/or unionists (Keeler, 2002; Alperovitz, 2005).

But more than 90% of *Fortune* 500 companies appear in "socially responsible" investing portfolios, which use the Dow Jones Industrial Average as their metric! From worthy origins in opposition to *apartheid*, the American War in Vietnam, and polluting firms, many of these funds have turned into corporate shills whose massive secrecy belies their claim to ethical conduct. The World Economic Forum's list of the "100 Most Sustainable Companies in the World" includes firms that bribe officials, provide false accounts, and are mass polluters—but are deemed appropriate for progressive investment (Hawken 2004 and 2005).

Absent an ongoing fabric of democratic control, consumer activism will always be an irritant rather than a systemic counter to corporate destructiveness (Hutton in Giddens and Hutton 2000: 47). For one thing, "consumer democracy" gives the wealthy more votes than the poor. Most US activists are affluent and highly educated (Keeter *et al.* 2002: 21), so the practice also ironically mirrors the unrepresentative plutocracies of the IMF and the World Bank. The impact on and inclusion of working people in such actions is frequently problematic (Frank 2003). And ethical consumption is difficult to sustain when, for example, numerous items with distinct production histories are bundled together, as in electrical equipment (Monbiot 2003: 56–8). Secondly, the right's glorification of consumers rarely endorses organized political action. When the *Economist* proudly announces that consumers "are kings" because of new technology and transparent pricing (does that mean see-through tags?) it is referring to an "All-seeing, All-knowing", surveillant, selfish, shopper – not a socially engaged collective force (Markillie 2005: 3). Eulogies to public opinion and rational choice do not carry over to endorsements of collective activism – people are sovereign when they purchase, but magically transmogrify into "special interests" when they lobby (Baudrillard 1999: 55; Micheletti 2003). Hence the formation of the Business Roundtable in the 1970s to combat consumer movements from the very top levels of executive action, rather than through discrete trade associations (Hutton 2003: 84) and the ready corporate uptake of campaigns like "Buy American." Consider this 2004 holiday-season pitch made by the outdoor-equipment company, Patagonia, based on the fact that it allocates 1% of its sales to conservation:

> There's no such thing as a free lunch. The air we breathe in big gulps. The snow we slide on every chance we get. We can't take any of it for granted. This holiday season, when you give the gift of Patagonia to your near and dear ones, you'll also be giving back to the environment. Since 1985, we've donated 1% of our sales to grassroots enviro groups. Shop Patagonia and give back. (www.patagonia.com)

Finally, boycotts and buycotts require high levels of organization and sustained commitment. They often end with apparent success, only for corporations to resume their nefarious activities in a quietly efficient manner (Shaw 1999: 111).

So what should cultural studies be up to? Our core word, "culture", derives from the Latin "colare", which implied tending and developing agriculture as part of subsistence. With the emergence of capitalism's division of labor, culture came both to *embody* instrumentalism and to *abjure* it, via the industrialization of farming, on the one hand, and the cultivation of individual taste, on the other. In keeping with this distinction, culture has usually been understood in two registers, via the social sciences and the humanities – truth versus beauty. This was a heuristic division in the sixteenth century, but it became substantive over time. Eighteenth-century German, French, and Spanish dictionaries bear witness to a metaphorical shift into spiritual cultivation. As the spread of literacy and printing saw customs and laws passed on, governed, and adjudicated through the written word, cultural texts supplemented and supplanted physical force as guarantors of authority. With the Industrial Revolution, populations became urban dwellers – food was imported, cultures developed textual forms that could be exchanged, and consumer society emerged through horse racing, opera, art exhibits, masquerades, and balls. The impact of this shift was indexed in cultural labor: *poligrafi* in fifteenth-century Venice, and hacks in eighteenth-century London, wrote popular and influential conduct books, works of instruction on everyday life that marked the textualization of custom, and the emergence of new occupational identities. Anxieties about cultural invasion also date from this period, via Islamic debates over Western domination.

Today, culture is a marker of differences and similarities in taste and status, explored interpretatively and methodically. In the humanities, culture is judged by criteria of quality and meaning, as practiced critically and historically. In the social sciences, the focus is on the socio-political norms of culture, as explored psychologically or statistically. So whereas the humanities articulate population differences through *symbolic* means (for example, which class has the cultural capital to

appreciate high culture, and which does not) the social sciences articulate population differences through *social* ones (for example, which people are affected by TV
messages, and which are not). Somewhere between those tasks is where cultural
studies makes its claims and does its work. At a moment when the First World uses
culture as a selling point for deindustrialized societies, and the Third World does so
for never-industrialized ones, our focus must be on a nimble, hybrid approach
governed not by the humanities or the social sciences, but by an agenda of *cui bono*?
Who benefits, who complains about the fact, and how can we learn from them?

Notes

1   The Director-General of the BBC at the time television was introduced, William
    Haley, refused to have a set in his own home, and instructed TV executives to ensure
    viewers did not watch it much (Airey 2004).
2   I am thinking of such US-based writers as Dave Andrews, Stanley Aronowitz, Michael
    Bérubé, Ben Carrington, Paula Chakravartty, CL Cole, Michael Curtin, Susan G
    Davis, Susan Douglas, John Downing, Philomena Essed, Rosa-Linda Fregoso, Faye
    Ginsburg, David Theo Goldberg, Herman Gray, Larry Gross, Lawrence Grossberg,
    Ed Guerrero, Michael Hanchard, Doug Kellner, Robin DG Kelly, Laura Kipnis,
    Mariam Beevi Lam, George Lipsitz, Cameron McCarthy, Anne McClintock, Lisa
    McLaughlin, George Marcus, Jorge Mariscal, Randy Martin, Rick Maxwell, Rob
    Nixon, Vorris Nunley, Constance Penley, Dana Polan, Andrew Ross, Dan Schiller,
    Ellen Seiter, Ella Shohat, Lynn Spigel, Bob Stam, Tom Streeter, and George Yúdice.
    Despite their prominence, their work is often taken to be apolitical-economic, or not to
    stand for cultural studies in dominant public characterizations. Hmm.

References

Airey, Dawn. (2004). "RTS Huw Wheldon Memorial Lecture." Royal Television
    Society.
Alperovitz, Gar. (2005). "The New Ownership Society." In *The Nation* (27 June): 30–2.
Babb, Florence E. (2004). "Recycled *Sandalistas*: From Revolution to Resorts in the New
    Nicaragua." In *American Anthropologist* 106, no. 3: 541–55.
Baudrillard, Jean. (1999). "Consumer Society." In *Consumer Society in American History:
    A Reader*, ed. Lawrence B. Glickman. Ithaca: Cornell University Press. 33–56.
Baum, Matthew A. (2002). "Sex, Lies, and War: How Soft News Brings Foreign Policy
    to the Inattentive Public." In *American Political Science Review* 96: 91–110.
Beck, Ulrich. (1999). *World Risk Society*. Cambridge: Polity Press.
Cordasco, Paul. (2002). "ISS Swinging Shareholder Votes toward Social Issues." In
    PRWeek (10 June): 9.
Costanza-Chock, Sasha. (2002). *White Paper #1: Background and Context for the Application
    of coyBOTt Software to Systematic Analysis of Branding, Boycott, and Cultural Sponsorship.*
Curtis, P. (2002). "Creative Accounting." *Guardian* 22 Jan.
Day, Gary. (2002). "A Brief History of how Culture and Commerce Were Really Made
    for Each Other." In *Critical Quarterly* 44, no. 3: 37–44.

Dreher, C. (2002). "What Drives U. S. Cities." In *Hamilton Spectator* 20 Jul.

Frank, Dana. (2003). "Where are the Workers in Consumer-Worker Alliances? Class Dynamics and the History of Consumer-Labor Campaigns." In *Politics & History* 31, no. 3: 363–79.

Greider, William. (2005). "The New Colossus." *The Nation* (28 Feb.):13–18.

Giddens, Anthony and Will Hutton. (2000). "In Conversation." In *Global Capitalism*. Ed. Will Hutton and Anthony Giddens. New York: New Press. 1–51.

Hawken, Paul. (2004). "Green is Good." *AlterNet.org.* 8 Oct.

Hawken, Paul. (2005). "The Truth about Ethical Investing." *AlterNet.org.* 29 Apr.

Hutton, Will. (2003). *A Declaration of Interdependence: Why America Should Join the World.* New York: W. W. Norton.

Keeler, Dan. (2002, May). "Spread the Love and Make it Pay." In *Global Finance*: 20–5.

Keeter, Scott, Cliff Zukin, Molly Andolina, and Krista Jenkins. (2002). *The Civic and Political Health of the Nation: A Generational Portrait.* Center for Information & Research on Civic Learning & Engagement.

Klaasen, Abbey. (2005). "2005 Ad Spending to Increase 3.4%." *Advertising Age* 28 Jun.

Maitland, Alison. (2002). "How to Become Good in all Areas." In *Financial Times* (11 Sept.): 10.

Markillie, Paul. (2005). "Crowned at Last." In *Economist* (2 Apr.): 3–6.

Marlowe, Chris. (2005). "NL Site Lets Movie Fans Crash Trailer." In *Hollywood Reporter* (18 Jul.): 18.

Martin-Barbero, Jesús. (2001). "Colombia: Ausencia de Relato y Desubicaciones de lo Nacional." In *Imaginarios de Nación: Pensar en Medio de la Tormenta*. ed. Jesús Martin-Barbero. Bogotá: Ministerio de Cultura. 17–28.

Maxwell, Richard. (2002). "Citizens, you are what you Buy." In *Times Higher Education Supplement* 20 Dec.

Micheletti, Michele. (2003). *Political Virtue and Shopping: Individuals, Consumerism, and Collective Action.* New York: Palgrave Macmillan.

Monbiot, George. (2003). *The Age of Consent: A Manifesto for a New World Order.* London: Flamingo.

Mosco, Vincent. (2004). *The Digital Sublime: Myth, Power, and Cyberspace.* Cambridge, Mass.: MIT Press.

Newell, Peter. (2001). "Environmental NGOs, TNCs, and the Question of Governance." In *The International Political Economy of the Environment: Critical Perspectives.* ed. Dimitris Stevis and Valeire J. Assetto. Boulder: Lynne Rienner. 85–107.

Rajagopal, Arvind. (2002). "Violence of Commodity Aesthetics." *Economic and Political Weekly* 5 Jan.

Sattar, M. G. (2001). "Responses to Franck Amalric." In *Development* 44, no. 4: 12.

Schell, Jonathan. (2005). "Faking Civil Society." *The Nation* (25 Apr): 6.

Shaw, Randy. (1999). *Reclaiming America: Nike, Clean Air, and the New National Activism.* Berkeley: University of California Press.

Stevenson, Deborah. (2004). " 'Civic Gold' Rush: Cultural Planning and the Politics of the Third Way." In *International Journal of Cultural Policy* 10, no. 1: 19–31.

Winocur, Rosalía. (2002). *Ciudadanos Mediáticos: La construcción de lo publico en la radio.* Barcelona: Editorial Gedisa.

Zaller, John. (2003). "A New Standard of News Quality: Burglar Alarms for the Monitorial Citizen." In *Political Communication* 20, no. 2: 109–30.

Chapter 1

What it is and what it isn't: Introducing . . . Cultural Studies

Toby Miller

Cultural studies is magnetic.[1] It accretes various tendencies that are splintering the human sciences: Marxism, feminism, queer theory, and the postcolonial. The "cultural" has become a "master-trope" in the humanities, blending and blurring textual analysis of popular culture with social theory, and focusing on the margins of power rather than reproducing established lines of force and authority (Czaplicka et al. 1995: 3). In place of focusing on canonical works of art, governmental leadership, or quantitative social data, cultural studies devotes time to subcultures, popular media, music, clothing, and sport. By looking at how culture is used and transformed by "ordinary" and "marginal" social groups, cultural studies sees people not simply as consumers, but as potential producers of new social values and cultural languages.

This amounts to a comprehensive challenge to academic business as usual. And the investment in the popular makes waves in the extramural world, too, as the humanities' historic task of criticizing entertainment is sidestepped and new commercial trends become part of cultural studies itself.

Cultural studies is a tendency across disciplines, rather than a discipline itself. This is evident in practitioners' simultaneously expressed desires to: refuse definition, insist on differentiation, and sustain conventional departmental credentials (as well as pyrotechnic, polymathematical capacities for reasoning and research). Cultural studies' continuities come from shared concerns and methods: the concern is the reproduction of culture through structural determinations on subjects versus their own agency, and the method is historical materialism (Morrow 1995: 3, 6). Cultural studies is animated by subjectivity and power – how human subjects are formed and how they experience cultural and social space. It takes its agenda and mode of analysis from economics, politics, media and communication studies, sociology, literature, education, the law, science and technology studies, anthropology, and history, with a particular focus on gender, race, class, and sexuality in everyday life, commingling textual and social theory under the sign of a commitment to progressive social change.

The political significance of popular cultural practices is perhaps best exemplified in subcultures. Subcultures signify a space *under* culture, simultaneously opposed to, derivative of, and informing official, dominant, governmental, commercial, bureaucratically organized forms of life – a shift away from culture as a tool of domination and towards culture as a tool of empowerment. This move wants to find out how the socially disadvantaged use culture to contest their subservient position. Historical and contemporary studies conducted through the 1960s and 1970s on slaves, crowds, pirates, bandits, and the working class emphasized day-to-day noncompliance with authority. For example, UK research into Teddy Boys, Mods, bikers, skinheads, punks, school students, teen girls, and Rastas had as its magical agents of history truants, drop-outs, and magazine readers – people who deviated from the norms of school and the transition to work by entering subcultures. Such research examined the structural underpinnings to collective style, investigating how their *bricolage* subverted the achievement-oriented, materialistic, educationally driven values and appearance of the middle class. The working assumption was that subordinate groups adopt and adapt signs and objects of the dominant culture, reorganizing them to manufacture new meanings. Consumption was the epicenter of such subcultures; paradoxically, it also reversed members' status as consumers. They become producers of new fashions, inscribing alienation, difference, and powerlessness on their bodies. The decline of the British economy and state across the 1970s was exemplified in punk's use of rubbish as an adornment: bag-liners, lavatory appliances, and ripped and torn clothing. But then commodified fashion and convention took over when capitalism appropriated the appropriator. Even as the media announced that punks were folk devils and set in train various moral panics, the fashion and music industries were sending out spies in search of new trends to market (Leong 1992).

Awareness of this double-edged investment in commodities, as objects of resistance whose very appropriation is then recommodified, makes socio-economic analysis via critical political economy a good ally of representational analysis via cultural studies. But a certain tendency on both sides has maintained that they are mutually exclusive: one approach is concerned with structures of the economy and the other with structures of meaning. But this need not be the case. Historically, the best critical political economy and the best cultural studies have worked through the imbrication of power and subjectivity at all points on the cultural continuum. Graham Murdock puts the task well:

> Critical political economy is at its strongest in explaining who gets to speak to whom and what forms these symbolic encounters take in the major spaces of public culture. But cultural studies, at its best, has much of value to say about . . . how discourse and imagery are organized in complex and shifting patterns of meaning and how these meanings are reproduced, negotiated, and struggled over in the flow and flux of everyday life. (1995: 94)

Ideally, blending the two approaches would heal the division between fact and interpretation and between the social sciences and the humanities, under the sign of a principled approach to cultural democracy. To that end, Lawrence Grossberg calls on cultural studies to provide a dynamic way of "politicizing theory and theorizing politics" that combines abstraction and grounded analysis. This requires a focus on the contradictions of organizational structures, their articulations with everyday living and textuality, and their intrication with the polity and economy, refusing any bifurcation that opposes the study of production and consumption, or fails to address such overlapping axes of subjectification as class, race, nation, and gender (1997: 4–5, 9–10).

This book has been designed with that goal in mind. To specify what such work involves, this Introduction examines the lineage to cultural studies, its current manifestations and preoccupations – in short, what it is and what it isn't.

Fathers and Other Origins

Richard Maxwell has provided a useful representation of global cultural studies (figure 1). Four founding parents of British cultural studies are listed, all of them postwar English-based intellectuals: Richard Hoggart, E. P. Thompson, Stuart Hall, and Raymond Williams. These men were adult educators and university professors on the left who wanted to understand the intersection of class and nation at the level of lived experience and social structure by foregrounding "the culture and sensibilities of industrial workers" (Maxwell 2000: 282).

Hoggart was a left Leavisite who favored uplift of the working class through literary study at the same time as he took their popular pursuits seriously. His classic work *The Uses of Literacy* appeared in the 1950s, after which he became a celebrated member of various review bodies into public culture, a star defense witness at the trial of Penguin Books for publishing *Lady Chatterley*, and in the mid-1960s the founder of the Centre for Contemporary Cultural Studies (CCCS) at the University of Birmingham. Hoggart went on to be a senior culturecrat at UNESCO and latterly a memoirist.[2] Thompson's key contribution came through his work on the history of the English working class (1968), a focus on the view of the past from "below" rather than on-high that eschewed theory in favor of ordinary people's accounts of their lives. This rejection of theory involved strong opposition to structuralist Marxism (Thompson 1978), which had entered British cultural studies of the 1970s under the sign of Louis Althusser (1977). Thompson was also active in Britain's Campaign for Nuclear Disarmament in its 1960s heyday and 1980s revival. Hall started as a left Leavisite and worked as Hoggart's deputy at the CCCS for some years, ultimately running the Centre for a decade from 1968 and marking out its classic period of collaborative, engaged Gramscian scholarship that investigated state stereotyping and ritualistic resistance. Hall continued his career at the Open University with a shift towards Foucauldianism and the postcolonial, brokering

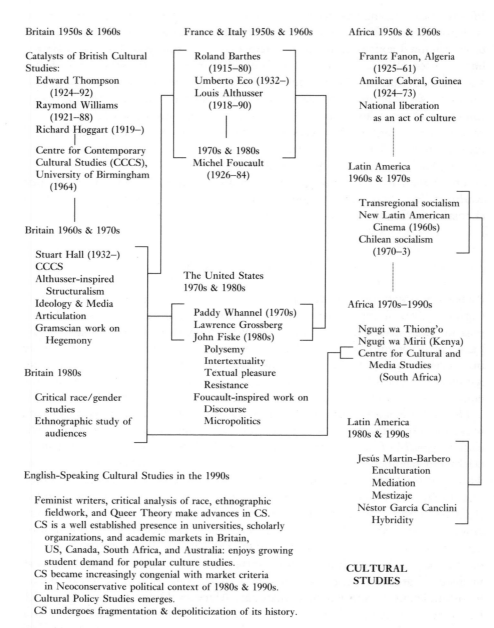

Figure 1 Global Cultural Studies

Source: copyright©Richard Maxwell 2000; reproduced with permission.

cultural studies' relationship to sociology and media studies, co-editing numerous works of theoretical exegesis, and becoming a key influence in the US. Throughout, Hall has sought a means of analyzing signs, representations, and ideology.[3] Williams drew heavily on his experiences growing up in Wales to make sense of cultural change and power dynamics. He has provided the largest body of theory for ongoing cultural studies work, via a wide array of noted volumes on literary history and theory, media and communications, culture, and society. That work models a hybrid between critical political economy and cultural studies, so I shall dedicate some space to its concerns and methods.

Williams is critical of idealist conceptions which assume that culture is a march towards perfection measured by universal values that are basic to the human condition, as if these were timeless rather than grounded in particular conditions of possibility. He also questions documentary conceptions of culture that record artistic work to preserve specific insights and highlight them through criticism. Instead, Williams proposes that we concentrate on the ways of life and values of particular communities at particular times, noting benefits and costs in how they are represented (1975: 57).

Williams' method, cultural materialism, works with Karl Marx's insight that people manufacture their own conditions of existence, but often without a conscious or enabling agency. Social practices, not nature, genius, or individuality, make a way of life and change it over time. This insight directs us away from any view of historical and contemporary culture that privileges aesthetic civilization, the experiences of rulers, or the impact of religion delivered from on-high (Williams 1977: 19). Instead, we should engage culture by reading its products and considering their circumstances of creation and circulation. Art and society – Williams calls them "project" and "formation" respectively – intertwine, with no conceptual or chronological primacy accorded to either term. The relations of culture, their twists and turns, the often violent and volatile way in which they change, are part of the material life of society. For example, language neither precedes nor follows the social world, but is part of it. That means allowing a certain autonomy to intellectual work from the prevailing mode of economic production, but not from its own microeconomies of person, place, and power (1989: 151–2, 164–6). Rather than an organic community that produces a culture of artworks, or a culture of artworks that reflects an organic community, each site has its own internal politics and is connected to the wider economy.

Cultural materialism articulates material culture (buildings, film, cars, fashion, sculpture, and so on) with sociohistorical change, explaining how the culture produced *by* ordinary people is repackaged and sold *to* them. Williams divides culture into *dominant* versus *residual* and *emergent* forms, as per Antonio Gramsci's (1971) model of hegemony, a process of securing consent to the social order that makes dominant culture appear normal and natural, alongside extant residual cultures, which comprise old meanings and practices that are no longer dominant but still influential, and emergent cultural practices, which are either propagated by a new class or incorporated by the dominant, as part of hegemony. These maneuvers find expression in what Williams terms a "structure of feeling": the intangibles of an era that explain or develop the quality of life. Such indicators often involve a contest – or at least dissonance – between official culture and practical consciousness. In short, Williams' view of culture insists on the importance of community life, the conflicts in any cultural formation, the social nature of culture, and the cultural nature of society.

Of course, there are many other sources of today's cultural studies apart from these four men. Manthia Diawara has provided a multicultural trace of UK–US developments that complicates the standard fatherly narrative, albeit foregrounding the later work of Hall. Diawara connects the Birmingham CCCS with London-based black cultural workers and people of color in black and feminist studies areas of US colleges. This trajectory involves certain key transformations of perspective. The initial animating force to cultural studies came from a desire to understand British culture in terms of class dominance and resistance, and the search for an agent of history that could propel radical politics. But that agency fell into doubt, with masculinity and Britishness/Englishness up for debate in ways that criticized sexism and white nationalism (Diawara 1994: 262–3; also see Women's Studies Group 1978). And as per Maxwell's schema, other, semi-autonomous forces have shaped cultural studies. Latin American influences include the socialism manifested in New Latin American Cinema and the pedagogy of the oppressed in the 1960s and 1970s, the Marxist media analysis done for Salvador Allende's Chile by Michèle and Armand Mattelart (1986, 1992), the hegemony studies of Colombian Jesús Martín-Barbero (1993), and the Mexican sociologist Néstor García Canclini's (1990) integration of social and cultural theory (Maxwell 2000: 286–7). In Africa, Ngugi wa Thiong'o, Ngugi wa Mirii, and others at the Kamiriithu Centre linked cultural critique to production (Wright 1996: 355–6, 361). In South Asia, the work of subaltern studies intellectuals such as Ranajit Guha (1982–) and Partha Chatterjee (1993) has been pivotal for postcolonial and historical research.

What it is (and what it isn't)

What do these different legacies mean for cultural studies today? John Frow and Meaghan Morris contrast the view of hegemonic powerbrokers, who see culture as a route to economic efficiency, with cultural studies, which questions power and subjectivity rather than using them to extract surplus value from ordinary people or educate them into obedience. Frow and Morris want to audit the denial, assimilation, and invention that occur each time such words as nation, community, or society are brought into discourse, moving away from essentialist definitions of national identity and towards plural accounts of person and polity (1993b: viii–ix, xv). Morris (1992) glosses the concerns of cultural studies as "racial, ethnic, sexual, gender, class, generational and national differences (roughly in that order), as these are produced and contested in history," along with "a critique of cultural universals."

At the same time as categorical devices from the social sciences are deployed here as grids of investigation, their status as machines obliterating difference is brought into question, the result being a productive intellectual polyphony that draws out contradictions and dissonances. If we link this to Frow and Morris's (1993b) litany of interdisciplinarity, we can specify a desirable cultural studies as a mixture of economics, politics, textual analysis, gender theory, ethnography, history, postcolonial theory, material objects, and policy, animated by a desire to reveal and transform those who control the means of communication and culture, and undertaken with a constant vigilance over one's own *raison d'être* and *modus operandi*. This could be connected to Grossberg's (1993) map of cultural studies along twin axes of cultural method and social theory on a grid comparing five methods (literary humanism, dialectical sociology, culturalism, structuralist conjunctures, and postmodern conjunctures) with eight theories (epistemology, determination, agency, social formation, cultural formation, power, specificity of struggle, and the site of the modern) to produce historicized cultural analyses.

So what is cultural studies *not*? Clearly, attempts to list what does and doesn't count as cultural studies are fraught, especially when they engage in an absolute binarization (cultural studies frequently disavows binary oppositions for failing to acknowledge the logocentric interdependence of supposed opposites, such as that whiteness depends for its sense of self on blackness, for example). But binaries are good to think with and good to tinker with, like any form of inclusion and exclusion. So here goes my list of what's in and what's out (table 1).

The *left* side of the table demonstrates a commitment to articulate knowledge with social change. It represents a will to link the professoriat with social movements as a primary *locus* of power, authorization, and responsibility. The *right* side demonstrates a commitment to articulate knowledge with social reproduction. It represents a will to link the professoriat with universities and professions as a primary *locus* of power, authorization, and responsibility. One is about a transformation of the social order, the other about its replication.

We can see the force of this divide in a raft of journal publications that stand for the recent and profound impact of cultural studies on a host of disciplines.[4] Journals provide a site for investigating the difference between cultural studies and its other, so here I'm going to repeat this binarism. There is a rough bifurcation in academic publishing between journals of tendency and journals of profession, each seeking to establish hegemony within particular spheres. They operate in binary opposition to one another, although there can be an overlap of topics and authors in certain cases. A schema of this opposition is presented in table 2.

Table 1   Cultural studies

What it is	What it isn't
Ethnography	Physical anthropology
Textual analysis of the media	Literary formalism and canon formation
Social theory	Regression and time-series analysis
Science and technology studies	Mathematics, geology, and chemistry
Political economy	Neoclassical economics
Critical geography	Planning
Psychoanalysis	Rational-choice theory and cognitive psychology
Postmodern art	Art history
Critical architecture	Engineering and quantity surveying
Environmentalism	Industrial development
Feminisms	Human biology
Queerness	Deviance
Globalization	Nationalism
Postcolonialism	World literature
Continental philosophy, structuralism, and poststructuralism	Analytic philosophy
Popular music	Musicology
Social semiotics	Formalist linguistics
Fashion	Technical design
Cultural and social history	Political history
Critical public health	Medical training
Critical legal studies and critical race theory	Legal training and legal formalism
Subcultural study	Interest-group study

Table 2   Cultural journals

Journals of tendency	Journals of profession
Avowed political project seeking to make interventions, situated in time and space	Avowed truth project seeking a universalist pursuit of knowledge
In-house manuscript reviewers who argue for and against authors' MSS along grounds of politics and cohesiveness	External manuscript reviewers who engage in double-blind review of MSS in terms of disciplinary competence and falsifiability
Open calls for MSS, theme issues, response to contemporary social questions	Access restricted to members of professional associations, lengthy period of review and revision
Seeks hegemony of a position across disciplines	Seeks hegemony over entry and success within a discipline
Editorial collective that is self-selecting	Editors chosen by association
Prone to inefficiency, sudden bursts of energy and newness, and an eventual sense that the "moment" of the journal has passed	Prone to efficiency, "normal science," and a fate that is joined at the hip to its sponsoring discipline
Social Text, Public Culture, Socialist Review, camera obscura, Radical History Review, History Workshop Journal	*PMLA, American Sociological Review, Cinema Journal, Journal of Communication, American Historical Review, Current Anthropology*

As noted above, journals on the right-hand side of the grid are refereed. Double-blind refereeing (where the author's identity is hidden from reviewers and *vice versa*) arose in the social sciences as compensation for not being as methodologically falsifiable or amenable to utilitarian auditing as paymasters and hegemons might wish. The system gradually spread across universities, although some of the sciences have stayed with single-blind review (where the author's identity is revealed to reviewers). Most refereed journals are financially and intellectually supported by professional organizations. *PMLA* only publishes papers submitted by dues-paying members of the Modern Language Association, and all such offerings are read by fellow initiates. Your work is not even reviewed unless you're a member of the club. The results leave many of us ambivalent. An editor of *Nature*, for example, has bemoaned the fact that refereeing would have prevented publication of the letter announcing the double-helix which appeared in the journal in 1953, while research on peer review shows that it generates caution and reproduces an "invisible college" of elite scholars and disciplines (Clemens et al. 1996; Maddox 1989; Willis and McNamee 1990). This college is prepared to be *very* political, as required: the editor of the American Medical Association's journal was sacked for daring to print a paper during the Clinton impeachment controversy that showed 60 percent of undergraduates at "a large mid-Western university" (how many times have we read that expression in survey research?) in 1991 did not think they had "had sex" if it involved oral contact rather than intercourse.

Some journals cross the divide. In five years, *Continuum: A Journal of Media & Cultural Studies* was transmogrified from a handful of faculty in Western Australia obtaining manuscripts, editing them, and putting in desktop codes, to a journal that had a senior editor, an editor, a photography editor, 2 reviews editors, 4 corresponding editors, 7 members of an editorial collective, 59 editorial advisers, and a British commercial publisher, with only 2 of those earlier artisans numbered among the above. So this schema is not a comprehensive divide. The editors of the journal *Cultural Studies* in fact "welcome" the academic formalization of cultural studies. They view publishing growth in the area as "signs of its vitality and signature components of its status as a field," but continue to call for "knowledge formations" that are "historically and geographically contingent" rather than obedient to disciplines (Grossberg and Pollock 1998: 1). For its part, the inaugural issue of the *International Journal of Cultural Studies* promised to localize knowledge, be "*post-disciplinary*," consider "academic research itself" as an object of inquiry, and engage the fact that "'cultural studies' is now a management and marketing skill" (Hartley 1998: 5–7).

The brigands on the left of the grid have gathered force in book publishing, too. The 1990s saw the appearance of numerous cultural studies anthologies, such as feminist readers edited by Sarah Franklin et al. (1991), Terry Lovell (1995), and Morag Shiach (1999), an omnibus internationalist survey (During 1993), a volume on black British cultural studies (Baker, Jr. et al. 1996), and national mixtures of solid gold and future memories from Australia, Germany,

France, Spain, Italy, Asia, Russia, Canada–Australia, and the USA.[5] Textbooks have been available for some time.[6] The gigantic *Cultural Studies* collection (Grossberg et al.) came out in 1992, and family-resemblance volumes exist in lesbian/gay/queer, legal, multicultural/postcolonial, regional, sports, political, and alterity studies, while there is a call within biomedicine to adopt a cultural studies research agenda, and notable contributions have been made in areas such as AIDS.[7] Several "Cultural Studies at the Crossroads" conferences have been held, and Honolulu convened a major event in 1993, with one block dedicated to cultural studies journals from New Zealand/Aotearoa, Australia, India, the Philippines, and the US. Major scholarly bodies have been transformed from within by cultural studies tendencies, notably the International Communication Association, the International Association for Mass Communication Research, and the National Communication Association. Finally, there is the inevitable raft of websites (Berry and Miller 2000).

Cultural studies has not avoided the eyes of academic and political invigilators, and the right-hand side of the publishing grid has analogs on the right of politics. Cultural studies' concerns with identity, and its struggles against a canon of supposedly elevating aesthetic work, lead to accusations of a fall from the grace of connoisseurship. Kenneth Minogue polemicizes in the *Times Literary Supplement* about this "politico-intellectual junkyard of the Western world" (1994: 27), while neoconservative readers of *Partisan Review* and the *New Criterion* are alert to the danger as well (Wolfe 1996; Kimball 1996). Chris Patten, a former Conservative Member of the UK Parliament and the last Governor of Hong Kong, calls cultural studies "Disneyland for the weaker minded" (quoted in Morley 1998: 478), and Simon Hoggart, son of Richard and a notable journalistic maven, is an implacable foe. He could be seen on British television in February 2000 chiding local universities for wasting time on this nonsense when they should be in step with Harvard and MIT. As there have been several conferences at Harvard Law School about cultural studies, and MIT is forever promoting these areas, cultural studies has obviously hit some hallowed targets in complex ways. Perhaps this is no wonder, for some right-wing libertarians welcome cultural studies. Virginia Postrel, editor of *Reason* magazine, wrote a 1999 op-ed piece for the *Wall Street Journal* in which she described cultural studies as "deeply threatening to traditional leftist views of commerce" because notions of active consumption were so close to the sovereign consumer beloved of the right: "The cultural-studies mavens are betraying the leftist cause, lending support to the corporate enemy and even training graduate students who wind up doing market research."

In the US, some sociologists, confronted by departmental closures, amalgamations, or a transmogrification into social policy, bury their heads in methodological anguish when confronted by cultural studies, or claim the turf and terminology as their own. What do you get when you cross Talcott Parsons with Émile Durkheim and Harold Garfinkel? "A New Proposal for Cultural Studies" (Alexander and Smith 1993). This position says Marxism has been overtaken by a revised functionalism that uses interpretative cultural anthropology and "subjective perceptions" to link meaning with social structure. Symbols and ideals, not power relations, are the appropriate focus. To underline the point, Cambridge University Press's "Cultural Social Studies" series is an avowedly Durkheimian project. It echoes both the "Editor's Note" (Salzman 1975) that inaugurated *Prospects: An Annual Journal of American Cultural Studies* over 25 years ago as an attempt to "elucidate the essential nature of the American character," and claims that cultural studies is just symbolic interactionism (Becker and McCall 1990). So conventional critics either throw up their hands in horror, or seek to incorporate the upstart hybrid as normal science.

On the left, cultural studies' concerns with identity have led to accusations of a fall from the grace of "real" politics (recalling Don DeLillo's character in the postmodern novel *White Noise*, who complains of his university that "There are full professors in this place who read nothing but cereal boxes"). *New Yorker* journalist Adam Gopnik has accused radicals in the US of being overcommitted to abstract intellection and the assumption that "consciousness produces reality," such that the "energy on the American left is in cultural studies, not health care" (1994: 96). But processes of consumption should include questions of pleasure and resistance as well as banality and domination, and debates over healthcare are partially conducted through the popular. In any event, the supposed distance between cultural studies and "real" politics is spurious: cultural studies in the US, for example, has been in the forefront of apparel-industry sweatshop activism and the documentation of contemporary labor conditions in education (Ross 1997; Nelson 1997; Martin 1998). This is no "flaky" area, thank you very much.

But the longstanding cultural studies journal *Social Text* (1979–) became mired in public controversy over social constructionism and scientific truth claims in 1996–7 when a physicist published a paper there stating things he did not believe, then announced this in a populist academic magazine, claiming his duplicity as a sign of the area's sloppy thinking and its weakness as a site for radical politics. There was massive media attention. Given the deceitful nature of this conduct, we can see why it is necessary for the US government to house a full-time bureau dedicated to scientific fraud by holders of Federal research grants, but it is still worth asking the question: what is going on with these critiques?

It seems as though cultural studies occupies the space of 1960s British sociology – an irritant to hegemonic forces because of its radical anti-elitist critique. This antagonizes both traditional academic disciplines and media mavens, who see it as the humanities' sacred duty to elevate the population (or at least segments of it) through indoctrination into a sacred array of knowledges carefully removed from the everyday. The DeLillo quip about full professors reading cereal boxes is funny and pointed. Of course, it is odd to turn away from high-cultural pursuits and invest one's academic capital in the banal, to shift direction from the Bauhaus to the Brillo box. The Patten quip about "Disneyland for the feeble-minded" is also funny and pointed. But in each case, there is something behind the remark. Understanding the iconic significance and material history of American food is of great importance, while acknowledging the pleasures of ordinary people rather than privileging the quasi-sacerdotal pronouncements of an elect may not be so much "feeble-minded" as threatening to cultural elites.

Conclusion

This volume is designed to show where cultural studies exists and what it does there, reflecting a significant diversity of interests and methods. We reach across disciplines, places, issues, and sources, in keeping with the postdisciplinary project of cultural studies – and do so in the interest of deprovincialization (contributors reside in five different continents). Part I, *Disciplines*, looks at the ways that cultural studies has intersected with an array of knowledges. After all, cultural studies must always find "a home . . . within specific disciplines even as it challenges the legitimacy of the disciplinarization of intellectual work" (Grossberg 1997: 5). Mark Gibson and Alec McHoul investigate what has constituted interdisciplinarity from Hoggart's time to our own. Rosemary Coombe asks whether there is a cultural studies of the law. Randy Martin lays out the terms on which American social theory has encountered cultural studies and Frank Webster does the same for the UK. Cultural studies' febrile relationship with science is addressed by Marianne de Laet. Richard Maxwell confronts the ongoing dialogue between political economy and cultural studies, arguing for their profound connectedness, while Douglas Kellner does the same for intersections with the Frankfurt School of critical theory. Silke Morgenroth surveys archaeology and George Marcus looks at anthropology, twin disciplines with quite distinct experiences of cultural studies – the former has remained aloof, to its cost as argued here, while the latter has seen its terrain and method both criticized and "borrowed." The section concludes with John Nguyet Erni's summary of cultural studies' most significant home, media and communication studies.

Part II, *Places*, locates the impact of cultural studies on transnational and national levels, a necessary move given the speed and depth of its diversification and its claims to be an emancipatory, inclusive project. George Yúdice contrasts the US and Latin American experiences, while Jorge Mariscal homes in on US cultural studies' attitude to Hispanic specificity and diversity. The New Zealand/Aotearoa and Australian encounters with cultural studies are addressed by Graeme Turner, and Eric Kit-wai Ma explains how the geopolitical and disciplinary changes experienced in Hong Kong in recent years have staged the advent of cultural studies. Ben Carrington offers an account of the UK's origin myths and Paul Moore inquires into European cultural studies.

Part III, *Issues*, grounds cultural studies practice in particular topics and struggles. Cultural studies' ongoing investment in youth culture is considered from a pedagogic point of view by Justin Lewis. Paul Smith calls for a renewed engagement with Marxism and C. L. Cole connects sport to science and political culture, while cultural policy is foregrounded as a pragmatic site of political intervention by Tony Bennett and problematized by Ana María Ochoa Gautier in the Colombian context and Andrea Fraser via a performance piece. Melissa Deem uses cultural studies methods to engage the current status of US feminism in popular culture, taking the 1999 impeachment crisis as a case study, and Jason King peers into the body via dance music. Fashion is the backdrop to Sarah Berry's essay, Robert Stam looks at cultural studies' vital connections to race, and Geoffrey Lawrence and I analyze globalization. The section is rounded out by Suvendrini Perera on diasporic identities. Part IV, *Sources*, concludes the volume with a bibliography, critical to so dispersed an intellectual field as this one.

Any undertaking that aims to map cultural studies is partial and potentially controversial, because the terrain is up for grabs in definitional and power terms, and is avowedly political. Let it be so. My own view? For what it's worth, I maintain that cultural studies should look at social movements and actionable policy as lodestones and direction-finders. In recognition of this, we must turn our gaze onto shifts in public discourse between self-governance and external governance, and track the careers of the commodity sign and the state sign as they travel through time and space – Hall's "circuit of culture" that focuses on practices of representation, identity, production, consumption, and regulation (1997: 1). This means recalling Foucault's provocation that the modern has as much to do with the governmentalization of the state as of the social. Then we shall have something to say about the institutional control of culture and the democratic potential of everyday life, pointing out erasures in the former and the potential of the latter. As Justin Lewis puts it, a concern with political power exercised over majorities need not be at the expense of specificity and marginality; rather, it should be regarded as a precondition to empowering the marginal (1999: 199–200). Maxwell stresses articulations between the two:

> People work to make culture. Not only the writers, technicians, artists, carpenters and all those who put together movies, books and such; culture is also made by labour not directly involved in the culture industries. Consider your own daily works of judgement and interpretation about a film plot, your grammar or a classmate's joke. Think of all those whose efforts built the bridges you have crossed, the roads travelled, the means of transport and human relationship . . . your love story, a brief encounter . . . and all the hardship, strikes, solidarity, death, wage negotiations, debt and satisfaction embodied in those structures. (2000: 281)

I recall my excitement when I first saw the front cover of the Birmingham Centre's *Working Papers in Cultural Studies 4* of 1973. Alongside a *bricolage* graphic of a thoughtful cherub, some compass-points with dollar and pound signs, and a few printers' codes, the bottom center-left read like this:

LITERATURE SOCIETY

MOTOR RACING

It seemed natural to me for these topics to be together (as is the case in a newspaper). But of course that is not academically "normal." To make them syntagmatic was *utterly sensible* in terms of people's lives and mediated reality, and *utterly improbable* in terms of intellectual divisions of labor and hierarchies of discrimination. Bravo.

Notes

1   Thanks to Marie Leger for her comments.
2   The inaugural issue of the *International Journal of Cultural Studies* features an interview with Hoggart and a bibliography of his work (Gibson and Hartley 1998).
3   The *Festschrift* entitled *Stuart Hall: Critical Dialogues in Cultural Studies* (Chen and Morley 1996) collects some of his work, reacts to it, and provides a useful bibliography.
4   On the journals front, there have been special issues of *Critical Studies in Mass Communication* ("Cultural Studies," 1989), *Critical Studies* ("Cultural Studies: Crossing Boundaries," 1991), the *Journal of Communication* ("The Future of the Field – Between Fragmentation and Cohesion," 1993), the *Canadian Review of Comparative Literature/Revue Canadienne de Littérature Comparée* ("Cultural Studies/Les études culturelles," 1995), the *University of Toronto Quarterly* ("Cultural Studies in Canada," 1995 and "Cultural Studies: Disciplinarity and Divergence," 1996), *Callaloo* ("Rethinking Black (Cultural) Studies," 1996), the *Southeast Asian Journal of Social Science* ("Cultural Studies in the Asia Pacific," 1994), *boundary 2* ("Asia/Pacific," 1994), *Politics & Culture* ("Cultural Studies and Cultural Politics," 1994), and *South Atlantic Quarterly* ("Ireland and Irish Cultural Studies," 1996). The *Quarterly Journal of Speech* asks whether "neo-Marxism as a metadiscourse" is "alien to rhetorical sensibilities" in evaluating the impact of the *arriviste*, while *Victorian Studies* is anachronistically moved to run a review symposium on work about the 1980s and 1990s (Rosteck 1995: 397; "Review," 1993). The journal *Cultural Studies* was relaunched in the US, its origins in Australia quickly wiped from the slate of history, the *Review of Education* redesignated itself a *Review of Education/Pedagogy/Cultural Studies* (Shannon and Giroux 1994), and *African Literatures and Cultures* transformed into the *Journal of African Cultural Studies*. Other significant related journals included *French Cultural Studies, Social Semiotics, Social Identities, UTS Review, Strategies: Journal of Theory, Culture & Politics, Pretexts: Literary and Cultural Studies*, and *Travezia: The Journal of Latin American Cultural Studies*, while the turn of the twenty-first century saw the launch of the *International Journal of Cultural Studies*, the *European Journal of Cultural Studies*, the *Journal of Spanish Cultural Studies, Inter-Asia Cultural Studies, Nepantla: Views from South*, and *Feminist Media Studies*.

5 Frow and Morris 1993a; Turner 1993; Jordan and Morgan-Tamosunas 2000, Forbes and Kelly 1996; Le Hir and Strand 2000; Graham and Labanyi 1996; Forgacs and Lumley 1996; Chen 1998; Kelly and Shepherd 1998; Blundell et al. 1993; Hartley and Pearson 2000.
6 Brantlinger 1990; Punter 1986; Turner 1990; Dirks et al. 1994; Gray and McGuigan 1993; Jenks 1993; Storey 1993; McGuigan 1992; Inglis 1993; Chaney 1994; Tudor 1999.
7 Abelove et al. 1993; Leonard 1995; Redhead 1995; Baker and Boyd 1997; Martin and Miller 1999; Good 1995; Treichler 1999; Dean 2000.

References

"Asia/Pacific as Space of Cultural Production." (1994). *boundary 2* 21, no. 1.

"Cultural Studies." (1989). *Critical Studies in Mass Communication* 6, no. 4.

"Cultural Studies in the Asia Pacific." (1994). *Southeast Asian Journal of Social Science* 22.

"Cultural Studies: Crossing Boundaries." (1991). *Critical Studies* 3, no. 1.

"Cultural Studies/Cultural Politics: Articulating the Global and the Local." (1994). *Politics & Culture* 6.

"Cultural Studies/Les études culturelles." (1995). *Canadian Review of Comparative Literature/ Revue Canadienne de Littérature Comparée* 22, no. 1.

"The Future of the Field – Between Fragmentation and Cohesion." (1993). *Journal of Communication* 43, no. 3.

"Rethinking Black (Cultural) Studies." (1996). *Callaloo* 19, no. 1.

"Review Forum on Cultural Studies." (1993). *Victorian Studies* 36, no. 4: 455–72.

Workplace. (1999). 2, no. 2. <http://www.louisville.edu/journal/workplace/ issue4/ contents22.html>.

Abelove, Henry, Michèle Aina Barale, and David M. Halperin, eds. (1993). *The Lesbian and Gay Studies Reader.* New York: Routledge.

Alexander, Jeffrey C. and Philip Smith. (1993). "The Discourse of American Civil Society: A New Proposal for Cultural Studies." *Theory and Society* 22, no. 2: 151–207.

Althusser, Louis. (1977). *Lenin and Philosophy and Other Essays,* trans. Ben Brewster. London: New Left Books.

Baker, Aaron and Todd Boyd, eds. (1997). *Out of Bounds: Sports, Media, and the Politics of Identity.* Bloomington: Indiana University Press.

Baker, Houston A., Jr., Manthia Diawara, and Ruth H. Lindeborg, eds. (1996). *Black British Cultural Studies: A Reader.* Chicago: University of Chicago Press.

Becker, Howard S. and Michael M. McCall, eds. (1990). *Symbolic Interaction and Cultural Studies.* Chicago: University of Chicago Press.

Berry, Sarah and Toby Miller. (2000). *Blackwell Cultural Theory Resource Centre.* <http://www.blackwellpublishers.co.uk/cultural/>.

Blundell, Valda, John Shepherd, and Ian Taylor, eds. (1993). *Relocating Cultural Studies: Developments in Theory and Research.* London: Routledge.

Brantlinger, Patrick. (1990). *Crusoe's Footsteps: Cultural Studies in Britain and America.* New York: Routledge.

Chaney, David. (1994). *The Cultural Turn: Scene Setting Essays on Contemporary Cultural Theory.* London: Routledge.

Chatterjee, Partha. (1993). *The Nation and its Fragments: Colonial and Postcolonial Histories*. Princeton: Princeton University Press.

Chen, Kuan-Hsing, ed. (1998). *Trajectories: Inter-Asia Cultural Studies*. London: Routledge.

Chen, Kuan-Hsing and David Morley, eds. (1996). *Stuart Hall: Critical Dialogues in Cultural Studies*. London: Routledge.

Clemens, Elisabeth S., Walter W. Powell, Kris McIlwaine, and Dina Okamoto. (1996). "Careers in Print: Books, Journals, and Scholarly Reputations." *American Journal of Sociology* 101: 433–94.

Czaplicka, John, Andreas Huyssen, and Anson Rabinach. (1995). "Introduction: Cultural History and Cultural Studies: Reflections on a Symposium." *New German Critique* 22, no. 2: 3–17.

Dean, J., ed. (2000). *Cultural Studies and Political Theory*. Ithaca: Cornell University Press.

Diawara, Manthia. (1994). "Black Studies, Cultural Studies, Performative Acts." In *Race, Identity and Representation in Education*, eds. Cameron McCarthy and Warren Crichlow. New York: Routledge, 262–7.

Dirks, Nicholas B., Geoff Eley, and Sherry B. Ortner, eds. (1994). *Culture/Power/History: A Reader in Contemporary Social Theory*. Princeton: Princeton University Press.

During, Simon, ed. (1993). *The Cultural Studies Reader*. London: Routledge.

Forbes, Jill and Michael Kelly, eds. (1996). *French Cultural Studies: An Introduction*. Oxford: Oxford University Press.

Forgacs, David and Robert Lumley, eds. (1996). *Italian Cultural Studies: An Introduction*. Oxford: Oxford University Press.

Franklin, Sarah, Celia Lury, and Jackie Stacey, eds. (1991). *Off-Centre: Feminism and Cultural Studies*. London: Routledge.

Frow, John and Meaghan Morris, eds. (1993a). *Australian Cultural Studies: A Reader*. Sydney: Allen and Unwin.

Frow, John and Meaghan Morris. (1993b). "Introduction." *Australian Cultural Studies: A Reader*. eds. John Frow and Meaghan Morris. Sydney: Allen and Unwin, vii–xxxii.

Garcia Canclini, Néstor. (1990). *Culturas Híbridas: Estrategias para Entrar y Salir de la Modernidad*. Mexico, DF: Editorial Grijalbo.

Gibson, Mark and John Hartley. (1998). "Forty Years of Cultural Studies: An Interview with Richard Hoggart, October 1997." *International Journal of Cultural Studies* 1, no. 1: 11–23.

Good, Mary-Jo Delvecchio. (1995). "Cultural Studies of Biomedicine: An Agenda for Research." *Social Science and Medicine* 41, no. 4: 461–73.

Gopnik, Adam. (1994). "Read All About It." *New Yorker* 70: 84–102.

Graham, Helen and Jo Labanyi, eds. (1996). *Spanish Cultural Studies: An Introduction: The Struggle for Modernity*. Oxford: Oxford University Press.

Gramsci, Antonio. (1971). *Selections from the Prison Notebooks*, trans. Quentin Hoare and Geoffrey Nowell-Smith. New York: International Publishers.

Gray, Ann and Jim McGuigan, eds. (1993). *Studying Culture: An Introductory Reader*. London: Edward Arnold.

Grossberg, Lawrence. (1993). "The Formations of Cultural Studies: An American in Birmingham." In *Relocating Cultural Studies: Developments in Theory and Research*, eds. Valda Blundell, John Shepherd, and Ian Taylor. London: Routledge, 21–66.

Grossberg, Lawrence. (1997). *Bringing it all Back Home: Essays on Cultural Studies*. Durham: Duke University Press.

Grossberg, Lawrence and Della Pollock. (1998). "Editorial Statement." *Cultural Studies* 12, no. 3: 2.

Grossberg, Lawrence, Cary Nelson, and Paula Treichler, eds. (1992). *Cultural Studies*. New York: Routledge.

Guha, Ranajit, ed. (1982–). *Subaltern Studies*. Delhi: Oxford University Press.

Hall, Stuart. (1997). "Introduction." In *Representation: Cultural Representations and Signifying Practices*, ed. Stuart Hall. London: Sage, 1997, 1–11.

Harris, David. (1992). *From Class Struggle to the Politics of Pleasure: The Effects of Gramscianism on Cultural Studies*. London: Routledge.

Hartley, John. (1998). "Editorial (with Goanna)." *International Journal of Cultural Studies* 1, no. 1: 5–10.

Hartley, John and Roberta Pearson, eds. (2000). *American Cultural Studies: A Reader*. Oxford: Oxford University Press.

Hoggart, Richard. (1957). *The Uses of Literacy: Aspects of Working-Class Life with Special Reference to Publications and Entertainments*. Harmondsworth: Penguin.

Inglis, Fred. (1993). *Cultural Studies*. Oxford: Blackwell.

Jenks, Chris, ed. (1993). *Cultural Reproduction*. London: Routledge.

Jordan, B. and R. Morgan-Tamosunas, eds. (2000). *Contemporary Spanish Cultural Studies*. London: Arnold.

Kelly, C. and D. Shepherd, eds. (1998). *Russian Cultural Studies: An Introduction*. Oxford: Oxford University Press.

Kimball, Roger. (1996). "'Diversity,' 'Cultural Studies' & Other Mistakes." *New Criterion* 14, no. 9: 4–9.

Le Hir, Marie-Pierre and Dana Strand, eds. (2000). *French Cultural Studies: Criticism at the Crossroads*. Albany: State University of New York Press.

Leonard, Jerry D., ed. (1995). *Legal Studies as Cultural Studies: A Reader in (Post) Modern Critical Theory*. Albany: State University of New York Press.

Leong, Laurence Wei-Teng. (1992). "Cultural Resistance: The Cultural Terrorism of British Male Working-Class Youth." *Current Perspectives in Social Theory* 12: 29–58.

Lewis, Justin. (1999). "The Opinion Poll as Cultural Form." *International Journal of Cultural Studies* 2, no. 2: 199–221.

Lovell, Terry, ed. (1995). *Feminist Cultural Studies Volumes I and II*. Aldershot: Elgar.

Maddox, John. (1989). "Where Next with Peer-Review?" *Nature* 339: 11.

Martin, Randy, ed. (1998). *Chalk Lines: The Politics of Work in the Managed University*. Durham: Duke University Press.

Martin, Randy and Toby Miller, eds. (1999). *SportCult*. Minneapolis: University of Minnesota Press.

Martín-Barbero, Jésus. (1993). *Communication, Culture, and Hegemony: From the Media to Mediations*. London: Sage.

Mattelart, Armand and Michèle Mattelart. (1992). *Rethinking Media Theory: Signposts and New Directions*, trans. James A. Cohen and Marina Urquidi. Minneapolis: University of Minnesota Press.

Mattelart, Michèle. (1986). *Women, Media and Crisis: Femininity and Disorder*. London: Comedia.

Maxwell, Richard. (2000). "Cultural Studies." In *Understanding Contemporary Society: Theories of the Present*, eds. Gary Browning, Abigail Halci, and Frank Webster. London: Sage, 281–95.

McGuigan, Jim. (1992). *Cultural Populism*. New York: Routledge.

Minogue, Kenneth. (1994). "Philosophy." *Times Literary Supplement* Nov. 25: 27–8.

Morley, David. (1998). "So-Called Cultural Studies: Dead Ends and Reinvented Wheels." *Cultural Studies* 12, no. 4: 476–97.

Morris, Meaghan. (1992). *Ecstasy and Economics: American Essays for John Forbes*. Sydney: E. M. Press.

Morrow, Raymond A. (1995). "The Challenge of Cultural Studies." *Canadian Review of Comparative Literature/ Revue Canadienne de Littérature Comparée* 22, no. 1: 1–20.

Murdock, Graham. (1995). "Across the Great Divide: Cultural Analysis and the Condition of Democracy." *Critical Studies in Mass Communication* 12, no. 1: 89–95.

Nelson, Cary, ed. (1997). *Will Teach for Food: Academic Labor in Crisis*. Minneapolis: University of Minnesota Press.

Postrel, Virginia. (1999). "The Pleasures of Persuasion." *Wall Street Journal* 2 Aug.

Punter, David, ed. (1986). *Introduction to Contemporary Cultural Studies*. London: Longman.

Redhead, Steve. (1995). *Unpopular Cultures: The Birth of Law and Popular Culture*. Manchester: Manchester University Press.

Ross, Andrew, ed. (1997). *No Sweat: Fashion, Free Trade, and the Rights of Garment Workers*. New York: Verso.

Rosteck, Thomas. (1995). "Cultural Studies and Rhetorical Studies." *Quarterly Journal of Speech* 81, no. 3: 386–403.

Salzman, Jack. (1975). "Editor's Note." *Prospects: An Annual Journal of American Cultural Studies* 1: iii.

Shannon, Patrick and Henry A. Giroux. (1994). "Editor's Comments." *Review of Education/ Pedagogy/ Cultural Studies* 16, no. 1: v.

Shiach, Morag, ed. (1999). *Feminism & Cultural Studies*. Oxford: Oxford University Press.

Storey, John. (1993). *An Introductory Guide to Cultural Theory and Popular Culture*. Athens: University of Georgia Press.

Thompson, E. P. (1968). *The Making of the English Working Class*. Harmondsworth: Penguin.

Thompson, E. P. (1978). *The Poverty of Theory*. London: Merlin.

Treichler, Paula. (1999). *How to Have Theory in an Epidemic: Cultural Chronicles of AIDS*. Durham: Duke University Press.

Tudor, Andrew. (1999). *Decoding Culture: Theory and Method in Cultural Studies*. London: Sage.

Turner, Graeme. (1990). *British Cultural Studies: An Introduction*. Boston: Unwin Hyman.

Turner, Graeme, ed. (1993). *Nation, Culture, Text: Australian Cultural and Media Studies*. London: Routledge.

Williams, Patrick and Laura Chrisman, eds. (1993). *Colonial Discourse/ Post-Colonial Theory*. New York: Columbia University Press.

Williams, Raymond. (1975). *The Long Revolution*. Harmondsworth: Pelican.

Williams, Raymond. (1977). *Marxism and Literature*. Oxford: Oxford University Press.

Williams, Raymond. (1989). *The Politics of Modernism: Against the New Conformists*, ed. Tony Pinkney. London: Verso.

Willis, Cecil L. and Stephen J. McNamee. (1990). "Social Networks of Science and Patterns of Publication in Leading Sociology Journals." *Knowledge: Creation, Diffusion, Utilization* 11: 363–81.

Wolfe, Alan. (1996). "The Culture of Cultural Studies." *Partisan Review* 53, no. 3: 485–92.

Women's Studies Group of the Centre for Contemporary Cultural Studies. (1978). *Women Take Issue: Aspects of Women's Subordination*. London: Hutchinson.

Wright, Handel Kashope. (1996). "Take Birmingham to the Curb, Here Comes African Cultural Studies: An Exercise in Revisionist Historiography." *University of Toronto Quarterly* 65, no. 2: 355–65.

PART I

Disciplines

Chapter 2

Interdisci plinarity

Mark Gibson and Alec McHoul

Hoggart's Fundamental Departure

Who can guess the full extent of the impact on university English departments, in February 1957, of Richard Hoggart's breakthrough work in what was later to be called "cultural studies" and whose full title reads: *The Uses of Literacy: Aspects of Working-class Life, with Special Reference to Publications and Entertainments*? Even a glance at the table of contents shows a fundamental departure from the routine objects of English literary criticism: the established canon and the works of emergent "serious" writers. In place of the "life and work" of famous authors (an approach which was itself, by the 1950s, already suspected of being too sociopolitical and, so, aesthetically unresponsive), the scene shifts to the working class, the family, the home, the parents, the neighborhood – as all of these touch upon the concrete lives of average everyday workers, men and women. Big literary history is replaced by the detail of the little histories of ordinary life. Instead of serious "literature," we find repeated references to popular art (*Peg's Paper* and "Club-Singing"). And the word "art" itself switches adjectives, away from "serious," "high," and "fine" and towards "popular," "commercial," and "mass." Then perhaps more significantly still, the word "art" is, in the final parts of the book, effectively replaced by "culture." So literary studies comes, chapter by chapter, to be transformed into something else. The something else, though, is not quite sociology or politics. Hoggart's uncompromisingly ordinary prose, his personal attachment to what he is addressing, his overt identifications, make the book almost but not quite social science, even in its "softest" form, and especially by the standards of the 1950s.

No. This is something new and different and something that offers insight into the peculiar interdisciplinary mix that cultural studies has become, should we care to return and look and not shy away from the idea that cultural studies is old enough to *have* a history – an idea that is currently unfashionable, despite the fact that cultural studies equally insists on historicizing many another discipline in an effort to unhinge its authority. And when we make such a return, we find a set of unique conditions that allow for the possibility of a Hoggart and his nascent interdisciplinary attachment to culture and the popular.

By the mid-1950s, the postwar British universities were just starting to open up in new ways to intakes based on talent and ability as well as those based on class, money, and ancestry. This was on nothing like the scale of the post-Newsome boom of the late 1960s and early 1970s which saw a number of new universities established across the country in such otherwise academic backwaters as Lancaster and Brighton. That second boom was, as is now well known, to become the central impetus behind cultural studies' adolescence, its great period of growth, popularity, and prosperity. It was also to mark cultural studies as a revolutionary curricular alternative to the traditional humanities and social science disciplines; as, in effect, an antidiscipline – for a moment at least. But Hoggart's own earlier decade was the crucial period of infant development and so the initial platform for cultural studies' shaping and uniqueness as an inter-discipline. And true to the pattern of many later writings, Hoggart also, in semi-autobiographical mode, narrates the conditions for this emergence. His famous section on the "Scholarship Boy" tells the story in no uncertain terms.

Cultural studies, in a sense, had to happen, if Hoggart is to be believed, when he tells us that a new type of student was – perhaps for the first time – to be encountered in the British universities. And here we have to remember that until about the time of Hoggart's own university life, most of the academics, the dons, were the social inferiors of their students. Who was this new arrival, the Scholarship Boy? Hoggart includes a particularly telling passage – and one whose sources are impeccable, for what we are reading here is Hoggart's own generalized experience:

> [H]e is not a "creative genius." He is clever enough to take himself out of his class mentally, but not equipped, mentally or emotionally, to surmount all the problems that follow. He is denied even the "consolations of philosophy," of acquiring such comfort as there is, in part at least, from assessing his situation. Even if he achieves some degree of culture, he finds it difficult to carry it easily, as easily as those who have not had to strain so much to get it, who have not known like him the long process of exploitation of "brains." (Hoggart 1957: 248)

Being neither of the "creative minority" (the English dons and their traditional students) nor of the "uncreative majority" (the class from which he comes and with which he cannot but identify), the Scholarship Boy is caught in a paradox, in a version of what Toby Miller (1993) calls the incompleteness of the self. This self is incomplete because it can't disavow "cleverness" or "brains"; all of its training and social-selectedness points to that. Yet at the same time, these "brains" are, surprisingly enough perhaps in an academic environment, insufficient for participation in its own "culture" (or perhaps "culturedness"), stemming as it does from a long and abiding upper-class and aristocratic history of

24

knowing just what to *do* with one's own intelligence. The Scholarship Boy – and here we could be tempted take this figure as standing for nascent cultural studies itself – cannot, and yet must, exist within an academic environment: striving for a respectability, a disciplinarity, it simply cannot have.

Given this paradox or aporia, the only rational alternative was for him (or it) to find ways in which cultures other than those of the universities themselves could become at least semi-respectable within them. This was, for Hoggart, and in some places still is, an uphill battle. Cultural studies, then, is not interdisciplinary for the *sake* of being so; interdisciplinarity is not its willed departure, the volunteered flag of its curricular radicality – at least not at this moment. Interdisciplinarity, on the contrary, arises out of structural institutional necessity. The primary ingredients of its own mix, literary studies, sociology, and autobiography, then, represent points of a triangle which bound the early form of the discipline. But none of these three alone could easily be adopted by the Scholarship Boy as "his" discipline. Literary studies (in either its aestheticist or historicist mode) simply refers back to the deep and abiding class culture of the "old" academic demographics. Sociology simply affirms the fact of technique or "brains" and uses them to do empirical studies – but without any sense of art, popular or otherwise. Autobiography suggests experience (what we would now call "identity politics"), easier writing from memory and anecdote, the absence of analytic distance and hence of the very "brains" that define the Scholarship Boy's main strength. But at the same time, these are the only equipments he has, at least as far as the humanities are concerned. What he must do is synthesize and combine them into something new, something that can then, as it were, "speak for itself" and, eventually perhaps, wear that interdisciplinarity as a badge of pride, as if it had been purposefully created out of his own volition towards radical institutional reform.

This is Hoggart, then, in 1957, already on the cusp of professional academic success, but still in touch with the process by which he had to struggle for that success as a very different kind of university student. We move now, on a decade or so, to Raymond Williams writing as a fully-fledged university teacher, describing yet another proto-cultural-studies "clientele": adult education.

Williams and Adult Education

The recognition of a new kind of subject in early British cultural studies opened the possibility of developing a new kind of pedagogy, and it is here that a commitment to interdisciplinarity begins to be articulated more explicitly than it was by Hoggart. In Raymond Williams' account, the most challenging context was extramural education – again, a precursor to the expansion of the tertiary system in the late 1960s and early 1970s – where students were held by little more than the interest, or capacity to explain, of the material presented to them:

> These people were, after all, in a practical position to say "well, if you tell me that question goes outside your discipline, then bring me someone whose discipline *will* cover it, or bloody well get outside of the discipline and answer it yourself." It was from the entirely rebellious and untidy situation that the extraordinarily complicated and often muddled convergences of what became Cultural Studies occurred. (Williams 1989: 157)

This early and embryonically interdisciplinary project of cultural studies was defined not so much by a particular problem or subject-matter as by an understanding of fields of academic specialization being constantly in dialogue with intellectual and practical interests beyond themselves. It was, for Williams, a project of:

> taking the best we can in intellectual work and going with it in this very open way to confront people for whom it is not a way of life, for whom it is not in any probability a job, but for whom it is a matter of their own intellectual interest, their own understanding of the pressures on them, pressures of every kind, from the most personal to the most broadly political. (Williams 1989: 162)

The motivation for interdisciplinarity in this context is, again, a recognition of incompleteness – but this time, and the shift is important, an incompleteness felt on the side of the teacher and a curriculum divided into disciplines. In its encounter with interests, ways of life and ethical practices outside itself, formal academic knowledge is forced into an awareness of its own status as partial, contingent, and distanced from the (literally) extramural world of a very different will to know, a very different set of "structures of feeling."

In Williams' case, this proto-interdisciplinary awareness of the incompleteness of the humanities academy was closely related to a particular view of language, most clearly outlined in the introduction to his *Keywords* as "historical semantics." This deliberately counters strong claims to authority made on the basis of specialized disciplinary vocabularies. While, in certain delimited areas, disputes may be resolved by reference to dictionary definitions or "proper meanings," for many of the terms most central to the discussion of culture and society such a procedure is impossible. Meanings, in this field, are more complex than the ideas of "discipline" and "definition" can allow, for the reason that they may vary according to active life circumstances, to what Williams here calls "relationships":

> [I]t is necessary to insist that the most active problems of meaning are always primarily embedded in actual relationships, and that both the meanings and the relationships are typically diverse and variable, within the structures of particular social orders and the processes of social and historical change. (Williams 1976: 22)

There is little justification, from this perspective, for that "familiar, slightly frozen, polite stare" which often meets "improper" usage. This is not to say that specializations of language are not valuable, "but in any major language, and particularly in periods of change, a necessary confidence and concern for clarity can quickly become brittle, if the questions involved are not faced" (Williams 1976: 16). Williams' position is in no way *anti*disciplinary, then (whatever cultural studies may have thought itself to be in later periods), but it is insistent in its emphasis on the *limits and incompleteness* of disciplinary forms of knowledge and their historical formation.

This ethics of knowledge, developed in the context of adult education, is also reflected in one of Williams' most enduring and widely-used concepts: that of "structures of feeling," alluded to above. The originality of the concept lies in its short-circuiting of familiar dichotomies which associate formal institutions, disciplines, and discourses simply with "structures" and areas of life outside them with "feeling" (sometimes identified with "agency"). "Structures of feeling" are not quite fully-articulated forms in the sense of academic disciplines, but more like *proto*disciplines still in the process of formation. In *The Long Revolution*, Williams explains this via the metaphor of the precipitation of chemicals from solution (Williams 1965: 63; see also Pickering 1997: 23–53). In the course of historical change, certain structuring processes are exhausted or become neglected while others assume the solidity of established institutions. The recognized academic disciplines of any period, along with political and social institutions, are clearly among the latter. There is never any question, for Williams, that a certain respect is owed to them as historical achievements, but the project of cultural studies is to cultivate a sensitivity to structures of feeling which have not yet found (and which may never find) a precipitate form. The point in this is not an abstract and critical progressivism or a principled opposition to structure as such; it is a more specific and directed concern for what disciplinary knowledge unavoidably excludes and how it is thereby rendered incomplete in the face of actual social and cultural "relationships." What it excluded, principally, for Williams, was the actuality of class-based (and perhaps regional) experiences – as it was for Hoggart. But something similar (though by no means identical), as we shall see, could apply equally to what is now called "diversity."

Appadurai: Diversity and Discipline Today

Coming closer to the present then – 1996 – and shifting continents, it is significant to find a paper that, in its own historical and political context, echoes at least some of the themes of incompleteness-in-the-face-of-difference to be found (again slightly differently) in the foundational work of Hoggart and Williams. We refer here to a *compte rendu* of the state of cultural studies in the American university by Arjun Appadurai (1996). Indeed the debt is partly acknowledged when Appadurai writes:

In general, English departments have been the spaces in which cultural studies has grown and thrived. Recalling the origins of cultural studies in England and the work of Richard Hoggart and Raymond Williams (both students of literature), this is perhaps understandable. It was also doubtless inevitable that it would be in the space of English that Matthew Arnold's sense of culture (as civilizing process) would encounter the revenge of popular culture as a subject fit for literary study. (1996: 28)

While Arnold's "civilizing process" was the very obstacle that Hoggart's Scholarship Boy's "brains" had to overcome, the new vanguard (which, arguably, Appadurai represents) sees "civilizing" as an essential part of the equally new amalgam of diversity and disciplinarity which, as it turns out, is yet another take on incompleteness. Clearly, then, a sense of class difference is no longer the single driving force. Its place in the overall structure is taken by diversity. In one of many binaries, for example, Appadurai distinguishes between diversity as an effect of sheer numbers – "the presence of students of color, faculty of minority background, and a vaguely international milieu" – and diversity as a real change to the underlying university culture (1996: 25). Again, on the one side (sheer numbers) a "clientele" or demographic from outside the traditional academic habitus and, on the other, an institutional culture faced with the problem of reaching some kind of *rapprochement* with it. The numbers are "there," but the *rapprochement* has not been made; an incompleteness of a new and different (but parallel) kind thus emerges:

While the American university has managed to put into its official life (job advertisements, faculty and student recruitment, and courses of study) the principle that more difference is better, it has not succeeded in creating a habitus where diversity is at the heart of the apparatus itself. (1996: 26)

This is still slightly redolent of both Hoggart and Williams: the university opens its doors to different social and cultural sectors in larger numbers (in the first case bright working-class boys and adult learners; in Appadurai's case a much broader nontraditional intake), but does not quite know what to do with them once in, does not quite know how to be more "user-friendly" towards them, does not quite know how to alter either its own or its students' traditional "culturedness." If we have here another and altered version of what Williams called an "entirely rebellious and untidy situation," its "solution" again seems to be a relatively similar congeries of "extraordinarily complicated and often muddled convergences" (Williams 1989: 157). But the difference between demographic numbers and institutional culture, in this new case, seems to leave *both* the new entrants *and* the academic curriculum incomplete. And once more, the incompleteness in question has to do with the question of discipline.

Appadurai, then, puts his finger on something that Hoggart and Williams, historically, could not have emphasized. They clearly saw, in their different ways, the disciplinary limits of the English department and its culture. But the newer "minoritarian" is able to complement this with a connection between two finer senses of disciplinarity. After Foucault, perhaps, Appadurai distinguishes between the two "main senses" of disciplinarity: "(a) care, cultivation, habit and (b) field, method, subject matter" (1996: 30). Appadurai then turns towards the first and more traditional sense of discipline as a site to be won by the new cohort of persons from diverse backgrounds. Accordingly, Appadurai favors the liberal arts college (for undergraduates) over the research schools (for postgraduates). He envisages (in what he refers to as a "utopia") the former as training a cosmopolitan self, with the latter only leading to reliable knowledge and a more restricted and technically competent self (mere "brains" perhaps, to revert to Hoggart).

Appadurai, then, has a new solution to this new version of incompleteness: an insistence upon the minoritarian as part and parcel of a liberal arts education. This idea(l) includes "area studies" along with anything that might count as " 'minors,' 'minorities,' and 'minor literatures' " (1996: 34). So his "positive" conclusion is that:

> The critical revitalization of the cultural study of other parts of the world (area studies) is thus at least one way in which to restore the primacy of the liberal-cosmopolitan ideal of discipline over the later, research-driven ideal of disciplinarity. (1996: 35)

Perhaps paradoxically, in the light of the earlier moments of cultural studies we have examined – or perhaps not, because neither Williams nor Hoggart, as we have seen, completely rejected "the liberal-cosmopolitan ideal of discipline"[1] – what appears to have returned with the incorporation of "area" and other "minoritarian" studies is an insistence on an older and more traditional cultivation of the self:

> The idea of discipline in the liberal arts aims to cultivate a certain sort of cosmopolitan liberal self among students. The idea of discipline that underpins the practice of research has very little to do – normatively – with any sense of a morally weighted sense of a liberal self, and has everything to do with the means and techniques for scrutinizing the world and producing knowledge that is both new and valid. (1996: 32)

Here, then, is a "liberal self" not completely dissimilar from that which Williams describes when he writes of "people for whom [intellectual work] is not a way of life, for whom it is not in any probability a job, but for whom it is a matter of their own intellectual interest, their own understanding of the pressures on them, pressures of every kind, from the most personal to the most broadly political" (Williams 1989: 162). Here again, a certain politics of identity and a set of life pressures traditionally disconnected with the academy is met by a humanities curriculum that "aims to cultivate a certain sort of cosmopolitan liberal self among students." This last expression could almost have issued from Arnold's own pen when he defines "culture" as "the disinterested and active use of reading, reflection, and observation, in the endeavour to know the best that can be known" (1889: 137).

Clearly, then, while there are parallels between the formative moments of cultural studies (in Hoggart and Williams) and more recent concerns elsewhere, we must still wonder whether Appadurai's "minorities" are a simple paradigmatic substitution for, say, Hoggart's Scholarship Boy. They may actually be working with quite different models of the relation between the traditional university and its "others." For Hoggart, it's a question of *translation* and the ethics of translation: between the "foreign" world of the universities replete with their "snail-eating Frenchmen" (1957: 183) and the boy from Leeds learning how to communicate on "civil" terms. For Appadurai and the "new vanguard," it's a question of political *representation*: majorities in the academy being forced to make way (first numerically, then culturally) for minorities in what is imagined as a universal and utopian forum.

In both cases however, and for all these important differences, we can notice that the resultant position on (inter) discipinarity – again, qualitatively different in each case – emerges not as a willed and radical curricular choice but as a vital structural response and solution to the *necessary incompleteness* that must arise when any self undergoes the rigors of institutional transformation; whether this self is the one who, for Hoggart, is "clever enough to take himself out of his class mentally, but not equipped, mentally or emotionally, to surmount all the problems that follow," or whether it's Arnold's or Appadurai's "certain sort of cosmopolitan liberal self."

Bennett: The End of Incompleteness?

A contrasting example to Appadurai of the shifting sense of (inter)disciplinarity in cultural studies is a recent series of interventions on the question by Tony Bennett (1993, 1998a, 1998b). The point of difference needs to be set against the background of some basic similarities. Like Appadurai, Bennett sees the new "diversity" of the university as requiring the issue to be thought in different terms from the early work of Hoggart and Williams (1998b: 37). Like Appadurai, he also works with a distinction among rationales for the humanities' academy between a "cultivation of selves" and the development of more abstract principles of theory and method. But where Appadurai favors the first of these, Bennett opts instead for the second. In doing so, he makes what is probably the strongest case to date for a full acceptance by cultural studies of a distinct disciplinary status. Rejecting what he sees as a romantic aversion to "technical competence," Bennett calls for the field "to lay claim to a definite set of knowledge claims and methodological procedures that will be convertible...into clearly defined skills and trainings that will prove utilisable in a range of spheres of practical life" (1998b: 52).

Bennett's target, then, is effectively *half* of Appadurai's double sense of the term "discipline." He rejects what Foucault (1970) would call the "transcendental" side of the double: discipline as "care, cultivation, habit" – but he positively values what Foucault calls the "empirical" (or perhaps, technical) side: discipline as "field, method, subject matter," to repeat Appadurai's definitions. What we might ask – and we will take this up in our conclusion below – is whether this turn to discipline as an empirical–technical mono-concern "solves" the problem of the structural (and, as we shall see, the equally ethical) incompleteness that we have found in various and very distinct forms in the work of Hoggart, Williams, and Appadurai. Before we can do this, however, we need some background to Bennett's intervention.

Bennett's position on disciplinarity emerges out of more general criticisms of an understanding of cultural studies as fundamentally grounded in "marginality" or "resistance" (for which see Bennett 1992, 1998b). Such an understanding, he argues, is both historically inaccurate and an obstacle to any realistic assessment of possibilities for the field. In the British case at least, cultural studies did not develop outside or in opposition to established institutions but within pedagogical spaces marked out by government – in the secondary school system, the extramural sector of the universities, then later within the universities themselves. Drawing on a Foucauldian understanding of governmentality, particularly as mediated through the work of Ian Hunter (1988, 1992, 1994), Bennett concludes that "the enabling conditions of cultural studies are located in precisely that sphere, the sphere of government and social regulation, to which cultural studies has usually supposed itself to be opposed" (Bennett 1998b: 46).

Bringing this perspective to bear on the question of disciplinarity, Bennett detects a certain bad faith in a continuing reluctance of cultural studies to characterize itself as a discipline. If we survey the scene today, he points out, the field has all the expected institutional trappings of a discipline. It has a recognizable and increasingly prominent place in university curricula in Australia, the United States, Canada, and Britain and to some extent also in the Asia-Pacific region and South Africa. There are a number of international refereed journals in the field as well as professional associations, conferences, and research centers: "Viewed in terms of the nature and extent of its institutionalization, then, there is little to distinguish cultural studies from many other areas of work in the humanities" (Bennett 1998a: 532). It is quite normal, Bennett argues, for systems of thought to begin their careers by "creating some elbow room for themselves within the existing array of disciplinary knowledges" (1998b: 41). But to claim a permanent aura of exceptionality – as somehow "outside" or "beyond" the disciplines – is merely evasive: "the need ... to define precisely how an emerging system of thought draws on and combines the techniques and methods of existing disciplines into distinctive new configurations cannot be indefinitely deferred" (1998b: 41).

The costs, for Bennett, in resisting a disciplinary normalization are twofold. It means, first, that intellectual authority tends to take, in Max Weber's sense, traditional or prerational forms: "The lack of a clear set of methodological precepts and theoretical principles has made cultural studies particularly prone to the organization of forms of authority based on the personal qualities of intellectuals" (Bennett 1998a: 533). In his distaste for personalized forms of authority, Bennett is sharply at odds with Appadurai's weaker sense of discipline – which he might even see as *anti*discipline – as a "cultivation of liberal-cosmopolitan selves." But he is also at odds with the senses of interdisciplinarity which emerge from the early work of Hoggart and Williams. This can be seen most clearly in a new interpretation given to the recurrent theme of incompleteness. For Bennett, following Hunter, the relevant context in which to understand this theme is not the structural position of cultural studies (which is how we have looked at incompleteness so far) but a form of romantic aesthetics, a concern with the fully-rounded development of a self that can balance its outward functional duties as citizen and its inward ethical duties towards itself. Implicit in this idea of incompleteness is an "epistemological norm of totality" which is established in opposition to the partializing effects of disciplinary divisions: "the constant demonstration of . . . incompleteness is . . . the means by which the case for wholeness is advanced" (1998b: 59; see also Miller 1993).

The second cost of refusing a disciplinary status is that it places cultural studies in a double bind. Any move towards such a status appears as a failure, betraying a process of institutional co-option and a consequent loss of critical potential. But as Bennett points out, this comes close to placing the field in a position in which it *cannot* succeed. If nothing is done to specify and consolidate its techniques, principles, and methods then it will also fail. The options become "institutionalize and perish, don't institutionalize and perish anyway" (1998a: 534).

Bennett's position is, however, a complex one, for he recognizes a number of ways in which cultural studies has cut across boundaries between the established disciplines. This is partly because of the nature of its concerns: the adoption of a broad definition of culture, the contextualization of cultural forms, and the address to broad themes of power and subjectivity have all involved building bridges, particularly between the humanities and social science disciplines. But there have also been institutional factors: the shift away from an expensive "researcher-in-the-archive" model of training in the humanities to a collective, group-based process of deciphering cultural documents has been a response partly to the vast increase in student numbers (1998b: 46). Balancing these observations against his desire to "discipline" cultural studies, Bennett suggests that the field might be seen as a kind of "interdisciplinary clearing house within the humanities" or, more paradoxically, an "interdisciplinary discipline" (1998a: 535). But, for all that, a discipline first and foremost.

Conclusion: Incompleteness as Structure and Ethics

Bennett's intervention into the (inter)disciplinarity debate, then, might help us pause to consider whether the *structural* incompleteness we have located in the developments from Hoggart to the present is not, in fact, related to an *ethical* incompleteness. Hunter (1993) (whose work, as we have seen, clearly informs Bennett's) has argued for this theme in relation to the history and (perhaps most importantly) the prehistory of cultural studies in and as a form of romanticism. For Hunter, this romantic project involves the development of a post-Kantian self that, ideally, would reach a position of equipoise between its empirical (practical, alio-ethical) and its transcendental (abstract, auto-ethical) capacities, producing "a well-bred, partly sensuous and partly ethicointellectual human being" (Kant 1978: 185). In effect, this self is "man," the "empirico-transcendental doublet" announced as our condition under modernity by Foucault towards the end of *The Order of Things* (1970: 303–43). That condition, particularly after Kantianism, is one of a doublet in eternal ethical imbalance seeking an impossible homeostasis of its two parts. Hence: eternal incompleteness. Although Hunter's use of this figure is complex and too detailed to be rehearsed here, we can readily draw up a table, using "empirical" and "transcendental" as proxies for the many names of this (essentially romantic) doublet, to show how – from a Hunterian perspective – our various forms of *structural* incompleteness could relate to this ethical form (table 3).

One interest of the Bennett–Hunter position, then, is that it shows how the *structural necessity* of incompleteness which prompts a parallel necessity of interdisciplinarity (as argued for in the present chapter) could map onto an *ethical* field of incompleteness, resulting in a particular type of trained subject which Hunter (1993) calls the "critical intellectual." Equally necessarily, then, if the Bennett–Hunter model's only radical intervention is, effectively, to delete one side of this ethical binary (rather in the way that, more than a century ago, Nietzsche deleted the similarly transcendental side of the famous Platonic binary), then, structurally, it is *bound* to return to a version of disciplinarity.

The question that remains – for us, in another paper; for cultural studies, as a pressing matter – is whether this return to disciplinarity, this technical-empirical-governmental exclusion zone, is sufficient to see cultural studies out of its alleged complicity with the post-Kantian "romantic" cultivation of the self and its necessary structural and ethical incompleteness. Is half a binary any more of a radical solution than a full one? Is half a binary even a possibility?

Table 3 Cultural studies: empirico-transcendental doublets

	Empirical	*Transcendental*
Hoggart (Scholarship Boy):	"brains"	"habitus"
Williams (structures of feeling):[2]	"structure"	"feeling"
	"institution"	"agency"

Appadurai (discipline):
"field, method,
subject-matter"
"care, cultivation, habit"
Bennett:
"technical competence"

–

What we might argue instead is that cultural studies, historically, empirically, through a series of what we might think of as "genetic" changes and alterations – particularly concerning new and distinct populations coming to inhabit the humanities academy over the course of the second half of the twentieth century – is *structurally overdetermined* to become interdisciplinary.[3] That condition being the case, cultural studies then becomes liable not just to being accounted for *ex post facto* as a variation on a theme of romantic aesthetics but also to being colonized or overtaken by romantic aesthetic discourses in actual institutional practice. However, while this double liability is a matter of historical fact and can be documented, it is by no means (as Bennett and Hunter appear to think) a necessary or intrinsic part of cultural studies as such. Foucault reminds us, in this case, of two important factors. First, if the "man" of modernity is indeed the empirico-transcendental doublet, it is always (at least until after modernity) going to be wishful thinking to keep either side of the doublet pure and alone. (And we should note that any attempt to do so, even in the name of historical contingency and the piecemeal, will always risk its own form of totalization.) Secondly, in all historical and disciplinary scenarios, including the history of cultural studies, things must remain contingent and could always have been otherwise.

Notes

1 As Andrew Milner reminds us, while Hoggart saw cultural studies as fundamentally interdisciplinary in itself, he nevertheless believed, quite contrary to Appadurai, that it should be a field of *postgraduate research* taking in undergraduates with "an initial discipline outside Cultural Studies ... an academic and intellectual training, and a severe one," preferably in "the social sciences, history, psychology, anthropology, literary study" (Hoggart 1995: 173; Milner 1999: 273).
2 Note that the terms "institution" and "agency" are not Williams' own but our own gloss. Also, as we have pointed out above, Williams refuses an oppositional relation between "structure" and "feeling" by concatenating them.
3 This argument confirms that of Readings in *The University in Ruins* (1996). Readings argues that, to quote Culler's useful summation, "cultural studies is made possible by a recent shift in the governing idea of the university" (1999: 343).

References

Appadurai, A. (1996). Diversity and Disciplinarity as Cultural Artifacts. In C. Nelson and D. P. Gaonkar, eds., *Disciplinarity and Dissent in Cultural Studies*. New York: Routledge.

Arnold, M. (1889). *Culture and Anarchy: An Essay in Political and Social Criticism* (popular edn.). London: Smith, Elder & Co. (Originally published 1869.)

Bennett, T. (1992). Putting Policy into Cultural Studies. In L. Grossberg, C. Nelson, and P. Treichler, eds., *Cultural Studies*. New York and London: Routledge.

Bennett, T. (1993). Being "In the True" of Cultural Studies. *Southern Review* 26, 2: 217–38.

Bennett, T. (1998a). Cultural Studies: A Reluctant Discipline. *Cultural Studies* 12, 4: 528–45.

Bennett, T. (1998b). *Culture: A Reformer's Science*. Sydney: Allen & Unwin.

Culler, J. (1999). What is Cultural Studies? In M. Bal, ed., *The Practice of Cultural Analysis: Exposing Interdisciplinary Interpretation*. Stanford: Stanford University Press.

Foucault, M. (1970). *The Order of Things: An Archaeology of the Human Sciences*. London: Tavistock. (Original work, *Les Mots et les choses*, published 1966.)

Hoggart, R. (1957). *The Uses of Literacy: Aspects of Working-class Life, with Special Reference to Publications and Entertainments*. London: Chatto & Windus.

Hoggart, R. (1995). *The Way We Live Now*. London: Chatto & Windus.

Hunter, I. (1988). *Culture and Government: The Emergence of Literary Education*. London: Macmillan.

Hunter, I. (1992). Aesthetics and Cultural Studies. In L. Grossberg, C. Nelson, and P. Treichler, eds., *Cultural Studies*. New York and London: Routledge.

Hunter, I. (1993). Setting Limits to Culture. In G. Turner, ed., *Nation, Culture, Text: Australian Cultural Studies*. London: Routledge.

Hunter, I. (1994). *Rethinking the School: Subjectivity, Bureaucracy and Criticism*. Sydney: Allen & Unwin.

Kant, I. (1978). *Anthropology from a Pragmatic Point of View*, trans V. L. Dowdell, rev. and ed. by H. H. Rudnick. Carbondale: Southern Illinois University Press. (Original work, *Anthropologie in pragmatischer Hinsicht*, published 1798.)

Miller, T. (1993). *The Well-tempered Self: Citizenship, Culture and the Postmodern Subject*. Baltimore: Johns Hopkins University Press.

Milner, A. (1999). Can Cultural Studies be Disciplined? Or Should it be Punished? *Continuum: Journal of Media and Cultural Studies* 13, 2: 271–81.

Pickering, M. (1997). *History, Experience and Cultural Studies*. London: Macmillan.

Readings, W. (1996). *The University in Ruins*. Cambridge, Mass.: Harvard University Press.

Williams, R. (1965). *The Long Revolution*. Harmondsworth: Penguin.

Williams, R. (1976). *Keywords: A Vocabulary of Culture and Society*. London: Fontana.

Williams, R. (1989). The Future of Cultural Studies. In R. Williams, *The Politics of Modernism*. London and New York: Verso.

Chapter 3

Is there a Cultural Studies of Law?

Rosemary Coombe

To address the question of whether there is a cultural studies of law, I will explore contemporary scholarship that assumes cultural perspectives on law by focusing on some of its most recent thematic preoccupations: identity, narrative, and justice. This survey is representative rather than comprehensive and concludes with an assertion and an agenda. The assertion is simple: although there are numerous cultural legal studies, no cultural studies of law is easily discernible. Although legal texts, legal forums, and legal processes have been analyzed as cultural forms, no substantial body of work demonstrating the methodological commitments, theoretical premises, and political convictions that characterize the interdisciplinary field of cultural studies has yet appeared with respect to law. The agenda I propose is more complex and, at this point, somewhat enigmatic. I suggest that a cultural studies of law will only emerge as a distinctive field of academic inquiry when scholars stop reifying law and start analyzing it as culture.

Defining the cultural studies of law is no easy task. Over the last 20 years, we have witnessed a proliferation of legal studies that borrow methods and approaches from the humanities and focus quite self-consciously on law's textuality. During this time we have seen the scholarship from the "sister" field of law and society adopt a less behavioralistic and richer interpretive approach to the social life of law, resulting in law's effects being understood less instrumentally and more constitutively: as legitimating the meanings, shaping the identities, and defining the perspectives through which we understand ourselves in the world. Finally, a revitalized legal anthropology continues to explore and develop these propositions in a wide variety of ethnographic studies (Darian-Smith 1999; Maurer 1997; Riles 1999). These three streams – legal humanities, interpretive sociolegal studies, and legal anthropology – primarily constitute the body of cultural legal studies. As with other scholarly fields in the 1980s and 1990s, this field embraces a social-constructionist framework where the law is seen not simply as applying to a preexisting social world but as actively creating the social world as we experience it.

The cultural study of law, then, is an interdisciplinary enterprise involving sociologists, anthropologists, literary scholars, and legal academics. Its traits clearly distinguish it from traditional legal scholarship. As Paul Kahn argues in *The Cultural Study of Law* (1999), conventional legal scholarship has been a remarkably undertheorized discipline precisely because most of its students have never stood outside of its practice. Legal critique has been pervasively tied to the empirical project of legal reform and legal scholars have come to the study of law with deep commitments to continue as citizens of law's republic to seek its improvement (Kahn 1999: 7). Because theory and practice are conceptually inseparable in this kind of intellectual work, nothing separates the conventional legal scholar from the object of her study and even those legal scholars who borrow from other disciplines largely do so in order to rationalize legal judgment, to better analyze social policy issues, and to expose particular ideological positions in order to achieve clarity and integrity in legal thought. Many critics argue that legal scholarship has been impoverished by the almost exclusive mandate directed at legal reform as well as the predominant assumption that scholarly work should be oriented towards judicial edification (Schlag 1996).

Cultural legal studies may be distinguished from conventional legal scholarship by a lack of commitment to the traditional legal scholar's main motivation for critical study: the perfectibility of legal reasoning. Moreover, cultural studies of law look at legal sites in ways that differ from the institution's own self-understandings and self-descriptions. For example, in a representative collection entitled *Law's Stories*, editor Paul Gewirtz tells us that: "Books about law typically treat it as a bundle of rules and social obligations. This book is different. It looks at law not as rules and policies but as stories, explanations, performances and linguistic exchanges – as narratives and rhetoric" (1996: 2). Questions about legal representation – the images, conventions, and narratives used in legal reasoning – preoccupy those working in the cultural study of law. Some of the earliest constructionist work focused on the way in which the law operates as a particular form of world-making. Anthropologist Clifford Geertz (1983) showed us that the law never simply finds facts but actively creates those facts to which it seemingly applies universal and neutral rules. Critical legal studies demonstrated early on that the way in which the law constructs legal facts results in the legal recognition of some harms but not others (Kelman 1981). Kim Lane Scheppele, for example, has explored the legal treatment of rape in terms of men's and women's conflicting understandings of events, the way facts are deemed relevant or irrelevant, and the process by which appellate-level opinions engaged in determinations of consent arrive at an understanding of the "truth" often through the manner in which the event is recounted (1992). Through her analysis, Scheppele successfully shows that law is biased not simply in terms of doctrine, but in its very construction and reading of the facts. Similarly, Gary Peller (1985) has considered the ways in which the existence or non-existence of consent in rape cases turns upon the expansion or contraction of the time frame or the perceived relevance of surrounding circumstances. All are astute readings

37

of how the law works through selective representations that construct legally relevant facts. Purely textual readings of judicial opinions that consider legal representation of bodies (Hyde 1997) – which I will discuss below – and sexualities (Colker 1996) provide similar insights.

The studies discussed above can be described as analyses of legal constructionism. Because they see law as having cultural form and consequence, each is a cultural study of law. Nonetheless, none of them provides much evidence of a cultural studies of law as a distinct field of legal inquiry.

Identity

We can best understand the insights of legal constructionism by considering how it contrasts with more conventional approaches in a particular field of inquiry. The development of feminist concerns with sexual inequality and gendered injustice provide an apt illustration and historical precedent for the growing understanding of law as constituting social identity. For many years, feminist legal scholarship assumed a modern instrumentalist understanding of law as a set of rules that could be transformed through reform to better serve all women's interests. The law was seen as the impartial instrument offered by the state to mediate and arbitrate neutrally. According to liberal feminists, both the state and the law could be amended incrementally through feminist reform to promote women's equality and to instill a gender-neutrality that would open public spheres to women. For radical feminists, on the other hand, law operated as a tool of patriarchy maintaining male dominance through the imposition of false dichotomies such as the public/private that maintained the invisibility of women's subordination. Law reform efforts were seen by most radical feminists to be misguided projects likely to be co-opted until women, through consciousness-raising, came to see the artificiality of these dichotomies and took direct control over sexuality and reproduction through separatist strategies. Although the radical feminist realization that legal structures were neither impartial nor objective but contained fundamentally androcentric biases was important, many feminists became frustrated by the theoretical and practical obstacles inherent in both the radical and liberal approaches as well as their lack of politically workable strategies:

> Two main problems have been identified, both of which stem from the instrumentalist, dichotomous analytical focus of liberal and radical feminisms. First, abstract concepts such as law and state are reified. That is, "things" are materialised and transformed into determining and controlling "actors"; for example, law becomes either the liberator or oppressor of (passive) women. Second, liberal and radical feminisms are characterised by essentialism or the attribution of an innate meaning to concepts, such as law, state, and sex/gender, which unifies the concepts and leads to dichotomization (e.g., male versus female). If we consider women and men to be homogenous groups, for instance, both intra-gender

differences and inter-gender commonalities are erased. In efforts to avoid reifica-
tion and essentialism, feminists have developed a diversity of theoretical
approaches to law that collectively have shifted the analytical focus from law as
an instrument to law as a gendering practice. (Chunn & Lacombe 2000: 6–7)

Approaches to law as a gendering practice are inspired by a "social constructionist
conception of law as a hegemonic discourse that can be deconstructed and
reshaped through the mobilisation of feminist counter-discourses" (Chunn &
Lacombe 2000: 2). Both Marxist and Foucauldian approaches have been influential in this understanding. Marxist legal history showed not only how law operated
historically to create and maintain power differentials in society, but that it also
afforded ideological resources and opportunities to simultaneously challenge
these structures of inequality. Socialist feminists came to understand that Law's
influence in maintaining female subordination was more complex and shifted over
time: sometimes law played an overt role through legislation and criminalization
but, in other historical periods, law's role might be more ideologically indirect in
its legitimizing and sustaining of male supremacy. Carole Smart's work (1989,
1992, 1995) was important in developing the distinction between law as adjudica-
tion and legislation and the law as practice. Her work also illustrated the ways in
which formal legal gains may actually disadvantage women to the extent that
women's class positions are not fully taken into account. In the social world, law
does not apply evenly and the law's "uneven development" is a consequence of
the law's formal application of equality to women who are differently situated
socially. Smart's "woman-in-law," or the "gendered subject position which legal
discourse brings into being" (1992: 34), has, however, been criticized by contemporary feminists as too monolithically constructed by too unidirectional a
process emanating from a too-limited articulation of law as a site and a practice.

A recognition of the legal construction of identity is perhaps most fully
developed in current feminist scholarship. Today's feminist cultural studies of
law reject liberal understandings of the subject as an autonomous, intentional,
and freely operating agent and share the social-constructionist insight that
subjectivities are shaped by legal structures that constrain agency even as that
agency may, in turn, transform these same structures (Coombe 1989). As discussed above, the law as structure is better understood in Foucauldian terms as
both a discourse (a coercive web of interconnecting disciplines of knowledge
governed by a particular conception of rationality) and a set of institutions and
institutional practices through which the discourse is made manifest. The law,
therefore, is no longer conceived as a power that resides exclusively with the state
but participates in the creation of diffuse and pervasive forms of power that
constrain and enable agency in social life. This view of social relations significantly informs a poststructuralist feminism that draws upon both Foucault and
Bourdieu as theoretical touchstones. Judith Butler's (1990) poststructuralist anti-
essentialism has been particularly influential in this respect. Her work reverses
traditional wisdom that saw gender as the social interpretation of natural sexual

differences and asserts instead that the sexed body is an artifact of legal and medical impositions of gender. Similarly, Chunn and Lacombe write that "[u]nderstanding the role of law in the production of gender is all the more important today because law is so pervasive, having penetrated every corner of our lives" (Chunn & Lacombe 2000: 17).

Many poststructuralist and anti-essentialist theoretical premises connect a growing body of American identity-based legal scholarship (Aoki 1996; Chang 1999; Delgado 1995a; LatCrit 1997) which shares the understanding that:

> The law functions as one of the principal social forces constructing individual and collective identities in direct and indirect ways. The legal system's role in defining and often circumscribing the meaning of race, color, ethnicity, national origin, and other such categories forms, conforms, and deforms the identities of racial and ethnic minorities. This process has been a central theme in critical race theory, Asian American legal theory, and most recently LatCrit theory. The legal system's role in defining gendered identities has been a central theme in radical legal feminism and its role in defining sexual identities has been a central theme in queer legal theory. (Montoya 1998: 37; citations omitted)

As Margaret Montoya further notes: "courts often choose to validate or to invalidate characteristics pertaining to individual and collective identities that are inconsistent with the way individuals see and define themselves. In its hegemonic reinforcement of a majoritarian identity as normative, the legal system confounds the attempts by Chicanos/as and other Outsiders not to be seen as aberrant, deviant, or Other" (1998: 140). However, the attempt by such outsiders to voluntarily "racialize" themselves, by adopting such signs of otherness as their own expressions – as affirmative markers of their consciousness of difference – is often prescribed by courts and legislatures who have upheld the rights of employers and others to prohibit certain styles of clothing, speech, and hairstyle (Montoya 1998: 141–2).

The limited ability of legal categories to acknowledge multiple forms of social subordination was one of the early insights from identity-based scholarship and nurtured the now burgeoning literature on intersectionality. The concept of intersectionality developed from the understanding that persons rarely occupy just one legal category of identity and that the law fails to recognize the complexity of their situations as a consequence (Crenshaw 1989, 1991). A disabled woman of color, for example, experiences gender oppression differently because of her race and experiences racial discrimination differently because of her gender and disability. Many women of color complain that white feminists still do not recognize that these dimensions of women's lives are not mutually exclusive but operate as intersecting and often invisible matrices of domination (Agnew 1996). More recently, national, cultural, and historical contexts have been added to those factors which combine to create subject positions. Ratna Kapur (1999) advocates the use of a concept of hybridity to understand post-colonial identities in her reading of India's cultural wars as a means of countering the longing for purity in cultural groups, values, and traditions. The desire for substantive essentialism manifested in the search for authentic cultural identities inevitably becomes reactionary and exclusive and effects a form of conceptual violence that may be actualized in physical violence against ethnic, sexual, and racial others. Intersectionality and hybridity have become the basis for a variety of politics – a strategic intersectionality – which "attempts to substitute analysis of differences based on essences for those based on political and cultural contexts, thereby creating the possibility for deeper comprehension and political alliance between feminists" and other potential political coalitions (Belleau 2000: 22).

Although much of this identity-based scholarship allegedly professes to understand the ambiguity of identity, ambiguity is too often merely asserted rather than described and explored. Moreover, much of this literature projects a possessive individualism onto subjects in the attribution of their identities. People always already "have" and possess awareness and ownership over their identities even when these are constructed or intersectional. An allegedly social-constructionist stance is often disarmingly coupled with a humanist insistence upon the centrality and unimpeachability of "lived experience" and the individual capacity to excavate one's authentic or "hidden self" (Montoya 1998: 139). The transparency of experience assumed here belies the very tenets of social constructionism, such as its understanding of the unrelenting social shaping of consciousness and the cultural forms of experience which are branches of knowledge molded by multiple fields of power.

Indeed, identity-based scholarship may overemphasize the law as a form of discourse without paying adequate attention to the material and institutional techniques of governmentality through which subjectivities are constituted and self-governance inculcated. Cultural studies that deploy the Foucauldian framework of governmentality explore law as a "legal complex" that intersects with other domains (e.g., economy, welfare, education) and their logics (e.g., health, longevity, death), sites (e.g., family, school, business), and modes of governance:

> Foucault suggested [that] the workings of this legal complex had become increasingly pervaded by forms of knowledge and expertise that were non-legal. Its regulations, practices, deliberations and techniques of enforcement increasingly required supplementation by the positive knowledge claims of the medical, psychological, psychiatric and criminological sciences, and the legal complex thus enroled a whole variety of "petty judges of the psyche" in its operations. Further, the legal complex had itself become welded to substantial, normalizing, disciplinary and bio-political objectives having to do with the reshaping of individual and collective conduct in relation to particular substantive conceptions of desirable ends. The legal complex, that is to say, had been governmentalized. (Rose & Valverde 1998: 542–3)

As a methodological approach, governmentality asks why, for instance, homelessness or prostitution emerge as a focus for government attention and action and what role is played by legal institutions, officials, and rationalities in this process. In other words, how does a problem become the object of legislation and who are the authorities that define the problem? Sean Watson (1999) uses the lens of governmentality to understand the affective milieu of the collective social life particular to police officers, characterized by a kind of paranoia centered on the "thin blue line between chaos and order" (p. 234). The institutional and social consequences of a cultural milieu that cannot deal with ambiguity, complexity, or difference and which highly valorizes authority, control, rightness, stability, security, dominance, and masculinity manifest themselves in discriminatory beliefs and practices directed at particular social groups such as black youth and gays and lesbians and the contrasting lack of concern about and punishment of white-collar criminals (Watson 1999: 236).

Indeed, the "new penology" is considered the quintessential area for sociolegal cultural studies:

> The project of new penology is to identify the kinds of persons who pose risks to others, and to render them harmless through exclusion (from certain venues such as public houses, football grounds, shopping malls or residential areas, or from society as a whole through long-term incarceration); surveillance (CCTV, electronic tagging); or by rendering them harmless through chemotherapy or allied techniques (compulsory medication of psychiatric patients).
>
> With its changed objectives, new penology uses techniques such as actuarial calculation of population characteristics and crime rates, and computer mapping of crime locations. Statisticians and geographers become the new criminologists, displacing sociologists, whilst psychologists engage in factor analysis of populations of offenders rather than analysis and therapy with individuals. (Hudson 1998: 556)

Governmentality has colonial origins and implications. Duncan Ivison (1998) discusses the significance of the nation and its "biologized state racism" which operated to identify, contain, or erase "degenerates" or "abnormals" conceived of ethnically, physically, or psychologically in colonial regimes of power (p. 564). Conceptions of citizenship, rights, and liberty formed the self-image of the colonizers who carried these emergent logics with them. Given the ongoing relationship of aboriginal peoples to a history of colonial administration, this is one area of legal study where the governmentality framework is considered especially promising.

As the governmentality literature suggests, considerations of identity rooted in an understanding of law as discourse often ignore the importance of institutional matrices, technologies of power, and material constraints that have historically shaped subjectivities. In identity-based scholarship, the "legal system" appears to refer exclusively to appellate-level courts and their reported reasons for judgment. This is not altogether surprising given the combined effect of the location of these scholars – in the legal academy – and their disciplinary expertise – primarily consisting of the interpretation of authoritative legal texts. Within anthropology and sociolegal studies, however, the law's construction of social identities is more likely to be explored empirically and in its inception in local legal disputes. For example, a 1994 symposium issue of the *Law and Society Review* devoted to "Community and Identity in Sociolegal Studies" contained three articles about Native American peoples' struggles to shape and influence the legal categories of identity used to define them. In this symposium, Wendy Espeland, Carole Goldberg-Ambrose, and Susan Staiger Gooding all recognized that "the potential of legally mediated categories to mark difference, shape consciousness, and inform the actions of those who confront them is a crucial form of power" (Espeland 1994: 1176). These ethnographically based studies give us a richer understanding of the processes through which the cultural self-understandings of a people confront the structures of definition that characterize Western legal systems.

As a growing body of law and society scholarship illustrates, the law itself plays an important role in shaping consciousness. These scholars share a commitment to examine legal structures and relationships in people's everyday social experience – often referred to as the "commonsense." David Engel (1998) outlines two widespread and overlapping approaches to the study of legal consciousness:

> At one end of the continuum, the power and resistance model sees law as significant because of its capacity to organize the categories, structures, meanings, and practices which less powerful people must then negotiate as they attempt to reclaim some portion of social space for their own. At the other end of the continuum, the communities of meaning model sees law as significant because of its symbolic centrality in the struggle among social groups to develop authoritative definitions of community, of social order and belonging, of appropriate behavior, and of law itself. (p. 138)

The most important, and arguably the most undertheorized, aspect of legal consciousness is the link between structure and agency. Culture and consciousness, writes Peter Fitzpatrick (1998), link structure and agency, yet social-constructionist and identity-based scholarship rarely problematize the basic claim that law, as a social construct, permeates and is inseparable from everyday living and knowing but nonetheless is tempered by human agency which can avoid, resist, invoke, or reconstruct this structure (pp. 188, 198). We need a dialogic and dynamic understanding of legal consciousness, then, that can address how ordinary citizens become knowing and effective agents who challenge and transform aspects of particular forms of structural domination (Fitzpatrick 1998: 191–4).

Given the proliferation of identity-based scholarship in the past decade, it would be premature to anticipate its demise. A transmutation is more likely given that scholars who are engaged in identity-based work express an evident desire to link studies of identity-formation to a larger set of issues and a wider field of contexts that will shed light on historically specific forms of power and knowledge. Thus, for example, Robert Chang (1999) considers the "Asian-American" in relation to the racialized and sexualized narratives of an American national imaginary and the history of nativism, and advocates a move away from identity politics and towards political identities based upon shared political commitments "using the goal of a radical and plural democracy as an organizing principle" (p. 8). Similarly a group of scholars call for a "postidentity scholarship" that attempts to "articulate a set of strategies that acknowledge our simultaneous and ambivalent desire both to affirm our identities and to transcend them" (Danielson & Engle 1995: xv). Despite the desire to transcend identity, however, few would concur with Kenneth Karst's assertion (1995) that racial and sexual orientation identities are myths and that social groups identified thereby are mere metaphors that need to be destroyed. Nor would many agree with Walter Benn Michaels (1997), who argues that all cultural identities are essentially racial and therefore must be dismantled. More typical is Dorothy Roberts' position (1999) that identity is an activity rather than an essence, a history, or a property and serves as a political act of identification that remains open to critique in ongoing movements for social change.

An understanding of law "as a hegemonic process, an apparatus, or ensemble of practices, discourses, experts, and institutions, that actively contributes to the legitimation of a social order" (Chunn & Lacombe 2000: 10) may be more promising for considerations of identity. Legal arenas and legal discourses are important sites for the construction of hegemony because they provide spaces and resources for struggles to establish and legitimate authoritative meanings (Coombe 1989, 1991). Conversely, law will be key to counterhegemonic political struggle as movements like LatCrit begin to offer what Francisco Valdes (2000) calls a "postsubordination" vision that "goes beyond critique, beyond unpacking and deconstructing . . . [and] . . . entails articulation of substantive visions about reconstructed social relations and legal fields . . . Postsubordination vision as jurisprudential method therefore calls for some hard thinking and honest talking about the type of postsubordination society that 'we' are struggling toward" (p. 839; see also Harris 1999). Elsewhere I have argued that law not only provides the generative conditions and prohibitive boundaries for hegemonic articulations (Coombe 1998b, 2000a) but also constitutes one of the means and media for the cultural politics that articulates the social. The law provides the very signifying forms that constitute socially salient distinctions, adjudicating their meanings, and shaping the practices through which such meanings are contested or disrupted. The law invites and shapes, but never determines, activities that legitimate, resist, and potentially rework and transform the meanings that accrue to these public discourses (Coombe 1998b: 35–7). From this position, identities may be seen as no more than temporary and unstable resting points in longer and heterogeneous political quests for recognition, inclusion, legitimation, and identification.

Narrative

Since the 1980s, sociolegal scholars have turned their attention increasingly towards the study of the power of language in legal processes. I cannot do justice here to all of the various approaches and perspectives upon legal language, but will point to particular themes that are likely to be of most interest to those working in cultural studies. For many scholars, law's hegemonic power is located in its forms of discourse, with narrative being recognized as one of its most powerful.

Paul Gewirtz asserts that scholars and the public are drawn to law as a theater where vivid human stories are played out – and where they are told and heard in distinctive ways and with distinctive stakes (1996). As they came to recognize the analogies between law, literature, and drama, sociolegal scholars increasingly turned to theories of narrative to understand law's rhetorical and epistemological power. Gewirtz points to the growing disenchantment with law's claims to the superiority of its own forms of reason as motivating the narrative turn and relates this to a wider loss of faith in objectivity (and other metanarratives) as well as the embrace of social constructionism.

Martha Minow offers Hannah Arendt's methodological commitment to narrative over more conventional forms of social-science exposition to buttress the claims of those scholars who study the narratives law offers and occludes (Minow 1996). Although Arendt felt that social science was necessary to describe human behavior, she also argued that narrative was necessary to capture the often ineluctable meaning of human action. In the aftermath of totalitarianism, storytelling was for Arendt the proper communicative mode for political theory, rather than the rational discourse of the social sciences which conventional legal scholarship aspires to replicate:

> Storytelling can disrupt the illusion that social sciences create in the service of rational administration, the illusion that the world is a smoothly managed household. Storytelling invites both teller and listener to confront messy and complex realities – and to do so in a way that promotes communication and thinking about how to connect the past and the future by thinking about what to do. Rather than taking the view that only experts understand and act in the political world the political theorist who tells stories thinks about politics in a way that remains faithful to the capacity of citizens to act together. (Minow 1996: 33)

Following Arendt, Minow sees the narrative form as having a particular moral resonance that connects past to present as well as author to reader and thereby has an innate capacity for rendering evident that plurality of perspectives at play in any given event or phenomenon. Stories, she suggests, do not articulate principles, provide consistency, guide future action, or provide firm grounds for evaluation or judgment; nor do they replace legal doctrine, economic analysis, jurisprudence, or sociological explanation. Instead, the revival of narrativity should be welcomed as a healthy disruption and dialogic challenge to the certainties of these other forms of approaching the law (Minow 1996: 36).

> Examining law as narrative and rhetoric can mean many different things: examining the relation between stories and legal arguments and theories; analyzing the

45

different ways that judges, lawyers, and litigants construct, shape, and use stories; evaluating why certain stories are problematic at trials; or analyzing the rhetoric of judicial opinions, to mention just a few particulars . . . it means looking at facts more than rules, forms as much as substance, the language used as much as the idea expressed . . . how it is made, not simply what judges command but how the commands are constructed and framed . . . It sees laws as artifacts that reveal a culture, not just policies that shape the culture. And because its focus is story as much as rule, it encourages awareness of the particular human lives that are subjects or objects of the law, even when that particularity is subordinate to the generalizing impulses of legal regulation. (Gewirtz 1996: 3)

The trial is seen as a particularly important arena where multiple actors (lawyers, witnesses, and judges) compile and communicate stories; it is also a forum in which particular kinds of stories are rendered out of bounds – confessions and some victim impact statements, for instance. Scholars believe that "focusing on the trial process as a struggle over narratives can give even familiar trial phenomena a fresh look" (Gewirtz 1996: 7). The recognition that trials have multiple audiences, e.g., juries, judges, fellow counsel, potential clients, the media, the public, and that audiences themselves have an impact upon how narratives are presented, adds new interpretive dimensions to our understanding of legal processes. I would suggest, however, that a more fully interpretive and historically contextualized scholarship might explore the ways that courtroom narratives intersect, refract, and compete with broader social narratives (Coombe 1991; Ferguson 1996; Weisberg 1996), and that a fuller understanding of the role of narrative in the legal process must attend to the full range of pre-trial processes. Few disputes are litigated, and of those cases that are, few go to trial; nonetheless legal narratives are shaped and shape consciousness and behavior at every step along the way.

In much of the work on legal narrative, however, the object of study seems to become its own subject or agent of powers that appear rather magical. Marianne Constable (1998) cites Douglas Maynard's study of plea bargaining, in which narrative forms "shape and narrow the range of what kind of truths can be told" (1990: 89). In his view, the characteristics of a case, or the legal niceties it poses, are not irrelevant to the plea bargaining process, but they "are talked into being by way of narrative and narrative structure" that "clearly affects the course of negotiations" (1990: 92). Indeed, Maynard even suggests that "narratives and their components may be devices for 'doing' the identities by which principal actors in the discourse are known" (1990: 87). Similarly, in Bennett and Feldman's work on the representation of the real in courtrooms, the ability of people with very different relationships to the law to communicate meaningfully about the issues in legal cases has to do with the fact that "stories produce a clear definition of an action and the conditions surrounding it" (1981: 10). This is because juries transform evidence into stories that create the contexts for social action and frameworks for judgment (Bennett & Feldman 1981: 3, 7). Other, less deterministic studies suggest that "jurors come to the trial with a set of stock stories in their minds and that they try to fit trial evidence into the shape of one of those stock stories. Lawyers, then, will have an easier time persuading a jury that their side's story is true if they can shape it to fit some favorable stock story" (Gewirtz 1996: 7). Joseph Sanders' work (1993) on pharmaceutical product liability trials tends to support this; he found that plaintiff's lawyers, despite the legal merits of the case and good scientific evidence that suggested that the drug was not the cause of the injury, nonetheless presented stories of corporate malfeasance. Juries seemed to find statistical evidence of probabilities unsatisfactory and discounted it because it didn't provide the comfort of narrative closure (Munger 1998: 48). Like most people, they "are not good at thinking statistically or probabilistically; they are much more comfortable thinking literarily, teleologically, religiously, narratively" (Dershowitz 1996: 104).

Indeed, Alan Dershowitz argues that such stock stories are both powerful and deceptive. Everyday life, after all, is rarely structured by the canons of dramatic narrative and is filled with irrelevant actions, coincidences, and random events: "In Chekhovian drama, chest pains are followed by heart attacks, coughs by consumption, life insurance policies by murders, telephone rings by dramatic messages. In real life, most chest pains are indigestion, coughs are colds, insurance policies are followed by years of premium payments, and telephone calls are from marketing services" (Dershowitz 1996: 100–1). To the extent that juries come to trials with expectations shaped by Chekhovian (or television) dramas, then, the truth finding function of the adjudicative process is imperiled: "A good defence lawyer – at least one with a client who has a motive and an opportunity – will not offer a competing narrative, but instead refute the narrative form by convincing the jury that the narrative is an uninformed fantasy and that the crime is random, inexplicable and perhaps, from an aesthetic point of view, disappointing" (Dershowitz 1996: 101).

The majority of scholarship on narrative in the legal process, however, focuses upon legal judgments, which are increasingly read as literary texts. It is impossible to review the entire body of law and literature scholarship that focuses on the US Constitution and its interpretation, but, as Peter Brooks reminds us, such cases provide obvious opportunities for rhetorical analysis.

> The story of the case at hand must be interwoven with the story of precedent and rule, reaching back to the constitutional origin, so that the desired result is made to seem an inevitable entailment. If narrative may be said to start at the end – in that we know an end is coming and that beginning and middle will retrospectively make sense in its terms and seem an enchainment of cause and effect – constitutional adjudication claims to start from the beginning, in first principles laid down in the Constitution itself. Constitutional adjudication is always in some measure a story of origins, reaching back to our founding text and ur-myth…As in Sartre's description of narrative, the story really proceeds in the reverse: its apparent chronology, from beginning to end, may cover up its composition, from end to beginning. (Brooks 1996: 21)

However, as Robert Weisberg asserts, there may be "some dangerously unexamined ethical and political consequences of 'narrative affirmance'" (Weisberg 1996: 63). The law engages the aesthetic strategies of narrative in the service of an authoritative version of the cultural identity of a nation, and to that extent, enshrines ethical and political values. Drawing upon Hegel, he represents the desire to narrate as the desire to represent authority and history as "the relation that the state has established between a public present and a past that a state endowed with a constitution made possible." The state requires narrative for the representation of its particular politics of community; "a nation emerges into political rationality through narrative – with its textual strategies and 'metaphorical displacements'" (Weisberg 1996: 78). The social authority of the nation is the basis of law, but the devices of law are continually required to represent the nation and its authority. Narrative study in legal scholarship should, according to Weisberg, attend to this unstable relationship. Weisberg points to a deeper subtext of historical cultural narratives that are reenacted in important trials as the community itself is put on trial and reconstructs itself poetically.

As well as a body of scholarship that attends to the influence of narrative in shaping legal forms of power, there is also a revival of the use of narrative in the self-conscious scholarship of law professors who identify with minority communities and seek to redress the injustices visited upon these communities by legal structures. This work uses stories or defends storytelling as having a distinctive power for those who stand in opposition to legal regimes and for outsider groups in general: "Telling stories (rather than simply making arguments), it is said, has a distinctive power to challenge and unsettle the status quo, because stories give uniquely vivid representation to particular voices, perspectives, and experiences of victimization traditionally left out of legal scholarship and ignored when shaping legal rules" (Gewirtz 1996: 5; Dalton 1996). Such "outsider scholarship" includes critical race theory (Delgado 1989, 1990, 1995a, 1995b; Johnson 1991; Matsuda et al. 1993; Williams 1991), Asian-American thinking (Aoki 1996; Chang 1999), LatCrit scholarship (Montoya 1998), and new variants of gay and lesbian scholarship (Fajer 1992; Valdes 1995), all of which draw upon personal histories, parables, chronicles, dreams, poetry, and fiction that help to reveal and undermine the law's dominant structures.

These scholars understand narrative as central both to identity formation and to activities that resist and challenge traditional forms of legal knowledge. Dwight Conquergood's conception of narrative is an apt description of the concept of narrative that informs this type of work:

> Narrative is a way of knowing, a search for meaning, that privileges experience, process, action, and peril. Knowledge is not stored in storytelling so much as is enacted, reconfigured, tested, and engaged by imaginative summonings and interpretive replays of past events in the light of present situations and struggles. Active and emergent, instead of abstract and inert, narrative knowing recalls and recasts

experience into meaningful signposts and supports for ongoing action. (Montoya 1998: 130; citing Conquergood 1993)

Margaret Montoya, for instance, offers narrative as "mediating" the constructionist effects of law and as offering an expressive counterpoint to the legal categories that minorities are forced to occupy. She draws on the critical pedagogy of Peter McLaren, who argues that "border identities" are created out of empathy for others through means of a passionate connection that is furthered by narrative. For such identities to be created, however, it is necessary to forge critical connections between "our own stories and the stories of others" (Montoya 1998: 134). Evidence of such linkages is, unfortunately, still quite rare in this literature. Nor is it clear what "mediation" is being accomplished and in what fashion. "Narratives, and especially autobiographical stories, can be acts of resistance and acts of transformation," we are advised (Montoya 1998: 142). But when, and how, will this occur?

By speaking personal truths to institutional powers, these "outsider scholars" attempt to strengthen their ties to their communities of identification, publicly affirm an othered identity, and give cultural specificity and experiential dimension to the histories of legal identification and categorization. For example, Montoya puts historically important cases involving Latinas/os into narrative form and juxtaposes these with more personal narratives to make manifest the relation between individual and collective experience; in so doing, she asserts that the effects of a [legal] discourse that has been used to disempower Latinas/os are somehow mitigated. Montoya herself is unsure to what extent these narratives are "subversive" and draws upon Patricia Ewick and Susan Silbey's (1995) distinction between hegemonic and counterhegemonic narratives. A hegemonic story depicts understandings of particular persons and events while effacing the connections between the particular and the social organization of experience, whereas a counterhegemonic narrative is one that is narrated from a position of social marginality, reflects upon how the hegemonic is constructed as an ongoing concern, and is told in circumstances that "reveal the collective organisation of personal life" (Ewick & Silbey 1995: 220–1). A good storyteller, it would appear, is simply a good sociologist.

As Gewirtz notes, there are many questions about this scholarship that remain unaddressed (1996: 6). When do stories compel and when do they repel audiences? What attributes of "outsider stories" enable them to have an impact upon listeners who are otherwise unreachable by traditional arguments? The legal storytelling movement tends to valorize narrative as more authentic, concrete, and embodied than traditional legal reasoning. But, Brooks insists, "storytelling is a moral chameleon, capable of promoting the worse as well as the better cause every bit as much as legal sophistry. It can make no superior ethical claim" (Brooks 1996: 16). Chang (1999) would appear to agree. He validates the use of narrative in critical scholarship not because he believes in the existence of a unique and unquestionably authentic voice that belongs to people of color, but because narrative self-consciously introduces the issue of social perspective into a scholarly field that has traditionally denied its significance. He does not believe that personal narrative can be validated on the basis that it challenges the current formulation of legal objectivity, reveals its biases, and provides the means to reconstruct it to make it more inclusive (Chang 1999: 69). Instead, he assumes a more radical, poststructuralist approach that rejects "standpoint epistemology" and favors an antifoundationalism that permits value judgments only from within particular social contexts and recognizes that no external or fully inclusive social standard for legitimation may in fact exist. Narrative's chief purpose is to persuade, and since it is the existence, nature, scope, and variety of forms of social oppression and subordination that outsider scholarship aims to make visible and have redressed, narrative is compelling for this limited, but still vitally significant, goal (Chang 1999: 75).

An emerging group of scholars use narrative analysis as a means of rethinking the nature of the sexualized, racialized, and gendered subject. Their work is distinctive in its emphasis upon corporeality. For example, both Alan Hyde and Peter Brooks attend to the body as a bearer of narratives: "the private body is a kind of narrative total or all the moral choices made by the subject that owns the body, the individual protagonist of the narrative: the crimes committed, the drugs ingested. Such bodies are narrative texts that the law relates to as a reader" (Hyde 1997: 152–3). Hyde asks how legal discourse constructs the body as a holder of legally relevant evidence, and examines the process through which such evidence is legally extracted, presented, and analyzed. He notes that this public use of the body is jurisprudentially balanced against and ultimately limits the privacy of any given person's body (Hyde 1997: 158–61). Invasive procedures like body cavity searches, medical diagnoses of sexual offenders, and medical testing for drug use are publicly acceptable forms of embodied violence. It is impossible, however, to maintain that more justice will result from the endorsement of a more "privatized" body because this simply operates to condone the varieties of "domestic" violence that are often publicly ignored.

Rather than accept the legal tendency to render judgment upon spurious categorizations of bodily practices as public or private, Hyde attempts to "denaturalize" social constructions of the body by highlighting the instability and incoherence of the categories in actual social life. He contrasts, for example, the legal treatment of nudity, and particularly female exposure and the relative acceptance of strip clubs and newspaper pin-ups, with the ambivalence or rejection of breastfeeding in public, topless sunbathing, or Mapplethorpe portraits of male body parts (Hyde 1997: 131–50). In feminist scholarship, Frances Olsen points out that not only has the traditional juridical subject been male but the universal "unproblematic body" has also been male (Olsen 1996: 211–12). Often corporeality, associated with the feminine, comes to signify the uncontrollable, disruptive, irrational, and expansive. Social fears become located in and represented by the female body (Bumiller 1998: 151) and nurtures scapegoating and loathing while fostering a concurrent repressed desire for this conceptualized opposite.

Pheng Cheah and Elizabeth Grosz (1996) go so far as to propose that "[p]lacing the body, rather than consciousness, intention or interiority in the center of legal focus ... may help account for and perhaps even transform the existing social inequities which make an abstract system of law participate in and reproduce these inequities" (p. 25). The widespread acceptance of rape as a war crime or crime against humanity is one instance where an understanding of the narrativization of corporeality in forging ethnic and national identities has helped to influence a major shift in the international legal order and its treatment of women. Attending to the body in these theoretical and practical projects has produced, incrementally yet hopefully not minimally, an opportunity for realizing greater justice.

Justice

In most of the cultural studies of law we have explored, the power of language in constituting legal power, and the power of certain linguistic forms to challenge that power, is flatly assumed. As Marianne Constable notes, language in this work is conceived of as resolutely social, and the social, it would appear, is all-encompassing (Constable 1998). In these texts, there is nothing outside of the social world, or beyond its representations, therefore the social world can fully represent itself. A certain metaphysics of social presence pervades these works. Consequently, they cannot adequately address the phenomenon of justice; though arguably a sense of injustice motivates many of these studies. Constable remarks that the lack that is injustice appears always to be located in silence – in the absence of story and voice, the absence of an articulable relation with the past, traditions which cannot represent their knowledge of themselves – such that the law speaks and the other is mute before it. An absence of voice is presumed to mean both an absence of power and an absence of justice; conversely, to posses voice is to be fully empowered and to realize justice (Constable 1998: 30). This inattention to justice issues, she suggests, is due to the very positivity of law (whether it is glossed as the legal system or legal discourse) that so much of this work assumes. Rather than emphasize the law's complete presence, she proposes that considerations of justice compel us to articulate the law's historical indeterminacy – the "eternal deferral of the coming-into-existence of any actual positivist legal system" (Constable 1998: 25).

The equation of voice with power and justice, as Constable suggests, affirms a particular constellation of legal positivism, liberalism, and a positivist social science which sociologizes law and accepts without question liberalism's construction of subjects who are compelled to speak in order to legitimate government. The speaking subject, she reminds us, is a liberal imposition, and liberal theory must constantly project speech onto silence in order to find in this silence

51

messages of consent or resistance. Invoking the work of poststructuralist legal theorists such as Drucilla Cornell (1992) and Peter Fitzpatrick (1992), Constable urges scholars to attend to "the limits of speech and to places where the texts of liberalism, positive law, and sociolegal study fall silent. In these places one encounters the limits of liberalism, legal positivism, and sociolegal study: the justice of which they do not speak" (Constable 1998: 32). To grasp law exclusively as a powerful social discourse is to fail to comprehend its limits and to encounter its others.

There is now a large scholarly literature deploying the methods or techniques of deconstruction. Although most of it engages in purely philosophical and doctrinal analysis, some of this scholarship takes seriously the claim that "deconstruction is justice" (Derrida 1992: 15) because it addresses the limits of law's rationality and its constitutive absences. Deconstruction is a means of making visible those others who are invisible in legal discourse and the dominant narratives it reproduces. Shannon Bell and Joseph Couture, for example, discuss the moral panic over child pornography that gripped a Canadian city in 1993 and show how the court – in conjunction with the psychiatric/psychological/social work professions, the police, and the media – "gendered the young male hustlers as victims and their gay male clients as abusers in a hegemonic narrative of justice . . . premised on homophobia, ageism, and whorephobia" (Bell & Couture 2000: 40), This narrative ignored the high incidence of physical abuse visited upon female teenage prostitutes, denied the active desire and consent expressed by male teenage hustlers, and excluded the very possibility of hebephilia (love for the young man who has passed the age of puberty). By using testimony, victim impact statements, and media interviews, Bell and Couture resurrect the representations of these interactions offered by the boys and young men involved. By uncovering complex relationships in which the interplay of power, desire, need, and pleasure exceeded the law's categorical imperatives, their study also recovered evidence of police pressure deployed to compel these boys into characterizing their activities in legally recognizable forms of culpability and injury that reinforce heterosexual normativities.

If legal processes and determinations effect characteristic forms of social repression, such repressions, according to Robert Ferguson (1996), never die but return to haunt legal consciousness. If Freud equates the rule of law with the development of civilization and civilization with creating a force-field of repression, then the performance of the rule of law, not surprisingly, sees the return of the repressed in the form of the uncanny (Ferguson 1996: 89). Unfortunately, Ferguson provides little explanation or elaboration for the underlying proposition that the law can be understood using a psychological dynamic, and we are given no basis to comprehend how the law comes to be structured psychically. An anthropological explanation for the institutional creation of shadowed places as well as the analysis of structural amnesia, however, is offered as an alternative approach that places the emphasis upon ascertaining "the impossible thoughts" and "the principles of institutional coherence that allow some repressed thoughts to escape oblivion" (Ferguson 1996: 89). In a remarkable reading of a brief trial following an 1800 slave insurrection, Ferguson effectively makes the case that because processes of public memory are enacted in courts of law, trials enable and invite the return of the repressed:

> [A] story wrongly refused by the law will return in the republic of laws as cultural narrative and, often enough, as renewed legal event. The law does not get beyond what it has not worked through. The pendulum swings back because the culture has made an ideological commitment to social justice and because the expectation of justice causes injustice to loom large. (Ferguson 1996: 97)

A consideration of law as a site of memory is an important recent theme in cultural studies of law. Like Ferguson's work, many of these studies draw upon psychoanalytic theory to focus upon trials as sites of commemoration and remembrance in which past trials are drawn upon, and key hidden or repressed elements in national historical cultural dramas return to contemporary consciousness (Sarat & Kearns 1999). Reva Siegel, for example, compares race and sex discrimination claims and shows how the former, inevitably linked to memories of slavery and segregation, always recall dramas of national shortcoming in a fashion that the latter do not (Siegel 1999).

Shoshana Felman explores the law's limits and the return of the repressed in her demand that cultural studies of law respect "the absolutely fundamental relation of the law to the larger phenomenon of cultural or collective trauma":

> the law remains professionally blind to this phenomenon with which it is nevertheless quite crucially and indissociably tied up. I argue that it is because of what the law cannot and does not see that a judicial case becomes a legal trauma in its own right and is therefore bound to repeat itself through a traumatic legal repetition...Legal memory is constituted, in effect, not just by the "chain of law" and by the conscious repetition of precedents, but by a forgotten chain of cultural wounds and by compulsive or unconscious legal repetitions of traumatic, wounding legal cases. My analysis will show how historically unconscious legal repetitions inadvertently play out in the historical arena the political unconscious of the law (the unconscious of past legal cases). These traumatic repetitions illustrate, therefore, in legal history, the Freudian notion of "a return of the repressed"; in the ghost of the return of a traumatizing legal case, what compulsively, historically returns from the forgotten legal past is the repressed of the judicial institution. (Felman 1999: 30)

She perceives the O. J. Simpson trial (although she appears to restrict her analysis to media reports and their interpretations of the trial) as reenacting national traumas of interracial and gendered violence. Cases like these, she suggests, inadvertently trigger the movement of a repetition or the dynamics of legal recall (i.e., the Simpson case reviving the Rodney King trial which itself may have conjured up the Dred Scott case). In such repetition the trial tries to resolve the trauma, but through such repetitions the trauma repeats itself by reopening an unconscious legal memory that, as Ferguson asserted, is ever bound to resurface. The O. J. Simpson trial, in her reading of it, revolved around something that could not be seen and that in fact was not seen – the invisible relation between marriage and domestic violence (Felman 1999: 58). The (black) jurors were unable to see the victim's battered face, her bruises or the husband's blows, just as (white) jurors in the Rodney King case could not see the beating or police abuse. The inability to see abuses of power is, she insists, "inscribed in culture as a trauma" (Felman 1999: 63). Felman assumes that trauma may be collective as well as individual, that traumatized communities, including oppressed groups, suffer repeatedly beyond the shock of the initial act of wounding, and that these repetitions are paradoxically both a reenactment of the injury and a form of psychic survival. Trauma is precisely that which cannot be seen – even within the law's penetrating gaze. Nonetheless, trauma is constitutive of law:

> Despite its topicality in modern thought, trauma theory has not yet penetrated jurisprudential studies. Since the consequence of every criminal offense (as well as of its legal remedy) is literally a trauma (death, loss of property, loss of freedom, fear, shock, physical and emotional destruction), I advance the claim that trauma – individual as well as social – is the basic underlying reality of the law. (Felman 1999: 35)

Such psychoanalytically informed work is promising from the perspective of a critical cultural studies of law because it provides analytical means for moving beyond law's positivity and presents avenues for exploring legal ambiguity and the absences, blindnesses, and characteristic failures that shape fields of legal power and knowledge. Still, a number of issues remain vexing. So much of this work centers upon American race relations that one cannot help but wonder whether it has wider applications. "The law," moreover, seems to have a unitary and reified quality in this scholarship that tends to narrowly focus on either constitutional cases or highly publicized criminal trials. References to a national cultural unconscious may be justified in this context, but how helpful will such an approach be in other doctrinal areas and other legal forums? Is it entirely illegitimate to pose questions about the representivity of such cases when they are offered up as representing the basic underlying reality of law? Isn't the very idea of an institution as complex as law having a singular, basic, underlying reality a structuralist claim incongruent with the very tenets of poststructuralist theory and deconstructionist methods? What other cases were considered in the process of arriving at this assertion? Now that cases are recognized as possessing an unconscious, the work of reading them has no doubt doubled in terms of the effort it requires, but surely the task needs to be undertaken if generalizations about the law are going to be made. Whether generalizations about "the law" should be made on the basis of singular cases, even if they can be shown to be representative, is a larger and perhaps more significant question.

In a more nuanced and more thoroughly researched study of the use of chain gangs in Arizona prisons, Joan Dayan (1999) reminds "us that the commemorative sites of law are not simply textual, but may also involve particular kinds of materialization of legal power. The memory that is encoded in the materializations of law's power found in chain gangs is the memory of slavery" (p. 19). The spectacle of contemporary chain gangs, which she relates to prison isolation units, conditions of confinement, and executions, reproduces a peculiar specularity in which the judicial non-existence of particular (black, male) bodies is marked by and attached to a historical regime of hypervisibility which, nonetheless, the law does not see by virtue of a blind adherence to precedent that denies the inmate any civil status. Through historical investigation, textual analysis, and ethnographic inquiry, Dayan's work points to the constitutive absences in the law's fields of vision as she explores the material realities of contemporary correctional practices and the ruses state officials deploy to justify their denial of inmate rights in knowing relation to the law's symbolic power. This work is especially welcome for its variety of sources and its diversity of analytical methods as well as for providing a rare example of cultural materialism in legal studies. It points in the direction of a cultural studies of law by attending to meaning and materiality as these are produced in a multiplicity of social sites.

Conclusion

The interdisciplinary field of cultural studies is distinctive and valuable because of its potentially careful consideration of the local complexities in the relations between power and meaning in everyday life. If the cultural study of law were to treat law the way the field of cultural studies has learned to approach culture, a critical cultural studies of law might become a meaningful, robust, and exciting field of intellectual inquiry (Coombe 1998b and 1998c; Coombe & Cohen 1999). Rather than applying a formalist approach to cultural artifacts as discrete works or self-contained texts, cultural studies focuses upon the social power of textuality. However, in many – if not most – cultural studies of law, the approach to law is as a body of discrete works (appellate cases) or singular texts (usually trials) which are simply read internally for an understanding of their cultural effects. In too many instances we get little or no inkling of the specific histories of these texts' production, consumption, reception, or circulation. Moreover, we are not given any sense of the social power of forms of legality or their meaning in forms of life that exist anywhere outside of the legal trial or the reported case. A cultural studies of law should become more attentive to social fields of inscription and the social life of law's textuality. With the emergence of identity-based scholarship and work on legal consciousness, however, this work is beginning to get done. Some of these texts give us more understanding of how some of law's dominant forms of representation are experienced by those in subordinate positions.

Cultural studies, however, requires multiple and shifting perspectives through the diverse contexts of a cultural form's social being in the world:

> [W]e cannot know how a text will be read simply from the conditions of its production, any more than we can know which readings of a text will become salient meanings within people's everyday lives. Scrutinizing texts in terms of their formal qualities tells us nothing about their conditions of production of consumption, the basis of their authority, or their likely interaction with existing ensembles of cultural meanings in the experiences of specifically situated subjects. These "reservoirs of discourses and meanings are in turn raw material for fresh cultural production. They are indeed among the specifically cultural conditions of production." If we think about law as central to the cultural conditions of producing everyday life we would recognize that we· need to augment the interpretive strengths of textual analysis with sociological methods of tracing networks of actors and considerations of the political economy of seeking justice. (Coombe 1998b: 47; citing Johnson)

Whereas cultural studies has showed us that the privileged canon of the humanities – literature – was not a discrete form of discourse that could be clearly distinguished, segregated, and elevated, but shared properties and relationships with a variety of discourses including travel-writing, medical texts, radio talk-shows, and mass media, many of those who study law culturally make vague references to "legal discourse" that serves to avoid any need to go beyond a Lexus database of cases, statutes, and legal doctrine. When such scholarly acts of traveling and "transgression" do occur (as with comparative readings of literature and film), they often skim the theoretical surfaces, providing brief if entertaining enlightenment of discrete texts, but often leaving unexplained the rationale for the textual comparison or its social consequence.

The starting-point for cultural studies is that culture is contested, fractured, marred by contradictions, and therefore the site of social struggle. Feminist and gay and lesbian legal studies in particular (Bower 1994) have made substantial headway in exploring the ways in which legal terms and categories contain fissures and faultlines that become the sites for political mobilization. Too many cultural studies of law treat contradiction as if it were purely an internal and resolvable property of legal discourse. The politics of producing and maintaining legal structures of meaning cannot be explored in many of these works because no agents of production are ever identified. I would agree with Austin Sarat's contention that, even in legal scholarship that attempts to treat law culturally, "[l]aw acts, law rules. There are no people, no actors, no agency" (2000: 139). The law too often appears as a monolithic, undifferentiated, univocal power akin to some sort of totalizing *deus ex machina*. Legal pluralism is rarely acknowledged, and the social situation and motivations of those actors who act within specific legal institutions and local legal structures are seldom considered. And, while cultural studies articulates relationships between cultural meanings and social and material inequalities, the cultural studies of law largely avoids any investigation into the material dimensions of legal meaning. As I have elsewhere implored:

> It is important that in the turn toward understanding law culturally . . . we do not lose sight of the political stakes at issue, the material domains of signification, or the distributional impacts consequent upon having one's meanings *mean something*. The role of law in institutions itself must be addressed – not simply as an overarching regulatory regime, or a body of institutions to which disputes are referred, but as a nexus of meaningful practices, discursive resources, and legitimating rhetoric – constitutive features of locally specific social relations of power. (Coombe 1998b: 45)

The scholarly transition from seeing the law as fully representing and shaping a social world that is transparent to the legal system, to acknowledging the significance of the repressed, the silenced, and the misrecognized in law, is a change long overdue and most welcome. For a critical cultural studies of law, however, this movement might suggest more than the postulation of a national repressed or the unconscious of a legal case and point more specifically to spaces of social marginality. We might consider that the law's greatest cultural impact may be felt where it is least evident, that the law is working not only when it is encountered in its most authoritative spaces, but also when it is consciously and unconsciously apprehended. The moral economies created in the shadows of law, the threats of legal action made as well as those that are carried out, people's everyday fears and anxieties about the law, are all loci where the law is doing cultural work (Coombe & Herman 2000b). The law shapes social identities and forms of politics even when it fails to recognize identities (Bower 1994) and, as I show elsewhere, a politics of non-identification based on non-identity has been legally engendered (Coombe 1998b). Law's absences may have presences elsewhere, but these traces will not be revealed to those who study law culturally but do not move beyond legal texts and media accounts of legal proceedings.

Although we can discern a large and engrossing body of legal studies that assumes cultural perspectives and considers law as a cultural phenomenon, there is as yet no substantial body of work that can be identified as a cultural studies having law as its subject-area of inquiry. Until scholars attend to the social life of law's textuality and address law's multiplicity and multivocality in creating fields of cultural politics, the cultural study of law is likely to remain a predominantly formalist and politically irrelevant branch of the humanities.

Suggested Reading (in addition to the References below)

Alfieri, A. (1991). Speaking Out of Turn: The Story of Josephine V. *Georgetown Journal of Legal Ethics* 4: 619–53.
——. (1991). Reconstructing Poverty Law Practice: Learning Lessons of Client Narrative. *Yale Law Journal* 100: 2107–48.

Binder, G. and Weisberg, R. (2000). *Literary Criticisms of Law*. Princeton: Princeton University Press.

Gilkerson, C. (1992). Poverty Law Narratives: The Critical Practice and Theory of Receiving and Translating Client Stories. *Hastings Law Review* 43: 861–945.

Guttierrez-Jones, C. (1995). *Rethinking the Borderlands between Chicano Culture and Legal Discourse*. Berkeley: University of California Press.

Haney López, I. (1996). *White by Law: The Legal Constructions of Race*. New York: New York University Press.

Hunt, A. (1993). *Explorations in Law and Society: Towards a Constitutive Theory of Law*. New York: Routledge.

Kelman, M. (1987). *A Guide to Critical Legal Studies*. Cambridge, Mass.: Harvard University Press.

Minda, G. (1999). *Boycott in America: How Imagination and Ideology Shape the Legal Mind*. Carbondale: Southern Illinois University Press.

Sousa Santos, B. de. (1995). *Toward a New Common Sense: Law, Science, and Politics in the Paradigmatic Transition*. New York: Routledge.

Wildman, S. M., et al. (1996). *Privilege Revealed: How Law, Language, and the American Mind-set Uphold the Status Quo*. New York: New York University Press.

References

Agnew, V. (1996). *Resisting Discrimination: Women from Asia, Africa, and the Caribbean and the Women's Movement in Canada*. Toronto: University of Toronto Press.

Aoki, K. (1996). Foreign-ness and Asian-American Identities: Yellowface, World War II Propaganda and Bifurcated Racial Stereotypes. *Asian Pacific American Law Journal* 4: 1–60.

Bell, S. and Couture, J. (2000). Justice and Law: Passion, Power, Prejudice, and So-called Pedophilia. In Chunn, D. and Lacombe, D. (eds.), *Law as Gendering Practice*. Don Mills, Canada: Oxford University Press.

Belleau, M. C. (2000). Intersectionalité: Feminisms in a Divided World (Quebec–Canada). In Chunn, D. and Lacombe, D. (eds), *Law as Gendering Practice*. Don Mills, Canada: Oxford University Press.

Benn Michaels, W. (1997). The No-drop rule. *Critical Inquiry* 20: 758–69.

Bennett, W. L. and Feldman, M. (1981). *Reconstructing Reality in the Courtroom*. New Brunswick, NJ: Rutgers University Press.

Bower, L. (1994). Queer Acts and the Politics of "Direct Address": Rethinking Law, Culture, and Community. *Law and Society Review* 28: 1009–33.

Brooks, P. (1996). The Law as Narrative and Rhetoric. In Brooks, P. and Gewirtz, P. (eds.), *Law's Stories: Narrative and Rhetoric in Law*. New Haven: Yale University Press.

Bumiller, K. (1998). Body Images: How does the Body Matter in the Legal Imagination? In Garth, B. and Sarat, A. (eds.), *How Does Law Matter?* Chicago: Northwestern University Press.

Butler, J. (1990). *Gender Trouble: Feminism and the Subversion of Identity*. New York and London: Routledge.

Chang, R. (1999). *Disoriented: Asian Americans, Law, and the Nation State*. New York: New York University Press.

Cheah, P. and Grosz, E. (1996). The Body of Law: Notes Toward a Theory of Corporeal Justice. In Cheah, P. et al. (eds.), *Thinking Through the Body of the Law*. New York: New York University Press.

Chunn, D. and Lacombe, D. (2000). Introduction. In Chunn, D. and Lacombe, D. (eds.), *Law as a Gendering Practice*. Don Mills, Canada: Oxford University Press.

Colker, R. (1996). *Hybrid: Bisexuals, Multiracials and Other Misfits under American Law*. New York: New York University Press.

Constable, M. (1998). Reflections on Law as a Profession of Words. In Garth, B. and Sarat, A. (eds.), *Justice and Power in Sociolegal Studies*. Chicago: Northwestern University Press.

Coombe, R. (1989). Room for Maneuver: Toward a Theory of Practice in Critical Legal Studies. *Law and Social Inquiry* 14: 69–121.

——. (1991). Contesting the Self: Negotiating Subjectivities in Nineteenth-century Ontario Defamation Trials. *Studies in Law, Politics, and Society* 11: 3–40.

——. (1998a). *The Cultural Life of Intellectual Properties: Authorship, Appropriation and the Law*. Durham: Duke University Press.

——. (1998b). Contingent Articulations: A Critical Cultural Studies of Law. In Sarat, A. and Kearns, T. (eds.), *Law in the Domains of Culture*. Ann Arbor: University of Michigan Press.

——. (1998c). Critical Cultural Legal Studies. *Yale Journal of Law and Humanities* 10: 463–86.

—— with Cohen, J. (1999). The Law and Late Modern Culture: Reflections on *Between Facts and Norms* from the Perspective of a Critical Cultural Legal Studies. *Denver University Law Review* 76: 1029–55.

——.(2000a). *Between Law and Culture*. Minneapolis: University of Minnesota Press.

—— and Herman, A. (2000b). Transforming Trademarks: From Mass to Popular Culture on the World Wide Web. *DePaul Law Review* 49, forthcoming.

Cornell, D. (1992). *The Philosophy of the Limit*. New York: Routledge.

Crenshaw, K. (1989). Demarginalizing the Intersection of Race and Sex: A Black Feminist Critique of Antidiscrimination Doctrine, Feminist Theory, and Antiracist Politics. *University of Chicago Legal Forum*: 139–67.

——. (1991). Mapping the Margins: Intersectionality, Identity Politics, and Violence against Women of Color. *Stanford Law Review* 43: 1241–99.

Dalton, H. (1996). Storytelling on its Own Terms. In Brooks, P. and Gewirtz, P. (eds.), *Law's Stories: Narrative and Rhetoric in Law*. New Haven: Yale University Press.

Danielson, D. and Engle, K. (1995). Introduction. In Danielson and Engle (eds.), *After Identity: A Reader in Law and Culture*. New York: Routledge.

Darian-Smith, E. (1999). *Bridging Divides: The Channel Tunnel and English Legal Identity in the New Europe*. Berkeley: University of California Press.

Dayan, J. (1999). Held in the Body of the State: Prisons and the Law. In Sarat, A. and Kearns, T. (eds.), *History, Memory, and the Law*. Ann Arbor: University of Michigan Press.

de Certeau, M. (1984). *The Practice of Everyday Life*, trans. Steven F. Rendall. Berkeley: University of California Press.

Delgado, R. (1989). Storytelling for Oppositionists and Others: A Plea for Narrative. *Michigan Law Review* 87: 2411–41.

———. (1990). When a Story is Just a Story: Does Voice Really Matter? *Virginia Law Review* 76: 95–111.

———(ed.) (1995a). *Critical Race Theory: The Cutting Edge*. Philadelphia: Temple University Press.

———. (1995b). Rodrigo's Final Chronicle: Cultural Power, the Law Reviews, and the Attack on Narrative Jurisprudence. *Southern California Law Review* 68: 545–75.

Derrida, J. (1992). Force of Law. In Cornell, D. et al. (eds.), *Deconstruction and the Possibility of Justice*. New York: Routledge.

Dershowitz, A. (1996). Life is Not a Dramatic Narrative. In Brooks, P. and Gewirtz, P. (eds.), *Law's Stories: Narrative and Rhetoric in Law*. New Haven: Yale University Press.

Diprose, R. (1996). The Gift, Sexed Body Property and the Law. In Cheah, P. et al. (eds.), *Thinking Through the Body of the Law*. New York: New York University Press.

Engel, D. (1998). How Does Law Matter in the Construction of Legal Consciousness? In Garth, B. and Sarat, A. (eds.), *How Does Law Matter?* Chicago: Northwestern University Press.

Espeland, W. (1994). Legally Mediated Identity: The National Environmental Policy Act and the Bureaucratic Construction of Interests. *Law and Society Review* 28: 1149–79.

Ewick, P. and Silbey, S. (1992). Conformity, Contestation, and Resistance: An Account of Legal Consciousness. *New England Law Review* 26: 731–49.

———. (1995). Subversive Stories and Hegemonic Tales: Toward a Sociology of Narrative. *Law and Society Review* 29: 197–226.

Fajer, M. A. (1992). Can Two Real Men Eat Quiche Together? Storytelling, Gender-role Stereotypes, and Legal Protection for Lesbians and Gay Men. *University of Miami Law Review* 46: 511–651.

Felman, S. (1999). Forms of Judicial Blindness: Traumatic Narratives and Legal Repetitions. In Sarat, A. and Kearns, T. (eds.), *History, Memory, and the Law*. Ann Arbor: University of Michigan Press.

Ferguson, R. A. (1996). Untold Stories in the Law. In Brooks, P. and Gewirtz, P. (eds.), *Law's Stories: Narrative and Rhetoric in the Law*. New Haven: Yale University Press.

Fitzpatrick, P. (1992). *The Mythology of Modern Law*. London and New York: Routledge.

———. (1998). Missing Possibility: Socialization, Culture, and Consciousness. In Sarat, A. et al. (eds.), *Crossing Boundaries: Traditions and Transformations in Law and Society Research*. Chicago: Northwestern University Press.

Geertz, C. (1983). *Local Knowledge: Further Essays in Interpretive Anthropology*. New York: Basis Books.

Gewirtz, P. (1996). Narrative and Rhetoric in the Law. In Brooks, P. and Gewirtz, P. (eds.), *Law's Stories: Narrative and Rhetoric in Law*. New Haven: Yale University Press.

Goldberg-Ambrose, C. (1994). Of Native Americans and Tribal Members: The Impact of Law on Indian Group Life. *Law and Society Review* 28: 1123–48.

Gooding, S. S. (1994). Place, Race, and Names: Layered Identities in *United States* v. *Oregon, Confederated Tribes of the Colville Reservation, Plaintiff-Intervenor*. *Law and Society Review* 28: 1181–229.

Harris, A. (1999). Building Theory, Building Community. *Social & Legal Studies* 8, no. 3: 313–25.

Hudson, B. (1998). Punishment and Governance. *Social & Legal Studies* 7, no. 4: 553–9.

Hyde, A. (1997). *Bodies of Law*. Princeton: Princeton University Press.

Ivison, D. (1998). The Technical and the Political: Discourses of Race, Reasons of State. *Social & Legal Studies* 7, no. 4: 561–6.

Johnson, A. M. (1991). The New Voice of Color. *Yale Law Journal* 100: 2007–64.

Johnson, R. (1987). What is Cultural Studies Anyway? *Social Text* 16: 38–80.

Kahn, P. (1999). *The Cultural Study of Law: Reconstituting Legal Scholarship*. Chicago: University of Chicago Press.

Kapur, R. (1999). "A Love Song to Our Mongrel Selves": Hybridity, Sexuality and the Law. *Social & Legal Studies* 8, no. 3: 353–68.

Karst, K. (1995). Myths of Identity: Individual and Group Portraits of Race and Sexual Orientation. *UCLA Law Review* 43: 263–370.

Kelman, M. (1981). Interpretive Construction in the Substantive Criminal Law. *Stanford Law Review* 33: 591–673.

LatCrit Symposium. (1997). Under Construction: LatCrit Consciousness, Community and Theory. *California Law Review*, 85.

Matsuda, M. J. et. al. (eds.) (1993). *Words that Wound: Critical Race Theory, Assaultive Speech and the First Amendment*. Boulder: Westview.

Maurer, B. (1997). *Recharting the Caribbean: Land, Law, and Citizenship in the British Virgin Islands*. Ann Arbor: University of Michigan Press.

Maynard, D. W. (1990). Narratives and Narrative Structure in Plea Bargaining. In Levi, J. and Walker, A. (eds.), *Language in the Judicial Process*. New York: Plenum Press.

Merry, S. E. (1990). *Getting Justice and Getting Even: Legal Consciousness among Working-class Americans*. Chicago: University of Chicago Press.

Minow, M. (1996). Stories in Law. In Brooks, P. and Gewirtz, P. (eds.), *Law's Stories: Narrative and Rhetoric in Law*. New Haven: Yale University Press.

Montoya, M. (1998). Border/ed Identities: Narrative and the Social Construction of Legal and Personal Identities. In Sarat, A. et al. (eds.), *Crossing Boundaries: Traditions and Transformations in Law and Society Research*. Chicago: Northwestern University Press.

Munger, F. (1998). Mapping Law and Society. In Sarat, A. et al. (eds.), *Crossing Boundaries: Traditions and Transformations in Law and Society Research*. Chicago: Northwestern University Press.

Olsen, F. (1996). Do (Only) Women Have Bodies? In Cheah, P. et al. (eds.), *Thinking Through the Body of the Law*. New York: New York University Press.

Peller, G. (1985). The Metaphysics of American Law. *California Law Review* 73: 1151–290.

Riles, A. (1999). Wigmore's Treasure Box: Comparative Law in the Era of Information. *Harvard International Law Journal* 40: 221–83.

Roberts, D. (1999). Why Culture Matters to Law. In Sarat, A. and Kearns, T. (eds.), *Cultural Pluralism, Identity Politics, and the Law*. Ann Arbor: University of Michigan Press.

Rose, N. and Valverde, M. (1998). Governed by Law? *Social & Legal Studies* 7, no. 4: 541–51.

Sanders, J. (1993). From Science to Evidence: The Testimony on Causation in the Bendicton Cases. *Stanford Law Review* 46: 1–86.

Sarat, A. (1990). "...The Law is All Over": Power, Resistance, and the Legal Consciousness of the Welfare Poor. *Yale Journal of Law and the Humanities* 2: 343–79.

——. (2000). Redirecting Legal Scholarship in Law Schools. *Yale Journal of Law and the Humanities* 12: 129–50.

Sarat, A. and Kearns, T. (1999). Writing History and Registering Memory in Legal Decisions and Legal Practices: An Introduction. In Sarat A. and Kearns, T. (eds.), *History, Memory, and the Law*. Ann Arbor: University of Michigan Press.

Scheppele, K. L. (1992). Just the Facts Ma'am: Sexualized Violence, Evidentiary Habits, and the Revision of Truth. *New York Law School Law Review* 37: 123–72.

Schlag, P. (1996). *Laying Down the Law: Mysticism, Fetishism, and the American Legal Mind*. New York: New York University Press.

Siegel, R. B. (1999). Collective Memory and the Nineteenth Amendment: Reasoning about "the Woman Question" in the Discourse of Sex Discrimination. In Sarat, A. and Kearns, T. (eds.), *History, Memory, and the Law*. Ann Arbor: University of Michigan Press.

Smart, C. (1989). *Feminism and the Power of Law*. London: Routledge.

——. (1992). The Woman of Legal Discourse. *Social & Legal Studies* 1: 29–44.

——. (1995). *Law, Crime, and Sexuality: Essays in Feminism*. New York: Routledge.

Valdes, F. (1995). Queers, Sissies, Dykes and Tomboys: Deconstructing the Conflation of "Sex," "Gender" and "Sexual Orientation" in Euro-American Law and Society. *California Law Review* 83: 3–377.

——. (2000). Outsider Scholars, Legal Theory and Outcrit Perspectivity: Postsubordination Vision as Jurisprudential Method. *DePaul Law Review* 49: 831–45.

Watson, S. (1999). Policing the Affective Society: Governmentality in the Theory of Social Control. *Social & Legal Studies* 8, no. 2: 227–51.

Weisberg, R. (1996). Proclaiming Trials as Narratives: Premises and Pretenses. In Brooks, P. and Gewirtz, P. (eds.), *Law's Stories: Narrative and Rhetoric in Law*. New Haven: Yale University Press.

Williams, P. (1991). *The Alchemy of Race and Rights*. Cambridge, Mass.: Harvard University Press.

Chapter 4

The Renewal of the Cultural in Sociology

Randy Martin

Many are the ways to think the link between cultural studies and sociology. A map of their institutional location would reveal a dense network of interdependencies, a separate department formed in one place, a unit or program that casts a wide net over existing resources in another (Berry & Miller 1999). This exercise in transdisciplinary cartography would also show tremendous regional variation (Forbes & Kelly 1996; Forgacs & Lumley 1996; Kelly & Shepherd 1998; Graham & Labanyi 1996; Turner 1992). A sociologist could be "doing" cultural studies as much as a renowned figure from the new field could grace a sociology faculty (Aronowitz 1993; Clough 1992; Gray 1997; Morley & Chen 1996; Bennett 1998). At times competition for monies would generate tensions, while at other moments political affiliations would allow cooperation to rule (Grossberg 1997; Striphas 1998).

While establishing propinquity, such a map would not necessarily tell us much about the fields of knowledge that these two terms are meant to designate (Gaokankar & Nelson 1996; Long 1997). One would be hard put to sort out which research methods belonged to which domain (McGuigan 1997). Ethnography? Historical Comparison? Content Analysis? Ethnomethodology? Survey Research? Yes please! Less satisfying still would be to claim that one took its object of study to be culture and the other society – if for no other reason than that both fields take the relation between these terms to be foundational to their endeavors. But it is precisely in the way that this relation is imagined that the impact of cultural studies on sociology can be most fruitfully expanded and specified.

My emphasis in what follows therefore will be on cultural studies as a theoretical intervention in sociology that brings new life to the latter's core questions. To treat cultural studies thus is not to address all the work that has gone by that name, but to focus on the conceptual innovations made available when a range of critical endeavors are clustered together that have permitted a fundamental rethinking of the meaning of the cultural. It is worth recalling that sociology came into being in the nineteenth century as an amalgamation of other fields (Brown 1993). No less today, its renewal rests upon an influx of critical reflection from the outside. Conceived of in the broadest terms, cultural studies is the conduit through which this flow of transdisciplinary energy has taken place. Since discipline is the organizational currency of the academy, the often internecine battles over intellectual and institutional properties need to be responsibly engaged. But lest these be left as merely local skirmishes over the banners under which we march, we need to keep the conceptual stakes of our interests close to hand. The tale I want to tell here is how the culture–society question came to be understood within sociology, how it was transformed by cultural studies, and what prospect this new embrace holds for the way in which we orient ourselves to our world.

Cultural Animations

Given all the entrances and exits to the big house called sociology, it is tough to claim that all the residents think alike even if they are subject to the same house rules or discipline. The same would have to be said for the somewhat smaller domicile called cultural studies. Imagining what the idea of sociology might be, well that's a different story – for any dweller is likely to offer up an account of what life is really like. Sociology textbooks frequently provide a linear narrative of the field with a tryptich of founding fathers: Karl Marx, Emile Durkheim, Max Weber; and a trilogy of schools: conflict, interactionist, functionalist. The two trinities don't really correspond. More importantly, origins are irrepressible, and the margins remain wider than the center.

Culture itself is given various inflections by sociologists active in the 1920s and 1930s. Robert Park and Ernest Burgess (1921: 52) argue that the cultural process shapes the forms and patterns inherited from prior generations. Charles Horton Cooley (1933) sees culture as the accumulated result of association. For William Graham Sumner (1927), it is an adjustment to the environment, and for Florian Znaniecki (1952) sociology is itself a cultural science. Yet concurrent with this scientific inflection is an interpretive enterprise as suggested by Alfred Schutz (1932: 214) with a privileging of "spontaneous activity," a perspective consonant with George Herbert Mead's emphasis on the "social creativity of the emergent self" (1934: 214). While these figures indicate a range of perspectives to early sociology in the United States, their work is seldom subject to significant revisitation.

Max Weber's legacy is more illustrative of how earlier threads get rewoven. Weber's consummate concern is to place the conduct of society on a rational basis. Because people take account of each other in doing what they do, their actions are both meaningful and oriented. Sociology is a science devoted to the "interpretive understanding of social action" (Weber 1978: 4). But action is divided between the means people acquire to conduct their affairs (instrumental reason) and the ends to which these techniques are put (substantive reason, or more prosaically, values). Society, in this light, is a historical project that rests upon certain value orientations held in common. The sum of these shared values is what typically passed as culture. Because action can lead societal development in any number of directions, and Weber details the various types, culture is left to play a compensatory role in providing purpose to the myriad ways people are able to behave. Parsons picks up on this notion of culture as a basically inert orientation that binds people together. Parsons describes culture as "transmitted," "learned," and "shared" (Parsons 1951: 15). Society is a "system" that has "dynamics" but whose normal state is static, leaving activity in opposition to culture as the thing needing to be explained.

In these accounts, sociology is separated between a statics and a dynamics. From this split a host of dichotomies issues that are frequently taken to organize the field conceptually – structure and process; macro and micro; norm and deviance. It is common to find figures like Durkheim read to be principally concerned (in his case via his concept of solidarity) with problems of order rather than change (Giddens 1972: 41). Change is the effect of the passage of still or synchronic moments transpiring in an abstract medium of time. Temporal succession is given and need not be explained by sociological law. Because change is a property of distance from the present and not the latter's internal condition, sociology is a predictive science that must measure what transpires against fixed expectations of what is possible. Under the assumption that explanation is predictive, seminal thinkers like Marx can be dismissed as irrelevant when a putative system change fails to take place.

The rationalization of culture achieved by sociologists should not be dismissed out of hand. Routine affairs of the common folk are made reasonable, where hitherto the actions of the mass were treated as intrinsically irrational (Le Bon 1895; Ortega y Gassett 1932). But this normalization of societal mundanities came at the expense of the very creative, generative aspect of daily life that would make it of interest to those who live it. Here cultural studies would have something to say.

Already by the mid-sixties when cultural studies was getting underway, the correction was occurring within sociology – and from Parsons' own students (Becker & McCall, 1990). Erving Goffman (1959; 1963) turned to dramaturgical models of human activity to explore how identity was accomplished through the avoidance of normalizing judgment (stigma). Harold Garfinkel (1967) explored the implied communicational maneuvers in conversational exchanges in his ethnomethodology to study how people passed themselves off as accomplished in quotidian situations. The latent cultural norms now became strategic and solidarity was proven to be an active complicity of self with others. Harvey Sacks (1995), John O'Neill (1972), Alan Blum and Peter McHugh (1984) mined the intricate sociality of what would come to be called the popular – the fundamental creativity with which common activities were invested. But for the system-theoretic model, these alternate sociologies were relegated to occupying the place of the micro in the very syntax they were meant to disturb. As Michael

Brown has shown, the incessant judgment without reference to value that characterizes a passing self-presentation is a feature of all capitalist social relations and therefore consistent with Marx's critique (Marx 1967; Brown 1986). This critical reengagement with Marxism (again already detectable among so-called maverick sociologists like C. Wright Mills (1959), Alvin Gouldner (1970), and Daniel Bell (1976)), is precisely what articulates cultural studies and sociology.

Twentieth-century Marxism was profoundly taken up with questions of culture and consciousness. In what initially was a hallmark of the west, leisure, private life, social reproduction were caught up in market relations to further expand the reign of the commodity. This brought the inner life of labor into the den of capital. At the same time, the cooperative and creative traditions of laboring people gave a different weave to the life made of commodified exchange, this was the basis for the study of popular culture. Animated by the rise of German fascism, Frankfurt School theorists Theodor Adorno and Max Horkheimer (1944) saw Weber's instrumental reason eclipsing the critical faculties that would allow people to see how capitalism compromised their most basic human interests. Herbert Marcuse's (1963) notion of repressive desublimation saw in the restrictive pursuit of pleasure a channeling of energies away from political activity. Jürgen Habermas (1989) saw the domain where community values were advanced being colonized by the universalization of technically driven specialized self-interest. For all of these theorists, whereas the commodification of culture served as a principle arena of social control, critical consciousness also held the promise for societal transformation. The enthusiasm for their work culminated in the widespread adoption of Habermas's concept of the public sphere (self-representing social practices evident in newspapers or coffee houses, as distinguished from state, market, and domestic life) as one of the signal ideas of current sociological thinking. Above all, the public sphere became a watchword for the intervention of critical participation in reasoned communication, guided by rules to facilitate the exchange of different perspectives, as itself a transformative societal force.

Concurrent influxes of Marxist-informed thought also supported this shift in the conception of culture from inert preservation of sameness to generative agent of difference. The reception of Gramsci (1971) was key for a range of explorations of what came to be known as counterhegemonic or resistant practices. Gramsci's suggestion that popular consent to capitalist rule meant devising modes of participation in dominant ways of life, spawned equal interest in the ways that culture might refuse the prevailing logic. For this to happen working-class culture had to be resistant or different at its core, as Paul Willis (1981) showed in his ethnographic study of British working-class kids' classroom misbehaviors. The subcultural was held out as a domain of creative refusal and could be deployed to describe stylistic innovation that embodied cultural differences along the lines of youth, race, sexuality, and the like (Hall et al. 1990; Williams 1977; Hebdige 1979). The relation between domination and opposition was treated as actively contested and therefore productive of politics. Three concepts were especially significant here. Althusser's (1971) notion of interpellation, the way in which people become subjected to authority through their recognition of themselves through what the state demands of them (to be good citizens, workers, parents, etc.), extended the reach of the state beyond its traditional institutional sites. Foucault's (1979) double meaning of discipline, as molding the body for certain acceptable practices and generating the capacity to act in ways that are socially legible, enabled repression and resistance to be understood as two features of the same process. Bakhtin's (1981) heteroglossia and polyphony found an unruly and uncontainable proliferation of different voices as the vital source of the popular. Each of these lines of analysis suggested that there was no unitary core to the self, but rather a whole field of contending subjectivities. The sociological category of role would have to yield to the more complex problematic of identification (Castells 1998). The definition of a particular self could no longer be read off from their position or location in a social structure. Identity was an effect of forces and flows already in motion. Cultural strife could not be seen as an artifact of failed normalization as in the older language of deviance, but now had to be treated as resulting in a transformative process that was less a deficiency in need of amelioration than a novel articulation of human activity that was fundamentally productive. Cultural production became the term of preference within sociology and was meant to amalgamate who people were with what they made (Peterson 1976; Barrett 1979; Blau 1989; Bourdieu 1993). This distinction between symbolic and material, once thought of as discrete activities, sectors, or spheres, could only be appreciated as a conceptual clarification of social practice that was both reflexive and generative, self-making and world-building.

It would certainly be inaccurate to say that all these refashioned ideas belonged to cultural studies. The linguistic turn which harkened in semiotics held the promise of treating the social as both structure and practice (*langue* and *parole*), neither outside nor inside the speaker's head but existing only through a community of speakers capable of introducing new meaning and value (Saussure 1966; Voloshinov 1973). These developments, known collectively as structuralism, promised a universal science of meaning that was capable of recognizing the shared complexity and capacity for innovation evidenced in human activity across cultural differences defined both ethnologically and hierarchically. Yet for this expansion of cultural value to occur, the limits to language, representation, structure had to be noted and the currents known as poststructuralism generalized the intensities of aesthetic practices to get at sublime, embodied, unspeakable dimensions of cultural accomplishment (Dosse 1997). Cultural studies directed these intellectual energies to a program of social research that was in coalition with what it studied (Grossberg 1997; Johnson 1986/7). Sociologists wasted no time incorporating the work of individual writers of these tendencies into the pantheon of social theory. But in the enthusiasm to operationalize the insights of a Foucault or Althusser, the context that gave these writers their nuance and impact was lost (Wright 1979). To the extent that cultural studies could not be pinned to a particular genealogy, it promised a more programatic and dramatic effect on sociological habits. Hence it could be seen as something to be kept outside or made redundant with extant work in sociology, rather than serving as a vehicle to renew the commitment to advancing the society/culture problem. This would require different ways of reading and attending to sources than was typical of protocols for data collection. An opportunity was presented to reflect upon representation in a dual key: as the metonymic issue of how a part might stand for a whole raised by the relation between sample and population in survey research, and question of resemblance posed when one looks for the world in a given object or work. The idea of text as developed by Barthes (1979) was especially useful as a means to get at the interwoven relations between the single case and the multitude of connections taken as context. These relations were inscribed or written onto what could be called a textual field made available through a self-critical practice of reading (Derrida 1998). Textualization meant being disturbed by details and not simply positioning them to affirm or deny hypotheses. Cultural studies did offer a shift in orientation toward extant methodologies rather than establishing a new paradigmatic method that would usurp the plurality of devices for research that reign in sociology. Within this more restricted dilemma, the limit to representation meant that epistemological issues could not be resolved by methodological fiat.

Dispersions Within

It would be a mistake to see sociology as a frictionless surface upon which all ideas glide evenly. The texture of susceptibility to influence varies greatly and the receptivity to the cultural turn has been concentrated in several areas. Sociology has long admitted a cultural dimension to every site and practice. There is a culture of the economic, the political, the family, you name it – making it easy to suggest that there is no resistance to what is already there. At issue, however, is not the presence of culture, but its concept, and here the interest in generative, creative activity has nestled selectively where existing perspectives have been most strained. As culture became privileged as the means to register social change, the questions of what it was and how it came to be were also enlarged. Among the traditional disciplines, what could count as an object of study was dramatically magnified. While sociology thrived in this climate along with the humanities, it made sense that the very approach to culture would be transformed along the way. That the functioning of society was questioned at the very moment when the vision of modernization heralded by sociology seemed to be realized, could only lead to tremors within the conventional understanding of social theory. These challenges were not simply attributable to the routine realization of logical inconsistencies that a community of expertise would learn to assimilate. Rather, there was a way in which the popular mobilizations implied a practical critique of society's operations that sociologists had to attend to. How social movements themselves incarnated critique would have to be rethought. These three areas where cultural studies has proven most effective are clearly intertwined. To see what this influence has entailed, I want to unravel the strands a bit between cultural sociology itself, by which I intend the whole range of areas from media, arts and the popular, social movements, especially those studies that have had to grapple with emergent forms, and theory.

It would be reasonable to expect art studies to have the greatest affinity with the turn to intrinsic generativity described here. Yet the thrust of much of this work has been to demonstrate that art too is a kind of rational action organized with a definite occupational structure (Becker 1984) and institutional dimension (Wolff 1981; Zolberg 1990). No longer simply a critical idea, but now a material force in its own right, the affinities between aesthetic and social form received less attention. Missing in this earlier work was the insight that the attention to design might advance the discussion of research design more broadly by providing a language to analyze the relation between knowledge's expressive form and its now inseparable content. When, for example, Attali (1985) argued that societal arrangements took audible form in music before they could be seen in more conventional measures of change, the aesthetic took on a special methodological and espistemological significance beyond any transformative capacity that could have been claimed for art itself.

This idea that one could think society through culture could be seen pointedly in developments in media studies. Against the kind of technological determinism that media increased information access without regard to interest and therefore indexed freedom and openness in society, seminal media studies located interest in ownership (Schiller 1973) through which media epitomized corporate dominance (Parenti 1986). The more radical implications of these studies for the fact–value distinction in sociology had to await further developments (Inglis 1990). When the concept of mediation was taken seriously, what appeared as discrete message transmissions could be treated as revealing the integration between production and circulation that allowed for a rethinking of economic relations (Baudrillard 1981). The notion that audiences had to be actively constituted granted agency to the otherwise passive domain of consumption. The study of the popular pushed this active force still farther, not only demanding that the artifacts employed in mundane affairs be appreciated through more expansive evaluative criteria (Frow 1995), but that the impact of the people as makers of history could never be reduced to the standard measures of accomplishment through which progress has typically been rendered (Brown 1986/7). The popular came to embody value-giving modes of rational action that were irreducible to the profit-taking dictates of exchange. Pleasure could become a political category that expressed this counterlogic (Jameson 1988). Symptomatic of these shifts, two recent developments are of note. One is the creation of a new special interest group of the American Sociological Association, "Consumers, Commodities and Consumption," with a new *Journal of Consumer Culture* edited by George Ritzer, whose own work (1993) has helped delimit the field. The formation accepts that consumption is "production for use," but does not want to diminish the significance of property and purchase that are dominant in a market-driven culture (Butsch 2000). Secondly, the journal of reviews for the American professional association, *Contemporary Sociology*, has renamed the section that attends to the above topics "cultural production." This new designation by the only genuinely nontechnical and consistently comprehensive registry of the field suggests an interesting change in syntax. While sequestered as a new speciality, cultural production nonetheless betokens an assimilation of the new turn. Production already denoted more active participation in what was made and what could be taken as fixed or given than construction, which was typically contrasted with essence or nature (Fuss 1989; Taussig 1993). At the heart of the distinction between production and construction lies another – that of the sensuous human activity that makes itself as it creates its world (Marx's conception of labor), versus construct, a contingent code or meaning that nonetheless begs the question of how it comes to be. A social construct operates by being momentarily naturalized as an inert truth, while production, properly construed, is a process that attempts to realize the capacity of forces that are uneasily brought together. Construct brings us back in the direction of codes, norms, and law from which the notion of cultural production beats a path of escape.

The case of cultural production suggests that once-familiar terms get freighted with new meanings and that what appeared to be a subspeciality of the discipline turns out to address it as a whole. What could be said for the study of culture *per se*, applies as well to sociological theory. For theory is meant to be the means through which one reflects on the general features of a situation. That it would be seen as one area of knowledge among others within sociology and not what is foundational to all avenues of research (Calhoun 1998) already speaks to a core problem for the field that cultural studies could be seen to rectify. Without appreciating the radical insight that one can grasp the whole otherwise by attending to what seems to be a particularity, the various critical currents applied to sociology look like abandonments of the aspiration to understand all of society. In actuality, the view from the concrete particular can make unexamined assumptions newly available. This decentering reveals what is contingent about the hitherto fixed center. This is where the attribution of a critical perspective to a particular identity or group interest proves so unhelpful. When gender, sexuality, race, or colonial relations are no longer blank constructs that organize people into groups but optics from which to make sense of the entire world, the approach to any comprehensive analysis cannot remain untouched. Here the distinction made by Eve Sedgwick (1990) between minoritarian and majoritarian uses of queer theory is worth bearing in mind. By attending to the sexual subjectivity of what appears outside normal practice, the diverse ways that sexuality is lived get uncloseted. What is illuminated as truth rests upon something kept in the dark, out of view, is what Peggy Phelan (1993) calls the unmarked.

It becomes evident that a position typically denoted as minority actually contains the key to the expansion of a whole domain of cultural expression and societal relations. As such, putatively natural categories such as sexuality and race are denaturalized, and identities pluralized so as to embrace a more inclusive view of human affairs. In addition, the creative and expansive work done over the kinds of available social relations is amplified.

We could say that what traditionally appear as issues of exclusion from nonnormative expressions that would be seen in terms of prejudice and discrimination, can be seen instead as a matter of the ambivalent desire to draw upon the creativity or pleasure of these newly articulated forms. For example, racism and homophobia are both barriers to equal treatment and ways to concentrate value (positively or negatively) in a category formally defined as other but practically constitutive of what a self might be (Mercer 1994; Berlant 1998). Cultural appropriation is the twin of hatred, for the theft of what is coveted, covers its tracks of being where it was not supposed to be (Lott 1993; Ziff & Rao 1997). This is not simply because there is pleasure in transgression, but because this is where a now socially expressible range of practices attains its fullest scale and scope. This is where cultural expression assumes the proportions of societal dynamics. The theorized voices of others point to the production of a social surplus in the sense of an elaboration of social forms and relations that extend what once would have been referred to as complexity. Because this last term assumes as its alter the simple or primitive, it has rightly been criticized by anthropologists (Lévi-Strauss 1966; Trouillot 1991). Society is not simply differentiated as Parsons would have understood the term, as further specialization and particularization of what is done by people – a kind of division of labor for social reproduction.

The various poststructural interventions exert a new transdisciplinary effect on sociology in which questions of power and domination are not simply distributional exclusions, but different ways to craft society when the means for producing social life (and not simply products) are considered historical resources. Sociology always had the potential to treat society as both subject and object, self-made and self-positing. Yet foundational concepts such as structure and process, macro and micro tended to uncouple what is in fact an indissolvable unity. The theoretical resources marshaled by cultural studies complicate these terms that would fix social positions and behaviors expected to flow from them and offer a recognition of both representation and its limits. The inclusion of the normally excluded must be conveyed by a rationalization or extension of rule to what was hitherto outside the pale. But the progressive force of the newly included is not simply assimilated, absorbed, and neutralized. Subalterns, as Gayatri Spivak (1988) would put it, do not suddenly speak as if they would be relieved of the burden of otherness to become a normal self. Little of the creativity of society would be realizable if such a predictable path to normalization could actually take place. Limitation becomes a sign for continued but contingent influence, for an expansive capacity whose effects can not simply

71

be named to be further sequestered by instrumentalities of control. Culture comes to embody the dynamism that is an ongoing feature of the accomplishment of society that is nonetheless incompletable.

As was the case with the influences of Marx, Weber, and Durkheim, social theory attains its greatest advances when its protagonists are actively engaged and affiliated with the societal projects they imagine. Marx helped organize and critically addressed an array of worker organizations and parties. Durkheim was active in the professional politics of the French sociologists. Weber worked to draft the legislation he felt would best rationalize society. It is therefore no accident that the theoretical innovations discussed here share the activist trajectories of the classical figures while bringing activist sensibilities into the process of theorizing itself. To appreciate these connections requires a look at the popular mobilizations and their renewed appreciation through a cultural studies lens. This takes us to the discussion of social movements.

While social change was always a central problematic of sociology, the question of how it came about remained vexing. A century of sociology had established the rationality of informal and mundane activity, but the market-driven optimization of self-interest produced a conception of individualism that rendered collective action an exceptional condition in need of explanation (Olson 1965). The common person engaged in transforming the social environment was a kind of decision-maker modeled on an executive of government or business. Collectively, social movements followed the Weberian split of means and ends that characterized all rational acts. Resources such as information or money were gathered or mobilized to achieve clearly articulated goals.

The gains of the resource mobilization approach were undeniable. What appeared inchoate and ephermeral could have lasting institutional effects as the goals of social movements became legislated or addressed as social goods. Further, the meaning of democracy was enlarged to emphasize participation as a value in itself, and not simply electoral or policy outcomes. Power was an effect of gathered critical publics, and not simply a perquisite of state to be distributed on demand. But beyond serving as an index of societal type, it remained unclear why people would affiliate with movement organizations if time for other pursuits was lost and the gains would be disbursed whether any given individual had participated or not. On closer inspection, it was the assumption that self and social interest were necessarily at odds that required revision. Participation did not so much meet an interest as generate a sense of self that was already social. When social movements were treated as culture-making bodies, participation could be playful and pleasurable, identity-giving and space-producing. As a grip on a narrow conception of politics was loosened, recognition and resource were no longer monopolized by the state. This did not mean that the state had withered, but that regulation of domestic life was a response to the politicization of what was once considered outside of politics, namely the matters of identity, consumption, development, thought to be merely private. By politicizing the quotidian, by extending the culture of movements beyond the measurement of formal goal attainment, by insisting on mobilization as the normal condition of life, cultural studies aimed to make what was scarce and exceptional abundant. This was a complication of the field that would introduce its own confusions.

If politics was everywhere and movements abounded, how to assess or evaluate their tendency so as to sustain the commitment to intervention and advocacy. The study of right-wing social movements and their statist assimilations by neoliberal governments suggested that these confusions were not simply issues of relativism. Just as one could no longer assume self-interest prior to activism, the collective will of the people could not just be read off of the presence of movement organizations. As more and more features of human life were set in motion as fungible features of what could be made of history, the fact of this development would come into conflict with the assessment of its tendency. Hints of a direction for society would have to be located in the cultural dynamics of the movement itself. For this to occur, close attention would have to be paid to the conflicting principles embodied in particular practices. The local was not autonomous from but a complex effect of global forces differentially condensed or "scaled" (Smith 1992). The question of how to read movements did not simply entail interpreting their ways of representing themselves. It meant seeing how changes already in process were being reflected upon and directed by those innovating ways of living together. This mobilization outside the organizational entailments of the movement approached the enactments shared by strangers that make it possible to speak of society. While a social movement is knowable through its cultures, it makes known what can be called society (Touraine 1981).

Between Project and Principle

As cultural studies has percolated through sociology, the internal conceptual affinity of culture and society has deepened. Some of the critical work that is the fruit of this relationship has been reported on here. The collaboration has not proceeded without suspicion. Substantive issues notwithstanding, it is tempting to fan the flames of disciplinary xenophobia if we do not have a place from which to imagine the mutual insinuation of fields and concepts. To this end, mere description is unsatisfying. It is important to argue on behalf of a politics for the relation of society and culture. Engagement with the politics would then help orient conceptual stakes and positions. Because of the connotations of society with system and the statics of bounded structures, some work to have come through poststructuralism has avoided terms deemed to be totalizing (Laclau & Mouffe 1985). On the other hand, the cultural turn has been treated as generating its own indulgences that must be corrected, most commonly an avoidance of institutional analysis that would incorporate the state and political economy (Bonnell & Hunt 1999).

While one could identify a list of candidates that bear these sins of omission, it is curious that the work that best overcomes these divides is not considered the benchmark that most effectively characterizes recent developments. The point is that cultural studies and sociology are as much known for the general impressions they give as for what could be said to be grouped empirically by each. They organize trajectories from which future work can be imagined. What do we want to imagine the relation of culture and society to be – beyond an inventory of pitfalls to be avoided? If society is to again have purchase as an orienting concept it would have to be taken up in critical analysis as a project, an endeavor to be realized, an image of what can be. A society organized on behalf of those who create what is valuable within it, that treats social value as a resource to be fostered, that provides a means to address how relations among us are to be configured and how our creativity of social form can be furthered, these are formulations of a society in and for itself, one that advances its own social means.

For this project, the term socialism (however battered it has been) is still the best fit. To achieve its unprecedented accumulation of wealth capitalism depends upon cooperation on a grand scale, but has difficulty abiding the conditions for collaborative interdependence. The reign of capital can be further extended and elaborated but it is difficult to postulate as an ideal. Conversely, socialism is always in part a project, someplace to get to from here, something other we could get in the move from present to future than dizzy accumulation without reflection on the quality of what has been amplified. If socialism is indeed the substantive reason, the ends of our societal project (a self-expanding aspiration, not a destination), we need equally to rework the question of means. Weber found endless technical mastery disenchanting. Implicitly, one could feel impelled to get good at something, but in the end it really wasn't all that much fun.

Culture, as used here, is not leisure, a break from work, but a "sensuous activity" that is pleased by having more of itself. It is the pleasure of labor that makes this last such a target for appropriation. Wanting more is a notion tainted by that angel called progress (McClintock 1992). But this is also an historical desire that once put in motion is not easily sated. Culture in this reckoning is less a whole way of life than a demand made on living, a critical principle that insists that more can be made out of what is to hand. This excess or social surplus is the material embodiment of participation that gives us democracy in more than name alone. Culture is a tangible capacity or agency to gather together human energies that are already on the move. This unceasing motion invites a reflection on where it is headed, and assumes an expanding appetite for what could be made from the thicket of associations. This amalgamation of socialism and democracy, of societal project with critical principle, should be enough to keep sociology and cultural studies mutually interested for some time to come. Society is not something whose boundaries can be described, nor its shape predicted. Its possibilities are a demand on present capacities that our critical moves must hope for.

References

Adorno, T. and Horkheimer, M. (1944). *The Dialectic of Enlightenment*. New York: Seabury, 1973.

Althusser, L. (1971). "Ideology and Ideological State Apparatuses." In L. Althusser, *Lenin and Philosophy*. New York: Monthly Review Press.

Aronowitz, S. (1993). *Roll Over Beethoven*. Middletown: Wesleyan University Press.

Attali, J. (1985). *Noise: The Political Economy of Music*. Minneapolis: University of Minnesota Press.

Bakhtin, M. (1981). *The Dialogic Imagination*. Austin: University of Texas Press.

Barrett, M. (1979). *Ideology and Cultural Production*. London: Croom Helm.

Barthes, R. (1979). "From Work to Text." In J. Harari (ed.), *Textual Strategies: Perspectives in Post-Structuralist Criticism*. Ithaca: Cornell University Press.

Baudrillard, J. (1981). *For a Critique of the Political Economy of the Sign*. St. Louis: Telos.

Becker, H. (1984). *Art Worlds*. Berkeley: University of California Press.

—— and McCall, M. (1990). *Symbolic Interaction and Cultural Studies*. Chicago: University of Chicago Press.

Bell, D. (1976). *The Cultural Contradictions of Capitalism*. New York: Basic Books, 1996.

Bennett, T. (1998). *Culture: A Reformer's Science*. Thousand Oaks, Calif.: Sage.

Berlant, L. (1998). *The Queen of America Goes to Washington City*. Durham: Duke University.

Berry, S. and Miller, T. (eds.) (1999). *Blackwell Cultural Studies Resources*: www.blackwellpublishers.co.uk/cultural/

Blau, J. (1989). *The Shape of Culture*. Cambridge: Cambridge University Press.

Blum, P. and McHugh, P. (1984). *Self-Reflection in the Arts and Sciences*. Atlantic Heights, NJ: Humanities Press.

Bonnell, V. and Hunt, L. (1999). *Beyond the Cultural Turn*. Berkeley: University of California Press.

Brown, M. E. (1986). *The Production of Society*. Totowa, NJ: Allen and Littlefield.

——.(1986/7). "History and History's Problem." *Social Text* 16: 136–61.

——.(1993). "The Future of Marxism and the Future of Theory." In C. Polychroniou (ed.), *Socialism, Crisis, Renewal*. New York: Praeger.

Bourdieu, P. (1993). *The Field of Cultural Production*. Cambridge: Polity Press.

Butsch, R. (2000). "Culture, Cultural Studies, and Consumption." *Consumers, Commodities and Consumption* 1, no. 2: 1–2.

Calhoun, C. (1998). Editor's Comments. *Sociological Theory* 16, no. 1: 1–3.

Castells, M. (1998). *End of Millennium*. Oxford: Blackwell.

Clough, P. (1992). *The End(s) of Ethnography*. Newbury Park, Calif. Sage.

Cooley, C. H. (1933). *Introductory Sociology*. New York: Charles Scribner's Sons.

Derrida, J. (1998). *The Politics of Friendship*. London: Verso.

Dosse, F. (1997). *History of Structuralism*, 2 vols. Minneapolis: University of Minnesota Press.

Forbes, J. and Kelly, M. (eds.) (1996). *French Cultural Studies*. Oxford: Oxford University Press.

Forgacs, D. and Lumley, R. (eds.) (1996). *Italian Cultural Studies*. Oxford: Oxford University Press.

Foucault, M. (1979). *Discipline and Punish*. New York: Vintage.

Frow, J. (1995). *Cultural Studies and Cultural Value*. Oxford: Oxford University Press.

Fuss, D. (1989). *Essentially Speaking: Feminism, Nature and Difference*. New York: Routledge.

Gaokankar, D. and Nelson, C. (eds.) (1996). *Disciplinarity and Dissent in Cultural Studies*. London: Routledge.

Garfinkel, H. (1967). *Studies in Ethnomethodology*. New York: Prentice-Hall.

Giddens, A. (ed.) (1972). *Emile Durkheim: Selected Writings*. Cambridge: Cambridge University Press.

Goffman, E. (1959). *Presentation of Self in Everyday Life*. New York: Doubleday.

——.(1963). *Stigma: Notes on Spoiled Identity*. New York: Simon & Schuster.

Gouldner, A. W. (1970). *The Coming Crisis of Western Sociology*. New York: Basic Books.

Graham, H. and Labanyi, J. (eds.) (1996). *Spanish Cultural Studies*. Oxford: Oxford University Press.

Gramsci, A. (1971). *Selections from the Prison Notebooks of Antonio Gramsci*. New York: International.

Gray, H. (1997). *Watching Race: Television and the Struggle for the Sign of Blackness*. Minneapolis: University of Minnesota Press.

Grossberg, L. (1997) *Bringing It All Back Home: Essays on Cultural Studies*. Durham: Duke University Press.

Habermas, J. (1989). *Structural Transformation of the Public Sphere*. Cambridge Mass: MIT Press.

Hall, S. et al. (1990). *Resistance Through Rituals: Youth Subculture in Britain*. London: Routledge.

Hebdige, D. (1979). *Subculture: The Meaning of Style*. London: Methuen.

Inglis, F. (1990). *Media Theory*. Oxford: Blackwell.

Jameson, F. (1988). "Pleasure: A Political Issue." In F. Jameson, *The Ideologies of Theory*, vol. 2. Minneapolis: University of Minnesota Press.

Johnson, R. (1986/7). "What is Cultural Studies Anyway?" *Social Text* 16: 38–80.

Kelly, C. and Shepherd, D. (eds.) (1998). *Russian Cultural Studies: An Introduction*. Oxford: Oxford University Press.

Laclau, E. and Mouffe, C. (1985). *Hegemony and Socialist Strategy: Towards a Radical Democratic Politics*. London: New Left Books.

Le Bon, G. (1895). *The Crowd: A Study of the Popular Mind*. New York: Penguin, 1977.

Lévi-Strauss, C. (1966). *The Savage Mind*. Chicago: University of Chicago Press.

Long, E. (ed.) (1997). *From Sociology to Cultural Studies: New Perspectives*. Oxford: Blackwell.

Lott, E. (1993). *Love and Theft: Black Face Minstrelsy and the American Working Class*. New York: Oxford.

Marcuse, H. (1963). *One-Dimensional Man*. Boston: Beacon.

Marx, K. (1967). *Capital*, 3 vols. New York: International.

McClintock, A. (1992). "The Angel of Progress: Pitfalls of the Term 'Postcolonialism.' " *Social Text* 31/2: 84–98.

McGuigan, J. (1997). *Cultural Methodologies*. London: Sage.

Mead, G. H. (1934). *Mind, Self and Society*. Chicago: University of Chicago Press.

Mercer, K. (1994). *Welcome to the Jungle: New Positions in Black Cultural Studies*. London: Routledge.

Mills, C. W. (1959). *The Sociological Imagination*. New York: Oxford University Press.

Morley, D. and Chen, K.-H. (eds.) (1996). *Stuart Hall: Critical Dialogues in Cultural Studies*. London: Routledge.

Olson, M. (1965). *The Logic of Collective Action*. Cambridge Mass: Harvard University Press.

O'Neill J. (1972). *Sociology as a Skin Trade: Essays Towards a Reflexive Sociology*. New York: Harper & Row.

Ortega Y Gassett, J. (1932). *The Revolt of the Masses*. New York: Norton, 1957.

Parenti, M. (1986). *Inventing Reality: The Politics of News Media*. New York: St. Martin's Press.

Park, R. and Burgess, E. (1921). *Introduction to the Science of Society*. Chicago: University of Chicago Press.

Parsons, T. (1951). *The Social System*. Glencoe Ill.: The Free Press.

Peterson, R. A. (1976). *The Production of Culture*. Beverly Hills, Calif.: Sage.

Phelan, P. (1993). *Unmarked: The Politics of Performance*. London: Routledge.

Ritzer, G. (1993). *The McDonaldization of Society*. Newbury Park, Calif.: Pine Forge.

Sacks, H. (1995). *Lectures on Conversation*, 2 vols. Oxford: Blackwell.

Saussure, F. (1966). *Course in General Linguistics*. New York: McGraw-Hill.

Schiller, H. (1973). *The Mind Managers*. Boston: Beacon.

Schutz, A. (1932). *The Phenomenology of the Social World*. Evanston Ill.: Northwestern University Press, 1967.

Sedgwick, E. (1990). *Epistemology of the Closet*. Berkeley: University of California Press.

Smith, N. (1992). "Contours of a Spatialized Politics: Homeless Vehicles and the Production of Geographical Scale." *Social Text* 33: 54–81.

Spivak, G. C. (1988). "Can the Subaltern Speak?" In C. Nelson and L. Grossberg (eds.), *Marxism and the Interpretation of Culture*. Urbana: University of Illinois Press.

Striphas, T. (ed.) (1998). *Special Issue: The Institutionalization of Cultural Studies*. *Cultural Studies* 12, no. 4.

Sumner, W. G. and Keller, A. G. (1927). *The Science of Society*. New Haven: Yale University Press.

Taussig, M. (1993). *Mimesis and Alterity: A Particular History of the Senses*. New York: Routledge.

Touraine, A. (1981). *The Voice and the Eye: An Analysis of Social Movements*. Cambridge: Cambridge University Press.

Trouillot, M.-R. (1991). "Anthropology and the Savage Slot." In R. Fox (ed.), *Recapturing Anthropology: Working in the Present*. Santa Fe: School of American Research.

Turner, G. (1992). *British Cultural Studies*. London: Routledge.

Voloshinov, V. N. (1973). *Marxism and the Philosophy of Language*. New York: Seminar.

Weber, M. (1978). *Economy and Society*, vol. 1. Berkeley: University of California Press.

Williams, R. (1977). *Marxism and Literature*. Oxford: Oxford University Press.

Willis, P. (1981). *Learning to Labor*. New York: Columbia University Press.

Wolff, J. (1981). *The Social Production of Art*. New York: New York University Press.

Wright, E. O. (1979). *Class, Crisis and the State*. London: New Left Books.

Ziff, B. and Rao, P. (1997). *Borrowed Power: Essays on Cultural Appropriation*. New Brunswick NJ: Rutgers University Press.

Znaniecki, F. (1952). *Cultural Sciences*. Urbana: University of Illinois Press.

Zolberg, V. (1990). *Constructing a Sociology of the Arts*. Cambridge: Cambridge University Press.

Chapter 5

Sociology, Cultural Studies, and Disciplinary Boundaries

Frank Webster

Introduction

Thirty-seven years ago Richard Hoggart delivered his inaugural lecture at the University of Birmingham university.[1] He presented it as a Professor of Modern English Literature, and he well deserved this title, having published a book-length study of the poet W. H. Auden a decade earlier.[2] But even before he began to address his audience there in 1963 it was clear that Professor Hoggart did not fit the orthodox mold of literary scholarship. Though still only in his early forties, much of Hoggart's reputation rested on achievements other than the Auden book, and these marked him as one who moved outside the boundaries of literary criticism. Let me signal just three of these:

1) His memorable role in the much-publicized trial, late in 1960, of Penguin Books (under the terms of the then new Obscence Publications Act) over the publication of *Lady Chatterley's Lover*. In this trial, and in face of hostile cross-examination which turned time and again to sexually explicit passages from the novel, Hoggart's defense of D. H. Lawrence as a "British non-conformist Puritan" whose concern was profoundly "decent," was widely regarded as crucial to the acquittal of Penguin Books.[3] Hoggart's sincerity, dignity, and calmly reasoned responses to the Prosecution marked him out as an especially effective advocate for the Defense (there is a notable exchange when Hoggart compares sexual expression in *Paradise Lost* with that in *Lady Chatterley's Lover*).

2) At around the same time as this, Hoggart had served as a member of the Pilkington Committee, the Royal Commission on broadcasting which had been examining the record of commercial television (ITV) and the BBC since the mid-1950s, and which was pivotal in the allocation of the new third channel to the BBC.[4] In the production of this landmark report (which marked, I think, the high point of public service broadcasting), it is widely acknowledged that Hoggart played a decisive part.[5] Those familiar with Hoggart's writing will easily enough recognize his distinctive formulations in sections of the finished report,

notably the critique of advertising and the resistance to commercial television's claim that TV ought to "give the audience what it wants." From another direction an anecdote tells of Hoggart's contribution. A year or two after Pilkington's completion, T. S. Eliot, who had given evidence to the Commission, observed that of its members he recalled only Hoggart and the "glass manufacturer." Hoggart had distinguished himself already beyond the realm of literature.

3) Most prominently, in 1957 Hoggart had published, after working at it for most of the decade, *The Uses of Literacy: Aspects of Working-class Life with Special Reference to Publications and Entertainments*. The book is still in print. It had been very widely reviewed and debated, though it was very difficult – indeed impossible – to categorize in terms of any discipline. Hoggart himself recollected that "Many people I knew in internal departments of English kept fairly quiet about it, as though a shabby cat from the council house next door had brought an odd – even a smelly – object into the house."[6] Sociologists recognized that it addressed their interests, but felt it was something of an intrusion onto their turf, and they were also suspicious of its autobiographical emphasis.

The Uses of Literacy was divided into two parts. The first examined pre-Second World War working-class life in and around Leeds, in a deeply felt and personal way. The second half contained an onslaught on various new phenomena such as juke boxes, pop music, "spicy" magazines, and sex and violence novels which were allegedly undermining working-class ways of life. There was little of orthodox sociology in this exercise, since so much of the account was recollected and reconstructed from Hoggart's own experiences and memories and filtered through a decidedly judgmental frame – yet the subject itself, as was the whole of the book, was undoubtedly sociological in its concerns. (Incidentally, and not surprising given that Hoggart, orphaned early, was reared by his grandmother, there was, to the sociologists of the time if not today, an unexpected concern for the domestic and feminine aspects of 1930s working-class life in Hunslet. This feature is especially evident if one contrasts *The Uses of Literacy* with what has become a sociological classic that appeared just the year before Hoggart's book. *Coal is Our Life: An Analysis of a Yorkshire Mining Community*, is so much more decidedly male in orientation – the pit, the club, the union, and the family in that order form that study. And this, be it noted, a book whose subject is life in Featherstone, scarcely ten miles from Hoggart's Hunslet.)

The Uses of Literacy remains, unmistakably, the product of a literary critic, yet its subjects were much wider matters than fiction, being working-class characteristics, mass media, consumerism, youth, and so on. I think that, if we cannot place it readily in any disciplinary sense, we can agree that, *from* literature, it was breaking out into new areas, areas which were having a palpable effect on everyday life in postwar Britain. For all this, and while it was obviously grappling with social change (the central concern of Sociology), *The Uses of Literacy* was not Sociology. It disqualifies itself at least because there is an absence of theory and the method is decidedly inappropriate for Sociology. (And yet here I am moved to cite a wonderful student whom I came across very early in my career, in 1975. Frank McKenna, was not long out of the labor movement adult education center, Ruskin College, Oxford, which he had attended, in his mid-forties, after working on the railways from the age of 15. He later wrote a marvellous book, *The Railway Workers*, based on studies he undertook at Ruskin.[7] I was talking to Frank about working-class life and we were exchanging views about sociological studies of this subject that was so close to us. Hoggart's name, and his *Uses of Literacy*, came into the conversation. Frank's eyes lit up and, learning forward while cupping his ear, he told me that, with Hoggart, "you can hear it," you can hear the voices of flesh and blood people and feel their presence, you can *be there* in a way in which most Sociology sadly misses.)

In view of these aspects of Hoggart – upright opponent of prudish censorship, the advocate of public service broadcasting, the analyst of working-class life before and after the War – it comes as no surprise that, in his inaugural lecture at the University of Birmingham, he "set out his stall" for what he wanted to accomplish as a Professor, and this wasn't to plot a career straightforwardly *inside* English Literature. What Richard Hoggart proposed was the formation of a Center for Contemporary Cultural Studies (actually he called it, revealingly, "Literature and Contemporary Cultural Studies"), and he urged that this be a locus for studying "popular arts" such as pop songs, photography, fashion, advertising, and television shows (for the nostalgic, his examples included *Candid Camera*, *Z Cars*, and *This is Your Life*).

And yet it should be noted that this project was to remain decidedly literary in orientation. The Centre for Contemporary Cultural Studies was to come *out of* literature since, as Hoggart himself put it, he was "for widening the boundaries of English as it was offered at universities,"[8] not for abandoning them. In this respect it is interesting to see that Hoggart's inaugural was published in volume 2 of his essays, *Speaking to Each Other*, which carries the revealing subtitle *About Literature*.[9] CCCS, as the Centre became known, opened in the Spring of 1964 with two staff, Richard Hoggart and Stuart Hall. This was a formidable combination, with the latter himself also an English Literature graduate, from Jamaica via Oxford, who had started a doctorate on Henry James before abandoning it in favor of editing *New Left Review*. (And even with Hall, who led CCCS to the heights during the 1970s, the literary legacy was telling. Listeners to *Desert Island Discs* on Radio 4 Feb. 18, 2000 will know that the one book he chose to take with him to the desert island was Henry James's *The Portrait of a Lady*.) Later that decade this duo was joined by Michael Green, who remains with us to this day, and he too came out of Literature, having studied the subject at Cambridge.

I would emphasize the ambition to extend the field of literary criticism during these early days of CCCS. Richard Hoggart argued that in the CCCS enterprise literature constituted "the most important"[10] element for at least two reasons. First, it was in literature and the literary approach that one found "absorbed attention to the detail of experience": in literature one could get beneath surface appearances, beyond the superficial, and into the rich texture of life as it is actually lived. As Hoggart put it in that lecture of 1963, "how well would we be able to apprehend, let alone express, the complexity of personal relations, if it were not for literature working as literature? I do not mean that we all need to have read the best books; but what has the fact that they have been read, and their insights ... to some extent passed into general consciousness, contributed to our understanding of our own experience?"[11] Second, in the literary critical approach, in what one might call a literary sensibility, a place could be found for key terms such as "significant" and "illuminating" when one tried to come to terms with the meanings of contemporary cultural expression.

It will not come as much of a surprise to many people to hear this said. The critic F. R. Leavis (and his wife Queenie[12]), important but embattled during their lives (in death largely forgotten and, where remembered, dismissed as naive, dogmatic, and authoritarian[13]), were an obvious influence on Hoggart at this time. Indeed, it is commonplace to regard Hoggart (as with the early Raymond Williams) as "Left-Leavisite," to highlight in their work a concern for close reading of texts, for a supposition that literature had some special claims of access to how we live and how we might better understand life, and for a willingness to judge that which one examines, not in some hurried or thoughless way, but as a serious responsibility which ought not to be shirked.

If Hoggart wanted to move literature into the study of contemporary culture, and in the process to retain important aspects of a literary approach, he was aware that this involved a trespass onto the terrain of Sociology. In his inaugural he acknowledged the significance of the "sociological" to his concerns, though he felt there was only limited value in the discipline of Sociology. To be sure, Hoggart saw a need for studies of audiences, of authors' circumstances, and the like, and therefore some sociological contribution was necessary, but when he looked at the work then available in the Sociology of Culture and Literature, he concluded that Sociology was reductive and external to literature, thereby a dismal science of limited use to CCCS.

I review these concerns and characteristics of Hoggart to provide a context for my own observations. In what follows I want to reflect more on Hoggart's – and his successors' – moves from Literature to Cultural Studies, and on the connections of Sociology with this. More particularly, though in no neat order, I want to comment on:

i)   the issue of evaluation and judgment in the enterprise of social and cultural analysis.
ii)   aspects of the recent history of Sociology in Britain.
iii) the emergence and development of Cultural Studies, especially in terms of its relation with Sociology.
iv)   the character of academic disciplines and the closing (and opening) of boundaries that this implies.

Preliminary: The Necessity of Discrimination

I now want to be more personal in my comments. In the human sciences we have learned that too often the author's voice is disguised. So I will bring out my own directly, though I shall endeavor to situate these thoughts in a wider context. I took a first degree in Sociology and immediately followed this with a master's in Social History, but then moved into the Sociology of Literature for my doctorate during the mid-1970s. I have often wondered why I made this shift, though I wondered much more, and with anguish, while I was doing the Ph.D.! One reason was undoubtedly that I had come to Sociology steeped in literature – my imagining of social relationships, past and present, was deeply influenced by immersion in fiction. Another was, I suppose, that I was Leavisite, and had been so since school days in which I had been taught by a passionate, but undeclared, Leavisite. Above all, that meant I was drawn to literature because it seemed to speak to me about the society in which I lived and which I yearned to better understand, because I was attracted by the emphasis on close textual analysis, and because such criticism also offered sensitivity to the social milieu of cultural works.

1974 was not a propitious time for a novitiate Sociologist to come to literature, especially one with Leavisite dispositions. This for at least two reasons. One was that Sociology at this time had reacted sharply against "empiricism" of all kinds ("positivism" was then a term of abuse, and remained so for far too long). In these terms, any concern for empirical materials on literature (say, sales, costs, readerships, literacy rates, and so forth) was of little interest to the by then dominant mode of thought in Sociology of Literature. Thus far, one might suppose, with the literary critics, since they didn't think so much of such things either. But against this must be set the fact that the reaction of Sociology to dull empiricism was accompanied by a call to put Theory above all else. On this ground, it wasn't only empirical sociologists who were to be pushed aside; it was also the atheoretical literary critics – notably F. R. Leavis and his acolytes – who were to be jettisoned. Leavis, famously unwilling and perhaps incapable of theorizing (how we ridiculed his rhetorical declarations that "it is so, is it not?"), was readily pigeonholed as an anachronism, left with nothing to offer we the theoretically empowered.

Looking back, it seems to me that just about everything was Theory then, anything but engagement with the substantive, whether a literary text or even something as mundane as the preferences of readers. We moved in the heady company of Georg Lukács, Pierre Macherey, and above all, Louis Althusser, whose "theoretical practice" had great appeal in (and far beyond) the Sociology of Literature. There one theorized everything, doing anything but engage with the work itself (that was far too gauche, as if one could seriously presuppose theoretical innocence). I might add that an important instigator of this "theoretical turn," Perry Anderson, editor of *New Left Review* for many years, was himself a judicious assessor of Leavis. Anderson, in the process of castigating British intellectual culture for its lack of theoretical sophistication, nonetheless declared that "Leavis's personal achievement as a critic was outstanding, his rigour and intelligence establishing new standards of discrimination."[14] The trouble was that most of us were carried away with the prioritization of theory: we missed Anderson's nuance, we rushed to theorize, and thoughtlessly jettisoned Leavis and his ilk.

In my view, this was an especially barren time for Sociology. Personally, I completed a doctorate late in 1977, but it wasn't on literature. It was on Theory. And what strikes me now about this Theory was that it was always so smugly "correct" and "superior," always at the ready to tease out the hidden or tacit theory of those thinkers who might write substantial accounts of Joseph Conrad or Charles Dickens, but because they failed to theorize were laughably "simplistic."

Here one may also note that one of the commonest targets of Theory was "reductionism." We intoned, over and again, that it was folly to reduce a text to a particular socioeconomic relation. But the irony was that Theory itself was reductionist with a vengence, since everything was "read off" *from* Theory. This was theoreticism at its worst: Theory being the alpha and omega of analysis, to which everything must defer.[15]

Looking back, I wish that I had had the determination to stay closer to Leavis (which is not of course the same as endorsing the Leavisite project – I have no desire to rehabilitate that). This for several reasons, including:

i) the concern with close attention to the substantive (to texts and subjects), which can be a strong counter to theoreticism (of which more below).

ii) the prioritization, in all things educational – in universities especially – of the question "what we are and what we might be." This may seem to be a simple question, but it is a bold and essential task for the human sciences, and one which Leavis posed recurrently.[16] I think that keeping this question to the fore of our minds, the pursuit of which is the primary task of universities, can be of inestimable help to us when we get into difficulties of disciplinary boundaries (of which more below).

iii) the unavoidable responsibility of intellectuals to discriminate in what they study.

I want here to say a little more about the latter since it seems to me a principle that is especially difficult to uphold in recent times, when evaluation is readily dismissed as a manifestation of prejudice. At the outset I want to say that my own journey through the Sociology of Literature and Theoreticism was not so singular as my preceding comments may suggest. Michèle Barrett, a graduate of the same university department as myself, took a similar trajectory, and, though both of us were well away from Birmingham University, it is clear that many similar influences were being felt here. Michèle went on to Sussex where she took a doctorate on Virginia Woolf. In her recent and important book, *Imagination in Theory* (1998),[17] Michèle – who during the 1990s became President of the British Sociological Association, and one of the very few world-ranked British sociologists[18] – records difficulties she had in undertaking her thesis on one of the twentieth century's most important British writers and critics. A recurrent dissatisfaction was the inability of Sociology to engage with matters of art, aesthetics, and the imagination (matters close, of course, to Virginia Woolf herself). Michèle observes that Sociology still has to come to terms with these issues, ones which are inextricably connected to questions of evaluation. And on the way she observes in Cultural Studies, the rise of which she generally celebrates, the same inability to deal with the questions of value and discrimination. I share Michèle Barrett's concerns. It is also, for me, sobering that Professor Barrett moved recently from her Chair in Sociology to join Lisa Jardine in a Department of Humanities in another university, I suspect exasperated with Sociology's continued failure to come to grips with art and the imagination.

One can certainly adduce reasons for avoiding making judgments. In some Sociology circles the emphasis may be on the nonjudgmental because this is seen as being in accord with the value-neutrality that must accompany a properly scientific attitude. There is, of course, much to be said in favor of this, and Max Weber[19] expressed it a great deal better than I might do.[20] I would agree unhesitatingly that detachment is a requisite of doing Sociology, but I do not think this means Sociology ought not to be asking serious questions of what it examines, and that amongst those questions should be matters of quality. Again, the admirable impulse to be inclusive can encourage us to avoid making judgments. Hoggart elsewhere posed the problem of the "ungifted taxi-driver"[21] in this regard. What he meant to highlight was that, while is pleasing, to the good-hearted at least, when the ordinarily excluded – such as taxi drivers – gain entry to restricted arenas – perhaps to literary or scholarly circles, the question of the quality of their output in those circles cannot be ignored because of delight in doors having been opened. More generally, there is the pervasive insistence that judgment is all a matter of disposition, of "each to his or her own," in these postmodern times. A corollary is a deep-seated relativism which finds expression within and without the academic realm.

Nevertheless, I do feel that the bypassing, for whatever reason, of the question of judgment is a weakness. I would not want to see Sociology or Cultural Studies lining up to announce "one true way" about the things that they study, but I do insist that we try to make reasoned arguments (on grounds of logic and of evidence) about the better and the worse. This also seems, I must say, a key ingredient of *critical* work, which surely must move beyond asking questions about a particular approach or phenomenon, towards identifying strengths and weaknesses. In this regard I am glad to be able to quote the following authority:

> In the end we are . . . back to a qualitative definition based on critical judgement of individual pieces of work. Such judgements are often dismissed . . . as "subjective" or "impressionistic"; but there is a difference, surely, between vague opinion and the considered view based on close analysis which presents itself for debate or discussion controlled by "evidence" from the work in question.[22]

It is commonplace nowadays to shy away from making judgments between the serious and the trivial, the worthy and the unworthy, the enduring and the ephemeral, the beautiful and the ugly, as it is from making the necessary discriminations that lie somewhere in between these poles. I concede that it is a difficult task, and today it is much easier – so much more inclusive – to bypass the responsibility to discriminate. And yet I do not feel that the issue should be shied away from since it is a task of life, indeed a duty of thinking beings. It is also a central responsibility of any university insofar as a university is charged with thinking especially hard about what goes on in the world. For sure, it ought not to be something which we do only in the privacy of our own homes (though, sadly, this is indeed often the case), while in public we gain easy assent by advocating "each to his own taste." Making judgments can seem contemptuous when done insensitively, but it is also a particularly insidious form of contempt to refuse judgments of any kind – I think here of the contempt evident in those who say that "your taste is for the *Oprah Winfrey Show*, mine for *Newsnight*; they're different but equal."[23] In this regard, I can only praise the candor of Mr. Gerald Ratner, who in 1991 came clean to a conference of businessmen when he announced that his firm's profits came from selling "crap" to people with no taste for anything better. I do not condone Mr. Ratner's conduct of his business, but there is something about his directness and ingenuity which must embarrass today's relativists who rarely if ever practice what they preach.

The Recent History of Sociology

At this point I should like to turn more directly to my own subject area, Sociology, to make some observations on the course of its history over recent decades. During the late 1960s Sociology in Britain began to break out of its dependency on US scholars – in the form of the structural functionalist theory and quantitative methodology which were so often its professional accompaniment[24] – that had been manifest for at least two decades. Clearly, the onset of political radicalism influenced this development, though it ought to be said that more tentative conflict theorists had already made the case for drawing on European traditions of thought.[25]

An intriguing development of this time was that two dominant paradigms emerged to face one another in British Sociology, namely Weberian versus Marxist approaches. There were, of course, heated exchanges between these schools of thought, but it does seem to me that, broadly, we can now see that there was a general consensus in British Sociology that the subject was fundamentally about *class* (closely followed by work and production). These were the key organizing concerns of the discipline, to which most writers returned. *Class analysis* predominated – one may even say it was hegemonic – in British Sociology, and, though definitions varied quite widely (from an occupational hierarchy, position in terms of ownership of property, to location in the labor market), there seemed to be agreement that class analysis was the prime concern of sociologists. Frank Parkin's wry observation at the time, that "inside every neo-Marxist there seems to be a Weberian struggling to get out,"[26] hints at the consensus beneath what were often heated debates. Incidentally, it is worth adding that class analysis was both singularly male at this time (class was typically taken by sociologists to be a quality of and from men), and there was a broad "leftist"[27] consensus amongst sociologists that class inequalities were a bad thing (it took the New Right in the 1980s to surprise British sociologists with the claim that class inequality was present but was also by and large just).[28]

Simplifying perhaps too much, one can say that, during much of the 1960s and the 1970s, class was the major relationship drawn by sociologists between matters such as educational attainment, voting behavior, leisure pursuits, and social mobility opportunities. What was offered was an account of Britain in which phenomena were apparently "read off" from one's social class. Looking back, it seemed that just about everything of significance could be understood in terms of a great divide between (that gross simplification) the "middle class" and the "working class" (though it was the latter which was much the most observed by sociologists). The working class had opportunities stacked against them, their marital relationships, political dispositions, and leisure habits were expressive of their class location, and even their tastes in food and entertainment were reducible to their class.

We can see that this consensus around class analysis came under attack during the later 1970s because of substantive developments and conceptual criticisms. The assault has continued throughout the past generation, culminating in Ray Pahl's dramatic assertion in 1989 that "class as a concept is ceasing to do any useful work for sociology."[29] Let me signal some aspects of this:

- Changes in the *occupational structure* became increasingly evident as traditional industries rapidly declined. There was nothing "natural" about this development, and it should be remembered that the destruction of the miners, a momentous event in British twentieth-century history, in the 1980s was an outcome of their being attacked by Mrs. Thatcher and the organized might of the state.[30] Ralph Miliband interpreted this as "class struggle from above,"[31] and it is a salutary reminder when we hear commentators referring to an "evolution" to an "information society" and "knowledge economy." But the outcome of the decline of male, manual jobs, and the parallel spread of service occupations, have had an important influence on the feel and experiences of inequality and much else besides. Today over 70 percent of jobs are in the service sector, and the shape of the stratification system has markedly changed (though, contrary to some presumptions, there is a greater degree of inequality at the extremities). With jobs becoming increasingly white collar and information based, then there are, to put it mildly, difficulties in continuing with established forms of class analysis. At the least the older division of "middle" and "working" class, always crude, is problematized.

- Closely associated with this has been the much observed *feminization* of the workforce which, in combine with the spread of *feminist thought*, has posed serious problems for those wanting to hang on to class analysis categories.

- There has developed an *increased concern for consumption* as a close corollary of sustained rises in living standards for the majority. Since the start of 1970 these have risen, on average, and in real terms, by about 100 percent, and results are evident all around us – in large-scale car ownership, in entertainment equipment in people's homes, in home furnishings and facilities, in styles and ranges of dress ... Combined, this expansion of consumption has acted as a counter weight to the one-time centring of analysis on production and work (and the classes which were presumed to stem from this).

- Relatedly, there has been an *explosive growth of media*, especially of the television, but also of course including video games, PCs, and teletext.

- This is integrally connected with the huge expansion of the *symbolic realm* and the import of "signs" that is continuing. Television is now around-the-clock and there are multiple channels available, and added to this must be the increase in music, in fashion and style, in design (from trainers to electric kettles, from T-shirts to mobile phones), as well as in advertising and marketing.

- We need to add to this the *growth of leisure*, notably in time off and in the relative ease of travel that has been an accompaniment of rising living standards and declining costs of transport, helping vault tourism into a major employer in many areas.[32] This demands attention from sociologists, though of a kind that, at least in important ways, defies earlier forms of class analysis.

- The growth and experience of what one might call, uncomfortably and clumsily, *cultures*, evident in, for instance, the development of variegated youth cultures, and also amongst multicultures which have come about through migration, ease of travel, and globalization. This is in evidence pretty well everywhere, whether in cuisine, in the supermarket, in street talk and styles, or the football squads of English soccer clubs.

- The increase in *new social movements* and what have been called lifestyle or identity politics (animal rights, environmental protests, feminism) which are unclearly connected with class relations.

These are very diverse phenomena, but together they promote the significance of culture and, as this more and more emerged as something important in its own right, so rose a chorus of denial that culture could be explained by Sociology's master concept, class. And so, of course, did class analysis's hold in Sociology begin to loosen its grip, many sociologists becoming convinced that it could not do justice to the complexities of these new forms of relationship.[33] It ought to be said that sociologists at Nuffield College especially have fought a powerful rearguard action to retain class analysis, and their findings, supported by meticulous conceptual thinking and empirical data, remain salient.[34] Such accounts insist that there was little or no increase in relative social mobility opportunities over the twentieth century. But they can sustain this only because they measure, not what is most striking about inequality today (i.e. the remarkable changes in its overall shape), but only the *relative* opportunities of people to move from one class category into another (i.e. they show that origins have remained, *relative* to one another, a huge effect on one's life chances). In short, the Nuffield research demonstrates and emphasizes that kids from the bottom of society still have a very hard time compared to those from the top, but they underplay – but do not deny – that the overall shape of society has radically changed. I cannot go along with the claim of two postmodern sociologists, that we have witnessed the "death of class,"[35] but it does seem to me difficult to refuse the view that we need to reassess the prioritization it had during the early 1970s. Class analysis does have very considerable difficulties in accounting for important issues such as sexualities, identities, lifestyle choices, race and ethnicity, as well as the conduct of everyday relationships in a thoroughly mediated world.[36]

The Emergence of Cultural Studies

A good deal of the discontent that was expressed against class analysis from within Sociology was echoed in the emergence of Cultural Studies. Indeed, while this has a complicated and wide-ranging genesis, the refrain of the Sociology of Literature – that reductionism of art to class relationships should be spurned – merged with the antireductionist insistence that was so much a part of the rise of Cultural Studies. Hoggart's legacy was important in this, but pride of place must surely go to Stuart Hall and the remarkable group of postgraduates who gathered in Birmingham in the 1970s.

I shall say little about this here. It is sufficient to observe that the Birmingham School took culture very seriously, and as such was at the forefront of path-breaking studies of youth, race, ethnicity, and gender (in addition to Hall, the names of Paul Willis, Angela McRobbie, Dick Hebdige, David Morley, and Paul Gilroy merit special mention in this context, but there was a host of very impressive others). Birmingham also promoted analysis of media to great effect. It was not alone in this, and scholars at Leicester and Glasgow especially played a key role, but it can scarcely be denied that *Policing the Crisis*, when it appeared in 1978, was a compelling read. It brought together politics, race, and a close account of the operation of media in Britain. Birmingham also insisted on the importance of ideas in politics, and from this emanated influential work on

89

the "authoritarian populism" of Margaret Thatcher, work which refuses to "read off," to reduce, politics to class.[37] As Stuart Hall insisted,[38] ideology had to be seen as a power in itself, the struggle for ideas in civil society being a prelude to political change. Here we had the sphere of ideology taken very seriously indeed – and who cannot but acknowledge Hall's prescience in conceiving the phenomenon of Thatcherism *before* her electoral victory in 1979?[39]

There was much more than this to the Birmingham School of this time, and it is easy enough with hindsight to see that some intellectual blind alleys were entered. For myself, I cannot but feel that the dalliance with Althusserianism was such an alley, however useful it seems to have been in allowing scholars at Birmingham to reflect on an autonomous sphere of ideology.[40] Nonetheless, what cannot be ignored is the significance of the "cultural turn" and the Birmingham School's central part in that tendency. It fed into the rise of Cultural Studies itself as an independent area of study (and the subject has soared in the United States especially, where it responds to different, and more propitious, circumstances), but it also had a profound influence on Sociology as it penetrated much of the mainstream through the efforts of the journal *Theory, Culture and Society* as well as those of Birmingham School members. The "cultural turn" helped fill an absence in British Sociology. I like to think this has been recognized by the wider community of Sociology. The award of a chair in sociology to Stuart Hall himself in 1979, his inclusion in a recent textbook on "key sociologists,"[41] and the distinction of being chosen as a recent President of the British Sociological Association, all suggest that this is so.

I shall return to the influence of the "cultural turn" on Sociology, but would now make some further remarks about the recent history of Cultural Studies. This developed as a hybrid subject, as we have seen drawing heavily on Literature, but happily raiding and contributing to anything which helped it better understand what was going on. As Hall put it, much of the strength of Cultural Studies stemmed from its being "a focal point for interdisciplinary studies and research."[42] There is much to be said for this, even for regarding Cultural Studies as consciously *antidisciplinary*, for insistently working on the frontiers of more fixed subject areas, for being what Michael Green calls "resolutely 'impure.'"[43] However, a price of success, especially in the United States,[44] has been Cultural Studies' institutionalization and – its corollary – the formation of disciplinary borders, which brings with it attendant risks. In this formation classic texts become identified (Hoggart, Williams, Hall, and so on) and core concepts and methods come to be taught as part of a canon. There have been dangers here for Cultural Studies, on which many critics have seized (though it should be noted that the Birmingham scholars themselves seemed acutely aware of them[45]). These include:

- The risk that antireductionism becomes translated into an uncritical celebration of diversity (difference) which is devoid of any emancipatory and evaluative elements. In this, particularly where postmodern approaches predominate, concern for material factors as well as for structured inequalities can be lost sight of.

- Enthusiasm for the creativity of people, so much a part of Cultural Studies' antireductionist ethos, runs a risk of underestimating the influence of constraints on actors.

- This emphasis on agency often comes associated with a mantra of "pleasure" in some quarters, a term which can easily slide into unthinking and indiscriminate celebration of the most superficial of cultural products.[46]

- The notion of a "cultural circuit" that has been developed by Hall and colleagues at the Open University has much to commend it. The division between Production, Representation, and Reception has found its way into many accounts of how Cultural Studies might proceed. I like very much the tacit notion here that some form of integration of all of these elements – some conception of totality – is needed if we are to make sense of the world. Yet it is striking that, in Cultural Studies, the realm of production appears still to be underexamined, relegated in favor of the remaining two elements of the "cultural circuit."[47]

- An excess of theory risks rekindling the sort of theoreticism which was so much in evidence in the mid-1970s. As Cultural Studies has been institutionalized, so there has been an invasion of theory which can become excessive and self-engrossing.[48] As I have said, Sociology itself has had a surfeit of this, especially that which is overconcerned with epistemology and with getting the theory right *prior* to engaging with the substantive. Here I would mention the old chestnut of political economy versus the active audience, which can be debated until the cows come home without getting anywhere nearer a resolution. At the back of this lies the old saw, objectivity versus subjectivity, which had been theorized to death. We really do need to get beyond these tired arguments and dualisms, perhaps into thinking, like Castells, of "disposable theory"[49] which we may jettison when it stops helping us better reveal what's going on in the world, and – here I am with Andrew Tudor[50] – we might acknowledge that Tony Giddens[51] has made a good fist at overcoming the dualism and move on.

The Discipline of Sociology

I have already commented on some of the ways in which Cultural Studies influenced Sociology. I think that one other important lesson for Sociology that has been underlined in this encounter is that knowledge itself is an outcome of negotiation. The authorities we revere, and the issues we address, are not self-evidently *there*, but express changeable priorities and concerns. On one level this is an easy point to concede: after all, the "holy trinity" of founding fathers in Sociology – Marx, Weber, and Durkheim – are a relatively recent creation. Marx was not much more than a shadowy presence before the late 1960s, and even

Durkheim became established only a few years earlier.[52] The process of nego-tiating over the canon continues to this day – one of my colleagues, David Parker, only recently and pointedly asked (in the journal *Sociological Review*), "Why bother with Durkheim?"[53]

Another way of putting this is is say that academic disciplines, while they are essential insofar as they provide us with tools of analysis, concepts with which to think, and points of orientation, cannot be set in aspic. They are, in intricate but inescapable ways, products of culture themselves and, as such, have no guaran-teed right of existence.[54]

This may be an easy point to admit on an intellectual level, but on the ground disciplines are powerful factors in the distribution of resources and the location of academic identities (think for a moment of the influence of the British government "Research Assessment Exercise" here). In this light, consider a response – one that I have encountered often – to the "cultural turn" in Sociology and to Cultural Studies with which this is closely associated. This regards interest in culture, especially when it mentions the word "postmodern," as a *threat* to the professionalization (and associated respectability) of Sociology, a discipline which ought to work only with "verifiable conjecture" and "testable propositions," in which a key requirement is a capability to undertake "social arithmetic" and handle the log linear analysis which promises to allow Sociology to provide definitive answers to questions that are empirically examinable.[55] From such a perspective the work of Zygmunt Bauman, Bruno Latour, Ulrich Beck, Hall, even that of Anthony Giddens (in my opinion Britain's most important sociologist since Herbert Spencer), scarcely qualifies as Sociology (it may appear speculative, untestable, even journalistic), and Cultural Studies itself is a diversion from more important tasks of professional-ization.

What we can see here is an attempt to establish foundations for a discipline of Sociology which has strongly policed boundaries. In this vision there is a strong core to the discipline – to caricature, a dose of the classical thinkers, rational choice theory, and a strong technical training especially in quantitative analysis. I have little doubt that this provides for a sense of group identity amongst those practitioners who seek to have a proper discipline of Sociology. I also have little doubt that it is deeply exclusionary of those who might dare to trespass into Sociology or even lay claim to the title.[56] In practice, proposals for a strong core are a minority position, since the majority of Sociology departments are more pragmatic in forwarding, at least in their undergraduate curriculums, a "weak core" in their courses – some classical theory, a range of methods, and some substantive analyses. This is also the welcome recommendation of the recently published *Benchmark Statement for Sociology*.[57]

Nevertheless, and with Cultural Studies in mind, I want to make a number of warnings against endeavors to erect boundaries in Sociology, against those who would have us identify disciplinary borders that might be patrolled by accredited professional agencies.

First off, I would urge Sociologists to "lighten up" out of respect for colleagues in other university departments. The exclusionary language one occasionally hears – "they can't even conduct multivariate analysis in 'x,'" "they wouldn't recognize a null hypothesis if it jumped out at them" – is offensive, perhaps on occasion deliberately so.

Second, I would remind the disciplinarians that it is not just a foible that leads government to encourage *interdisciplinary* work. I well appreciate that we often feel most comfortable speaking to people like ourselves, but the fact is that – recalling that the primary purpose of the human sciences as a whole is to understand and explain what's going on in the world – reality is intrinsically interdisciplinary. To make sense of it is not the prerogative of any single discipline or even a particular version of the discipline. If one seeks for an instance of this, I would urge as an exemplar Manuel Castells' great trilogy, *The Information Age*, interdisciplinary through and through, yet remarkable in its achievement.[58]

Third, Sociology has always been a markedly "fuzzy"[59] subject that has been easily entered by outsiders (historians especially, but there are plenty of others) and which happily incorporates the contributions of outsiders when it suits. It is as well to recall here that many of the classics refused the title sociologist (one thinks especially of Marx, but Weber himself – the one undisputed "master" – was trained in Law, and did his doctorate in the legal framework of medieval business organizations). To be sure, one could insist that this is an outcome of their writing prior to disciplinary formation (a scarcely persuasive argument), but I would reply that some of the most productive contemporary Sociologists come from outside the discipline (for example, Hall from Literature, Martin Albrow and Michael Mann from – or with Mann perhaps to – History, Gary Runciman and Ralph Dahrendorf from Classics). Moreover, some of the most interesting contributions to Sociology have come from those working outside the subject. There are many examples, so I simply highlight a couple of my favorites – E. P. Thompson's *Making of the English Working Class* (1963) played a key role in debates within Sociology throughout the sixties and seventies on a host of issues, from class analysis and conceptualization, to the causes and character of change; Barrington Moore's (another Classicist) *Social Origins of Dictatorship and Democracy: Lord and Peasant in the Making of the Modern World* (1966) was central in the thinking of sociologists about the part played by the peasantry in bringing us to where we are today.

Fourth, I would encourage us to stay with a conception of Sociology which emphasizes its openness by referring to the Gulbenkian Commission's *Report on the Restructuring of the Social Sciences*. This commission, chaired by Immanuel Wallerstein,[60] and whose report was published in 1996 as *Open the Social Sciences*, is at once an analysis of the development of knowledge and an advocate on new directions for the social sciences. In brief, it argues that, up until the 1960s, there were three branches of knowledge, one was the natural sciences, another the humanities, and – pitched in the middle of these "two cultures" –

were the social sciences, though these were disposed towards emulation of the natural science model (since this gave disciplinary credibility). But what has happened since then is that these boundaries have become markedly less clear, due to developments that have come from different directions. On the one hand, there has been, within natural science, an ongoing assault on what one might call Newtonian presuppositions, powered essentially by the difficulties that were being encountered by older scientific theories in solving problems concerning ever more complex and unstable phenomena. An upshot has been a developing stress on nonlinearity, chaos theory, and complex systems analysis. Relatedly, there has been the continual questioning of natural science from the social constructionists who, while they may have instigated the "Science Wars" backlash, have I think succeeded in raising serious questions about the practices of natural science.[61] On the other hand, the Commission suggests that Cultural Studies, especially in the United States, has pulled the Humanities into the Social Sciences, evidenced in, for instance, the promotion of once-excluded matters like gender, sexuality, and ethnicity, and non-Eurocentric issues, not to mention (in what one might call the strong program of postmodernism) the problematization of just about all kinds of knowledge. In the US we have had, in response, vigorous "Culture Wars," but few can deny there can be no turning back from this social scientization of the Humanities, to days when "Literature was Literature." All this is not to claim that we all meet in a muddy middle. Not at all, but with Wallerstein, I would celebrate the genuine fruitfulness of knowledge production that can break out of fixed borders. If one seeks an example of what I mean, just let me instance Edward Said's wonderful book, *Orientalism: Western Conceptions of the Orient* (1978), a work that is impossible to categorize by any established discipline, yet indispensable for those seeking to understand how we live today. In particular, I would commend here just two of the Gulbenkian's recommendations – encourage research programs that cut across traditional disciplinary boundaries and work for compulsory joint appointments of staff across departments (in this respect it is worth noting that Castells, to whom I have just referred as the author of what is indisputably one of the best analyses of late twentieth-century civilization, has long held a position at Berkeley of Professor of Sociology and Planning).

So it is clear that I am drawn to an open conception of Sociology. I have a bit more to say on that, but this reference to Wallerstein allows me to make another point which is more programatic. The Gulbenkian Report stresses that, to understand the world of today, a world of connectedness, of migration without historical precedent, a world of multiculturalism and hybridity, social scientists must become more linguistically able. It may frighten some of us (it frightens me!) that Wallerstein[62] suggests, in all seriousness, that our graduate students should aim to become adept in five or six of the major languages of the world today if they are going to be equipped to make sense of it (it is the extraordinary good luck of native English speakers that theirs is the world's *lingua franca*).

I am not quite sure what to make of this suggestion, but it does lead to observe that Sociology to a large extent, and Cultural Studies still more, predominate in particular locations, in the USA, the UK, and Australia (i.e. the English-speaking and Western centers of publishing). There are a number of ironies about this, but observing them is insufficient. I would urge that we make special efforts to extend the reach, appreciatively and sensitively, of Cultural Studies and Sociology into areas previously sidelined, usually in preference to the United States. This is not an easy task because of our linguistic deficits, and because resources are not likely to flow from places such as China, India, and Africa. That this is so makes particularly gratifying that the Department of Cultural Studies and Sociology at Birmingham, if small, has such a reach of expertise – having colleagues working on (and often coming from) Latin America, North Africa, India, and China is a great asset.

I would add that it is important for British Sociology and Cultural Studies to reach deeper into the continent of Europe. We in Britain suffer as a nation in being what Norman Davies describes as always "semi-detached"[63] with regard to our closest neighbors. Davies puts Poland at the center of his history of Europe, and here Warsaw, Prague, and Kiev are as prominent as Paris, London, and Rome. Last year I read Mark Mazower's disturbing book, *Dark Continent: Europe's Twentieth Century*.[64] I commend it to anyone who might mistakenly believe, "democracy" and "civilization" having been cradled in this arena, that in consequence intellectuals can leave out of their scrutiny a region which is comfortably "settled," devoting their energies instead to more obviously "troubled" or even "exciting" areas. But this – Europe – is the arena in which the greatest conflicts of the twentieth century were waged, where communism and fascism faced one another and went to the limit, where the ideologists fought between themselves in appallingly and unprecedentedly bloody ways, where genocide was conceived and implemented. Still today there are issues here in Europe, perhaps especially in central and eastern Europe, which command the urgent attention of Cultural Studies and Sociology – ethnic hatreds, the reemergence of fascism, the turmoil of socioeconomic restructuring, cultural differences, political integration, variable identities, changing informational environments, forced and unforced migrations, "fuzzy" nationhoods (to adopt Judy Batt's apposite terminology).

Conclusion

In conclusion, let me restate my conviction that Sociology ought to work with the "cultural turn" in thought, welcoming rather than resisting the emergence of Cultural Studies. I have little sympathy for those Sociologists who feel that Cultural Studies has left them by, still less for those who would expel it from the academy. We are currently enjoying pretty good times in social sciences in general, and Sociology in particular. Of course, resources are tight, but Sociologists should remember the cold years of the 1980s, when there were abusive attacks from people in power (remember Sir Keith Joseph and his abhorrence as regards the SSRC, accusations of "marxist bias" at the Open University, and fevered talk of the "decomposition" of Sociology?[65]). Today Sociology is at the heart of "Third Way" debates, while conceptions and issues such as "information society," "families of choice," social inclusion and exclusion, "globalization," "identity," "welfare," and "multiculturalism" find a ready ear in influential circles which recognize the value of social research. The Chair in Sociology at Birmingham University, lost in the 1980s, has even been restored! Being in this positive position, I would urge Sociology not to turn its back on Cultural Studies. The latter has made too many contributions to sociological thinking, and has so much more to give, to deserve this.

To this end, Sociology needs to resist the temptations of disciplinary closure and the exclusions that readily accompany such a move. Of course, to do anything requires that some frontiers be established, but it needs to be remembered that these are always subject to change and we need to keep them as open as we possibly can. Having open access to Cultural Studies is a crucial element of this. We need to insist on the primacy and collective endeavor of the human sciences to "tell it like it is." There is no royal route to that end. Hoggart set the style of breaking disciplinary boundaries back in 1963 when he announced the Centre for Contemporary Cultural Studies. Hall and his colleagues continued with that tradition, along the way opening areas and asking questions that too much Sociology appeared incapable of addressing. But Birmingham was not alone in welcoming the "cultural turn." From a different direction came John Urry, a sociologist at Lancaster since 1971, and long the lead in what is one of only two 5* Sociology departments in the UK. Back in 1981 Urry[66] advocated Sociology as a "parasitic" discipline, one happy to be informed by social movements such as feminism and environmentalism and open to contributions from other disciplines. This is a Sociology with no core, or at least if it has a core it is a protean one. But what we can be sure about is that Lancaster has led the way in British Sociology in being open to the "cultural turn." The proof of this is in the pudding. Skeptics may want to reflect on some of the work that has come out of that department in recent years – pioneering studies on tourism, on Heritage industries, on the culture of places such as the Lake District, on economies of signs and space, and on the development of "disorganized capitalism."[67]

Cultural Studies can also learn from Sociology, not least to resist unthinking celebration of the popular as well as to critically address questions of the validity and reliability of evidence.

Finally, both disciplines can, I hope, return to a concern with evaluation. I have no doubt that this is a fraught task, moving dangerously between elitist dismissal and banal populism, maintaining a commitment to the disinterestedness that is crucial to good academic work while still being willing to criticize and discriminate what is being examined. Nonetheless, I believe this to be an essential ingredient of the human sciences for the twenty-first century.

Notes

1 Thank you to Ann Gray, David Jary, and Liz Chapman for comments on a first draft of this chapter, which was originally my inaugural lecture as Professor of Sociology at the University of Birmingham.

2 Richard Hoggart (1951), *Auden: An Introductory Essay*, London: Chatto and Windus.

3 C. H. Rolph (1961), *The Trial of Lady Chatterley: Regina v. Penguin Books Limited*, Harmondsworth: Penguin, pp. 91–104.

4 Postmaster-General (1962), *Report of the Committee on Broadcasting, 1960*, Cmnd 1753, London: HMSO [Pilkington Report].

5 See, for example, Michael Tracey (1983), *A Variety of Lives: A Biography of Sir Hugh Greene*, London: Bodley Head, p. 189; Anthony Smith (ed.) (1974), *British Broadcasting*, Newton Abbot: David and Charles, p. 117.

6 Richard Hoggart (1990), *A Sort of Clowning, Life and Times, 1940–1959*, London: Chatto and Windus, p. 147.

7 Frank McKenna (1980), *The Railway Workers, 1840–1970*, London: Faber and Faber.

8 Richard Hoggart (1992), *An Imagined Life, Life and Times 1959–1991*, London: Chatto and Windus, p. 93.

9 Richard Hoggart (1970), *Speaking to Each Other, vol. 2, About Literature*, London: Chatto and Windus.

10 Ibid., p. 255.

11 Ibid., p. 249.

12 Her book (1932), *Fiction and the Reading Public*, London: Chatto and Windus, 1965, was in several respects a forerunner of early CCCS concerns.

13 David Hamilton Eddy (1992), "A Forgotten Embarrassment of Riches," *Times Higher Education Supplement*, April 24, p. 15.

14 Perry Anderson (1992), "Components of the National Culture" [1968], in *English Questions*, London: Verso, p. 97.

15 Those who recall E. P. Thompson's magnificent essay, (1978), *The Poverty of Theory*, London: Merlin, which demolished the Althusserian theoretical edifice, may appreciate the liberatory feelings this engendered.

16 F. R. Leavis (1943), *English and the University*, London: Chatto and Windus, (1969), *English Literature in Our Time and the University*, London: Chatto and Windus.

17 Michèle Barrett (1998), *Imagination in Theory*, Cambridge: Polity.

18 Anthony Giddens (1995) wrote that "British sociology ... can offer a clutch of individuals with a worldwide reputation, such as John Goldthorpe, Steven Lukes, Stuart Hall, Michèle Barrett, Ray Pahl, Janet Wolff and Michael Mann"; "In Defence of Sociology," *New Statesman and Society*, April 7, p. 19.

19 Max Weber (1949) [1917], "The Meaning of 'Ethical Neutrality,' and 'Objectivity' in Social Science and Social Policy," in *The Methodology of the Social Sciences*, trans. and ed. E. A. Shils and H. A. Finch. New York: Free Press.

20 See also Alvin Gouldner's contrasting essays, "Anti-Minotaur: The Myth of a Value-Free Sociology" and "The Sociologist as Partisan: Sociology and the Welfare State," in A. W. Gouldner (1973), *For Sociology: Renewal and Critique in Sociology*, London: Allen Lane, pp. 3–68.

21 Richard Hoggart (1980), "The Crisis of Relativism," *New Universities Quarterly* 35(1): 21–32.

22 Stuart Hall and Paddy Whannel (1964), *The Popular Arts*, London: Hutchinson, pp. 35–6.

23 Richard Hoggart (1995), *The Way We Live Now*, London: Chatto and Windus.

24 Though this is an oversimplification. See Jennifer Platt (1996), *History of Sociological Research Methods in America, 1920–1960*, Cambridge: Cambridge University Press.

25 For example, John Rex (1961), *Key Problems of Sociological Theory*, London: Routledge and Kegan Paul; Ralph Dahrendorf (1968), *Out of Utopia*, London: Routledge and Kegan Paul.

26 Frank Parkin (1979), *Marxism and Class Theory: A Bourgeois Critique*, London: Tavistock, p. 25.

27 John Rex observes "an almost complete absence in Britain...of a systematic conservative sociology" (p. 1007) which must have contributed to this orientation, as did an interpretation of Max Weber which downplayed his pro-capitalist and conservative characteristics. John Rex (1983), "British Sociology 1960–80: An Essay," *Social Forces* 61: 999–1009.

28 See David Marsland (1988), *Seeds of Bankruptcy: Sociological Bias against Business and Freedom*, London: Claridge Press; Peter Saunders (1990), *Social Class and Stratification*, London: Routledge; (1995), *Capitalism, A Social Audit*, Buckingham: Open University Press; Peter Berger (1987), *The Capitalist Revolution*, London: Gower.

29 Ray Pahl (1989), "Is the Emperor Naked? Some Questions on the Adequacy of Sociological Theory in Urban and Regional Research," *International Journal of Urban and Regional Research* 13(4) Dec.: 709–20.

30 See Seumas Milne (1994), *The Enemy Within: The Secret War Against the Miners*, London: Verso.

31 Ralph Miliband (1980), "Class War Conservatism," *New Society* 19 June, pp. 278–80.

32 See John Urry (1990), *The Tourist Gaze*, London: Sage.

33 Cf. Harriet Bradley (1996), *Fractured Identities: Changing Patterns of Inequality*, Cambridge: Polity.

34 Cf. Gordon Marshall (1997), *Repositioning Class: Social Inequality in Industrial Societies*, London: Sage.

35 Jan Pakulski and Malcolm Waters (1996), *The Death of Class*, London: Sage.

36 Though see the insightful piece by David B. Grunsky and Jesper B. Sorenson (1998), "Can Class Analysis be Salvaged?," *American Journal of Sociology* 103(5) March: 1187–234.

37 Though the class analysts at Oxford responded thoughtfully to this (and other) claims with their usual blend of rigorous argument and empirical evidence. See Anthony Heath, R. Jowell, and J. Curtice (1985), *How Britain Votes*, Oxford: Pergamon.

38   Stuart Hall (1988), "The Toad in the Garden: Thatcherism among the Theorists," in C. Nelson and L. Grossberg (eds.), *Marxism and the Interpretation of Culture*, Basingstoke: Macmillan, pp. 35–73.

39   Stuart Hall (1979), "The Great Moving Right Show," *Marxism Today*, Jan., pp. 14–20.

40   Stuart Hall (1986), "Cultural Studies: Two Paradigms," in N. Garnham et al. (eds.), *Media, Culture and Society: A Critical Reader*, London: Sage, pp. 33–48. Cf. E. P. Thompson (1981), "The Politics of Theory," in Raphael Samuel (ed.), *People's History and Socialist Theory*, London: Routledge, pp. 396–408.

41   Rob Stones (ed.), (1998), *Key Thinkers in Sociology*, London: Macmillan.

42   Stuart Hall, "Race, Culture and Communication: Looking Backward and Forward at Cultural Studies," *Rethinking Marxism* 5(1): 11–18.

43   Michael Green (1996), "The Centre for Contemporary Cultural Studies," in John Storey (ed.), *What is Cultural Studies?* London: Arnold, p. 53.

44   Rick Maxwell (2000), "Cultural Studies," in Gary Browning, Abigail Halcli, and Frank Webster (eds.), *Understanding Contemporary Society: Theories of the Present*, London: Sage, pp. 281–95.

45   See David Morley (1998), "So-called Cultural Studies: Dead Ends and Reinvented Wheels," *Cultural Studies* 12(4): 476–97.

46   See Angela McRobbie (1991), "New Times in Cultural Studies," *New Formations* (13) Spring: 1–18.

47   See Jim McGuigan (1992), *Cultural Populism*, London: Routledge.

48   Terry Eagleton observes that Stuart Hall has often objected to abstract theorization himself, but adds that this is a bit rich given the flirtation of Hall with high theory – Althusser, Gramsci, deconstruction – through the years. See Terry Eagleton (1996), "The Hippest," *London Review of Books*, March 7, pp. 3–5.

49   Manuel Castells (2000), "Materials for an Exploratory Theory of the Network Society," *British Journal of Sociology*, 51(1) Jan./March: 5–24.

50   Andrew Tudor (1999), *Decoding Culture: Theory and Method in Cultural Studies*, London: Sage.

51   Anthony Giddens (1984), *The Constitution of Society: Outline of the Theory of Structuration*, Cambridge: Polity.

52   R. W. Connell (1997), "Why is Classical Theory Classical?," *American Journal of Sociology* 102(6) May: 1511–57.

53   David Parker (1997), "Why Bother with Durkheim? Teaching Sociology in the 1990s," *Sociological Review* 45(1) Feb.: 122–46.

54   See Steven Seidman (1998), *Contested Knowledge: Social Theory in the Postmodern Era*, Oxford: Blackwell.

55   The quotations are from the present head of the ESRC, Gordon Marshall, and A. H. Halsey, the doyen of Oxford/Nuffield Sociology.

56   Joan Huber, in her Centennial Essay in the *American Journal of Sociology*, would expel from the discipline "antirationalists" (postmodernists, constructivists, and the like) who threaten the disciplinary center of Sociology. See Joan Huber (1995), "Institutional Perspectives on Sociology," *American Journal of Sociology* 101(1) July: 194–216.

57   Quality Assessment Agency (2000), *Benchmark Statement for Sociology*, Bristol, HEFCE, Jan.

58 Manuel Castells (1996–8), *The Information Age*, 3 vols., Oxford: Blackwell.
59 T. Becher (1989), *Academic Tribes and Territories*, Buckingham: Open University Press.
60 Gulbenkian Commission (1996), *Open the Social Sciences: Report on the Restructuring of the Social Sciences*, California: Stanford University Press.
61 There is a huge literature on this. My favorite is Donald McKenzie (1990), *Inventing Accuracy: A Historical Sociology of Nuclear Missile Guidance*, Cambridge, Mass.: MIT Press; (1996), *Knowing Machines*, Cambridge, Mass.: MIT Press.
62 Immanuel Wallerstein (2000), "From Sociology to Historical Science: Prospects and Obstacles," *British Journal of Sociology* 51(1) Jan.–March: 25–35.
63 Norman Davies (1996), *Europe: A History*, London: Pimlico, p. 13.
64 Mark Mazower (1998), *Dark Continent: Europe's Twentieth Century*, Harmondsworth: Penguin.
65 Irving L. Horowitz (1993), *The Decomposition of Sociology*, New York: Oxford University Press.
66 John Urry (1981), "Sociology as a Parasite: Some Virtues and Vices," in Philip Abrams et al. (eds.), *Practice and Progress*, London: Allen and Unwin. Reprinted in John Urry (1995), *Consuming Places*, London: Routledge, pp. 33–45.
67 One might consult the Lancaster Sociology Department's website: http://www.comp.lancs.ac.uk/sociology/ See also John Urry (1990), *The Tourist Gaze*, London: Sage; (2000), *Sociology beyond Societies: Mobilities for the 21st Century*, London: Routledge; Scott Lash and John Urry (1987), *The End of Organized Capitalism*, London: Sage; (1994), *Economies of Signs and Space*, London: Sage; Phil Macnaughten and John Urry (1998), *Contested Natures*, London: Sage.

Chapter 6

Notes on the Traffic between Cultural Studies and Science and Technology Studies

Marianne de Laet

1   Representation: On the Nature of the Universal

> When someone talks to me about a universal, I always ask what size it is, and who is projecting it onto what screen. I also ask how many people maintain it and how much it costs to pay them. I know this is in bad taste, but the king is naked and seems to be clothed only because we believe in the universal. (Bruno Latour 1988: 4.4.5.1)

Universality and representation

We tend to believe in the universal; we believe in the universality of scientific facts and technological artifacts, of surveys and overviews and of scholarly practices. Universals furnish our cultural space.

In this chapter I introduce the academic field of science and technology studies (STS), which has made it its business to learn about the social, material, and cultural conditions that make and maintain the universal. While the object of the scientific enterprise is to *produce* universals – and it is notorious for its success in generating quite a few of them – STS, the field that engages in the (social) study of science and technology, can be cast as tracing *how*, exactly, particulars become universals in this arena of scientific and technical knowledge. Put another way: STS is – among other things – interested to trace the strategies of representation that form the trajectory from local theory or vision to universal (arti)fact.

This is an unorthodox way to frame STS. As the name of the field implies, STS has science and technology as its objects of study. An alternative name by which the field is referred to, social studies of science and technology, points to the attention to science and technology's relationship with society and culture; their nature as social (or human) accomplishments; and/or the social structure of their enterprises. In the 30 years of its existence the field has made "culture" a central, though problematic, analytical category. While it is acknowledged that culture needs to be part of any kind of understanding of the processes and practices of technology and science (Pickering 1992), there is no consensus on how to conceptualize the role it plays. Does the world of science constitute a separate culture? Should the main concern be how science and technology shape culture and/or vice versa? Is it only a particular type of culture that can develop and sustain the scientific mode? If science and technology turn out to be culturally grounded, what does this imply for the universals they aspire to produce?

Inquiry into the universal may come with the STS territory. For in tracing the origins, the genesis, or the building of universals, one acquires a view of the social, cultural, and material particulars that go into their making. I suggest that this inquiry into the universal is at the heart of STS. It is a major source of difficulties between STS practitioners and their objects of study: those who engage in the practices of technology and science. For the quest for *universal* knowledge, which after all motivates the pursuit of science, seems at odds with the proposition, offered by STS, that the creation of such knowledge depends on culturally specific – and hence *particular* – routines. And while not *every*one who engages with the social or humanistic study of science and technology endorses such skepticism towards the universal (some philosophers and historians of science, especially, would not agree), I suggest that most of those who identify themselves with the field of STS, in some way or other, share this interest in how it – the universal – comes about.

Linkages of STS and cultural studies (from now on, CS) are obvious. Not only is there a joint interest in the relations of science, technology, and culture; like those who work in the field of STS, scholars in cultural studies are interested in how the universal grows out of particularities. Moreover, the skepticism towards the universal, the general, or the overview that can be found in STS, is even more apparent, for slightly different reasons, in CS. For even though general statements suggest universality, they are always partial – or so CS claims – and they are always made from a particular location or point of view. Surveying is not only a descriptive, but also a normative act: while reviewing, one reviews from the perspective of one's own intellectual and institutional alliances and thereby affirms the interests of those alliances. Or one surveys from one's geographical, ethnic, and/or political location, and thus is partial in another sense (Haraway 1997).

This skepticism towards the strategies of representation that need to be mobilized in order to produce a universal or an overview becomes even more urgent when one considers the *multicultural spaces* in which scientific knowledge and technical artifacts operate – which STS is increasingly requested to take into account. While in CS cultural difference has long been a central theme, in STS the relation between culture and science is a problematic issue and diversity, of cultures and so also of the cultures of science, has only recently begun to be seriously considered. Knowledge, especially scientific knowledge, and technology, especially "high" technology, despite their diffuse manufacture, their travel, and their use in a variety of heterogeneous locations, are still regarded as in, and of, and carrying one, homogeneous (but mythical) culture – the "culture of the West."

Overview

While many scholars in STS trade in skepticism of the universals that science and technology generate, they equally suspect the knowledge that they produce themselves. Trained to be "reflexive," they are aware that the knowledge that is produced in the field *itself* can be problematic on account of precisely its suggestion of universal applicability (Ashmore 1989) – and that thus caution is called for. Annemarie Mol, a Dutch science studies scholar, puts it as follows: "I want to avoid the idea that I am – or am in – a knowing *center* from which the various *elsewheres* in this large world may be *overseen*. I don't think that the *overview* is a proper mode of knowledge in a complex world where, or so it seems to me, the crucial political and intellectual challenge is to find ways of living with difference" (Mol 2000).

Caution is required. For while Mol is talking here to a heterogeneous audience about her discomfort in portraying the unifying role of the intellectual, and in a development context at that, what about my present commission to provide a (homogeneous?) portrait of a field as mixed as science studies? Suspicion towards the ways in which one might represent STS itself is in order, too. For STS is a diverse, a complicated, and an international field, which is made out of at least four disciplines, a plethora of case studies, a number of explanatory models, serious intellectual debates, and a few major controversies. I do not wish to provide a summary overview of this field; of its place in a cultural studies environment and in a world fraught with differences in knowledges, technologies, and their uses. And yet, for a Blackwell Companion, the overview seems to be an apt mode of representation. It is an uncomfortable responsibility, the responsibility of having to represent. What to do?

Framing the chapter

Here is what I propose. I organize what follows not around *differences* between STS and CS, nor do I attempt to give an overview of what STS is *all* about. Rather, I focus on the common interest in CS and STS in the work of culture, in the work of representation, and in the work of making universals out of particulars – in order to bring into view the traffic across the two fields, their exchanges with the arenas of science and technology themselves, and the ways in which all learn from each other. And I do so in what I hope is an appropriate fashion. By telling you a small story about a particular case, in which a printing machine with its appending practice of and knowledge about printing – a machine that is thought to be a universal technological object – travels to Zimbabwe and turns out not to be quite so universal at all, I show how STS might be *done* rather that *summarizing* or *overviewing* what it consists of.

Before we turn to this story, let me organize some of the convergences and differences between STS and CS around the issues of universality, representation, and culture. For these themes, I suggest, provide insight in what the relations between STS, CS, and the practices of science and technology are all about.

2   Science and Technology Studies and Cultural Studies

Universality, representation, culture; those are the issues around which I frame this chapter. It seems fair to say that – counter to the practices of science – CS and STS are not about producing universals; they are about understanding how universals come to be.

STS

Unlike CS, which is after the interpretation of cultural signs, artifacts, and symbols, unearthing their deeper (but culturally specific or local) *meaning* and which, as Andrew Ross frames it, is out to "show how the powerful language of science exercises its daily cultural authority in our society" (Ross 1996: 10–11), a leading motif in STS is to deconstruct the universal by asking about its *materiality*, its workings, and its use. How does a universal come about? What is it made out of? What does it cost to make it stick? What are the mechanisms by which scientific language and technological artifacts are given such authority in our society? These are the kinds of questions that are asked in STS – not only of universals but, more specifically, about the scientific facts and technological artifacts that are often taken to universally apply.

The field of STS emerged in the late 1970s, out of what hitherto had been three separate disciplinary interests in the nature of science and, to a lesser degree, of technology: history, philosophy, and sociology of science. An influx of anthropological studies of the workings and practices of the scientific and technological enterprise sealed the orientation of the field towards empirical, detailed, case-based, studies of the innards of scientific and technological practice and culture (Pickering 1992; Latour & Woolgar 1986; Knorr Cetina 1981; Traweek 1988).

A social studies approach is thus assumed and an interest in culture implied; the (many) historians and (fewer) philosophers of science who identify with the field of STS have the "social" or the "cultural" (whatever the precise content of the terms) in mind, as factors that help explain (in the latter case), or that need to be taken into account in the understanding of (in the former), the workings of technology and science. However, it is not the case that STS is a homogeneous project, organized around culture – or that it has fully assimilated the separate disciplines of history, philosophy, sociology, and anthropology of science. Each of these disciplinary tracks still flourishes in its own right, and not everyone who is active in them would identify him or herself with the STS field.

To apply a bit of STS analysis: there is a sociological explanation for this. The matter of disciplinary identity is still a major factor in the academic market for jobs, publications, and awards. One might give a historical explanation: each of these disciplines has developed a canon, a set of topics, and perhaps not a method but in any case a general approach to the subject-matter. A philosophical consideration: culture is a concept that is hard to approach with rigor and so for many philosophers this disenfranchises the enterprise of either pursuing a cultural approach to science, or to taking culture seriously as a factor to be considered in its development. Politically, STS has recently been identified, whether justified or not, with an insistence to not only recognize that the universal is partial, but to request that scientific methods learn to take such partiality seriously into account. And while anthropologists of science and cultural analysts usually subscribe to this project to democratize science as a political motivation for doing science studies work, this does not apply to everyone who works in the general area of studying technology and science. And so it has come to depend on the measure of comfort with this political and cultural orientation whether historians, philosophers, or sociologists associate themselves with STS – there is some apprehension about the current tendency to converge with cultural studies. For both the degree to which social and cultural factors are assumed to be responsible for the development of technology and science, and the political thrust of STS, remain divisive points (Ross 1996).

So STS is characterized by its object: technology and science. It distinguishes itself by its method: the empirical investigation of practices, workings, and materialities of technology and science. Also on the level of method, there is an ethnographic sensibility in sections of STS, bringing new challenges to the anthropological enterprise, such as that of studying one's "own" culture: the culture of science and technology of which the STS enterprise is an element (Ashmore 1989); and that of "studying up": studying powerful institutions (Fujimura 1991). Some unifying themes that run through all of STS will reemerge in what follows: the texture and materiality of scientific representation; the enabling constraints on innovation and technical development; the (political) use and ideological status of scientific facts and technical artifacts; the reconsideration of social, material, and cultural arrangements that ground, enable, and institutionalize knowledge.

CS and STS

Meanwhile, with the emergence of a consensus that contemporary (Western) society is dominated and shaped by scientific knowledge and technical in(ter)-ventions (Knorr Cetina 1999: 5), technology and science have gained legitimacy, or even urgency, as objects of study in CS. The further acknowledgment that "technoscience" – a term which flags the merger of science and technology

(Haraway 1997) – and the hazards of advanced industrialized life are closely knitted forces that frame turn-of-the-century culture as what Ulrich Beck calls a "risk-society" (Beck 1992), defined not only by the presence of environmental and technoscientific risk but also the formation of institutions that are centered around its management, gives CS its political thrust. Add to this mix the matter of what we call globalization and its consequent insistence to absorb diversity, and the question of the relations of science, technology, and culture becomes even more pressing – as a conceptual as much as political issue that frames the connections between CS and STS.

Changes that have taken place in STS over the past decades (in focus, subject-matter, theoretical stakes) are to some extent a response to its exposure to CS. Or, if not a response, then at least these changes coincide with theorizing in CS. The traffic between the fields is mediated by their objects, which flow back and forth: CS takes on science while STS takes on culture and both are interested in the issue of an increasingly global but irremediably partial spread of technoscientific cultures. There is political convergence: both fields have incorporated and elaborated the ideology critique of the 1970s, and a call for democratization of technoscience motivates at least portions of CS as well as STS.

Methodologically, both fields have been influenced and changed by the influx of cultural anthropology and CS more overall, STS partially, have taken in semiotics (the study of how humans organize the systems and articulate the processes of meaning: Fabbri & Perron 1990: vii) as a way of reading, respectively, texts and objects. Conceptually, the leading rule in both fields seems to be to make strange the taken-for-granted, by interrogating the images and objects that frame our daily lives. The traffic with CS is embodied by the emergence of a flourishing and highly visible new "cultural" stream in STS. This stream has the material and conceptual connections between culture and science as its central theme. (Some examples: Alpers 1983; Biagoli 1993; Downey & Dumit 1996; Haraway 1989, 1991, 1997; Hartouni 1997; Helmreich 1998; Hess 1995; Knorr Cetina 1999; Lave 1988; Mol forthcoming; Traweek 1988.)

Universality and representation. Both CS and STS are concerned with the work of representation. But while one asks what does it mean to represent, the other asks what resources does representation require and what are its effects? Whereas CS is primarily interested in the ways in which science and technology inform and shape culture, in the ways in which they are represented in contemporary culture and how, through such representations, they shape the cultural imagination, STS is rather interested in the question of how culture shapes technology and science. So the latter takes apart the universal – and hence universality! – by looking at the materialities that are required in order to sustain it.

Of course the differences between the fields are forged. For STS is not homogeneous. Neither is CS. Their shared interest in the entanglements of culture, technology, and science makes the two fields converge in certain ways; many scholars in science and technology studies are cultural observers, too. And of course in practice those who are interested in one question often find themselves dealing with the other as well, and so there is an area where CS and STS blend together and where both questions are addressed – as sides of the same coin. Nevertheless a disclaimer is in place here: convergence does not imply merger, and despite their shared interests CS and STS remain quite separate fields, with different perspectives, different methods, and a different set of questions that motivates them.

The point of my disclaimer is to stress that although culture has become an important analytic concept in STS, and although STS is increasingly (but inappropriately) identified with a cultural approach to technology and science, a generalized "cultural" take on technology and science is not representative of the field of STS as a whole. My treatment evokes *an* approach to studying science and culture in tandem; it does not "represent," or stand for, the whole of STS. But it does provide a glimpse of what STS and CS may do for each other.

3 Science and Culture: Fusions?

Resisting the separation of science and technology, the word *technoscience* itself makes clear that category fusions are in play. There is one other category separation, in particular, that seems ill fitted to do much useful work in representing technoscience: that between science and politics, science and society, or science and culture. (Haraway 1997: 62)

This is, in a nutshell, where science studies and cultural studies merge: in finding its object taken up by cultural studies, science studies is pushed to reconsider the ways in which culture and technoscience matter to each other.

It is appropriate to say that STS *re*considers the relation between science and culture. For the field has struggled with the relations of science, technology, and culture from its inception in the late 1970s. Coming out of a critical movement that wanted to assess how science and society (or culture) influence each other, the matter of how to frame those relations – what kind of model to propose for them – has issued in heated debate. Roughly four positions can be distinguished.

In the first place there is the nineteenth-century tradition in which science is considered the equivalent of art and treated as its counterpart in constituting high culture. Art and Science are the sophisticated accomplishments of Western civilization, by which it distinguishes itself from other locations – where primitivity reigns. In this view science and technology are kept separate, one taken as a part of "high" culture, the other as "low." While this position on science and culture has been criticized and discarded by sociologists and historians (of science) throughout the most part of the twentieth century, some early work in the field of STS has taken explicit position against the remnants of this view. So in early STS one finds the argument that the great (hierarchical) divide between the cultured and the primitive that is inscribed in this view is not so much an articulation of how matters stand between cultural realms, but rather an artifact of how culture, science, and knowledge are defined. This way of parsing things, it argues, is itself a cultural idiosyncrasy: by positioning science as an exclusively Western European enterprise it becomes unthinkable to include Chinese, Babylonian, or Bushman accomplishments in what might count as knowledge (Foucault 1970; Latour 1993).

In the second place there is the position that science and technology develop according to a dynamic entirely their own, and without reference to culture. In this frame the development of science is usually the prime focus (given primacy over the consideration of technology, that is) and this development is mostly rather unreflectively understood as progressing, unencumbered by cultural or societal constraints. It is in early history and philosophy of science – precisely the targets of science studies critique in the late 1970s – that this position can be found. *Boundaries* are strict, and are strenuously policed, in this approach, not only as a matter of fact (science and technology *are* separate, and they *are* strictly demarcated from culture and society, for the adherents to this approach), but also as a matter of intellectual policy: the act of separation guarantees analytical rigor. To add a reflective note on this practice of investigating science and technology, borrowed from early STS critiques: it might be the case that it is this very policy of strict analytical separation which leads to the recognition of strict separations in the reality to which the analysis is applied.

In the third place there is the position that considers culture the ambience for the development of technology and science; culture (or society) provides *context* and enabling constraints which mold the shape that technology and science can assume. (Staudenmaier 1985: 1–2). Pushed further, this position assumes a constructivist view, where science and technology are thought to be fully *determined* by such cultural and societal constraints. While much present history of science (and technology) falls into the former category, the second is more frequently adopted by sociologists of science. The emergence of STS as a trans- (or inter-) discipline, encompassing contributions from the history, the sociology, the philosophy and, a bit later, from the anthropology of science (and, to a lesser extent of technology), marked the transition to this more contextual or constructivist approach. One of the motives of the new orientation towards technology and science was, to find an alternative to the "progress" talk of the previous generation; one of its results, that the science–technology–culture relationship came to be understood as intrinsically mutual. A reflective note: culture, in this framework, is considered to be a known entity; more often than not science and technology are treated as its dependent variables.

Finally there is the position where STS and CS converge – a take on the matter that has come out of developments within STS, as well as in response to conversations with (for instance) cultural studies. Here, while the frame of mutual and intrinsic relationships is maintained, neither culture, nor technology, nor science are taken to be fixed, certain, known entities; or, for that matter as an ultimate determining factor in explaining developments in either realm (Latour

1987). Science and technology are treated as emergent effects, brought about by those who engage in them in conjunction with the (cultural) institutions that enable them. Likewise, culture is considered an emergent effect of the forces that operate on it – of which technoscience is (a significant) one. Rather than insisting on separating the realms of science and technology, many of those who operate in this mode prefer to use the term "technoscience" to indicate that science studies has become sensitized to the ways in which technology and science blend into each other. And rather than assuming that relations between technoscience and culture act according to a set model, those who operate in this mode are interested to (1) sort out the variety of models that may be, and that have been, applied to understand these relations, and (2) to map out the variety of ways in which they hold together. This attention to what might be called the *fluidity* of both technoscience and culture is – in these or in other terms, such as blurring boundaries, reflexivity, heterogeneity, hybridity, implosion, simultaneous production of the technical and the social – a feature of much recent work in or around STS (Beck 1992; Latour 1996, 1999; Haraway 1989, 1991, 1997; Bowker & Star 1999; De Laet & Mol 2000).

In this latter approach, a suspension of judgment about what constitutes (and separates) culture and technoscience is held in balance by an insistence on investigating the *materials* of which they are made up. Entities, even seemingly abstract ones such as culture, are held together by material objects. Their relations are mediated by concrete things – rather than by abstractions such as structures, institutions, or policies. This is not to say that structures, institutions, or policies do not exist; it is to say that they can only be understood by sorting out the materials that constitute them. Research in STS of the past 30 years – with its focus on case studies, laboratory studies, empirical research of scientific practices – has brought this materiality of relations – consisting of paper traces, spatial arrangements, laboratory rats, experimental assays, techniques to test for anemia to name a few – squarely into view (Latour & Woolgar 1986; Callon 1998; Mol & Law 1994). Materiality, then, stands out as another crucial feature in contemporary STS. And so in this fourth approach, as culture and technoscience move and modulate in tandem, so do they need to be followed – that is, investigated – as fluid but tangible categories that mutually shape one another. Obviously, my own reluctance to represent STS in terms of overviews and universals, and my choice to, in what follows, present some stories and possible ways of taking a cut at things, comes out of this approach.

Learning to Print in Zimbabwe: Universals, Representation, Culture

Universals

It is June 1997. I am looking at a photographic, electronic printer in a polytechnical school in Harare; it is about 6 months old, a state-of-the-art printing device. "Looking at it" is as much as one can currently do with this machine – and that without learning much about it – since it has been out of order almost from the day it arrived. This printer has cost what in Zimbabwe is a fortune. Luckily it didn't have to be paid for with a Zimbabwean fortune; it was donated by a Danish aid organization and cost what in Denmark constitutes much less than a fortune. The teacher, who was donated by a Dutch aid organization – but who will have to leave Zimbabwe short after my visit because even so she costs the Zimbabwean government too much – shows me around.

When a Danish aid organization sends a state-of-the-art printing machine to Zimbabwe it assumes that the technology is universal: that it will work elsewhere, no matter where this elsewhere is. Good machines are supposed to hold their own, whatever the circumstances in which they operate. For such a printing machine to be universal, does its size matter? Does it count who is bringing it where? How many people are needed to maintain it, and how much it costs to pay them? In other words, what is needed for it to be a universal? What are the costs and benefits to the expectation that this technological object is universally applicable? What are its materiality, its workings, and its use? How does a universal come about? What is it made out of? What does it cost to make it stick?

Universals. The machine does things: it prints. But in Zimbabwe it doesn't. Material issues count for this. In the case of the printing machine in Zimbabwe – as is the case with many machines that end up, with the best of intentions, in other worlds – the assumption of universality turns out to be wrong. In new, intractable environments, machines often break down. Such breakdowns can be "technical" (in which I include "mechanical": a wire breaks, a lamp gets displaced); it can be social (it is not used, or it is used for other purposes than it was intended for; as a footstool, for instance); it can be something in between. This in-between is the interesting space: what might be located there? Culture, perhaps?

Representation

The words that represent this printer – its operation manual – have disappeared. They have been lost. Perhaps they are stolen. They never meant much, anyway: they didn't really instruct the Zimbabwean polytechnical printing students on how to operate this machine. For they tell about switches and buttons, but not about hows and whys. So (and this "so" deliberately forges a causal link) even while the words were still around, the machine was out of operation. One of its lamps has been out of whack almost from the day the printer arrived. It may have been used as a footstool, or something. This is rather a typical state of affairs, according to the teacher; in and to Zimbabwe, things do not always travel well. The school's other state-of-the-art printing machine fell off a truck, the other day, on the way back from a trade fair demonstration. "*Aju paraplu*," she says in laconic Dutch vernacular. Which means so much as: "oh, well..."

110

Representation. The manual "represents" the printing machine in multiple ways: it *holds* its knowledge and it *stands* for it, hidden behind lock and key in the closet of the principal's office. Command over the manual means command over the machine. In order for the printing machine to be a universal the manual for the printing machine has to be a universal as well. The knowledge about the machine that is represented in the manual should be transparent, and should be as transportable as the machine itself. But like the machine, the manual is not. In new, intractable environments, like a polytechnical school in Harare, knowledge often breaks down. It breaks down because the carrier of knowledge fails to carry it effectively to these places. Such failure can be "technical" (it is not readable, for instance, because manuals are notoriously dense); it can be "social" (the manual ends up behind lock and key in the principal's office because that is where written text goes); or it can be somewhere in between. Again: the in-between is interesting. What might be happening with the manual, there? Might it perhaps arrange its own cultural space around it?

Culture

Usually words are kept behind closed doors, in this place in Zimbabwe. For they do get stolen. They mean much in that respect: they are sufficiently desirable to be unlawfully appropriated. Such appropriation happens on a regular basis. Even a useless manual to a useless printing device is a much sought-after collection of words. As a consequence (or is it the reason?) the principal keeps most words under lock and key. It is quite possible that these particular words – the ones that might make the printer work, the ones that describe and operate the apparatus – are in the principal's office as well. To all purposes that would be the same as if they were stolen. For, once in the principal's closet they are not accessible to anyone else. Here is another way in which facts – and things – break down. The words that capture them disappear into someone's private domain.

Culture. The machine moves through cultures: from Denmark to Zimbabwe; from high-tech laboratory to low-tech educational environment; from designer to user; from material space to world of representations. We are used to thinking of "culture" as the thing that is outside: it is nationality, it is context, it is environment; it is what sets the stage. "Culture," then, might explain what happens to the printing machine in Zimbabwe: we are quick to assume that worship sanctifies the written word and places it behind bars. That in certain cultures (cultures much like ours in this respect), status and collections of texts go together. That there is a culture that doesn't know – doesn't care to know? – about this particular machine. But maybe, maybe, culture is "inside." A "culture" that places high stakes on the written word may *result* from the realization that without the written word the printing machine will never work. A particular cultural arrangement may result from the way in which technologies travel – and from the ways in which they break down.

111

Materiality: an STS approach

So the teacher, who is responsible for the education of the public domain, decides to do without the words. "Let 'em stick their heads in a machine," she says. "That's much better for them, anyway. Go into the machine, look at it, take it apart, draw it. See what is made up of." The machine they stick their heads in is another one, an older one, though; and it won't ever work again, that much is for sure. "Sticking your head in" is not something that can be done with just any machine, and it is not done without consequence. It can not be done with little machines, nor with machines that consist mainly of chips – like the Danish Multi-Million-Zim-Dollar one. And you don't do it easily with a brand-new, freshly delivered one. But in the case of the older machine, or with the one-that-fell-off-the-truck, it is possible: these machines are out of use anyway, for one reason or another. So they offer students a chance to do without words, now, and in the future, when they – the students – will be printers, "originators" as they will be called, themselves. Maybe there is even a chance that, through sticking their heads into these machines, the students will learn some things about the Danish thing as well. That its lamps are not footstools, perhaps, because a print is as good as the angle of its light.

An STS approach has its eye on practices. It asks, for instance, how a machine that is not working can teach about printing; how in a new environment a machine – a printer for instance – assumes different tasks than the ones for which it was sent elsewhere – to Zimbabwe for instance. It has an eye on materialities: it is small, material things that decide whether the machine will work or not. Maybe our printer has to go to a trade show because it is the only machine in Zimbabwe. Maybe it falls off a truck on the way back. Maybe its manual stays with it so that someone can try to learn how to operate it. Maybe the manual disappears on day one. Maybe it is the culture of respect for written words that forces them to be placed behind lock and key and that so decides that this machine does not turn out to be a universal; or maybe, maybe it *is* a cultural idiosyncrasy that it works here and not there. And an STS approach has an eye on effects: maybe other things than learning to print emerge from sending a printer to Zimbabwe. Maybe it is a new cultural arrangement; a cultural arrangement that is sociotechnical in nature, that emerges from the travel of this machine. Perhaps culture is context but content; perhaps it is not already there but an emergent effect of the travel of technologies into new space.

5 Musings at the End

I would have been happy to give only particulars about STS and its differences and convergences with CS. But of course I have done a bit more. After all, the format of a chapter on STS and CS in the Blackwell Companion to Cultural

Studies requires that it *represent* universals, generalities, an overview; it is supposed to be a presentation of dependable matters of fact. You have been reading this because you wanted to know what STS is "all" about. So I have told you one of various versions of the history of the field, of its roots and developments, of its achievements and battles, of its findings and established facts; all this organized around a series of efforts in STS, in the course of its existence, to *grapple with the matter of culture*, around the issues of representation about the practice of making universals.

But you should keep in mind that a chapter written in this way should also be viewed as a way to *build* universals. For if I have given you a particular overview of what STS is all about, you now carry this overview with you, take part in its diffusion – and in the process its particularity disappears from view and the overview becomes more of a universal than it was before. My *partial* view may have gained more *general* viewing and thereby it has perhaps become – an *overview*. A tricky proposition, to write such a chapter, you will now understand. The writing of a universal is a performative act, that contributes to its making.

There are costs and benefits to the making of such a universal. I have been interested here to sort out what such costs and benefits, in a particular case, of certain universals – namely of the mission of STS and the travel of a printing device – might entail. I have wanted to keep in mind the costs and benefits of writing a story about STS in a volume like this. So here is how to read what I have written. I have organized what came before not around *differences* between STS and CS, nor have I attempted to give an overview of what STS is *all* about.

Rather, I have focused on the common interest in CS and STS in the work of culture, in the work of representation, and in the work of making universals out of particulars – in order to bring into view the traffic between the two fields and the ways in which they learn from each other. And I have done so in what is hopefully an appropriate fashion: by telling you a small story about a particular case, in which what is thought to be a universal technological object travels and turns out not to be quite so universal at all. In this story I have sorted out the cost and benefits to the expectation that a technological object is universally applicable. And so by following this object I have pursued the classic anthropological project of tracing the materiality of culture, which becomes a fresh pursuit when we try to understand what happens when the facts of science and the artifacts of technology travel into other worlds.

References

Alpers, S. (1983). *The Art of Describing: Dutch Art in the Seventeenth Century*. Chicago: University of Chicago Press.

Ashmore, M. (1989). *The Reflexive Thesis: Wrighting Sociology of Scientific Knowledge*. Chicago: University of Chicago Press.

Barnes, B. (1977). *Knowledge and Social Imagery*. Chicago: University of Chicago Press.

Barnes, B. and Bloor, D. (1982). "Relativism, Rationalism, and the Sociology of Knowledge." In M. Hollis and S. Lukes (eds.), *Rationality and Relativism*. Oxford: Blackwell.

Beck, U. (1992). *Risk Society*. London: Sage.

Biagioli, M. (1993). *Galileo Courtier*. Chicago: University of Chicago Press.

Biagioli, M. (ed.) (1999). *The Science Studies Reader*. New York and London: Routledge.

Bijker, W. (1995). *Of Bicycles, Bakelite and Bulbs: Towards a Theory of Sociotechnical Change*. Cambridge, Mass.: MIT Press.

Bijker, W. and Law, J. (eds.) (1992). *Shaping Technology/Building Society: Studies in Sociotechnical Change*. Cambridge, Mass.: MIT Press.

Bijker, W., Hughes, T., and Pinch, T. (eds.) (1989). *The Social Construction of Technological Systems: New Directions in the History and Sociology of Technology*. Cambridge, Mass.: MIT Press.

Bowker, G. and Star, L. (1999). *Sorting Things Out: Classification and its Consequences*. Cambridge, Mass.: MIT Press.

Callon, M. (ed.) (1998) *The Laws of the Markets*. Oxford: Blackwell.

De Laet, M. and Mol, A. (2000). "The Zimbabwe Bushpump: Mechanics of a Fluid Technology." *Social Studies of Science* 30(2): 225–63.

Downey, G. and Dumit, J. (1996). *Cyborgs and Citadels: Anthropological Interventions in Emerging Sciences and Technologies*. Santa Fe: SAR Press.

During, S. (ed.) (1993). *The Cultural Studies Reader*. London and New York: Routledge.

Fabbri, P. and Perron, P. (1990). Foreword to A. J. Greimas, *The Social Sciences: A Semiotic View*. Minneapolis: University of Minnesota Press.

Foucault, M. (1970). *The Order of Things*. New York: Random House.

Fujimura, J. (1991). in D. Maines (ed.), *Social Organization and Social Process*. Hawthorne, NY: Aldine de Gruyter.

Gross, P. and Levitt, N. (1996). *Higher Superstition*. Baltimore: Johns Hopkins.

Haraway, D. (1989). *Primate Visions: Gender, Race, and Nature in the World of Modern Science*. New York and London: Routledge.

Haraway, D. (1991) *Simians, Cyborgs, and Women: The Reinvention of Nature*. London: Free Association Books.

Haraway, D. (1997). *Modest_Witness@Second_Millennium. FemaleMan©_Meets_Onco-Mouse™*. New York: Routledge.

Hartouni, V. (1997). *Cultural Conceptions: On Reproductive Technologies and the Remaking of Life*. Minneapolis: University of Minnesota Press.

Helmreich, S. (1998). *Silicon Second Nature: Culturing Artficial Life in a Digital World*. Berkeley: University of California Press.

Hess, D. (1995). *Science and Technology in a Multicultural World: The Cultural Politics of Facts and Artifacts*. New York: Columbia University Press.

Hess, D. and Layne, L. (1992) *Knowledge and Society, vol. 9: The Anthropology of Science and Technology*. Greenwich: JAI Press.

Jasanoff, S., Markle, G. E., Petersen, J. C., and Pinch, T. (eds.) (1995). *Handbook of Science and Technology Studies*. Thousand Oaks: Sage Publications.

Knorr Cetina, K. (1981). *The Manufacture of Knowledge: An Essay on the Constructivist and Contextualist Nature of Science*. Oxford: Pergamon.

Knorr Cetina, K. (1999). *Epistemic Cultures: How the Sciences Make Knowledge*. Cambridge, Mass.: Harvard University Press.

Knorr Cetina, K. and Mulkay, M. (eds.) (1983). *Science Observed: Perspectives on the Social Study of Science*. London: Sage.

Latour, B. (1999). *Pandora's Hope: Essays on the Reality of Science Studies*. Cambridge, Mass.: Harvard University Press.

Latour, B. (1987). *Science in Action*. Cambridge, Mass.: Harvard University Press.

Latour, B. (1988). *The Pasteurization of France, followed by Irréductions*. Cambridge, Mass.: Harvard University Press

Latour, B. (1993). *We Have Never Been Modern*. Cambridge, Mass.: Harvard University Press.

Latour, B. (1996). *Aramis, or the Love of Technology*. Cambridge, Mass.: Harvard University Press.

Latour, B. and Woolgar, S. (1986). *Laboratory Life: The Construction of a Scientific Fact*. Princeton: Princeton University Press.

Lave, J. (1988). *Cognition in Practice: Mind, Mathematics, and Culture in Everyday Life*. Cambridge: Cambridge University Press.

Lynch, M. and Woolgar, S. (1988). *Representation in Scientific Practice*. Cambridge, Mass.: MIT Press.

Mol, A. (forthcoming). *The Body Multiple: Artherosclerosis in Practice*. Durham: Duke University Press.

Mol, A. (2000). "Things and Thinking. Some Incorporations of Intellectuality." *Lecture for the Conference on the Role of the Intellectual in the Public Sphere*. Beirut, Feb.

Mol, A. and Law, J. (1994) "Regions, Networks, and Fluids: Anemia and Social Topology." *Social Studies of Science* 24(4): 641–71.

Nelkin, D. (1992). *Controversy: Politics of Technical Decisions*. Newbury Park, Calif.: Sage.

Pickering, A. (ed.) (1992). *Science as Practice and Culture*. Chicago: University of Chicago Press.

Ross, A. (ed.) (1996). *Science Wars*. Durham: Duke University Press.

Serres, (ed.) M. and Latour, B. (1995). *Conversations on Science, Culture, and Time*. Ann Arbor: University of Michigan Press.

Shapin, S. (1994). *A Social History of Truth: Civility and Science in Seventeenth-Century England*. Chicago: University of Chicago Press.

Shapin, S. and Schaffer, S. (1985). *Leviathan and the Air-Pump: Hobbes, Boyle, and the Experimental Life*. Princeton: Princeton University Press.

Star, L. (ed.) (1995). *Ecologies of Knowledge: Work and Politics in Science and Technology*. Albany: SUNY Press.

Staudenmaier, J. M., Sj. (1985) *Technology's Storytellers: Reweaving the Human Fabric*. Cambridge, Mass.: MIT Press.

Traweek, S. (1988). *Beamtimes and Lifetimes: The World of High Energy Physics*. Cambridge, Mass.: Harvard University Press.

115

Chapter 7

Political Economy within Cultural Studies

Richard Maxwell

The attainment of critical consciousness is not an ultimate destination, but an ongoing process whose unfolding will continually surprise and confound the patterns of thought and habit that prevail at each point along the historical road of human development. Current efforts at communications–cultural policy making must be seen and understood in this way. However advanced or primitive the formulations may be, they are only markers on an endless road to the realization of human potential.

Herbert I. Schiller (1919–2000)[1]

Introduction

Much labor within critical communication and cultural studies has been devoted to pondering, provoking, and prolonging the rivalry between critical approaches of political economy and cultural studies (CS). Most of this effort has focused on CS and political economy as if these were entirely incommensurate, if not antagonistic, worlds of thought. Characteristic descriptions of their differences include terms such as "separate spheres" and "the great divide," and, as McLaughlin (1999) has recently pointed out, analogies reminiscent of the "unhappy marriage" days of Marxism and feminism. Though much of the war of words has subsided, the framework for thinking about the differences has left little for those involved to do but search nostalgically for the sweet old theoretical rendezvous (under the tree of Antonio Gramsci, Louis Althusser, or *The German Ideology*) or find a pragmatic reason to meet at the contested border between these two academic territories, either for technocratic (doing cultural policy) or technical reasons (ethnography   political economy   methodology).

This chapter heads in another direction, proposing instead that writers who are self-identified with either political economy or CS ought to strive to locate their rival already residing within their work. In a sense, McGuigan (1997), an advocate of cultural studies, made this move when he argued that John Fiske's writing on active audiences was consistent with assumptions of classical Liberal political economy. However, his attempt may have unhelpfully derided Fiske's work instead of raising awareness about the political economy that is everywhere to be found inside CS.

Political economy already features in CS work in two ways: as an empirical problem and as a set of theoretical propositions and background assumptions. The empirical political economy can be described as the dynamic interaction of politics and economy, a relationship whose effects reach into all parts of life where power relations determine economic arrangements and outcomes and, simultaneously, where economic forces delimit political thought and action. As an empirical problem, the main question confronting CS writers has been how the political economy defines, organizes, and regulates cultural industries and cultural labor, the latter encompassing the work of cultural production, distribution, and consumption.

The theoretical political economy (hereafter PE, to distinguish it from empirical political economy) can be broken down into three families of thought: Mercantilist, Liberal, and Marxist. Although the three family lines have crossed and mixed, strictly speaking, some form of Marxist (a.k.a. critical) PE has been CS's most significant other, in particular for CS writers aiming to identify and critically analyze the ideological links between national popular cultures and prevailing political structures. However, it is misleading to think that CS writers exclusively draw on Marxist PE, as McGuigan's critique of "cultural populism" suggested. Moreover, once extended to the international level, much CS writing appears to be in theoretical agreement, or at least in dialogue, with critical and mainstream variants of neo–Mercantilism and Liberalism. This chapter examines these aspects of political economy within CS to draw out both the empirical and the theoretical political economy already residing within cultural studies. In mapping the major families of theoretical PE, I hope to raise awareness of the present and potential uses of PE within CS.

Confronting the Political Economy: The Persistent Instance

While they did not write as theoretical political economists, the founders of British CS began with key empirical problems that the political economy of British capitalism had posed in their intellectual and political work. They stressed the conditions of the working class in Britain *vis-à-vis* media, education, and other cultural industries that were changing with the expansion of the welfare state, growing affluence, and the rise of consumer capitalism in the post-Second World War era.

Richard Hoggart, for example, attempted to show how these changes in the postwar political economy affected the traditional sites of working-class culture, focusing, for example, on the ways that consumer capitalism was destroying the matrix of authentic working-class sentiments and attitudes. Hoggart's study may have emphasized anthropological understanding of working-class culture, but his insights were still about the political economy within culture. In contrast,

117

Raymond Williams and Edward Thompson were more engaged with questions of ideology and politics, though each took on the changing political dynamics in the postwar period from different angles. Thompson confronted the political economy by addressing the ways that workers generated traditions, beliefs, ideas, and their own institutions through their struggle for survival in and emancipation from the capitalist political economy. Where Thompson emphasized class conflict in his notions of culture, Williams challenged the prevailing political economy for limiting the working class's participation and presence in the common culture. Rather than focus on the way that the contemporary political economy eroded traditional life-ways of the working class, as did Hoggart, or on the way it generated incommensurable cultures through class experience, as did Thompson, Williams sought to understand and remake culture as an inclusive realm of cultural labor. This effort was initiated in *Culture and Society*, where Williams showed that contemporary usage of terms like "art" and "culture" were descriptions of cultural labor undergoing processes of particularization and stratification during the transition to modern industrial society.[2]

Much of British CS continued to develop its politics of writing as a challenge to the empirical political economy's pressures and limits upon culture. Areas where this was most evident included work on inequality in the education system, efforts to understand the link between media and political ideology, in particular to improve the fortunes of the labor movement (with or without the Labour Party), and analyses about the barriers of access to both the means of cultural production and capacities of cultural consumption. These efforts to generate a critique of the political economy of culture and communication helped to distinguish CS from value-neutral cultural analysis, subjectivist Leavisite literary criticism, as well as the ahistorical and empiricist sociology of communication and mass culture coming out of American social science.

These interests overlapped and were deepened in important ways with the advances that feminists and critical analysts of race and racism brought to a second wave of British CS in the 1960s and 1970s. It was at this time that a coherent and arguably more culturalist set of theories began to define CS's approach to the empirical political economy. Eventually some CS writing began to avoid empirical description and analysis, especially in the 1980s and 1990s, but CS refuted this trend (see Morley 1992, 1997); even CS writers unfriendly to the theoretical work of political economists of culture have been critical of idealist CS (see Grossberg 1995 and Carey 1997). What perhaps better and more fairly typifies latter-day CS is its tendency to confront the empirical political economy as a separate realm of power and social organization that can be provisionally linked to cultural forms via ideological or institutional-discursive analysis (articulation theory).

On an international scale, CS has had to confront the empirical political economy in its neocolonial and imperialist forms. CS writing in Africa, Asia, and Latin America can be traced to revolutionary and transitional conditions that accompanied post-Second World War nation-building, decolonization, and national liberation struggles. Fanon, Cabral, and Nkrumah were important influences in the African struggle against colonial rulers, and they sought to link questions of national culture to the emancipation of their peoples from the prevailing colonial political economy. Latin American writers on cultural imperialism were not merely concerned with dethroning the hemispheric rule of the US political economy, but were imagining socialist societies through new forms of cultural expression. This was manifest in the pan-regional efforts of the New Latin American Cinema and work of associated intellectuals, Freirean theories of knowledge and pedagogy, as well as in cultural studies inspired by the Cuban revolution and in the endeavors of the international team of critical media scholars who worked in Chile during the Allende years (especially Armand and Michèle Mattelart). In Canada and Australia, CS not only drew on British theoretical influences but also grew from critical engagement with US cultural and economic imperialism.

The global expansion of the capitalist political economy during the postwar era, under US military and commerical direction, led to a number of crucial shifts in awareness in British and American CS. The protests against the Vietnam war in the 1960s and early 1970s highlighted questions of the cultural supports of imperialism. Civil rights and farm workers movements put the historical experiences of African Americans and Chicanos on the agenda of radical American cultural analysis. A countercultural wave of protests and celebrations helped galvanize CS's abiding interest in the relation between youth subcultures, rebellion, identity, and political ideology. Important political economic issues that subsequently came under the CS radar in the 1970s and 1980s included cultural domination through the import of US and British cultural goods to Third World countries, race and gender representation in media and politics, the superpower politics defined around cold war enmities, the displacement of cultural policy from the realm of national political economies to global economies driven by transnational corporate agendas, and the demographic changes that required an expansion of studies on diasporic and minority cultures within first world nations.

By the year 2000, the empirical political economy had further developed along these same faultlines. Millions more people were brought into the ranks of the working class around the world, as the industrial and information economies expanded and displaced many people from traditional modes of agricultural production. This economic transition has also increased levels of poverty and hunger around the world, as many national economies have failed to provide an equitable distribution of resources and support for large sectors of their populations still living in subsistence farming conditions, working in the impoverished primary commodity sector, or unable to make the adjustment to market economies. Many of the worst conditions could be found in sub-Saharan Africa, eastern Europe, and parts of the former Soviet Union. Workers in developed countries have also experienced setbacks in their basic conditions of survival. The revival of extreme free-market policies eliminated restrictions on global

119

corporate concentration, via mergers and acquisitions and vertical integration, setting off a series of massive layoffs in all sectors of the economy. These policies also encouraged the removal of the social protections of workers, cheapening and destabilizing labor markets in order to attract transnational capital investment. One result of this attack on working conditions everywhere has been a renewal of the labor movement worldwide accompanied by a revival of CS's critical interest in the labor movement.

In addition, in the richest parts of the world, the information technology sector, the late century motor of capitalist expansion, has shown significant signs of massive racial and class divisions separating information haves and have-nots. The so-called digital divide has a striking international character, as illustrated in the United Nations Development Program's (UNDP) 1999 *Human Development Report*. According to the summary report, by the late 1990s OECD countries made up 19 percent of the world's population, but accounted for 91 percent of the world's Internet users (p. 3). Such a cultural divide had long been reflected in international audiovisual markets, but by the end of the 1990s the tremendous economic power accumulated by US cultural industries crossed a remarkable threshold. As the *Report* put it, "The single largest export industry for the United States is not aircraft or automobiles, it is entertainment" (p. 6). The *Report* further noted the extreme affluence and consumption enjoyed in North America, the European Union, and Japan. There, the richest fifth of the world's population lived and consumed nearly 90 percent of the world output, taking 82 percent of exports of goods and services, and 68 percent of foreign direct investment. The income gap in 1997 between the richest fifth and the poorest fifth of the world's population "was 74 to 1, up from 60 to 1 in 1990 and 30 to 1 in 1960" (p. 3). The grotesque disparity in wealth in the capitalist political economy of 2000 confronts CS with ever worsening class divisions on a global scale. Consider that the "assets of the top three billionaires are more than the combined GNP of all least developed countries and their 600 million people" (p. 3). If you combine the assets of 358 of the world's billionaires you would have assets that equal those of 2.3 billion of the world's poorest, roughly the total assets of 38 percent of the global population (Harvey 1999: xv).

In sum, the main storyline connecting political economy and cultural studies should find CS writers confronting the empirical political economy – now globally – as a regulator and shaper of the general conditions and purposes of cultural labor (from production to consumption, and from the local to the national and the global scales of life). However, it should be noted that the political economy has also pounded, regulated, and shaped the work of cultural studies itself. It has therefore become increasingly important for CS writers to contemplate how the political economy affects their own attitudes and critical projects. The neo-Liberal contraction of the capitalist state's social support for education and the subsequent rise in the market-based demand to think of students as retail customers and academic programs as revenue streams has provoked a certain degree of professionalization, entrepreneurialism, and narrowing of the scope of academic CS – conditions which, in part, led throughout the 1990s to a less politically engaged formation of CS writers and greater willingness to write works that were congenial with a market-conforming popular culture. This political economic pressure on higher education during the last 15 years has arguably been one of the root causes of the growing feeling of job insecurity among CS educators (and all educators in the humanities for that matter). Bringing out their confrontations with the empirical political economy should alert CS writers to sources of resentment within the conditions of their own cultural labor. Such an avowal should also make it easier to speak openly about CS's partnership with theoretical PE.

The Fundamental Things

It is widely accepted among CS scholars that they belong to the family of theoretical Marxist PE. The evident links between CS and Marxist PE have been around studies of ideology, the state, class, civil society, and differentials of power. The obvious discursive connection is that both understand and write about culture in political terms, rather than in the narrowly apolitical terms of professional economics and liberal humanist cultural inquiry. There is a broad range of topics that fall within Marxist PE's critical approach to culture, including propaganda, ideology, telecommunication and media policy, international communication, film and electronic media industries, labor, music and the recording industry, intellectual property, advertising, marketing research, tourism, fashion, urban structures, and information technology. Within academic approaches to the political economy of culture, the study of communication and media industries tends to dominate the literature largely because these are easily understood as holding a strategic position in the political and economic life of modern societies. In addition, these subjects stand out for the quality of recent theoretical elaboration devoted to them, especially the work of Vincent Mosco (1996) and Dan Schiller (1996).

So while political economists often appear to be working on matters that emphasize economics, commerce, labor, and industrial structures, their outlook will almost always have a political horizon where economics confronts ethical questions of justice, equality, differential power, resource distribution, and social well-being. CS shares this with PE. Where CS and PE part ways is when CS suggests that politics and economics are separate realms. PE takes a holistic view of interdependent political and economic spheres, while CS theory tends to compartmentalize these areas of life as semi-autonomous spheres of activity. Of course, distinct schools of political economy do not agree on the exact relation between politics and economics nor about which realm counts more in that relation, but these tend to be disputes not about epistemology or facts but over normative theory. In general, the holistic approach to political economy applies to PE studies of culture as well, inasmuch as most political economists can agree that culture, politics, and economics are empirically interdependent, while at the same time arguing about the extent of each area's normative influence over the others.

At any rate, if CS's deep kinship with Marxist PE is assumed, the story about the growing divergence between CS writers and PE can be depicted as a dispute mostly among Marxists. Objects of CS's internal critique of Marxism have come to include mass culture theory of the Frankfurt School sort, problems in mechanistic models linking economic infrastructure to cultural superstructure, dominant ideology theory, neglect of culture in state theory, overemphasis on large social structures of class and nation at the expense of subnational and subcultural formations, the illusions of scientificity and objectivism, etc. Some have seen this history as proof of an ever widening gap between Marxist PE and CS (cf. Grossberg 1995). This, it seems to me, is misleading for at least two reasons. First, most CS writers engaged in rethinking Marxist theory have been as committed to a critique of the empirical political economy as are the advocates of academic Marxist PE – both have therefore drawn from each other (and should continue to do so) and from as many other available sources as they can find in order to modify their theories and advance their critiques of capitalist political economy. However, there is a second reason to reject the claim that there's a growing gap between CS and PE. The claim paves the way for the normative installation of a fundamentalist desire, namely, the internal purity of CS's intellectual identity. Such a fundamentalist urge would suppress the pluralizing drive that CS writers, in particular Raymond Williams, had long ago devised and that set CS apart as a transdisciplinary field. There is the related, self-diminishing aspect of theoretical fundamentalism: that is, it takes away CS's ability to make meaningful changes within theoretical PE. For when CS writers abide by a belief in their fundamental difference, they are encouraged to externalize (expel) all theoretical PE living within their work and deride it, thereafter constructing PE as incommensurable with CS. Of course, this works both ways (cf. Ferguson and Golding 1997; McChesney 1996).

To begin to turn down this fundamentalizing drive, this chapter asks CS writers to think about theoretical PE as a part of their own project again. PE is already inside CS, perhaps only in the background assumptions, perhaps in explicit ways that need to be drawn out for closer examination. What follows is a broad conceptual map of academic PE, divided into three families of thought: Mercantilist, Liberal, and Marxist. These families have crossed and produced offspring, the most notable ones being Institutionalism and the French Regulation School, and each has different sorts of concerns: some overlap, others have been modified to meet new empirical challenges. All this chapter can do is present an overview of PE and discuss continuities of the family lines that appear in CS. The present story of PE within CS cannot avoid saying something about CS within PE, though regrettably not as much as it should. Still, this chapter can indicate where there might be slopes and turns in that road too.

122

Theoretical Political Economy

Mercantilist PE developed between the sixteenth and nineteenth centuries to explain how wealth and well-being were achieved by making economic activity subservient to the interests of state power. Originally, Mercantilism served the interests of the absolutist state by justifying policies of government intervention in the domestic economy and protectionism in international economic relations. The enrichment of the state treasury was understood as the source of power in world affairs as well as the basis of whatever general welfare existed in the territories administered by the state. From this perspective, Mercantilist political theory argued that social order depended on producers devoting their work to the reproduction of the political authority of the state (Crane and Amawi, 1997: 5–6).

Liberalism reversed this idea of politics and the problem of order by arguing that political authority should be devoted to ensuring the reproduction of producers, the latter understood as merchants and small commodity producers. A new center of power and authority based upon growing commodity production and the rise of merchant wealth lay behind this theoretical challenge to the Mercantilist view of politics and economy. In *The Wealth of Nations* (1776), Adam Smith (1723–90) attacked Mercantilism on the grounds that state intervention and protectionism were actually counterproductive of economic activity and wealth accumulation, and hence contrary to the state's interests. Smith's liberal theory of political economy argued instead for limited state intervention in the domestic economy and free trade in the international economy. The state should maintain order but without interfering in the economic affairs of producers, for example, by defending property rights. In this sense, the answer to the question – for whom is order a problem? – shifted from the state to the property-owning producers who were nevertheless happy to leave enforcement of order (as long as it was in their interest) to political authorities. The doctrine of free trade also came to offer crucial ideological support to Britain's and, in the twentieth century, the US's military and commercial global expansion, bolstering the imperial aspirations of these modern hegemons.

Liberal PE underwent a series of modifications, first with David Ricardo's (1772–1823) efforts to narrow the purview of political economists around a rigorous methodology focusing more on the question of the interrelationships among individual economic actors (producers, consumers, nations) and less on politics. Ricardo also sharpened certain ideas that can be traced to Locke about the moral and political rights of producers by arguing that labor (of merchants and commodity producers), as opposed to land and rents, was the fount of value creation and therefore the lawful basis for the private accumulation of capital, or income-generating property. Ricardo extended Smith's ideas of free trade by taking account of how weaker economies could benefit from free trade through their comparative advantage, modifying Smith's argument that global trade only benefited those nations who possessed the absolute advantage of being able to produce something more efficiently than anyone else (Crane and Amawi 1997: 6–7).

At the same time, Mercantilists adjusted their theory to fit the aspirations of emerging national economies and states in America and Europe, in effect arguing that some kind of protectionism was necessary to defend infant industries until, and unless, they grew strong enough to compete in the open global market dominated at the time by Britain. After studying Hamiltonian Mercantilism in the United States, Friedrich List (1789–1846) elaborated Mercantilist theory in terms that were suited to, and helped advance, Germany's aims of becoming a modern industrial nation-state (Crane and Amawi 1997: 35–54; Hobsbawm 1992). List could not develop a sufficiently strong theoretical challenge to the logic of free trade and comparative advantage, but his thinking inspired the German Historical School, which adopted the nationalist position that political power should reign over economic processes. While the German historicists failed to solidify a theoretical foundation to support nationalist PE, they nevertheless devised conventions for determining the significance of policy and the organization of institutional ensembles in the history of national economies. These strains of Mercantilism (nationalism) and historicism underpin much of Max Weber's advances in historical sociology, especially his analyses of the interaction of markets with the national state and modern bureaucracies (Crane and Amawi 1997: 17; Mosco 1996: 54).

By the late nineteenth century, these concerns with the historical interdependence of national institutions, politics, and economics had spawned an offshoot of political economic thinking known as Institutionalism. Institutional PE emerged from an American matrix of pragmatism, historicism, socialism, and Mercantilism (the latter in the idiom of American national exceptionalism). Thorstein Veblen (1857–1925) is often credited with innovations that introduced Institutionalism into theoretical PE (Ross 1991: 204–16; Mosco 1996: 55; Babe 1993). His *The Theory of the Leisure Class* (1899) combines PE and cultural analysis, in part to explain how the working class experiences consumption under capitalism. He argued that consumption was motivated largely by envy, emulation, and a striving to better one's neighbors – seeing the leisure class as a kind of institutional identity, or "habit of mind," engendered by economic activity. However, the "institution of the leisure class" is ultimately counterproductive of economic activity and social progress, said Veblen, because it robs workers of money and energy (the means to consume) "to such a point as to make them incapable of the effort required for the learning and adoption of new habits of thought" (quoted in Ross 1991: 209). From an evolutionary and psychologistic view of history, Veblen predicted that emulative consumption would pass from this stage of false consciousness and impoverishment, to one dominated by feelings of "injured justice," and eventually provoke class conflict and socialism (p. 206).

Veblen's socialism was rooted in his readings of Marx and the German and Italian Marxists, from whom he developed a materialist understanding of consciousness as a force that is not only shaped within social institutions but one that

124

can also determine an institution's organization and aims, a trajectory that led Dorothy Ross to describe Veblen as the American Gramsci (1991: 207). Later Institutionalists modified Veblen's theory of historical change into a kind of structural explanation and his socialism into "a call for liberal social control" (1991: 216). One contemporary Institutionalist is John Kenneth Galbraith, whose book *The Affluent Society* (1958) examined the institutional role that advertising played in creating desire for consumer goods, an argument that struck a blow against Liberal PE's presumption that consumers are rational and free thinking (Mosco 1996: 55).

Also in the late nineteenth century, Liberalism was transformed from within by Marginalism, which servered the study of economics from politics as well as from political and ethical considerations of social conflict, labor, and institutional influences. After the Marginalist "revolution," economics (or neoclassical economics) defined social issues and institutions as external to economic processes, assigning them a separate logic that was irrelevant to economic theory. Marginalism instead focused on developing a mathematical model that would eliminate subjectivity from the marketplace interaction of supply and demand which set prices (and, it was hoped, set aside the questions of social conflict, moral judgment, difference, and order).[3] Marginalism professionalized economics, striving to make it a mathematical science and to elevate its influence within the social sciences and government policy, mostly to the detriment of Mercantilism. In addition, by putting aside questions of politics and society, Marginalist economics abandoned a significant part of Liberal PE's intellectual field, which was subsequently occupied by the disciplines of sociology and political science, in particular around the study of formal politics, the state, social action, order, and conflict (Clarke 1982). One feature of Marginalist thought that migrated back into liberal political theory was the mathematical modeling of rational choice to explain the causes of individual and organizational behavior in relations of power and exchange (they will always seek to maximize their own self-interest, etc.).

Crane and Amawi (1997: 8) explain Marginalist economics' success as the result of its seemingly progressive empiricism. In other words, it appeared to explain in a rigorous scientific manner how and why world capitalism advanced. Marginalist theory seemed to be tested empirically when its predictions of Britain's and the US's economic success (ignoring external causes) proved to be correct, as was its prediction of the failure of protectionist trade conflicts that contributed to the Great Depression of the 1930s. In contrast, Simon Clarke (1982) argues that Marginalism and its complementary social sciences did not, in fact, provide a scientific basis for understanding capitalism at all. Instead, Clarke offers a critical interpretation of why the Marginalist "revolution" succeeded: it was a simple and polished ideological fix for classical Liberalism's failure to explain the persistent problems of social order, class conflict, and inequality in the capitalist political economy. Moreover, as William Melody (1994: 28) puts it, "neo-classical market theory can justify equally well virtually any result. What it does tend to reflect in reality is the existing distribution of market power."[4]

Indeed, it is hard to ignore the fact that Liberalism's doctrinaire separation of economics and politics could not be sustained without numerous internal modifications throughout the twentieth century, starting with John Maynard Keynes' (1883–1946) challenge to the foundational belief that unfettered markets will always tend to produce universal benefits. An economist in the Liberal tradition, Keynes argued for neoclassical economics to accept a larger role for the state in managing the economy, in particular during cyclical business crises but in general as an ongoing complement to global market forces. Keynes' macroeconomic approach gave wider scope of influence to regulatory instruments and institutions, at both the domestic and international levels of governance. Such a shift in thinking allowed Liberalism to modify certain assumptions about free trade, comparative advantage, and equilibrium of benefits to take into account imperfect competition, underdeveloped economies, and unemployment. Still, as Crane and Amawi (1997: 12) argue, neoclassical economic orthodoxy successfully resisted the Keynesian "onslaught," defending economistic approaches, deriding any talk of the politicization of markets as "irrational" (rather than, as Keynes attempted, to deal with Liberalism's inability to explain how markets are shaped by politics), and becoming the dominant "theoretical tool used by institutions such as the World Bank and the International Monetary Fund."

The central ideas of classical Liberal PE – methodological individualism, subservient state, free trade, comparative advantage – remained opposed to the Institutionalist perspective as well, despite the anomalies in the liberal market economy that Institutionalist continued to reveal, in particular the observable interdependence of economy, politics, cultural experience, social inequality, and social institutions. As for classical theoretical Mercantilism, it did not survive the challenge from Liberal economic theory, though it still managed to maintain a significant presence in policies of economic nationalism up to the Second World War. Afterwards, Mercantilism had a few reprieves but overall diminished in influence among national policy-makers until it was virtually snuffed out by neo-Liberalism at the end of the twentieth century (Crane and Amawi 1997: 5–8).

Nevertheless, many of the central concerns of Mercantilism have maintained a residual presence in political economic thought, mostly in modified forms that overlap in varying degrees with Liberal and Marxist projects. For example, since the Second World War, Liberal economic policy has been linked with a form of Mercantilism in military and foreign policy, expressed most clearly in the realist vision of international relations, which sees sovereign national states locked in a power struggle within an anarchic world environment (Crane and Amawi 1997: 18). Likewise, after the Second World War, secular nationalist ideals of social peace, social progress, and economic development were provisionally reworked under Marxist PE thanks to the struggle of socialist internationalism against fascist imperialism. Many writers of Marxist international PE, in particular Lenin, Stalin, and Rosa Luxemburg, came to influence the theories and movements of national liberation and decolonization in the Third World (Hobsbawm 1992). Out of this mix grew socialist–inspired models of nationalist economic and cultural development, which opposed Liberal theoretical advocacy of US-led imperialist expansion of free-market capitalism. Some of these studies would overlap with Marxist-inspired PE studies of underdevelopment, world systems theory, and dependency.

While political theorists like Michael J. Shapiro, James Der Derian, and David Campbell have contributed CS writing on military and diplomatic cultures, it is still an area in which most CS writers in the humanities have made few inroads. However, there has been a good deal of CS work touching on issues of cultural protectionism, especially as this has been discussed by writers challenging PE's approach to cultural imperialism. Neo-Mercantilism certainly resides in political economists' demands for *ad hoc* applications of protectionist rules that regulate political, financial, and commercial aspects of national cultural industries. And any CS writer who has addressed policies affecting national culture, or the question of cultural imperialism, has also absorbed or confronted these ideas. Some, like John Tomlinson (1991), have challenged the Mercantilist assumptions in protectionist (nationalist) policies associated with critics of cultural imperialism from a position consistent with Liberal doctrine. Recently, Scott Olson (1999) has proposed the wholesale adoption of a comparative advantage model in order to explain the universal demand of Hollywood cinema in divergent national reception contexts – suggesting further links between Liberal PE and CS textual and audience research models. Other CS writers have resisted the draw of Liberal PE, but have incorporated assumptions drawn from neo-Mercantilist thought. Toby Miller (1998), for example, has confronted a number of the neo-Mercantilist ideas that emerged in the period following the crisis of the liberal world economy in the 1970s. At that time, there was a burst of effort to elaborate new theories of the state, theories of autonomous development or delinking, and nationalist cultural policy. Miller has been rethinking the problems of cultural consumption and citizenship without resorting to Liberal notions of consumer sovereignty, drawing on PE that intermixes concerns of Mercantilism, Institutionalism, and internationalist Marxism.

Mercantilism's residual influence was (and remains) clearly a part of cultural and communication policy where arguments about the defense of cultural identity, pro and con, have required historical and theoretical sources from outside both the Liberal orthodoxy of free trade and the Marxist tradition that sees the state as epiphenomenal. In international communication, Marxist and institutional political economists modified the Listian nationalist agenda during the 1960s and 1970s, within frameworks known as dependency and world systems theory, to elaborate anti-imperialist policies in support of cultural and information autonomy in less-developed national and regional economies. This approach to cultural autonomy was most explicitly developed in Cees Hamelink's *Cultural Autonomy in Global Communications* (1983), which drew on neo-Listian theories to promote protectionism of cultural industries in the Third World. And, throughout the work of Dallas Smythe (1907–1992) and Herbert I. Schiller (1919–2000), the founders of American political economy of culture and communication, strains of neo–Mercantilist thought mix with Institutionalism and Marxism. These writers were concerned with identifying and analyzing how market criteria stifled the emancipatory potential of communication; both were dedicated to freeing up human development from exploitation, oppression, and other forms of economic and social injustice (Lent 1995). Smythe's notion of the audience commodity (1981) and Schiller's work on cultural imperialism (1969/ 92 and 1976, among others) remain standard references for many CS writers interested in the effects of commercialization within culture.

Finally, whatever the ultimate heading of individual CS writers, Marxism, or at a least Marxist inflected theory, has always been an important point of departure for them. A central feature of Marx's analysis of the capitalist political economy was a critique of the institution of private property and its social byproducts, including the structured inequality in the relations of production (class), the preeminence of exchange-value over labor-invested value and use-value (life under the money sign: wages and status), the money form's role in the estrangement of value from both use-value and labor (commodity fetishism), and a mode of comprehending the world that derides and subordinates noncommercial ways of living (social and economic imperialism).

Marx's critique of property relations had two important basic features. One was to demonstrate how the institution of private property engendered a class of property holders (the bourgeoisie) whose control over resources and the technical means of making their property productive grew only by virtue of their command over the labor of a non-property-holding class (the proletariat). As workers fight to free themselves from this relationship, and the bourgeoisie works to reinforce the proletariat's subjugation, each class becomes increasingly aware of itself as a class. British CS, in particular E. P. Thompson, Richard Hoggart, and later writers using ethnographic techniques to study working-class youth cultures, drew out some of the cultural implications of this basic relation to understand the sources of expressive differences and interpretive conflicts in British popular culture. How people made sense of differential power in societies stratified by class became the stuff of early CS ideology research. With advances made by feminist and antiracist activists within CS, this line of inquiry became increasingly attentive to the aspects of property relations that fostered both gendered and racialized stratification.

While Marxist PE showed how capitalist property relations made objective enemies of workers and property-owners, it also demonstrated how this fraught relation in the capitalist political economy could become naturalized by the Liberal discourse of moral and political rights accorded to property-owning individuals. This cultural expression or story linking moral right, property, individualism, and sovereignty not only became the standard way Liberalism made sense of the new political economy. The story also developed into a formidable ideological system that served to justify the domination of the bourgeoisie over the proletariat (and by extension, capitalist over the noncapitalist regions of the world). CS developed a critique around the edges of this ethico-political dimension of capitalism in the Gramscian idiom of cultural hegemony to understand some of the ways dominant media and political actors worked within civil society to win the consent of working-class people to programs and policies that were structurally opposed to their interests.

The other basic feature of Marx's critique of capitalist property relations was the discovery of divergent forms of value that come into being during capitalist processes of production, circulation, and exchange. In its basic form, a commodity did not possess a fixed and inherent value, but was filled with value by the effort that goes into making it; in this humanist framework Marx saw, and celebrated, labor as the substance of value. But Marx added that once a commodity becomes available for others, its value is understood in a fresh, supplementary way as an aspect of its usefulness. Marx identified disparate interpretations of a commodity's value flowing from diverse needs, wants, and desires, referring to this dynamic quality as the use-value of a commodity (we can think of a commodity in contemporary terms as any good or service). Use-value describes the material side of a good or service. If labor gives substance to a commodity's value, the diversity of social uses gives products their meaning, or use values, in our lives.

Many CS writers have delighted in and deepened the stories of the way distinct groups of people use consumer goods, media products, services, and shopping to enhance or make sense of their lives. Use value is not always discussed in the technical terms employed by Marx, but the number of studies that touch on issues of consumption is enormous. The question CS must ask is how their background assumptions connect to those elaborated in Marxist PE – remaining alert, that is, to the different and competing social presences and meanings of value, use-value, and exchange-value (discussed below). Likewise, CS writers might think how Liberal PE makes value intelligible as the utility in a good or service. It would be especially important to do so when treating value in terms of pleasure or displeasure, thereby looking in their work for discursive continuities with Jeremy Bentham's utilitarianism and its modified version in Marginalism. Further, it might be worthwhile considering if the ideas linking consumption and identity have remained consistent with institutional PE, in particular with Veblen's views on the (fraught) institutional identities that can be formed in a semi-autonomous realm of consumption. Of course, heeding these lines of influence is something that PE writers ought to take seriously as well. When it comes to considerations of value and evaluation, many PE writers choose to ignore the distinctions Marx made – in part because the technical terminology can easily become confusing – and instead rely on ideas that are easily suited to Liberal or, more often, Institutionalist frames of PE thought.

One of the most important distinctions Marx made in his critique of capitalist property relations concerned the form of value engendered by exchange, which is the dominant mode of sociability under capitalism. Recall that according to the Liberal doctrine, free trade (uninhibited exchange) creates wealth, and trade is predicated on individual sovereigns holding private property. A harmonious social order is supposed to flow from the universal assumption that every individual involved in exchange sees their counterpart, and imagines their own self seen by their counterpart, as the rightful owner of the property in question. This recognition of personhood-in-exchange endows individuals with the associated right of a sovereign to decide freely when to sell and with whom to enter into exchanges of privately held properties. Non-property-holders, or people living life in noncommercial ways, could achieve only semi-sovereign status, at best, having failed to qualify for full personhood under the property rules of social encounter. With the institution and institutional identities of private property in place, the individual accumulation of income-generating property, or capital, form a dynamic system of wealth creation. Capitalists put their capital into production to make more capital. A commodity produced with the fundamental goal of capital accumulation will of course have to have a use-value, or multiple use-values, but will be launched into circulation with a price attached to it. The price that adorns the commodity helps secure a presence for exchange-value, the third, and most rapacious, form of value.

Marx's distinctions of value have helped PE and CS writers alike to recognize the artifice of value in cultural products and practices. Value does not occur in nature, but is a socially generated presence with socially constructed meanings that flow alternately from work, daily efforts to make sense of and to satisfy material needs, and from the relations of exchange that support private property. Each kind of sociality generates different forms of value, and each provides a distinctive ground for interpreting the value of people, things, and even the value of being social. However, for Marxist PE, while value and use-value (work and meeting material needs) might be seen in playful and creative competition with each other, exchange-value comes into being in an avaricious form suited to the reproduction and growth of capital. Indeed, capitalism elevates exchange value as the preeminent mode of understanding and judging the labor in the product (value) and the product's material side (use-value).

The key point from the perspective of Marxist PE is to be alert to the conflict over the interpretation of value that pits the worthiness of life derived from exchange against values that come from noncommercial forms of living. While much CS writing has focused on contests of meaning at the heart of culture, for example, where popular culture resists or challenges dominant value systems, some technical details are needed here to distinguish how Marxist PE would define this interpretive struggle. For Marx, there is no getting around the alienation of value from labor: both use-value and exchange-value pull goods and services far from the specificity of their source of value, the original effort, and press their own interpretations of value upon labor-invested value. However, as long as they are saved from exposure to exchange, labor-invested value and use-value are theoretical equals, in a sense, because both involve an equality of effort to bring value into being. Culture is made, at least in theory, when labor that gives substance meets labor that gives meaning. That is why, as an abstract principle, the belief that cultural producers must be responsive to the needs, tastes, and desires of cultural consumers is such an attractive one. For it implies that value remains in open negotiation: both producers and consumers work to generate new value and meaning in goods and services in an ongoing if agonistic way. If we heed this relation we can better perceive and cultivate an ethical regard for how people work to bring value into existence and how that value undergoes an inevitable alienation from the labor that originally brought it into being.

This rosy picture is, of course, too rosy. Once exchange-value comes into the relation, it separates consumers from producers of value, attempts to overtake the interpretation of value, and pressures those under its influence to see value in terms of price, status, and profit. As capitalism propagates faith in exchange as a legitimate form of sociability, the price of things and the money-form hammer their way into people's daily lives with such force that the ability to recognize the structured inequality of property relations, labor-invested value, and use-value is diminished. For Marxist PE, the experience that results from the social imperialism of exchange-value is explained by the theory of commodity fetishism. In *Capital*, Marx suggested that once exchange-value, and exchange relations, dominate the political economy, it became possible for commodities to appear to gather value – taking on the commodity form – without labor-invested value. Things can acquire a commodity form by simply being priced and sold. Price not only misrepresents itself as equal to value; it hides the qualitative value of labor generally and the material, particular side of value in daily life. If this is true, said Marx, then "price ceases altogether to express value." And,

> Objects that in themselves are no commodities, such as conscience, honour, &c., are capable of being offered for sale by their holders, and of thus acquiring, through their price, the form of commodities. Hence an object may have a price without having value. The price in that case is imaginary. (Marx 1967: 102)

If I were to relate to this imaginary system in which commodities, their prices, and money appear as the complete infrastructure of consumption, then, according to Marx, I would be susceptible to the fetishism of commodities. In addition to denying me full exposure to the political economy in which I live, commodity fetishism also naturalizes value in terms of exchange. Money and exchange-value not only alienate value from the labor that made it, but induce a kind of slumber, a feeling of enchantment, that makes it hard to sustain an ethical regard for the strife of labor's alienation from value. When labor is prohibited from serving, or disappears altogether, as a source of ethical responsiveness, the primary cultural resources available for making sense of the world of commodities flow from a contest between exchange-value and use-value. Such a contest is fixed in favor of exchange. For if use-value multiplies with the diversity of social needs and desires of goods and services, exchange-value narrows a commodity's use to satisfy one overarching and imperious need: to accumulate capital (Maxwell 1996).

131

Many CS writers, including Judith Williamson and Raymond Williams, have sharpened Marxist PE's perception of commodity fetishism by showing how advertising and marketing reinforce exchange-value through the manipulations of signs that endow goods and services with magical power. Critical PE analyses of commodity fetishism also overlap in interesting ways with other non-Liberal approaches that have endeavored to unfreeze arrested forms of value and interpretation buried in modern institutions and discourses, in particular CS work inspired by Foucault, Derrida, and other post-Nietzscheans. More often CS writers have extended Marxist PE's perception of commodity fetishism through a mix of institutional-historical studies of consumerism, shopping, and so on. This story usually tells of the transition from traditional, small-town market relations to mass-market exchange relations in which mass-produced goods are disseminated to an anonymous mass of consumers.

Property relations not only create conditions that make a miserly and mystical form of value possible but also help to advance the process that transforms value into profit. This process of transformation takes time, however, and so an obsession with shortening turnover time – the time it takes to realize a profit – became an essential feature of capitalism. In a famous passage from the *Grundrisse*, Marx (1973: 524) identified the role that communication networks would play in resolving this problem of profit realization:

> The more production comes to rest on exchange value, hence on exchange, the more important do the physical conditions of exchange – the means of communication and transport – become for the costs of circulation. Capital by its nature drives beyond every spatial barrier. Thus the creation of the physical conditions of exchange – the means of communication and transport – the annihilation of space by time – becomes an extraordinary necessity for it.

For Marxists, communication technologies have been employed for their power to overcome the temporal barriers to profit realization by eliminating the spatial obstacles that hinder exchange (time annihilates space). In the sixteenth and seventeenth centuries, profits were realized on an average of four times a year; in the nineteenth century, by contrast, turnover occurred once daily (Braudel 1986: 607–8). Consider that by the late twentieth century satellite communication in combination with digital, computerized networks allowed for the instantaneous turnover of capital into profits in global financial and commodities markets. The drive to shorten turnover time not only made communication technology a strategic asset in maintaining property relations and amplifying capital accumulation. Wage-labor has also been forced to adopt work rhythms that are synchronized with the ongoing speed-ups of capital circulation.

Thus Marxist PE tracks the links between private property and social inequality, conflict, and order. Marxist PE turns down the moral codes of Liberal political economy, in particular the legitimacy of privilege accorded to owners of income-generating property, the so-called means of production. Marx also analyzed the ever-widening relations of exchange, the inherent tendencies toward crises in capitalist accumulation, the inevitability of interfactional struggle among capitalists, and the subordination and intermittent destruction of labor. Marx demonstrated the profound contestability of classical Liberalism's fundamentals (methodological individualism, a normatively subservient state, and free trade), and revealed the internal instabilities of the capitalist system. Later Marxists, starting most notably with Lenin, extended this work to examine the geographical expansion of capitalism, its imperialist forms, and its impact on noncapitalist regions, further challenging Liberalism's faith in free trade and comparative advantage. The sources here for CS are multiple, not least of which is the basis for understanding differential power structured into capitalist property relations. More importantly, perhaps, has been CS's attempts to bring out the experiential details of consumption and strive to link the daily lives of consumers to a critique of differential power, not only in terms of class but also related to axes of power that are structured by gender, race, and nation. In addition, there have been recent examples of CS's renewed interest in labor as a source of ethical and political responsiveness to questions of culture, conflict, inequality, and the public good (see Miller 1998).

Final consideration should be given to the French Regulation School of PE and its resemblance to the families of PE thought discussed above. The regulation approach understands capitalism as a general system of wealth creation, or regime of accumulation. But within that system there are inherent crises which create conditions that make new modes of regulating the system possible. One can envision these modes of regulation as so many pillars holding up the regime of accumulation; each successive crisis, or round of destruction, eliminates some pillars while erecting others. Cultural patterns are part of the substance of each of these pillars, so shifting conditions of culture go hand in hand with changing modes of regulation. While capitalism is viewed as a superordinate political economy, on-the-ground reproduction of the political economy depends on particular regional or national ensembles of economic and state institutions (markets, exchange, money, regulatory agencies, prisons, military, etc.). This approach arguably draws on a mix of neo-Mercantilism (recognition of the state power and national political economies), Liberalism (neo-Keynesian role for regulatory instruments), Marxism, and Institutionalism (accounts of systemic instability, inequality, historicism, institutional identities and roles for organizations and bureaucracies); there are additional resemblances with the Liberal-Institutionalist approach found in the work of Joseph Schumpeter, who wrote of the destructive cycles in capitalist development.

In the 1980s and 1990s, the Regulation School came to feature prominently in CS writing. One of the most recognizable themes concerned the passing of a mode of regulation called Fordism, a term Gramsci gave to the factory discipline of serial production that replaced direct force as a mode of regulating both productivity and control over labor. Webster and Robins (1986: 48–51) identified four broad and interrelated areas that distinguish Fordism as a mode of regulation. First, Fordism pushed the capitalist form of sociability into the "non-work" areas of leisure, the family, and everyday life; this was accomplished in part through the spread of consumerism (Ewen 1976). Second, the state managed society through economic planning, fiscal policies, scientific research and development, welfare and social policies. "The third and fourth aspects of Fordism are related and involve the attempted capitalist annexation of time and space respectively" (Webster and Robins 1986: 50). Fordism did not reach a relatively solid form until after the Second World War, at which time the labor movement had been purged of socialist and communist programs, and Keynes had resigned Liberalism to accepting, at least provisionally, a significant role for the state.

Fordism peaked in the late 1960s as a stable regime of accumulation, but grew more rigid in the four areas described by Webster and Robins. Harvey (1989) suggests that it was the rigidity of Fordist institutions that initiated the global economic crisis in the early 1970s. The shake-up of the recession of 1973, sharply extended by the oil crisis, created conditions for "experiments in the realms of industrial organization as well as in political and social life" (Harvey 1989: 142–5). Regulationists dubbed this phase of restructuring "postfordism." It was a time characterized by the emergence of entirely new sectors of production, new financial services, markets, and speed-up in technical and organizational innovations (1989: 147). There was also a shift in economic geography with the rise of so-called Newly Industrializing Countries, accompanied by the revival of sweatshops and domestic labor under patriarchal discipline and amplified job growth in the "service sector." Deepening structural unemployment engendered a highly flexible labor market in which part-time and unskilled labor reserves began to keep wages low and weaken the traditional role of organized labor under Fordism. And, finally, the large-order production system of Fordism was modified to make room for more pliable small-batch production and subcontracting, what some have suggested represent a long-term shift toward a regime of flexible accumulation (1989: chapter 9).

According to this approach, the crisis of Fordism brought cultural and communication industries into the center of economic activity. Greater flexibility in production entailed an acceleration in product innovation which demanded the speed-up of turnover time. PE and CS writers began to take notice of the repositioning of the cultural industries to satisfy these demands for flexibility and acceleration. Technology and organization innovation extended the geographical reach of the "physical means of exchange." They also enabled the production of cultural objects with an incredibly brief, if not non-existent, shelf life (digitally stored audiovisual products and computer software are exemplary), which cost almost nothing to store or distribute, and which have the advantage that their values can be turned into profits almost instantaneously. David Harvey (1989: 157) pointed out that the primary "need to accelerate turnover time in consumption has led to a shift of emphasis from production of goods (most of which, like knives and forks, have a substantial lifetime) to the production of events (such as spectacles that have an almost instantaneous turnover time)." Harvey saw this shift from the consumption of goods to the consumption of entertainment, information, and images as a godsend for capitalism. Capital accumulation will always suffer intermittent crises of overaccumulation when capitalists cannot get a portion of their surplus capital back into circulation because of overproduction; and capital must be moving or it doesn't grow. So the arrival on the scene of a volatile, ephemeral image in the commodity form provided one way to keep capital in motion (Cf. Ewen 1988; H. Schiller *passim*). This process occurs through the conversion of all sorts of cultural forms, popular identities, and expression into commercialized image innovations. From a Regulationist perspective, then, entertainment and information industries offered a novel fix within the post-Fordist mode of regulation, and, once recognized as such in older pockets of industrial capital, initiated a wave of unprecedented investment, growth, and concentration in the cultural and information industries. Finally, it could be argued that post-Fordist restructuring gave greater currency to the commodity form and exchange-value as it amplified the role of informational-cultural commodities as well as the marketing of tangible goods (Maxwell 1991 and 2001).

Conclusion: Culture Works

The purpose of this chapter has been to introduce ideas from theoretical PE which may already inform a good deal of thinking in CS, hopefully broadening the way CS writers imagine PE within their own work. Liberalism survives in CS writing that uses notions of consumer sovereignty and comparative advantage to explain cultural consumption. Some neo-Mercantilism and a lot of Institutionalism can be found in both Marxist PE and CS writing that looks for causes and alternatives to the global inequalities in communication and information. And Marxist and Institutional PE continue to inspire ways of identifying and analyzing the changes in the empirical political economy, especially in the midst of the present post-Fordist restructuring. There are clear applications of all these families of PE throughout CS, far too many than can be acknowledged in one essay. What I have tried to show here is that while the effort to disassociate CS from PE, or vice versa, may help to secure an academic identity in confusing times, it encourages writers to be disdainful of sources that already constitute a part of their thinking. Perhaps it would be too disturbing for proponents of a pure CS or PE to do otherwise. After all, to admit that the thing you have derided is inside, muddying up your supposedly coherent identity, might derail your writing. But the times may demand that PE and CS do just that.

To conclude, I want to suggest that the defense of the contest between labor-invested value and the multiple forms of use-value – to use the technical terms of Marxist PE – can serve as a formidable challenge to commercialization, the latter understood as the tendency within capitalism to convert life, and the interpretation of life's value, into commerce. The interpretive struggle between labor-invested value and use-value is not only productive of culture, it is a condition of possibility for open negotiation where both producers and consumers work to generate new value and meaning in goods and services. In that sense, it has the potential of dissolving the difference between the institutional identities of producer and consumer, offering instead a vision of culture work as the interdependent efforts in production, distribution, and consumption that bring value and meaning into the world. Yet it is crucial to remember that this interdependence is characterized by the strife that necessarily accompanies the alienation of culture work from the value and meaning it creates. So if PE and CS writers strive to defend the fundamental openness of the encounter between value and use-value, and remember that this is a fraught relationship calling for a good deal of mutual forbearance among competing interpretations over the value and meaning of things, they might also be able to cultivate an ethical responsiveness to the inevitable alienation of labor from value.

This is not easy in a world in which the story of private property and the interpretive agenda of exchange-value are dominant. Exchange is the only form of value that is brought into being to make other value sources conform to its standards of judgment, utility, meaning, and interpretation. It inscribes itself as value in a totalizing story of earnings, prices, money, and commodities; this is an enchanted story that induces a kind of forgetting that makes it hard to respond ethically to the strife inherent in bringing value into the world. Exchange also splits cultural labor between production and consumption. As long as labor is ensnared in an exploitative relation with productive private property, there is a formal though unstable separation between compulsory and voluntary effort, the latter defined paradoxically within Liberalism as nonwork effort in the realm of consumption. This view of passive or unproductive consumption has been widely refuted by CS and PE writing on the culture of work that takes place in supposedly nonwork times, when we make meaning and make the system run by reproducing ourselves in the infrastructure of consumption. Nevertheless, the association within Liberalism of productive property and productive labor recapitulates the moral and political problematic of productivism, which tends to elevate the work of production over the work of consumption. Moreover, it offers a mode of comprehending the world that derides noncommercial and nonproprietary forms of making a living. Finally, it makes the work we do to make culture appear to be divided into the separate activities of textual production and reception. If this is the way things are, then perhaps the wedge of exchange has also played a part in fostering an intellectual division of labor that has kept CS and PE from recognizing their common cause.

Notes

1 *Communication and Cultural Domination*, 1976, pp. 96–7.

2 This section draws on a number of historical accounts about cultural studies, including Schiller (1996), Turner (1990), and parts of Curran, Morley, and Walkerdine (1996), During (1993), and Gray and McGuigan (1993).

3 The eponymous "marginal" is the outermost point before people stopped wanting something, that imaginary margin in which people still find some rational utility in having the last and least desirable unit (the marginal unit) of some good or service. Marginal utility would also determine the last and least desirable point at which a supplier would pay for the cost (capital and labor) of producing more and more of that good or service.

4 Melody, an Institutionalist, gives an example of how Marginalist economics has been used to rationalize the disconnection of phones in poor communities where there is no significant business loop, even when, according to Marginalism's own mathematical model, there is equivalence between what the poor subscriber is willing to pay and the marginal utility (short-term social costs) of having the phone; and, at the same time, no measurable cost benefit for the phone company in disconnecting the lines of subscribers who are unable to pay (1994: 28–9). What matters most in this case is the power that the telecommunications industry has to dominate the interpretation of the "facts" generated by the neoclassical model, given that local residential customers are rarely in a position to put forward their own favorable interpretation of the same economic facts.

5 Parts of this section on Marxist PE have been derived from Maxwell (1991).

References

Babe, R. (1993). "Communication" Blindspot of Western Economics," in J. Wasko et al. (eds.), *Illuminating the Blindspot*. New York: Ablex.

Braudel, F. (1986). *Civilization and Capitalism, 15th–18th Century: The Perspective of the World*, vol. 3, trans. Sian Reynolds. New York: Harper and Row.

Carey, J. (1997). "Reflections on the Project of (American) Cultural Studies." In Ferguson and Golding 1997: 1–24.

Clarke, S. (1982). *Marx, Marginalism and Modern Sociology: From Adam Smith to Max Weber*. London: Macmillan.

Crane, G. T. and A. Amawi (eds.) (1997). *The Theoretical Evolution of International Political Economy*, 2nd edn. Oxford: Oxford University Press.

Curran, J., D. Morley, and V. Walkerdine (eds.) (1996). *Cultural Studies and Communication*. London: Arnold.

During, S. (ed.) (1993). *The Cultural Studies Reader*. London: Routledge.

Ewen, S. (1976). *The Captains of Consciousness*. New York: McGraw Hill.

Ewen, S. (1988). *All Consuming Images*. New York: Basic Books.

Ferguson, M. and P. Golding (eds.) (1997). *Cultural Studies in Question*. London: Sage.

Gray, A. and J. McGuigan (eds.) (1993). *Studying Culture*. London: Arnold.

Grossberg, L. (1995). "Cultural Studies vs. Political Economy." *Critical Studies in Mass Communication* 12(1): 72–81.

Hamelink, C. (1983). *Cultural Autonomy in Global Communications*. New York: Longman.

Harvey, D. (1989). *The Condition of Postmodernity*. New York/Oxford: Blackwell.

Harvey, D. (1999). *The Limits to Capital* new edn. London: Verso.

Hobsbawm, E. J. (1992). *Nations and Nationalism since 1780*, 2nd edn. Cambridge: Cambridge University Press.

Lent, J. (ed.) (1995). *A Different Road Taken*. Boulder, Colo.: Westview Press.

Marx, K. (1967). *Capital*. New York: International Publishers.

Marx, K. (1973). *Grundrisse*, trans. Martin Nicolaus. New York: Vintage Books.

Maxwell, R. (1991) "The Image is Gold – Value, the Audience Commodity, and Fetishism." *Journal of Film and Video* 43(1 & 2), Spring and Summer.

Maxwell, R. (1996). "Out of Kindness and Into Difference: The Value of Global Market Research." *Media, Culture and Society* 18(1), Jan.

Maxwell, R. (ed.) (2001). *Culture Works: Essays on the Political Economy of Culture*. Minneapolis: University of Minnesota Press.

McChesney, R. (1996). "Is There Any Hope for Cultural Studies?" *Monthly Review* 47 (March): 1–18.

McGuigan, J. (1997). "Cultural Populism Revisited." In Ferguson and Golding 1997: 138–54.

McLaughlin, L. (1999). "Beyond 'Separate Spheres': Feminism and the Cultural Studies/Political Economy Debate." *Journal of Communication Inquiry* 23(4): 327–54.

Melody, W. (1994). "The Information Society: Implications for Economic Institutions and Market Theory." In E. A. Comor (ed.), *The Global Political Economy of Communication: Hegemony, Telecommunication and the Information Economy*. New York: St. Martin's.

Miller, Toby (1998). *Technologies of Truth*. Minneapolis: University of Minnesota Press.

Morley D. (1992). *Television, Audiences, and Cultural Studies*. London: Routledge.

Morley, D. (1997). "Theoretical Orthodoxies: Textualism, Constructivism and the 'New Ethnography' in Cultural Studies." In Ferguson and Golding 1997: 121–37.

Mosco, V. (1996). *The Political Economy of Communication*. London: Sage.

Olson, S. (1999). *Hollywood Planet*. Totowa, NJ: Lawrence Erlbaum.

Ross, D. (1991). *Origins of American Social Science*. Cambridge: Cambridge University Press.

Schiller, D. (1996). *Theorizing Communication*. Oxford: Oxford University Press.

Schiller, H. I. (1969/92). *Mass Communication and American Empire*. Boulder, Colo.: Westview, 2nd edn. 1992. Originally published by A. Kelley Publishers, 1969.

Schiller, H. I. (1976). *Communication and Cultural Domination*. White Plains, NY: M. E. Sharpe.

Smythe, D. (1981). *Dependency Road: Communication, Capitalism, Consciousness, and Canada*. Norwood: Ablex.

Tomlinson, J. (1991). *Cultural Imperialism*. London: Pinter.

Turner, G. (1990). *British Cultural Studies*. Boston: Unwin Hyman.

United Nations Development Program (1999). *Human Development Report*. Oxford: Oxford University Press.

Webster, F. and K. Robins (1986). *Information Technology: A Luddite Analysis*. Norwood, NJ: Ablex.

138

Chapter 8

Cultural Studies and Philosophy: An Intervention

Douglas Kellner

Since cultural studies has become a global popular in the past two decades, philosophy has been an unthematized and often suppressed dimension of the enterprise. While many trained in philosophy, such as myself, have engaged in the practice of cultural studies, few have reflected on the philosophical dimension and the role of philosophy within the project. The lack of reflection and debate over the function of philosophy within cultural studies and general suppression of such concerns have rendered cultural studies vulnerable to problematic philosophical positions and/or have vitiated the enterprise due to inadequately developed philosophical dimensions.

Accordingly, in this entry I will argue for three specific roles for philosophy in: (1) reflecting on the method, assumptions, and metatheory of cultural studies; in (2) articulating the normative standpoint of critique; and (3) in developing the moral and aesthetic dimensions which are currently, in my opinion, not adequately at work in the dominant versions of cultural studies now circulating. Yet I do not want to exaggerate the importance of philosophy and my argument will be that cultural studies today should pursue its transdisciplinary project by combining philosophy, political economy, social theory, cultural critique, and a multiplicity of critical theories in the effort to develop a cultural studies adequate to the challenges of the present age.

Conceptualizing Cultural Studies

Cultural studies has today become a contested terrain with a variety of competing versions. In this fragmented and conflicted field, it is useful to sort out competing models and notions of cultural studies, to delineate their presuppositions, and to appraise the strengths and limitations of competing models. This is the job of metatheory which attempts to grasp the presuppositions of an enterprise, to critically analyze and appraise them, and to defend one's own perspective and position if one is advancing a substantive concept of one's own – as I will do in this intervention.

While the diversity of cultural studies currently proliferating is vast, the movement that has been a global phenomenon of great importance over the last decade was inaugurated by the University of Birmingham Centre for Contemporary Cultural Studies in 1964, led at the time by Richard Hoggart and then by Stuart Hall from 1965 to 1979. Hence, our metatheoretical inquiries will begin with delineation of the presuppositions of British cultural studies during its initial period of gestation and development. During its now classical period, the Centre developed a variety of critical approaches for the analysis, interpretation, and criticism of cultural artifacts. Through a set of internal debates, and responding to social struggles and movements of the 1960s and the 1970s, the Birmingham group came to focus on the interplay of representations and ideologies of class, gender, race, ethnicity, and nationality in cultural texts, including media culture. They were among the first to study the effects of newspapers, radio, television, film, and other popular cultural forms on audiences. They focused on how various audiences interpreted and used media culture in varied and different ways and contexts, analyzing the factors that made audiences respond in contrasting ways to media texts.

From the beginning, British cultural studies systematically rejected high/low culture distinctions and took seriously the artifacts of media culture, thus surpassing the elitism of dominant literary approaches to culture. Likewise, British cultural studies overcame the limitations of the Frankfurt School notion of a passive audience in their conceptions of an active audience that creates meanings and the popular. Building on semiotic conceptions developed by Umberto Eco, Stuart Hall argued that a distinction must be made between the encoding of media texts by producers and the decoding by consumers (1980b). This distinction highlighted the ability of audiences to produce their own readings and meanings, to decode texts in aberrant or oppositional ways, as well as the "preferred" ways in tune with the dominant ideology.

The now classical period of British cultural studies from the mid-1960s to the early 1980s initially adopted a Marxian approach to the study of culture, one especially influenced by Althusser and Gramsci (see, especially Hall 1980a and Centre for Contemporary Cultural Studies 1980a and 1980b). Although members of the school of British cultural studies usually omit the Frankfurt School from the narrative of its genesis and history, some of the work done by the Birmingham group replicated certain classical positions of the Frankfurt School, in their social theory and methodological models for doing cultural studies, as well as in their political perspectives and strategies (see Kellner 1997b). Like the Frankfurt School, British cultural studies observed the integration of the working class and its decline of revolutionary consciousness, and studied the conditions of this catastrophe for the Marxian project of revolution. Like the Frankfurt School, British cultural studies concluded that mass culture was playing an important role in integrating the working class into existing capitalist societies and that a new consumer and media culture was forming a new mode of capitalist hegemony.

Both traditions focused on the intersections of culture and ideology and saw ideology critique as central to a critical cultural studies (Centre for Contemporary Cultural Studies 1980s and 1980b). Both saw culture as a mode of ideological reproduction and hegemony, in which cultural forms help to shape the modes of thought and behavior that induce individuals to adapt to the social conditions of capitalist societies. Both also interpreted culture as a potential form of resistance to capitalist society, as well as a mode of social reproduction, and both the earlier foreruners of British cultural studies, especially Raymond Williams (1958 and 1961), and the theorists of the Frankfurt School, conceived of high culture as forces of resistance to capitalist modernity. Later, British cultural studies would valorize resistant moments in media culture and audience interpretations and use of media artifacts, while the Frankfurt School tended, with some exceptions, to see mass culture as a homogeneous and potent form of ideological domination – a difference that would seriously divide the two traditions.

Despite their differences, like the Frankfurt School, the work of the Birmingham school of cultural studies is transdisciplinary in terms of their metatheory and practice. It thus subverts existing academic boundaries by combining social theory, cultural analysis and critique, and politics in a project aimed at a comprehensive criticism of the present configuration of culture and society. Moreover, it attempts to link theory and practice in a project that is oriented toward fundamental social transformation.

Both traditions thus deployed theory as a mode of conceptualizing the general contours of the established mode of historical development and analyzed the conjunctions of culture and society in specific historical contexts. Max Horkheimer and T. W. Adorno's concept of the culture industry can be seen broadly as a philosophical analysis of the configuration of society and culture that was emerging in the era of state and monopoly capitalism in the 1930s and 1940s in Europe and the United States; the analyses of the decline of working-class culture, the rise of a commercialized mass culture, and emergence of new oppositional cultures within British cultural studies can likewise be seen as a form of broad theoretical discourse often associated with philosophy – or a philosophically-mediated social theory. Both schools, however, were resolutely historicist, seeing concepts and methods, as well as social forms, as developing in specific historical contexts and within specific modes of production. Both were influenced by Marxian modes of theorizing, though the Frankfurt School was more influenced by forms of Hegelian Marxism, such as had been developed by Georg Lukács and Karl Korsch, whereas British cultural studies attempted to merge the historicist and activist perspectives of Gramsci with Althusser's more structuralist Marxism (see Hall 1980a).

From the beginning, British cultural studies was highly political in nature and focused on the potentials for resistance in oppositional subcultures, first, valorizing the potential of working-class cultures, then youth subcultures, to resist the

141

hegemonic forms of capitalist domination. Unlike the classical Frankfurt School (but similar to Herbert Marcuse), British cultural studies turned to youth cultures as providing potentially new forms of opposition and social change. Through studies of youth subcultures, British cultural studies demonstrated how culture came to constitute distinct forms of identity and group membership and appraised the oppositional potential of various youth subcultures (see Jefferson et al. 1976 and Hebdige 1978). Cultural studies came to focus on how subcultural groups resist dominant forms of culture and identity, creating their own style and identities. People who conform to dominant dress and fashion codes, behavior, and political ideologies thus produce their identities within mainstream groups, as members of specific social groupings (such as white, middle-class conservative Americans). Individuals who identify with subcultures, like punk culture, or black nationalist subcultures, look and act differently from those in the mainstream, and thus create oppositional identities, defining themselves against standard models.

As it developed into the 1970s and 1980s, British cultural studies successively appropriated feminism, race theory, gay and lesbian theory, postmodern theory, and other fashionable theoretical modes. Thus, they turned to examining the ways that cultural texts promoted sexism, racism, homophobia, and other forms of oppression, or promoted resistance and struggle against these phenomena. This approach implicitly contained political critique of all cultural forms that promoted oppression and domination while positively valorizing texts and representations that produced a potentially more just and egalitarian social order.

With a postmodern turn in cultural studies, there was an increasing emphasis on the audience and how audiences produce meanings and how cultural texts produce both popular pleasures and forms of resistance (Fiske 1989a, 1989b, and 1993). Critics of this phase of cultural studies claim that the project has been losing its critical edge, has fallen into a postmodern cultural populism (McGuigan 1992), and has surrendered the political radicalism and critical thrust of the original project (Kellner 1995). Defenders of the turn toward cultural populism argue that the original, more critical model tended to be overly elitist and excessively critical of popular pleasures, while neglecting the complex ways that cultural texts can be appropriated and used.

The fetishism of the popular also leads dominant trends in British and North American cultural studies to slighting high culture and the engagement of modernist and avant garde movements, such as distinguished the work of the Frankfurt School whose analyses extended from the most esoteric modernist art to the most banal artifacts of media culture. It appears that in its anxiety to legitimate study of the popular and to engage the artifacts of media culture, cultural studies has turned away from so-called high or elite culture in favor of the popular. But such a turn sacrifices the possible insights into all forms of culture and replicates the bifurcation of the field of culture into a "popular" and "elite" (which merely inverts the positive/negative valorizations of the older high/low distinction). More important, it disconnects cultural studies from attempts to develop oppositional forms of culture of the sort associated with the "historical avant-garde" (Bürger 1984). Avant-garde movements like Expressionism, Surrealism, and Dada wanted to develop art that would revolutionize society, that would provide alternatives to hegemonic forms of culture (see Bronner and Kellner 1983).

The oppositional and emancipatory potential of avant-garde art movements was a primary emphasis of the Frankfurt School, especially Adorno and Walter Benjamin, and it is unfortunate that British and North American cultural studies have largely neglected engaging avant-garde artforms and movements. This is connected with a failure of many versions of cultural studies and the sociology of culture to develop philosophical perspectives on aesthetics as found in the Frankfurt School. But the turn away from high culture, modernism, and aesthetics also points in British cultural studies to a failure to develop a radical cultural and media politics, such as is found in the works of Brecht and Benjamin, concerned with activist cultural politics and the development of alternative oppositional cultures. The ignoring of modernist and avant-garde art and intense focus on the popular was aided and abetted by the postmodern turn in cultural studies which disseminated key positions and strategies of British cultural studies throughout the world, but also helped produce an important mutation in the cultural studies project.

In addition, I would argue that critical social theory is necessary to adequately develop cultural studies. Earlier models in the Frankfurt School and British cultural studies made the relationship between culture and society the center of their analysis, utilizing the methods of social theory and more literary and cultural analysis to contextualize the production, distribution, and consumption of culture and to critically analyze cultural texts. As British cultural studies developed, it brought more and more theories into its purview, but as its project became globalized and absorbed into a multiplicity of disciplines the connection with social theory has often been attenuated. In some of the ludic, postmodern forms of cultural studies, context, text, and the constraints of everyday life disappear in descriptions of the pleasures of consumers or of the surfaces of texts. Thus, the relationship between cultural studies and social theory is itself complex, shifting, and variable.

In this context, I would propose that cultural studies utilize a synthesis of philosophy and critical social theory to develop a multiperspectivist approach which includes investigation of a broad expanse of artifacts, interrogating relationships within the three dimensions of: (1) the production and political economy of culture; (2) textual analysis and critique of its artifacts; and (3) study of audience reception and the uses of media/cultural products. This metatheory involves suggesting, first, that cultural studies itself be multiperspectivist, getting at culture from the optics of political economy and production, text analysis, and audience reception. I would also propose that textual analysis and audience reception studies utilize a multiplicity of perspectives, or critical methods, when engaging in textual analysis, and in delineating the multiplicity or subject positions, or perspectives, through which audiences appropriate culture. Moreover, the results of such studies need to be interpreted and contexualized within critical social theory to adequately delineate their meanings and effects.

Of course, there are dangers in championing the importance of the philosophical dimension in cultural studies. One of the hazards of cultural studies is the proclivity toward theoreticism, in which culture and society are reduced to discourse and in which one discourse is privileged above all others. This tendency leads to the problematic notion of a purely Baudrillardian, Foucauldian, Deleuzean, Habermasian, or (fill in the blanks) other form of cultural studies in which analysis is reduced to the problematics of the theorist in question. Of course, deploying any given theory in an imaginative way can yield novel and important insights. But reducing cultural studies to one theoretical problematic, or transcoding cultural studies into the language of a specific theory, can itself be highly destructive of the broader project.

One can obviously not deploy the full range of methods and perspectives noted above in each distinctive project that one undertakes and the nature of particular projects will determine what perspectives are most productive. But one should nonetheless see the dimensions of political economy, textual analysis, and audience research as complementing each other rather than as constituting separate domains. I am not, therefore, making the impossible suggestion that one adopt this comprehensive multiperspectivist approach every time that one sets out to do cultural studies or a piece of sociological cultural research. Obviously, intensely focusing on political economy, on audience reception, or on close textual reading and criticism, alone can be very valuable and yield important insights. But exclusively and constantly highlighting one of these dimensions to the omitting of others can be destructive for a sociology of culture or cultural studies that aims at developing comprehensive and inclusive approaches to culture and society, which interrogates culture in all of its dimensions.

The Standpoint of Critique

Hence, I would argue for metatheoretical perspectives within cultural studies to combine philosophy, critical social theory, political economy, and a variety of methods of textual analysis and audience study to capture the full wealth of the forms and effects of culture, ranging from high culture and modernism to media culture and oppositional subcultures. Philosophy would thus secure the metatheory of cultural studies, question and defend its assumptions, articulate its values, refine its concepts, and provide standpoints of critique – topics that I will take up in this section.

A postmodern turn in cultural studies, however, has led to a surrender of articulation of a normative critical standpoint for cultural studies and has often substituted a predominately textualist or ludic approach for the earlier activist political thrust of cultural studies. The populist turn in audience reception has

144

led to a sense that audiences alone produce meaning, that the polysemic overflow of cultural texts and diversity of audiences produces a multiplicity of meanings and effects that undermine attempts to provide privileged readings or to delineate audience response. Ludic textualism sees texts as polysemic proliferaters of meanings which elude hermeneutical delimitations. While it is true that indeterminacy of meaning in both texts and audiences undermines attempts to provide textual readings or analyses of effects that are anything more than provisional and probablistic, it is also true that extreme relativism is both disabling and itself problematic.

Stuart Hall's earlier theorizing of audience decoding stressed a "preferred reading" toward which the text attempts to direct its reader while acknowledging the possibility of negotiated, oppositional, and resistant readings (1980b). As David Morley points out, the concept of a preferred reading points to a structured polysemy, and concern with correspondences between texts and readings. Morley worries that the "new audience research" has gone too far toward relativism, romanticism of audience-decoding, indeterminancy of meaning, and occlusion of media power, and argues that cultural studies should return to a sociological materialism, a methodological pragmatism, and epistemological realism (1997: 122). His critique points to the need for philosophical perspectives to examine the various presuppositions of specific versions of cultural studies and to provide a standpoint for critique of textual idealism, extreme relativism, or ludic perspectives that merely celebrate textual pleasures and diverse audience readings to the exclusion of concern with meaning, truth, value, and other epistemological concerns.

I want, therefore, to articulate several standpoints of critique within cultural studies ranging from political to ethical and aesthetic critique. For the now classical period of the Birmingham School, political critique was privileged over other modes of cultural analysis and criticism. British cultural studies engaged the politics of representation, analyzing representations of class, gender, race, ethnicity, subculture, sexual preference, and nation. Especially in the late 1960s and into the 1970s, British cultural studies focused on critical dissection of the norms, values, role models, and negative and positive representations in cultural artifacts. Rather than focusing on ethics *per se*, British cultural studies and its later variants tended to engage the politics of representation. Employing Gramsci's model of hegemony and counterhegemony (see Gramsci 1971 and 1992), British cultural studies attempted to specify forces of domination and resistance in order to aid the process of political struggle and emancipation from oppression and domination. Their politics of representation thus entailed a critique of cultural representations that promoted racism, sexism, classism, or any forms of oppression. Representations that promoted domination and oppression were thus negatively valorized, while those that promoted egalitarianism, social justice, and emancipation were positively valorized.

In this optic, ethics tends to be subordinated to politics and the moral dimension of culture tends to be underemphasized or downplayed. Thus, one could

145

argue for a cultural studies that more explicitly stresses the importance of ethical/moral analysis, scrutinizing cultural texts for the distinctive ethical norms, ideals, and values portrayed and then evaluating the work accordingly. Or one could explore in more detail and depth than is usually done in cultural studies the moral and philosophical dimensions of cultural texts, the ways that they carry out moral critiques of society and culture, or embody moral concerns regarding good and evil, and right and wrong, while constructing – or deconstructing! – models of moral and immoral behavior or phenomena.

I have used the terms "ethics" and "moral" in the preceding paragraph, and for the purposes of this discussion I would like to distinguish between "ethics" and its cognates and "morality" and its family of terms. In ethical analysis, one is concerned with norms, values, models, and what Hegel called *Sittlichkeit*, the established ethical discourses and practices of a given society. Morality, by contrast, concerns ideals of the good and the ought which terminate in imperatives, articulating that realm described by Kant as *Moralität*. Within cultural studies, then, ethical analysis and critique dissects the norms, values, and societal models embedded in specific cultural representations, discourses, and texts which are subjected to critical scrutiny in the light of specific moral, political, or aesthetic values.

I am not advocating, however, moralistic critique of culture in which one condemns certain representations, texts, or even genres (i.e. pornography) as "immoral" or harmful in some way. What I am calling for is critical dissection of the ethical and moral discourses and effects of specific texts, carrying out spirited discussion of the norms, moral and otherwise, in which we critically analyze and perhaps judge specific cultural texts or artifacts. I am thus against moral dogmatism and absolutism, but am concerned to promote discussion of representations of ethical phenomena in cultural studies and the norms and ideals of moral critique.

Indeed, ethical concerns permeated earlier versions of cultural studies (see Hoggart 1957 and Williams 1958). Culture is, among other things, a major transmitter and generator of values and a cultural studies sensitive to the very nature and function of culture should be aware of its ethical and moral dimension. Thus, concern with ethics and with how cultural texts transmit specific ethical values and moral ideals should be a central and fundamental consideration of cultural studies, as it was with classical literary studies. While it is unlikely that the texts of media culture have the ethical/moral depth and complexity of great literary texts, it is clear that ethical and moral concerns are of fundamental importance to the sort of popular cultural artifacts that have been the domain of cultural studies.

Likewise, it is important to raise the issue of ethical and moral judgment and critique in order to engage in critical discussion of what precise values, norms, and ideals are not only represented in cultural texts, but also operative in the specific work of cultural studies itself. Raising the issue of the ethical and moral dimension of cultural studies obviously brings up the issues of what values one uses and justifies in doing cultural critique. That is, while a merely descriptive account of ethical values in cultural texts does not commit one to specific moral positions, if one criticizes media culture for ethical or moral failures – i.e. depicting excessive sex and violence, propagating pornography, prejudicial representations of women or people of color, glorifying war, etc. – then one needs to justify one's critical standpoint. This issue, of course, opens the door for passionate philosophical disputation and I think that the absence of such vigorous ethical and philosophical debate within cultural studies has vitiated the project. Although one wants to avoid ethical absolutism and dogmatism, it strikes me as healthy to discuss precisely what ethical values are being deployed in carrying out critiques of artifacts of media culture. It also strikes me as salutary to force those making ethical judgements to defend their values and presuppositions, making clear why they are advancing such judgments.

If philosophical argumentation involves putting in question presuppositions and assumptions, giving reasons for one's position, engaging in critical dialogue, then such discourse, I believe, would only strengthen cultural studies, providing more robust interpretations and debates. The relative neglect of ethical–moral critique and disputation is another symptom, then, of the avoidance of hard philosophical issues in dominant versions of cultural studies, a neglect that I believe undermines the project.

As noted above, British cultural studies has also tended to eliminate aesthetics concerns from its project – a move that I suggested above was both theoretically and politically disabling. British cultural studies never really theorized, à la Frankfurt School, the contradictions of culture, i.e that culture is an ordinary part of everyday life, of social reproduction; but also transcendent, constituting another dimension that can serve as a locus of critique and opposition. British cultural studies has focused on culture and cultural experience as a means of reproducing or opposing the existing society, and in the latter has tended to ignore the possibilities of art as transcendence, especially the ways that certain art forms can produce critical visions of existing reality or alternative representations of a better world. The neglect of aesthetics in cultural studies leaves out the transcendent dimension of culture, of culture that surpasses ordinary experience and everyday life, of art that presents visions of another world and alternative modes of thought and being. Likewise, British cultural studies tends to ignore the potential shock effects of aesthetic modernism and the avant-garde, the ways that art can shake up ordinary modes of perception, awaken individuals to perceive ugly or frightening realities often suppressed.

A dialectics of culture such as is found in the works of Adorno, Benjamin, or Marcuse sees culture as both affirmative and negative, as both reproducing and opposing the established social reality. Thus, while on one hand culture is ordinary, constituting shared common experiences of familiar modes of everyday life, on the other hand, culture is extraordinary, providing another dimension to existing reality, one of transcendence, autonomy, and potential opposition. Culture can generate meanings that help transform life as well as idealizing and

147

stabilizing existing forms. It can help shape subcultures of resistance and provide critical perspectives on existing reality that provide an impetus to personal or social transformation. Art, in its manifold guises and forms, is important and should not be neglected by cultural studies.

Yet aesthetic critique and opposition has its limitations and I do not want to propose a wholesale aestheticizing of cultural studies, although I believe critically taking up issues of aesthetics can strengthen the enterprise. The initial distancing from aesthetics within British cultural studies probably had to do with a desire to renounce the idealism and elitism of many aesthetic approaches; British cultural studies emerged as an overcoming of the textualism and aestheticism of literary analysis, but in reacting against its excesses, I would argue, went too far in throwing issues of aesthetics out of cultural studies altogether.

With the postmodern turn in culture, in which aesthetics becomes a more salient aspect of every domain of life, from packaging and advertising of commodities to the creation of identity and lifestyle, one needs to realize that aesthetics are a key ingredient of everyday life and require serious scrutiny. Of course, the absorption of aesthetics into everyday life renders claims for a critical and transcendent dimension of culture problematic – as Jameson argues in his famous article on postmodernism (in 1991: 47ff). Yet precisely the question of what forms of art do and do not have critical and oppositional potential, as well as questions of the intersection of art and politics, and of aesthetics and everyday life, continue to be relevant and important to the project of understanding and transforming existing societies and cultures. Thus, I would argue that concerns with aesthetics should be an important part of a revitalized cultural studies for the next millennium.

Cultural Studies, Pedagogy, and Politics: Some Concluding Comments

A critical cultural studies would thus pursue certain aesthetic, ethical, and political ends. Yet understanding the origins, locations, and effects of cultural studies also involves a concern with pedagogy. While the early development of British cultural studies was closely connected to adult education and pedagogy, later cultural studies became more academic and disciplinary. In recent years, however, there has been a call to return cultural studies to articulation with a critical pedagogy, a project that I endorse (see Giroux 1994; Grossberg 1997; and Kellner 1995). Since media culture itself is a potent from of pedagogy, cultural studies should develop a counterpedagogy that teaches audiences how to read cultural texts, how to critically decode and produce oppositional readings, and thus to understand the effectivity of cultural texts in socialization, the construction of identity, and the reproduction of social relations.

Questions of pedagogy inevitably involve questions of value, thus the political, ethical, and aesthetic concerns I discussed above would be a key aspect of a pedagogy of cultural studies. I would also argue that critical pedagogy involves what Paolo Freire (1972 and 1998) calls reading the world through reading the text, so that gaining critical literacy, the ability to read the word, involves at the same time learning to read the world through the word and text. This injunction is parallel to a basic tenet of critical cultural studies that operates with a dialectic of text and context, situating and reading texts through their social contexts and better understanding context through critical reading of texts. From this perspective, gaining critical media literacy involves learning to read texts through the world and the world through texts. Hence, just as politics is a form of pedagogy, a critical pedagogy is a form of politics, teaching individuals how to situate their forms of culture and their everyday lives in the context of the social and political system in which they live.

Developing critical media literacy also requires development of a postmodern pedagogy that takes seriously image, spectacle, and narrative, and thus promotes visual and media literacy, the ability to read and critically analyze images, stories, and spectacles of media culture. Yet a postmodern pedagogy is concerned to develop multiple literacies, to rethink literacy itself in relation to new technologies and new cultural forms, and to develop a cultural studies that encompasses a wide array of fields, texts, and practices, extending from popular music to poetry and painting to cyberspace and multimedia like CD-ROMs (see Kellner 1998 and Hammer and Kellner 1999).

The particular pedagogy employed, however, should be contextual, depending on the concrete situation, interests, and problems within the specific site in which cultural studies is taught or carried out. For it will be the distinctive interests of the teachers, students, or critic that will help determine what precise artifacts are engaged, what methods will be used, and what pedagogy will be deployed. Just as a cultural studies research problem and text is necessarily contextual, flexible, and open-ended, so too must be its pedagogy and its politics.

Such a transdisciplinary and political project involves a synthesis of the Frankfurt School, British cultural studies, postmodern theory, and other critical approaches, combining empirical research, theory, critique, and practice. A revitalized cultural studies would reject the distinction between high and low culture and would study a broad expanse of cultural artifacts. It would use the concept of an active audience and valorize resistance, but also explore manipulation and more passive reception, detecting both the ruses of media power and the tactics of audience resistance. A political cultural studies would follow earlier trends of British cultural studies with detailed consideration of oppositional subcultures and alternatives to mainstream culture, but would also devise strategies of developing alternative media and an activist cultural politics. It would combine the Frankfurt School focus on political economy, on media manipulation, and on the ways that culture reproduces domination, with scrutiny of the emancipatory potential of a wide range of cultural artifacts extending from modernism and the avant-garde to critical and subversive moments in media culture.

A critical sociology of culture and oppositional cultural studies would also draw upon feminist approaches and multicultural theories to fully analyze the functions of gender, class, race, ethnicity, nationality, sexual preference, and so on which are so important in constituting cultural texts and their effects, as well as being fundamentally constitutive of audiences who appropriate and use texts. British cultural studies progressively adopted a feminist dimension (see McRobbie 1994 and 1997; and Gray 1997) and paid greater attention to race, ethnicity, nationality, and sexuality, as various discourses of race, gender, sex, nationality, and so on circulated in responses to social struggles and movements. Earlier forms of cultural studies sought to articulate analysis of the thematics and effects of its artifacts with existing political struggles, and I would defend returning to this project. There indeed continues to be a significant number of attempts to connect cultural studies with oppositional political movements and, more recently, with more pragmatic involvement in policy issues and debates (see McGuigan 1996 and Bennett 1992 and 1997). There are thus a heterogeneity of political articulations of cultural studies and, as with its pedagogy, its politics will necessarily be conjunctural and contextual, depending on the particular site and moment of a certain form of cultural studies.

Moreover, it is of crucial importance for a theoretically responsible cultural studies to continually appropriate the latest theoretical discourses and to modify its assumptions, program, and discourses in response to critiques of its previous work, the emergence of new theories that can be used to strengthen one's future work, and in response to oppositional social movements which produce novel critical political discourses and practices. Both the Frankfurt School and British cultural studies continually modified their work in response to new theoretical and historical developments and in a period of rapid social-historical change and the proliferation of new theories, cultural practices, and forms of political struggle, engagement with theory and history is of fundamental importance for cultural studies today.

To capture the novelties of the present moment, bold vision is needed. Adorno and Horkheimer's critique of the culture industry, for example, provides a provocative philosophical overview of the production, nature, circulation, and reception of products of the culture industry as it had developed into the 1940s (1972 [1947]). Jameson's magisterial sketch of the contours of postmodernism provides a highly suggestive mapping of contemporary culture that has generated a wealth of debate and insight (1991). Technological revolution and the emergence of new forms of cyberculture, new identities, new public spheres, and new politics require similar daring philosophical vision today.

Hence, a contemporary cultural studies would be open to new theoretical impulses and would be prepared to engage new subject-matter. We are currently living in a proliferating image culture in which new technologies are changing every dimension of life from the economy to personal identity. In a postmodern media and computer culture, fresh critical strategies are needed to read narratives, to interpret the conjunctions of sight and sound, words and images, that are producing novel cultural spaces, forms, and experiences. This project also involves exploration of the emergent cyberspaces and modes of identities, interaction, and production that is taking place in the rapidly exploding computer culture, as well as exploring the new public spaces where myriad forms of political debate and struggle are evolving (Kellner 1997c). Finally, a future-oriented sociology of culture should look closely at the development of the media and computer industries, the mergers and synergies taking place, and the syntheses of information and entertainment, computer and media culture, that are being planned and already implemented. A global media and cyberculture is our lifeworld and fate, and we need to be able to chart and map it accordingly to survive the dramatic changes currently taking place and the even more transformative novelties of the rapidly approaching future.

References

Ang, Ien (1991). *Desperately Seeking the Audience*. London and New York: Routledge.
——(1996). *Living Room Wars: Rethinking Audiences for a Postmodern World*. London and New York: Routledge.
Agger, Ben (1992). *Cultural Studies*. London: Falmer Press.
Aronowitz, Stanley (1993). *Roll Over Beethoven*. Hanover, NH: University Press of New England.
Benjamin, Walter (1969). *Illuminations*. New York: Shocken.
Bennett, Tony (1982). "Theories of the Media, Theories of Society." In Gurevitch et al. (eds.), *Culture, Society, and the Media*. London: Macmillan.
——(1992). "Putting the Policy into Cultural Studies." In Grossberg et al. 1992.
——(1997). "Towards a Pragmatics for Cultural Studies." In McGuigan 1997b: 42–61.
Best, Steven and Douglas Kellner (1991). *Postmodern Theory: Critical Interrogations*. London and New York: Macmillan and Guilford Press.
——(1997). *The Postmodern Turn*. New York: Guilford Press.
——(forthcoming). *The Postmodern Adventure*. New York: Guilford Press.
Blundell, V. et al. (1993). *Relocating Cultural Studies*. New York: Routledge.
Bronner, Stephen and Douglas Kellner (eds.) (1983) *Passion and Rebellion: The Expressionist Heritage*. Universe Books and Bergin Publishers (USA) and Croom Helm (England); 2nd edition, Columbia University Press 1988.
——(1989). *Critical Theory and Society: A Reader*. New York: Routledge.
Bürger, Peter (1984). *Theory of the Avant-Garde*. Minneapolis: University of Minnesota Press.
Centre for Contemporary Cultural Studies (1980a). *On Ideology*. London: Hutchinson.
——(1980b). *Culture, Media, Language*. London: Hutchinson.
Davies, Ioan (1995). *Cultural Studies, and After*. London and New York: Routledge.
During, Simon (ed.) (1993). *The Cultural Studies Reader* London and New York: Routledge; 2nd edn. 1998.
Dworkin, Dennis (1997). *Cultural Marxism in Postwar Britain: History, the New Left, and the Origins of Cultural Studies*. Durham: Duke University Press.
Ferguson, M. and P. Golding (eds.) (1997). *Cultural Studies in Question*. London: Sage.

Fiske, John (1989a). *Reading the Popular*. Boston: Unwin Hyman.
—— (1989b). *Understanding Popular Culture*. Boston: Unwin Hyman.
—— (1990). *Introduction to Cultural Studies*. London: Routledge.
—— (1993). *Power Plays. Power Works*. New York and London: Verso.
Freire, Paulo (1972). *Pedagogy of the Oppressed*. New York: Herder and Herder.
—— (1998). *The Paulo Freire Reader*. New York: Continuum.
Giroux, Henry (1994). *Disturbing Pleasures: Learning Popular Culture*. London and New York: Routledge.
Gramsci, Antonio (1971). *Selections from the Prison Notebooks*. New York: International Publishers.
—— (1992). *Prison Notebooks*, vol. 1. New York: Columbia University Press.
Grossberg, Lawrence (1997). *Dancing in Spite of Myself. Essays on Popular Culture*. Durham and London: Duke University Press.
—— Cary Nelson, and Paula Treichler (eds.) (1992). *Cultural Studies*. New York: Routledge.
Hall, Stuart et al. (eds.) (1980). *Culture, Media, Language*. London: Hutchinson.
—— (1980a). "Cultural Studies and the Centre: Some Problematics and Problems." In Hall et al. 1980: 15–47.
—— (1980b). "Encoding/Decoding." In Hall et al. 1980: 128–38.
Hammer, Rhonda and Douglas Kellner (1999) "Multimedia Pedagogical Curriculum for the New Millennium." *Journal of Adolescent & Adult Literacy* 42(7): 522–6; longer version in *Journal of Religious Education*, 1999.
Hebdige, Dick (1978). *Subculture: The Meaning of Style*. London: Methuen.
Hoggart, Richard (1957). *The Uses of Literacy*. New York: Oxford University Press.
Horkheimer, Max and T. W. Adorno (1972). *Dialectic of Enlightenment*. New York: Seabury. First published 1947.
Jameson, Fredric (1991). *Postmodernism, or the Cultural Logic of Late Capitalism*. Durham: Duke University Press.
Jefferson, Tony et al. (1976). *Reistance through Rituals*. London: Hutchinson.
Jensen, Joli and John J. Pauly (1997). "Imagining the Audience: Losses and Gains in Cultural Studies." In Ferguson and Golding 1997: 155–69.
Johnson, Richard (1986/7). "What is Cultural Studies Anyway?" *Social Text* 16: 38–80.
Kellner, Douglas (1992). "Toward a Multiperspectival Cultural Studies." *Centennial Review* 26(1) (Winter): 5–42.
—— (1995). *Media Culture: Cultural Studies, Identity, and Politics between the Modern and the Postmodern*. London and New York: Routledge.
—— (1997a). "Overcoming the Divide: Cultural Studies and Political Economy." In Ferguson and Golding 1997: 102–19.
—— (1997b). "Critical Theory and British Cultural Studies: The Missed Articulation." In McGuigan 1997b: 12–41.
—— (1997c). "Intellectuals, the New Public Spheres, and Technopolitics." *New Political Science* 41–2: 169–88.
—— (1998). "Multiple Literacies and Critical Pedagogy in a Multicultural Society." *Educational Theory* 48(1): 103–22.
Mepham, John (1991). "Television Fiction – Quality and Truth-Telling." *Radical Philosophy* 57 (Spring): 20–7.
McGuigan, Jim (1992). *Cultural Populism*. London and New York: Routledge.

——(ed.) (1997a). "Cultural Populism Revisited." In Ferguson and Golding 1997: 138–54.

——(1997b). *Cultural Methodologies*. London: Sage.

McRobbie, Angela (1994). *Postmodernism and Popular Culture*. London and New York: Routledge.

——(1997). "The Es and the Anti-Es: New Questions for Feminism and Cultural Studies." In Ferguson and Golding 1997: 170–86.

Morley, David (1992). *Television, Audiences, and Cultural Studies*. New York and London: Routledge.

——(1997). "Theoretical Orthodoxies: Textualism, Constructivism and the 'New Ethnography' in Cultural Studies." In Ferguson and Golding 1997: 121–37.

O'Connor, Alan (1989). "The Problem of American Cultural Studies." *Critical Studies in Mass Communication* (Dec.): 405–13.

Steele, Tom (1997). *The Emergence of Cultural Studies 1945–65: Adult Education, Cultural Politics and the English Question*. London: Lawrence & Wishart.

Stevenson, Nick (1997). "Towards a Pragmatics for Cultural Studies." In McGuigan 1997b: 62–86.

Tester, Keith (1994). *Media, Culture and Morality*. New York and London: Routledge.

Turner, Graeme (1990). *British Cultural Studies: An Introduction*. New York: Unwin Hyman.

Williams, Raymond (1958). *Culture and Society*. New York: Columbia University Press.

——(1961). *The Long Revolution*. London: Chatto and Windus.

——(1976). *Keywords*. New York: Oxford University Press.

——(1981). *Communications*. London: Penguin.

Chapter 9

"X" never, ever, marks the spot: Archaeology and Cultural Studies

Silke Morgenroth

> Archaeology is the search for fact. Not truth.... So forget any ideas you've got about lost cities, exotic travel, and digging up the world. We do not follow maps to buried treasure and "X" never, ever, marks the spot. Seventy percent of all archaeology is done in the library. Research. Reading. We cannot afford to take mythology at face value.
>
> Prof. Indiana Jones, *Indiana Jones and the Last Crusade*, dir. Steven Spielberg, 1989

The subject of archaeology is the investigation of the material relics of human cultures and societies of the past where there are few if any written records available.

It covers a timespan from the earliest evidence of hominid existence at least three million years ago to the recent past (e.g. indigenous, nonliterate peoples or industrial archaeology). The first written records appear around 3000 BC in western Asia and considerably later in most other parts of the world. Consequently archaeology is the only means to explore about 99 percent of human history.

The central questions of archaeology are: How was the past? How did people live? Why did they live in a certain way and why did these ways change? But these questions only matter because they are directly connected to us, the asking subject: How did the present evolve?

A modern image might illustrate the archaeologist's view: you switch to a film on TV, just a few minutes before the end. You won't be able to grasp the context of plot and conflict, which you would easily had you seen the whole film. These last minutes of a film can be compared to our conscious lifespan: The technical, economical, and social structures of today's world can be better understood if we regard the whole historic development – the whole film. In that sense archaeology tries to discover and picture developments from the very beginning onwards, to help explain problems of the present (Ziegert 1990: 55). That archaeologists are concerned about the present might appear a rather strange notion: the public picture of the archaeologist seems to be rather cloudy and outdated, even to members of fellow disciplines.

In the following I will therefore start with a brief view into archaeological terminology and sketch the theoretical discussions of the last decades. After that I examine in what ways archaeology is contributing to present problems, and if there are actual or possible connections to the field of cultural studies.

Archaeological Key Terms

The central concern of the archaeologist is the interpretation of *artifacts* – objects used, modified, or made by people.[1] Some of them are of material and artistic value, but the vast majority is waste, like broken stone tools or potsherds. Many of them can only be recognized or interpreted if the environment is taken into account. Therefore non-artifactual organic and environmental remains, *ecofacts*, e.g. animal bones, plant remains, or ashes, are another basic category of evidence. Archaeological structures that can't be carried, like postholes or storage pits, are called *features*. A structure of features and artifacts forms a *site*.

The digging of a site is the classic image of archaeological work. The aim of a dig is to understand its context – the finds, their *association* with other finds, and their horizontal and vertical position (*provenience*) in the surrounding sediment. Ideally an excavation would enable one to identify any possible feature, map and describe it, so that the site could be totally reconstructed, in all three dimensions. In recent decades, with the development of geophysical and geochemical survey techniques, interest in excavating a site has diminished, because it reveals and destroys archaeological evidence at the same time. There are voices demanding only to dig where absolutely necessary and to preserve as many sites as possible for future generations of archaeologists, when methods might have been developed that make it possible to answer questions we can't even think of today.

Generally, and in contrast to what museums teach us, the find itself is secondary, its context primary. The value of an artifact is less important than what its context can tell us. Connected to this is the analysis of the *formation processes* of the archaeological record. Finds do not represent the whole of past existence. They are a selection which does not show the complete picture. Faunal, floral, climatic, and chemical influences affect material in many different ways. But the archaeological record is also formed by our ability to recognize and identify it.

An important task for the excavation of a site is the recognition of the *stratigraphy*. That is valid for any excavation, whether it is a paleolithic cave or the underwater remnants of a lake dwelling. Identifying stratigraphy implies a temporal relation of the finds: lower layers mean older finds. That allows the creation of an age scale, the *relative dating* of objects or events, according to their

155

stratigraphic position, to describe evolutions or developments. The basic achievement in relative dating was the establishment of the three-part organization for the Old World into stone, bronze, and iron ages. This establishes a hierarchy of tools as well as an evolution of cultures. This categorization has proved to work quite well, but it is misleading when considered as a description of past reality.

Ideally the stratigraphy of a site can produce stratigraphically sorted artifacts which can be arranged in a *typology*. Important as these relative methods are, the final goal of dating is achieving *absolute dates*. They tell us about the speed of developments or whether things happened at the same time or must be seen in a relation. Until the development of scientific methods (best known are radiocarbon dating, tree-ring dating) historical dating was the only way to do this. Historical dating is possible because we can link the calenders of the Romans, the Egyptians, and the Maya to our dating system. If you now find a Roman coin (absolute date) in the same context (*sealed deposit*, e.g. a grave) with a celtic pot, you can cross-date the pot with the coin. Still, you don't really know if the two artifacts have the same circulation. The coin, for example, could be far older, having been used as a lucky charm for generations, before it was laid down with the pot. The pot would then be dated older than it actually is.

As Trigger has noted, "prehistoric archaeology is the only social science that has no direct access to information about human behaviour" (1989: 357). The relics do not speak by themselves, we have to interpret them. Interpretation means asking questions. The answers vary greatly, depending on what we are looking for. A clay pot, for example, can be tested chemically to give a date of its manufacture and therefore a date for the location where it was found; the quality of the clay can indicate its origin and give clues about the range of contacts. The form of the pot can be interpreted in a typological sequence and give information about beliefs. Analysis of the shape and residues might give information about the use of the pot.

Anthropology or History?

Because of the vast field it tries to cover, and because of restrictions in the nature of its subject, archaeology has to connect to several humanities and sciences like history, ethnography, and biological anthropology as well as chemistry, geography, and others. It shares techniques and methods and needs to communicate results: Archaeology is so interdisciplinary that the scientific basis of archaeology itself has been questioned.

In the European tradition (and the former colonies that are influenced by its university traditions) archaeology is mostly linked to historical or culture-historical departments, usually called prehistory (*préhistoire* or *Vor- und Frühgeschichte*). In the United States, in contrast, archaeology is one of four subdisciplines that form the departments of anthropology (along with sociocultural, biological/physical, and linguistic anthropology). This disciplinary difference is far more than a mere bureaucratic procedure: it mirrors the development of quite remarkably different methods and theories in Europe and the US.

For almost the first half of the century archaeology was dominated by the culture-history paradigm, based on Gustaf Kossinna and his influential book *Die Herkunft der Germanen*, published in 1920. It sought to locate the origin of present or historically known ethnic groups by tracing them backwards and connecting them to archaeologically documented material cultures. This led to a major crisis, as his approach was misused by fascist regimes, prominently the Nazis: archaeology was used to prove that Germans were offspring of the Indo-German Aryans. Furthermore, it was argued that Poland in fact "belonged" to the nordic Aryans; archaeology thus supplied Nazi Germany with the scientific backup for the invasion of Poland and Russia (Hodder 1991: 1). Without being a Nazi himself in the literal sense Kossinna laid an important foundation for being used by this "master race ideology." As a reaction to political abuse, German archaeology became insignificant, trying to avoid any politically misusable statements (see Härke 1991).

In the sixties, a new paradigm was established by the (mainly) American "New Archaeology" or processual archaeology (see Binford & Binford 1968).[2] It tried to get rid of the old culture-historical burden by introducing mathematical purity into archaeology. The definition of ahistoric models was the new goal. If results could be empirically proven, there would be no danger of ideological misuse. Archaeology should be able to produce facts and truth, not merely hypotheses and interpretations.

Analogical models were taken from ethnography as a basis for making inferences about past societies. Processual archaeology spread widely, and led to the development of highly usable new methods and techniques, like the stronger importance of experimental procedures and ethnographic archaeology. This paradigm is still dominant in the US.

In the United Kingdom it was conquered by postprocessual archaeologies in the eighties. Postprocessual has become a collective name that emphasizes the rejection of processualist theories, but is in itself a rather incoherent bundle of structuralist (e.g. Yates 1989), poststructuralist (e.g. Hodder 1989), neo-Marxist (e.g. Miller and Tilley 1984) and feminist (e.g. Gero and Conkey 1991) approaches. Their common concern was the processualists' tendency to be scientific-positivist, evolutionist, and functionalist, and to disregard the socio-cultural relevance of archaeology.

Postprocessualism is based on the idea that all truth is subjective, because every decoding of a message is inevitably another encoding (Tilley 1990: 338). Through this, relativism is seen as an absolute principle. Shanks and Tilley have concluded that the goal of research must be political (1987: 195). Archaeological discourse should help to disempower political and intellectual elites by verifying relativism, and therefore validating all explanations of the past. Especially feminist and Marxist approaches demand that archaeological theories be connected with a specific interest in present society.

Postprocessualism still is an almost entirely British phenomenon, but derives considerable prestige from the preeminence of postmodernism in comparative literature and its dissemination throughout the humanities and social sciences (see Hunt 1989).

Archaeology Studies Culture

The strictly archaeological definition of culture is rather specific, because it is limited to material characteristics. An archaeological culture is "a constantly recurring *assemblage* of artifacts assumed to be representative of a particular set of behavioural activities carried out at a particular time and place" (Renfrew and Bahn 1991: 485). As straightforward as this appears to be, it is of course not a sufficient definition, because after all we are interested in people, not pots. In fact, all archaeological inferences about past societies hinges critically upon an understanding of the relationship between material and nonmaterial aspects of culture. The basis for this is the anthropological notion that man, in contrast to animals, is obviously inadequately fitted for survival in natural surroundings (Gehlen 1997) and, hence, has to adapt by creating tools. "Culture, however we define it, is manmade production, creative doing, by which man can overcome his dependence on his inner and outer nature" (Greverus 1987: 60).

These means, tools, values, and rules can be transmitted as cultural objectifications of a material or immaterial nature: synchronically from generation to generation, diachronically between social spaces and within groups or classes. Material culture is the primary aspect of human adaptation to environment: food, housing, clothing. To start looking at these primary aspects of staying alive can make it easier to recognize the more hidden forms of cultural objectivizations, in which the direct connection between needs and their fulfillment cannot be as easily seen.

Culture is constructing much more than mere survival would demand. The ability to symbolize and add meaning to things that they do not carry in themselves are connected issues of discussion. An example is a house: it facilitates survival and social interaction, and tells of its inhabitants' values via their aesthetics of living (Schultz and Lavenda 1990: 360ff). In that sense archaeology can make interferences about far more than just material culture.

We know that there are symbolic meanings but we can only comprehend them in a comparative way: we look for analogy, which in the case of a house, seems quite simple, because the concept is still familiar to us. But that might be misleading: different cultures might have totally different values; the range of possible human behavior exceeds our specific horizon. We have to accept this, there is no way out. That reminds us of the historic dimension of culture.

Inasmuch as there is an awareness for the broad range of possible human behavior it is necessary to use analogy: we can only perceive the past if we posit that there is a common perception between the people of the past and ourselves. But this implies the transfer of our values into the past: we automatically think that the biggest and most decorated houses belong to the rich and powerful, as in our present society – not to the poor and underprivileged. Historical imagery is always dependent on the historian's social and economic circumstances or surroundings:

> I'm convinced that history actually is the dream of a historian, and that this dream is mostly determined by the environment the historian lives in. (Duby and Lardreau 1982: 48)

Archaeology and Cultural Studies

Archaeological statements are therefore always and inevitably also statements about the culture of the archaeologist. In that sense they are political and of interest to cultural studies. The connection of the two is still far from obvious. They are both concerned with culture. But there seems to be hardly any mutual interest, none that could be proven by the printed word, after all. Seemingly the two had to travel too far to have reached each other by now. Cultural studies is traditionally concerned with the study of contemporary culture, texts, and mass media, explicitly avoiding historic dimensions that stretch before capitalism, interested in individual voices and sociopolitical investigations. None of these interests could easily be connected with archaeology. Since archaeology cannot refer to written records, it is furthest away from modern society and has been rather opposed to political inferences in the last five decades.

But there has recently been an orientation of anthropology towards cultural studies and vice versa (During 1993; Vincent 1996). This affected archaeology as well, on a small scale that is nevertheless recognizable. As shown above, post-processual archaeologists have become interested in political impact, the construction of knowledge, identity, and society. Thus archaeology moves towards the interests of cultural studies.

The same applies to cultural studies. During recent decades historical dimensions got more important. For example, it is seen as a problem that cultural studies has a simplified view of premodern societies. Historical research is here explicitly demanded (Lutter and Reisenleitner 1998: 63). There is also the problem of hegemonic developments, like the social evolution of popular and high culture. The inscription of certain cultural forms is a complex sociohistoric process, which might be better understood by taking archaeological perspectives into account. The growing impact of gender or race studies demands a historical or anthropological perspective as well: it adds aspects to the constitution of identities and to the range of alternatives to euro- and androcentric views.

159

Archaeology and cultural studies meet in the opposition to positivist and behaviorist understandings of the humanities. They meet in the perception of post-structuralist and deconstructive ideas. Cultural studies can communicate with archaeologists when they want to see the world not as naturally given, but socially and culturally constructed (Carey 1997: 12). Likewise there is the warning, that the isolated interpretation of singular cultural practices loses awareness of culture as a whole way of living (e.g. Kellner 1997).

After all, one shouldn't forget that one of the typical descriptions of cultural studies suggests that it "is a discipline constantly shifting its interests and methods, both because it is in constant and engaged interaction with its larger historical context and because it cannot be complacent about its authority" (During 1993: 20). Maybe without yet really noticing, postprocessualist archaeology and cultural studies have reached common ground.

The following examples illustrate some of the places of mutual interest.

Archaeology and Nationalism

> Archaeological sites are such potent symbols of national identity (e.g. Masada in Israel, or Zimbabwe in, significantly, Zimbabwe) that peoples today are frequently willing to fight over them. Archaeology and ancient history help define a people as distinct and occupying (or claiming) territories that were historically theirs. (Kohl and Fawcett 1995: 11)

Archaeology cannot ignore that its theories were and will be used for building a sense of nation or territory. It has been argued that there is an almost natural relationship between archaeology and nationalism, and archaeology thus may always be an unavoidably political enterprise (Silberman 1995). Moreover archaeology often appears to be a discipline that almost invites state interference. Dependent upon considerable support for their primary research, archaeologists seem peculiarly vulnerable to state pressures.

National identities are constructions, in the sense of Anderson's imagined communities (1983). The contribution of archaeology is important in the construction of cultural identity and claims on territory, because its material evidence can be used to symbolize a historical unified nation with common values. For many peoples in the world, their archaeological past is much more important than is commonly appreciated.

Not long ago the wish of the "Former Yugoslav Republic of Macedonia" to name itself simply "Macedonia" led to a major political crisis, because the Greeks felt that to be an assault on their history and felt threatened by possible territorial claims connected to ancient Macedonia (Kohl and Fawcett 1995: 10). A less hostile example might be the European celebration of the Celts during the last decade. Major exhibitions like "I Celti – La prima Europa" (The Celts – The First Europe, Venice 1991) generated tremendous public awareness – several popular books and TV documentaries – indicating interest all over Europe. This is clearly connected to the political idea of a European nation. But the notion of the Celts as the first Europeans is a modern concept. It definitely has nothing to do with anything the Celts might have been communicating.

Archaeology also plays a crucial role for countries or peoples who seek pre-colonial self-esteem or minorities looking for their history without a written record. In Australia, for example, written records do not exist before AD 1788. And they can only teach us the history of European colonists, providing a blurred image of the Aborigines, whose culture stretches more than 23,000 years beyond that point. The "natives" have developed a sense of their own history as a means of opposing the oppression of the colonial heritage.

Many countries claim their antiquities, many peoples object to archaeological excavation of their burial grounds or religous sites. A recent and very problemat-ical case is that of the Kennewick Man, skeletal remains found in July 1996 on the banks of the Columbia River in Kennewick, Washington (see Thomas 2000, Downey 2000). It has been radiocarbon dated to approximately 9,400 years of age. This makes it one of the oldest human finds in North America – an archae-ological sensation. But five northwestern tribes claim the body as their ancestor and demand a stop to scientific investigation, which they see as an ongoing violation of their cultural and religious beliefs. They want to bury him according to tribal rituals. In 1990 the Native American Graves Protection and Repatriation Act was passed, and they have the legal right to do so. Theoretically a cultural connection to the remnants has to be proven, but practically all finds older than 500 years (i.e. pre-Columbian) were returned. But in the case of Kennewick Man, scientists started legal action, denying the possibility of a cultural connec-tion bridging almost 10,000 years. In their view, the freedom of science was in danger.

By high court decision a DNA test was carried out, in order to determine which Indian tribe Kennewick man may have belonged to, so that the bones could be returned to the rightful descendants. This procedure, the notion that culturally or socially constituted units like tribes or nations can be traced back-wards through genetic examination or skull measurement, is a misconception that reminds one of Kossinna's attempts to link the Germans to the Arayans, with dreadful consequences.

Kennewick Man is thought not only to be more than 9,000 years old but of Caucasian origin. If this is true, then a momentous scientific and cultural discovery has been made. But such a discovery does not fit the Left's ideological view of the US. In keeping with this view, Clinton ordered the site destroyed and the bones vandalized in the hope of destroying any possibility of determining the remains' racial origins. This is a calculated Orwellian attempt by the Left, through Clinton, to try and control the present, and hence the future, by destroying historical evidence. There is no clearer evidence of the Left's power, influence and malice, especially in the media. (James Henry: "The Left's War Against America," *New Nation News*: www.newnation.org/NNN-Kennewick-man.html)3

And here again one can see the dangers of importing anthropological reasoning into sociopolitical debates. This conflict is not about bones, but power in a present society. Perhaps what Kennewick Man can indicate after all is that the US has been an immigrant country for at least 10,000 years.

Archaeology has to take notice of the growing diversity of views and questions. An example of this is archaeological investigation of the life-conditions of African-American slaves in the eighteenth and early nineteenth centuries. Archaeologists were surprised to be told by African Americans they contacted that they were sick of hearing about slavery. Instead of that, they were interested in finds showing their ancestors' cultural connection to Africa. One can prove that the inhabitants of houses in the southeastern US were African American via finds in a specific corner, below the hearth. A similar pattern can be observed in West Africa. This issue was relevant for African Americans because it proves a cultural connection to Africa, but also cultural cohesion across a huge region of the United States: slaves were not simply desocialized workers, but had a distinct group identity, that can be traced to a particular African region (Leone 1996).

Archaeology and Gender

> Cultural studies merges into those modes of history-writing which reconnect us to the world in ways that cannot be taken for granted, and in which our given identities, our "origins" begin to seem less secure. (During 1993: 25)

This applies also to myth and ideology, inasmuch as myth is an arrangement of the past in patterns that create and reinforce archetypes so familiar that they seem like eternal truths – which in the context of Roland Barthes also means ideology, because it promotes the interests of dominant groups in society. In that sense archaeology plays a crucial role in constructing myths.

An obvious example is the question of sex and gender. Within this discussion archaeology plays a prominent role; a major argument in this context is taken from archaeology in the form of long-range hominid development and genetic distinction. In applying archaeological arguments the relevance of cultural determination for gender questions is denied.

As an example for how gender-driven stereotypes receive scientific backing I want to take some quotes from *Wir Neandertaler* (We Neanderthals), a German book from 1988, by the renowned journalist and author Wolf Schneider. It was a bestseller with a high reputation for its scientific accuracy and daring way of introducing new perspectives.

> When the men returned to the camp from hunting, laden with loot, they were greeted by the women with the fruits of job-sharing: with the nuts, berrys, roots, which the women had collected and picked. (p. 85)

It is remarkable that the author tries to find comfort in the fact that the relation of the sexes seems stable over at least 3.7 million years. Family life at the home of *homo erectus* is identical to the stereotype of the *bourgeois*, postcapitalist pattern: daddy comes home from work, mummy and the children greet him cheerfully and they sit down to have supper. Darling, how was your day?

> Why did men get involved in so many duties, instead of living free like the male chimpanzees? Probably because there was a reward: sex – permanent female readiness, whereas all other animal females are only willing and fertile at distinct rutting seasons. To chain a roving hunter and involve him in the care of the brood, was achieved best by the women, who could offer him permanent pleasure, after all, three out of four weeks [*sic!*] – whereas the women who were in an animal rhythm had a smaller chance of finding a protector, and therefore diminished the chances of survival of their children. Consequently sexuality for hundred thousands of years has not only meant producing children, but likewise binding a partner and protecting the brood. (p. 87)

In what duties did men get involved? Did they care for the brood? Were they roving hunters? How could you prove any of those assumptions? What is the basis for such interpretations? Archaeology isn't alone in facing this problem, that the social context of the scientist will always be found in his answers.

It is as questionable to compare early humans with chimpanzees, as it is to compare them with indigenous peoples. The few hunter-gatherer societies that could be ethnologically described represent only a very small aspect of all the possible forms of society. The myth of the monogamous women and the promiscuous man has lately been challenged: women didn't need a protector, the social group provided all the protection they needed; you do not necessarily need a father to raise a child. But because women are fertile for only a day per month, promiscuity, gathering as many sperm as possible, proves a valuable means of reproduction – for the women. That early men were hunters is another common myth. It seems more likely that man started his meat-eating career with scavenging (Binford 1981). The picture of the proud hunter, erect king of the creatures, is so much more what we want ourselves to be than a humble scavenger, scraping bones for the bits hyenas left behind.

It's common knowledge that the first human was "Lucy," skeletal remains of an about 3.6 million-year-old ancestor in the African desert. But why did the find of almost half a skeleton (no skull) lead to the assumption that it was a female? (Did she carry a handbag?) It seems to fit into some mythological picture of the seventies, when Lucy was found, that the first human is a great-grandmother. Actually the interpretation is quite questionable: it is not at all easy to distinguish male and female skeletons just by the bones; usually it is the context that leads to

163

the definition of sex. And there isn't a context that could be referred to in Lucy's case.

In archaeology, gender as well as sex are theoretical constructions. The analysis of skeletal remains is not an objective procedure: often female and male characteristics can be found at the same time, and it is then a mere subjective decision: the one with the sword is male, the one with the necklace is female. Ethnography tells us about cultures of the Native Americans who knew a third gender: biologically men, culturally women. Archaeology wouldn't have been able to recognize that in the skeletal remains (Bernbeck 1997: 329)

The Past and the Present

Inasmuch as archaeology is interested in past culture, it is also part of present culture. Archaeologists are fictional heroes in films (*Indiana Jones*) and computer games (Lara Croft), and archaeological settings are the background for thrillers and love stories (Agatha Christie, Barbara Woods). Documentaries in TV and reports in print get quite considerable attention, not to forget the thousands of museums that reach a lot of visitors.

There is a tremendous gap between what is discussed inside archaeology and what is being communicated as common knowledge of the past. Let's take Indiana Jones as an example. His job is nothing less than saving the world from evil ("Nazis! I hate these guys!"), fact-izing the mythology of two major religions by finding the ark of the covenant (which Lara claims to have found as well in 1993) and the Holy Grail. In *The Temple of Doom*, his Western rationality masters the misuse of religious belief and saves an illiterate tribe. So in any case he has to deal with mythology which is of tremendous importance: "The quest for the grail is not archeology, it's a race against evil. If it is captured by the Nazis the armies of darkness will march all over the face of the earth" (Henry Jones, *Indiana Jones and the Last Crusade*).

Without a sense of doing wrong, Indiana Jones plunders the temples of South America, India, and Egypt, searching for materially precious artifacts first hand. The undeveloped natives can't see the value of the objects. They are merely afraid because of some superstitious belief system. That the Indiana Jones trilogy is a festival of escapism is nothing surprising. It is not the adventure aspect that makes Indiana Jones so annoying (nobody wants to see a one-to-one depiction of boring archaeologists), but the hidden messages of hegemony and ideology which are very well understood by the public.[4]

Museums act very much the same way. The vast majority of exhibitions represent a merely art-historical view of the past. The famous collection from ancient Egypt in the Metropolitan Museum of Art in New York, for example, displays most of its holdings dispersed and out of context. The aim is the experience of the precious and exotic, awe at the past and the status of the museum itself. There is no possibility of getting a picture of how the society might have worked, what their problems were. Learning in a sociocultural way is not encouraged, just gathering an unquestionable knowledge.

The overall public picture of archaeology is quite outdated. The setting of Indiana Jones in the 1930s is probably not a coincidence: Archaeology seems backward and preserved in history. Many archaeologists feel threatened by these escapist tendencies. The enormous popularity of magical, extraterrestrial, or other fringe perceptions of the past seems to be directed against archaeology itself. An example might be the Swiss author Erich von Däniken (*Chariots of the Gods*), who is enormously popular and spreads the thesis that all achievements in human cultural or technical development were brought to us by aliens from outer space.

Probably this is not only the fault of archaeologists: the public seems to prefer the opportunity to escape the complexity of postmodernism in the archaeological timeslot. How comforting to go to the Met and relax in a decent culture with proper hierarchy and a simple structure, easy to grasp with a few sentences attached to the show-case.

But still, archaeology could be doing the opposite: adding to our understanding of variety and giving us the opportunity to learn about sociocultural life-forms, encouraging the individual to imagine, be critical, and develop openness. This is what archaeology has to offer public culture: a playground for the practice of critical, historical thinking.

The Past and the Future

Present archaeology, as dispersed as it it is in a worldwide perspective, is generally dominated by two major positions. Processualists claim their interpretations are provable and therefore criticizable. Postprocessualists doubt the capacity for objective knowledge and demand awareness of the social and intellectual background of archaeological interpretation.

They both have a place in archaeology: processual methods cannot be substituted in the practice of field archaeology. Conducting an excavation with a clearly defined scientific vision is of great value. But the time for a wider concern with the implications of archaeological work is due: postprocessualism introduced valuable new perspectives into the range of cultural behavior – past and present. And through these new concerns, archaeology moves towards cultural studies and can benefit from its tradition of critique and disciplinary openness. Archaeology still needs encouragement to participate in and contribute to not only academic knowledge but to sociocultural reality, willingly and fearlessly.

Until now archaeology in general has been stuck with internal discussions and has only minimally been concerned with social implications. Cultural studies, on the other hand, has lately moved towards historical views and can expand its interest in anthropology towards archaeology. There is a lot archaeology can contribute: an insistent concern with cause and process and a notion of the antiquity of human cultural development; a realization of the dynamic record of continual social and cultural change in prehistory that belies notions of static, pristine, "traditional" cultures. For people without written records, archaeology provides the possibility of gaining access to their own history. Archaeology has the potential to show the dynamics of societies before the colonial encounter. It can also contribute to the theoretical understanding of the expansion of the modern capitalist world-system.

Whether one likes it or not, archaeological argumentation plays an important role in modern politics and societies. It is used to claim territory, build identity, question the status quo. It is displayed in museums, schoolbooks, and the mass media. Its influence is quite strong because of its exotic appeal on the one hand, and its terminological complexity on the other.

Archaeology has to be challenged and questioned. It is not physics – X never, ever, marks the spot. In that sense it has to be seen as one of the humanities and treated in the same way: with critical empathy and the awareness that it is always us, being entwined in a specific social context in the present, looking for answers in the past. What we'll find will not be antique reality, but might be enriching and add new perspectives to our present.

Notes

1 I can only remark on very global aspects of archaeology. For an adequate look into techniques and methods, theories and practice see for example Renfrew and Bahn 1991; Trigger 1989.

2 In Great Britain David L. Clarke was working on similar but not identical ideas; see Clarke 1978.

3 One basic misconception in this is the confusion of "caucasian" and "caucasoid": the former being a cultural or linguistic term for peoples in eastern Europe (often racially misused), the latter being an anthropological term for south to southeastern Asian features. The skull of the Kennewick Man was labeled caucasoid by anthropologist James Chatters, who first examined the bones (at that time he was convinced he was dealing with a 100-year-old trapper).

4 "I loved this movie because it is really believable. It makes you see how cruel the Nazis really were and how they were dealt with. It also makes you believe that you have to be careful who you trust because it could be a life and death situation. I definitely give this movie a 10/10" (Comment on the messageboard in the Internet movie database for *Indiana Jones and the Last Crusade*).

References

Anderson, Benedict (1983). *Imagined Communities: Reflections on the Origins and Spread of Nationalism*. London: Verso.

Barnard, Alan, and Jonathan Spencer (eds.) (1996). *Encyclopedia of Social and Cultural Anthropology*. New York: Routledge.

Bernbeck, Reinhard (1997). *Theorien in der Archäologie*. Tübingen: Francke.

Binford, Lewis R. (1981). *Bones – Ancient Men and Modern Myths*. New York/London: Academic Press.

Binford, Lewis R. and S. R. Binford (eds) (1968). *New Perspectives in Archaeology*. Chicago: Aldine Publishing Company.

Campbell, Neil and Alasdair Kean (1997). *American Cultural Studies: An Introduction to American Culture*. New York: Routledge.

Carey, James (1997). "Reflections on the Project of (American) Cultural Studies." In *Cultural Studies in Question*, eds. Marjorie Ferguson and Peter Golding. London/Thousand Oaks/New Delhi: Sage.

Châtelet, François (1962). *La naissance de l'histoire: La formation de la penseé historienne en Grece*. Paris.

Childe, V. Gordon (1949). *Social Worlds of Knowledge*. Oxford: Oxford University Press.

Clarke, David L. (1978). *Analytical Archaeology*. New York: Columbia University Press. First published 1968.

Downey, Roger (2000). *Riddle of the Bones: Politics, Science, Race, and the Story of Kennewick Man*. New York: Copernicus.

Duby, Georges and Guy Lardreau (1982). *Geschichte und Geschichtswissenschaft*. Frankfurt am Main: Suhrkamp.

During, Simon (ed.) (1993). *The Cultural Studies Reader*. New York: Routledge.

Eggert, Manfred K. H. and Ulrich Veit (eds.) (1998). *Theorie in der Archäologie: Zur englischsprachigen Diskussion*. Münster: Waxmann.

Etcoff, Nancy (1999). *The Survival of the Prettiest: The Science of Beauty*. New York: Doubleday Books.

Gehlen, Arnold (1997). *Der Mensch, seine Natur und seine Stellung in der Welt*. Wiesbaden: Quelle & Meyer. Originally published 1962.

Gero, J. M. and M. W. Conkey (eds.) (1991). *Engendering Archaeology: Women and Prehistory*. London: Blackwell.

Greverus, Ina-Maria (1987). *Kultur und Alltagswelt: Eine Einführung in Fragen der Kulturanthropologie*. Frankfurt am Main: Institut für Kulturanthropologie und Europäische Ethnologie der Universität.

Härke, Heinrich (1991). "All Quiet on the Western Front? Paradigms, Methods and Approaches in West German archaeology." In *Archaeological Theory in Europe: The Last Three Decades*, ed. Ian Hodder. London: Routledge.

Hodder, Ian (1989). *The Meanings of Things*. London: HarperCollins.

Hodder, Ian (1991). "Archaeological Theory in Contemporary European Societies: The Emergence of Competing Traditions." In *Archaeological Theory in Europe: The Last Three Decades*, ed. Ian Hodder. London: Routledge.

Hunt, Lynn (1989). "Introduction: History, Culture, and Text." In *The New Cultural History*, ed. Lynn Hunt. Berkeley: University of California Press.

Jenkins, Keith (1995). *On "What is History?"* New York: Routledge.

Kellner, Douglas (1997). "Overcoming the Divide: Cultural Studies and Political Economy." In *Cultural Studies in Question*, eds. Majorie Ferguson and Peter Golding. London/Thousand Oaks/New Delhi: Sage.

Kohl, Philip L. and Clare Fawcett (eds.) (1995). *Nationalism, Politics, and the Practice of Archaeology*. Cambridge: Cambridge University Press.

Kossinna, Gustaf (1920). *Die Herkunft der Germanen: Zur Methode der Siedlungsarchäologie*. Leipzig: Verlag C. Kabitzsch.

Leone, M. P. (1996). "A Historical Archaeology of Capitalism." *American Anthropologist* 97(2): 251–68.

Lutter, Christina and Markus Reisenleitner (1998). *Cultural Studies: Eine Einführung*. Wien: Turia und Kant.

Miller, D. and C. Tilley (eds.) (1984). *Ideology, Power and Prehistory*. Cambridge: Cambridge University Press.

Murdock G. P. and C. Provost (1973). "Factors in the Division of Labor by Sex: A Cross-Cultural Analysis." *Ethnology* 12: 203–25.

Renfrew, Colin, and Paul Bahn (1991). *Archaeology: Theories, Methods, and Practice*. London: Thames and Hudson.

Schiffer, Michael B. and Skibo, James M. (1987). "Theory and Experiment in the Study of Technological Change." *Current Anthropology* 28(1): 595–622.

Schneider, Wolf (1988). *Wir Neandertaler: Der abenteuerliche Aufstieg des Menschengeschlechts*. Hamburg: Gruner and Jahr.

Schultz, Emily A. and Robert H. Lavenda (1990). *Cultural Anthropology: A Perspective on the Human Condition*. St. Paul, Minn.: West Publishing Company.

Shanks, Michael and Christopher Tilley (1987). *Social Theory and Archaeology*. Albuquerque: University of New Mexico Press.

Silberman, Neil Asher (1995). "Promised Lands and Chosen Peoples: The Politics and Poetics of Archaeological Narrative." In *Nationalism, Politics, and the Practice of Archaeology*, eds. Philip L. Kohl and Clare Fawcett. Cambridge: Cambridge University Press.

Thomas, David Hurst (2000). *Skull Wars, Kennewick Man, Archaeology, and the Battle for Native American Identity*. New York: Basic Books.

Tilley, Christopher (1990). "Michel Foucault: Towards an Archaeology of Archaeology." In *Reading Material Culture*, ed. Christopher Tilley. London: Blackwell.

Tong, Enzheng (1995). "Thirty Years of Chinese Archaeology (1949–1979)." In *Nationalism, Politics, and the Practice of Archaeology*, eds. Philip L. Kohl and Clare Fawcett. Cambridge: Cambridge University Press.

Trigger, Bruce G. (1989). *A History of Archaeological Thought*. Cambridge: Cambridge University Press.

Trigger, Bruce G. (1995). "Romanticism, Nationalism, and Archaeology." In *Nationalism, Politics, and the Practice of Archaeology*, eds. Philip L. Kohl and Clare Fawcett. Cambridge: Cambridge University Press.

Vincent, Joan (1996). "American Anthropology." In *Encyclopedia of Social and Cultural Anthropology*, eds. Alan Barnard and Jonathan Spencer. New York: Routledge.

White, Leslie (1973). *The Concept of Culture*. Minneapolis: Burgess Publishing.

Yates, T. (1989). "Habitus and Social Space: Some Suggestions about Meaning in the Saami (Lapp) Tent ca. 1700–1900." In *The Meanings of Things*, ed. Ian Hodder. London: HarperCollins.

Ziegert, Helmut (1990). "Vom Kuriositätensammeln bis zur historischen Basiswissenschaft: Die Archäologie will zur Lösung heutiger Probleme beitragen". *uni hh Forschung: Beiträge aus der Universität Hamburg* 24: 46–56.

Chapter 10

The Unbalanced Reciprocity between Cultural Studies and Anthropology

George E. Marcus

The simple fact is that cultural studies has meant a lot more to anthropology than anthropology has meant to cultural studies. The same could not perhaps be said for the relationships between cultural studies and the disciplines of history, literature, and sociology, in which many key participants in the former arose from training in the latter. Further this unbalanced reciprocity, which it is the aim of this chapter to explore, holds mainly for the relationship between an efflorescing cultural studies and an anthropology somewhat resentful and suspicious but open to it during the past two decades in the United States. American anthropology (often designated as *cultural* anthropology) has identified itself strongly since the time of Franz Boas with a version of the culture concept, whereas British anthropology, including its Australian and other imperial variants (often designated as *social* anthropology), did not make culture a key concept or identification for itself. While the ethnographic method central to anthropology generally remained attractive as one of the modalities of cultural studies, enhancing modes of textual interpretation, it is primarily the quite separate minor key tradition of ethnography in sociology (especially, British sociology) that provided the proximate model for cultural studies' use of the ethnographic method.

Much as some have tried to find explicit links and references to anthropology in the genealogy of cultural studies, in its British origins, or Amerian expansion, these have been rather paltry. Cultural studies for a long time has been concerned with the affairs of the West (and with particular English-speaking nationalisms within the West), and anthropology with the Rest. In the past two decades, this partition of concerns has changed dramatically as changing demographics, and issues of diversity and multiculturalism, and of academically produced theories more specifically, have become very explicit concerns in the West, and as the Rest has been decolonized, globalized, and transcultured. Still the palimpsest of disciplinary and interdisciplinary origins continues to mark the practice of cultural studies and anthropology and to keep the engagement between them unbalanced and productive, but less productive than might be imagined.

In this chapter, my concern will be with the relationship between cultural studies and anthropology in the United States, and particularly with the present situation after a decade of clear mutual perception of cross influence.[1] Further, appropriate to my sense of both the affinity and the primary direction of unbalanced reciprocity between cultural studies and cultural anthropology, my emphasis will be on what cultural studies has done for anthropology.

In early discussions among anthropologists with awareness (from the end of the 1980s on) of the rising tide of cultural studies, I recall that their most vivid response was of being appropriated, of having their *de facto* (customary?) intellectual property hijacked, even of being violated! I think milder versions of this attitude toward cultural studies are now fairly widespread among anthropologists and have mostly to do with insecurities about how well they have done their task of cultural critique in relation to their own home society as they have studied others, a task practiced inconsistently since at least the time of Franz Boas. Anthropologists' *sotto voce* sense of resentment and anxiety in the face of cultural studies may go something like this then: "If we have not done it well enough, now maybe it is too late with more chic and certainly more energetic upstarts on the scene who seem to have discovered the verities that we have long claimed and developed in the culture concept . . . and without even an acknowledgment!"

We will have little more time in this chapter for such expressions of resentment about an appropriation that never really happened. In *Keywords* (1976), Raymond Williams gives us a sense of the complex branching genealogies of the culture concept in European thought of which the anthropological genealogy is just one. While it may have ended up with a similar overlapping version of the culture concept as in anthropology (culture as common, culture as accessible through the study of everyday life), cultural studies has had its own genealogy, moving in reaction to the idea of culture with a capital "C" (more the French-derived civilization notion that cultural anthropology never embraced) toward culture with a small "c" (more the German-derived notion of the concept), that as distinct forms of life experienced and created by the masses, by middle and working classes in modern industrial societies.[2]

Cultural studies conceives of culture much like anthropology, but this conception is rooted in a sense of the developing class nature of modern societies, with which cultural anthropology in its various repatriations as it shifted from a predominant study of small encapsulated societies elsewhere has only lately caught up. Thus, in figuring the actual and potential relationships of cultural studies and anthropology, it is best to consider each to have separate genealogies within the complex history of the culture concept. And while the divide of the West and the Rest deeply marks the history of the two intellectul projects, still continuing to differentiate their basic orientations, we should not let envy, insecurity, or overweening ambition as a part of the normal politics of disciplines or interdisciplines overcome the potential analytic strength and fascinating questions for research that are offered by the fortuitous circumstance that these two projects now occupy roughly the same overlapping space in scholarship and critique. In the considerable positive influence that this overlap has had on anthropological research in what I have characterized as a relationship of un-balanced reciprocity, this potentiality is even now apparent.

First, What Is Cultural Studies? . . . For My Purposes

There is by now a voluminous and still growing self-regarding literature about cultural studies, asking always "what is it?," "who are we?," monitoring the field's origins, its recent proliferation, and its present prospects. Each further act of writing on cultural studies gets caught up in this dense discourse of self-concern with the always unsettled question of how the field is to be defined and bounded. While there is no doubt about the British origins of cultural studies, which have become iconic and even mythic for further developments, what it has become in the United States has been a grounds for describing it as a project of *unlimited* alternative possibility to standard academic disciplinary practices. Perhaps the easiest position in defining cultural studies is the one favoring bounding cultural studies and restricting further directions in relation to its British origins, leaving well-defined narrow channels for understanding its evolution. The other position is one that encourages open-endedness, inclusivity, and even a certain unruliness in the development of the field – one that refuses to define the clear boundaries of cultural studies, but encourages "a family of resemblances" among various intellectual movements that preceded it. This refusal of clear bounding can be seen even as a political statement, one that adopts a radical open view of interdisciplinarity as nondisciplinarity, refusing to conceive of an interdisciplinary field evolving toward the model of disciplines. This position is argued at the potential cost of institutional definition and support. Thriving in the long term in academia depends upon the creation of departments, programs, hierarchies, emblematic methods and objects of study, professionalization, and gatekeeping of various kinds, and these all depend on statements of purpose, boundary, and specification, sensitive to an ecology of other such reigning statements.

For my purpose, then, which is to define the environment in which cultural studies and anthropology have been mutual but unbalanced sources of influence for each other during the last decade's proliferation of cultural studies in the United States, it is best to view cultural studies with a specific origin but as a current unbounded space of eclectic discussion among those with diverse dis-ciplinary trainings seeking common problems of cultural analysis. In this en-deavor, there is on the one hand a strong ideological urge to leave the project open and unbounded, and on the other hand, a counter-urge to establish a strong institutional identity for the project with aspirations for resources and recogni-tion within the academy.

Today, the styles and agendas of inquiry of cultural studies permeate inter-disciplinary programs in the social study of science and technology, media

171

studies, women's studies, postcolonial studies, gay and lesbian studies, and various ethnic studies. It has been an influence and identity that some in each of these fields embrace, but that many others do not; it is a stimulus that both repels and sticks, and either way, generates an important, shaping influence on the rhetorics and practices of prominent contemporary interdisciplinary undertakings.

Indeed, the massive 1992 volume *Cultural Studies* (edited by Grossberg, Nelson, and Treichler) is an excellent marker at the high point of the proliferation of cultural studies in the United States of these tendencies toward both the desire for boundedness and the unruly and ambitious desire to encompass all of the preceding ferment in the academy. Distinct disciplinary styles are legible in the many pieces of this collection, but it is bad form for their authors to speak in their name or to evoke disciplinary identities other than to indicate that they are transcending them. There are rather repeated efforts to evoke the senses of culture in the variously interpreted British tradition of cultural studies (itself not so easy to homogenize, as Stuart Hall's piece demonstrates) to find spaces of articulation free of older disciplinary authorities, just as the editors in the introduction attempt to define a central tendency in the burgeoning world of cultural studies of the early 1990s.

The implication of this unruly condition of the proliferation of cultural studies for developing the next two sections is that the channels by which cultural studies' influence flows into anthropology and vice versa are a messier matter than if cultural studies were a more bounded phenomenon tied closely to its originary British manifestation. For example, such channels of influence may be traceable in anthropology not to Stuart Hall, but rather through postcolonial studies of one variety or another, where cultural studies in its British lineage had been a more explicit influence. As classical anthropology itself has taught, in all processes of diffusion, the lines of influence are rarely direct or one-way, but go through numerous, fascinatingly complex mediations.

Finally, the recent proliferation of cultural studies can also be seen as the effort to consolidate and give an explicit political weight and relevance, in the Marxist and liberal tradition of leftist thought, to all of the preceding interdisciplinary discussions and intellectual movements of radical critique of disciplines of the 1970s and 1980s, primarily stimulated by the models of feminism and postmodernism. The critical movements of the 1970s and 1980s were often criticized for having ambiguous politics, a certain hermeticism, and a lack of social responsibility or engagement. Cultural studies accented and marked the political in these movements and gave it clarity in terms of its own origins in forms of British and so-called western Marxism (the work of Gramsci, the Frankfurt School, and Althusser being major theoretical inspirations). The apparent irresolutions about politics were replaced under cultural studies by a more defined, but generic left-liberal doctrine of critique (often referred to as "the cultural left").

Here there is an affinity of the political definition offered by cultural studies with the often unmarked political articulation in the embedded critical dimension of American anthropology especially since the 1960s. This involves not only an anticolonialism (which is very characteristic of British anthropology of the same period), but also the influence of the same Marxist theory which provided the anthropology of the 1960s with a means of critiquing the American state and domestic culture in protest to the Vietnam War and the unraveling of liberal policies and programs of the post–Second World War period. The most important critique by American anthropology of colonialism was thus finally a critique of American culture and politics themselves, 1960s style (as reflected in the volume *Reinventing Anthropology*, Hymes 1969), rather than the more direct critique of explicit colonialism and empire (but not of the British domestic scene) in the parallel endeavor within British anthropology (see Asad 1973). In order for American anthropology to criticize US involvement abroad it had to repatriate its research and make explicit its critical side earlier and more directly than did British or even French anthropology. This was formative in giving cultural anthropology an explicit politics not unlike the development of Marxist thought and identifications in cultural studies. It also accounts for some of anthropology's sense of competitiveness with cultural studies in delivering critical messages about American culture from the standpoints of relativism and theories of difference, a terrain that anthropologists felt that they should occupy, but never did fully. Thus, it is the left-liberal critique of the pretensions of modern societies to Culture in the face of culture as difference and as common everyday life that both unites and divides cultural studies and cultural anthropology, forming the basis, especially from the period of the 1980s on, for the reciprocities, an account of which follows.

Second, What Have Been the Connections of Anthropology to Cultural Studies?

What is it that cultural studies scholars could specifically recognize in anthropology as relevant to their work and as different from so much of the traditional practice of the discipline in which they largely had no interest? What came to be recognized as relevant in anthropology to cultural studies was determined by how anthropology had related to and participated in the preceding and broader movement of intellectual shift and the critique of disciplines in the United States – the more diverse and less organized so-called postmodern movement. This movement included all of the criticial interpretative tendencies of the late 1970s and early 1980s led by feminism and by literary studies trying to broaden itself through the stimulus of French poststructuralist theories of the 1960s into a more socially, historically, and politically aware cultural studies.[3] I would argue that this channel into cultural studies was largely constituted in anthropology by first, the "Writing Culture" critique (see Clifford and Marcus 1986) of the early to mid 1980s, and then by the *Public Culture* project which followed it through the late 1980s and early 1990s (see Appadurai 1996). Feminist scholarship within anthropology (see di Leonardo 1991, and Gordon and Behar 1995) has always provided vital overlaps with the self-identified tradition of cultural studies and its expansion in the United States, but feminism as an intellectual movement in universities, I believe, had an earlier and more strongly cultivated interdisciplinary identity of its own, and consequently scholarship done in its name (as in anthropology) has been much less likely to conceive of itself channeling or merging into a burgeoning interdisciplinary space under the name of cultural studies. Because it was "first," so to speak, feminist scholarship has had greater stakes in holding itself apart from later movements, partially modeled on its styles.

The Writing Culture *critique*

The volume *Writing Culture*, published in 1986, was the result of a week-long 1984 seminar at the School of Research in Santa Fe, and reflected discussions within anthropology and across its boundaries in the preceding years regarding the critique of the discipline's core modes of representation and discourse. In the above-noted broad-based interdisciplinary trend of critique that swept the humanities and social sciences in the 1980s, *Writing Culture* represented the alliance between scholars of literature (often comparative literature) refining the theoretical means for undertaking the critique of discourses (particularly modes of realist representation) and cultural anthropologists who understood the critique of their own discursive forms of representing others to be the most powerful means to articulate a self-critique of the discipline that had been brewing in various expressions since at least the 1960s (see Marcus & Fischer 1999). From the perspective of scholars, trained in other disciplines such as literature, law, architecture, philosophy, history, art and art history, film/media studies, and sociology, and who were themselves participating in the interdisciplinary movement stimulated by literary studies trying to become cultural studies, *Writing Culture* had the following special attractions:

It became a model of *effective* rhetorical critique that demonstrably shook the established practices and conventions of a discipline and suggested new questions and genres of analysis in the direction of the interdisciplinary movement which inspired it. History, for example, had had much earlier a provocative and systematic critique of its rhetoric by Hayden White, but it failed to have a decisive impact on the research and writing practice of historians. The relative success of a similar critique in anthropology at a time when the interdisciplinary movement was gaining strength made *Writing Culture* more than just a book focused on anthropology, but a morale-building exemplar of the transformative possibility of rhetorical critique.

Relatedly, the collective, cooperative effort that produced *Writing Culture*, and the fact that this effort was the result of an interdisciplinary alliance central to the broader movement itself, made it particularly attractive as well. It was this cross-disciplinary character that gave it particular strength as a *disciplinary* critique.

That is, anthropologists would not have had to take the critique very seriously if it were merely produced by literary scholars seeking imperialistically to expand their interests. Indeed, and quite unfairly, some anthropologists have frequently diminished the cogency of the critique by telling themselves that after all Jim Clifford is not an anthropologist. But they also had to remind themselves that others were involved in the volume with quite strong past credentials as anthropologists. At the same time, the anthropologists involved in the critique could never have carried it off without the sophistication and knowledge of those in the volume, like Clifford, who brought to it previous training in theory, history, and literary studies. It was this collaboration across disciplinary boundaries in the critique of a particular discipline that gave *Writing Culture* a certain exemplary power.

In the general interdisciplinary movement, *Writing Culture* gave anthropology a progressive voice or position, which it might not otherwise have had, and thus gave it an influence in the general trend that it might not otherwise have had. There were indeed crucial inputs that were desired of anthropology in this trend of postmodernist, and then cultural studies, critique. First, while the critique of ethnographic rhetoric had undermined the notion of its emblematic object of study as "the primitive" or "the exotic," it still authoritatively spoke or wrote for, however qualified by self-critique, the nature of radical difference outside Western contexts. And, I would argue, the figure of the primitive or the exotic remained crucially important in the broader interdisciplinary movement, albeit in nuanced and conflicted ways. Anthropology's struggle with its own object of study, as expressed in *Writing Culture*, kept the "space" of the exotic alive in postmodernist discourses but under severe critique. Maybe not to Edward Said's satisfaction, the self-critique of anthropology did represent in critical discourses the problem of other cultures until it merged, by the early 1990s, with the outpouring of writings in the US on postcolonialism.

The other aspect of traditional anthropology that was broadly attractive in interdisciplinary arenas was its emblematic method of ethnography, and this genre and practice of inquiry was of course the focus of *Writing Culture*. The fascination with ethnography exhibited by disciplines and an interdisciplinary movement that are fundamentally text-oriented and rely on reading as a research practice derives from an anxiety about lack of connection – empirical and experiential – with the social realities to which their analyses refer. Taking on ethnography as an allied method of inquiry in cultural studies – whether done naively or far too easily from the perspective of anthropological rectitude – is ideologically an important aspect of practice that was given considerable mystique by the elaborate focus and reflection on this genre and method in *Writing Culture*. Again, similar to the trope of the primitive, the simple inspired borrowing of ethnography from anthropology within the trend of interdisciplinary critique would not have worked, but the borrowing of an ethnographic ethos *under strong critique*, such as *Writing Culture* offered, was powerfully attractive.

175

The fate of *Writing Culture* outside the discipline of anthropology is probably tied to the fate of the interdisciplinary trend of critique in which it was in origin embedded. The 1980s in the US were a fascinating time for theoretical modes of thought and reflection, a variegated and deep shift in the purposes of scholarship and the nature of knowledge, performed through powerful undoings of authoritative rhetorics. The 1990s were far less interesting in the sense of discovering new theoretical ideas, but the world itself has become far more interesting – the stories of globalization, the "new world order," the much reported demise of the nation-state, *fin-de-siècle* ends and beginnings, the triumph of science and technology in the areas of biogenetics and information, the profound return of fundamentalist religiosity, etc. The challenge is to deploy in committed, original, and patient ways the ideas of the 1980s, but it is very unclear whether there is the will or even inclination to shift modes from the quick surface takes of the avant-garde thirst for the new and the shocking, which was definitely the style of the 1980s interdisciplinary movement in academia, to the much more painstaking and careful exploration of the salience of these same ideas in understanding unfolding events and processes. In this, *Writing Culture* and the ways that is has been received in interdisciplinary trends of critique struggling to maintain their edge, remain one bellwether of attitude and possibility among scholars reared in older left/liberal intellectual traditions, but living in politically very conservative, yet dynamically uncertain times.

The Public Culture Initiative

As cultural studies was emerging in the late 1980s as the central tendency or designation of the unruly interdisciplinary field that had preceded and overlapped with it, the world of post-*Writing Culture* cultural anthropology was given a further channel into what were becoming the emblematic topics, styles, and concerns of cultural studies research by the *Public Culture* initiative, undertaken by Arjun Appadurai and Carol Breckenridge. This project first took shape in the late 1980s as a newsletter and an international network of scholars with common interests, then as a prominent, award-winning journal (beginning in 1988) with an unusually active collective editorial group, two book series (at Duke University Press and the University of Minnesota Press), and a connection to the independent Center for Transcultural Studies in Chicago, which funded and sponsored a series of workshops and international conferences over several years. With thoroughly multidisciplinary participation but with anthropology (through predominant ties among graduates of the University of Chicago anthropology department) at its core, this project was a powerful presence during much of the expansion of cultural studies in the United States.

For United States academia, *Public Culture* in its publications and conferences was a unique forum for the exposure of discussions and debates among non Euro-American intellectuals and scholars, especially from China, India, and the Soviet Union. It was precocious in terms of focusing the study of culture within the transformations that now are captured by the label globalization (see Appa-durai 1996). As such, it provided a needed critique of the area studies establish-ments which had dominated the study of the non–Western world in Cold War academia. It sought to explore the ways in which the geographically situated understandings of cultures must adapt to the essentially transcultural processes in which both situated and mobile cultural imaginaries were being formed everywhere in the world of the 1990s. "Public Culture" was indeed the concept employed to label this sphere, and it was filled in analytically by a heady mixture of scholarly and theoretical trends of the 1980s and 1990s that, uniquely to this forum in the West, were articulated in versions and authorial voices from many different places.

The *Satanic Verses*/Salman Rushdie controversy in 1989 first provided the *Public Culture* project with a newsworthy event of major proportions and one that fortuitously materialized a token example of the sphere of transcultural processes to mass public view. It provided a crucible of widespread discussion in the West and other places in the world that brought attention to the *Public Culture* initiative. At the same time, this initiative participated in and provided an additional forum for the rapid rise of so-called postcolonial schorlarship, produced most emblematically by South Asian writers in American universities. Political by nature, sharply analytical, and highly sophisticated in its reception and adaptation of Western cultural theories, postcolonial scholarship became its own field, but also a major influence in the "worlding" of US cultural studies.

The publications and conferences of *Public Culture*, however, were the venues for the broadest and most diverse critiques and applications of the ideas and movements that had been developing and reorganized under the aegis of cultural studies. Besides early takes on globalization, it introduced and furthered import-ant discussions of diaspora and exile, the relation of identities to transcultural public spheres and "imagined communities" (after Anderson 1983), the issue of the viability of the state in various places, the role of history and memory in nationalist commitments, the conditions of civil societies and human rights, the comparative and cross-cultural meanings of the ideas of modernity and post-modernity themselves. It was not only eclectic in the range of topics, places, and contemporary issues it addressed, but it was also eclectic as to method. It borrowed much from media studies, film criticism, and the study of popular culture. Often ethnographic in sensibility, it did not limit itself to the traditional methods of any one discipline, but combined virtually the entire range of techniques of cultural analysis.

Thus, the *Public Culture* initiative provided the most important cross- (and of course, trans-) cultural arena for the examination of the intellectual capital that was otherwise being developed with only the West in mind. In terms of the emerging interest in gathering up the earlier trends of critique under the rubric of cultural studies, it became the most obvious channel in the early 1990s through which to listen to and absorb anthropology, among other scholarly concerns with non–Western worlds. After the *Writing Culture* critique, which opened spaces

177

for new work in anthropology rather than defined what that work would be, the *Public Culture* initiative actually facilitated the predominant directions of research that anthropology might take consistent with the range of questions, theories, and discussions associated with the emergence of the cultural studies arena in the US academy. From the point of view of cultural studies scholarship, then, it is little wonder that it could see its own reflections in the anthropology that the *Public Culture* initiative so powerfully encouraged through the 1990s, thus providing the second and successor channel of recognition for anthropology after the *Writing Culture* critique.

Third, What Have Been the Connections of Cultural Studies to Anthropology?

Because of the complex organization (assemblage?) of knowledges which the recent proliferation of cultural studies in the United States has encompassed, it is much more difficult to define the specific channels of cultural studies' influence on contemporary research projects in cultural anthropology. These have been differential, dispersed, multiply mediated, but unquestionably substantial (through, for example, the *Writing Culture* critique and the *Public Culture* initiatives as channels in reverse direction, back toward disciplinary rather than interdisciplinary realms). For example, through the virtual clearing-house function of the *Public Culture* initiative just discussed, cultural studies came into anthropology through postcolonial scholarship, or popular culture studies, among other fields. It has come into anthropology through the evolution of feminist studies into gender studies, along with the rise of gay and lesbian studies. The effort to transform the previously narrow pursuit and study of ethnographic film into a more encompassing field of ethnographic and indigenous media has also brought a strong influence of cultural studies styles of inquiry and topics of interest into anthropology. Indeed, cultural studies in terms of its iconic, originary British formation has seemingly had very little direct influence on anthropology, but through mediations, characteristic of the reorganization of a previously developing interdisciplinary space as generically cultural studies in the 1990s, its impact on anthropology in the United States has been profound.

Perhaps the best way to focus in on the way that cultural studies has influenced cultural anthropology in overview during the past decade is to explore the irony that many students are attracted to graduate training in cultural anthropology these days, not because of their knowledge of or exposure to the specific past of the discipline, but because of the influence on them of interdisciplinary trends, crystallized in such fields as feminism, postcolonial studies, and cultural studies, that have swept across the organization of knowledge production over the past two decades. Within these trends, as we have described, anthropology – its ethos, its methods, and its subject-matter – has been a key figure of influence at various moments through the *Writing Culture* critique and *Public Culture* initiatives. This has stimulated the influx of extraordinarily talented graduate students into anthropology, driven sometimes more by the prestige of how anthropology has been evoked in say, literary and cultural studies, as a discipline that proceeds by a thorough self-critique – a signal achievement indeed – than by the actual situation of pedagogy that they encounter nowadays, especially in elite departments of graduate training in anthropology. They are pulled (inspired?) into graduate school by certain exemplars of how anthropology either is used in the work of non-anthropologists (as in the case, for example, of Bruno Latour, Donna Haraway, Jim Clifford, or Andrew Ross) or is developed by noted anthropologists deeply identified with interdisciplinary trends (for example, Renato Rosaldo, Emily Martin, Dorinne Kondo, among many, many others, and increasing all the time). More specifically the beacons that draw the students to particular departments, perhaps as ever, are the impressively original works of ethnography of senior professors made prominent by them, and who are in the transitional early forties to mid-fifties generation. Yet, these same students, inspired by cultural anthropology's external face, find themselves in a more complicated situation once inside the regime of training, defined by the unresolved binds and ambivalences of the trends that have been remaking anthropology since the 1980s.

So what defines this unresolved situation of pedagogy that faces students when they arrive in virtually every graduate department nowadays? Here, I invoke a perspective that I have developed from both my own observations in directing a graduate program over the years – admittedly, one more heavily identified with interdisciplinary trends than with the central traditions of anthropology – and from many conversations with faculty involved with training graduate students. At the heart of this perspective is an observation about an interesting break in the research careers of a number of the senior professoriat of anthropology, which in turn reflects a key bind that is being sorted out and negotiated in a variety of ways in all major graduate programs in cultural anthropology. A survey of this variety would tell much about changes in the ideology of research practice in anthropology today, and in turn about the fate of the discipline's commitments and traditions.

Among the most noted anthropologists within my own and adjacent cohorts, I have noted a distinct break between first and second projects of research. First projects of such anthropologists can be fully understood within the frame of stable disciplinary practices in place for the past fifty years and which still define at least formally the categories by which choices of dissertation projects are channeled, jobs are defined, and curricula – especially undergraduate curricula – are shaped. Fieldwork with the aim of making a contribution to the world ethnographic archive divided into distinct culture areas, each with a distinctive history of anthropological discourse and trajectory of inquiry, still orients graduate training. The initial training project of ethnographic research – two or more

179

years of fieldwork in another language, dissertation write-up, followed by the publication of a monograph – constitutes the capital on which academic appointments are attained and then secured through tenure. While projects within this traditional regime of doing anthropology are still dynamic in their own terms, the regime itself – certain attitudes about ethnography and what it should be, a professional ethos about the proper concerns and sensibilities of an anthropologist – remains institutionally powerful, tradition-bound, and a deep component of anthropological fellowship.

Then there are the second projects of such senior scholars, which reflect the equally powerful legacy within anthropology of the interdisciplinary trends of the past two decades. These second projects define a zone of experimentation, which are developed in the shadow of the traditional regime but depart in various distinctive ways from the longstanding models of training and career that do in fact remain powerfully in place as the foundation of contemporary senior professors' identities within the organization of anthropological knowledge and as the base of their professional ethos. The problem at the heart of these second projects is precisely that of resignifying the conventions of ethnography for unconventional purposes, sites, and subjects – particularly moving beyond the settled community as site of fieldwork toward dispersed phenomena that defy the way that the classic ethnography has been framed and persuades. The importance of complex theories of culture in modernity and postmodernity, and the use of diverse methods, especially ones that focus on texts, and the analysis of cultural artifacts, are central to these second projects. How to preserve the core disciplinary ethos and commitment to ethnography within these second projects is a major and exciting challenge for senior scholars. To the extent that they wish, these scholars are beyond the specific constraints of training models and expectations in the production of ethnography, the apparatus of disciplinary legitimacy which remains shaped by these models, and the trial of establishing a successful career which still depend on them. Senior scholars have many options and are relatively free to make their bargains with the bimodal, or even schizoid, regimes that shape first and second projects.[4]

But graduate students often drawn, as noted, into anthropology today by the example of their professors' second projects, in turn powerfully stimulated by the references and works of interdisciplinary trends, are not so free as their professors to play with the binds that are remaking anthropology itself. They force their professors to come to terms with their own ambivalences and commitments to models that they themselves enacted in their first projects and now may be lost in their students if these models are not skillfully negotiated into what students present them with as research ideas. The traditional regime of training is thus directly at stake in students' desire to pursue work more like what their professors are currently doing, where this regime is not directly at stake in the personal research practices of senior scholars and graduate teachers themselves. In the case of the latter, the crisis of the discipline's traditions has been deferred or evaded, while it is confronted head on in negotiating research projects with graduate students who want to pursue dissertations for which there is no training model, but only exemplars.

It is in this scene of negotiation and how it is played out in every department – and not particularly in the privileged bargains that senior scholars make with themselves in their own work – that the key shifts of the discipline are being enacted. New ideologies of research emerge fitfully in this primal scene of generational transition – in some places smoothly and with decorum, in others torturously.

What to teach graduate students, what to have them read of the tradition outside of the frame of a "history of anthropology" course are crucial issues in most doctoral programs. My impression is that the weighting has shifted in core courses from older work to more contemporary work by anthropologists, and the thorough mixing of interdisciplinary literatures. What seems to me central, however, in training students today is the negotiations over the meaning and value of what is to be counted as ethnography in new work, given both the immense symbolic and literal capital that ethnography has had for anthropologists themselves and the prestigious mystique that it has created for anthropology (as the master of this practice) in the interdisciplinary realms where its identity has circulated. It is precisely over the issue of acceptable ethnography where anthropologists have most often been cranky about the way their identity, or even their central practice without attribution, has been appropriated in fields such as cultural studies. I often hear among anthropologists, for instance, how a set of interviews or casual contacts with subjects is not "ethnography," how so-called ethnography generated by cultural studies scholarship is overwhelmed by theory, that there is nothing of the native point of view in these works. Yet, within anthropologists' own disciplinary domain, it is precisely these sorts of projects that many of their most talented graduate students are bringing to them, in which ethnography as it has been known and valued in anthropology threatens to be subordinated to the primacy of certain kinds of topical interests, theoretical arguments, and other methods. Indeed, within the primal scene of negotiation to which I referred, even those senior anthropologists who have defined their current work deeply within the realm of interdisciplinary influences and styles of research and have been the ones to attract new kinds of students to anthropology are sometimes pushed to conservative positions of disciplinary boundary-making ("But this is not anthropology!"), or are at least forced to define for themselves the limit of what they will accept as the effacement of the explicit and traditional training models of anthropological dissertation research by the orientations and research ideas of the very students that they have attracted.

The more positive side of the pedagogical task, of course, in contemporary graduate training is to make the necessary accommodations, in league with students, to the intellectual influences of the past two decades which have reshaped social and cultural anthropology. And the more optimistic view is that this is precisely what is happening everywhere. For me, though, the most important task in this ongoing process is to rethink explicitly, or translate, if you will, the ethos and methods of ethnography so constitutive of the training model into the new forms of research such that anthropologists will be able to persuade themselves that in these arenas, they do good ethnography by their own standards, that in turn have direct and deep links with their past. Only then do I believe that anthropologists will be able to revive stimulating debates among themselves about their own new works, which I see as sorely lacking, instead of the aestheticist assessments and admiring dismissals of brilliant ethnographies that now reign in arenas of work relatively new for anthropology. Instead of exemplars – impressive work for which we have no basis for extended discussion and debate within the discipline – they will be the centers of deeper and more sustained discussions, admired of course, but recreating a gravity of argument within the current rather vacant public sphere inside the discipline. This will await the current remaking of projects at the crucial phase of professional initiation that is now being negotiated by professors and students in their misrecognitions and new understandings.

Despite all of the sophisticated discussions of recent years about representation in ethnographic research, it seems to me that what is at the core of the ambivalence among otherwise sympathetic professors in response to projects that are conceived in cultural studies terms, is the absence in them of the ideal of thickness, or even the presence of flat-footed literalness, in ethnographic reporting. Much of the ethos of "good" ethnography lay in the ability to be thick or literal on demand about one's fieldwork. It seems to me that when professors call for more "anthropology" in their students' projects, this has something to do with attaining a thorough enough observer's knowledge of a site or field of study such that the ethnographer can offer thicker or at least more literal descriptions when queried by other anthropologists. Probably this arises from a deep suspicion that theory-discourse and certain prepackaged tropes and frames of analysis and writing are alibis for what any good ethnographer should know or be able to say, regardless of the written form that the ethnography takes.

How this demand for thickness or literalness amid projects in new terrains and of quite baroque theoretical complexity can be met is really not a matter of articulating new rules of anthropological method, as such, but rather of doing the ethnography itself of the actual negotiations of dissertation projects that are ongoing.

The key fact is that there is virtually no space or scene of fieldwork that contemporary ethnographers enter that has not been already thoroughly mediated by other projects of representation. There is no longer any question of fieldworkers entering these spaces as if these other layers and competing sectors of representation did not exist. The freshness of ethnographic perspective thus depends not on the recreation of an unmediated site of discovery of an "other" (good literary journalists are already likely to have been there). Rather, any direct, experiential sense of others as subjects – remaining a distinctive contribution of anthropology – must be accompanied by negotiating through dense webs of already existing representations. Ethnography thus becomes a kind of "writing machine" among others, and ultimately the literal events, actions, and behaviors that are habitually the descriptive foci of study of ethnography must be negotiated as also already having been heavily represented, inscribed, and written about.

Ethnographers employ a rather primitive and even naive organization or economy of writing in their work, and for them, there is perhaps something intimidating in being overwhelmed by other structures of power and organization, understood as writing machines, with much more complex productions of representation (as in, for example, the production of legal opinions, corporate reports, news copy, or journalistic pieces with their elaborate divisions of labor for research, fact-checking, and editorial control). The image is of the lone anthropologist with his notebook, tape-recorder, and word-processor, working amidst the massive corporate structures of law, media, science, and contemporary political movements. "Writing Culture" today means overcoming the naive model of writing in anthropology as ethnographers find themselves involved in other kinds of writing machines, not as a separate function of intellectual work – separate from the fieldwork – but as an integral, inseparable part of it. This overlapping of highly structured projects of representation – writing machines – in which the ethnographic process becomes engulfed is finally what it means to include institutional and everyday lifeworlds as parallel, complexly connected objects of study in the same frame of ethnographic inquiry. The idea of a writing machine is not just one interesting way to think about this more complex object of ethnography, but is a defining feature of fieldwork reflexive enough *not* to sustain the primitive writing machine of traditional anthropology in splendid isolation.

The writing function of ethnography is thus what ultimately ties anthropologists reflexively to their contexts of study, in which they increasingly find themselves and their writing in uncertain environments of response, reaction, reception, and competition as they provide their classic forms of knowledge amid other modes of representation. "Writing Culture" thus becomes a much broader exercise that signifies not just the production of texts in a certain controled genre, but a metaphor for the distinctive research process of fieldwork itself in this brave new world of changed locations of research.

So the cultural studies influence at the moment meets a certain post-*Writing Culture* crisis of anthropology, not so much focused any longer on what the published ethnography will look like but on what fieldwork itself is to be on topics largely situated in the realm of cultural studies theory and debate and that are hard to grasp with the old paradigm of ethnographic research (see Marcus 1999). As we have seen in the present double bindings of mentors and their students in graduate programs, the shape of research and its relation to the training model is highly contested. Indeed, certain established styles of cultural studies research which mix textual analysis and the practice of ethnography in the study of genres of popular culture and their reception, culture industries, media, social movements, and gender and identity politics hold the ground in the meantime, but the future of the discipline of anthropology requires new practices of its own, crucially modified from the classic conception of ethnographic research still at least ideologically in place, for which models do not really exist in cultural studies itself. Cultural studies provides an expansion of topical interests in the study of culture for anthropologists after *Writing Culture* and in the frame of such influential initiatives as *Public Culture*, but anthropology is now in pursuit of new methodological practices, and this evolution is likely to take place within its own self-conceived disciplinary space rather than under the sign of interdisciplinary play and license. In the meantime, the styles of work in cultural studies are more an inspiration than a model and are absorbed by anthropologists with a mixture of suspicion and ambivalence.

Notes

1 For some years, I have been meaning to complete a partially written account of my experience of the ferment in the United States humanities and social science disciplines with forms of cultural analysis, beginning in the early 1980s and evolving into the now maturing cultural studies movement. But I probably won't. As the years passed, the ground was always shifting too quickly; I have abhorred being possibly bogged down in answering for what I would have had to say for years after; and besides, the things I have wanted to say have already been said – numerous times. This work was not to have been a review of the ideas, virtues, or sins of cultural studies from a distanced perspective or commentary, but actually an ethnographic memoir of what it was like to be involved in this energetic, rather exotic world, with a focus on its habits, customs, and practices with all of the stylized reflexive moves of contemporary ethnographic participation. The sense of what I intended is given in a 1988 article (Marcus 1992) which stimulated the editor of a university press to ask me to write a short book in this style, when such commentaries on the "moment" were in high demand. In any case, at least the angle of my essentially ethnographic approach to writing about cultural studies, particularly at its boundary with anthropology, is very much in evidence in what I am writing here.

2 What the overlapping notion of culture in cultural studies lacked was the idea of holism so important to the anthropological concept. For anthropologists, culture was focused on the everyday, the common, and the average, but it also encompassed the totality of culture through the study of the functional interrelations of processes, beliefs, customs, and rituals. The holism of the anthropological concept, which does not fit the cultural studies usage at all, of course comes from the predominant focus of anthropology upon small-scale, so-called tribal societies that were viewed as isolated wholes in space and time, and as discrete objects of study. This habit of conceptualization has declined markedly in anthropology, making the holistic style of analysis less relevant, and bringing the anthropological notion of culture into an even greater overlap with that of cultural studies.

3 This ambition of literary studies to become cultural studies in the United States is to be distinguished in its initial phases from the British originary moment of cultural studies (beginning in the 1950s) as the now more specific icon and locus of inspiration

for the current proliferation of cultural studies in the United States. As noted, this proliferation is the attempt to give definition to all of the preceding ferment of critique during the 1980s. When the role of literature was regnant as the font of theory for cultural studies in the early 1980s, the precedent of British cultural studies was present, but only as a variant, not as a dominant influence. By the late 1980s, however, when the label cultural studies had become a generic identification for the ferment of the previous years, the tradition of British cultural studies gained iconic and more substantive significance, while the earlier interest of literary studies in conceiving of itself as cultural studies flowed into this more general reorganization of this evolving interdisciplinary space of critical ferment amid the traditional humanities and social science disciplines.

4   In the wake of the influence of interdisciplinary trends on anthropology since the 1980s, this bimodal state of the discipline is frequently registered in a variety of venues, albeit expressed with striking differences of opinion about how important this influence has or has not been. For example, recently I found the following sentiments in a brief *TLS* review by a British anthropologist of a collection of popular anthropology, appearing in a publication of the Smithsonian Institution (David Gellner, *TLS* Oct. 30, 1998, p. 32):

> Anthropology in Britain is a low profile discipline . . . Things are very different in North America, where, unlike in Britain, there is considerable consensus about what counts as anthropology, and what fledgling anthropologists must pass before they can proceed to their Ph.D. research, namely, the "four fields" of cultural anthropology, biological anthropology, archaeology and linguistics . . . The book [*Anthropology Explored*] provides a sense of a massive anthropological profession, secure in the use of basic concepts, largely unruffled by the deconstructive, postmodern concerns that are some of its elite members' most influential exports, both to neighboring disciplines and to anthropology elsewhere.

This comment is seemingly in line with at least the sense of the distinction that I drew between a discipline that is still deeply embedded institutionally and ideologically in its traditional identifications, but what excites or provokes discussion among its exemplars (its contemporary "elite"?) is moving in other, not yet well-defined directions that threaten the appearance of coherence and perhaps morale amidst the "massive anthropological profession." This contradiction, I argue, is what graduate students must deal with most directly and keenly in the formulation of their research. Indeed, if the current trend of splits in departments continues resulting in entities identified as engaging in only social and cultural anthropology, apart from the other subfields and most often defining themselves in terms of the so-called elite trend of interdisciplinarity (as has just happened dramatically at Stanford, previously at Duke, and exists on a *de facto* basis in many leading departments), then one has to question the accuracy of the observation in the last statment of the above review.

185

References

Anderson, Benedict (1983). *Imagined Communities*. London: Verso.

Appadurai, Arjun (1996). *Modernity at Large: Cultural Dimensions of Globalization*. Minneapolis: University of Minnesota Press.

Asad, Talal (ed.) (1973). *Anthropology and the Colonial Encounter*. New York: Humanities Press.

Clifford, James and George E. Marcus (eds.) (1986). *Writing Culture: The Poetics and Politics of Ethnography*. Berkeley: University of California Press.

Gordon, Deborah and Ruth Behar (eds.) (1995). *Women Writing Culture*. Berkeley: University of California Press.

Grossberg, Lawrence, Cary Nelson, and Paula Treichler (eds.) (1992). *Cultural Studies*. New York: Routledge.

Hymes, Dell (ed.) (1969). *Reinventing Anthropology*. New York: Pantheon Books.

di Leonardo, Micaeola (ed.) (1991). *Gender at the Crossroads: Feminist Anthropology in the Postmodern Era*. Berkeley: University of California Press.

Marcus, George E. (1992). "A Broad(er)side to the Canon, Being a Partial Account of a Year of Travel Among Textual Communities in the Realm of Humanities Centers, and Including a Collection of Artificial Curiosities." In *Rereading Cultural Anthropology*, ed. George E. Marcus. Durham: Duke University Press.

Marcus, George E. (ed.) (1999). *Critical Anthropology Now: Unexpected Contexts, Shifting Constituencies, Changing Agendas*. Santa Fe: School of American Research Press.

Marcus, George E. and Michael Fischer (1999). *Anthropology as Cultural Critique: An Experimental Moment in the Human Sciences*, 2nd edn. Chicago: University of Chicago Press. First published 1986.

Williams, Raymond (1976). *Keywords: A Vocabulary of Culture and Society*. New York: Oxford University Press.

Chapter 11

Media Studies and Cultural Studies: A Symbiotic Convergence

John Nguyet Erni

By most accounts in the United States and Britain, the integration of the theories and methods of cultural studies to the field of media studies has been swift and far-reaching.[1] This integration has also been recognized as a transatlantic movement, as witnessed in numerous historical reflections provided by American (and American-based) mass communication scholars on how the field encountered and, in different degrees, absorbed British cultural studies (see Carey 1997; Delia 1987; Hardt 1992; Heyer 1988; Levy & Gurevitch 1994). Indeed, over the years, the shift from "mass communication research" to "media studies" – as both epistemological and bibliographic tags – has been an evolution marked indelibly by cultural studies.

Yet media studies and cultural studies are not synonymous, despite their mutual accessibility, shared methods, and common attention to the production and reception of cultural texts and commodities. Each of them arose from a different historical, disciplinary, and intellectual trajectory. The most significant difference lies in the Marxist intervention infused with Continental philosophy (most relevantly the structuralist tradition and its subsequent mutations), which has enabled cultural studies to reconfigure the field of media studies through (*a*) a repositioning of "mass media" to the critical study of "popular culture" (with special attention to the culture of the "popular class"; (*b*) an intellectual and political investment in semiology and ideological criticism (of media texts and audiences); (*c*) a heightening of identity-based media criticism; and as a result, (*d*) a paradigmatic fragmentation produced – or constructed – between the political-economic critique of the media and cultural studies of the media.

In this chapter, I survey these transformations in the field of media studies in the United States over the past three decades. My contention is that the rapid and successful integration of cultural studies to media studies suggests that mass communication research (especially in the United States) has been aware of, and sufficiently receptive to, media as a *political social practice*. Indeed it is important to note that prior to the "arrival" of British cultural studies, American media research has already seen a vibrant concern about the political functions and consequences of media use, a debate that would subsequently be captured in the contrast between so-called "administrative" and "critical" media research. Another important reason why British cultural studies has been successfully adopted is that a strong intellectual current within mass communication theory and research, which has been elegantly articulated in the work of James W. Carey, has already laid the foundation for a "cultural" approach to media and society. Carey's position has been most closely associated in the field with "American cultural studies." Toward the end of the chapter, I shall consider some exemplary works in media studies, particularly those concerned with global media culture. These works will be drawn from a non-US context.

The Historical and Intellectual Legacy of Media Studies

We are fast approaching the twentieth anniversary of "Ferment in the Field" (1983), a special issue of the *Journal of Communication* offering a landmark occasion for a debate over the epistemological forces that had impacted mass communication research in the US. "Ferment in the Field" pointedly assessed the legacy of positivism and neobehaviorism that formed the foundation for much of American mass communication research since the Second World War, and offered a significant alternative paradigm broadly known as "critical theory." The operating term in that assessment was "alternative," signaling, interestingly, more of an intention to exhibit a different tradition than a thorough engagement with past traditions. Many of the 35 essays in the issue outlined the challenge of critical Marxist-oriented media research whose central concerns were with the questions of power and control. Here, according to the essay by Jennifer Daryl Slack and Martin Allor, critical scholarship was translated from European Marxism and more specifically critical theory of the Frankfurt School (1983: 208–9), and according to the essay by Dallas Smythe and Tran Van Dinh, from political economy that "requires that there be criticism of the contradictory aspects of the phenomena in their systems context" (1983: 123).

To be sure, "Ferment in the Field" was an occasion for a transatlantic encounter. In the broadest sense, "mass communication" was – and is – the locus of an historical and intellectual encounter between an America steeped in the social and political spirit of Progress, Pragmatism, and liberal pluralism and a Europe distinguished by the historical experience of Fascism, exile, fragmentation, and antagonism (Carey 1985, 1991, 1997). The notion of mass media as producing a "democratic order," securing "consensus," or even supporting "behavioral determinism," came under radical suspicion. Thus in many ways, "Ferment in the Field" was more than a challenge to the tradition of American mass communication research; implicitly it was an attack on American nationalism. Yet as many scholars have argued in hindsight, the posture in "Ferment" of polarizing what was famously called the "administrative" versus "critical" studies of mass communication too quickly denied the *historicity* of the American tradition, as if the very questions of power and control were blind to the practitioners in that tradition. In order to properly see how the theories and methods of cultural studies percolate through "Ferment," it would be instructive to lay out some of the representative research questions in American mass communication research since the 1940s and those in the alternative paradigm originating in the 1960s from Europe and Britain. I say percolate because what was proposed in "Ferment" as the alternative paradigm only represented one version of cultural studies that was tailored for the discipline of communication, which is not to be confused with the whole intellectual project of cultural studies at large. I shall return to this point later.

Broadly, some of the central research questions examined in, and intellectual inquiry underlying, the American mass communication tradition include: what is the relationship between communication and the organizing process of community? (e.g. Dewey 1927; Bryson 1948; Burke 1945); how does mass communication, particularly the press, commercial advertising, television, and political propaganda, participate in, and alter, the social reality of modernization in the US? (e.g. Enzensberger 1970; Lasswell 1927; McLuhan 1964; Meyrowitz 1985; see also Peters 1989, 1996); what is the science of mass communication, and its methods, that can be quantitatively, rather than speculatively, studied in order to calibrate its social effects, particularly in shaping public opinion? (e.g. Hovland et al. 1949; Schramm 1948, 1949, 1954; Berelson & Janowitz 1950); how is the individual, and more broadly the atomized public, stimulated by the intent of the message of the media producer? (e.g. Lasswell 1948; Klapper 1949); how does the individual utilize mass communication in order to maintain himself or herself as a functioning member of society? (e.g. Wright 1986; Blumler & Katz 1974); how can media research techniques, such as those of radio and advertising, be trained and linked to the professional world, and more broadly to the media market? (e.g. Lazarsfeld 1938; Lazarsfeld & Stanton 1949); how does the media, particularly television content, cultivate long-term effects on the audience and society? (e.g. Gerbner et al. 1980; Morgan 1989). In sum, the American mass communication tradition in the period since the 1940s has been a social-scientific enterprise shaped by emerging functional and "practical" research objectives to measure media effects, resulting on the one hand in a professionalization of mass communication research and, on the other hand, in a positivist sociological understanding of mass media (albeit influenced by an interpretive tradition present in the Chicago School of Sociology). Especially from the 1940s to 1960s, the notion of media "criticism" largely involved methodological issues and thus, according to Hanno Hardt (1992), "was bound to threaten creative or innovative modes of inquiry" (p. 122). The behavioral scientific orientation became both the source and result of inquiry, thereby binding the specialization of the field to a "monadic circle" (Hardt, p. 122).

By now, students of media studies are familiar with the encounter between Paul Lazarsfeld and Theodor Adorno in the late 1930s, whose joint but flawed radio research in Princeton funded by the Rockefeller Foundation marked a major fork on the path of mass communication research. Their encounter would stand in for the divergence of the so-called "administrative" tradition from the "critical" tradition. Lazarsfeld's 161-page memorandum to Adorno accused him of "disregard of evidence and systematic empirical research" (Lazarsfeld 1938). Adorno, on the other hand, remembered the radio project as being merely interested in reactions within the dominant commercial system, so that "the structure and implications of the system itself are not analyzed" (Adorno 1976: 71). The impact of Adorno and other members of the Frankfurt School who emigrated from Nazi Germany to the United States in the 1940s has been profound, for they imported German *Sozialforschung* to the American social science research tradition. Their attention was to the historical character of mass culture and to the possible rift between the (individualistic) values posed by the consumption of mass culture on the one hand and sociopolitical reality on the other. Their theoretical formulation was decidedly Marxist. Their key challenge was to the abstracted empiricism of what Max Horkheimer called "the assiduous collecting of facts . . . the gathering of great masses of detail in connection with problems" present in American social scientific research (Horkheimer & Adorno 1972: 190–1).

Important works in communication studies influenced by this critical tradition of the Frankfurt School have asked two major sets of questions: first, is the industrialization of mass media, with its concentrated ownership and control, desirable for American society? (e.g. Horkheimer and Adorno 1972; Schiller 1989; Smythe 1981; Lowenthal 1984). Second, what is the "emancipatory potential" of public communication when it is reconceptualized not only as commercial culture but also as a shared arena of public participation and deliberation, a reconceptualization necessitated by the historical experience of totalitarianism? (e.g. Habermas 1979; see also Arendt 1951; Levinas 1989). Overall, the reconfiguration of media studies by critical theory has enriched the theoretical discourse by pressing American communication research to confront the undemocratic character of mass culture, and by extension, to deal with the possible collusion of research with the dominant political and economic system. *Broadly put, the transformation from "American mass communication research" to "critical media studies" demanded a radical critique of society and of positivist philosophy and functional, neobehavioral social theory.* Such was the collective spirit embodied in "Ferment in the Field," a spirit that captured the biting philosophical elaboration of the Frankfurt School. Today, almost twenty years later, the field of media studies continues to operate in the shadow of a bifurcated terrain, even as the social-scientific character of research has been thoroughly informed, in different degrees, by the critical neo–Marxian paradigm.[2]

"Ferment in the Field" opened the door for the incorporation of British cultural studies by way of the latter's intellectual relations with critical theory. Interestingly, however, the neo-Marxist orientation shared by British cultural studies and the Frankfurt School has produced another bifurcated terrain from within, a terrain often marked by the split between cultural studies and political economy. This divergence has often been referred to as the contrast between the attention given to textual matters and audience pleasure on the one hand and the attention given to the production apparatus of the media on the other. The doorway opens into two chambers. The character and consequences of this division will be discussed in more detail at a later point of this chapter. What is important here is that the absorption of cultural studies into the field of media studies was marked by a distinct, emerging construction of cultural studies in the image of "communication," and more specifically, in the (crass and mechanistic) image of a production–text–consumption process.[3]

Lawrence Grossberg (1997b) has suggested that "historically and genealogically, the discipline of communication was the site of the first major opening for an obvious and explicit cultural studies project in the United States" (p. 279). Reflecting on the development of the Centre for Contemporary Cultural Studies in Birmingham, Stuart Hall (1969–70) also remarks on the *de facto* perception of the Centre's work as the site of media studies: "The notion that the Centre, in directing attention to the critical study of 'contemporary culture', was essentially to be a centre for the study of television, the mass media and popular arts . . . though never meeting our sense of the situation . . . nevertheless came by default, to define us and our work" (qtd. in Grossberg 1997b: 281–2). In addition, many in the field of media studies took Richard Johnson's essay, "What is Cultural Studies Anyway?" (1986–7), to be the paradigmatic framework for a cultural studies approach to media. Johnson's essay provides a model of cultural studies that resembles the tripartite focus in conventional communications theory, namely the attention to the *separate* dimensions of production, textuality, and reception (Grossberg 1997b: 286). As a result, the broader project of cultural studies initiated by Raymond Williams, Richard Hoggart, and Stuart Hall entered into media studies in the United States by way of a reductivism of "culture" to "communication" (Grossberg 1997b: 282). On the other hand, Grossberg has pointed out that a certain misreading of Hall's essay "Encoding/Decoding" (1980), and by extension a misreading of Marx's introduction to *Grundrisse*, has also contributed to the field's desire to tailor cultural studies according to the measure of a conventional, often apolitical, model of communication (see ibid., pp. 283–6).

Interestingly, thus, whether by design or by default, the sea-change experienced in the field of media studies in the US over the years pivots on the ambiguous (and admittedly controversial) term "culture." By this I mean a development of the field that can be witnessed through three "fulcrums" that pivot around "the cultural." A whole intellectual transformation would move from the notion of "progressive society" (in the US) through that of the "public sphere" (in Europe) to that of "civilization" (in England), and then would be captured under the empire of "culture" (transatlantic). This was the first pivoting in the field. The second pivotal change entails the translation between "culture" and "communication" as discussed above. The third would involve

191

yet another translation: that between "culture" and "ideology." Correspondingly, the absorption of cultural studies into the field of media studies can be said
to operate in a geohistorical plane, a methodological plane, and a theoretical plane
all at once. These three levels find the swiveling term "culture" to be a common
denominator, thereby enabling the hitherto shift from "mass communication
research" to "media studies" to continue to mutate into research on "media
culture."[4] I have touched on the first two fulcrums above. Now let me briefly
turn to the third one.

In the 1970s and early 1980s, media studies as practiced in the Birmingham
Centre and Open University (re)turned to the "repressed," as it were, through
what Stuart Hall (1982) called the "rediscovery of ideology." At the base of this
rediscovery was the dictum that the media did not reflect, but constructed,
"reality." Hall and his colleagues (Tony Bennett, James Curran, Graham Murdock, Janet Woollacott, and others) re-indicted the positivistic tradition in media
studies for (*a*) falsely presuming the production of an integral and organic
"consensus" by the media and for (*b*) lacking a sophisticated theory of power.
Turning first to the interpretive sociology of Howard Becker, Durkheim, and
Weber, they restored the critical concept of "deviance" in a hierarchical society.
They incorporated Stephen Lukes' *Power: A Radical View* (1975) and Roland
Barthes's work, so as to elaborate a model of consensus creation driven by
(mythologized) power. Interestingly, this model would prefigure the Foucauldian moment of contribution, since his model of power too addresses the matter
of consensus production. Through these theoretical elaborations, a Marxist
framework resting on a specific radical ideological critique was formally introduced to media studies. This ideological critique examined two central questions: "How does the ideological process work and what are its mechanisms?
How is 'the ideological' to be conceived in relation to other practices within a
social formation?" (Hall 1982: 65). The preoccupation was with print and
television news, its central problematic was class struggle, and its main philosophical thrust "structural-conjuncturalist" (see Grossberg 1997a: 220ff). This
ideological critique of the media meshed the diverse theoretical repertoire of
Althusser, Gramsci, and Volosinov and outlined a serious intellectual and political commitment to a reconceptualization of "culture" as structural signification, as hegemonic formation, and as a site of (class) struggle. James Curran et
al.'s *Mass Communication and Society* (1977) and Michael Gurevitch et al.'s
Culture, Society, and the Media (1982) are two important collections that summarized the ideological position in this newly conceptualized media studies at
that time.

Scholars would quickly note the shift in cultural studies from the "culture and
society" tradition most closely associated with Raymond Williams, Richard
Hoggart, and E. P. Thompson, to that of "culture and ideology." In this
instance, a "communicational cultural studies" (Grossberg 1997b) is sutured
into an "ideological cultural studies." James W. Carey went on to point out the
radical reduction of "culture" to "ideology" in the cultural studies of language,

media, work, subcultures, and the whole social formation. According to Carey, this reductivism has drawn considerable "resistance" to cultural studies:

> [R]esistance to centering the question of ideology or of adopting cultural studies as a point of view toward the mass media is that it seems to commit oneself in advance to a moral evaluation of modern society – American in particular, the Western democracies in general, the mass media above all – that is wholly negative and condemnatory. It seems, therefore, to commit one to a revolutionary line of political action or, at least, a major project of social reconstruction. (Carey 1985: 33)

Here, Carey only associates the ideological critique with the so-called "pessimistic" impulse of cultural studies,[5] and therefore does not foresee the redeployment of ideological critique in later times surrounding reception studies of the media. Still he argues that this resistance to the question of ideology is misplaced, even as it casts a spotlight on a reductivist cultural studies. Even as "culture" is phenomenologically diverse in essence as well as effects, the ideological critique of culture reveals the diminished role of "coercion" in modern life, while the description of the ideological state apparatus points to the displacement of a repressive state apparatus (Carey, p. 36). Above all, Carey argues that to overcome resistance to the ideological critique is to keep open the possibility of a productive comparative dialogue between British and American brands of cultural studies.

Indeed, Carey was the first scholar in communication to seriously integrate the intellectual legacy of British cultural studies to the American context (see Carey 1975, 1983; Grossberg 1997b). As early as the 1950s, his displeasure with communication research as conducted in the mode of positivistic science led him to propose a cultural studies as an alternative paradigm (see Carey 1985). Carey's American version of cultural studies used the ideas of Max Weber, John Dewey, Robert Park, C. Cooley, and Kenneth Burke to build a framework consistent with American Progressivism in which modern communication and the media could be usefully situated. Carey also took Raymond Williams' notion of the "long revolution" seriously, enabling a conceptualization of "culture" as a ceaseless, continuous transformation of economic, political, and community life. Finally, Carey's project revisited both Chomsky and Althusser, and both Harold Innis and Gramsci, to chart the integrated relations of symbols, rituals, and social structure in "communication." Too often, contemporary media studies in postpositivist times have not fully ascertained the impact and usefulness of the tradition of American cultural studies. Too often, we fail to acknowledge the structural humanism common to British and American cultural studies. We have yet to re-imagine this common ground as a symbiotic relation.

In the above, I have attempted to chart the historical and intellectual formations responsible for the development of media studies into a critical paradigm informed by cultural studies. I surely do not claim comprehensive coverage. In addition, I have not made analytical distinctions between diverse media forms, such as news, television, film, radio, advertising. Such distinctions will be alluded to below when I turn to the specific manner in which cultural studies has transformed the field of media studies, namely (*a*) the shift toward the study of the politics of "popular culture"; (*b*) the primacy of the ideological critique of texts and audience; (*c*) the proliferation of "identity politics" in media studies, such as gender politics, racial politics, and sexual politics; and (*d*) the creation of a perpetual schism developed between political economy and cultural studies.

Media Studies and Cultural Studies: Points of Engagement

In an essay in Nelson and Gaonkar's (1996) *Disciplinarity and Dissent in Cultural Studies*, Arjun Appadurai observes that the ongoing debates about cultural studies reveal an "overdetermined landscape of anxieties" that he describes as an "omnibus characterization about its 'theory' (too French), its topics (too popular), its style (too glitzy), its jargon (too hybrid), its politics (too post-colonial), its constituency (too multicultural)" (p. 30). While Appadurai's tone is sarcastic, he nonetheless points to the inflated ways by which opponents of cultural studies have caricatured it. Surely, the field of media studies has produced its own resistance to, and caricature of, cultural studies over the years. Perhaps the most aggressive attack seen recently can be found in Ferguson and Golding's *Cultural Studies in Question* (1997).[6] It therefore comes as no surprise that in the 1970s, the integration of cultural studies into the field of media studies was largely about a politics of legitimation.

In this section, my purpose is twofold. Besides reviewing the various points of engagement through which cultural studies has redefined the field of media studies, I will also consider how that engagement has increasingly encountered a politics of resentment. Understanding this backlash is today part of the necessary point of engagement from within and without.

Popular culture without guarantee

[T]o imagine that popular culture is *not* "already politics," is it seems to me, politically disastrous. (Morley 1998: 487)

The first point of contact between cultural studies and media studies has been about the transformation of mass media studies to the study of the politics of popular culture. Shaped by the general cultural upheaval of the 1960s and the formation of the New Left, British cultural studies saw the terrain of popular culture, or the ordinary, messy culture of everyday life and its flexible sensibilities, as an important site of political and social conflict. Attention to mass media would be shifted to this larger, more politicized, terrain of popular culture. More specifically, it was a shift toward a formal engagement with the high-culture versus low-culture debate (see MacCabe 1986). As early as 1964, Stuart Hall and Paddy Whannel argued in *The Popular Arts* that "the struggle between what is good and worthwhile and what is shoddy and debased is not a struggle *against* the modern forms of communication, but a conflict *within* these media" (p. 15). Television, music, and cinema continue to be arenas where the distinction between the tasteful and the disdained is marked. Through an assumed equation between popular culture and working-class culture, cultural studies in the 1970s and early 1980s maintained that understanding. The political motivation (the hegemony) that marginalized the "popular class" and the "debased culture" they consumed was a key aspect of a repoliticized media studies.

This politics of legitimation, as I would want to put it, however, produces contradictory effects in media studies. On the one hand, it was a response to the manipulation thesis proposed by, and an orthodox Marxism underlying, the Frankfurt School. The study of popular media becomes legitimate once its "opium effects" are dispelled, as it were. On the other hand, the legitimation impulse spurs a nostalgic idealization of the (precommercial) lost past thought to have formerly belonged to an "authentic" working-class culture. Tony Bennett (1986) calls this a "walking backward into the future" (p. 18), whereby any form of communication consumed by the working class, such as community newspaper and radio, is assumed to prefigure revolution! Integrating Gramsci's treatment of the "national-popular," Iain Chambers (1980) proposes a corrective by leaving open the possible articulation and disarticulation between popular culture and working-class culture in a larger political context (especially in Britain) where the "popular" can be (and has been) actively appropriated into the erection of (hegemonic) nationalism. In this respect, the whole subculture debate in England surrounding working-class youth's relation with popular culture in the 1970s, especially Hall and Jefferson's *Resistance Through Rituals* (1976), Hebdige's *Subculture* (1979), Willis's *Profane Culture* (1978), and McRobbie's *Feminism and Youth Culture* (1991), remains an important opening for looking at the complex and often *contradictory* negotiations offered by popular *cultures*.

The theorizing of popular culture thus provides a robust opportunity for rethinking media power in the existing historical and social structure. In production studies of popular music, for instance, it allows for a differentiation of the "gradation" of commercialization between, say, independent local music production and the core music industry dominated by large music companies (see Robinson 1986; Ross & Rose 1994; Shore 1983). Even music charts and market sales are relatively open spaces for negotiating the extent to which commercial music penetrates the public. The bargaining of taste, identity, and affect is of course an active dimension of popular music consumption. The work of Lawrence Grossberg, Simon Frith, and Dick Hebdige, and more recently, of Tricia Rose, Sarah Thornton, Michael Dyson, and George Yúdice, to name only a few, are familiar to us in this regard. Similarly, the study of television daytime dramas and soap operas, which has necessarily intersected with feminist theorizing of

195

popular media, has seen the balance between celebration and condemnation (let alone campy readings that converge the two) as the hallmark of political ambivalence in the project (see Allen 1995; Grisprud 1995). The examination of media power is therefore reconstituted, to paraphrase Stuart Hall, into a "popularity" without guarantee (see also Bennett et al. 1986; Garafalo 1987; Miller & McHoul 1998; Stallybrass & White 1986; Williamson 1986).

By the early 1990s, popular culture research, courses, and books abounded. Yet the politics of legitimation continues to pervade the field of media studies; the ground has still to be guarded. This is because a certain uncharted auto-celebration of anything popular, the opponents would have it, has gone too far. On the one hand, for them, consumption is forever suspect. On the other hand, theories that support the passion for the popular are seen as offering the new old tricks so reminiscent of the liberal-pluralist ethos that plagued American mass communication research of the past. However, this charge of a "new revisionism" (Curran 1977) in studies of popular culture, it seems, requires fixation on certain examples or figures in cultural studies (e.g. the highly repeatable target of a John Fiske) or a certain disdain of "soft science" (e.g. constructed for feminist ethnographic studies of interpretive communities). The disingenuous spirit arises when the question of historical limits is easily forgotten; attackers of popular culture studies today operate with a willful amnesia about the hard-won space pried open only two decades ago.

The primacy of ideological criticism in media studies

I have stressed above that historically for cultural studies, the key to reconstitute the field of media studies, so that it would be responsive to historical conditions and to mechanisms of social power, has relied on a Gramscian approach. It is important to note that it is not that theories of ideology and hegemony are deployed to supplant that of culture and communication; rather, they provide the necessary scaffolding for building a broader *historicized* articulation of media effects. To this end, cultural studies in the 1970s showed us a key piece of empirically based media research that exemplified the primacy of the ideological critique. It is instructive to briefly revisit Hall et al.'s *Policing the Crisis* (1978).

A robbery – labeled a mugging – was committed in Handsworth, England, in 1972. The crime excited a massive response from the media, the judicial system, and the public. Although the crime was familiar to London streets from at least the 1860s, the press and the police described it as "a frightening new strain of crime." In a short time public debates over this "new" crime renewed panic over the moral fabric of the "British way of life," as well as over an apparent softening or even collapse of British law and order. By 1976, the debates seemed to have condensed around a single effective "origin": black youth in the inner city. By then, mugging and blacks had become synonymous terms in the public imagination.

196

The fear surrounding the Handsworth case grew into something much larger, much more menacing; the social control prompted by such fear therefore became much more severe, much more "justifiable." Taking a skeptical view of this constructed "newness" of such crime, the authors of *Policing the Crisis* suggest that the analysis of the Handsworth case unearths a whole terrain of contested forces, shaping the incident from outside, behind the scenes, and linked to a certain hegemonic struggle for the power of the state to step up control, not of crime *per se*, but of the social group thought to be unmistakably associated with the crime: black youth.

Policing shifts the study of ideology from a transactional model to a structural and historical model; "mugging" is not treated as a fact consumed in the circuit of public communication, but a relation "in terms of the social forces and contradictions accumulating within it . . . or in terms of the wider historical context in which it occurs" (Hall et al. 1978: viii). The historical issues, they argue, are precisely the "critical forces which *produce* 'mugging' in the specific form in which it appears" (p. 185; emphasis theirs). The Handsworth case therefore illustrates a crystallization of the operation of the media, so that through one case we can observe the shape of the whole news process and its relation to hegemony. The theory of articulation so central to the ideological critique offers a useful method to examine the apparent convergence of the press and the legal institutions in their attempt to maintain the stability and cohesion of society through the (hyper) control of crime and of black youth. *Policing* therefore discovers a repressed terrain of discourses, attitudes, and practices against blacks, all of which predated the Handsworth case and subsequently structured the way the incident was interpreted and how it was then "appropriately" responded to, contained, and policed.

The implications of the methods and theories used in *Policing* have been far-reaching. The key shift has been to scrutinize mediatized events in their discursive relations as a complex web of information, achieving prominence in the public imagination ("common sense") and asserting the possibility of altering social policies and realities. The 1988 grisly true-life murder story–the "preppy murder" – for instance, became a major media event and was studied by Charles Acland in his *Youth, Murder, Spectacle* (1995), for its ideological content about racialized youths and police work. In *Unstable Frontiers*, Erni (1994) unpacks the media discourse surrounding the "invention" of an AIDS drug (AZT) and explains how its ideological significance lies in a certain rejuvenation of medical authority and management of the deviant body. Examples such as these exemplify the impact of cultural studies' theories and methods on understanding news. It is obvious that the ideological critique found in these examples is not limited to matters of textuality, contrary to the view of many opponents of cultural studies.

At the same time, this ideological approach somehow overcommits to the notion of "preferred reading" derived by Hall, who never meant to limit reading only to texts. As media studies veered toward the ideological model over the

197

years, we have also moved from studies of "preferred reading" to the other (autonomous) moments in Hall's model of media effects, namely the negotiated and oppositional readings of texts and contexts. Hence the continuous growth of audience reception studies in media studies (e.g. Ang 1995; Morley 1986, 1992; Radway 1988; Seiter et al. 1989, to name just a few) and the theoretical revisions underpinning such studies (e.g. Allor 1988; Erni 1989; Grossberg 1997c), which attempt to conceptualize and trace the multiple relations audiences find within the media's consumptive environment.

Not unlike the politics of legitimation surrounding the study of popular culture, audience studies of the media as conducted in the name of cultural studies have seen their share of disapproval from the intellectual arbiters of the ethnographic tradition (e.g. Ferguson & Golding 1997; see also Nugent & Shore 1997). Some of this objection fails to see the media consumption environment as a *distinct* social formation, with its own organization of interpretive community, openness of intertext, centrality of gossip and other everyday practices, and so on. The effort to rethink the "field" in fieldwork in media studies has led to the effort to rethink ethnography and its methods. At a time of media consumption in a hyperinformational surrounding, just as cultural studies is facing the task of inventing new methods for studying the users of media, it seems counter-productive to call for a return to more "secure disciplinary foundations" and their "established methodological procedures," be it anthropology, sociology, or political economy (see Morley 1998).

Difference, identity, and performativity in media studies

Since the 1970s, significant scholarship in the field of media studies has focused on the politics of difference – social, signified, discursive differences. Media studies research quickly got organized around a list of identity-based investigations of the way the media represents diverse differences. Correspondingly, various new and established political and intellectual movements articulating diverse identities came to shape specific domains in the field: feminist media studies, media studies of race and ethnicity, queer media studies, national and regional media studies, and so on.[7]

The political and intellectual foci of these studies can be gleaned from the questions they ask, which broadly include: What is an adequate theory of subjugation of marginalized identities? How are identities of different social groups represented in the media, and transformed into non-identity-based discourses (such as those linked to questions of technology, cultural citizenship, nationalism, religion, etc.)? How are cultural representations of subordinated identities linked to material, economic constraints and other mechanisms of control? What is the relationship within, between, and across different identities, and how are they linked to the categories of agency, power, resistance, and performativity? How do we imagine alternative representations? Examples of relevant media studies works are too numerous to cite here.[8]

An exciting effect of this broad proliferation of media studies tradition from the 1970s to the present, is the formation of a crossover between academic studies and activist-oriented media works. Identity-based media studies theorize a set of concerns often shared by media activists in more practical terms: inclusion versus exclusion, public versus private, positive versus negative visibility, accommodation versus resistance, and a whole host of other political and historical concerns linked to specific events, locales, representative figures, judicial decisions, and so on, and to specific relations with various social institutions, such as medicine, technology, citizenship, nationalism, other political regimes, and so on. The tapes produced by the Media Education Foundation, for instance, represent a forging of a direct linkage among academic treatments of media theory, educational training of a critical media literacy, and possible activist use.[9] Moreover, independent and activist film and video makers concerned with identity politics in the media, such as those concerned with sexual and racial representations (e.g. Marlon Riggs, Deidre Pribam, Richard Fung, John Greyson, Jennie Livingston, and many many others, some of whom crossover to the academic world), have made films and videos that resemble print work in the field of media studies. Although they may not share the label of cultural studies, these works exemplify the nature and character of a field committed to social change. Given the public nature of such critical works, there is little wonder that they continue to be entangled with a backlash surrounding the broader discourse of "political correctness" (see "Symposium" 1992).

Borderlands in media studies: cultural studies and political economy

The critique of the media from both cultural studies and political economy stems from a shared sense of political struggle. Meanwhile, the division in methods of investigation between the two is sometimes falsely dichotomized. Rather, on the one hand, sophisticated analysis of industrial practices and structures of the media often involves interpretive procedures and a thorough understanding of how capital–be it capital in its Fordist or post-Fordist moments – restructures social, economic, and discursive relations in media practices (e.g. Burnett 1996; Geuens 1999; Gitlin 1986; Hannerz 1996; Sussman 1995). On the other hand, well-grounded studies of media as cultural discourse, including its moments of circulation and consumption, often begin with a thorough survey of the material conditions surrounding, if not constituting, the discourse and its related ideological context, including historical, economic, and policy conditions (e.g. Ang 1995; Daley & James 1998; Gripsrud 1995; Lewis & Jhally 1998; Miller 1998b; Morley & Robbins 1995; Tullock & Jenkins 1995; Spigel & Curtin 1997). Clearly, communication and media are complex systems with cultural, political-economic, and policy dimensions.

Yet there are real differences. But they cannot be captured in the serial sloganeering of such polarities as concrete versus abstract, plain versus jargonistic, research versus theory, objective versus narcissistic, and so on.

199

The initial integration of cultural studies into the field of media studies saw an important adjustment of the legacy of orthodox Marxism, especially its "economic determinism" of social life. This adjustment, seen through various attempts to reread Marx's theory of base and superstructure, was made in a framework and a time preoccupied with class concerns. The role of ideology and language in media culture was ignored by an economic deterministic theory in media studies. At the center of what needed adjustment was the whole way of thinking about media consumers.

First, cultural studies proposed that the assertion of media consumers as "cultural dopes" narcotized by the process of commodification had led to a bankrupt political project, especially for the Left. Cultural studies argued that the social could not be collapsed into the economic. Seen in this way, the shift to the critical study of the politics of popular culture "without guarantee" as well as to an ideological orientation, was to turn our attention to a major blindspot in the political-economic approach. The capitalist media were integrated into social life while people encountered the media, but in ideological conditions not of their own making. Cultural studies suggested that unless this theorizing was taken seriously, communication and media studies would degenerate into a tyranny of political certainty, whereby the logic of commodification would be seen to over-whelmingly define all aspects of our (presumably passive) relations with the media.

Second, cultural studies proposed that media studies needed a more expansive view of the media consumers and media workers beyond their class orientation. Political economy failed to theorize social difference even at a time of what Laclau and Mouffe (1985) had called "the surplus of the social." To take an example, for a long time, political economic analyses of the movie industry only focused on the economic structure of expansion, labor exploitation, and regulatory practices, without recognizing that these dimensions of the industry had differential impact on women and cultural minorities. Even in Douglas Gomery's (1992) sophisticated study of the history of movie theaters in the US, movie theaters for black Americans and other ethnic groups are separately considered as "alternative operations." Movie-going practices and the business aspects of the industry are examined under the (easy) assumption of a direct correspondence between the concentration of capital and the reality of a segregated movie-going public. In other words, capital movement and interests unproblematically *explain* the social reality of segregation in media consumption. *Broadly put, the political-economic approach to the media conflates business with history. Cultural studies maintains that "the social" within history is constituted by forces well beyond "the economic."* Even labor issues, being one of the main points of investigation in political economy, are *social* issues. Even the exploitation of labor in the increasingly integrated, deregulated media industry requires the promotion of a whole social and cultural discourse espousing the ideological virtues of "autonomy," "local control," Taylorist "efficiency," "global down-sizing," and so on.

200

In recent years, the divergence between cultural studies and political economy has been deepened. I will forgo a rehashing of the battle here.[10] Instead, I share the view of Vincent Mosco, a senior scholar in the political-economic tradition, who summarizes the relation between the two sides with extraordinary lucidity and potential for dialogue. It is worth a lengthy quotation:

> [C]ultural studies reminds political economy that the substance of its work, the analysis of communication, is rooted in the needs, goals, conflicts, failures, and accomplishments of ordinary people aiming to make sense of their lives, even as they confront an institutional and symbolic world that is not entirely of their own making and which, in fact, appears more often than not as an alien force outside of their own control. Cultural studies has also contributed to the expansion of critical work beyond class analysis to include research inspired by feminism and those newer social movements committed, for example, to peace and environmentalism. This work has served to remind political economy that, though social class is a central dividing line, or, from the perspective adopted here, a starting point, multiple overlapping hierarchies constitute the process of structuration. Moreover, though its extreme formulations celebrate the politics of contemporary life as a search for particular identities that fragment oppositional politics, cultural studies has recognized the energizing potential of multifaceted forms of social agency, each of which brings with it dimensions of subjectivity and consciousness that are vital to political praxis and which have received too little treatment in political economic analysis. (Mosco 1996: 251–2)

Global Media Studies: Some Recent Works

I would like to work toward a conclusion with a discussion of media studies conducted outside of the US context, particularly in the current hothouse atmosphere of global media studies. In this chapter, I do not claim thorough coverage of the different ways cultural studies has impacted the field of media studies, especially that in different national and regional traditions. Nonetheless, cultural studies, in its current phase of internationalization, has yet to produce an assessment of its reception in contexts other than the US and UK, and other than English-speaking areas. Analysis of global media, it seems, has emerged from all corridors of social sciences as well as from the telecommunication industries. The current enthusiasm surrounding critical global media studies in the English language has come from scholars commenting on the globalization (and various degrees and dimensions of internationalization) of the media from the vantage point of the US, UK, Europe, and Australia (e.g. Downing 1996; Miller 1998a; Shohat & Stam 1994, 1996; Sinclair et al. 1996; Trent 1998). I want to discuss two related works at some length, so as to identify some directions that media and cultural studies seems to be taking today.[11]

By and large, global media studies has proceeded with a common theoretical premise that in the vast space of global capitalism, *what* identity we have has increasingly become a question of *where* and *when* our identity is situated along the shifting traffic of global media. This argument makes possible a theory of "wired identity" experienced in the transnational trafficking of (dis)orienting images and narratives (see Erni 1996). Crucial to this theory is the configuration and distribution of power in temporal and spatial terms. David Morley and Kevin Robins' *Spaces of Identity* (1995) and McKenzie Wark's *Virtual Geography* (1994) represent two important works in cultural studies that, in their own ways, work through the implications of this notion of "wired identity." Their assessment has effectively destabilized normative, official discourse about the relationships among world territories, especially in light of the aftermath of international events such as the formation of the European Community, the rise of Asian Pacific capitalism, the German reunification, and the creation of NAFTA, GATT, and the WTO. As a result of an emerging postmodern global remapping of the world along lines of telecommunications, which cannot be simply collapsed into lines of capital and wealth, such relationships have to be reassessed. In addition, these two works can be used here to point to two parallel, and somewhat contradictory, impulses within a media studies today, increasingly articulated with questions of transnationalism in geographical, political, and cultural terms.

These works connect closely with the large and influential body of critical writing that explores the contour of colonization conceptualized in spatial and temporal terms. Since the 1970s, this growing body of work has been an important voice in the examination of transnational development projects and the globalization of capital and communications. Key texts include, for instance, David Harvey's *The Condition of Postmodernity* (1989), Henri Lefebvre's *The Production of Space* (1991), Neil Smith's *Uneven Development: Nature, Capital and Production of Space* (1990), Edward Soja's *Postmodern Geographies* (1989), Doreen Massey's *Space, Place and Gender* (1994), and so on. Of course, Edward Said's important writings, including *Orientalism* (1978) and *Culture and Imperialism* (1993), have laid the foundation for a conceptualization of colonization in terms of the imaginary production of the dazzling, exotic space of Orientalism. In addition, the recent renaissance in Canadian critical theory of the important work of Innis attests to the centrality of "critical geography" as a focus of social theory concerned with the power of colonization derived from mobile forms of communication (e.g. see Acland & Buxton 1999). Thus, *Spaces of Identity* and *Virtual Geography* may be properly considered postcolonial media and cultural studies.

Situated in western Europe, Morley and Robins write out of a tradition of British cultural studies that in part has historically been a project about dismantling the hegemony of Western, particularly Eurocentric, systems of knowledge and power. In contrast, Wark sees the world from Sydney, Australia, what he dubs a "simulated America" (p. 14). Sydney cultural studies therefore in part represents a confluence of intellectual responses to the simulation effect, making it quite sensitive to the transnational dynamic of media, culture, and identity (e.g. Turner 1993).

Like Fredric Jameson, Morley and Robins in *Spaces of Identity* reformulate the question of global culture not only in terms of the economic order within which the cultural object takes form but also of the psychic processes that engage in its creation and reception.[12] They attend to the articulation of transnational European culture and identity as a "political unconscious" that erects European supranationhood as a historical, political, and economic regime as well as mediated psychic fantasy. Wark's *Virtual Geography*, on the other hand, addresses the question of political fantasy in the global media by suggesting that the subjective and objective dimensions of cultural production are *effects*, not the substance, of globalization. Rather than positing the subject/object designations in cultural relations, Wark focuses on the pathways – what he calls "vectors" via Paul Virilio's work – that constitute such designations in the first place. Ultimately, the "political unconscious" of global capitalism and transnational cultural production appears as *a map of vectoral pathways* that consist of mobile lines of economics, distribution of natural and human resources, historical memories, electronic and digital signals, advertising images and sounds, and so on. These mobile vectors thus wire the globe with differential power, setting up an uneven transnational flow of resources, desires, and identities. In sum, Wark postulates that to be a "subject" of culture, to have identity in the global sphere, means finding the coordinates of vectors that form a certain narrative charged with meaning of subjecthood that can only be discerned in topographical, relational terms.

In *Spaces of Identity*, Morley and Robins mark the emergence of the "European Community" or "European Union" in the 1980s as a historical moment of crisis. They argue that this project of forming a trans-European economy has been couched in official terms as a matter of cultural adjustments by people of various local regions: "The new *culture of enterprise* enlists the *enterprise of culture* to manufacture differentiated urban or local identities" (p. 37; emphasis added). This agenda, they suggest, is accomplished by sweeping telecommunications initiatives or directives that would link disparate regions and territories into what they call "audiovisual geographies" that are detached from the spaces of national culture, and are realigned "on the basis of the more 'universal' principles of international consumer culture" (p. 11). Given the inherent diversity of national cultures and identities across Europe, how can this new media order possibly create social, political, and psychic coherence for the diverse inhabitants of Europe? They ask: "What does the idea of Europe add up to when so many within feel that they are excluded?" (p. 3). According to them, there are two levels of hegemonic exclusion: internal exclusion through the production of "false local cultures and economies" within Europe, and external exclusion through the symbolic demarcation of non-European Otherness. To cohere, to be "Europe," thus means the persuasion of a core, "organic" European identity postulated on retrieving "common memories" of nationhood and empire across vast terrains. This is where the media come in.

While Morley and Robins agree that global capitalism has not annihilated all spaces and places (p. 30), they argue that differentiated local identities are manufactured in the media "around the creation of an image, a fabricated and inauthentic identity, a false aura, usually achieved through 'the recuperation of history'" (p. 37). They take up the intense cultural debate in Europe opened up by Edgar Reitz's 1984 film, *Heimat*, which was subsequently developed in his sequel *Die Zweite Heimat* (1990). According to Morley and Robins, Reitz's films served as a lightening-rod for a continental debate all over Europe regarding its future. Through this "German story," passionate debates about who owned the franchise on the representation of the past coincided with the proliferation of the discourse of the European Union, thereby constituting the ideologically charged notion of the "homeland" as the symbolic condensation point of European identity. Given that in the discourse of European Union, "the longing for home is not an innocent utopia" (p. 90), Morley and Robins provocatively ask: "Can we imagine an identity, an awareness, grounded in the experience of not having a home, or of not having to have a home? Can we see home as a necessarily provisional, always relative, truth?" (p. 103). If *Heimat* is a precarious form of European fundamentalism, the critical issue confronting Europe since the 1980s, the authors assert, is whether it can be open to "the condition and experience of homelessness" (p. 103).

Their conceptual conclusion is this: the European Union accords symbolic coherence to a Europe as an economic, technological, and cultural leader in world affairs. Such a symbolic coherence is achieved by reasserting European modernity as unique compared to the "overdevelopment" of the United States and Japan on one side, and the "underdevelopment" of Islamic countries, Africa, and Central Asia on the other side. Hence, European modernity supplies a happy medium to world civilization in late capitalism. This European order is largely about the serial demarcation of maps and territories, including physical and imaginary or psychic borderlines between Self and Other. Meanings of identity thus reside in the designations of subject/object relations according to economic and cultural power. Morley and Robins see the Eurocentric project as largely regressive and reactionary. In the end, it promotes fear and anxiety more than feelings of unity. In contrast, Wark's *Virtual Geography* proposes an alternative model of analyzing the phenomenon of globalization that refuses the model of subject/object relations.

Wark's study, with a subtitle of "Living with Global Media Events," discusses the question of globalization by theorizing it as a problem about how to experience the media events that link distinct sites and separate time zones in the world. How do we reconcile the dazzlingly confusing situation of watching the Gulf War in 1991 or the handover of Hong Kong to China in 1997, as something so far and yet so near, so recent yet so prone to forgetfulness at the same time? On a daily basis, the high rate of repetition of information, images, historical narratives, recent memory, economic tales, and mediated moralism in these global

204

media events alone can produce such a disorienting effect as to deprive us of rational discourse. How *does* one live with such a strange mediated experience?

Wark focuses on four recent important global events that have been so thoroughly mediated across vast spaces and time zones as to render their status a function and effect of the movements of media vectors. In fact, he does not call the Persian Gulf War of 1991, the fall of the Berlin Wall in 1989, the Beijing Tiananmen Square massacre in 1989, and the "Black Monday" stockmarket crash of 1987, events *per se*. In the vectoral field, these highly charged international stories are termed "sites," "intersections," "lines," and "noises." He moves back and forth between "objective" re-reporting of these events and plots the coordinates that link and shape them on the maps of transnational media. He argues that our everyday experience of global media spectacles crucially depends on *where* and *when* they are distributed to various sites in the world along established but shifting "power-lines." These power-lines are the trajectories along which information, technologies, capital, and even warheads can potentially pass. They disrupt the normative distance and temporal relations between different geographical locales. The experience of living with these global media events conceptualized here as media vectors means observing not so much the "events" as such, but the movements of media vectors across geographical and temporal spaces. Watching the Gulf War or the Hong Kong handover, therefore, becomes a kind of concrete abstraction, taking in information and meanings that fall from the sky, integrating them into the constantly shifting (and perpetually revising) local interpretations, and expecting that they will change from day to day and from locale to locale. According to Wark, such is the technomythical reality of living with global media events.

In this way, Wark's study offers a new way of "doing" media studies that is grounded in the everyday realities of a world remapped by media vectors. Researchers will become postmodern map-makers. How does the mediated, vectorial map of the world today tell the story of uneven development along class, racial, and gender lines that *are* the objective mainstay of global conditions? Better yet, to adopt a Warkian language, *where* and *when* do global media events fix, anchor, and concentrate global power relations so that our everyday experience in this context is both magically surreal yet, *at a given time and space*, painfully "real"? For every vector that transgresses national and historical lines, there are, *in the first and last instance*, the material spheres of national and historical structures from which to transgress. There are also all the material, historically determined trappings of mostly economic reality – and economic devastation – that vectors can pass through, but cannot (at least have not) effectively transformed. Throughout his study, Wark has only a tangential discussion of material power in relation to vectoral movements. At best, he has an antimaterialist theory of power. Power is defined only as the problem of access to the vectoral field: "Rapid and effective access to useful information is a vector . . . Access to these vectors is a form of power, and hence a line along which the struggle in and around events takes place" (p. 18).

205

Ultimately, in a rapidly globalizing world, we confront the dialectics of the global/universal and the local/particular. Whether it is the question of the European, American, or Japanese utopias or the Middle East or Chinese dystopias, the strong tendency for the telecommunication industry to transport and transgress cultural borders will always have to confront the global–local nexus. Because the media are simultaneously global and local, it becomes critically important for media studies scholars to talk about both the possibilities and limitations of the "wired identity." Morley and Robins' *Spaces of Identity* and Wark's *Virtual Geography* can be treated as a type of media broker, projecting two parallel, but ultimately diverging, views on how the global–local complex of the New World Order transforms the materiality of everyday life in late capitalism.

To conclude, I juxtapose two brief passages from the conclusions of these two recent examples of global media studies to point out, at the risk of simplification, the bewildering difference in their view of the global–local media complex. Wark argues:

> Events are in a sense fractal. Each event appears as a confluence of noise in the matrix of vectors, but examine that event on a smaller scale and it appears to be made up of little events, all in a certain sense self-similar with the bigger event discovered at a larger scale . . . Hence it seems appropriate to name what can be quite vast and global phenomena after something which takes place in the microscopic scale of electrons, nestling next to each other in a program of immaterial information. (Wark 1994: 228)

On the other hand, Morley and Robins write:

> The point is simply that "we" are *not* all nomadic or fragmented subjectivities, living in the same "postmodern" universe . . . Many writers have referred to the contemporary dynamic of simultaneous globalisation and localisation. However, for some such people, the globalising aspect of the dynamic is the dominant one, while for others it is very much the localising aspect which is increasingly operative, as their life-chances are gradually reduced, and they increasingly remain stuck in the micro-territories in which they were born. (Morley & Robins 1995: 218)

"Microscopic electrons" of information or "micro-territories" of historical agents? "Immaterial information" or "life chances"? To be certain, these are the points of departure between these two important works. They are also points of political contention for those of us who study the transformation of cultures and identities in the age of global communication. As cultural studies steers between these two poles, it will significantly shape the future practice and politics of media studies.

In this chapter, I have confined my discussion to the most visible lines of inquiry in media and cultural studies in the US. Some important strands have not been addressed, including, for instance, film studies, new (multi)media studies, media and cultural policy research, and the non-English-speaking media studies traditions. My hope is that this map I am sketching will be useful for opening up more work on the histories of media and cultural studies.

Notes

1   I would like to thank Patrick Daley and Vamsee Juluri for their insightful comments on an earlier draft, and Toby Miller for his encouragement.
2   For more recent reflections of the history and trajectory of mass communication research, see the essays collected in these anthologies: Levy and Gurevitch (1994), Hanson and Maxcy (1999), Marris and Thornham (1996).
3   Even Marris and Thornham's (1996) enormously useful anthology on media studies is explicitly framed by the model of production–text–reception. See their introductory chapter.
4   These transformations are presented here only for heuristic purposes. They are clearly not linear transformations.
5   More recently, Carey has expressed his view of the current proliferation of cultural studies: "I think this is a false prosperity. Intellectually and politically cultural studies is not very healthy and I believe its days are numbered except as an irrelevant outpost in the academy" (1997: 15). Readers are encouraged to read his entire essay to understand Carey's despair in context.
6   For a recent well-argued, if slightly sardonic, reply to the various forms of attacks on cultural studies, see Morley 1998.
7   Some important examples: feminist media studies (Valdivia 1995; Treichler & Wartella 1986), media studies of race and ethnicity (Gray 1995; Hamamoto 1994), queer media studies (Henderson, forthcoming), national and regional media studies (Chen 1998; Downing 1996; Miller 1998a; Turner 1993). See also other relevant chapters in this volume.
8   Besides browsing through publisher lists, readers interested in sources on a wide variety of identity-based media studies works can visit these useful websites and listserv sites: *wwwculturalstudies.net*; *www.cas.usf.edu/communication/rodman/cultsutd*; *www.blackwellpublishers.co.uk/cultural*; *www.eserver.org/gender*; *www.popcultures.com/internat.htm*; *www.newmediastudies.com*.
9   See the Media Education Foundation's website: *wwwmediaed.org*.
10 For a particularly aggressive challenge to cultural studies from the perspective of political economy, see Ferguson & Golding 1997. As for cultural studies' challenge and reply to the attacks, see Grossberg 1995 and Morley 1998.
11 This last section of the chapter contains a revised portion of a previously published essay. See Erni 1996.
12 In writing about Jameson, Colin MacCabe (1986) suggests that the Jamesonian analysis sees every cultural production as "at its most fundamental level a political fantasy which in contradictory fashion articulates both the actual and potential social relations which constitute individuals within a specific political economy" (p. xi).

References

Acland, Charles R. (1995). *Youth, Murder, Spectacle: The Cultural Politics of "Youth in Crisis."* Boulder, Colo.: Westview Press.

Acland, Charles and William Buxton (eds.) (1999). *Harold Innis in the New Century: Reflections and Refractions.* Montreal: McGill-Queens University Press.

Adorno, Theodor W. (1976). "Sociology and Empirical Research." In T. Adorno et al. (eds.), *The Positivist Dispute in German Sociology.* New York: Harper & Row.

Allen, Robert (ed.) (1995). *To Be Continued . . . : Soap Operas Around the World.* London and New York: Routledge.

Allor, Martin (1988). "Relocating the Site of the Audience." *Critical Studies in Mass Communication* 5: 217–33.

Ang, Ien (1995). *Living Room Wars: Rethinking Media Audiences for a Postmodern World.* London and New York: Routledge.

Appadurai, Arjun (1996). "Diversity and Disciplinarity as Cultural Artifacts." In C. Nelson and D. P. Gaonkar (eds.), *Disciplinarity and Dissent in Cultural Studies.* London: Routledge.

Arendt, Hannah (1951). *The Origins of Totalitarianism.* New York: Harcourt Brace.

Bennett, Tony (1986). "The Politics of 'the Popular' and Popular Culture." In T. Bennett et al. (eds.), *Popular Culture and Social Relations.* Milton Keyes: Open University Press.

Bennett, Tony et al. (eds.) (1986). *Popular Culture and Social Relations.* Milton Keyes: Open University Press.

Berelson, Bernard and Janowitz Morris (eds.) (1950). *Reader in Public Opinion and Communication.* Glencoe, Ill.: Prentice-Hall.

Blumler, Jay G. and Elihu Katz (eds.) (1974). *The Uses of Mass Communications.* London: Sage.

Bryson, Lyman (ed.) (1948). *The Communication of Ideas: A Series of Addresses.* New York: Harper & Row.

Burke, Kenneth (1945). *A Grammar of Motives.* New York: Prentice-Hall.

Burnett, Robert (1996). *The Global Jukebox: The International Music Industry.* London and New York: Routledge.

Carey, James W. (1975). "A Cultural Approach to Communication." *Communication* 2: 1–22.

Carey, James W. (1983). "The Origins of the Radical Discourse on Cultural Studies in the United States." *Journal of Communication* 33(3): 311–13.

Carey, James W. (1985). "Overcoming Resistance to Cultural Studies." In M. Gurevitch and M. Levy (eds.), *Mass Communication Review Yearbook*, vol. 5. London: Sage.

Carey, James W. (1991). "Communications and the Progressives." In R. Avery and D. Eason (eds.), *Critical Perspectives on Media and Society.* New York and London: Guilford Press.

Carey, James W. (1997). "Reflections on the Project of (American) Cultural Studies." In M. Ferguson and P. Golding (eds.), *Cultural Studies in Question.* London: Sage.

Chambers, Iain (1980). "Rethinking 'Popular Culture.'" *Screen Education* 36: 113–17.

Chen, Kuan-Hsing (ed.) (1998). *Trajectories: Inter-Asia Cultural Studies.* New York and London: Routledge.

Curran, James et al. (eds.) (1977). *Mass Communication and Society*. London: Sage.

Daley, Patrick and Beverly James (1998). "Warming the Arctic Air: Cultural Politics and Alaska Native Radio." *Javnost/ The Public* 5(2): 50–60.

Delia, Jesse (1987). "Communication Research: A History." In C. Berger and S. Chaffee (eds.), *Handbook of Communication Science*. Newbury Park, Calif. Sage.

Dewey, John (1927). *The Public and Its Problems*. New York: Minton, Balch & Co.

Downing, John (1996). *Internationalizing Media Theory*. London: Sage.

Enzensberger, Hans Magnus (1970). "Constituents of a Theory of the Media." *New Left Review* 64: 13–36.

Erni, John Nguyet (1989). "Where is the 'Audience'? Discerning the (Impossible) Subject." *Journal of Communication Inquiry* 13(2) (Summer): 30–42.

Erni, John Nguyet (1994). *Unstable Frontiers: Technomedicine and the Cultural Politics of "Curing" AIDS*. Minneapolis: University of Minnesota Press.

Erni, John Nguyet (1996). "On the Limits of 'Wired Identity' in the Age of Global Media." *Identities* 2(4): 419–28.

Ferguson, Marjorie and Peter Golding (eds.) (1997). *Cultural Studies in Question*. London: Sage.

Garafalo, Reebee (1987). "How Autonomous is Relative: Popular Music, the Social Formation and Cultural Formation." *Popular Music* 6(1): 77–92.

Gerbner, George et al. (1980). "The 'Mainstreaming' of America: Violence Profile No. 11." *Journal of Communication* 30(3): 10–29.

Geuens, Jean-Pierre (1999). *Film Production Theory*. New York: State University of New York Press.

Gitlin, Todd (ed.) (1986). *Watching Television*. New York: Pantheon Books.

Gomery, Douglas (1992). *Shared Pleasures: A History of Movie Presentation in the United States*. Madison, Wis.: University of Wisconsin Press.

Gray, Herman (1995). *Watching Race: Television and the Struggle for "Blackness"*. Minneapolis: University of Minnesota Press.

Gripsrud, Jostein (1995). *The Dynasty Years: Hollywood Television and Critical Media Studies*. London and New York: Routledge.

Grossberg, Lawrence (1995). "Cultural Studies versus Political Economy." *Critical Studies in Mass Communication* 12.

Grossberg, Lawrence (1997a). "The Formation(s) of Cultural Studies: An American in Birmingham." In *Bringing It All Back Home: Essays on Cultural Studies*. Durham, NC: Duke University Press.

Grossberg, Lawrence (1997b). "Toward a Genealogy of the State of Cultural Studies." In *Bringing It All Back Home: Essays on Cultural Studies*. Durham, NC: Duke University Press.

Grossberg, Lawrence (1997c). "The Context of Audiences and the Politics of Difference." In *Bringing It All Back Home: Essays on Cultural Studies*. Durham, NC: Duke University Press.

Gurevitch, Michael et al. (eds.) (1982). *Culture, Society, and the Media*. London and New York: Methuen.

Habermas, Jürgen (1979). *Communication and the Evolution of Society*. Boston: Beacon Press.

Hall, Stuart (1969–70). Introduction to *The Annual Report of the Centre of Contemporary Cultural Studies*. Birmingham, England.

209

Hall, Stuart (1980). "Encoding/Decoding." In S. Hall et al. (eds.), *Culture, Media, Language*. London: Hutchinson.

Hall, Stuart (1981). "Notes on Deconstructing the 'Popular.'" In S. Raphael (ed.), *People's History and Socialist Theory*. London: Routledge and Kegan Paul.

Hall, Stuart (1982). "The Rediscovery of Ideology: Return of the Repressed in Media Studies." In M. Gurevitch et al. (eds.), *Culture, Society, and the Media*. New York: Methuen.

Hall, Stuart and Tony Jefferson (eds.) (1976). *Resistance Through Rituals*. London: Hutchinson.

Hall, Stuart et al. (1978). *Policing the Crisis: Mugging, the State and Law and Order*. New York: Holmes and Meier Publishers.

Hamamoto, Darrell (1994). *Monitored Peril: Asian Americans and the Politics of TV Representation*. Minneapolis: University of Minnesota Press.

Hannerz, Ulf (1996). *Transnational Connections: Culture, People, Places*. London and New York: Routledge.

Hanson, Jarice and David Maxcy (eds.) (1999). *Notable Sources in Mass Media*, 2nd edn. Guilford, Conn.: Dushkin/McGraw-Hill.

Hardt, Hanno (1992). *Critical Communication Studies: Communication, History & Theory in America*. London and New York: Routledge.

Harvey, David (1989). *The Condition of Postmodernity*. Oxford: Blackwell.

Hebdige, Dick (1979). *Subculture: The Meaning of Style*. London: Routledge.

Henderson, Lisa (2000). "Queer Communication Studies." In B. Goodykunt (ed.), *Mass Communication Review Yearbook*. Thousand Oaks, Calif.: Sage.

Heyer, Paul (1988). *Communications and History: Theories of Media, Knowledge, and Civilization*. New York: Greenwood Press.

Horkheimer, Max and Theodor Adorno (1972). *Dialectics of Enlightenment*. New York: Herder & Herder.

Hovland, Carl et al. (1949). *Experiments in Mass Communication*. Princeton: Princeton University Press.

Johnson, Richard (1986–7). "What is Cultural Studies Anyway?" *Social Text* 34: 17–52.

Klapper, Joseph (1949). *The Effects of Mass Media*. New York: Bureau of Applied Social Research, Columbia University; mimeographed.

Laclau, Ernesto and Chantal Mouffe (1985). *Hegemony and Socialist Strategy*. London: Verso.

Lasswell, Harold (1927). *Propaganda Technique in the World War*. New York: Peter Smith.

Lasswell, Harold (1948). "The Structure and Function of Communication in Society." In L. Bryson (ed.), *The Communication of Ideas*. New York: Harper & Row.

Lazarsfeld, Paul (1938). Unpublished letter, undated, response to Theodor Adorno's manuscript, "Memorandum." Music in Radio, Princeton Radio Research Project, June 26, 1938.

Lazarsfeld, Paul and Frank Stanton (eds.) (1949). *Communications Research, 1948–49*. New York: Harper Brothers.

Lefebvre, Henri (1991). *The Production of Space*, trans. Donald Nicholson-Smith. Oxford: Blackwell.

Levinas, E. (1989). *The Levinas Reader*. Oxford: Blackwell.

Levy, Mark R. and Michael Gurevitch (eds.) (1994). *Defining Media Studies: Reflections on the Future of the Field*. New York: Oxford University Press.

Lewis, Justin and Sut Jhally (1998). "The Struggle over Media Literacy." *Journal of Communication* 48(1) (Winter): 109–20.

Lowenthal, Leo (1984). *Literature and Mass Culture: Communication in Society*, vol. 1. New Brunswick: Transaction.

Lukes, Stephen (1975). *Power: A Radical View*. London: Macmillan.

MacCabe, Colin (ed.) (1986). *High Theory/Low Culture: Analyzing Popular Television and Film*. Manchester: Manchester University Press.

Marris, Paul and Sue Thornham (eds.) (1996). *Media Studies: A Reader*. Edinburgh: Edinburgh University Press.

Massey, Doreen (1994). *Space, Place and Gender*. Minneapolis: University of Minnesota Press.

McLuhan, Marshall (1964). *Understanding Media*. London: Routledge & Kegan Paul.

Meyrowitz, Joshua (1985). *No Sense of Place: The Impact of Electronic Media on Social Behavior*. New York: Oxford University Press.

Miller, Toby (1998a). *Technologies of Truth: Cultural Citizenship and the Popular Media*. Minneapolis: University of Minnesota Press.

Miller, Toby (1998b). "How do you turn Indooroopilly into Africa? *Mission Impossible*, Second World Television, and the New International Division of Cultural Labor." In his *Technologies of Truth: Cultural Citizenship and the Popular Media*. Minneapolis: University of Minnesota Press.

Miller, Toby and Alec McHoul (1998). *Popular Culture and Everyday Life*. London & Thousand Oaks, Calif.: Sage.

Morgan, Michael (1989). "Television and Democracy." In I. Angus and S. Jhally (eds.), *Cultural Politics in Contemporary America*. London and New York: Routledge.

Morley, David (1986). *Family Television: Cultural Power and Domestic Leisure*. London: Comedia.

Morley, David (1992). *Television, Audiences, and Cultural Studies*. London: Routledge.

Morley, David (1998). "So-called Cultural Studies: Dead Ends and Reinvented Wheels." *Cultural Studies* 12(4): 476–97.

Morley, David and Kevin Robins (1995). *Spaces of Identity: Global Media, Electronic Landscapes and Cultural Boundaries*. London and New York: Routledge.

Mosco, Vincent (1996) *The Political Economy of Communication*. London: Sage.

Nelson, Cary and Dilip Parameshwar Gaonkar (eds.) (1996). *Disciplinarity and Dissent in Cultural Studies*. London: Routledge.

Nugent, S. and C. Shore (eds.) (1997). *Anthropology and Cultural Studies*. London: Pluto Press.

Peters, John Durham (1989). "Satan and Savior: Mass Communication in Progressive Thought." *Critical Studies in Mass Communication* 6: 247–63.

Peters, John Durham (1996). "The Uncanniness of Mass Communication in Interwar Social Thought." *Journal of Communication* 46(3) (Summer): 108–23.

Radway, Janice (1988). "Reception Study: Ethnography and the Problems of Dispersed Audiences and Nomadic Subjects." *Cultural Studies* 2(3): 359–76.

Robinson, Deanna (1986). "Youth and Popular Music: A Theoretical Rationale for an International Study." *Gazette* 37: 33–50.

Ross, Andrew and Tricia Rose (eds.) (1994). *Microphone Fiends: Youth Music and Youth Culture*. London and New York: Routledge.

Said, Edward (1978). *Orientalism*. New York: Random House.

Said, Edward (1993). *Culture and Imperialism*. New York: Knopf.

Schiller, Herbert I. (1989). *Mass Communications and American Empire*. New York: Augustus M. Kelly.

Schramm, Wilbur (ed.) (1948). *Communications in Modern Society*. Urbana: University of Illinois Press.

Schramm, Wilbur (ed.) (1949). *Mass Communications*. Urbana: University of Illinois Press.

Schramm, Wilbur (ed.) (1954). *The Processes and Effects of Mass Communication*. Urbana: University of Illinois Press.

Seiter, Ellen, Hans Borchers, Gabriele Kreutzner, and Eva-Maria Warth (1989). *Remote Control: Television, Audiences and Cultural Power*. London and New York: Routledge.

Shohat, Ella and Robert Stam (eds.) (1994). *Unthinking Eurocentrism: Multiculturalism and the Media*. London and New York: Routledge.

Shohat, Ella and Robert Stam (1996). "From the Imperial Family to the Transnational Imaginary: Media Spectatorship in the Age of Globalization." In R. Wilson and W. Dissanayake (eds.), *Global/Local: Cultural Production and the Transnational Imaginary*. Durham, NC: Duke University Press.

Shore, Lawrence (1983). *The Crossroads of Business and Music: A Study of the Music Industry in the United States and Internationally*. a Doctoral dissertation, Stanford University.

Sinclair, John, Elizabeth Jacka, and Stuart Cunningham (eds.) (1996). *New Patterns in Global Television: Peripheral Vision*. New York: Oxford University Press.

Slack, Jennifer Daryl and Martin Allor (1983). "The Political and Epistemological Constituents of Critical Communication Research." *Journal of Communication* 33(3): 208–18.

Smith, Neil (1990). *Uneven Development: Nature, Capital and the Production of Space*. Cambridge, Mass.: Blackwell.

Smythe, Dallas W. (1981). *Dependency Road: Communications, Capitalism, Consciousness, and Canada*. Norwood, NJ: Ablex.

Smythe, Dallas W. and Tran Van Dinh (1983). "On Critical and Administrative Research: A New Critical Analysis." *Journal of Communication* 33(3): 117–27.

Soja, Edward (1989). *Postmodern Geographies: The Reassertion of Space in Critical Social Theory*. New York: Verso.

Spigel, Lynn and Michael Curtin (eds.) (1997). *The Revolution Wasn't Televised: Sixties Television and Social Conflict*. London and New York: Routledge.

Stallybrass, Peter and Allon White (1986). *The Politics and Poetics of Transgression*. Ithaca, NY: Cornell University Press.

Sussman, Gerald (1995). "Transnational Communications and the Dependent-integrated State." *Journal of Communication* 45(4) (Autumn): 89–106.

Symposium: Communication Scholarship and Political Correctness (1992). *Journal of Communication* 42(2) (Spring): 56–149.

Treichler, Paula and Ellen Wartella (1986). "Intervention: Feminist Theory and Communication Studies." *Communication* 9: 1–18.

Trent, Barbara (1998). "Media in a Capitalist Culture." In F. Jameson and M. Miyoshi (eds.), *The Cultures of Globalization*. Durham, NC: Duke University Press.

Tulloch, John and Henry Jenkins (1995). *Science Fiction Audiences: Watching Star Trek and Doctor Who*. London and New York: Routledge.

Turner, Graeme (ed.) (1993). *Nation, Culture, Text: Australian Cultural and Media Studies*. New York and London: Routledge.

Valdivia, Angharad (ed.) (1995). *Feminism, Multiculturalism, and the Media*. London: Sage.

Wark, McKenzie (1994). *Virtual Geography: Living with Global Media Events*. Bloomington & Indianapolis: Indiana University Press.

Williamson, Judith (1986). "The Problems of Being Popular." *New Socialist*, 14–15.

Wright, Charles R. (1986). *Mass Communication: A Sociological Perspective*, 3rd edn. New York: Random House.

PART II

Places

Chapter 12

Comparative Cultural Studies Traditions: Latin America and the US

George Yúdice

Allow me to begin with a disclaimer: I can speak of several cultural studies traditions but it would be impossible for me, even for a team of researchers, to exhaustively cover the terrain implied by "Comparative Cultural Studies Traditions: Latin America and the US." Even in the best of circumstances, that is, assisted by an efficient system of dissemination for cultural studies work, as in the US, one runs into the problem of uneven access: to subaltern public spheres within the boundaries of the nation-state, comprised of peoples who have to deal not only with poor life conditions but also with problematic representations of those life conditions; and uneven access to the panoply of cultural practices of these diverse groups on the part of researchers. The difficulty of learning about the cultural life of diverse groups is multiplied geometrically in Latin America, and not only for US and European researchers; it is equally difficult for local researchers to gain access.

I would like to focus on this differential difficulty and extrapolate from it a larger frame that I will adopt in discussing Latin American and US cultural studies traditions. This frame involves examining the differences in state structures, global market relations and their impact on national consumer economies, the university and culture industry systems, and so on. My reason for beginning this chapter with this frame is that it makes the discussion more manageable, a trade-off, however, for greater specificity. I shall attempt to be more specific in some of the examples I give, which are not to be taken as representative of the entirety of the comparison but rather as illustrative of some significant similarities and differences.

Without such a frame – which focuses on the different circumstances for the study of culture in the two regions – it would be hard to assess how the similarities in the analysis of culture have different functions respective to each region. If I were to limit myself to the legacy of the Birmingham Centre in US cultural studies and to many Latin American cultural-political and research projects, I would have to remark on the saliency of work on the popular and its relationship with mass

An earlier version of this chapter appeared as "Tradiciones comparativas de estudios culturales: América Latina y los Estados Unidos" in *Alteridades* 3:5 (1993): 9–20.

culture industries. Of course, the popular can be construed and analyzed from many perspectives, but what both traditions, at least as I have generally character-ized them, have in common, is the shift in the definition of culture from special-ized practices, particularly of elites, to everyday life. And in this regard, the methodologies do not differ greatly. In the late sixties and seventies there was a turn to poststructuralist and especially an Althusserian framework for construing the place of the popular. Class was increasingly displaced by the focus on everyday life, especially as the focus of analysis shifted from the ways in which economic and social forces determined the consciousness of subordinate groups to the ways in which, even under the most colonized of circumstances, these groups challenged and resisted these forces, leading to what more recently has become a politics of identity and representation. Ethnography became, for example, an important instrument in determining how this resistance took place. So, without the larger frame of analysis, it would seem that these tendencies had the same significance in both regions. There may be recognition of an asymmetry in the sense that many of the new theoretical and methodological currents have tended to travel from North to South, which is not to say that there weren't perspectives developed in Latin American that traveled North: the consciousness-raising movement characteristic of Paulo Freire's "pedagogy of the oppressed" and of the Christian Base Com-munities made important contributions to pedagogical theory, as the work of Ira Schor, Henry Giroux, Peter McLaren, and others attests. The dominant tenden-cies, however, at least according to the frame I am sketching out, point, rather, to an *uneven flow* of knowledge and methodologies. Let me elaborate.

In the first place, as I have already suggested, the market for certain kinds of theory and research is much stronger in the United States and several countries in western Europe. This does not mean that US academics have easier access to Foucault or Bourdieu; on the contrary, certain prestige theorists that comprise some of the key texts of cultural studies, although comparatively more expensive, are readily available in Latin America, precisely because the intellectual cutting edge is still imagined to slice from the North.

Secondly, the reception of these texts, what David Bordwell has called the *SLAB Theory* (Saussure, Lacan, Althusser, and Barthes; we could add many more), differs in Latin America from what the process might be thought to be in the US, where these have had greater impact in the Humanities (particularly English), in which, together with Media Studies and Communications depart-ments, the transdiscipline of cultural studies tends to be housed. Generally the term "Cultural Studies" is rarely used in Latin America. However, there are many longstanding traditions of Latin American cultural analysis for which other terms are used: communications, intellectual history, discourse analysis, inter-disciplinary studies, and many other terms used in particular disciplines. Even the term "Humanities" means something else and is not generally used in the division of the disciplines in Latin America. More often than "Humanities," the term "Facultad de Letras" is used, but even that is of recent coinage, dating from the 1920s. The study of culture, including literary and artistic culture, is often addressed in what in the United States are considered social sciences. Furthermore, since interdisciplinarity has been initiated in regional social science networks like CLACSO and FLACSO, what we refer to here as "cultural studies" is most identified with sociological and anthropological analysis. For this reason, cultural analysis in Latin America is more directly part of the study of civil and political society than in the United States. Add to this the strong social bias in literary studies, as in the work of António Cándido and Angel Rama, which gives the US critic the impression that Latin American theory and criticism are more sociological than aesthetic.

Beyond these terminological and structural differences within the academy, there is also a difference between university-based cultural studies work and that carried on in an array of non-academic settings, sometimes associated with journals, radio stations, community organizations, women's groups, museums, municipalities, and even individual, independent scholars. Non-Governmental Organizations (NGOs) have been particularly important in making this work possible, since funding sources are scarce. In both these non-academic settings as well as social science-based interdisciplinary programs, there is a tendency to make use of quantitive methodologies for the study of culture, particularly those developed by Bourdieu, but also polling methods developed in the US. This is a reaction, in part, to the dominant tradition of cultural analysis, which is the intellectual essay, some of whose canonized exponents are José Martí, José Enrique Rodó, Gilberto Freyre, José Carlos Mariátegui, José Vasconcelos, Fernando Ortiz, and Ezequiel Martínez Estrada. It is notable, also, that this tradition, which forms part of national and continental self-understanding in Latin America, conspicuously excludes women intellectuals, as well as blacks or indigenous people. Mary Pratt has characterized this tradition as the "National Brotherhood," meaning by this that it had the effect of reinforcing hierarchies, for example, smoothing the cultural terrain for the construction of hegemony favorable to dominant classes and patriarchy.

In spite of these ideological tenets, it should be said that the essayistic tradition is an important forerunner of the new interdisciplinarity that could be characterized as cultural studies in Latin American contexts. The fact that these intellectuals sidestepped and straddled many discourses which are now codified as institutionalized disciplines, made it possible for them to draw the full range of philosophical, aesthetic, and everyday cultural practices into the analysis of social, political, and economic processes. Their weak point, however, was their excessive reliance on speculative approaches, which limited the practicality of their formulations. The lack of attention to questions of gender and sexual orientation continues, even to this day, for example in the work of Néstor García Canclini, the best-known exponent of what is now being called cultural studies in Latin America. Generally, the category of gender is making its way into various disciplines through the participation of feminists, but it does not have the salience that it does in the US. Perhaps this relative lack can be explained by turning to another part of my frame, the political one.

219

Here in the United States, cultural studies is quickly being consolidated around what has come to be called a *politics of representation* paradigm, which is to say that crucial issues like social injustice based in race, class, and gender discrimination are thought to be reparable at the discursive level. Conversely, certain popular cultural practices and forms, especially music and other highly technified forms such as film and video, as well as the more traditional practice of writing among racial minorities,[1] are thought to have, again on the discursive level, subversive effects *vis-à-vis* the status quo. On this view, multicultural representations are considered viable means to reverse the effects of discrimination. The practice of cultural politics in Latin America, on the whole, is quite different. Representations of certain subaltern groups – say, blacks in Brazil and indigenous peoples in Mexico – on the one hand, form part of the *mestizaje* or hybrid identity that constitutes the "national-popular," or, on the other, contribute to their stigmatization. There *is*, of course, a politics of representation of marginalized peoples, but this is not usually a politics in the service of redressing injustice. US scholars specializing in Latin America, however, are increasingly interpreting the cultural practices of such groups precisely in this way, that is, in keeping with the politics of representation paradigm. One has to wonder whether or not this tendency will make itself manifest in Latin America as well. After all, like other cultural transfers, it is a matter of transnationalization and globalization of prestigious discourses, in this case the projection of a US-inflected politics of identity onto the popular practices of Latin American subaltern groups. There are, however, limits to such a politics of representation, and these are much more obvious in the Latin American context.

In the first place, it must be recognized that a politics of representation is generally accompanied by some compromise at the material level, for example, universal participation in consumer capitalism, at least at the level of cheap commodities. Intervening at the level of representations can serve a compensatory function in societies like the US where, despite the problems of homelessness, lack of access to healthcare, and downward mobility, the basics of the vast majority of the population are met. That is not the case throughout Latin America. Secondly, while it is not the norm for the US state itself to manage cultural production (we are, supposedly, a society with relatively little state intervention, although we are certainly feeling the increasing presence of state power in decision-making on cultural issues despite conservative hype about the benefits of shrinking government), the state in most Latin American countries is *directly* involved in guiding the cultural, at both the elite and popular levels. In fact, it might be said that it has been a general practice of so-called developing countries to protect their cultural patrimony and their culture industries because that is one of the means by which "consensus" has been enforced. The refunctionalization of samba in the 1930s for the purposes of inscribing blacks and mulattoes into an obedient workforce in the project of Brazilian modernization is a case in point.

Although the formation of national identity differs from country to country in Latin America, there are some constants in the way modernization, representations of subaltern races, ethnic and immigrant groups, and what we might call dependency are articulated. This common form of articulation differs radically from the national solutions adopted in the US and makes all the difference in understanding the study of culture in Latin America. If in Britain Arnold, Leavis, and Eliot differentially privileged the power of high culture to form citizens, and in the US the emphasis came to fall on mass culture, in Latin America, the nation was a hegemonic culture with a base in the popular. This tradition goes back to the middle of the nineteenth century, and focused on literature as the means to create a culture autonomous from that of Europe. Andrés Bello (1847), like José Martí, argued that Latin America would have no proper culture until it had a clearly defined literature, based on local practices, that did not imitate European models. This tradition was still alive in the work of Angel Rama, who throughout the 1870s and early 1880s, until his death, strove to prove that Latin American culture was on a par with that of Europe and the US, for, according to him, ever since late nineteenth-century *modernismo*, Latin America was fully integrated into the global forces of capitalism, which he understood, in part, as the driving force to which culture responds. Of course, this response only expressed itself then, according to Rama, in the symbolic and therefore compensatory form of literature, for it was only in this sphere that a Latin American practice could be said to be on a par with that of the metropolitan countries.[2] Latin America's integration into capitalism had its own flavor which, anticipating such notions as that of reconversion or hybridity, he called *transculturation*, after Cuban anthropologist Fernando Ortiz.

If early on elite cultural studies focused on literature, race was the terrain on which the relationship between nation and state was negotiated in studies of popular culture. Actually, the problem of race as a complicating factor in the definition of Latin American identity and the main element of identity politics goes back to the moment of the conquest. (I must acknowledge, at least parenthetically at this point, that gender was as important a factor, in view of the fact that very few Iberian women accompanied the conquistadores and the colonizers, making the problem of miscegenation a markedly gendered one; however, this is ground that, with few exceptions, has lain fallow until the present.) More specifically since the twenties and thirties, when intellectuals in most Latin American countries began to examine the issue of race consistently as the major factor in the definition of culture – national culture (*la patria chica*) and continental culture (*la patria grande*) – new insights into the interaction of *race, popular culture*, and *North–South relations* (traditionally characterized as imperialism) developed which to this day are far from being recognized in other cultural studies traditions. The work of the Peruvian José Carlos Mariátegui, the Brazilian Gilberto Freyre, and the Cuban Fernando Ortiz – who coined the term "transculturation" as a corrective to the unidirectional notion of "acculturation" – involves a "holistic," if not organicist, kind of analysis which draws on class, regional economics, immigration, religion, popular music, literature, and other cultural practices, where "popular" refers, more etymologically, to "people" (of the working classes) than to market popularity, that is, mass culture. Interestingly, such "holistic" analysis of culture was possible in this essayistic tradition because modes of knowledge-production were not clearly and disciplinarily defined at the time in the Latin American context. Of course, many of the analysts of popular culture were also elites, organic intellectuals, as it were, in the service of the new national-capitalist projects of modernization; others, like Mariátegui, worked on behalf of the oppressed.

It was in the twenties and thirties that new state forms were being shaped for Latin America's entry into the post-First World War global economy as producers of import substitutes. This new role required a new interpellation of the citizen as worker, and since the most likely workers were of a different race (indigenous, black, or of mixed race) or ethnic (immigrants), the result was an authoritarian state (e.g, Peronism in Argentina, Varguism in Brazil) that drew its legitimacy for its modernizing projects from popular sectors in the face of opposition from the traditional oligarchy. Regarding cultural studies, the question is not so much whether this populism effectively empowered the "popular" sectors but rather that it put on the agenda of any social analysis and policy the issue of popular culture, even to this day when it is studied in terms of social movements rather than on the exclusive basis of class. The Latin American experience has in fact yielded a great contribution to contemporary social theory in the recognition, already expressed by Gramsci, that politics, "legitimate" knowledge and culture are wedded in the process of hegemony, which as Ernesto Laclau explains, functions basically as the *articulation* of "non-class contents – interpellations and contradictions – which constitute the raw materials on which class ideological practices operate." In other words, the "cultural" is the terrain of conflict and articulation of "legitimate" and contestatory knowledges. It should be pointed out that Laclau's early work on populism is inscribed within and revolutionizes an Argentine tradition of analysis of populist politics. It is only later that his work, in collaboration with that of Chantal Mouffe, is seen as inspired by the British cultural studies movement.

The other main cultural studies issue that derives from the Latin American experience is the notion of cultural flows, particularly North–South, as regards technology, science, information, the media, intellectual and artistic trends, and market relations. Already in the 1880s José Martí, wrote insightfully on the cultural shifts being produced in the North–South axis. Of course, Martí, like most other Latin American culture critics until recently, reduced this relation to one of "cultural imperialism." Lately a "transnational" analysis of cultural flows has yielded important insights into more general social and political processes. For example, US mass media, rather than simply being seen as colonizing Latin America, have in many cases been perceived to have the effect of producing contradictions in communities in which, say, gender equality just was not part of "common sense." This has led a new generation of cultural critics since the mid-seventies to coin such terms as "cultural reconversion" (Néstor García Canclini) and the "mediations" of differential reception (Jesús Martín-Barbero). By focusing, for example, on consumption and other means of cultural mediation, they have been able to gauge how and to what extent the diverse groups that make up Latin America's cultural heterogeneity interact with one another and what prospects there are for subaltern groups to gain a greater participation in the distribution of knowledge, goods, and services.

The study of the relation of culture to social movements also has a long history. In the early sixties there developed a trend known as *conscientización* throughout the continent. Its purpose was to challenge state policy, elitist institutions, and the social stratification which they fostered on the basis of "legitimate" knowledge and to further the cause of popular sectors of the population. This was done by creating alternative institutions and seeking the alliance of traditional institutions like the church and the educational establishment in legitimizing the knowledges embodied in popular practices. The movement was dedicated not only to the study of culture but even more to the redefinition of culture in keeping with non-elitist, popular criteria. As such it operated multidisciplinarily, encompassing pedagogy (Paulo Freire), political economy (Marxism), religion (Liberation Theology), grassroots activism (Base Christian Communities among urban and rural working classes and student organizations), ethnography, journalism, literature, and other cultural practices. Most significant was a new expressive mode that emerged from this movement: *testimonio*. Giving testimony involved the production of popular knowledge that touched on a range of what would be different disciplines in other cultural configurations: social history, ethnography, autobiography, literature, political analysis, and advocacy. Specifically, this knowledge countered the "legitimate" knowledge that justified modernization, that is, social, political, and economic restructuring after the model of European and North American development, a restructuring which was having deleterious consequences among popular sectors. This challenge to developmentalism, furthermore, underscores a longstanding epistemological resistance in Latin America to knowledge flows from North to South that function to integrate the region at a disadvantage and for the benefit of United States economic policies.

Much of the discussion in this chapter hinges on the question of value: that is, value in the production, circulation, reception, transformation, response, etc. of knowledge and cultural forms in general. Ultimately, how these processes are mediated in and through power relations determines value. And these power relations cut across class, race, gender, geopolitical, and other boundaries. Recognition of this is what constitutes the current crisis in knowledge and its legitimation, not only in the North but in the South as well.

Many are the Latin American social scientists and cultural critics who write about this paradigm crisis, often inserting it within the global crisis of modernity. One of the very few research centers currently dedicated to cultural studies in

Latin America, the ILET (Instituto Latinoamericano de Estudios Transnacionales), founded in Mexico in 1976, with annexes in Buenos Aires and Santiago, focused on transnational flows of communications, information, gendered identity images and lifestyles and their relation to the breakdown of formal politics, the new social movements, democratization, and the increasing importance of the cultural for integration into transnational ways of life. It could hardly be said, then, that culture corresponds to the "way of life" of the nation as a discrete entity separate from global trends. Chilean sociologist José Joaquín Brunner elaborates further, that what may seem like a crisis in modernity in the European or North American setting is in fact the norm in Latin America. He rejects the idea that modernization is inherently foreign to a supposedly novohispanic, baroque, Christian, and *mestizo* cultural ethos, which becomes inauthentic, according to Octavio Paz, as it is "colonized" by other ethical values. Brunner rejects such an essentialist notion of Latin America. Rather than an inherent magical realism, which the literati have put forward to legitimize the contradictory mixtures, these are generated by the differentiation in modes of production, the segmentation of markets of cultural consumption, and the expansion and internationalization of the culture industry. Latin America's peculiar forms of hybridity, then, are not to be celebrated for their marvelous qualities nor denounced as inauthentic; they are, rather, the features that characterize the emergence of a modern cultural sphere in heterogeneous societies (Brunner 1987: 4).

Mexican anthropologist Guillermo Bonfill also refers to a crisis in paradigms in assessing the viability of anthropology in the current context. He argues that anthropology in Mexico emerged as an adjunct of the Cardenista state's project of national integration. What, then, is the space for anthropology now that the state is brokering Mexico's integration into a transnational arrangement, most immediately the Free Trade Agreement, which was just the first stage in Bush the Elder's Enterprise for the Americas Initiative, courted by many Latin American governments?[3] So long as anthropologists were an integral part of the state's national project, they were able to have some leverage over policy decisions. Now, Bonfill suggests, anthropologists ought to "ally with society," that is, alter their relation to their informants and involve them in projects at the service of communities and social movements (Bonfill 1991: 88–9).

Such a "reconversion" of the anthropologist's practice has important repercussions on cultural studies. Bonfill's suggestion is already being carried out, in fact, by other social scientists who conceive of cultural studies not only as the study *of* culture, but the intervention in and collaboration with the struggles of the new social movements. Here the interrelations between politics, cultural politics, identity formation, institution-building, and the reconversion of citizenship come together. For example, Elizabeth Jelin (1991) and other members of CEDES (Centro de Estudios de Estado y Sociedad) have been working recently with victims of human rights violations in Argentina. Jelin's premise is that the concept of citizenship in a democratic culture must take into consideration symbolic aspects such as collective identity and not just a rationalized rights discourse. In this regard, she comes quite close to Nancy Fraser's concept of the correlation between identity and the struggle over needs interpretations. According to Fraser, the conflicts among rival needs claims in contemporary society reveal that we inhabit a "new social space" unlike the ideal public sphere in which the better argument prevails. The struggles over needs interpretations involve the viability of experts who oversee state bureaucracies and other institutions that administer services, the legitimacy of claims made by groups on the basis of a cultural ethos, and the " 'reprivatization' discourses of constituencies seeking to repatriate newly problematized needs to their former domestic or official economic enclaves" (Fraser 1989: 157). To Fraser's spheres we would also have to add the traditional aesthetic enclaves which would relegate individuals' practices, on the basis of taste, to elite or popular forms, regulatable by state apparatuses.

To continue with Jelin, she posits three domains in which citizenship is produced: (1) the intrapsychic, which is the basis for intersubjective relations; (2) public spheres; (3) state relations with society, from authoritarian to participatory ones, taking into consideration as well forms of clientelism, demagogy, and corruption. The main question is how to foment a democratic ethos. Jelin's answer is by expanding public spheres, that is, those spaces not controled by the state in which practices conducive or oppositional to democratic behavior are constrained or promoted. The proliferation of public spheres will ensure that more than one conception of citizenship (rights and responsibilities) prevails. As such, the task of the researcher is to work in collaboration with groups to create spaces in which the identity and cultural ethos of those groups can take shape. Such a cultural studies project, then, becomes part of the struggle to democratize society just as the state is brokering free-market policies, such as the privatization of all public and cultural space.

I will give one more example of cultural studies work which takes a different but complementary tack from that of Jelin. Néstor García Canclini (1991) and a team of researchers from the Universidad Autónoma Metropolitana carried out a study of the effects of the Free Trade Agreement on education and culture. It is a policy analysis which takes into consideration such aspects as political economy not normally included in the kind of cultural studies that predominate in the US. To give just one example from this work – which has separate sections on the free trade agreement's likely impact on education, diverse culture industries, technological innovation, intellectual property and author's rights, tourism, and border culture – Mexico's publishing industry will be adversely affected as the state opens up primary school textbook production (96 million per year) – which has been its responsibility – to competitive bidding. What complicates the matter is that bidding will be allowed to foreign publishers, thus making it unlikely that Mexican companies will be able to compete either in terms of cost or quality (1991: 111). More important on the level of the cultural is the decentralization of the educational system foreseen in the plans to privatize;

rather than the state providing subsidies the communities themselves will have to buy them for their students, as in the US. This means that the communities will control the content of the textbooks, an aspect of the plan which the Catholic Church is eager to see put into effect. The church has already launched an attack on sex education and other ethical matters that until now reflect a relatively liberal position.

As is evident from this one small example, the cultural repercussions of the free trade agreement are potentially enormous. Although taking a different approach, the group of artists, writers, culture industry executives, journalists, academics, etc. brought together by the Friedrich Ebert Foundation in Montevideo also assessed the impact of an impending trade agreement, the formation of MERCOSUR (a regional market initially comprised of Argentina, Brazil, Paraguay, and Uruguay) (Achugar 1991). I bring this up only to give another example of the increasing recognition that cultural studies must go beyond a politics of representations in which power is understood almost exclusively as a function of symbolic manipulation. If the example of the new cultural studies work in Latin America has anything to offer the Anglo-American traditions, it is this recognition that state and civil institutions, policy-making bodies, political economy, trade agreements, and so on are indispensable for a viable cultural studies. Furthermore, they underscore the role that the cultural critic can take: not just standing on the sidelines celebrating the supposed subversiveness of another media-manufactured rock star or sitcom, or condemning state policies without taking the trouble to intervene more directly in institutional politics. I am thus gratified to see in Routledge's *Cultural Studies* reader, an essay by Tony Bennett entitled "Putting Policy into Cultural Studies" which runs counter to just about every other essay in the book. Since cultural studies should be about "examining cultural practices from the point of view of their intrication with, and within, relations of power," Bennett advances "four claims regarding the conditions that are necessary for any satisfactory form of engagement, both theoretical and practical, with the relations between culture and power" (p. 23). I think these claims are quite consistent with the selection of Latin American cultural studies work that I have reviewed here. They are: "*first*, the need to include policy considerations in the definition of culture in viewing it as a particular field of government; *second*, the need to distinguish different regions of culture within this overall field in terms of the objects, targets, and techniques of government peculiar to them; *third*, the need to identify the political relations specific to different regions of culture so defined and to develop appropriately specific ways of engaging with and within them; and, *fourth*, the need for intellectual work to be conducted in a manner such that, in both its substance and its style, it can be calculated to influence or service the conduct of identifiable agents within the region of culture concerned" (p. 23).

Aside from cogent criticisms of this policy-oriented approach, such that it might become subordinate to state dictates, a problem that has certainly affected many Latin American cultural studies researchers, especially before the ongoing privatization, this approach can serve to strengthen the "politics of representation" typical in the US. It is not usually thought that so much of what constitutes identity is in part due to pressures from the state. If in Latin America the focus of cultural studies has moved to questions of citizenship in the wake of authoritarian dictatorships and a transition to democracy under the difficult circumstances of free-market policies, which heighten social conflicts, in the US in this same period, the state itself has collaborated in the shift from questions of citizenship based on rights discourse to one based on interpretability of needs and satisfactions, as I have argued above.

There have been numerous debates in the past two decades over whether identity is an essence or whether it is socially constructed. Generally, most cultural studies approaches subscribe to a constructionist view. However, the constructionist view has remained unsatisfying because it cannot account for experience. I am not speaking about experience in the sense in which Hoggart uses it to refer to working-class culture. His usage of the notion does smack of essentialism, about the authentic ways to be working class. The turn to subcultural work at the Birmingham Centre dispelled that approach by focusing on how identities are constituted in the process of hegemony. But that approach was not adequate enough to account for experience or the *performances of experience* which have become the most important artistic expressions of the day, replacing literature, concert music, and the "art" film as the preferred aesthetic practice of the cognoscenti.

It is very difficult at present, I think, to draw a clear line between the prevailing understanding of identity politics and what I am calling performance of experience. They coincide in many if not most instances. But let me try to distinguish. Identity politics in the United States has its origin in the struggles of the civil rights movement, which as Michael Omi and Howard Winant characterize it, was the first true expression of democratization in the United States.[4] By this they mean that unlike the pre-Second World War period in which racial minorities were limited to a *war of maneuver* – "a situation in which subordinate groups seek to preserve and extend a definite territory, to ward off violent assault, and to develop an internal society as an alternative to the repressive social system they confront" (p. 74) – civil rights transformed the character of racial politics to one of political struggle or a *war of position*, which necessitates the "existence of diverse institutional and cultural terrains upon which oppositional political projects can be mounted" (ibid.). Civil rights, in other words, became an emergent and established position in the struggle for hegemony, to the point that the transformation of the cultural-political matrix enabled other subordinated groups to wage their own wars of position. Of course, the state and the economy were implicated in this struggle for hegemony, with the result that many state institutions and policies were transformed and the consumer and culture industries learned to wage their own marketing of position. Identity groups in the United States, as we now understand them, began to enact or perform as such in the public spheres, "authoring themselves," as it were, in the process. Identity necessarily became a practice, a performance, a deployment across the institutionalized terrain of the social formation because performing it was the means to appropriate by reaccentuating or reconfiguring the genres available for social participation: forms for negotiating all aspects of life from health, education, and housing to consumption, aesthetics, and sexuality. In fact, as new theories of the public sphere hold, not only identity but the very understanding of "needs" and "satisfactions" is open to interpretability and performativity.[5]

Such an authoring process goes beyond the limits of the term constructionism, which emphasizes the pressures of institutions and economy. It also goes beyond the notion of interest group, whose already given self-knowledge enables it to seek social and political gains. Of course, identity groups engage in interest politics too, but the new or reinvented identity groups author and perform their identities contingently. What I have said up to here can, perhaps, hold for all identity groups in the US. However, part of the understanding of performing identities contingently means that different groups will do so on quite different bases. Michael Warner, the editor of a key book on queer theory, cautions against the knee-jerk disposition to "identity parallelism," that is, the idea that all groups marginalized on the basis of race, ethnicity, gender, sexual preference, class, etc. are somehow equivalent.

> Different conditions of power give rise to different strategies that cannot always be made homogeneous. Sometimes alliance politics can force important corrections; many themes and organizational efforts in gay politics have been used on the model of white, middle-class men in ways that are only beginning to be apparent. But strategic requirements may differ even where people act in the best faith. Because queer embodiment is generally invisible, for instance, it occasions a unique politics of passing and knowing, building into many aspects of the queer movement a tactics of visibility – classically in the performative mode of coming out, or "screaming," and more recently in "outing" and the in-your-face politics pioneered by Queer Nation and ACT UP. Considerable stress, both within these organizations and in relation to other political groups, has resulted from the fact that these new tactics of public display respond in a primary way to the specific politics of queer embodiment.[6]

Indeed, the particularity of embodiment is the crucial criterion in understanding performativity. I cannot imagine the same kind of display by a straight chicano male on the basis of his chicanoness or maleness or straightness. Generally, blacks and chicanos and women do not go through the ritual of "coming out" as such. However, there are different kinds of performativity that have to do with styles of dress, gesture, speech, and so on that are part of the performance of identity among all identity groups. The difference, I think, harks back again to the fantasies that underpin performance, what all of these aspects of display mean in relation to desire and fantasy.

Attending to fantasy helps shift the politics of identity from its emphasis on correcting representations to understanding that performativity is not just adopting a role (as in conventional sociology) nor becoming a simulacrum in the Baudrillardian sense. In the first place, fantasy is an "imaginary scene in which the subject is a protagonist, representing the fulfilment of [desire]."[7] In this regard, I would venture to argue that in contemporary US society, in which the media and consumer culture have placed the question of identity in the public and in which "needs" and "satisfactions" are not givens but phenomena to be interpreted and struggled over, fantasy is no longer limited to the private psyche but projected on the screen of the social. Desire is, precisely, the operator in this situation, "appear[ing] as the rift which separates need and demand" (Laplanche & Pontalis, p. 483). After all, identity groups attempt to satisfy their demand for recognition on the basis of how they can project their ethically legitimated needs across the social and political terrain. Secondly, since no group is in control of the politics of "needs interpretations," the process of this social fantasy must be ongoing, subject to the compulsion to repeat. Thirdly, the above would seem to indicate that fantasy as the process through which identity and politics interface is not easily made to produce the kinds of cognitivist and political readings sought by the more Marxist-oriented strains of cultural studies. Jacqueline Rose is helpful on this point:

> Fantasy and the compulsion to repeat – these appear as the concepts against which the idea of a more fully political objection to injustice constantly stalls. It seems to me that this is the ground on to which the feminist debate about psychoanalysis has now moved; but in doing so it has merely underlined a more general problem for political analysis which has always been present in the radical readings of Freud. Which is how to reconcile the problem of subjectivity which assigns activity (but not guilt), fantasy (but not error), conflict (but not stupidity) to individual subjects – in this case women – with a form of analysis which can also recognise the force of structures in urgent need of social change? (Rose 1986: 14)

It seems to me that identity politics has found a way of dealing with the impasses that have always frustrated political interpretations of aesthetic culture. The performativity that characterizes US identity politics and which is a prime, though undertheorized, object of analysis of cultural studies, is premised on the expansion of fantasy, the imaginative dimension that has always been attributed to art, to the entirety of public space. This, of course, comes at a cost, for the major result is, perhaps, the absolute eradication of the private, where traditionally aesthetic activity was supposed to inhere.

I don't have the space to elaborate on this, but suffice it to say that the culture wars in the US have to do with this transference of the performance of the aesthetic from private to public experience. Classical aesthetic theory defined artistic practice as constituting the realm of freedom. But that freedom is precisely what is at stake when fantasy becomes subject to political pressures. Of course, it has been argued, as has done Terry Eagleton, that such freedom was always an illusion that covered over bourgeois dominance, a kind of "prosthesis to reason" or a proxy for power.[8] But rather than think of it in terms of freedom, it may be more productive to characterize it as the signs of satisfaction and demand that structure fantasy, that structure identity.

I would like to conclude with a brief summary of the points I have tried to make. I have tried to characterize how several strains of the Anglo-American cultural studies tradition have construed aesthetic culture. Because it has always been an overriding concern of this tradition to attend to questions of politics and power, aesthetic culture has been variously understood in relation to class conflict, hegemony, resistance, subversion, and so on. In the tradition of German idealism that extends from Kant through Hegel and on to Lukács, Adorno, and Jameson, aesthetic culture has also been interrogated as a heuristic device for what Jameson calls "cognitive mapping," a heuristic device that allows subjects to know the structures of realities that are not permeable to experience.[9] I have tried to understand contemporary aesthetic experience in the US partly in relation to this political and cognitivist tradition, departing from it, however, in recognition of modes of experience that are not subordinated to these categories.

Notes

1   It is an interesting phenomenon that as traditionally prestigious cultural practices such as literary writing have over the past half century lost their pivotal position in shaping national identity, minority and other subaltern groups have increasingly adopted these practices. This is most evident in the United States, where the group-formative writing of Latinos and African-, Asian-, and Native Americans is at the center of the multicultural movement's attempt to deconstruct national culture and reconfigure it as manifold. This tendency, however, is also evident in many Latin American countries where, at least in the critics' views, the cultural practices of popular sectors – peasants, workers, shantytown dwellers, urban youth, and so on – should be put on a par with prestigious cultural forms. One important result of this movement has been the emergence of *testimonio* as a sanctioned literary form. See Yúdice 1990 and 1991.

2   See Angel Rama, *Los poetas modernistas en el mercado económico* (Montevideo: Facultad de Humanidades y Ciencias, Universidad de la República, 1967); *Rubén Darío y el modernismo (circunstancia socio-económica de un arte americano)* (Caracas: Universidad Central de Venezuela, col. Temas, no. 39, 1970); *Las máscaras democráticas del modernismo* (Montevideo: Fundación Angel Rama, 1985).

3   The eagerness to get on Bush the Elder's good side was so strong that President Carlos Menem of Argentina sent troops to the Gulf War, despite vociferous protests by the citizenry.

4   Michael Omi and Howard Winant, *Racial Formation in the United States: From the 1960s to the 1980s* (New York: Routledge, 1986), p. 75.
5   For an account of the politics of "needs interpretations" in the context of the public sphere, see Nancy Fraser, "Rethinking the Public Sphere," and George Yúdice, "For a Practical Aesthetics," *Social Text* 25/26 (1990): 56–80, 129–45.
6   Michael Warner, "Introduction: Fear of a Queer Planet," *Social Text* 29 (1991): 13. This special issue of *Social Text* on queer theory is comprised of a selection of essays published by the University of Minnesota Press in a book-length volume.
7   L. Laplanche and J.-B. Pontalis, *The Language of Psychoanalysis*, trans. Donald Nicholson-Smith (New York: Norton, 1973), p. 314.
8   Terry Eagleton, *The Ideology of the Aesthetic* (Oxford: Blackwell, 1990), p. 16.
9   Fredric Jameson, "Cognitive Mapping," in *Marxism and the Interpretation of Culture*, eds. Cary Nelson and Lawrence Grossberg (Urbana: University of Illinois Press, 1988), p. 349.

References

Achugar, Hugo, ed. (1991). *Cultura mercosur (política e industrias culturales)*. Montevideo: Logos.
Bennett, T. (1992). "Putting Policy into Cultural Studies." In L. Grossberg et al. (eds.), *Cultural Studies*. New York: Routledge.
Bonfill Batalla, Guillermo (1991). "Desafíos a la antropología en la sociedad contemporánea." *Iztapalapa* 11(24): 9–26.
Brunner, José Joaquín (1987). "Notas sobre la modernidad y lo postmoderno en la cultural latinoamericana." *David y Goliat* 17 (Sept.).
Fraser, Nancy (1989). *Unruly Practices: Power, Discourse and Gender in Contemporary Social Theory*. Minneapolis: University of Minnessota Press.
García Canclini, Néstor, ed. (1991). *Educación y cultura en el Tratado de Libre Comercio*. Mexico.
Jelin, Elizabeth (1991). "¿Cómo construir ciudadanía? Una visión desde abajo." Paper delivered for the CEDES project on *Human Rights and the Consolidation of Democracy: The Trial of the Argentine Military*. Buenos Aires, Sept. 20–1.
Rose, Jacqueline (1986). *Sexuality in the Field of Vision*. London: Verso.
Yúdice, George (1990). "For a Practical Aesthetics." *Social Test* 25/16: 129–45.
Yúdice, George (1991). "*Testimonio* and Postmodernism. " *Latin American Perspectives* 18(3) (summer): 15–31.

Chapter 13

Can Cultural Studies Speak Spanish?

Jorge Mariscal

What shall we do with such a miserable conglomerate of undesirable peoples based on an effete civilization?

> George Ticknor, founder of Spanish studies at Harvard University,
> on the eve of the Mexican War

It is hard not to wonder how much of the recent enthusiasm for cultural studies is generated by its profound associations with England and the ideas of Englishness.

> Paul Gilroy, *The Black Atlantic*

As a beginning graduate student in comparative literature at the University of California at Irvine, I was told by a senior faculty member that I could not receive credit for Spanish as one of my required languages because "there is no significant corpus of literature in Spanish. We accept only French or German." In the mid-1970s my experience was not an isolated one. At some University of California campuses, Spanish was simply not accepted; at other institutions across the country (Yale University, for example), one had to file a special petition in order to receive credit for it. Writings in Spanish did not emit the same amount of high cultural sheen that French, German, and even certain periods of Italian literature exuded for the academy in the United States.

To understand fully the history that produced this situation, it is necessary to go back several centuries in order to locate the beginnings of what has come to be called the "Black Legend." During the sixteenth century, a project was begun in English writing to construct a Spain so different, so other to what Elizabethans valued, that Spanish culture became a simple inversion of English culture (see Gibson; Maltby). This political agenda realized through writing functioned in tandem with shifts in the centers of economic power – Seville to London and Amsterdam – and worked to construct an imaginary identity called "Spanishness." It also contributed to the process by which "Englishness" was invented, and it was an early manifestation of future cultural and economic projects such as

232

nineteenth-century theories of racism and the contemporary international North–South dichotomy (Amin).

The potency of the opposition England/Spain (and after the Enlightenment, Europe/Spain) was so great that it has survived through countless historical periods and in countless national contexts. My anecdote from graduate school indicates one way it has functioned at a microlevel of knowledge production. At the level of state policy-making, it would be transported to the American continents and made to serve the imperialist ambitions of the United States in 1898. Modified by the insertion of Mexico in the place of Spain, it would underwrite US ambitions from 1848 to the present, that is, from the territorial conquest of the southwest to the North American Free Trade Agreement (NAFTA). In my first epigraph above, George Ticknor's question suggests that Mexico and other former colonies are the effete progeny of decadent Spain. As the founder of Spanish studies in North America, Ticknor initiates the century-and-a-half-long genealogy of the Black Legend in the US in which, in both the highest intellectual and policy-making circles and the popular imagination, the center – Spain – and its margins – Latin America and its disasporic populations – became interchangeable. It is because of the power of this opposition and the tendency for entities named "Spain," "Mexico," "Latin America," and, in the US context, "Hispanic" to function as essential categories in Anglophone thought that some of us who write on Spanish-language cultural topics are cautious about approaching any methodology with Anglophone origins. This caution extends to cultural studies now being institutionalized in university settings traditionally hostile to Spanish-speaking cultures.

It should go without saying that the Spanish-language traditions homogenized by Anglophone scholars and policy-makers constitute a wide spectrum of local histories and internal hierarchies. The histories of Puerto Rico, Cuba, Argentina, Peru, and so on are disparate and individually complex, although they share, together with the Philippines, the experience of having once been part of the Spanish empire. It is somewhat ironic, then, that despite the long shelf-life of Black Legend discourses, the cultural production of Spain was granted the highest prestige in US Spanish departments. Spain at least could claim some connection (albeit tenuous from the Anglo-Saxon point of view) to Europe. After all, English-speaking literary scholars were hard-pressed to exclude *Don Quixote* from the Western canon. To this day, advanced placement exams for Spanish used in college admissions privilege obscure texts by Spanish writers rather than including Latin American or US Latino authors. In most educational settings, Castilian Spanish was the preferred dialect in language classrooms for well into the 1960s, a situation that saw more than a few Chicano and Puerto Rican native-speaker students being told they did not know Spanish. The boom in Latin American literary studies in the US, fueled in part by foreign policy interests in the early 1960s, initiated a slow reconfiguration of the internal dynamics of departments. The carving out of an institutional space for US

233

Latino studies, however, would have to wait until the mass mobilizations of the early 1970s.

The field of Chicano studies, for example, founded by activist scholars during the height of the Chicano Movement, exploded in the late 1980s and early 1990s in large part due to the creation of "Hispanic" markets, the proliferation of literary and artistic production, and the influence of emergent cultural studies methods. In the early years of its existence, however, Chicano studies faced the open hostility of traditional Spanish departments where senior faculty from Spain referred to Chicano/a literature as "barrio trash." This unfortunate reality drove many Chicano studies programs, at least those unable to maintain curricular and budgetary self-sufficiency, to seek refuge in English and American studies programs, where they encountered a different but complementary set of residual prejudices that lingered on from the US colonial past. The Black Legend about Spain, the product of a northern European imaginary, became (depending on local conditions) either separated from or fused to a "Mexican/Latino Legend" whose origins resided deep in Manifest Destiny, scientific racism, and white supremacy. The early twentieth-century fantasy Spanish heritage in southern California architecture, for example, was in part an attempt by Anglo elites to recuperate a "Spanish past" that was white European and not *mestizo* Mexican. In this context, "Spanish" was considered superior to Mexican even though underlying racial prejudice continued to represent all contemporary forms of the Spanish language and "hispanized" ethnicities as less civilized than their English-based counterparts. If these ideological currents are now hopelessly intertwined and difficult to sort out, the consequences in a contemporary academic context are more easily discernible. Young Chicano scholars, many of whom do not incorporate Spanish-language materials in their research agendas, write papers on the Zapatista Movement in Mexico without citing a single Mexican historian. Others propose readings of US Latino hip hop culture through a North American black/white binary that is unable to account for Latin American processes of *mestizaje* and syncretism. Those critics claiming to do "radical" readings of "Hispanic" cultures pursue their research in the English language and rely predominantly upon non-Spanish-speaking authorities. In effect, the Black Legend wins again.

Jon Stratton and Ien Ang have traced the unchallenged hegemony of "Englishness" and "Britishness" in the early work of the Birmingham Centre. They convincingly argue that there has been little change during the ensuing years despite the global travels of the cultural studies project: "The international cultural studies 'society' is definitely not a European affair but, on the whole, confined to English-speaking constituencies. This doesn't mean that there is no cultural studies in other languages than English (there most definitely is) but by and large these other cultural studies traditions are ignored by Anglo-American dominated, English-speaking, cultural studies" (p. 389). It would be difficult to deny the overall dominance of English in US cultural studies. The state educational apparatus and media representations have expelled from the collective memory the fact that indigenous, Spanish, and Mexican languages and traditions historically preceded the Anglo-American nation and the English language. As Alfred Arteaga puts it: "US American culture presents itself as an English language culture; it espouses a single language ethos; it strives very actively to assert a monolingual identity" (1994: 13). Juan F. Perea cuts to the heart of the matter: "The mere sound of Spanish offends and frightens many English-only speakers, who sense in the language a loss of control over what they regard as 'their' country" (1998: 583). To remember that English is a belated newcomer to New Mexico, Texas, or California, therefore, is to recall the history of conquest and colonization that began in the 1830s. That the language identified with service and agricultural workers, busboys, gardeners, and domestic maids has a rich and diverse literary tradition spanning vast geographical spaces is a fact lost on the majority of those who continue to control the region's resources. In the 1990s, a resurgent nativism fueled by white fear about changing demographics led to the passage of Proposition 227 and the elimination of bilingual education. Such initiatives cannot be separated from the postconquest history of white supremacy that, to use Margaret Montoya's term, cast Spanish early on as an "outlaw language" within the public sphere. Montoya writes: "Claiming the right to use Spanish in academic discourse is an important form of resistance against cultural and linguistic domination. Reclaiming these 'outlaw' languages, taboo knowledge, and devalued discourses is a stand against cultural hegemony" (1998: 578). In many contexts in contemporary California, to speak Spanish is to engage in an act of defiance if not outright resistance, yet it is well to recall that US Latinos presently constitute the fifth largest ethnic-linguistic community in all of Latin America. Projections suggest that by 2050 they will be the third largest.

The globalization of cultural studies is an inescapable development given recent changes in capitalist production and consumption and the restructuring of the North American university along "interdisciplinary" lines. Because the official language of this new world order is unquestionably English, cultural studies workers will have to make a concerted effort to become fluent in non-English traditions if they are to realize the acts of "translation, rearticulation, transcoding [and] transculturation" outlined by Stuart Hall in a recent interview (Chen 393). I am assuming, of course, that one of our goals continues to be to intensify the critique of neoliberalism and neo-imperialism, and not merely to celebrate the act of "crossing borders" and the fact, for example, that the Japanese are fans of Freddy Fender. To the extent that cultural studies is willing and able to "speak Spanish," "speak" the hybrid languages of US Latino culture, "speak" the indigenous languages of the Americas, and in so doing allow sub-altern cultures to speak for themselves, the hegemony of "Englishness" and Anglo-American narratives of world and US history will be successfully challenged. Only then will a meaningful global cultural studies project come into being.

Cultural Feedback and the Transformation of Common Sense

> One must break down the historical barriers of collective psychology as well as the structures of power.
>
> Carlos Monsiváis, *Entrada libre*

What is at stake in the next century for people in the Spanish-speaking world transcends any methodology interested in stopping its analysis at what was called at the height of poststructuralism the struggle for the sign. In most of Latin America, the 1980s was a decade lost to foreign debt, unemployment, and inflation. Central America was the site of unprecedented economic and state violence, while Latinos in the United States watched many of the meager gains of the late 1960s and early 1970s rolled back. The number of incoming Latino students at major universities decreased, while high school drop-out rates remained high; undocumented workers were scapegoated for the economic crisis in the southwestern United States; neoconservatives put select minorities on display as examples of their commitment to diversity (from Richard Rodriguez, the MacNeil-Lehrer "expert" on Latino issues and a New Age romantic, to Linda Chavez, a former Reagan appointee and the author of the reactionary *Out of the Barrio*); in San Diego County, Anglo teenagers assaulted and robbed Mexican migrant workers as a form of entertainment.

Cultural studies workers committed to progressive change attempted to interpret the cultural production born of such unsettled circumstances and the circumstances themselves. The engagement of cultural studies with larger social issues depends upon a deliberate transgression of institutional and ethnic boundaries and a broadening of the collective project. Ideally, a comparative cultural studies method would complement research focused on single "national" groups. The "Chicano experience," for example, cannot be adequately understood unless it is read next to and through the history of Mexico and Spain and also juxtaposed to the history of Pilipinos, African Americans, Puerto Ricans, poor whites, and other disempowered groups in the United States. At certain critical junctures, the interconnectedness of such groups becomes particularly apparent: the Gold Rush in California, the Second World War, the period of the American war in southeast Asia, the union movement spearheaded by the United Farm Workers, and attacks on immigrants, affirmative action, and bilingualism in the 1990s. In urban centers like Los Angeles and New York, where hundreds of linguistic formations co-exist, Spanish-language cultural practices are best studied in juxtaposition to other traditions.

Contemporary forms of domination function best, it would seem, when the cultural production of diverse groups, and the groups themselves, are kept apart or reduced to simple dichotomies. The maintenance of a strict black–white opposition as the ground for US race relations – an opposition reinforced by texts ranging from Michael Jackson's "Ebony and Ivory" and "Black or White" videos to Spike Lee's movies to Toni Morrison's mediation on US national literature, *Playing in the Dark* (1990) – is conducive to the maintenance of the status quo, for it renders virtually invisible those groups that fall somewhere outside the traditional dualism, thereby making a heterogeneous collective subject more difficult to imagine. This kind of segregation has not always been the case. Chicano, Pilipino, and African American coordinating committees, chaired by both women and men, in California's trade union movement during the late 1930s are only one suggestive example of collaborative work. In the artistic sphere, the hope for a progressive hip hop movement has been deferred by a willingness on the part of many performers to reproduce market and patriarchal values. In the short term, those artists with explicitly progressive and pan-ethnic projects such as Wu Tang, Ozomatli, Blackeyed Peas, Salvadoran performance artist Quique Avilés, and the San Diego-based Taco Shop Poets deserve critical attention. If a North American cultural studies project is to understand and play some part in democratizing the future, a wide range of social and artistic circuits and past organizing models will have to be laid bare and objectively investigated for both their conservative potential and radical promise.

Because any simple continuity within or autonomy of the Spanish-speaking tradition is illusory, cultural studies gains most from foregrounding the ever-changing function of cultural objects according to context, that is, according to historical and geographical contingencies. Recent comparative analyses have been alert to spatial difference but less so to temporal difference, and the emphasis in much cultural studies work on contemporary mass and popular culture of the last thirty years has disconnected the field from the study of earlier periods. What gets lost in a presentist methodology is access to the diverse genealogical moments of Western racism, for example, or the ways patriarchal traditions reinscribe themselves in different historical settings. Writers who are actively intervening in the reproduction of cultural objects from earlier periods often display a better transformative sense than do most critics. An example is Luis Valdez, the Chicano playwright and film director, who in 1989 adapted a Spanish medieval nativity play to the conditions of late twentieth-century California. In *La Pastorela*, hell becomes a toxic waste site, and Christ the son of migrant workers.

What a cultural studies project might undertake in response to such an adaptation would be an analysis of how the transmission of that play – from fourteenth-century Spain to sixteenth-century Mexico to contemporary California – involved a complex genealogy of political and cultural, that is, community-specific, functions. In twentieth-century studies, one might investigate the ways in which Chicano subcultural styles, produced out of the contact with other elements of urban culture in the United States, are returned to Mexico and take up different functions. The Mexican essayist Carlos Monsiváis has written about how successive generations of subcultural styles that originated in the US southwest as counterhegemonic practices (*pachuco* and *cholo* dress, music, and language, for example) are stripped of their political and contestatory function in order to make the voyage south where they are reenacted by middle-class youth in the large cities of northern Mexico (Monsiváis 1981: 291–5). The Chicano/a children and grandchildren of Mexican immigrant families export to their "ancestral home" an uncanny and not always welcome (from a traditionalist point of view) cultural gift in a process performance artist Guillermo Gómez Peña calls the "Chicanization of Mexico." In the 1990s, this cross-border exchange continued through musical forms such as *quebradita*, *rock en español*, and *techno-banda*, but also through the culture surrounding drug-trafficking and gang violence. Because of Latino immigration patterns in the 1980s, the impact of US cultural forms and social ills now extended not only to Mexico but to Central America and beyond.

In his ethnographic survey of punk and *cholo* styles in Mexico and the United States, José Manuel Valenzuela outlines the political and economic relations as well as the transference between the two countries of subcultural styles and alternative subjectivities. In the conjuncture of US–Mexican unequal dependency, popular culture on the southern side of the border is driven by international market forces and US control of mass communication systems. Nevertheless, the contact between different subcultural communities can produce unexpected results, as in an anecdote recounted by a Mexican punk:

> [From Tijuana] I began to go to punk parties in San Diego . . . Once a band was playing and they had a gringo [US] flag so I went up between the instruments and pulled down the flag and said to my friend: Do you have any matches? Yeah, well light this and we burned the gringo flag in front of the gringo punks and some applauded and others got angry, A little of everything, no? There were some nationalist patriots, right? "We're Number One" and all the rest . . . [Later, one of the band members objects to the flag burning.] I asked him why he objected if they sang songs against the United States, and he said, "My brother died in Vietnam" and I told him, "Do you know who killed your brother? Your flag killed him. Your love for your country killed him, get it? And you should be against your flag because it killed your brother." (1988: 179)

The discourse of uncritical patriotism (what in a more precious language has been called the "national ontology") is radically critiqued by an alternative voice from the so-called Third World that at the level of style would seem to be part of the North American punk's cultural universe. The resultant contradiction likely did not lead to immediate politicization but may have unsettled the band member's passive acceptance of national myths of the United States long enough to view his own culture from the outside.

This kind of exchange, in which divergent perspectives are juxtaposed and problematized through a process of transculturation, is a relatively commonplace occurrence in all border communities. The relationships among various groups, however, continue to be complicated by nationalist and class biases. For example, one Mexican artist, Roberto Gil de Montes, who admits to incorporating graffiti in his work under the influence of Chicano street art, arrogantly insists on his own superior authenticity: "I certainly have nothing against Chicanos. After all, we gave birth to them. They come from what we are . . . When they did try to be like me, it seemed ridiculous. So how could I identify with them? They were trying to become what I already was" (Benavidez 1991: 6). Such statements are driven by the will to cultural purity, a belief in racial origins, and an inability to imagine complex identities and alliances. Like Octavio Paz before him, Gil de Montes reduces Chicano art and identity to a deracinated simulacrum of essential Mexicaness.

Transcultural exchanges might better be read as mechanisms of supplementarity. Social identities, cultural forms and styles, enter a new environment and either transform it immediately or produce the conditions for future change. As with the *indiano* in sixteenth-century Spain (a returnee from America with newly-accumulated wealth), who was symptomatic of an unsettled field of social relations and thus became a recurring figure in literature and a concretization of emergent subject positions, the *pícaro*, *cholo*, *pachuco*, *cha cha girl*, and other "characters" might be productively read as bearers of change (albeit not necessarily progressive change). In the final analysis, the *indiano's* wealth invigorated a declining aristocracy even as it prepared a space for an emergent middle class whose political power in Spain was not solidified until the late nineteenth century. Four hundred years later, transnational Mexican service workers return to small cities in Mexico with sufficient wealth to sustain a relatively "aristocratic" lifestyle (Marcum). It is not clear to what extent these workers may contribute, if at all, to the struggle to democratize the Mexican political system. In the historical *longue dureé*, these supplementary figures and cultural representations of them often reveal structures of experience barely discernible in the social field. Because each subcultural style or returnee figure is related differently to hegemonic forces in the new context, one ought not assume that the rearticulation of social relations they produce constitutes either "subversion" or "resistance."

James Clifford frames the issue this way: "How are national, ethnic, community 'insides' and 'outsides' sustained, policed, subverted, crossed – by distinct historical subjects – for their own ends, with different degrees of power and freedom?" (1997: 36). The recognition that Spanish is not a foreign language in a North American context but rather a necessary component of any future US national identity is a small step out of traditional ethnocentrism. In the face of changing demographics in California and elsewhere, the entire issue of "minority" discourse will have to be rethought in the light of a multilinguistic and multicultural community where those groups formerly in the majority are not excluded but are forced to relinquish their dominance in favor of a more egalitarian *convivencia* (living together).

Teaching for Progressive Social Change

The present is a labyrinth with no exit, but it is the teacher who must imagine possible solutions even though they seem far away.

José Vasconcelos, "Speech on Day of the Teacher"

Confronted by the "end of history," progressives around the world struggle to maintain the optimism of spirit prescribed by Gramsci. The academic phrase "late capitalism" rings hollow, yet we know the current order will prove disastrous for a majority of the world's people, for the environment, and for future generations. In an institutional setting, the demystification of origins, the reimagining of communities, the investigation of transnational cultural exchange, and the fashioning of alternative social visions to which cultural studies workers might contribute are directly linked to issues of pedagogy and activism. It is in the classroom that the status quo is either uncritically reproduced through the kinds of appropriations I have outlined or overturned in order to produce a new "common sense." But the desire to problematize accepted knowledge, which some poststructuralisms and cultural studies seem to share, is not easily realized by groups living within traditional cultural formations. I am thinking not only of working–class Latino communities, where discourses of Catholicism, Christian fundamentalism, and patriotism are strong, but also of the majority of the middle class in the United States, resigned to consumerism and civic inaction. The Brazilian educator Paulo Freire reminds us that "problematization does not come easily to passively receptive masses, no matter where they are – in the 'countryside' of the world or in the classrooms or before the television sets of the cities" (1988: vii). After the problematization of individualism, ethnic authenticity, and traditional knowledge production has begun, we are left with the difficult enterprise of imagining alternative social relations. Manuel Castells has called this trajectory the passage from a "resistance identity" to a "project identity" that "seeks the transformation of the overall social structure" (1997: 8). He defines "resistance identity" as "the exclusion of the excluders by the excluded," and therefore necessary for drawing the lines of struggle for disempowered groups. "Project identity" (which I take to be a gloss on Sartre's notion of the project) expands resistance identity "toward the transformation of society." In terms of practical politics, I would argue that both forms of identity can be usefully deployed according to specific contexts and objectives.

The question of whether or not Anglophone cultural studies is capable of generating multilinguistic and multicultural project identities remains unanswered. Put another way, is the privatized university (now public in name only) a site where a critical philosophy of praxis can be developed collectively? Neoconservative claims during the 1980s that US universities were being taken over by "Marxist faculty" were absurd but widely disseminated by media pundits and right-wing politicians. At the end of the 1990s, celebrity columnists like George Will (1999) reproduced the warning that "[higher education] is the niche where such Marxists as still exist have gone to earth." Pierre Bourdieu reminds us of "the incessant work of the neoliberal 'thinkers' aimed at discrediting and disqualifying the heritage of words, traditions, and representations associated with the historical conquests of the social movements of the past and the present" (1998: 103). It is not Marxism alone that revisionist intellectuals hope to disparage but every progressive tradition of the last hundred years.

In reality, the poststructuralist dispensation (and most of its ethnic and postcolonial studies progeny) turned a generation of scholars against socialist theory for its purported "totalizing and teleological" sins. That some faculty pose as "Marxists," especially those working primarily on aesthetic materials rather than economic or political, concerns no one in the corporate academy as long as classroom theories do not translate into praxis on campus, in struggles for graduate student unionization, for example, or in communities beyond campus walls. In short, administrators will tolerate even Marxist professors as long as the institutional boat remains unrocked.

The vast majority of faculty members and administrators continue to be committed to maintaining the status quo through managerial practices and liberal rhetoric now unabashedly determined by market values which include an array of "multiculturalist" agendas. The corporate world has been at the forefront of foreign-language instruction and "diversity" development, e.g. Dun and Bradstreet's ¡Hola! program (Hispanic Organization of Leaders for Action) and Aetna's Hispanic Network. The latest theory fashions – from border studies to its successor globalization studies – fit easily into modes of knowledge production as understood by privately funded thinktanks that are relatively autonomous vis-à-vis traditional departmental structures. In the corporate sphere, the CEO of General Electric may speak about building "diverse and global teams" who possess "the self-confidence to involve everyone and behave in a boundaryless fashion." On campus and off, the meaning of the term "diversity" has been co-opted beyond recognition by the new corporate-educational-military complex. Elite theory, interdisciplinary perhaps but articulated almost exclusively in English, cannot salvage the situation as even the most optimistic professors admit: "The institutionalization of any field or curriculum which establishes orthodox objects and methods submits in part to the demands of the university and its educative function of socializing subjects into the state" (Lowe 1998: 41). Lowe imagines that Ethnic and Asian American studies programs will serve as "oppositional forums," a gloss on Martin Carnoy's notion of "exploitable political space" within the privatized university. I would argue that the new corporate university can tolerate with impunity such forums or spaces as long as the elitism, personality cults, and generally antidemocratic nature of local institutional bureaucracies remain unchallenged. The grassroots project to dismantle institutional racism and sexism, a struggle not seriously pursued since the mid-1970s, will have to be renamed, new strategies imagined, and a new generation of student activists energized before the terrain lost during the last twenty years of conservative reaction can be won back.

Chicana writer Ana Castillo paints an accurate portrait of most faculty on the so-called academic left: "Very few among those very few will do very little toward challenging their institutions in any way. Or they will do it when there is clear personal advantage to be gained or when there is little to no risk, not a moment before. As for the rest whose interests are clearly invested in their careers and not social change in or out of the institution, there are far too many" (1995: 211). University of Minnesota student Anne Martinez corroborates Castillo's sentiments from an undergraduate perspective: "It has been my experience that very few faculty or staff members can or will go out on a limb for much of anything" (Wing 1999). While the attempt to separate academic life from politics has marked the entire history of the US university, it is particularly evident today when anyone questioning the status quo is quickly labeled "uncollegial" and a "loose cannon" intent on disrupting polite "conversations" (the idea of intellectual debate has been mostly discarded).

Faced with the carefully managed expansion of what Elizabeth Martinez calls "a buffer of colored elite," the assertion pronounced in the Chicano Movement's "Plan de Santa Barbara," sampled from Mexican thinker José Vasconcelos, is as necessary as it was in 1969: "At this moment we do not come to work for the university, but to demand that the university work for our people." They added: "It is the students who must keep after Chicano and non-Chicano administrators and faculty to see that they do not compromise the position of the student and the community" (Muñoz 1989: 200). Thirty years ago, Chicano students demanded (and continue to demand) nothing less than the kind of commitment that informed the Birmingham Centre in its earliest days. As Raymond Williams put it: "If you accept my definition that this is really what Cultural Studies has been about, of taking the best we can in intellectual work and going with it in this very open way to confront people for whom it is not a way of life, for whom it is not in any probability a job . . . then Cultural Studies has a very remarkable future indeed" (1989: 162). In California, where Spanish-speaking and African American communities have seen their opportunities to attend the state's most elite universities diminish because of a decrepit K–12 system, exclusionary admissions policies, and the statewide abolition of affirmative action programs (Proposition 209), it is incumbent upon those of us who work in higher education to establish connections between those communities and campus resources and expertise – in other words, to locate and intervene in what E. P. Thompson referred to as "a medium of practical engagement."

Cultural studies in the United States emerged at precisely the moment when racism and elitism reappeared in new and reinvigorated forms, and in a context of post-Cold War triumphalism, the massive redistribution of wealth upwards, and the subsequent hardening of US society whose symptoms can be traced from Clinton's "welfare reform" to military interventions aimed at civilian populations abroad to the violence perpetrated by the children of Reaganism in middle–class suburbs like Littleton, Colorado. At the end of the century, university officials in the name of bottom–line economics downsize humanities and ethnic studies programs, two of the only sites where sustained critiques of neoliberalism, patriarchy, sexism, and racism might take place. Even in those disciplines created by collective action in the 1960s and now under siege, the competition and lack of solidarity typical of the most crass forms of capitalism are rampant among young scholars, a situation exacerbated by celebrity culture in which academic theorists known only to small elite audiences are obscenely compared to historic populist artists like Aretha Franklin. The hyperprofessionalization inflicted upon students of color by faculty in marginalized fields such as ethnic studies in order to enforce artifically rigorous standards too often results in student alienation and failure. Unless we are willing to critique these market-inspired practices and debate our colleagues who engage in them, the struggle for a North American cultural studies project beyond neoliberalism, monolingualism, and ethno–centrism, in which individual and collective identities can be understood and nurtured in the service of a more equitable distribution of rights and resources, will be lost.

Notes

This chapter is a revised version of an essay written in late 1991 and published in 1994. Because of the changes in the political climate in the US since that time, particularly in California, I have had to rethink substantially the issues involved while attempting to stay true to the original argument. A slightly longer version of the revised essay will appear in Angie Chabram-Dernersesian, ed., *Chicana/o Cultural Studies* (Routledge, forthcoming).

References

Acuña, Rodolfo (1997). *Anything But Mexican: Chicanos in Contemporary Los Angeles*. London: Verso.

Alarcón, Norma. "The Theoretical Subject(s) of This Bridge Called My Back and Anglo-American Feminism." In Calderón and Saldívar.

Amin, Samir. (1989) *Eurocentrism*, trans. Russell Moore. New York: Monthly Review Press.

Arteaga, Alfred (1994). *An Other Tongue: Nation and Ethnicity in the Linguistic Border-lands*. Durham: Duke University Press.

Benavidez, Max (1991). "The Labyrinth of the North." *Los Angeles Times* "Calendar," Sept. 15.

Bourdieu, Pierre (1998). *Acts of Resistance: Against the Tyranny of the Market*, trans. Richard Nice. New York: The New Press.

Cabán, Pedro (1998). "The New Synthesis of Latin American and Latino Studies." In Frank Bonilla, Edwin Meléndez, Rebecca Morales, and María de los Angeles Torres (ed.), *Borderless Borders: US Latinos, Latin Americans, and the Paradox of Interdependence*. Philadelphia: Temple University Press.

Calderón, Hector and Jose David Saldívar (eds.) (1991). *Criticism in the Borderlands: Studies in Chicano Literature, Culture, and Ideology*. Durham: Duke University Press.

Castells, Manuel (1997). *The Power of Identity. The Information Age: Economy, Society and Culture*, vol. 2. Oxford: Blackwell.

Castillo, Ana (1995). *Massacre of the Dreamers: Essays on Xicanisma*. London and New York: Penguin.

Chen, Kuang-Hsing (1996). "Cultural Studies and the Politics of Internationalization: An Interview with Stuart Hall." In David Morley and Kuan-Hsing Chen (eds.), *Stuart Hall: Critical Dialogues in Cultural Studies*. London: Routledge.

Clifford, James (1997). *Routes: Travel and Translation in the Late Twentieth Century*. Cambridge, Mass.: Harvard University Press.

Davis, Mike (1999). "Magical Urbanism: Latinos Reinvent the US Big City." *New Left Review* 234: 3–43.

Freire, Paulo (1988). *Cultural Action for Freedom*. Monograph Series No. 1. Cambridge, Mass.: Harvard Educational Review.

Gibson, Charles (1971). *The Black Legend: Anti-Spanish Attitudes in the Old World and the New*. New York: Knopf.

Graham, Helen and Jo Labanyi (eds.) (1995). *Spanish Cultural Studies: An Introduction: The Struggle for Modernity*. New York: Oxford University Press.

Larsen, Neil (1995). *Reading North by South: On Latin American Literature, Culture, and Politics*. Minneapolis: University of Minnesota Press.

Lowe, Lisa (1998). "The International Within the National: American Studies and Asian American Critique." *Cultural Critique* 40 (Fall, 1998): 29–47.

Maltby, William S. (1971). *The Black Legend in England: The Development of Anti-Spanish Sentiment, 1558–1660*. Durham: Duke University Press.

Marcum, Diana (1997). "The Busboys of San Miguel." *Los Angeles Times Magazine*, Dec. 14.

Monsiváis, Carlos (1981). *Escenas de pudor y liviandad*, 6th edn. Mexico City: Grijalbo.

Montoya, Margaret (1998). "Law and Language(s)." In Richard Delgado and Jean Stefancic (eds.), *The Latino Condition: A Critical Reader*. New York: New York University Press.

Muñoz, Carlos, Jr. (1989). *Youth, Identity, Power: The Chicano Movement*. London: Verso.

Perea, Juan F. (1998). "American Languages, Cultural Pluralism, and Official English." In Richard Delgado and Jean Stefancic (eds.), *The Latino Condition: A Critical Reader*. New York: New York University Press.

Pratt, Mary Louise (1991). "Arts of the Contact Zone." In *Profession 91*. New York: Modern Language Association.

Saldívar, Ramón (1990). *Chicano Narrative: The Dialectics of Difference*. Madison: University of Wisconsin Press.

Sánchez, Rosaura and Beatrice Pita (1999). "Mapping Cultural/Political Debates in Latin American Studies." *Cultural Studies* 13: 290–318.

Spivak, Gayatri. "Bonding in Difference." In Arteaga.

Stratton, Jon and Ien Ang (1996). "On the Impossibility of a Global Cultural Studies: 'British' Cultural Studies in an 'International' Frame." In David Morley and

Kuan-Hsing Chen (eds.), *Stuart Hall: Critical Dialogues in Cultural Studies*. London: Routledge.

Thompson, E. P. (1978). *The Poverty of Theory and Other Essays*. New York: Monthly Review Press.

Valenzuela, José Manuel (1988). *A la brava, ese!* Tijuana: El Colegio de la Frontera Norte.

Will, George (1999). "What To Do With All Those Ph.D.s." *Sacramento Bee* webpage, April 25.

Williams, Raymond (1989). "The Future of Cultural Studies." In *The Politics of Modernism: Against the New Conformists*. London: Verso.

Wing, Bob (1999). "Multiculturalism and the Struggle for Ethnic Studies." *Colorlines: Race, Culture, Action*, May 17.

Further Reading

Acuña, Rodolfo (1998). *Sometimes There Is No Other Side: Chicanos and the Myth of Equality*. Notre Dame: University of Notre Dame Press.

——(1988). *Occupied America: A History of Chicanos*, 3rd edn. New York: Harper and Row.

Anzaldúa, Gloria (1987). *Borderlands/La Frontera: The New Mestiza*. San Francisco: Spinsters/Aunt Lute.

Cantú, Norma Elia (1995). *Canícula: Snapshots of a Girlhood en la frontera*. Albuquerque: University of New Mexico Press.

García, Alma M. (ed.) (1997). *Chicana Feminist Thought: The Basic Historical Writings*. New York–London: Routledge.

García, Ignacio M. (1997). *Chicanismo: The Forging of a Militant Ethos among Mexican Americans*. Tempe: University of Arizona Press.

Gutiérrez, David (1995). *Walls and Mirrors: Mexican Americans, Mexican Immigrants, and the Politics of Ethnicity*. Berkeley: University of California Press.

Leclerc, Gustavo, Raúl H. Villa and Michael J. Dear (eds.) (1999). *Urban Latino Cultures: La vida latina en L.A.* Thousand Oaks–London: Sage Publications.

Martínez, Elizabeth (1998). *De Colores Means All of US: Latina Views for a Multi-colored Century*. Cambridge, Mass.: South End Press.

Monsiváis, Carlos (1982). *Amor perdido*. Mexico City: Ediciones Era.

——(1987). *Entrada libre: crónicas de la sociedad que se organiza*. Mexico City: Ediciones Era.

——(1997). *Mexican Postcards*, trans. John Kraniauskas. London–New York: Verso.

Montejano, David (ed.) (1999). *Chicano Politics and Society in the Late Twentieth Century*. Austin: University of Texas Press.

Reyes, David and Tom Waldman (1998). *Land of a Thousand Dances: Chicano Rock 'n Roll from Southern California*. Albuquerque: University of New Mexico Press.

Sánchez, George J. (1993). *Becoming Mexican American: Ethnicity, Culture and Identity in Chicano Los Angeles, 1900–1945*. Berkeley: University of California Press.

Chapter 14

Australasia

Graeme Turner

"Australasian Cultural Studies"

It makes geographic sense to deal with the development of cultural studies in Australia and New Zealand through the label of "Australasia." However, it would be wrong to allow this to carry with it an assumption of uniformity or homogeneity among either the various practices of cultural studies within Australia or New Zealand or between the dominant traditions in the two countries. Despite their geographic proximity to each other (and their lack of proximity to just about anyone else), and despite their common colonial origins, the Australian and New Zealand traditions have been very different. While Australian cultural studies has benefited from a range of fortuitous developments both within the university system and the media industries, cultural studies in New Zealand has had to deal with a less hospitable university environment and an extremely limited potential market of students and readers. Both traditions have been determinedly local or national in their focus, and have accepted the responsibility to make their academic knowledges matter to their societies. However, this task has been much easier for those working in Australian conditions than for their New Zealand counterparts and this is reflected in the scale of cultural studies' development in Australia and its implication in international debates. Interestingly, however, Australia's level of participation in New Zealand debates has not been high. Contrary to what one might expect, there has not been a thriving intellectual trade between the two countries in cultural studies or related fields and only infrequently has there been a sense of their contributing to a common, postcolonial or "Antipodean" counterdiscourse to northern hemisphere orthodoxies. While each might claim such a contribution for their own, there have been few moments of solidarity in a common cause.

This means that one cannot deal with Australian and New Zealand cultural studies as a joint enterprise. What follows will necessarily privilege Australian cultural studies as the larger, more developed, and more complex academic and intellectual field which also enjoys more widespread international recognition as a specific cultural formation. There are good reasons for this. It should be understood, since one can't rely on this being known outside Australasia, that there is an enormous disparity in the size of the populations of New Zealand and Australia (3 million in New Zealand to 19 million in Australia) which significantly affects such things as the size of the university system, the potential market for academic books and student textbooks, and the opportunities for a group of like-minded scholars to develop the critical mass required to make their work visible and significant.

The character of the two university systems is significantly different, too. The vast majority of universities in New Zealand reflect the Oxbridge traditions which have shaped most postcolonial university systems and remain overwhelmingly discipline based, even in instances where they serve what are clearly cross-disciplinary vocational objectives. Their counterparts in Australia have comfortably accommodated inter-or multi-disciplinary programs for more than two decades, so that there is a wider range of structural models in place – and, of course, the scale of the sector allows for this more easily than can be the case in New Zealand. The academic environment confronting cultural studies scholars in New Zealand has been, and is still to some extent, a little hostile; even a respectable but relatively new field such as film studies finds itself having to justify its existence against more traditional and established disciplines. As we shall see, New Zealand's massive political investment in economic rationalism – the deregulation of social institutions and the widespread application of the logic of the market to the provision of government services, in particular – has, somewhat ironically, improved matters over the last decade as cultural studies has demonstrated its attractiveness to the market. However, the scale of the operation possible, even in the most positive of environments one could imagine for New Zealand, makes it very difficult for scholars there to develop the kind of community most would like to see.

There are other, related, contextual considerations. Australia still owns its media industries, some of its films are able to return their budgets purely through local exhibition, and the export of Australian television productions has been on balance extremely successful. The existence of a film and media sector that is both sizeable and culturally significant has a direct relation to the comparative success of media and cultural studies programs within Australian universities, and to the public access enjoyed by academics from these disciplines to the newspaper opinion pages, talk radio, television news and current affairs programs, and to government institutions, reviews, inquiries, and other policy-making forums. While New Zealand academics are no less able or motivated, and while there are clear examples of certain New Zealand academics performing the role of the public intellectual to the hilt, the absence of the conditions outlined above means that they generally enjoy less widespread cultural or political influence than their counterparts in Australia.

An answer to some of these problems, one would think, would be for Australia and New Zealand to think of themselves as one community of scholars, one market for an Australasian or antipodean cultural studies. Something like that has happened, for instance, in communication studies through the peak professional body, the Australian and New Zealand Communication Association. It has not happened in cultural studies, for a variety of reasons. The most fundamental is that a key concern for media and cultural studies in both countries is the analysis of their specific national contexts – for the interrogation of the meaning of the nation, of the dominant constructions of national or racial identity, the examination of and participation in government sponsored processes of nation formation, and so on. This constitutes an impediment to collaborating with those working with another national tradition, even one so physically and historically close to one's own. Such an impediment is implicated in and strengthened by the current political relation between Australia and New Zealand. There are cultural issues – the trade in television programming across the Tasman Sea, for instance – upon which the interests of the two countries are opposed through what could easily be seen as a neocolonial politics. There have been a number of scholars on both sides who have been keen to break through this politics and extend academic debate across the Tasman – New Zealander Geoff Lealand wrote the chapter on New Zealand in Stuart Cunningham and Elizabeth Jacka's *Australian Television and International Mediascapes* (1996), for example – but such collaboration is still in the earliest stages and much development remains to occur. While theorists such as McKenzie Wark (1992) may talk of an "Antipodean" cultural studies, his examples are always drawn from two or three exponents of Australian cultural studies and provide no sense of ever having looked at the New Zealand tradition. To my knowledge, there is only Tara Brabazon's (1999) so far unpublished manuscript, *Tracking the Jack: A Retracing of the Antipodes*, which takes the comparison on directly as an intellectual project – and the fact that it is so far unpublished suggests what kind of obstacles confront such a project.

The Origins of Cultural Studies in Australia and New Zealand

The establishment of a local version of cultural studies in Australia was made possible by a variety of enabling conditions. These include a renewed interest in the analysis of Australian culture and Australian histories through an emerging field of Australian studies over the 1970s; the development of a nationally focused tradition of media and film studies supported by the establishment of government agencies for film and (later) television production; the introduction of a new sector in tertiary education which sought interdisciplinary and vocationally oriented programs to offer to a student base that was growing dramatically in response to the abolition of tuition fees; the 1980s influence of a group of British émigrés trained in what became known as cultural studies; the opening up of a publishing market for Australian cultural studies initially in Australia and then, eventually, internationally; and, finally, a degree of incorporation of cultural studies academics into government policy-making processes within a series of state and federal administrations.

The universities in Australia came rather late to the consideration of their own nation's literature, history, and culture. For many years, Australian history was taught as a footnote to British imperial history, while the idea of an "Australian literature" was regarded as an oxymoron. Increasingly, certainly from the mid-1960s onwards, this situation changed as history and literary studies in particular addressed their attention to issues of national identity, the delineation of "the national character" through national cultural production. In many cases, newly introduced theoretical perspectives from structuralism and narratology proved useful as scholars moved from defining the national character as an idealist or empirical exercise, and embraced the notion that such a character might be the product of cultural construction, of narrative, of invention, or a Barthesian notion of mythology.

By the early 1980s, scholars within history and literary studies were no longer in search of "the truth" about the nature of Australian society or its typical citizens. Rather, they found themselves addressing their analysis towards Benedict Anderson's "imagined community," and thinking about the meanings attached to the national culture, the patterns of inclusion and exclusion, and the interests served. Initially leading to a productive alliance between literature and history, these were new questions for the humanities in Australia which were ultimately about how "Australia" was or had been represented in all kinds of forms and media – and about the consequences and effects of these representations. To deal with these questions adequately, one had to think about the whole field of meanings within which the nation-building project made its sense and the systems of production and distribution that regulated the flow of meanings. What had come to be called "Australian studies" led to an inquiry into the operation of culture itself, into how the processes of cultural formation worked.

Clearly, if they were to gain any purchase on this, literary studies, history, and Australian studies were in need of some new advice. While these disciplines have never been comfortable with this fact, the raggedly hybrid version of Australian cultural studies which was developing out of Birmingham Marxism, Saussurean semiotics, and French poststructuralism turned out to be the best source of that advice. What cultural studies had, that Australian studies lacked, was a theory (or more correctly a repertoire of theories) about the way cultural processes worked, about how culture generated and shared its meanings, and ultimately how this affected the distribution of power. Cultural studies provided a rationale for the analysis of Australian culture that was more flexible, integrated, and critical than the multiperspectived but essentially descriptive approaches taken by Australian studies.

There is an alternative tradition running in parallel with the one just described. Since the government-funded revival of the Australian film industry in the early 1970s, a local tradition of film and media analysis had been developing. Initially dominated, again, by nationalist or at least antiimperialist

249

arguments aimed at defending the production of local cinema for local audiences, film and media studies benefited from the close temporal alignment between its development as a discipline and the film industry's commercial and critical legitimacy. Journals such as *Cinema Papers* and *The Australian Journal of Screen Theory* are creatures of the 1970s, and attest to the strength of interest in Australian film, as well as the level of theoretical sophistication of a critical tradition which was drawn towards Metzian film semiotics and Lacanian appropriations of Freud. Some contributors worked at a slightly more grassroots level as well; Meaghan Morris spent some years as a film reviewer for the mainstream press during this period. The concerns of this tradition were not, by and large, canonical in the way many film studies had been elsewhere; the connection between film and culture, and the cultural politics of the film text, dominated Australian screen theory at the time and directly informed the growing number of film and media studies courses becoming available. (For a discussion of the development of Australian film cultures, see Tom O'Regan 1996.)

Over time, it is probably this tradition – that of a political and cultural analysis of film and media texts and industries – which has been the most powerful influence on the directions cultural studies has taken in Australia. It is certainly directly implicated in the development of a specific form of cultural policy studies, because the analysis of media policy had been a fundamental component of Australian cultural studies, film studies, and media studies from the very beginning. Over the second half of the 1970s through to the middle of the 1980s, these two traditions – film and media studies, and studies of Australian culture – worked in a sometimes uneasy alliance which helped to push the field beyond the analysis of representation towards an understanding of the institutional and industrial means of cultural production while retaining the more traditional concern with texts such as film and television programs. The mix of approaches is well represented in Susan Dermody and Elizabeth Jacka's (1987, 1988) cultural history of the Australian film revival which divides its two volumes into treatments of the film texts and the film industry.

A key support to these developments came from changes to the structure of higher education in Australia. In 1972, tuition fees for tertiary education were abolished and shortly after a new sector of tertiary institution was established – the colleges of advanced education (CAEs). The result was a revolution in the academic structuring of humanities and social science teaching within Australia. The CAEs were intended to be more vocationally focused than the existing traditional universities, and were asked to offer geniune alternatives to their predecessors. At the same time, a group of new universities explicitly dedicated to interdisciplinary teaching and research further accelerated the pace of change and fueled interest for new academic and pedagogic projects. Among the most significant beneficiaries of these changes were the new interdisciplinary areas of media studies, communication studies, Australian studies, film studies, and, ultimately, cultural studies. A number of these institutions went on to play an enormously significant part in Australian cultural studies. Murdoch University and Curtin University in Perth, Griffith University in Brisbane, and the University of Technology (UTS) in Sydney all developed strong identities around cultural studies over these years; among those who worked in these institutions are John Frow, John Hartley, Tom O'Regan, Ien Ang, Meaghan Morris, Stephen Muecke, Ian Hunter, Stuart Cunningham, and Tony Bennett. Early journals such as *Interventions* (UTS), *Continuum* (Murdoch), and the *Australian Journal of Cultural Studies* (Curtin and Murdoch), which later became the Routledge Journal *Cultural Studies*, came from these institutional locations.

The expansion of the higher education system brought other benefits. As new programs in media, television, film, and cultural studies were planned, developed, and implemented, opportunities for new staff appointments opened up. Many of these programs had their counterparts in the UK, where the process had started much earlier and where the combination of the Birmingham Centre's publications, the Open University Popular Culture course readers, and the Methuen New Accents series had already established a readership as well as a much more sophisticated understanding of how this kind of material could and should be taught. A number of key appointments from the UK – among them, John Tulloch, Tony Bennett, John Fiske, and John Hartley – contributed significantly to course planning and to the development of both national and international publication opportunities for Australian scholars on Australian material.

The British theoretical influence was significant. Fiske, in particular, brought the Stuart Hall model of cultural studies to the attention of many Australians interested in new ways to teach popular culture. However, it would be wrong to see this as the only, or even an uncontested, influence. Certainly among those working at Murdoch University and Curtin University (then, the WA Institute of Technology), the Birmingham models were strongly influential. Even there, though, were countervailing pressures from what came to be called social semiotics, from phenomenology, and from Marxist literary theory. On the other side of the continent, it was the French influence which was most pronounced. For Sydneysiders working in media and communications studies in the early 1980s, the term "cultural studies" was itself suspect. Their alignments were more with Baudrillard than Stuart Hall, and their interest much less in analyzing cultural forms than in theorizing the politics of representation. A little later, those working at Griffith University in Brisbane were to champion a version of Foucauldian discursive analysis as the dominant mode of practice for cultural studies. There was, then, no single tradition of cultural studies in Australia over this period – or at any time since, for that matter – nor was cultural studies universally accepted by the full range of scholars working across critical and media theory at the time.

A common element within the various approaches, however, has been the focus on the local, the national, and contemporary politics. The nation has been a consistent but often bitterly contested term within Australian cultural studies. This, in all its guises: as idealist principle, as cultural construction, or as a regressive and essentializing force. Given the physical isolation of Australia, and given the brevity and accessibility of its white history, the category of the nation inevitably figures – either as the object or as the analytic ground – in large cultural debates. In the history of Australian cultural studies, that has been the case as well. Whether in arguments about the textual regimes of Australian films or the structure of the policy regimes which make them possible, definitions of the nation play a central role. (For further developments of this idea, see the introductory essays in both Frow and Morris 1993; and Turner, 1993.)

It is hard to move from this account of the origins of Australian cultural studies without making the account of New Zealand cultural studies seem like the negative version. Perhaps the point to emphasize is how arbitrary and fortuitous the enabling conditions in Australia have been, and how cruelly their absence in New Zealand has impacted on the development of the field. There was no parallel in New Zealand to the way the expansion of the Australian higher education system aligned itself with new interdisciplinary pedagogic and academic objectives. Cultural studies had to establish itself within existing disciplinary environments as a contribution to those disciplines. It was a different raft of disciplines, though. New Zealanders, at this point, tended to come to cultural studies from sociology rather than from film, media, or area studies – or even from English or history. As a result, there was a lot to argue about: about cultural studies as poor sociology, about the need for cultural studies within sociology, about "imported" sociology, and so on. Further, cultural studies came to New Zealand in a relatively singular form; the work of the Birmingham Centre for Contemporary Cultural Studies was taken as a very explicit point of departure and the evaluation of this paradigm occupied those working in New Zealand for most of the 1980s. There seems to have been no counterpart to the competing poststructuralist traditions that complicated matters in Australia – perhaps because the discipline of English had kept cultural studies pretty much at arms' length until the 1990s.

For most of the 1980s, while Australian cultural studies was developing new programs and attracting new students, cultural studies in New Zealand consisted of a group of academics centered around the journal, *Sites*, established in 1981 at Massey University in Palmerston North. According to Tara Brabazon's account (1999), the *Sites* project was explicitly an application of the work of the Birmingham CCCS to the New Zealand context, but it was also a relatively exclusive project to which contributions from other universities were discouraged. Intellectual trade between Australia and New Zealand was almost non-existent and the increasing emphasis on text and context, or issues of nationalism and identity, which marked Australian work at the time do not seem to have traveled across the Tasman. Indeed, where they did, they were held up as an example of what cultural studies in New Zealand must not become (Lealand 1988). In contrast, it is probably race – the central problem for this bicultural society – which has remained the core issue for New Zealand cultural studies (particularly in its more sociological guises) through arguments around the structures which produce the identities of Maori and Pakeha (the Maori term for white settlers).

The lack of an expanding institutional framework to encourage a more out-ward looking perspective, or simply a larger number of colleagues and students, held back cultural studies in New Zealand until the late 1980s. Until that time, the stranglehold of the disciplines had maintained a relatively conservative range of offerings within the university system and resisted the antidisciplinary ethic implicit in cultural studies. It is a deep irony that the aggressive economic rationalism of successive New Zealand governments through the 1990s, with the emphasis on market-driven services exerting a heavy influence over the university system's promotions to prospective consumers, actually assisted in the development of interdisciplinary subject areas such as cultural, media, and film studies. The academic conservatism of the universities was only overcome by economic necessity as government policy provided universities with little choice other than to pursue directions which were attractive to students. As a result, programs in film, cultural studies, and media studies have become much more familiar parts of the tertiary landscape – although there is evidence that they still have to combat entrenched opposition from traditional disciplines who are prone to regard them as cash cows rather than as legitimate and respectable enterprises in their own right. That said, it is also the case that cultural studies is now finding a place in a broader range of disciplinary locations than sociology: it is in English, politics, communications, and so on – much more like the models found in the US and the UK than had previously been the case.

The improvement this represents for the institutional location of New Zealand cultural studies is reflected in the fact that, over the 1990s, New Zealand-based cultural studies scholars have become far more visible internationally: the work of Roy Shuker (1994), Geoff Lealand (1996), Nick Perry (1994), and Claudia Bell (1996) not only contributes to the development of a national cultural studies tradition, but also to major international debates – including those with Austra-lia. The position at the end of the 1990s for cultural studies in New Zealand was much improved, then, although there is still a sense of slight embattlement that is reflected in such things as staff promotions and research resources. There is now something approaching a critical mass in terms of the individuals now involved in New Zealand cultural studies, but institutional respect or support cannot always be taken for granted.

There are some signs, too, of a growing intellectual trade between Australia and New Zealand particularly around issues of broadcasting regulation policy and local content in film and television production. In 1993, the Institute of Cultural Policy Studies (later to become the Australian Key Centre for Cultural and Media Policy) held a conference in Brisbane aimed at cultural studies scholars from Canada, Australia, and New Zealand, entitled "Postcolonial For-mations." As that title implied, the assumption behind this conference was that these postcolonial Commonwealth nations confronted similar issues in the formation of cultural policy, and that there was a need for some event at which this projected commonality might be further explored. This assumption had, in turn, emerged from the experiences of the Australian and Canadian delegates at the famous 1990 conference at the University of Illinois, "Cultural Studies: Now and in the Future," which eventually produced the Grossberg, Nelson, and Treichler collection, *Cultural Studies* (1992). These experiences had emphasized the difference between the kind of work required within the postcolonial national context, and that being done within the British and American contexts. This difference was taken up by a conference organized in Perth in 1991 by John Hartley and Ien Ang aimed at "dismantling" the sense of homogeneity perceived in Anglo-American cultural studies; it primarily addressed Australian scholars and resulted in a special issue of *Cultural Studies* called "Dismantling Fremantle" 3(6), 1992). The "Postcolonial Formations" conference took this initiative one step further, by offering the first direct invitation for cultural studies scholars from Australia, Canada, and New Zealand to meet and exchange ideas about the specificity of cultural studies in a postcolonial context.

The role of the state in the formation and implementation of cultural policy was a major theme in this conference, and it has underpinned something of a dialogue between researchers in Australia and New Zealand around broadcasting policy in particular. New Zealand's broadcasting sector, once dominated by traditional public-service broadcasters, is now one of the most radically deregulated in the world. Australia has moved some way towards deregulation without ever quite removing the distinction between the public and commercial sectors. The comparison between policy regimes and their effects in the two countries has proved to be a productive one and there is now a reasonably strong relationship between the research literatures from both countries.

Although the common thread which links studies of cultural policy in both countries is their resistance to cultural domination, especially, from the northern hemisphere, there have been occasions where the politics of the relation between Australia and New Zealand have themselves sparked debates. Currently, arguments over local content rules within the film and broadcasting industries have sparked considerable exchanges between Australian and New Zealand scholars – each defending what is ultimately a strategic but nationalist case (see, for example, the panel on "Project Blue Sky" in *Media International Australia*, Britton et al. 1997).

The Contribution of Australasian Cultural Studies

As the objective of the "Postcolonial Formations" conference implies, the primary contribution Australasian cultural studies made to international cultural studies in the first instance was to challenge the unspoken but nevertheless unmistakable assumption to emerge from the northern hemisphere boom in cultural studies during the latter half of the 1980s: that Anglo-American cultural studies was universally useful and exportable. Once challenged, of course, this assumption was quickly disavowed and the field responded very positively to the suggestion that cultural theory might itself be culturally specific. Australasian cultural studies writers were among the first to put this challenge and provide this suggestion by insisting on the difference of the Australian context, and the need for extensive modification of theoretical models developed elsewhere if they were to be useful in an Australian cultural studies (Turner 1992a, 1992b). Such a suggestion would now seem a truism as cultural studies has vigorously embraced the idea of its own decentering (see Ang & Stratton 1996), but this was not the case in 1990. The speed with which it was taken up in the northern hemisphere is reflected by the appearance in the one year of two Australian cultural studies readers – one published in Australia (Frow & Morris 1993) and one published by Routledge in the UK (Turner 1993) – as well as the Routledge *Relocating Cultural Studies* collection edited by a group of Canadians who had attended the "Postcolonial Formations" conference: Valda Blundell, John Shepherd, and Ian Taylor (1993).

Meaghan Morris (1988: 241–87) offered a model for the construction of an Australian cultural studies which indigenized materials taken from elsewhere in her discussion of the appeal of the 1986 Australian film, *Crocodile Dundee*. Seeing it as an example of the Australian, hybridizing, tactic of "positive unoriginality," Morris pointed out how the film both stole from and parodied its American models, admired and disdained American power, and asserted and undermined Australian nationalisms. In her account, appropriation of this level of complexity (or as she puts it, "dead cleverness") acquired the attributes of a measured resistance, even a postcolonial politics. To find such a politics ambivalently articulated within such a populist text is characteristic of Australian cultural studies, but the potential for such a politics remains fundamental to its work. Ironically, it is a potential which is released by maintaining some strategic interest in the idea of the nation – not as an ideal but as the most pragmatic point of focus for critical and political action – and this has also been acknowledged within New Zealand cultural studies (Horrocks 1995; 1996).

Strategic nationalism and cultural policy tend to go together in this history, and it is probably under the label of cultural policy studies that the contribution of Australasian cultural studies has been filed in recent years. The convenience of that location possibly slightly overestimates both its importance and its novelty, but it is certainly true that a strong body of research developed around the work of Tony Bennett (some of which is collected in Bennett 1998), Ian Hunter (1988, 1994) and Stuart Cunningham (1992) at what became the Key Centre for Cultural and Media Policy, which was jointly located at Griffith University, Queensland University of Technology, and the University of Queensland in Brisbane. As I said earlier, film and media policy had always been a concern within Australian cultural studies, but the range of interests broadened under Bennett's influence – coming to include the policy frameworks established for national museums and art galleries, schooling, and tourism, to name some.

The fortuitous alignment between the development of a highly sophisticated theoretical framework for cultural policy studies and the incumbency of a series of state and federal Labor governments – reform governments under whom both the established policy units and the demand for independent policy advice expanded dramatically – certainly played a part in the success of the cultural policy studies agenda. However, despite the initial, slightly heady, claims for it to be the *ur* discipline for cultural studies which offered the perfect opportunity to balance theory and practice, politics and policy, cultural policy studies has perhaps settled back into a more realistic role as a fundamental contributor to the mainstream of cultural studies research and practice.

The word "practice" here ushers in another consideration. In their editorial to a recent issue of *Continuum* 13(1), April 1999), Henry Jenkins, Tara McPherson, and Jane Shattuc (1999), described "the next generation" of cultural studies work in the US by, among other things, pointing to its preference for more case-oriented research – the models of practice taken from cultural history, say, rather than cultural theory. Australasian cultural studies is very sympathetic to such a redirection of cultural studies because so much of the work it has done in the last two decades has been applied, case studies aimed at uncovering a particular problem or arguing a particular position through a specific and detailed instance (see, for instance, Morris 1992; Johnson 1993; Turner 1994). The effect of the British influence – which seems to me to have this applied inflection too – may be responsible for this, or it may simply be that so much of the work is conscious of a national agenda and has a specific problem as its target. As I suggested at the beginning of this account, one of the key attractions to cultural studies in the first place was that it enabled Australians to study their own culture. It is not surprising that this, although in widely varying ways, is exactly how it has been put to use.

Developing a national profile for cultural studies – either within the academy or more broadly – has not been easy in either Australia or New Zealand. As is the case elsewhere, cultural studies' residual populism, its preference for the contemporary and the ephemeral, and the sophistication of its analytical discourses, makes it an obvious target for critiques of academic knowledges, of intellectual fashions, or simply of the usefulness of the academy. Establishing an international profile for individual researchers or for concentrations of researchers in Australasia, when so much of the work being done is advisedly culturally specific and explicitly local in its application, and when publishers selling primarily into European and American markets express understandable caution about Australian topics, has been a challenge. It is a testament to the energy and relevance of so much of Australasian cultural studies that so many of its contributors are well-known names in the international literature. It is also a testament to the ethical orientation of so many of the gatekeepers in cultural studies that they have remained alert to the appeal of what I have called elsewhere "central ideas from marginal places" (Turner 1993: 4).

References

Ang, Ien and John Hartley (eds.) (1992). "Dismantling Fremantle." Special issue of *Cultural Studies* 6(3).

Ang, Ien and Jon Stratton (1996). "Asianising Australia: Notes towards a critical Transnationalism in Cultural Studies." *Cultural Studies* 10(1): 16–36.

Bell, Claudia (1996). *Inventing New Zealand*. Auckland: Penguin.

Bennett, Tony (1998). *Culture: A Reformer's Science*. Sydney: Allen and Unwin.

Blundell, Valda, John Shepherd, and Ian Taylor (eds.) (1993). *Relocating Cultural Studies: Developments in Theory and Research*. London and New York: Routledge.

Brabazon, Tara (1999). *Tracking the Jack: A Retracing of the Antipodes*. Unpublished ms.

Britton, Anne, Jock Given, and Geoff Lealand (1997). "Forum: Are New Zealand Programs Australian?" *Media International Australia* 83: 38–50.

Cunningham, Stuart (1992). *Framing Culture: Criticism and Policy in Australia*. Sydney: Allen and Unwin.

Cunningham, Stuart and Elizabeth Jacka (1996). *Australian Television and International Mediascapes*. Melbourne: Cambridge University Press.

Dermody, Susan and Elizabeth Jacka (1987). *The Screening of Australia, Volume 1: Anatomy of a Film Industry*. Sydney: Currency.

Dermody, Susan and Elizabeth Jacka (1988). *The Screening of Australia, Volume 2: Anatomy of a National Cinema*. Sydney: Currency.

Frow, John and Meaghan Morris (eds.) (1993). *Australian Cultural Studies: A Reader*. Sydney: Allen and Unwin.

Grossberg, Lawrence, Cary Nelson and Paula Treichler (eds.) (1992). *Cultural Studies*. New York: Routledge

Horrocks, Roger (1995). "Strategic Nationalisms: Television Production in New Zealand." *Sites* 30: 85–107.

Horrocks, Roger (1996). "Conflicts and Surprises in New Zealand Television." *Continuum* 10(1): 50–63.

Hunter, Ian (1988). *Culture and Government: The Emergence of Literary Education*. London: Macmillan.

Hunter, Ian (1994). *Rethinking the School: Subjectivity, Bureaucracy, Criticism*. Sydney: Allen and Unwin.

Jenkins, Henry, Tara McPherson, and Jane Shattuc (1999). "Introduction." *Continuum* 13(9): 5–12.

Johnson, Lesley (1993). *The Modern Girl: Girlhood and Growing Up*. Sydney: Allen and Unwin.

Lealand, Geoff (1988). *A Foreign Egg in our Nest*. Wellington: Victoria University Press.

Lealand, Geoff (1996). "New Zealand." In Cunningham and Jacka, *Australian Television and International Mediascapes*, pp. 214–28.

Morris, Meaghan (1988). *The Pirate's Fiancée: Feminism, Reading, Postmodernism*. London: Verso.

Morris, Meaghan (1992). *Ecstasy and Economics: American Essays for John Forbes*. Sydney: emPress

O'Regan, Tom (1996). *Australian National Cinema*. London: Routledge.

Perry, Nick (1994). *The Dominion of Signs*. Auckland: Auckland University Press.

257

Shuker, Roy (1994). *Understanding Popular Music*. London: Routledge.

Turner, Graeme (1992a). "It Works for Me: British Cultural Studies, Australian Cultural Studies and Australian Film." In Grossberg et al., *Cultural Studies*, pp. 640–53.

Turner, Graeme (1992b). "Of Rocks and Hard Places: The Colonized, the National and Australian Cultural Studies." *Cultural Studies* 6(3): 424–32.

Turner, Graeme (ed.) (1993). *Nation, Culture, Text: Australian Cultural and Media Studies*. London: Routledge.

Turner, Graeme (1994). *Making it National: Nationalism and Australian Popular Culture*. Sydney: Allen and Unwin.

Wark, McKenzie (1992). "Speaking Trajectories: Meaghan Morris, Antipodean Theory and Australian Cultural Studies." *Cultural Studies* 6(3): 433–48.

Chapter 15

Peripheral Vision: Chinese Cultural Studies in Hong Kong

Eric Kit-wai Ma

If cultural studies exhibits the feature of radical contextualism, then any tale about the cultural studies of a particular locale will depend very much on the sociocultural location of the storyteller. As a local who was born and grew up in the formative years of colonial Hong Kong, my tale about Chinese cultural studies will be very much colored by my experiences in Hong Kong and my academic training in the UK. My discursive position enables me to map the forms of cultural studies in Hong Kong with an ethnographic closeness to the specificity of the local academic community. However, my rather restrictive sociocultural position is also preventing me from giving a balanced account of Chinese cultural studies in general terms. In doing so, I would have to erase the internal contradictions between Hong Kong and China, which are two drastically different historical formations. Although Hong Kong is now part of China, there are still strong tensions between centrifugal impulses of localization and inter-nationalization and the centripetal force of resinicization and renationalization (Ma 1999; 2000). Based on a dozen interviews with local scholars, this chapter is a small discursive fragment of Chinese cultural studies narrated from the vantage point of Hong Kong. Instead of recycling theses and bibliographies, I want to contextualize cultural studies in Hong Kong by talking about the ways in which it has been embodied in the biographies of academics and histories of institutions. Thus this is not a chapter about theoretical debates, but a map of how cultural studies has been fostered within and across institutional and cultural spaces. From the peripheral vision of Hong Kong, I will also briefly contrast the forms of cultural studies in Hong Kong with those practiced in Mainland China.

Specificity

Cultural studies in Hong Kong has emerged from the specific sociocultural contexts of decolonization and renationalization. It is carried by individuals who translate and revise cultural theories in their research and teaching in their particular habitats in Hong Kong. The various brands of cultural studies in the UK engage culture along the elite/popular, mainstream/subcultural, and national/local axes. These emphases have to be reworked to suit the specificity of the Hong Kong case. The first point of contrast is the question of the nation-state. In the postwar decades, Hong Kong was a colony without a nation. In order to avoid political antagonism, both the Chinese and British governments refrained from imposing strong nationalistic imperatives on local culture. This meant that, for many years, Hong Kong people did not have a strong historical or national narrative to situate their own subjectivity. Colonial politics was mysteriously disguised by administrative diversion (Law 1998; Chiu 1997). In the years before and after the sovereignty change, this suppression of national narrative has fueled the desire for reclaiming histories among the general public as well as local intellectuals (Ma 1998). As a result, cultural studies scholars in Hong Kong have been more concerned with articulating local identity and less with resisting state power. This is in quite sharp contrast with the major thrust of cultural studies in Mainland China, where state power is highly visible. Since the early 1990s, the Chinese state has consolidated its power by promoting a consumer culture that fosters and satisfies social desire (Wang 1999; 1998). It has absorbed the power of the market and shored up popular support by the dialectic of occasional coercion and winning of general consent (Ma 2000). Cultural studies in China, which has been gathering weight since the 1990s, has devoted much of its energy in negotiating a discursive space between strong state control and rising market forces.

The second point of contrast is the relevancy of class analysis. Hong Kong experienced a structural expansion in the postwar decades. Compressed economic growth and the opening up of professional sectors promoted upward mobility and obfuscated class lines. Working-class families were relatively less restricted to their class position because of the structural changes brought about by industrialization and technological advancement. Economic transformation and the sudden population increase led to a truncation of whatever class structure had existed previously (Leung 1996). Arguments of cultural studies that stress class resistance cannot be applied directly in the Hong Kong context. This can be contrasted with cultural studies in China, where class analysis is still a legacy of the Left and the recent opening up of capitalist markets has triggered some class related issues such as the exploitation of female workers in many coastal provinces (Tan 1999). However, since the 1990s, class issues have become more visible in Hong Kong as economic inequality has worsened and the structural expansion of the middle sectors has come to a halt after the Asian economic meltdown in 1997. Some social activists affiliated with cultural studies have recently been quite active in attending to issues related to the structural poverty of the Hong Kong working class (Ip & Lam 1999).

The third point of contrast is on the question of high culture. Hong Kong has been an immigrant society for many years. More specifically, in the late

1940s and the early 1950s, political refugees from China flooded into the colony, and as a result, the Hong Kong population was increased by more than half within a few years. Hong Kong as we now know it is comprised mainly of mainland migrants and their descendants. As an immigrant society, the cultural makeup of Hong Kong does not privilege an elite culture (Luk 1995). Or to put it in another way, elitist/traditional Chinese culture is recognized only as a remote cultural authority but does not have a dominant discursive power in the everyday life of Hong Kong people. Thus the painstaking valorization of popular culture against the hegemony of high culture in some of the now classic Birmingham projects is not readily relevant in the Hong Kong context. In Hong Kong, the mass culture debate has been less intense. Although the study of popular culture as a decent academic project has still been problematic, popular culture in itself hasn't attracted the kind of contempt from the elite as in other established cultures. In fact, popular culture cut across grassroot and elite classes to become the cradle of a collective local identity in the 1970s and the 1980s (Ma 1999). Without the discipline of and the resistive pressure against high culture, subcultural formations in Hong Kong are less visible. This means a very influential subfield of cultural studies cannot be easily translated into Hong Kong. In contrast, when I attended a cultural studies conference (entitled Media and Local Cultural Production) in Beijing for the first time in 1999, my impression was that cultural studies in China, as compared with cultural studies in Hong Kong, exhibits a stronger discursive struggle between elitist and popular culture. Cultural studies in China puts more stress on issues such as the cultural leadership of intellectuals, the legacy of literature and the avant-garde, and the archaeology of the notions of the "mass" and the "people." In contrast, in Hong Kong, the study of high culture and the less than influential role of intellectuals are at best marginal on the research agenda of cultural studies (see the special features on the problematic identity of Hong Kong intellectuals in *Hong Kong Cultural Studies Bulletin*, issue 6, 1996 and issue 2, 1995).

Indigenization

In Hong Kong, cultural studies has emerged in academic discourses and become very visible since the 1990s. However, it has merged with and been reinforced by the historical formation of the study of indigenous Hong Kong culture which has an earlier history than cultural studies. For many years, indigenous Hong Kong culture had been narrated from the point of view of the political and cultural centers of imperial China and, later, Britain. These early narratives of Hong Kong described Hong Kong as a cultural desert and as a barren rock (Wong et al. 1997). Seen as an unworthy academic subject, Hong Kong Studies did not have a visible presence in local colleges and universities. One notable exception was the anthropological tradition of studying the rural areas of Hong Kong (e.g. Ward

261

1983; Hayes 1983). The anthropological conception of culture as the everyday enabled early anthropologists to avoid the dominant discourse of Hong Kong as a place without (elitist) culture.

In the 1960s, the local generation, which began to experience a strong sense of collectivity, could not find a narrative space to situate their indigenous experiences. This started to change with the first generation of local academics who studied overseas and came back to Hong Kong in the late 1960s and the 1970s. Some of them started to develop research that focused more on local issues. Motivated by a strong identification with local culture, they struggled to find discursive spaces within and beyond academic institutions. Some of the pioneers in Hong Kong Studies fought guerrilla wars in formal universities which privileged established disciplines. They did research on local histories and cultural identities under departments such as education, history, anthropology, literature, and sociology. Their endeavors were not recognized as "decent" research. Nevertheless, in the late 1970s and the 1980s, universities were not policed by strict research assessment technologies, and these pioneers were pretty much left alone to do their own work (see Sinn 1995; Cheung & Tam 1999).

Thus in the 1970s and 1980s, Hong Kong Studies negotiated its path along various institutional inroads. But since the early 1990s, a small fraction of Hong Kong Studies has taken a new turn by merging with cultural studies. One moment of crystallization was a conference organized by Hong Kong University in 1991. The conference was entitled "Hong Kong Culture and Society," and was organized by a team headed by Elizabeth Sinn from the History Department. This was a very localized (conducted in Cantonese) conference, bringing together scholars from very diverse disciplines as well as professionals from the cultural industries. The conference transgressed academic boundaries and put Hong Kong culture on the research agenda. Participants recalled that the conference had indeed fostered a sense of a community of scholars doing Hong Kong Studies. Although not all papers presented at this conference could be generalized under the umbrella of cultural studies, some use the arguments and language of cultural studies. The introductory papers coined phraseology like "New Directions in Cultural Studies" (Ng 1995) and "Prolegomena on Cultural Studies in Hong Kong" (Chan 1995), calling attention to everyday cultural practices and the complicated articulation of local identities. The conference motivated further engagements, some of which have been developing along the lines of sociohistorical analyses, while others have incorporated cultural studies as a tool of teaching and research. Since the early 1990s, courses introducing cultural studies have been proposed and taught. Some have gathered weight to become cultural studies departments, which I will discuss in the next section.

As I pointed out earlier, in Hong Kong, British cultural studies is not readily applicable to resisting the power of the nation and the elite. However, the intellectual sentiment of cultural studies in valorizing resistance has been assimilated to the particular academic formation of Hong Kong Studies. This is not to say that cultural studies in Hong Kong is only the study of Hong Kong culture, and that Hong Kong Studies is only conducted in the language of cultural studies. There are many scholars doing Hong Kong Studies without any affiliation with cultural studies. But what is interesting is that, at a certain discursive moment, a number of people who have been studying local culture adopt and appropriate the language of cultural studies to articulate and empower their own work. In fact, a few local scholars tend to liberally and interchangeably use the labels "Hong Kong Cultural Studies," "Cultural Studies," and "Hong Kong Studies." Here, cultural studies is not deployed to deconstruct elitist culture or resist state power, but is adopted to open up the possibility of discussing and describing the once voiceless local culture. Furthermore, various theories of cultural studies have been utilized to make sense of the multifaceted identity politics of the political transition of the 1990s. During this transition period, the imagination of the end of Hong Kong unleashed a series of nostalgic desires and redemptive impulses to save local culture. Key concepts of cultural studies such as cultural imagination, overdetermination, articulation, hegemony, and resistance have triggered the chain reaction of inventing new words and expressions to capture the moment of disappearance and rearticulations of Hong Kong culture before and after 1997 (see Leung 1995; Chan et al. 1994a; Erni, forthcoming). Some local cultural studies scholars even try to rethink the marginalization of Hong Kong culture from the opposite end – they write about the exploitative capitalistic culture of Hong Kong which is fueled by a "northbound imaginary" reproducing itself in cities in mainland China (Law et al. 1997). These academic exercises and self-therapeutic writings have produced provocative papers, which have landed in international conferences and journals and, in return, reinforced further research on the local culture of Hong Kong.

Institutionalization

Since the late 1990s, cultural studies has been formally incorporated into academic institutions as departments offering undergraduate and postgraduate degrees. The process of institutionalization demonstrates an interesting pattern of complicated struggles with mixed imperatives. There are three major institutional initiatives to build cultural studies programs in local universities, and they are directly or indirectly related to English departments. The first, forerunning initiative was within the English Department at the University of Hong Kong. At first, new courses on local culture and cultural studies met with strong resistance on the ground that Hong Kong University, as the best in the colony, should maintain a high standard of English, especially in the flagship English Department. Research projects, such as those on Hong Kong popular novels and films, were seen as marginal at best and illegitimate at worst. Yet courses and postgraduate research projects on Hong Kong culture continued to be welcomed by students and finally gathered weight to spin off, in 1989, the new Comparative Literature Department, which is more liberal in redefining the boundaries of literature. The initial proposal of naming this new department a cultural studies department was rejected. Under the name of Comparative Literature, it has been offering cultural studies and literature courses since the early 1990s.

The birth of the Modern Languages and Inter-Cultural Studies Department at the Chinese University of Hong Kong followed a similar pattern. In the early 1990s, a very visible cultural studies project was initiated by a cross-disciplinary team with core members coming from the English Department at the Chinese University. The cultural studies project promoted interdisciplinary collaboration and published the bilingual *Hong Kong Cultural Studies Bulletin*. Selected papers from the bulletin were later published in a series of anthologies by Oxford University Press (e.g. Chan 1997a, 1997b; Law 1997). This was the first collaboration which officially bore the name cultural studies and was funded by a competitive institutional grant offered by the University Grants Committee. Yet work related to this big project was not recognized by the English Department. Conflicts intensified as research students and assistants started to develop more research on local culture. Since most of these studies analyzed cultural texts which were in written Chinese or spoken Cantonese, their legitimacy within the English Department was challenged. The disputes spilled over into a war of words within and outside the department, in the form of protest letters, billboard statements, and a proposal for a new department. Finally, a new department, the Department of Modern Languages and Inter-Cultural Studies, was set up to offer both postgraduate and undergraduate degrees in cultural studies.

A couple of interrelated imperatives motivated the split of cultural studies away from English departments in both universities. It was partly motivated by the colonial imperative to maintain the purity of the English language, but this argument was conflated with the administrative mandate of keeping up the competitive edge of Hong Kong as an English-speaking international city. Besides, the canon of exemplary English literature could not accommodate local culture as a legitimate academic subject. Disciplinary differentiation has become inevitable. However, in the case of the Chinese University, the establishment of the new cultural studies department was not just a heroic story of rebellion. In fact, its birth was partly a result of administrative calculation. The department now comprises different groups of people – members of the former European language sections and dissidents from the English department, all now merged and housed under one new department to streamline administrative resources.

The third initiative has resulted in the launch of the first full-blown cultural studies program in the territory. It is an outgrowth of the School of General Education at Lingnan College. This former college has recently been upgraded to a university and the new administration has positioned it as a liberal arts institute. Compatible with this new institutional positioning, cultural studies can serve as a niche for competing against established universities. Thus a new cultural studies department has evolved not as a threat to traditional disciplines but as an edge on the unique identity of the young institution. In contrast with those evolving from English departments, this department originated from General Education, which shares the same educational mandates of enlightenment and empowerment. The department now has faculty members from anthropology, sociology, media studies, comparative literature, and philosophy. Stephen Chan, one of the major architects of the department, was the group leader of the pioneering cultural studies project at the Chinese University of Hong Kong. He left the English Department there to join Lingnan's cultural studies program. In the initial stages, the administration might not thoroughly know the what, how, and why of cultural studies, but the simple fact is that it draws a large number of applicants and presents an alternative to classical studies. The setting up of the department is very much in line with the institutional needs of Lingnan University.

The recent institutionalization of cultural studies marks the partial differentiation between cultural studies and Hong Kong Studies. As noted in the previous section, the major form of expression of cultural studies in Hong Kong has been the convergence of cultural studies with Hong Kong Studies. Cultural studies has been appropriated as one of the many tools to legitimize indigenous culture. Yet the sense of urgency triggered by the sovereignty change in 1997 has diminished in recent years. Furthermore, the process of developing cultural studies into a program offering degrees suggests the unavoidable differentiation between a body of theoretical knowledge (cultural studies) and a topic of inquiry (Hong Kong Studies). There were initially two proposals for the cultural studies program at Lingnan University. One was smaller in scale and was a localized program on Hong Kong culture; the other was bigger and more integrative, treating cultural studies as a body of theories and practices and Hong Kong Studies as one of the many topics of cultural analysis. The second option has been adopted. Now the cultural studies program at Lingnan integrates cultural studies with traditional courses in sociology, history, and literature as well as courses in Hong Kong society and culture. On the other hand, the cultural studies department at the Chinese University is comprised of linguistics and European studies. The department tries to build a unique identity by naming itself "Inter-Cultural Studies" to mark the particular in-betweenness of the Hong Kong context. Inter-Cultural Studies, as explained by Kin-yuen Wong, the department chair, stresses the strength of navigating in between different cultures but not privileging any single dominant cultural frame of reference. These institutional setups redirect the attention of some local scholars into the building of courses and curriculums of cultural studies. In the coming years, cultural studies will continue to be a project which valorizes local culture, but there will be a new thrust to transform cultural studies into an education project for local university students.

Camouflage

One interesting observation that has emerged from the interviews is the metamorphism of cultural studies within institutional spaces. Besides those cultural studies programs mentioned above, there are people doing and teaching cultural studies in various departments which do not bear the name of cultural studies. In some departments of local universities, labels such as cultural studies, womens studies, postcolonial studies are still considered to be troublesome by the administration. However, young scholars can smuggle in cultural studies theories under different course titles. They can do cultural studies under the camouflage of traditional courses, general education electives, and topical studies without altering the basic setup of established academic programs. In canonized disciplines such as English and Chinese languages, the tactic of doing cultural studies without naming it provides a space for subversive maneuvering.

Cultural studies can be incorporated into the social sciences relatively more easily than into the humanities. A little bit of cultural studies is welcomed by the social science departments because it attracts students and can be translated into resources. Of course there are subtle resistances. Sometimes cultural studies is seen as soft "discursive" theory, which is fashionable but snoopy and speculative. Most receptive to cultural studies are general education units, which embrace cultural studies as one of the tools of empowerment. As noted, the first full-blown cultural studies program was initiated by the School of General Education at Lingnan College (now university). In 1999 the General Education Centre at the Hong Kong Polytechnic University started an annual conference on Hong Kong Culture. Cultural studies is staged as a competitive edge. Generally speaking, my informants can easily propose and teach cultural studies as general education courses.

Except for those who are now formally committed to cultural studies within institutional settings, many of my informants were ambivalent towards cultural studies. They did not mind doing cultural studies "part-time" and wearing that hat for a while, as long as the relevant theories and practices were useful in their own research and teaching. But they are more comfortable navigating in between disciplinary and institutional spaces, using cultural studies as theoretical leverage for their own pursuits. They take cultural studies as an enabler for them to give a voice to Hong Kong's marginal yet energetic local identity, to explore the academically illegitimate subject of popular culture, to take pleasure in transgressing disciplines, and to fuel their humanistic desire for social and cultural intervention. They are attracted to cultural studies because of its in-betweenness and ambiguity. However, their alliance with cultural studies is contingent and situational and some maintain a fairly critical distance. A few say they don't understand some esoteric forms of cultural studies but have participated in relevant collaborative projects anyway; others say they are happy with the cultural studies tag but do not want to commit to it because to them, cultural studies, as an academic fashion, may not last long. They are more concerned with their own research interests than committing to just one trend of thought. These tendencies of refusing to be defined are in fact compatible with cultural studies' basic tenets of flexible and reflexive incorporation of whatever is useful in the war of positions to make minute advances on various cultural fronts.

Transgression

It is difficult to disentangle biography and academic formation or the personal inclination of intellectuals and the discursive impact of cultural studies in the academic community of Hong Kong. Despite some very obvious differences, the dozen informants I interviewed exhibit a converging academic temperament. Most of them had impulses to transgress academic boundaries, negate the orthodox, redefine the canon, and reset the academic agenda. At the same time, they refrained from describing and prescribing a definition for cultural studies, especially when they referred to the kind of cultural studies they were doing.

A few of my informants were quite rebellious against the intelligentsia established in Hong Kong in their college years. The extreme form can be an outright dismissal of local university education. Some say that their formal training in Hong Kong universities was dull and irrelevant. One of them critically redefines his undergraduate training in philosophy by the theoretical language of cultural studies. He says that the well-respected neo-Confucianists at the Chinese University were actually intellectuals who migrated from the political center of China in the north to the peripheral colony in the south. From within the marginality of Hong Kong, they imagined, essentialized, idealized, and regenerated Chinese Culture under the name of neo-Confucianism. Of course, not many of my informants were as critical. Some were quite moderate in commenting on their academic training in Hong Kong. They came into contact with Western cultural theories by reading books outside the regular curriculum. Many of them were student activists. Their involvement in student publications, social movements, and public forums prompted them to borrow and apply theories old and new from various local and Western sources. Since there has been no formal cultural studies program in Hong Kong and abroad until very recently, cultural studies has been appropriated in very diverse ways, mostly in a contingent and do-it-yourself fashion.

Most of my informants also have an intellectual history of transgressing the boundaries of their own discipline. As I mentioned in the first section, they reset the research agenda by putting Hong Kong cultural studies into the map of colonial education. Most of them expressed the desire to borrow concepts and methods from other disciplines. They think that relying on just one discipline is too restrictive in the analysis and critique of cultural phenomena which are oftentimes multifaceted and interdisciplinary in nature. One informant, trained in comparative literature, started to do ethnography some ten years ago. She thought that textually based research was "dead." She has appropriated sociological and anthropological methods in her recent research and sees textual research as too speculative. Another informant, also from comparative literature, thought that limiting oneself to the study of classical texts is a dead end for the discipline since it cannot take care of the ongoing popular cultural texts of the times. People from media studies, including myself, are not satisfied with the professionalization of media studies which reduces the social aspects of communication issues into a mere mediacentric problematic. People in sociology are self-critical of the grand narrative of social theory; instead, they use cultural studies as a tool to explore the everydayness of sociocultural routines. Those committed to early critical theories find cultural studies fascinating because it enables them to deviate from the fixation on macropolitical economy and to engage in critique of elitist as well as consumer culture. Besides transgressing their own disciplinary boundaries, my informants tended to want to transgress the boundaries of academic institutions and engage culture in public forums. At different points of time in their career, they participated in cultural criticism, social networking, and all sorts of educational and civic projects.

Yet these initiatives should not be romanticized. As one of my informants aptly pointed out, the interdisciplinarity of cultural studies in Hong Kong is more personal than collective. It is a rather personal endeavor of traveling and temporarily dwelling in different theoretical terrains. Still a lone researcher, the interdisciplinary culturalist appropriates different approaches in different academic ecologies. Interdisciplinarity seems to be more of an individual reflexive act than a commitment to developing interdisciplinary networks. What really surprised me in those interviews was how little communication and interaction there was among peers. Some told me that there is virtually no academic exchange between colleagues. One talked about the frustration of organizing a big and "successful" cross-disciplinary conference but ending up without substantial exchanges between participants from relevant fields. Transgressing boundaries involves highly selective appropriation of a narrow range of exotic theories, leaving out the difficult and unfamiliar core, and then returning to the comfortable academic habitat of one's own discipline. The situation would change, as cultural studies departments are now formally appointing faculty members from diverse disciplines under the same roof. But it is always good to be reminded that academic transgression is more often an imagined ideal. This is not to negate interdisciplinary initiatives such as the cultural studies conferences and joint projects organized by various parties in Hong Kong. However, these joint ventures so far have mostly been effective in providing a space for cross-disciplinary awareness and fostering a sense of the collective identity of an imagined interdisciplinary community of cultural studies scholars.

Decontextualization

Most people doing cultural studies have a strong commitment to locality. Cultural studies is an academic commitment in the broadest sense. It involves funding, publication, circulation of ideas, and various sorts of cultural engagement. Some cultural studies people are more concerned with theoretical exploration; others are driven by the desire for social and cultural intervention. The imperatives of social intervention on the one hand and academic endeavors on the other can be mutually reinforcing. But in the particular context of Hong Kong, the two are sometimes contradictory and mutually negating. In recent years, academic activities in local universities have been monitored by very restrictive measures. There has been stronger pressure for academics to publish in English and in international journals rather than local and regional journals. Publishing in Chinese, in some cases, can be academically suicidal. This control of academic production has produced a very strange cultural studies contour in Hong Kong.

As an international city and a former British colony, English is taught in schools and used in the business sector. However, most people in Hong Kong speak Cantonese and Mandarin Chinese in their everyday life. The most vibrant forms of popular culture are mostly in Cantonese. English of course is an integral part of Hong Kong culture and is hybridized with the local dialect. Hong Kong people are quite famous for incorporating broken English expressions into their Cantonese. Thus we have a local culture which is embodied and expressed by the hybridized languages of Cantonese, Mandarin, and English. But if we map out the discursive power of these languages, Cantonese is most powerful in the everyday, and English, and increasingly Mandarin, are more powerful in the political and economic sectors. English has more cultural capital in the elitist sense, while Cantonese is more dynamic in the everyday.

Doing cultural studies, doing it in English, and writing for competitive international journals mean that one has to translate Hong Kong's hybrid culture into English and then generalize and exoticize it for the international academic community. This transnationalizing is neither necessarily good nor bad. Theorizing and generalizing cultural studies can add to the diversity of cultural analyses. These exercises encourage intercultural sensitivity by exoticizing the domestic and domesticating Western theories to explain local particularities (e.g. Abbas 1997). However, in the case of Hong Kong, the international pull is far greater than the commitment to locality. The disciplinary techniques of forced retirement, naming of inactive researchers, and denial of tenure are rewarding high theorization and punishing local commitment.

Thus there is a differential of visibility of different brands of Hong Kong cultural studies in the international and local academic communities. Those who are committed to the locality and conduct their work in Chinese are less visible, while those fluent in the dominant theoretical (and English) language are more visible on the international scene. Outsiders may not know much about the work

269

of activists in Hong Kong who write cultural criticism in newspapers, display exhibits, organize study groups, record and analyze the life histories of marginal communities, publish oral histories of old women and migrants, and map out the city space of old districts (e.g. Kowk 1999; New Women 1998; Choi 1998; Leung 1996; Man 1997). This work is committed to the local culture but is quite invisible and often not recognized as rigorous academic activities by the university administration.

Here I am not playing the card of identity politics by drawing lines between insiders and outsider. I simply want to point out a particular form of discursive contour quite different from, say, the early Birmingham trajectories, of which the research outputs were targeted primarily to engage and intervene in local culture, but of course had theoretical relevancy to international academic communities at large. In Hong Kong, the academic energies of cultural studies have been diverted to fit into the international picture. For instance, speaking from my personal experience, I channel my energy into writing, quite often with much difficulty, in English, and getting my works published in international journals. On the other hand, I am reluctant to accept invitations to write in Chinese. My habit is to reserve my best hours to write in English, and then write in Chinese when I am exhausted. And I usually reserve the "left overs" of my research for Chinese outlets. If cultural studies is a project which gives a voice to the voiceless, then doing cultural studies in Hong Kong is giving a very strange voice to Hong Kong indeed. The primary audiences of academic output are international journal reviewers and not local scholars and laymen.

My rather strange cultural studies engagement can be put into sharper focus when compared with the practice of a Beijing cultural studies group. I attended a Beijing cultural studies conference for the first time in 1999. I was very impressed by the work of the Beijing cultural studies group led by Dai Jinhua, who is well informed in Western theories but does her research, writing, and teaching in Chinese. She creatively invents and revises cultural studies concepts and theories and domesticates them into the Chinese language (Dai 1999; Wang et al. 2000). Her works are very influential in creating new discursive spaces in the specific locality of Beijing. At the same time, she has been engaging in academic exchanges with international academic networks outside China. In contrast, institutional pressure causes cultural studies in Hong Kong to lopsidedly privilege the international and undermine the local. The power of cultural studies to engage the local is hampered by the distorted dynamic of this form of academic decontextualization.

Postscript

I was asked to write a chapter on cultural studies in Asia. Soon I found that the task was beyond by ability. Asian countries have wildly different social, political, and cultural formations, and it is quite impossible to generalize the cultural studies of the criss-crossing cultures in Asia. In doing so, much would have to be generalized and flattened. Thus I have limited myself to a small fragment of Asian cultural studies as illustrated in the case of Hong Kong. However, the configuration of a fragment may be relevant to the imagination of the whole.

In the UK and the United States, the political economies of culture are relatively stable when compared with the Asian countries, where cultural formations are more dynamic and unstable. Cultural studies in the transitional societies of Asia may merge with the particular cultural formation in very specific ways in particular historical moments. In Hong Kong, the rise of local consciousness has been a primary cultural formation in the 1970s and the 1980s, and the study of this particular formation was partly triggered by, in Abbas's terms (1997), the cultural politics of disappearance in the runup to 1997. Thus cultural studies in Hong Kong have been articulated with this concern for local identity in prominence. But localized issues such as the institutionalization of cultural studies in universities, the potentialities of and barriers to interdisciplinarity, the tension between local commitment and international networking, and the mediation of cultural studies in the dominant international language of English, are not confined to the specific case of Hong Kong, and are of different degrees of relevance to cultural studies in other Asian countries.

I will end this chapter with a poem written by a cultural studies scholar in Hong Kong. For twenty some years, Ping-kwan Leung, a poet, novelist, columnist, and professor, has been transgressing disciplinary and institutional boundaries to talk about the story of Hong Kong through his creative and academic writing. In an exhibition in 1995, he placed his poems besides the fragments of a Northern Song Dynasty fish-shaped pot. This supposedly Northern pot is in fact dressed in the artistic style of the South. By creating this discursive space, he dramatically narrates a story of how the pottery of the marginalized South has been incorporated to become the art of the homogenizing North, how Hong Kong's locality can be erased by the Chinese totality, and how the rereading of a tiny fragment can contribute to the understanding of the whole.

"Fragments of a Northern Song Dynasty Fish-shaped Pot"

Were they excavated from Chaozhou mountain kilns in the south
Or from Ling Ding Isle off Tuen Mun [Hong Kong]
Salvaged?

A single fragment of fish scales leads us to imagine
Fins, jaw, and the mouth
The pot's maw wide open?

Did they set sail in those days from a southern harbor,
Along with incense, rhino horns, and elephants tusks,
To the country of the lions?

Did they rest beside a half chrysanthemum, or a finger of Buddha
Keeping company with the big ears of a cocker Spaniel
Other bits and pieces of history?

Those empowered to write history, with a stroke of the pen, incorporated
The southern kilns into those of the north, producing
A complete history

The fragments say: Please carefully study our grain
Don't read us into
Your history

Did the missing parts travel across the oceans, to be found
Perhaps on the Java seabed, or in the Philippines –
In the museum of art and artifacts?

With no respect for different developments, how can one trace the past?
With no understanding of the absent, how can one imagine
A whole fish?

Ping Kwan Leung, 1995 (trans. Martha Cheung)

Notes

I would like to thank the local scholars who were so generous in giving me their time for long interviews.

References

Abbas, A. (1997). *Hong Kong: Culture and the Politics of Disappearance*. Minneapolis: University of Minnesota Press.

Chan, H. M. (1995). "Popular Culture and Political Society: Prolegomena on Cultural Studies in Hong Kong." In E. Sinn (ed.), *Culture and Society in Hong Kong*. Hong Kong: Centre for Asian Studies.

Chan, S. C. K. (ed.) (1997a). *Cultural Imaginary and Ideology: Contemporary Hong Kong Culture and Politics Review*. Hong Kong: Oxford University Press (in Chinese).

Chan, S. C. K. (ed.) (1997b). *The Practice of Affect: Studies in Hong Kong Popular Song Lyrics*. Hong Kong: Oxford University Press (in Chinese).

Chan, S. C. K. et al. (eds.) (1994a). "Special Topic: Cultural Studies in Hong Kong." *Hong Kong Cultural Studies Bulletin*, 1: 4–12.

Chan, S. C. K. et al. (eds.) (1994b). "An Annotated Bibliography of Studies in Hong Kong Popular Culture in the Past Twenty Years (1974–94)." *Hong Kong Cultural Studies Bulletin*, 1: 13–19.

Cheung, S. C. H. and M. S. M. Tam (eds.) (1999). *Culture and Society of Hong Kong: A Bibliography*. Hong Kong: Chinese University of Hong Kong.

Chiu, F. Y. L. (1997). "Politics and the Body Social in Colonial Hong Kong." In T. Barlow (ed.), *Formations of Colonial Modernity in East Asia*. Durham and London: Duke University Press.

Choi, P. K. (ed.) (1998). *6:30 pm Every Evening – Female Workers in Evening Schools of the 1970s*. Hong Kong: Step Forward Press (in Chinese).

Dai, J. (1999). *You zai jingzhong* (still in the mirror). Beijing: Knowledge Press (in Chinese).

Erni, J. (ed.) (forthcoming). *Cultural Studies*, Special issue on Hong Kong.

Hayes, J. (1983). *The Rural Communities of Hong Kong: Studies and Themes*. Hong Kong: Oxford University Press.

Kowk, J. Y. C. (1999). *Ageing in the Community: Research on the Designing of Everyday Life Environment for the Elderly*. Hong Kong: School of Design, Polytechnic University of Hong Kong.

Ip, I. C. and O. W. Lam (eds.) (1999). *Street Corners* 1 (in Chinese), Special issue: poor people are lazy people?

Law, W. S. (ed.) (1997). *Whose City: Civic Culture and Political Discourse in Post-war Hong Kong*. Hong Kong: Oxford University Press (in Chinese).

Law, W. S. (1998). "Managerializing Colonialism." In K. H. Chen (ed.), *Trajectories: Inter-Asia Cultural Studies*. New York & London: Routledge.

Law, W. S. et al. (1997). "Northbound Imagery: Repositioning Hong Kong Postcolonial Discourse." In S. C. K. Chan (ed.), *Cultural Imaginary and Ideology: Contemporary Hong Kong Culture and Politics Review*. Hong Kong: Oxford University Press (in Chinese).

Leung, B. K. P. (1996). *Perspectives on Hong Kong Society*, Hong Kong: Oxford University Press.

Leung, P. K. (ed.) (1995). *Today Literary Magazine* 28 (in Chinese). Issue feature: Hong Kong Culture.

Luk, B. H. K. (1995). "Hong Kong History and Hong Kong Culture." In E. Sinn (ed.), *Culture and Society in Hong Kong*. Hong Kong: Centre of Asian Studies (in Chinese).

Leung, F. (1996). *Wenhua lache* (Cultural Chit Chat). Hong Kong: Hong Kong Humanities Press (in Chinese).

Ma, Eric Kit-wai (1998). "Re-inventing Hong Kong: Memory, Identity and Television." *International Journal of Cultural Studies* 1(3): 329–49.

Ma, Eric Kit-wai (1999). *Culture, Politics and Television in Hong Kong*. London: Routledge.

Ma, Eric Kit-wai (2000a). "Rethinking Media Studies: The Case of China." In J. Curran and M. J. Park (eds.), *Dewesternizing Media Studies*. London: Routledge.

Ma, Eric Kit-wai (2000b). "Re-nationalization & Me: My Hong Kong Story After 1997." *Inter-Asia Cultural Studies* 1(1): 173–9.

Man, S. W. (ed.) (1997). *Hong Kong Cultural Studies Bulletin* 7. Special issue: The Culture and Politics of Human Rights.

New Women Association (1998). *Laughters and Tears: Oral Histories of Old Ladies*. Hong Kong: New Women Association (in Chinese).

Ng, C. H. (1995). "New Directions in Cultural Studies." In E. Sinn (ed.), *Culture and Society in Hong Kong*. Hong Kong: Centre for Asian Studies.

Sinn, E. (ed.) (1995) *Culture and Society in Hong Kong*. Hong Kong: Centre for Asian Studies.

Tan, S. (1999). "Working Female Workers and their Personal Letters." Paper presented at the conference, Media and Local Cultural Production, Beijing, Dec. 13–15 (in Chinese).

Wang, J. (1998). "Public Culture and Popular Culture: Metropolitan China at the Turn of the New Century." Paper presented at the conference, Modern and Contemporary Chinese Popular Culture, Duke University, May 8–9.

Wang, J. (1999). "The State Question in Chinese Popular Cultural Studies." Paper presented at the conference, Media and Local Cultural Production, Beijing, Dec. 13–15.

Wang, J. et al. (eds.) (2000). *Cinema and Desire: Feminist Marxism and Cultural Politics in the Work of Dai Jinhua*. London & New York: Verso.

Ward, B. (1983). *Through Other Eyes: Essays in Understanding "Conscious models."* Hong Kong: Chinese University Press.

Wong, W. C. et al. (eds.) (1997). *Hong Kong Un-imagined: History, Culture and Future*. Taipei, Taiwan: Rye Field Publishing Company (in Chinese).

Chapter 16

Decentering the Centre: Cultural Studies in Britain and its Legacy

Ben Carrington

> Cultural studies has multiple discourses; it has a number of different histories. It is a whole set of formations; it has its own different conjunctures and moments in the past. It included many different kinds of work. I want to insist on that! It always was a set of unstable formations. It was "centred" only in quotation marks . . .
>
> Stuart Hall, "Cultural Studies and its Theoretical Legacies"

Introduction

Recently I wandered into the new multi-storey Borders bookstore and café in Brighton, England, where I live, and asked the sales assistant where I could find the sociology section. "Sociology?," she replied, apparently bemused by my inquiry into such an antiquated subject-matter, "would that be under Cultural Studies?" I checked for signs of postmodern irony in her voice but none could be found; "Sociology . . . *under* Cultural Studies."

Her comments made me reflect on the contemporary state of both sociology and cultural studies within Britain and their somewhat tempestuous relationship. It struck me that cultural studies *appears* to have achieved a dominant, I'm tempted to say hegemonic, position compared to its cognate sibling disciplines. Indeed even to think of cultural studies itself as a discrete discipline with its own methodologies, modes of address, forms of enquiry, boundaries, and history, is something that is often taken for granted, despite the inherently contradictory nature of such a claim. That is, cultural studies can more accurately be read as an explicitly *trans*disciplinary project that owes less to academic notions of bounded, specialized knowledge production, than it does to forms of engaged political critique.

There are as many students studying cultural studies and related disciplines – media studies and communication, film studies, sport and leisure studies, etc. – in Britain as there are students taking courses in "straight" sociology. Indeed there are now a number of joint cultural studies and sociology courses, seemingly a reaction on the part of some sociology departments to stay relevant to a cohort of students keen to learn more from Roland Barthes and Jean Baudrillard than from Robert Merton and Karl Mannheim. Put another way, cultural studies has become the cool and sexy subject, compared to its apparently dour and anachron-istic sociological bedfellow. The contemporary institutionalization of cultural studies, then, requires some critical reflection.

Georg Simmel once noted the impossibility of total knowledge for the modern subject in "being surrounded by an innumerable number of cultural elements which are neither meaningless to him [*sic*] nor, in the final analysis, meaningful. In their mass, they depress him, since he is not capable of assimilating them all, nor can he simply reject them, since after all, they do belong *potentially* within the sphere of his cultural development" (1968: 44). Standing in front of any large bookstore's cultural studies section, it is indeed easy to identify with Simmel's sense of being overwhelmed. So much work is now being produced that falls broadly under the category of "cultural studies" that it is difficult to highlight contemporary trends, or to note what is genuinely new or interesting amongst the waves of words produced.

In this context I will not attempt to map all the contours of cultural studies in Britain, or even suggest that the issues I highlight are the only ones in need of address. Instead I will point towards some key issues that need to be more fully considered than they have been hitherto in thinking about what cultural studies has to offer contemporary analyses of society. In particular I will question the unilinear accounts of the development of cultural studies in Britain that privilege a disengaged academic history and raise some concerns about its current university-institutionalization. Linked to the questioning of cultural studies' official history I problematize the lack of critical reflexivity concerning the embodiment of nationalist ideologies within cultural studies. Finally I look at some examples of contemporary cultural studies work, and ask whether or not cultural studies has really displaced sociology in the way some are prone to suggest, and as the sales assistant, implicitly at least, inferred.

From Hoggart to Hall . . .

There is now something approaching an official history of the development of cultural studies in Britain which has become established as *the* narrative of cultural studies. It is familiar to any teacher who has read student summaries of it and it normally runs something like the following:

Cultural studies started when Richard Hoggart wrote *The Uses of Literacy* in the late 1950s, and Raymond Williams wrote *Culture and Society, 1780–1950* and *The Long Revolution*. (Sometimes mention is also made of E. P. Thompson's *The Making of the English Working Class*, but not always, as it is rather long and few contemporary students seem to have the time or patience to actually read it in its entirety.) Then depending on how much the student has researched they will mention Hoggart's appearance in court in 1960 for Penguin Books (defending the obscenity case against D. H. Lawrence's *Lady Chatterley's Lover*). The story continues that after winning the case Penguin donated some money to Hoggart who then founded a centre at Birmingham University to study culture, which was then "taken over" by Stuart Hall (at which point Hoggart normally exits the story), who became the centre's Director, and who, along with some bright young students, read a lot of French social theory and Gramsci. The Birmingham Centre for Contemporary Cultural Studies (CCCS) thus, during the 1970s and early 1980s, allowed for neo-Marxist-inspired critiques of everyday life that sought to understand how ideology worked in and through popular culture, without privileging a crude Marxist reductionism, and how forms of cultural resistance might emerge – and the rest, as the essays invariably say, is history.

I do not wish to deny that something like the above did indeed happen – clearly certain individuals were important at specific moments and certain institutions did become the focus for particular sorts of intellectual activity. Indeed there are useful introductions to the field of cultural studies, particularly in Britain, that tell this story with some care (see Storey 1996; Turner 1996; Mulhern 2000). Rather than add yet another version to this now well-rehearsed fable I want instead to raise a few concerns about some of the omissions from this narrative.

One of the problems with such accounts is that they tend to highlight the publication of academic *texts* as "producing" cultural studies as an academic discipline taught within universities, rather than seeing such texts themselves as being the outcome of a wider sociopolitical process of education from the 1930s and 1940s aimed at social transformation, situated within adult and workers' education colleges. This is an important distinction, lost on many students, and indeed lecturers, when trying to understand the wider social formation of cultural studies and its purpose. Thus, although many would endorse Hall's view that trying to find *the* origins of cultural studies is "tempting but illusory," and that in "intellectual matters absolute beginnings are exceedingly rare. We find, instead, continuities and breaks" (Hall 1980: 16), most histories of cultural studies still date its start, more often than not, to sometime around 1957.

For many of the predominantly young, white, middle-class university students (for despite Britain's "expansion" of higher education the chances of working-class students reaching university have not increased for 30 years) cultural studies would appear to be little more than a method for deconstructing cultural "texts" using French poststructuralist theory. However, 60 years ago those engaged in trying to understand the political and ideological significance of culture, and in particular popular culture, within society were involved in a different project. For them "cultural studies," if they referred to it at all in that way, was initially concerned with the education of adult workers. It was the hope that a genuinely socialist democratic society could be created that led many tutors to see workers' education and the analysis of everyday life as a form of political struggle. Though there were tensions between those who wanted to promote an explicitly socialist, class-bound, form of teaching aimed at *workers'* education, as opposed to a more liberal and generic *adult* education for all, the key aim was a form of pedagogical praxis rooted in the day-to-day lived experiences of people for whom formal education had not provided. Though this utopian vision was never entirely fulfilled it did provide the context from which cultural studies could emerge. As Tom Steele succinctly puts it, "from 'the embers of the independent workers' education movement arose the phoenix of cultural studies" (1997: 9).

The key point to remember about Hoggart, Williams, and Thompson is not so much the books they produced at a particular moment but that they were all adult educators at the margins of, or outside, the formal higher education sector, engaged in this political process. Stuart Hall too was an extramural teacher for a while, and it is not a coincidence that he spent much of his professional life at the Open University for mature students, a place where he could teach and communicate with students who had not come from privileged backgrounds, thus continuing the ethos of cultural studies' educational praxis (see "The Formation of a Diasporic Intellectual" in Morley & Chen 1996). It is important to restate the fact that the formation of cultural studies was, first and foremost, a political project aimed at popular education for working-class adults (Steele 1997: 15). There was always a tension then with the provision of such education becoming incorporated – both ideologically and institutionally – within "bourgeois" university departments, which, for the most part, is what did happen. This shift from the autonomous spaces for adult and workers' education and political praxis, to the disciplinary logic of university-based teaching has contributed to narrowing our understandings about the origins of cultural studies and what it is, and could be, today. As Williams himself emphatically noted:

> it can hardly be stressed too strongly that Cultural Studies in the sense we now understand it . . . occurred in adult education: in the WEA, in the extramural Extension classes. I've sometimes read accounts of the development of Cultural Studies which characteristically date its various developments from *texts*. We all know the accounts which line up and date *The Uses of Literacy, The Making of the English Working Class, Culture and Society*, and so on. But, as a matter of fact, already in the late forties . . . even in the thirties, Cultural Studies was extremely active in adult education. It only got into print and gained some kind of general intellectual recognition with these later books. I often feel sad about the many people who were active in that field at that time who didn't publish, but who did as much as any of us did to establish this work. (Williams 1989: 154)

I do not claim this to be a new or original insight. Others have made similar points before in different contexts (for example see Dunn 1986; Laing 1986; Davies 1995; and Dworkin 1997). It is offered instead as a reminder of an aspect of cultural studies' formation that is in danger of becoming exorcised from the collective memory, with problematic results in how we are to conceive of cultural studies' contemporary relevance. When a commentator as astute as Chris Barker can claim that cultural studies' "main location has *always* been institutions of higher education and the bookshop" (2000: 7, emphasis added), then a degree of contestation is needed over those accounts which risk narrativizing cultural studies' historical purpose (and present location) into a depoliticized humanities discipline.

What this should alert us to is that although referring to "British cultural studies" *may* be a useful shorthand way to highlight some general concerns regarding the place and importance of understanding culture in relation to social reproduction, dominant ideologies, and power relationships, it tends to have the effect of implying a false unity and cohesion that does not exist. Certainly there is cultural studies work (broadly defined) that has taken place in Britain, a particular geographical-national location, but that is not the same thing as claiming there is *a* British cultural studies tradition, which some summaries tend to imply. The work around adult workers' education highlighted above, the more formative and orthodox analyses of society and culture found in Williams, the CCCS's interventionist work in the 1970s and 1980s and the important contributions of feminist analyses, the work of black British postcolonial theorists in the 1990s, the postmodernist influenced "new ethnographies" being produced by a number of "post-CCCS" researchers, or other centers, such as those at the Open University, University of East London, or Goldsmiths, could all claim to be engaged with cultural studies work.[1] Yet to describe them all as constituting "British cultural studies" as though their work shared core conceptual and methodological concerns regardless of time or location, stretches the signifier too far. It is to question such protonationalist imaginings that I now turn.

Questioning the "British" in British Cultural Studies

Whatever may be said in favor of the earlier intellectual engagement with popular culture by those concerned to create a better social environment for the working classes, and cultural studies' educative role in this transformation, certain issues remained marginalized. Feminist scholars in particular have clearly established how many of the studies assumed a normative male bias in their work and often failed to seriously address issues concerning the construction of gender identity, sexuality, and an adequate theorization of patriarchy (see Brundson 1996; Franklin et al. 1991; Gordon 1995; Gray 1997; McRobbie 1994, 2000; Nava 1992). Indeed, many of those who argued that the forms of knowledge taught with the workers' education associations should focus on the analysis of more serious "public" issues such as politics, international relations, and the economy, did so on the basis that the "soft" disciplines associated with the humanities would emasculate the workers' revolutionary project, revealing certain masculinist and patriarchal assumptions (cf. Steele 1997).

I want, however, to briefly discuss another "omission" by highlighting the ways in which some of the claims made defending forms of "authentic" working-class communities from the influence of American mass culture have operated from within particular racialized forms of nationhood. Many of the earlier key studies rarely addressed issues of how racial formation was central in articulating issues of British nationalism, or sufficiently problematized the fact that they often spoke to, and from, a particularly English, not British, sensibility. This theoretical neglect has allowed those who want to trace certain intellectual lineages from the early founding figures, to simply ignore "race" and racialization as core thematics within contemporary cultural studies.

The huge social, cultural, and economic changes that occurred in Britain during and immediately after the 1939–45 war provided the context within which cultural studies was to emerge. Cultural studies can thus be seen as an attempt to provide a set of answers to Britain's decline as a world "superpower" during this time (Hall 1980; 1992). The postwar period also brought with it wider sociocultural changes, especially when, due to acute labor shortages as it rebuilt its social infrastructure, Britain recruited skilled manual workers, as well as nurses and doctors, from its former colonies. The resulting migration of peoples from Asia, Africa, and particularly from the English-speaking Caribbean, was to decisively reshap the nature, content, and style of British politics (Solomos 2000). It was not so much that "race" had now been introduced into the British psyche – it had always been there shaping the customs, mores, and patterns of the metropolis – but rather that whereas Britain's colonial relationships could, at one level at least, be thought of as happening "out there," across the waves, Britain was now, at its center, confronted with the facts of its imperialist legacy – the "island race" no longer seemed so disconnected.

Despite the government's official welcoming attitude, at least until the early 1960s, Asian and black people faced a violent and hostile reception on the streets of Britain. Especially so when the 1970s saw a domestic economic downturn and a wider international recession, fueled by a rapid decline in Britain's manufacturing base, and a rise in unemployment which suddenly left Britain's Asian and black populations politically exposed as "enemies within," supposedly taking the jobs of indigenous British folk. The late 1970s and early 1980s also saw a political swing away from the corporatist politics of the postwar period towards the election of Margaret Thatcher's "New Right" government, which combined a "free-market" economic approach with a more explicitly nationalistic form of politics. "Race," now coupled with immigration, became one of the key political issues encapsulating as it did anxieties over the state of the nation – both economically and culturally – and the crisis of the body politic.

If Munt is correct in suggesting that "the principle that working-class identity emerged into a new self-consciousness after the [Second World] war is pivotal to comprehending the eventual consolidation of working-class cultural studies" (2000: 2), then it was surprising that the reconfigured nature of the working class, fractured, mediated and aligned across new "race" lines, during the 1950s and since, was so poorly theorized within cultural studies until the late 1970s and early 1980s. While Britain was gripped by this sociopolitical maelstrom, cultural studies, still wedded to notions of working–class life as it was thought to have existed in the 1950s, failed to adequately respond to and understand these changes, seeing any shift from analyzing cultural formation in purely class terms as being a negation of cultural studies' purpose (cf. Owusu 2000).

Notwithstanding the earlier important work of Dick Hebdige and indeed the CCCS's (1978) *Policing the Crisis*, one of the landmark exceptions to this was the publication in 1982 of *The Empire Strikes Back*, regarded by some as one of the CCCS's most important interventions (Solomos & Back 1996: 10; Hall 1996: 270). The book sought to explain how social struggles in Britain had to be set within the context of the political and economic crises of British capitalism, and the ways in which "race" was being used to articulate and "manage" these problems. Even here however the move to open up questions of "race" and nationalism met resistance. As Hall recalls, "getting cultural studies to put on its own agenda the critical questions of race, the politics of race, the resistance to racism, the critical questions of cultural politics, was itself a profound theoretical struggle . . . it was only accomplished as the result of a long, and sometimes bitter – certainly bitterly contested – internal struggle against a resounding but unconscious silence" (1996: 270). Discussing the context for the intellectual work behind the publication of *The Empire Strikes Back* itself, Hall continues, "Paul Gilroy and the group of people who produced the book found it extremely difficult to create the necessary theoretical and political space in the Centre in which to work on the project" (ibid.).

The concern, which underpinned much of the earlier cultural studies work, to rearticulate and empower forms of working-class resistance by retrieving the importance of culture, forming cross-class allegiances and the place of intellectuals within this, came of course from certain readings of Gramsci and his concept of the "national-popular" (Forgacs 1988; 1999). It is clear that while the national-popular allowed for a space within which critiques of the operation of the state in relation to political strategies could be developed, it also meant that the nation itself was often taken as a given. Hall has identified Gilroy's intervention as marking an important moment in the development of cultural studies away from this unproblematic embrace of "the nation" as a site of political struggle:

> The national-popular has some powerful elements in it, but it also has some worrying ones too . . . it [. . .] inserts us into a curious argument where we suddenly find ourselves at the edge of socialism in one country: the idea that you could create a national-popular conception of the UK which wouldn't have anything to do with anywhere else. It's a very tricky moment. We're only saved from that by the fact that I move out of the Birmingham Centre and Paul Gilroy moves in! If you go down that path too far, thinking that the privileged object of politics must be the nation – the national-popular, rather than the popular – what a bag that puts you in. (1997a: 29).

Certain "celebratory" accounts of the uniqueness of "British cultural studies" often replicate this very problem. That is they fail to note the inter cultural and transnational intellectual flows that helped shape the theoretical development of cultural studies in Britain, as well as ignoring how the wider globalized social conditions – colonialism and imperialism in particular – allowed for the class-situated form of politics that emerged to occur in the first place, and is presumably why the figure and work of C.L.R. James receives such negligible discussion in many histories.

Paul Gilroy, himself associated with the CCCS in the early 1980s through his co-authorship of the *Empire* book, has subsequently spent much of his career precisely trying to break free from the narrowing of the conceptual gaze in this respect and has therefore had something of an ambivalent relationship to cultural studies (see Smith 1999). In this context, one of the most important cultural studies books is Gilroy's (1987) *There Ain't No Black in the Union Jack*. Its blend of social theory, grounded empirical analysis, historical sensitivity, connections to progressive community-based politics, and originality of thought should have made it a key cultural studies text. Indeed many will often cite the book in such a fashion, yet it is often difficult to see that those who claim to have read it have fully taken on board the implications of its arguments. At his Professorial lecture Gilroy explicitly described his project as being unified by his "antipathy towards nationalism in all its forms and a related concern with the responsibility of intellectuals to act ethically, justly, when faced with the challenges nationalisms represent" (1999: 184). For Gilroy questions of "race" as well as the histories of colonialism and Empire are not epiphenomenal to the development of British society. Such processes are central in understanding how Britain's economy had been constructed and its class relations mediated, and subsequently how this affected the formation of its culture more generally, and its sense of national identity. Any cultural studies project had, therefore, to remain cognizant of how "race" acted as a modality through which class and nationalism were lived. In other words, black people, as agents, needed greater recognition in the socio cultural histories of Britain, and the racialized nature of the story itself had to be recognized. Gilroy wrote *There Ain't No Black in the Union Jack* as "a corrective to the more ethnocentric dimensions" (1987: 12) of cultural studies:

> I have grown gradually more and more weary of having to deal with the effects of striving to analyse culture within neat, homogenous national units reflecting the "lived relations" involved; with the invisibility of "race" within the field and, most importantly, with the forms of nationalism endorsed by a discipline which, in spite of itself, tends towards a morbid celebration of England and Englishness from which blacks are systematically excluded. (ibid.)[2]

Graeme Turner's otherwise comprehensive account of cultural studies in Britain is a case in point. It is only in the revised second edition, published in 1996, that there is any serious discussion of popular culture's place in the articulation of "race," racism, and nationalism, and only in later editions is there any serious engagement with Gilroy's critique of the "founding fathers'" submerged ethnonationalism. If Turner presents a somewhat late acknowledgment, a more worrying example of the disavowal of "race" and its centrality to the formation of cultural studies and the conceptual debates it subsequently followed can be seen in (yet another) recent introduction to cultural studies in Britain. In it the author makes the following perfunctory remarks:

> I shall not discuss [in this book] the emergence of "post- colonial" cultural studies, or the significant recent considerations of race and "otherness" in culture. This is not because I consider these issues unimportant. It is because, for all their undoubted importance, they are not addressed to the central analytic problems of the cultural studies tradition. (Tudor 1999: 7)

Were it not for the fact that such "authoritative" accounts have the potential, and institutionally-invested power, to shape how we understand what constitutes the appropriate field of study within cultural studies – and this relates ultimately to what is taught and who gets to teach the subject – it would be tempting to ignore such misconstrued and ethnocentric positions. However Tudor, and other similar myopic accounts, would do well to read, and *understand*, Gilroy's observations when he notes:

> Looking at cultural studies from an ethnohistorical perspective requires more than just noting its association with English literature, history, and New Left politics. It necessitates constructing an account of the borrowings made by these English initiatives from wider, modern, European traditions of thinking about culture, and at every stage examining the place which these cultural perspectives provide for the images of their racialised others as objects of knowledge, power, and cultural criticism. It is imperative, though very hard, to combine thinking about these issues with consideration of the pressing need to get black cultural expressions, analyses, and histories taken seriously in academic circles rather than assigned via the idea of "race relations" to sociology and thence abandoned to the elephants' graveyard to which intractable policy issues go to wait their expiry. (1993: 5–6)

Given such a climate within cultural studies in Britain it is not surprising that it took American-based authors Houston Baker, Manthia Diawara, and Ruth Lindeborg, and an American publisher, to acknowledge the distinctive contribution of black British scholars to cultural studies, in their 1996 book *Black British Cultural Studies*. Even today the distinctive contributions – tracing issues concerning postcoloniality, diasporic identity, the cultural politics of recognition and difference, and the syncretic nature of culture – found in the work of a new generation of scholars such as Chetan Bhatt, Barnor Hesse, Jayne Ifekwunigwe, Bobby Sayyid, and Lola Young, is still marginalized, with only token acknowledgment given to the likes of Kobena Mercer, Hazel Carby, and Gilroy himself.

An indication of the failure of the earlier cultural studies intellectuals to break free from such forms of ethnic absolutist thinking, and to question the nation-bounded aspects of their intellectual work, can be seen in a discussion of multiculturalism by Richard Hoggart. Hoggart repeats these mistakes in his conflation of nation identity with racialized ethnicity, and his subsequent inability to decouple discussions of immigration from the national-popular. Hoggart, as most accounts acknowledge, is rightly credited as central to cultural studies' history, so his current demise to that of an increasingly conservative commentator is a minor intellectual tragedy. In *The Way We Live Now* Hoggart rails against those who claim Britain to be a multicultural society ("This is simply not so," 1995: 165) because Britain's ethnic minority groups do not constitute a large enough percentage of the population to merit the description. He goes on to suggest that describing Britain as multicultural gives "ammunition" (ibid.) to white racists – who presumably would then feel justified in thinking that "their" culture was being eroded. Hoggart notes that there "have been large immigrations of people from different cultures in the last twenty or thirty years. These people should be accepted fully" (ibid.).

Hoggart's position fails to account for the protean and synthetic nature of culture generally and national cultures in particular. It is of course misleading, and tautological, to refer to national cultures as "multicultural" in the sense that *all* national cultures are inherently multicultural by the very fact that they will necessarily contain various linguistic, regional, and ethnic groupings as part of their constitution. As authors from Richard Jenkins to Edward Said have noted, diversity and cultural exchange, as regards ethnicity and national identities, is the norm. Yet this was not the point Hoggart was making. In juxtaposing a mythical monocultural Britain, Hoggart inadvertently aligned himself with British right-wing politicians such as Norman Tebbit, who have argued that Britain is, and always will be (assuming immigration is restricted, or even reversed), a mono-cultural, essentially white, Christian society.

As Hoggart should have known, our understandings about nationality, cultural identity, and difference are not framed by the numerical size of particular groups, but by the ways in which cultures are imagined, narrated, and re-presented in particular settings (see Hall 1999). This often means that migrant groups will have a "disproportionate" effect in changing the national sense of identity – particularly in cultural spheres such as youth cultures and other areas of popular culture – for all citizens in society, in a way that far outweighs their numerical size. Hence why many now reject the term "ethnic minority," for it implies both a homogenous "majority" culture, as well as a discrete and disconnected "minority" culture. If ethnicity is defined in cultural terms the notion of ethnic minority in situations where the supposed minority is culturally dominant – black youth culture being a case in point – becomes somewhat misleading and oxymoronic.

Writing less than ten years earlier about Williams' problematic construction of authentic and inauthentic types of national belonging (see Williams 1983), Gilroy argued that:

Williams combines a discussion of "race" with comments on patriotism and nationalism. However, his understanding of "race" is restricted to the social and cultural tensions surrounding the arrival of "new peoples." For him, as with the right, "race" problems begin with immigration. Resentment of "unfamiliar neigh-bours" is seen as the beginning of the process which ends in ideological specifica-tions of "race" and "superiority." Williams, working his way towards a "new and substantial kind of socialism," draws precisely the same picture of the relationship between "race", national identity and citizenship as [Enoch] Powell. (1987: 49)

A decade on, Hoggart had theoretically aligned himself, in much the same way, with Tebbit, revealing a problematic neglect and misunderstanding of theoretical conjunctures around "race," nationalism, and cultural formation that cultural studies is still struggling to adequately comprehend.

Contemporary Cultural Studies

If it were possible to trace certain contemporary trends as regards cultural studies work in Britain one would be an implicit, and occasionally explicit, rejection of some of the central concepts developed by the CCCS. For example, Andy Bennett's important studies of musical cultures distance themselves from the overly deterministic class-centered accounts of subcultural theory found within the "classic" CCCS tradition. With the perceived dissolution of Britain's static class structure, Bennett, and other "post-subculturalists" (see Muggleton 2000; and also Miles 2000), focus on understanding people's consumer identifications and lifestyle choices not in terms of "class resistance," and the "authentic" subcultures these social relations produced, but via the subjective accounts through which people give meaning to and construct their own lived experiences; what Muggleton refers to as "postmodern hyperindividualism" (2000: 6).

Ethnographic studies are used as a way of challenging "top-down" concepts such as subcultures, which are viewed as tied to outdated notions of bounded and rigid, class-inflected identities which no longer resonate with the fluid, tempor-ary, and heterogeneous lifestyle patterns of (post)modern groups. Thus Bennett in particular draws as much on Maffesoli's notion of "neotribes" and the work of postmodern cultural theorists such as Steve Redhead as on the earlier work of Hebdige or Hall (see Bennett 1999a, 1999b, 1999c, 2000). As Lovatt and Purkis argue, summarizing a position many of the post-CCCS researchers would identify with to some degree, "we take the view that understanding popular culture requires theoretical flexibility – putting empathy before explanation; thus avoiding the temptation to lapse into objectifying meta-theories of culture" (1996: 249). Where counterhegemonic practices are located they more often than not focus on the body as a site of a subversive, creative, and inherently polysemic form of "political" resistance, such as in Sweetman's ethnographic studies on tattooing and body piercing "subcultures" (1999a; 1999b). Sweetman argues that contemporary culture is marked by a move from stable, collective group identities to shifting, personalized identifications: "contemporary body modification appears to serve less as a marker of group identity, and more as an expression of the self" (1999b: 71). The strength of this work undoubtedly lies in the renewed interest in carefully constructed ethnographic methodologies that allow for grounded empirical and theoretical work to remain attuned to the subjects researched. What is less clear is whether such work will be able to link to the broader, structural changes within society, within which such cultural practices have to be located, or to discussions of power and inequality within and between these more diffuse social formations, which is something, to date, that often seems missing from these new studies.

However, while it could be argued that there is a "postmodern drift" away from the certainties provided by the neo-Marxist CCCS analyses, so there are also indications of a renewed interest in the class location of many of the subjects of cultural studies analysis. In attempting to rejoin debates influenced by feminism, postcolonialism, postmodernism, and queer theory, that in some accounts have rejected a class framework, Sally Munt argues that "Cultural Studies is above all the stories/study of everyday life, and it is axiomatic to claim that everyday life is saturated with class relations. The fact that not everybody believes this doesn't make it untrue, it merely alludes to the success of entrenched beliefs in liberal pluralism" (2000: 10). This is not based on a nostalgic longing for the "good old days" of Hoggart, Williams, and Thompson, but on a genuine attempt at *rethinking* – as opposed to merely revising or an outright repudiation of – the possibilities and problematics of traditional Marxist models for cultural analysis and the deficiencies of earlier work. Indeed her own work, which has carefully excavated the contours of lesbian identity and queer theory, has always been anchored within broader discussions of nationalism and class identity (see for example Munt 1998).

There are currently other trends within cultural studies that are more problematic and worth briefly noting, though these are clearly not tied to work in Britain alone. Influenced by the popularity of certain forms of deconstruction and the "linguistic turn" more generally within social theory – normally due to poor readings/translations of Derrida – certain philosophical perspectives have gained a degree of currency in reading and interpreting cultural forms in a way that often obliterates the social context within which such practices are embedded. Put another way, there is still much textual analysis of culture that is divorced from the material conditions of its production and consumption and that fails, therefore, to develop a sufficiently integrative mode of analysis – what McRobbie has referred to as the "textual trap" (1994: 39). Being able to deconstruct the dialogic processes of signification, intertextuality, bricolage, and intersubjective interpellation within a Nike commercial is one thing; connecting this to the exploitative economic production of the shoes themselves in southeast Asia, through to their consumption in the deprived inner-cities of the West, and the meanings this produces, is quite another, and a process too often not addressed. As Hall has warned, the institutionalization of cultural studies risks turning it into an esoteric academic pursuit, where "power" and "resistance" can reside everywhere (and therefore nowhere), removed almost entirely from the everyday experiences of people (see Hall's "Cultural Studies and its Theoretical Legacy," in Morley & Chen 1996, and also Hall 1997a). It is quite clear that cultural studies needs to remain attuned to the political and economic context for the production and formation of culture in the first place, the relationship of this to the articulation of particular ideologies within texts themselves, and how "audiences" read, understand, and make sense of such cultural practices in their day-to-day lives, linking how dominant ideologies attempt, and fail, to interpellate people through culture.

Sociology versus Cultural Studies: Is Anyone Else Bored With This Debate?[3]

Speaking as President at the 1996 British Sociological Association's annual conference, Stuart Hall remarked that he found it surprising that he had been given the honor as he had never considered, and still did not consider, himself to be a sociologist.[4] No doubt many others would have agreed. Hall then outlined the starting-point for the work done at the CCCS during his time at the Center. "We went to [Talcott] Parsons," he said, "and whatever he had rejected, we read." Though used as an amusing anecdote to situate the type of engaged, reflexive, and critical intellectual work done by the Centre it also spoke, perhaps unintentionally, to a tension that has been perceived at least to have existed between sociology and cultural studies. Whereas many sociologists have privileged a form of abstract theory building and knowledge gathering over engaged sociopolitical analysis and action, and have attempted to build a positivistic form of sociology, mirrored to a greater or lesser degree, on the objectives and assumed "objectivity" of the natural sciences, cultural studies has been seen as a debased and ideologically driven political project. As one commentator has noted, sociologists tend to "renounce the moral-critical role of cultural studies, maintaining the traditional social-scientific conception of the scholar as objective and value-neutral" (Wolff 1999: 505). Hall's comments would appear to give credence to such a view. That is, at least as Hall recounts, the work of cultural studies was not concerned to engage with Parsons and certain forms of functionalist theory, but to sidestep the debates altogether and raise other questions about power, ideology, subjectivity, and cultural resistance that could not be framed within the conventional sociological discourses of socialization, norms, and value consensus. Thus while Alvin Gouldner (1970) signaled the coming crisis of Western sociology at the start of the 1970s, and tried to answer that call via a critical engagement *with* Parsonian sociology, cultural studies located, instead, its debates around the very aspects of sociality – everyday life, popular pursuits, and laterally language and meaning – that sociology had failed to adequately analyze.

For some sociologists, cultural studies is almost antisociological in its intellectual approach, which far from helping us to better understand the dynamics of culture's role in the construction of social relations, has now become a "facile and useless" (Tester 1994: 9) enterprise that is, apparently, "incapable of confronting important questions of cultural and moral value in anything approaching a serious manner" (ibid.).[5] Bryan Turner, Professor of Sociology at Cambridge University, has similarly criticized contemporary cultural studies for being little more than "decorative theory," as opposed to the more substantive offerings grounded in social reality found within sociology and social (as opposed to cultural) theory. Turner rails against those who would privilege certain forms of cultural analysis that are not first and foremost situated within "the social." He does this by contrasting contemporary cultural studies in Britain against the "golden age" of its early development:

> The attempt to submerge the social in the cultural cannot produce an adequate understanding of power, inequality, and social stratification. Cultural studies have lost their roots in the critical tradition of Raymond Williams, Richard Hoggart, and the early Birmingham Centre for Cultural Studies [sic], a tradition that was crucially concerned with the loss of community and the power of the media. Cultural theory has become an end in itself – the narcissistic study of its own textual traditions – and has as a result lost its sense of the importance of empirical research. (Turner 2000: xv)

One of the problems in outlining the division in this way is that it necessarily distorts and homogenizes an entire area of enquiry. Many of the leading cultural studies theorists would themselves make similar criticisms about *some* of the work done within the field. Indeed the problems of theoreticism – theory for its own sake, disconnected from empirical engagement – are precisely some of the main problems with contemporary *sociology* and social theory (see Craib 1992; Mouzelis 1995; Seidman 1998). Turner continues his attack by arguing that cultural studies, due to its eclectic and multidisciplinary basis, lacks the intellectual depth and sophistication to "develop a range of concepts with the breadth, scope, and moral seriousness of Weber's notion of rationalization, Marx's concept of alienation, Durkheim's analysis of the sacred, Simmel's understanding of mental life and the city, or Parson's analysis of the democratic revolution in the education system" (2000: xvi).

It would be too easy to counter such a statement with a list of equally significant theoretical contributions from cultural studies theorists, but to do so would be to descend into a form of academic playground fighting ("our concepts are better than yours") which, as I want to stress here, is both unnecessary and counterproductive – even if we could resolve who should be on which "side"; no doubt Simmel would be argued over, though I expect cultural studies theorists would be happy to let the sociologists have Parsons.[6] The point rather is that cultural studies would not wish to deny the importance of such insights, but try to extend them by incorporating them within new frameworks – say in relation to issues concerning governance, cultural regulation, and discursive regimes of power. Such sentiments reveal a defensive and insecure attitude towards cultural studies, which more often speaks to the continuing ontological and epistemological crises of sociology in the twenty-first century, than it does to cultural studies' alleged moral and intellectual weaknesses. As one critic has lamented, sociology "looks poised to enter the final tragic-heroic Hegelian moment of 'sublation,' in which its immanent truths are in a way preserved, but also superseded, as new carriers of the Idea take flight" (McLennan 1998b: 61). "Is there a future for sociology?," asked Britain's leading sociologist, Anthony Giddens, in his 1996 book *In Defence of Sociology*. He answered; "don't despair! You still have a world to win, or at least interpret" (1996: 7) – hardly a rallying call. It would be difficult to think of a similar angst-ridden proclamation from within cultural studies.

This division between sociology and cultural studies is in many ways a false one, that overstates the extent of divergence and certainly their alleged incompatibility, and overlooks the fact that many of the founding classical theorists of sociology were concerned with aspects of culture and meaning, which to a degree were neglected in the more structural-functionalist approaches of modern sociology (Hall 1997b). Although proponents of cultural studies often claim to have a multi-, if not inter-, disciplinary base, drawing on history, politics, aesthetics, literary theory, and so on, it is actually sociology that provides the major metaconceptual framework for most of the work. Indeed many people who work within "cultural studies," actually do so from within sociology departments, or as Professors of Sociology *and* Cultural Studies (with the sociology normally coming first). Although many sociology departments have now adapted to the influences of cultural studies, in programs of study, Professorial titles, and new research centers, they have not, on the whole, and contrary to some more exaggerated claims, been replaced by cultural studies departments. (Though this is truer of older universities in the UK – the newer "red brick" and post-1992 universities tend to have created a more open space for cultural studies as a discrete area of work.)

To divorce the two makes little sense, distorts their inherently symbiotic relationship as well as failing to acknowledge the pivotal way in which cultural studies has decisively reshaped the theoretical, methodological, and conceptual concerns of sociology over the past 20 years in way which has given sociology new impetus, even as some of sociology's more conventional commentators try to deny this shift.[7] Even during cultural studies' incipient phase of development, figures who would later be seen as key intellectuals in the development of systems approaches to sociology were engaged in work that directly led into the formation of cultural studies. Karl Mannheim, for example, was attracted to the political aspirations behind the adult workers' education associations and their rootedness within working-class communities when he first migrated to England from Germany in the early 1930s. Mannheim's *Ideology and Utopia* was hugely influential on adult education tutors in defining a role for both themselves as educators and their relationship to teaching working-class emancipatory education, and who in many ways was an important conduit for importing European critical social philosophy into the rather empiricist aspects of British intellectual life at that time, which was to later prove so important to the New Left. As Steele notes, Mannheim's work during, and immediately after, the postwar period: "transformed the existing practice of academic sociology by making it confront the issue of culture and, by harnessing it to the interdisciplinary practices of adult education, paved the way for the post-war generation of cultural studies" (1997: 116).

The influence of cultural studies upon sociology can be seen in other ways too. Alan Tomlinson (1999: 79) notes that a survey of British sociologists in the early 1970s asking them to name their key sociological texts chose Durkheim's study *Suicide*, closely followed by Weber's *The Protestant Ethic and the Spirit of Capitalism*. Just under a decade later, while Durkheim had "slipped" to second, it was Paul Willis's (1977) study of how working–class males were schooled into working–class jobs that was deemed to be one of the best explanatory texts. Tomlinson further points out that Giddens himself when asked to specify an empirical study that best exemplified his theory of structuration – a concept which Giddens had actually "appropriated" from the psychologist Piaget (1971) – pointed to Willis's landmark cultural studies text (see Giddens 1984).

Indeed Giddens' *In Defence of Sociology* has a chapter dedicated to Raymond Williams' work. Gouldner's text too opens with an account of popular culture and uses The Doors' "(Come on Baby) Light My Fire" to illustrate the central thesis of his book – while the city of Detroit was being burned and looted the song was apparently being used by a car manufacturer to advertise their product. It was this "context of contradictions and conflicts that is the historical matrix of what I have called 'the Coming Crisis of Western Sociology'" (1970: xii), noted Gouldner.[8] Even a conventional sociological critic like Bryan Turner concedes that all that may be needed is a reconciliation rather than a divorce, when he notes that the solution to the division "is to make sociology more cultural and cultural studies more sociological" (2000: xiv).

For some, the distinction that Turner tries to draw is not only irrelevant, but unhelpful. Scott Lash, for example, has argued against those within cultural studies (or cultural theory in Lash's vocabulary) who have dismissed "the importance of forms of social life" (1999: 1), as well as those sociologists "who pay scant attention to culture – who neglect the cultural dimension altogether – in favour of the calculated and calculating rationality of actors, systems or massive matrices of quantitative data" (ibid.). Many would respond, no doubt, to both Turner and Lash by pointing out that such a "multidimensional" approach to analyzing culture is exactly what they have been doing all along.

If these dualisms are to be resolved they require more than pious pronouncements, but a genuine rethinking of the nature of sociological enquiry and its purpose. It may be that though they do clearly share common ground, the prioritizing by cultural studies of the constructed nature of language, subjectivity, and identity as a way to understand the operation of power, ideology, and the production of social hierarchies, as opposed to working the other way around – that is, by treating the social as a preexistent given and then trying to understand how various symbols are then used within that social system – reflects a different standpoint position that can co-exist and need not necessarily be seen as antithetical.

Conclusion

It would be misleading to assume that many of the issues I have highlighted are not currently being debated. The problem is that increased academic specialization often means that there are now large gaps between those who consider themselves "theorists," those who perceive themselves as, first and foremost, "grounded empiricists," and those who still view their roles more widely in terms of pedagogic praxis. While most would argue against this tripartite distinction, it is increasingly the case that forms of critical pedagogy are often seen as being a specialist concern for those interested in the promotion of better teaching and learning techniques. That is, forms of empowerment via the *teaching* of cultural studies are rarely joined up with the theoretical developments and grounded studies of various communities and even less connected to forms of progressive politics or policy concerns – "empowerment" now being reduced to improving teaching techniques so as not to disaffect students (see Buckingham 1998). The notion that cultural studies might form the basis for a democratic mode of emancipatory politics, and how we might reconvene the public sphere to address such pedagogic issues pertaining to cultural politics, is a question that needs to be more fully considered (Giroux 2000). Indeed, rather than seeing cultural studies as engaged in a project to expand our understandings of the scope and delimitations of politics, many on the left in Britain perceive cultural studies as being a form of "postpolitical" negation and disengagement *from* "real" politics, not a means to effect this end. Thus cultural studies is viewed with contempt for being little more than an intellectual Trojan horse allowing the infiltration of postmodern discourses of "difference," which has confused us as to the true (economic) determinants of politics (see Eagleton 1996).

The problem with such accounts is they fail to acknowledge the importance of new social movements to progressive politics, the genuinely radical nature of the "cultural turn" within social theory, and the extent to which it is no longer possible, theoretically or politically, to simply prioritize a reified conceptualization of "the economic" as always being the key determinant of social formation in the last instance. The lip-service given to the importance of nonclass subjectivities by *some* of the more orthodox political-economy approaches is little more than an attempt to recenter modes of analysis that have not developed since the 1970s, often by parodying new social movements as being factional, particularistic, and "merely cultural" (Butler 1998). Discussing this tension between political economy/mass communication scholars and Gramscian/cultural studies theorists, Morley notes that the former:

291

have lately been heard to say that, of course, they have always recognized that there was more to life than questions of class and economic determination; that questions of culture and meaning have always been important to them; that, of course, questions of race, gender and sexuality have always been prominent among their concerns; that, naturally, the analysis of low-status forms of fictional media production is important; and that, certainly, they have never thought of audiences as passive dupes or zombies... A look back at some early debates between these scholars and those working in cultural studies... shows quite a different story, in which all these things that now, it seems, mass communications scholars have "long recognized" have, in fact, had to be fought for, inch by inch, and forced on to the research agenda by those primarily within the cultural studies tradition, against the backdrop of much wailing and gnashing of teeth on the part of the political economists. (1998: 488)

It is doubtful whether those who taught within adult and workers' education colleges during the 1930s, 1940s, and 1950s and whose intellectual work was directly connected to political engagement and social change, would recognize what constitutes cultural studies today. This is not necessarily a cause for concern, and it is clearly important to avoid any nostalgic and uncritical notions of the "good old days" of cultural studies in Britain. To argue that cultural studies' emergence within radical adult education needs to be retrieved for the cultural memory need not be mistaken for a "romantic and heroic conceptualisation of cultural studies" (McGuigan 1997: 1) and its "revolutionary" past. To argue for a broader historical understanding of the wider social formation of cultural studies does not negate a critical appraisal of the problematic theoretical absences within earlier work, or suggest that contemporary cultural studies can *only* be about political pedagogical praxis. Nevertheless it does help us to question the ontological and ethical basis of contemporary cultural studies work. This necessitates greater emphasis to be put into thinking through the nature of much research, and its links to public policy concerns, if it is to remain purposeful, and avoid becoming both obscurantist and irrelevant, to the lives of those it seeks to understand. Graeme Turner (1996) is surely right when he argues that cultural studies has presented a radical challenge to the orthodoxies of the disciplines found within the humanities and social sciences, enabling a fuller, richer, and more complex understanding of the role of culture in society. Cultural studies' commitment to understanding and analyzing aspects of everyday life, Turner continues, "has the admirable objective of doing so in order to change our lives for the better. Not all academic pursuits have such a practical political objective" (1996: 234). In the current climate of increasing neoliberal managerialist ideologies saturating university and wider educational life, whether cultural studies in Britain will be able to fulfill its intellectual, political, and pedagogic goals remains, at present, unclear.

To return to my opening observations. I did eventually find the sociology section. It was tucked away at the back of the store next to a fire exit, and in between texts on business management, homeopathy, and a children's play area. And there was no cultural studies section. Make of that what you will.

Notes

1 Goldsmith's could now claim to be the new center of cultural studies in Britain, at least in terms of the numbers of cultural theorists working there. (That said I am cautious of reinscribing certain institutions as being "central" as this necessarily "marginalizes" other spaces of production. As Turner notes, regarding the neglect of work by those based at Cardiff by many histories, "the field of study has been subject to a degree of metropolitan control and that there are geographical margins as well as theoretical or ideological ones" (1996: 76); see also Schwarz (1994). Currently the University of East London has a number of important cultural studies theorists working across various departments and more formally the Manchester Institute for the Study of Popular Culture, based at Manchester Metropolitan University, has quickly established itself as one of the UK's leading centers for cultural studies research. Thus I certainly do not wish to imply we should necessarily see Goldsmith's-based lecturers' work as "better" than that currently being produced elsewhere.) Goldsmiths' Centre for Cultural Studies, directed by Scott Lash, modestly claims to be a "supradisciplinary center" which is "a locus of intellectual activity and fermentation," though it might well be argued that Goldsmith's less well-known Centre for Urban and Community Research actually comes closer to fulfilling the pedagogic and interventionist ambitions of earlier cultural studies.

2 Gilroy has suggested that "it seems impossible to deny that Hoggart's comprehensive exclusion of 'race' from his discussion of postwar class and culture represented clear political choices" (1996: 236).

3 With apologies to Lawrence Grossberg for paraphrasing this line – see the exchange between Grossberg and Nicholas Garnham over the relevance of more cultural-studies-inflected versions of media studies versus broader, political-economy, approaches in Storey 1998. Aspects of this debate were rehearsed in Ferguson and Golding 1997. Kellner dismissively refers to the earlier debate as "futile" as most of the participants "talked past each other and often substituted personal attacks for discussion" (Kellner 1997: 120). See McLennan 1998a for a survey of the increasingly heated nature of the sociology versus cultural studies debates; see also the essays collected in Long 1997, particularly the chapters by Steven Seidman and Richard Johnson. A convincing response to the criticisms leveled at cultural studies *vis-à-vis* sociology can be found in Morley 1998; see also McRobbie 1999.

4 This is of course a minor, but slightly amusing, occupational hazard for those early inter/multidisciplinary cultural studies scholars who now find themselves elevated through the higher education structure to senior positions, but sometimes within institutions that have not kept pace with the disciplinary changes. Simon Frith, for example, noted his surprise and embarrassment during his inaugural lecture at now being a "Professor of English," even though "I haven't studied English formally since I did O levels" (quoted in Wolff 1999: 499).

5 Such criticisms are not new. Hall, for example, recalls the "blistering attack specifically from sociology" (1980: 21) which was directed at the CCCS, when it was first

opened in 1964, in an attempt to seemingly put cultural studies in its place: "the opening of the Centre was greeted by a letter from two social scientists who issued a sort of warning: if Cultural Studies overstepped its proper limits and took on the study of contemporary society (not just its texts), without 'proper' scientific (that is quasi-scientific) controls, it would provoke reprisals for illegitimately crossing the territorial boundary" (ibid.).

6   It is significant, in this context, that Parsons, in his structural-functionalist approach to sociology, had such difficulty incorporating the types of phenomenological-sociological investigations of urban culture and everyday life that concerned Simmel, which would later be more fully explored by cultural studies, something which Turner here glosses over – see Levine 2000 on Parsons' difficulties with aspects of Simmel's sociology.

7   Or as Gilroy forcefully puts it: "In the field of Sociology, as in many other places, there is a very strong current of resentment which suggests that all of these arguments around culture and its complexities were things that were already known and already practised by Sociologists. I think that's bullshit, but it's very interesting that this position represents itself as common sense … What is more of an immediate issue for me is the kind of culturalisation, a novel sensitivity to the workings of culture that has been evident in the implosion and collapse of Sociology as a discipline. This disciplinary predicament has produced a political battle around culture and its workings" (Smith 1999: 18).

8   Some may object to these examples, pointing out that Giddens largely fails to develop any sophisticated analysis of the place of culture *per se*, and indeed that the chapter on Williams is one of the shortest in the book. Further, the first section of Gouldner's opening chapter is actually called "Sociology as Popular Culture," and certainly not a Sociology *of* Popular Culture, clearly a different thing. There are indeed no textual readings of popular culture to be found in either book. That said, both do open up the possibility at least for more sociologically informed analyses of culture and popular culture.

References

Baker, H., M. Diawara, and R. Lindeborg (eds.) (1996). *Black British Cultural Studies: A Reader*. Chicago: Chicago University Press.

Barker, C. (2000). *Cultural Studies: Theory and Practice*. London: Sage.

Bennett, A. (1999a). "Subcultures or Neo-Tribes? Rethinking the Relationship between Youth, Style and Musical taste." *Sociology* 33(3): 599–617.

Bennett, A. (1999b). "Hip-hop and Main: The Localization of Rap Music and Hip Hop Culture." *Media, Culture and Society* 21: 77–91.

Bennett, A. (1999c). "Rappin' on the Tyne: White Hip Hop Culture in Northeast England – An Ethnographic Study." *The Sociological Review* 47(1): 1–24.

Bennett, A. (2000). *Popular Music and Youth Culture: Music, Identity and Place*. Basingstoke: Macmillan.

Brundson, C. (1996). "A Thief in the Night: Stories of Feminism in the 1970s at CCCS." In D. Morley and K.-H. Chen (eds.), *Stuart Hall: Critical Dialogues in Cultural Studies*. London: Routledge.

Buckingham, D. (ed.) (1998). *Teaching Popular Culture: Beyond Radical Pedagogy*. London: UCL Press.

Butler, J. (1998). "Merely Cultural." *New Left Review* 227: 33–44.

CCCS (1978). *Policing the Crisis: Mugging, the State, and Law and Order*. London: Macmillan.

CCCS (1982). *The Empire Strikes Back: Race and Racism in 70s Britain*. London: Routledge.

Craib, I. (1992). *Modern Social Theory: From Parsons to Habermas*. London: Harvester Wheatsheaf.

Davies, I. (1995). *Cultural Studies and Beyond: Fragments of Empire*. London: Routledge.

Dunn, T. (1986). "The Evolution of Cultural Studies." In D. Punter (ed.), *Introduction to Contemporary Cultural Studies*. London: Longman.

Dworkin, D. (1997). *Cultural Marxism in Postwar Britain: History, the New Left, and the Origins of Cultural Studies*. London: Duke University Press.

Eagleton, T. (1996). *The Illusions of Postmodernism*. Oxford: Blackwell Publishers.

Ferguson, M. and P. Golding (eds.) (1997). *Cultural Studies in Question*. London: Sage.

Forgacs, D. (ed.) (1988). *A Gramsci Reader*. London: Lawrence and Wishart.

Forgacs, D. (1999). "National-Popular: Genealogy of a Concept." In S. During (ed.), *The Cultural Studies Reader*, 2nd edn. London: Routledge.

Franklin, S., C. Lury, and J. Stacey (eds.) (1991). *Off-Centre: Feminism and Cultural Studies*. London: HarperCollins.

Giddens, A. (1984). *The Constitution of Society: Outline of a Theory of Structuration*. Cambridge: Polity Press.

Giddens, A. (1996). *In Defence of Sociology: Essays, Interpretations and Rejoinders*. Cambridge: Polity Press.

Gilroy, P. (1987). *There Ain't No Black in the Union Jack: The Cultural Politics of Race and Nation*. London: Routledge.

Gilroy, P. (1993). *The Black Atlantic: Modernity and Double Consciousness*. London: Verso.

Gilroy, P. (1996). "British Cultural Studies and the Pitfalls of Identity." In H. Baker, M. Diawara, and R. Lindeborg, (eds.), *Black British Cultural Studies: A Reader*. Chicago: Chicago University Press.

Gilroy, P. (1999). "Between Camps: Race and Culture in Postmodernity." *Economy and Society* 28(2): 183–97.

Giroux, H. (2000). "Public Pedagogy as Cultural Politics: Stuart Hall and the 'Crisis' of Culture." *Cultural Studies* 14(2): 341–60.

Gordon, D. (1995). "Feminism and Cultural Studies: Review Essay." *Feminist Studies* 21(2): 363–77.

Gouldner, A. (1970). *The Coming Crisis of Western Sociology*. London: Heinemann.

Gray, A. (1997). "Learning from Experience: Cultural Studies and Feminism." In J. McGuigan (ed.), *Cultural Methodologies*. London: Sage.

Hall, S. (1980). "Cultural Studies and the Centre: Some Problematics and Problems." In S. Hall, D. Hobson, A. Lowe, and P. Willis (eds.), *Culture, Media, Language*. London: Hutchinson.

Hall, S. (1992). "Race, Culture, and Communications: Looking Backward and Forward at Cultural Studies." *Rethinking Marxism* 5(1): 10–18.

Hall, S. (1996). "Cultural Studies and its Theoretical Legacies." In D. Morley and K.-H. Chen (eds.), *Stuart Hall: Critical Dialogues in Cultural Studies*. London: Routledge.

Hall, S. (1997a). "Cultural and Power." *Radical Philosophy* 86: 24–41.

Hall, S. (1997b). "The Centrality of Culture: Notes on the Cultural Revolutions of Our Time." In K. Thompson (ed.), *Media and Cultural Regulation*. London: Sage.

Hall, S. (1999). "Whose Heritage? Un-settling 'The Heritage', Re-imagining the Post-nation." *Third Text* 49 (Winter): 3–13.

Hoggart, R. (1995). *The Way We Live Now*. London: Chatto and Windus.

Kellner, D. (1997). "Overcoming the Divide: Cultural Studies and Political Economy." In M. Ferguson and P. Golding (eds.), *Cultural Studies in Question*. London: Sage.

Laing, S. (1986). *Representations of Working-Class Life, 1957–1964*. London: Macmillan.

Lash, S. (1999). *Another Modernity, A Different Rationality*. Oxford: Blackwell Publishers.

Levine, D. (2000). "On the Critique of 'Utilitarian' Theories of Action: Newly Identified Convergences among Simmel, Weber and Parsons." *Theory, Culture and Society* 17(1): 63–78.

Long, E. (ed.) (1997). *From Sociology to Cultural Studies: New Perspectives*. Oxford: Blackwell Publishers.

Lovatt, A. and J. Purkis (1996). "Shouting in the Street: Popular Culture, Values and the New Ethnography." In J. O'Connor and D. Wynne (eds.), *From the Margins to the Centre: Cultural Production and Consumption in the Post-industrial City*. Avebury: Arena.

McGuigan, J. (1997). "Introduction." In McGuigan (ed.), *Cultural Methodologies*. London: Sage.

McLennan, G. (1998a). "Sociology and Cultural Studies: Rhetorics of Disciplinary Identity." *History of the Human Sciences* 11(3): 1–17.

McLennan, G. (1998b). "Fin de Sociolgie? The Dilemmas of Multidimensional Social Theory." *New Left Review* 230: 58–90.

McRobbie, A. (1994). *Postmodernism and Popular Culture*. London: Routledge.

McRobbie, A. (1999). "Afterword: In Defence of Cultural Studies." In *In the Culture Society: Art, Fashion and Popular Music*. London: Routledge.

McRobbie, A. (2000). *Feminism and Youth Culture*, 2nd edn. London: Macmillan.

Miles, S. (2000). *Youth Lifestyles in a Changing World*. Buckingham: Open University Press.

Morley, D. (1998). "So-called Cultural Studies: Dead Ends and Reinvented Wheels." *Cultural Studies* 12(4): 476–97.

Morley, D. and K.-H. Chen (eds.), (1996). *Stuart Hall: Critical Dialogues in Cultural Studies*. London: Routledge.

Mouzelis, N. (1995). *Sociological Theory: What Went Wrong?* London: Routledge.

Muggleton, D. (2000). *Inside Subculture: The Postmodern Meaning of Style*. Oxford: Berg.

Mulhern, F. (2000). *Culture/Metaculture*. London: Routledge.

Munt, S. (1998). *Heroic Desire: Lesbian Identity and Cultural Space*. London: Cassell.

Munt, S. (2000). "Introduction." In S. Munt (ed.), *Cultural Studies and the Working Class: Subject to Change*. London: Cassell.

Nava, M. (1992). *Changing Cultures: Feminism, Youth and Consumerism*. London: Sage.

Owusu, K. (2000). "Introduction: Charting the Genealogy of Black British Cultural Studies." In K. Owusu (ed.), *Black British Culture and Society*. London: Routledge.

Piaget, J. (1971). *Structuralism*. London: Routledge.

Schwarz, B. (1994). "Where is Cultural Studies?" *Cultural Studies* 8(4): 377–93.

Seidman, S. (1998). *Contested Knowledge: Social Theory in the Postmodern Era*, 2nd edn. Oxford: Blackwell Publishers.

Simmel, G. (1968). *The Conflict in Modern Culture and Other Essays*. New York: Teachers College Press.

Smith, M. (1999). "On the State of Cultural Studies: An Interview with Paul Gilroy." *Third Text* 49 (Winter): 15–26.

Solomos, J. (2000). *Race and Racism in Britain*, 3rd edn. London: Macmillan.

Solomos, J. and L. Back (1996). *Racism and Society*. London: Macmillan.

Steele, T. (1997). *The Emergence of Cultural Studies, 1945–65: Cultural Politics, Adult Education and the English Question*. London: Lawrence and Wishart.

Storey, J. (1996). *An Introduction to Cultural Theory and Popular Culture*, 2nd edn. Hemel Hempstead: Prentice Hall.

Storey, J. (ed.) (1998). *Cultural Theory and Popular Culture: A Reader*, 2nd edn. Hemel Hempstead: Prentice Hall.

Sweetman, P. (1999a). "Marked Bodies, Oppositional Identities? Tattooing, Piercing and the Ambiguity of Resistance." In S. Roseneil and J. Seymour (eds.), *Practising Identities: Power and Resistance*. London: Macmillan.

Sweetman, P. (1999b). "Anchoring the (Postmodern) Self? Body Modification Fashion and Identity." *Body and Society* 5(2): 51–76.

Tester, K. (1994). *Media, Culture and Morality*. London: Routledge.

Tomlinson, A. (1999). *The Game's Up: Essays in the Cultural Analysis of Sport, Leisure and Popular Culture*. Avebury: Arena.

Tudor, A. (1999). *Decoding Culture: Theory and Method in Cultural Studies*. London: Sage.

Turner, B. (2000). "Preface to the Second Edition." in Turner (ed.), *The Blackwell Companion to Social Theory*. London: Blackwell.

Turner, G. (1996). *British Cultural Studies: An Introduction*, 2nd edn. London: Routledge.

Williams, R. (1983). *Towards 2000*. London: Chatto and Windus.

Williams, R. (1989). *The Politics of Modernism: Against the New Conformists*. London: Verso.

Willis, P. (1977). *Learning to Labour: How Working Class Kids Get Working Class Jobs*. Aldershot: Gower.

Wolff, J. (1999). "Cultural Studies and the Sociology of Culture." *Contemporary Sociology* 28(5): 499–507.

Chapter 17

European Cultural Studies

Paul Moore

In 1995 a series of texts were published aimed at addressing the issue of cultural studies in Europe. They were specifically designed as an "introduction" to the area of study and each volume dealt with a specific geographical region – Spanish Cultural Studies, German Cultural Studies, French Cultural Studies, and so on. These texts came at a time when government agencies, politicians, administrators, and intellectuals were attempting to redefine the debates about the "New Europe." This redefinition was grounded in an understanding that culture could no longer be given lip-service in relation to European development, and needed to be placed center-stage with a policy-driven agenda.

An examination of these texts provides an insight into the difficulties associated with creating a cultural studies platform that will allow the different meanings of culture in the European context to be facilitated. *A Dictionary of Cultural and Critical Theory* (Payne 1996), for example, argues that cultural studies in western Europe is associated with departments of English and equates it with other, more established terms such as the French *civilisation*, the Scandinavian *civilisation*, and the German *Landeskunde*. The overview concludes that while there are large numbers of people involved in cultural studies work across Europe, it is evident that such work "remains the poor relation to study of language and literature, lacking space in the curriculum, status in the eyes of most professional staff, and an explicit theoretical and disciplinary space" (Payne 1996: 186).

The focus on the development of cultural studies within particular national contexts by these texts was clearly, then, prescient. Each volume opened with an introduction that set out the breadth of the task involved in developing an identifiable cultural studies dimension within the established cultural histories of the various nations. Hence Rob Burns, writing about German cultural studies, analyzed the development of cultural studies in Britain, drawing a distinction between aesthetic and anthropological definitions of culture and foregrounding Williams' conception of culture as a "whole way of life." This tradition is set against the "Critical Theory" writings of Adorno and Horkheimer and it is this

Frankfurt School which is seen as the main impetus for the study of culture in Germany. Burns concludes that the text attempts, therefore, "to reconcile the two paradigms of 'culturalism' (with its emphasis on cultural practice as constitutive and empowering) and the 'culture industry' (with its focus on a consensus mass culture saturated with imposed meaning)" (Burns 1995: 7).

In the introduction to the French volume Michael Kelly argues that the key issue for cultural studies in France is one of identity, and that identity in French culture is articulated through the cumulative interaction of class, gender, and nation. He concludes that "the richness and multiplicity of its cultural discourses are a guarantee that it will continue to find powerful and vivid ways of articulating new identities. And for this reason French culture is a precious resource not only for France, but also for others who are willing to listen" (Forbes & Kelly 1995: 7).

Finally, in the Spanish volume, Helen Graham and Jo Labanyi offer a definition of culture which involves "both lived practices and artefacts or performances" (Graham & Labanyi 1995: 5), and this definition is used to develop a synopsis of the major thrusts in Spanish culture from the mid-1800s to the present day. It is at the beginning of the synopsis, however, that the crucial question for all of these texts is posed: "The starting point of any volume that claims to have as its aim the establishment of Spanish cultural studies as a discipline must be to ask why the discipline has been so slow to develop" (Graham & Labanyi 1995: 1).

The answer is partly to be found in the main body of each of these volumes. Rather than offering analysis of cultural studies as everyday lived experience each volume offers a historical overview of the development of culture in each nation. The importance of cultural movements is set against the crucial political events of the period in question, and each volume is similar in its assumption that European culture equates with some undefined notion of "high" culture. The Spanish volume does attempt to offer an analysis of popular music, television, cinema, and gay and lesbian culture, but other than these notable exceptions the only reference to popular culture throughout the texts is in general comment on the mass media or the threat of Americanization. The result is a body of work that offers the reader a *study of culture in Europe* rather than *a European cultural studies*.

Why No European Cultural Studies?

An analysis of these cultural studies texts offers an indication as to why a European cultural studies has been so slow to develop. While each volume presents a detailed and rich overview of the cultural developments in the selected area (and poses the key questions in relation to the creation of a wider cultural studies agenda, hence advancing the debate), the space to challenge accepted notions concerning cultural worth is hindered generally in Europe by four underlying assumptions. The first is the assumption that cultural studies is an expression of national identity.

While all cultural behavior is destined to take place in some national context or other the majority of cultural studies research takes place at the local and regional levels and is interested in the ways in which people negotiate positions which often challenge and subvert national movements and concerns. The analysis of these negotiations was a major theme in the early work of the so-called Birmingham School, where subcultural behavior localized at street level was seen as an authentic expression of class resistance. Even when the "failings" of the researchers working with the Centre for Contemporary Cultural Studies were exposed (lack of attention to gender and race in particular), the resultant studies still emphasized the importance of the local and regional over the national. In the postmodern environment the work of commentators such as Harvey (1990) and Massey (1998) indicate that cultural behavior takes place across geographical boundaries while at the same time remaining localized and relevant on a daily basis. Places where cultural creativity manifests itself include the home (especially for females), the school, the workplace, the street, and, most recently, the club. This concentration on the local brings us back to the definition of culture proffered by Williams, a definition grounded in issues related to class, industrialization, and politicization. In this formation cultural studies focuses on the "lived experience" of people producing meanings and values through everyday social interaction. The goal of all serious intellectual work, therefore, according to Williams, ought to be the achievement of community or a democratic common culture (Williams 1963). None of this work denies the importance of the idea of national identity as a means of articulating the elements of local and regional cultural behavior, but crucially it recognizes that all national identity, as Anderson (1983) argues, is a social and cultural construct rather than a primordial given. In this sense even the idea of a British cultural studies emphasizes too strongly the notion of a unified state identity whereas, in fact, there is a large body of research to show that for peripheral areas (see Bell 1990) and marginalized groups (see Gilroy 1987) the idea of Britain is extremely complex and problematic.

The development of cultural studies in Europe has also been hindered by the belief that Europe is the repository for much of what is usually termed "high" culture. This tradition harks back to the days of the "Grand Tour," and it is a tourist myth perpetuated by those wishing to sell Europe as a vehicle for enrichment through the visiting of various cities associated with "high" cultural excellence – Paris for art, Vienna for music, Prague for architecture, and so on. Graham and Labanyi (1995) acknowledge, in relation to Spain, that notions of "high" and "low" culture are social constructs aimed at suggesting that some are imbued with ethical values while others are not, and they see the distinction as not one between high and low culture but one which has three facets – high culture, popular culture, and the masses. In this distinction, however, their definition of the popular relates to ideas of folklore while the masses refers to the culture of the proletariat formed during industrialization. This distinction confuses rather than clarifies the meanings popular culture has developed in relation to popular artforms such as cinema, music, and dress style and again insinuates, as they concede, an attempt by the established cultural commentators to create a connection between some mythical "volk," a peasant population linked with dignity to the land, and the modern state.

Evidently, what has developed here is a definition of "high" culture in the Arnoldian sense. Ang (1998a: 97) argues that the high/popular culture hierarchy is not only alive and well in European discourse on culture, but that "more importantly . . . the defense of 'high culture' takes on not just a conservative, but a critical value in European self-enunciation." This conservatism is also reflected in the nostalgia shown by George Steiner for the high intellectual culture of the coffee-house, "this particular space – of discourse, of shared leisure, of shared exchange of disagreements – by which I mean the coffee-house, does define a very peculiar historical space roughly from Leningrad to Kiev and Odessa" (quoted in Kearney 1992: 44).

Roman Horak (1999), in an article entitled "Cultural Studies in Germany (and Austria) and Why There Is No Such Thing," identifies the same prejudice against popular culture. Given that Rob Burns (1995) and Graham and Labanyi (1995) argue that the Frankfurt School played the key role in the developing study of culture in Germany it is significant that, having juxtaposed the work of the Birmingham School against an overview of the status of the social sciences in German/Austrian academia, he comes to the conclusion that, "even the most explicit critics of the Frankfurt School shared one thing with those they criticized – a disdain for, or even fear of, mass popular culture" (Horak 1999: 112).

This fear and disdain for the popular is, it could be suggested, linked closely to a fear of American culture. The threat of Americanization has been a constant theme in cultural studies and the early work of Hoggart and Williams was framed in the context of the celebration of a working–class tradition under threat from Hollywood films, Levis, Coca Cola, and McDonaldization. This threat takes on a greater significance in a Europe of "high" culture and becomes embroiled in debates about cultural imperialism. Tomlinson (1991) has shown that an unthinking acceptance of this thesis ignores the fact that cultural imperialism is itself a discourse, manufactured around five subdiscourses of dominance, media imperialism, nationality, global capitalism, and modernity. The apparent presence of each of these "problems" serves to reinforce conservative cultural policies and limit debate as to the *actual* significance and importance of the American influence in any particular country or region. Hence Steiner can define American influence as the "Culture of the Secondary," a form of parasitism which creates talk about talk and images of images, a culture which allows the development of the apparently mundane because there is nothing to offer in its place.

> Twenty-eight or thirty miles from Paris, they are building a Disneyland, the second largest in the world, and they expect three hundred thousand visitors in the first few months, and it will be followed by other theme amusement parks. Apparently, Russia is now equally eager to get in on this. I look on this with despair. (quoted in Kearney 1992: 46)

The fact is, however, that if Americanization is to be proved, it must be proved in the context of specific cultural practices and not assumed. As Webster (1988: 183) says, "there are still plenty of debates where American/popular culture is alluded to, and argued against, but not known."

All three of the preceding factors could be subsumed under the heading of Eurocentrism and it is this discourse which is the fourth assumption undermining the development of a European cultural studies. Eurocentrism assumes the superiority of Western history and sees Europe as the center for important progressive change in the modern world, a unique centre which is both the bearer of civilization and its protector. Ang (1998a) argues that this position has served to elide the discourse of Eurocentrism and the "real" Europe itself to the extent that Eurocentrism has been normalized as a kind of "common sense": "most Europeans are unthinkingly Eurocentric indeed because Eurocentrism is, in a fundamental way, formative of and crucial to the European sense of cultural identity" (Ang 1998a: 89). The result of this elision is an unquestioned and unquestioning assumption of superiority which permeates the European structure of feeling and prevents an analysis which could deconstruct the various aspects of this supposed superiority and allow important cultural debates to be opened and illuminated. The elision even challenges those intellectuals who, while aware of this Eurocentric straitjacket, continue to buy into the discourse through what Ang labels "reluctant Eurocentrism," a strategy which manifests itself as a belief that only Europeans can critique Europe.

Reasons to be Optimistic – Part One

If, as is argued, the development of a European cultural studies is being hindered by these four assumptions there needs to be a framework of strategies developed which will allow the evolution of a number of theoretical ways of examining aspects of European culture which remain hidden or unexamined.

One way this might be addressed would be to reject any notions of essentialism and apply an analytical model grounded in the concept of "hybridity." One such model is that suggested by Massey (1998: 123). Massey argues that all culture is subject to hybridity, emphasizing the idea that more mature peoples and places (for example Europe) have the capacity to draw on a variety of cultural influences. As she says, "this openness of cultural formations is not specific to the young. 'Hybridity' is probably a condition of all cultures" (Massey 1998: 124).

More significantly, Massey challenges the academic tradition of organizing cultural space in terms of hierarchical "scale" (body, home, community, region, nation, globe) and proposes instead a move from roots to routes which will create "a notion of space as organised, not into distinct scales, but rather through a vast complexity of interconnections" (1998: 124). One method of examining notions of "hybridity" and interconnectedness is through the metaphor of "border crossings."

This abstract idea has been grasped as a focus for discussions concerning the new forms of identity because it offers a concept that can accommodate (and appear to explain) the complexities of geographical areas where inhabitants are asked to belong to both a nation and a supranational state. It also serves to guard against any notion of essentialism while recognizing the importance of both the local and the global. As Ang puts it, "the borderland tends to be imagined as a utopic site of transgressive intermixture, hybridity and multiplicity, the supposed political radicalness of which mostly remains unquestioned" (Ang 1998b: 14).

This is a theme explored by a number of writers in *Border Crossing: Film in Ireland, Britain and Europe* (Hill et al. 1994), a collection of essays which discuss the economic and cultural significance of Europe for British and Irish filmmakers. Amidst discussions of creativity, film production in Northern Ireland, and the necessity of a Celtic cinema, the two essays most relevant to this discussion deal with whether a European cinema exists, and if so, what its future might be. In answer to the first of these questions Philip French argues that the recognition of the need for national cinemas was essentially a perception of dictators such as Lenin and Hitler and he reaches the conclusion that there is indeed a European cinema. It is a cinema, however, constructed from a complex intermingling (border crossings) of a complex range of national and regional influences. Hence, as French argues in the example of Jacques Tourneur, the distinguished maker of American B movies,

> He was the son of Maurice Tourneur, the first established European director to work in the United States – he went there in 1914 and became one of the major figures of American silent cinema. Jacques became an American citizen and apart from five years in France from 1928 to 1933, he worked in the USA and was a remarkable exponent of the low-key horror movies (especially in collaboration with the Russian-born producer Val Lewton), the Western and the film noir thriller. Such are the complexities and, indeed, ironies in the relations between European and American cinema. (Hill et al. 1994: 52)

As to the future of European cinema, Hill also takes up this notion of the creative intercourse between regions, arguing that the idea of a pan-European cinema is problematic because it fails to recognize the hybrid nature of cultural identities. For Hill, however, this does not mean the European and the national are locked in opposition. "Rather, it is to indicate that what common European identity there is, or might be, only exists alongside and intermeshed with the nationally and culturally specific. Ironically, therefore, the experience of 'being' or 'becoming European' might be precisely one of the areas which a national, or a nationally specific, cinema could and should address" (Hill et al. 1994: 72).

While the arguments of Hill, French, and others who contribute to the debates raised in *Border Crossing* are based on a concrete analysis of films, film-makers, and audience consumption, the view of border/cultural interchange taken by Chambers (1990) is more philosophical. Chambers attempts to find an answer to the problem of what it means to "be English" by journeying through the issues which underpin contemporary culture, philosophy, and criticism. He comes to the conclusion that no one idea can be understood without an analysis of how it fits into the network which is modern (postmodern) society and that this network can be accessed only through "border dialogues." In the final analysis this journey emphasizes the fact that acknowledgment of a European culture both reinforces and subverts the idea of "home" and undermines any notion of a "guaranteed context." "To point to limits and inhabit the border country of frontiers and margins robs discourse of a conciliatory conclusion" (Chambers 1990: 116).

Henry Giroux (1992) also shows that Europe can act as a "borderland" for global interaction when he argues that a discursive space can be created where a polyglot of languages and experiences can come together to intermingle in a way which emphasizes the multicultural nature of all cultural narratives. This notion is given worldwide expression in websites such as "Border Crossings" that attempt to show the impact various cultural positions have on both their local and global neighbors.

The role which the Internet will play in the development of a European cultural studies is significant. Stanley Hoffman (1981: 213) argues that "Europe remains a virtuality, the past is mere spectacle, and the future is a riddle," and it is telling that much of the recent work in cultural studies in Europe is Internet based. While one must be careful not to overestimate the importance and impact of the new communication technologies, Stratton is surely correct when he suggests that "the hyperspace of the Internet elides the geographical spatial formations of nation-states which underpin their claims to a national culture" (Stratton 2000: 725). In the context of a Europe struggling to articulate the tension between national and supranational identity this distinction is crucial because it allows an imagined cultural identity which is no threat to national boundaries. Remembering Appadurai's cultural "scapes" and the idea of flows of information, it is also the case that the Internet mediates any tension between center and periphery. It is not surprising, therefore, that some of the most interesting cultural studies debates are being promoted by those on what might be termed the periphery of Europe. Hence the work of the Research Institute for Austrian and International Literature and Cultural Studies (INST). This web-based research project operating under the title "Cultural Studies and Europe or the Reality of Virtuality" aims to address a number of key problematics in relation to cultural studies – multilingualism, education and scholarship, libraries and universities, the issue of art as a divisive force, and migration. These problems are debated through an online discussion forum named the "cultural collabatory" which has received contributions from Italy, Poland, Germany, Norway, and in a wider context, Japan and Africa. The website has a number of themed pages, again asking the key questions such as "Does Europe Exist? – History, Potentialities and Problems of European Identity on these Grounds." The importance of addressing the identified problematics is ultimately grounded in a commitment to cultural studies as a way forward.

> The cultural forms mentioned continue current divisions, although they are a step toward improving mutual understanding and counter the use of culture as a means of exclusion. While there are still no sound political concepts in relation to cultural processes, there is discussion on the theme of "cultural policies for Europe" which points in that direction. The political vacuum to date has meant that "culture" has been appropriated primarily by nationalistic and populist groups (with the exception of modern art, which not by chance represents a bête noire as much to Le Pen as to the Taliban, Jorg Haider and Vajpayee). However conditions have changed in comparison to a Europe of nation states, potentially weakening the political opportunities of nationalists. These new conditions are in essence the necessity of furthering peace (and with it those elements which link cultures), the common economic area, new work structures, opportunities for cross-border communications, the search for compromise between different interest groups in society, the need for a new dynamic between societies and nature, the opportunity for people to participate in developments at all levels, etc. (INST, 1998)

The recognition of the hybridity of European identitiy would also be encouraged through a challenge to the traditional European cultural construct which has served to silence debate about marginalized groups. The analysis of difference and the "other" has been a central feature of cultural studies research. Edward Said is adamant, however, that Europe has not only not come to terms with the other in its midst, but has, through its literature for example, engaged in a "kind of paranoid, delusional fantasy" (quoted in Kearney 1992: 111) which is both xenophobic and fundamentally racist. It is imperative, according to Said, that Europe develops an understanding of its "other," if only to allow them to live together as "complementary enemies."

> There is also complementarity between Europe and its others. And that's the interesting challenge for Europe, not to purge it of all its outer affiliations and connections in order to try to turn it into some pure new thing. (Kearney 1992: 105).

Ang (1998a) argues that his process can only succeed if the privileged status given to European intellectuals in the critiquing of Europe is challenged by those very others. Citing the work of commentators such as the Indian historian Dipesh Chakrabarty, she contends that a real cultural studies of Europe can only develop if the idea of Europe as a linear, homogenizing process is challenged: "The

Other, with no agency of its own, is always defined as being at the receiving end of processes of 'Europeanization' and 'Westernization'. What is not acknowledged is that those at the receiving end of these processes are actively making their own histories even if it is always inescapably in conditions not of their own making" (Ang 1998a: 102).

Morley and Robins (1995) are also convinced of the importance to European identity and culture of a recognition of the "other," and argue that the way to bring this internationalism about is to promote "solidarities" with Third World cultures. In so doing the rich diversity of European culture will be recognized. "European identity can no longer be, simply and unproblematically, a matter of Western intellectual and cultural traditions . . . The question is whether ethnic (and also gendered) differences are disavowed and repressed, or whether they can be accepted – and accepted, moreover, in their difference" (Morley & Robins 1995: 41, 42).

The presence of hybridity and the need for a recognition of the "other" in European debates has been given greater importance by the "liberation" of the eastern European states. The violence that has been a feature of much of the emancipation process in eastern Europe has signaled the fact that the idea of nationhood has not been replaced by the idea of a European identity. This has renewed debate about the ways in which a culture to which all nations of Europe can contribute and accept as representative can be constructed.

An understanding of the way in which these "new" European states have imagined themselves may be found in an analysis of the ways in which the concept of *place* has been rethought to provide insights into the processes whereby the everyday environment underpins notions of identity and culture.

Contemporary place has three interrelated contexts – the local, the national, and the transnational – and discussions about their relations center on arguments concerning globalization and homogeneity. Much of the discussion surrounding the process of globalization has related to the concept of Americanization and the threat this holds for European identity (see George Steiner in Kearney 1992). This discussion has also related globalization to traditional notions of modernization and linked them in a "symbolic hierarchy" (Featherstone 1993: 170), the assumption being that as nations modernize they will absorb and hence duplicate American cultural practices (as well as other financial and consumer ideals). Ultimately this would lead to a homogeneous culture, albeit through a corrosive rather than a constructive homogenization. Featherstone challenges this theory of homogenization on the grounds that it prioritizes time over space and assumes that history has some inner logic associated with progress, giving it a univeralizing force. Such a position ignores the postmodern challenge to theories of development, particularly claims concerning the end of history as a unitary process. He argues, "This secularisation of the notions of progress and the perfectibility of the world entails a greater awareness of the constructed nature of history, of the use of rhetorical devices and the capacity to deconstruct narratives" (Featherstone 1993: 171).

For Featherstone, then, the paradoxical consequence of the process of globalization is that people recognize the range and extensiveness of their local cultures, the result being an increase in diversity rather than homogeneity. Clearly, global process "involves both the particularisation of universalism and the universalisation of particularism" (Bird et al. 1993: 253).

The key problem, therefore, in exploring the increased intensity of cultural exchange between European nations and European locales is how to shift the debate away from the general (statements about flows of images, products, and people) and into the specifics of a model which will facilitate a mapping of activities undertaken by specific groups in specific contexts. A developing cultural studies of Europe has a key role to play in the articulation of such a model and both Giddens, and Appadurai have attempted to produce relevant models.

Giddens (1990) argues for four interconnected features in a world system. These are the world capitalist economy, the nation-state system, the worldwide diffusion of modern technologies with the associated division of labor, and the emergence of a world military order. The problems with this model, in the context of the present argument, are that the factors operate at the national rather than the transnational level, but more crucially, they focus on the economic rather than the cultural despite Giddens, claim that the cultural dimension is implicit.

Appadurai (1990) goes some way to addressing these problems with the concept of "scapes" as a pattern for globalization. Five scapes are identified – "ethnoscapes" which are created through the movements of people such as tourists, immigrants, or exiles; "technoscapes" created by the flow of machinery and industrial plant, national and transnational; "mediascapes" produced by the flow of images and information and distributed through the multiplicity of media forms; "financescapes" created by the rapid flow of money in all its forms around the world; and "ideoscapes" related to the flow of ideas between states, super-state organizations, and movements. While it has been suggested that these "scapes" represent merely the progress of the capitalist economy towards a world system (as described by Giddens), the concept of flow emphasizes Appadurai's conviction that the "scapes" are dynamic and that particular cultural groups are involved in a constant negotiation with combinations of scapes in the process of the construction of particular cultural identities. As Jarvie and Maguire point out, "Instead of endlessly arguing about whether homogeneity or heterogeneity, integration or disintegration, unity or diversity are evident, it is more adequate to see these processes as interwoven. Nor is it a question of either/or but of balances and blends" (Jarvie & Maguire 1994: 251).

If Appadurai's concept of "scapes" is applied to the New Europe it is apparent there is a clear dichotomy between the economic and the cultural. Postwar cooperation was inevitably concentrated on issues of reconstruction, and early agreements such as the Brussels Treaty (1948), the Council of Europe

(1949), and the Western European Union in the 1950s focused on the development of what might be termed the "technoscape" and the "financescape." It could be suggested that at this early stage in the process these organizations were intergovernmental rather than supranational (Hainsworth 1994: 9), but by the late 1950s more genuinely integrative bodies such as the European Economic Coal and Steel Community (1951), the European Atomic Community (1958), and the European Economic Community were all firmly established.

While there was a constant reference to the importance of cultural issues in a Europe undergoing reconstruction, there were no policies or agencies which addressed the creation of a European cultural identity directly. In other words the "Ideoscape," "mediascape," and "ethnoscape" elements were not progressing with the same urgency as the economic elements. Hainsworth (1994) has shown how, in relation to film, this has changed to some extent recently, but it is crucial that the importance of cultural capital is recognized in a more general sense. Traditional notions of business and politics are being challenged by patterns of consumption which have a cultural foundation. This challenge, usually described in stereotypical form as the move from Fordism to post-Fordism in the industrial economies of the West, signals a profound shift in emphasis which recognizes that the key factor in the culture industry is the industry, not the culture (Jameson 1991). Rather than being commodified à la the Frankfurt School, a point has been reached where industry is commodified through culture. "It is not just that the economic determines the cultural but, as a number of commentators have observed, economies are inflected culturally and industry in general comes to resemble cultural industry in particular" (McGuigan 1996: 88).

If the argument for a move away from static notions of "high" culture into forms of experience which recognize hybridity and the importance of practices associated with marginalized groupings, then it is necessary to identify the kinds of material and cultural behavior which might make up a cultural studies of Europe. The focal point for an identification of such formations is, again, the proposition that "everyday lived experience" should be the foundation principle on which various material practices are constructed. This concentration on "ordinariness" encourages the examination of the types of data and subjects that would be the key elements in such formations. Alan Durant (1997) offers an interesting typology of cultural studies resources in an article exploring the pedagogic possibilities of British Cultural Studies. Durant gives a range of resources and explains how they might be incorporated into the study curriculum. The resources cited include interaction with people, personal recorded testimony of others, visiting places, exposure to the country's media, social rituals, and customs, social institutions, surveys, statistics and charts, heuristic contrasts and oppositions, and reading signs and styles (Durant 1997: 24–30). Doubtless other suggestions could be added to this list, but its range illustrates an attempt to identify those ordinary practices that can underpin an developing cultural studies framework. The identification of a network of interlocking cultive facets relates to the concept of common culture outlined by Paul Willis in research undertaken, significantly, for the Gulbenkian Institute, in which he investigated cultural activities in relation to the cultural media. Willis revisited the research, originally undertaken in 1987, in 1998, and developed "Notes for a Common Culture." These notes argued that through the three processes of "symbolic work," "symbolic creativity," and "symbolic extension" the elements of a common culture emerge. This is a common culture that renders out of date older notions such as middle-class, working-class, or regional culture. It is a common culture that is not controled or directed by economic power.

> Common culture has continuities with, but has to be distinguished from, traditional and working-class cultures. Nor is common culture coterminous with popular culture. For me the former concerns ordinary, everyday practices, the latter the provided products. The same materials can either weigh down daily life with banality or be bent to its rhythms according to context and social practice. Popular culture is simply the surprising and unpredictable catalyst. Meanwhile ordinary culture, everyday sense and meaning-making, may be shifting in almost epochal ways from varieties of deference and parochialism to varieties of openness and profane independence. (Willis 1998: 169)

Ireland: A Case Study

The complex matrix of theoretical ideas of which hybridity, anti-essentialism, awareness of place, and an understanding of everyday lived experience form a central framework is only useful if it can be applied in specific locations with specific effects. One such specific context is Ireland, which despite its post-colonial status and dysfunctional political problems has managed to reimagine itself as a vibrant, (post)modern state with an aggressive economic standing built through the construction of a complicated network of global links. The so-called "Celtic Tiger" has not been constructed and reimagined at the expense of more traditional definitions of nationality. Rather, as Martin McLoone has shown, the New Ireland is a product of an intense debate about culture and identity which has touched every facet of Irish cultural life and been articulated through the changing position of the Irish economy.

McLoone identifies three distinct phases of economic development in Ireland: a first period of growth from 1958 to 1978, a second period of stagnation from 1978 to 1988, and the present period from 1988 which has heralded unimagined growth. "This economic success has given rise to the sobriquet 'the Celtic Tiger' to describe Ireland's increasingly vigorous and assertive presence on the world stage and needless to say has energised internal debate more completely than even the years of gloom had done" (McLoone 1994).

While McLoone is particularly interested in film, he illustrates how this economic ferment drove debates about culture and identity, and links the often acidic discussions taking place in Ireland at that time about film, television, national identity, and religious/moral issues with the various economic periods.

What is significant about McLoone's analysis is that although he rightly foregrounds the Irish film industry/culture's relationship with America and Britain, the implicit argument is that the solution to the postcolonial problem with those countries was to be found through reimagining Ireland in a European cultural context. Hence in relation to Britain he suggests that "in many ways, the *'Europeanisation' of Irish Identity came to be seen as the most effective way of breaking the close economic and cultural ties with Britain*" (my italics) (McLoone 1994). Or in relation to the 1976 Broadcasting Act he concludes that, "the changes [in the Act] here are profound and make a shift away from the old nationalist consensus *to a new orthodoxy built around a liberal, European sense of identity*" (my italics) (McLoone 1994).

The development of a non-essentialist definition of culture in Ireland (in this case Northern Ireland) has also been encouraged by studying the impact of popular culture on traditional identity positions. The accepted explanations for cultural difference in Northern Ireland tend to emphasize simplistic variations on the Catholic/Protestant divide. This emphasis fails to recognize, in a similar fashion to the European reluctance to recognize popular cultural expressions, that cultural articulation for many people, particularly the young, is grounded in the everyday. The construction of an alternative, anti-essentialist cultural paradigm, therefore, involves the recognition of cultural and subcultural activities which challenge embedded notions of cultural identity, while offering alternative identities based on an awareness of transnational movements such as rave culture, popular music, and New Age culture. In the Irish context two recent articles would suggest that this process has started. Martin McLoone (1994), in his analysis of Van Morrison, illustrates the ways in which the complexity of cultural influences are merged in the music he produces. In so doing, Morrison produces a music which for those from Northern Ireland transcends the particular in any given song. "*Astral Weeks* is, of course, about Belfast, not about the Derry of my roots nor the Dublin of my student days. But when I first heard it, I recognised it as being about the 'here and now' of where I then was and, even more crucially, about the past of where I had been" (McLoone 1994: 41). McLoone speaks of the pride he felt that Morrison was from Northern Ireland – "he was one of us" – and goes on to examine the outside influences which have impacted on Morrison's music and the complex manner in which the local and the global have been interrogated in the construction of his "rootedness." This process, McLoone concludes, has been crucial to the understanding of the development of popular cultural identity in Northern Ireland.

His achievements have set an example for peripheral indigenous cultures everywhere, demonstrating how an adherence to, and a transgression of, one's "rootedness" is not only possible but is actually the best way to guard against the dominance of trans-global popular culture. (McLoone 1994: 44)

In an examination of the study of culture in Northern Ireland, David Butler also argues against "narrowly cast" and "essentialist" models of cultural identity (Butler 1994). Having established that cultural identity is formed in society through the social relationships we negotiate day to day, Butler argues that it is the constant gathering of cultural reference points which ultimately creates rootedness. This is not to say that there is some given relationship between culture and identity; rather that cultural formations should be imagined as a "border crossing (social, geographic, economic, philosophical). Minimally, group identities are made in history: a social activity requiring wilful invention, imagination, and intent. Cultural practices are no more nor less than the embodiment of structured social relations, but, to be clear, there is no necessary relationship between culture and identity. We have to think ourselves into them" (Butler 1994: 32).

Butler argues, therefore, that "traditional" cultural practices do no more than reinforce the divisions in Northern Irish society, and he is particularly critical of attempts to create consensus, on the grounds that such attempts confirm the very aspects of sectarianism they are designed to undermine and that the concept of respect for all traditions may allow the worst excesses of sectarian behavior to go unchallenged on the grounds that it is representative. Ultimately, Butler calls for a widening of the definition of accepted/unacceptable cultural practice in order that the dissensual nature of Northern Irish society be recognized, a process which will challenge exclusivity and essentialism.

> I would propose an extensive understanding of the making and the meaning of cultural formations: that cultural identities are formed in the midst of a wide range of influences and constraints, in the contemporary world as much as in and by the past. Besides sectarian cultures there are, of course, limitless instances of overlap and inflow: from music, movies, broadcast television, in books and magazines, in the high street and other more or less exotic locations. These are the conditions of (post)modern life. Also, it is vital that we explode the fantasy of total and exclusive identities, which the dichotomous processes of balanced sectarianism inadvertently sustain. (Butler 1994: 55)

The importance of these analyses is that they are creating a foundation for the recognition that Northern Ireland is already building cultural identities which function outside the essentialist cultural identities promoted by the explanations of Northern Ireland which predominate. They recognize that in the operation of the young sectarian gangs, the punk movement, or the rave movement individuals and groups are producing cultural practices and formations which, while evidently informed by the context of conflict, do not represent themselves through traditional signs, customs, beliefs, and icons. Neither do they look only inward, being willing to ally on a transnational basis with other like-minded groups or individuals for whom a shared cultural practice creates a shared imagined community. As Colin Graham suggests, culture should be presented as a "process rather than in stasis; as ideological and conflictual rather than universal and medicinal; as an emanation from all parts of society, rather than stratified into 'high', 'low', or 'popular', and identifying movement across cultures as resourceful, ironic filtering across ideological monoliths" (Graham 1994: 74).

Ireland, then, can be seen as a specific example of the process which European leaders hope to promote, of a country using European economic links to initiate debates about culture which create a hybrid, multicultural society which, while not without problems (McLoone cites racism and the existence of a large disenfranchised urban underclass) can, nevertheless, produce globally recognized examples of "ordinary" cultural practices such as U2, the Corrs, Van Morrison, Riverdance, and, of course, many critically acclaimed films. The success of these ventures serves to underscore further the importance of an open, all-embracing cultural identity which is at once Irish, European, and Anglo-American.

Conclusion

To attempt an overview or analysis of European cultural studies is to be immediately reminded of Ien Ang's warnings concerning the privileged position European intellectuals construct whereby the proposition that self-doubt is a uniquely European quality excludes "others" from an analysis of Europe and underlines the conceit that Europe has the capacity to interrogate itself. Nevertheless, this self-examination is vital if Europe is to move from a form of cultural study which is static, conservative, and finds its intellectual force and relevance in replaying and reinforcing the mythical status of European "high" art and cultural iconography.

Having established exactly what is meant by European cultural studies, the move can then be made to create and articulate projects that will offer opportunities for advancement and progression where European economic and cultural policies can operate with a visionary complementarity. That definition will be facilitated if those working in European cultural studies create the conditions necessary to confront the key issues as outlined by Ang (1998a: 89):

> How are Eurocentric modes of thinking articulated within contemporary European culture itself as an "implicit (self)positioning," a lived structure of feeling? How does this structure of feeling inform the experience of being European in the late twentieth century? And what is the politics of European Eurocentrism today? These questions go some way towards what I would call a cultural studies of contemporary Europe – that is, an understanding of "Europe" not just as an abstract idea, but as a concrete, complex and contradictory social space where

particular forms of cultural practice and lived experience are shaped, negotiated, and struggled over.

References

Anderson, B. (1983). *Imagined Communities*. London: Verso

Ang, I. (1998a). "Eurocentric Reluctance – Notes for a Cultural Studies of 'the New Europe." In Kuan-Hsing Chen (ed.), *Trajectories – Inter-Asia Cultural Studies*. London: Routledge.

Ang, I. (1998b). "Doing Cultural Studies at the Crossroads: Local/Global Negotiations." *European Journal of Cultural Studies* 1 (Jan.).

Appadurai, A. (1990). "Disjunction and Difference in the Global Cultural Economy." *Theory, Culture and Society*, 7(2–3).

Bell, D. (1990). *Acts of Union – Youth Culture and Sectarianism in Northern Ireland*. London: Macmillan.

Bird, J., T. Putnam, G. Robertson, and L. Tickner (eds.) (1993). *Mapping the Futures – Local Cultures, Global Change*. London: Routledge.

Burns, R. (ed.) (1995). *German Cultural Studies*. Oxford: Oxford University Press.

Butler, D. (1994). "The Study of Culture in Northern Ireland." *Causeway* 1(3): 50–6.

Chambers, I. (1990). *Border Dialogues – Journeys in Postmodernity*. London: Routledge.

Durant, A. (1997). Quoted in G. Turner (1997). *British Cultural Studies*. London: Unwin Hymen.

Featherstone, M. (1993). "Global and Local Cultures." In J. Bird et al. (eds.), *Mapping the Futures – Local Cultures, Global Change*. London: Routledge.

Forbes, J. and M. Kelly (eds.) (1995). *French Cultural Studies*. Oxford: Oxford University Press.

Giddens, A. (1990). *The Consequences of Modernity*. Cambridge: Polity Press.

Gilroy, P. (1987). *There Ain't No Black in the Union Jack*. London: Routledge.

Giroux, H. (1992). "Resisting Difference: Cultural Studies and the Discourse of Critical Pedagogy." In L. Grossberg, C. Nelson, and P. Treschler (eds.), *Cultural Studies*. New York: Routledge.

Graham, C. (1994). "The Poet, the Shah and Alladin: Culture High and Low: Ideology and Understanding." *Causeway* 1(3): 71–4.

Graham, H. and J. Labanyi (eds.) (1995). *Spanish Cultural Studies*. Oxford: Oxford University Press.

Hainsworth, P. (1994). "Politics, Culture and Cinema in the New Europe." In J. Hill, M. McLoone, and P. Hainsworth (eds.), *Border Crossing – Film in Ireland, Britain and Europe*. Belfast: Institute of Irish Studies.

Harvey, D. (1990). *The Condition of Postmodernity*, Oxford: Blackwell.

Hill, J., M. McLoone, and P. Hainsworth (eds.) (1994). *Border Crossing: Film in Ireland, Britain and Europe*. Belfast: Institute of Irish Studies.

Hoffman, S. (1981). *Culture and Society in Contemporary Europe: A Casebook*. London: Allen and Unwin.

Horak, R. (1999). "Cultural Studies in Germany (and Austria) and Why There Is No Such Thing." *European Journal of Cultural Studies* 2(1).

Jameson, F. (1991). *Postmodernism, or, The Cultural Logic of Late Capitalism*. London: Verso.

Jarvie, G. and J. Maguire (1994). *Sport and Leisure in Social Thought*. London: Routledge.

Kearney, R. (1992). *Visions of Europe: Conversations on the Legacy and Future of Europe*. Dublin: Wolfhound Press.

Massey, D. (1998). "The Spatial Construction of Youth Cultures." In T. Skelton and G. Valentine (eds.), *Cool Places – Geographies of Youth Cultures*. London: Routledge.

McGuigan, J. (1996). *Culture and the Public Sphere*. London: Routledge.

McLoone, M. (1994). "From Dublin up to Sandy Row: Van Morrison and Cultural Identity in Northern Ireland." *Causeway* 1(3): 39–44.

Morley, D. and K. Robins (1995). *Spaces of Identity – Global Media, Electronic Landscapes and Cultural Boundaries*. London: Routledge.

Payne, M. (1996). *A Dictionary of Cultural and Critical Theory*. Oxford: Blackwell.

Stratton, J. (2000). "Cyberspace and the Globalisation of Culture." In D. Bell and B. M. Kennedy (eds.), *The Cybercultures Reader*. London: Routledge.

Tomlinson, J. (1991). *Cultural Imperialism: A Critical Introduction*. London: Pinter.

Webster, D. (1988). *Looka Yonder: The Imaginary America of Popular Culture*. London: Comedia.

Williams, R. (1963). *Culture and Society 1780–1950*. Harmondsworth: Penguin.

Willis, P. (1990). *Common Culture*. Buckingham: Open University Press.

Willis, P. (1998). "Notes on Common Culture: Towards a Grounded Aesthetics." *European Journal of Cultural Studies* 1(2).

PART III

Issues

Chapter 18

Let's Get Serious: Notes on Teaching Youth Culture

Justin Lewis

The lights in the lecture theater go down as 200 undergraduates' eyes flicker obediently towards the enlarged video screen. A fresh-faced John Lydon – Johnny Rotten as was – leers towards the politely attentive students. "God save the queen . . . She ain't no human bein'" he taunts, leaning into the camera with an expression that manages to be both half-crazed and whimsical. If most of the students enjoy this irreverent interruption, I am struck by the oddity of the moment, and it is at this point in my "Popular Culture and Cultural Studies" course that I am forced to confront the audacity involved in teaching youth culture to youth.

Although the lecture theater speakers keep the crashing sound of the old Sex Pistols ditty at a respectable volume, I like to think that they do not, even now, entirely contain the breezy, twinkle-eyed rudeness of the video clip. And yet this is, in the lifespan of popular culture, a piece of ancient history, one that has been plucked from dusty archives like a relic of a bygone age. Most of the students in the lecture theater are in their late teens or early twenties. This was the music I was listening to at their age, a time before they were born. I can't help wondering what on earth they make of it.

The aim of the lecture is to explore the connections and discontinuities between the economic structure of a cultural industry and the culture it pro-duces, but the video clip is too loud to be read merely as an illustration of a particular point. It symbolizes not only the gap between professor and student but the difficulty of being analytical about something so visceral without appear-ing to entirely miss the point. I am reminded of the quip that writing about music is like dancing about architecture.[1] But I am more painfully aware that the link between the clip and my own youth labels me, to use the historically appropriate vernacular, as "a boring old fart," a status compounded by my attempt to be serious about something so playful.

At the risk of making matters irretrievably worse, I shall, in this essay, briefly ponder some of the issues this raises about the purpose and pitfalls of teaching popular culture. My main concern is one of being taken seriously, since whatever

317

else it might be, popular culture is a serious business. I shall begin with the general obstacle that lies in the path of those who might want to teach popular culture – especially youth culture – at an institutional level. Having made it to the lecture theater or the classroom, I will then briefly consider two major pedagogical difficulties: the problems involved in persuading "youth" to view their own culture critically; and the problem of authority on a terrain which appears to be the student's territory.

This chapter thereby puts forward three distinct arguments. First, teaching popular culture and/or youth culture is something that has been forced upon the academy rather than embraced by it. Indeed, it is regarded with skepticism in many sectors of elite public discourse. We are therefore operating in a potentially hostile climate – one that requires us to be more forceful and less opaque than we have been in advocating the importance of teaching popular culture. Second, that one of the main issues involved in teaching popular culture is to address the politics of pleasure – and, in particular, the specific forms of investment that undergraduates bring to popular youth culture. Third, that we need to acknowledge the awkward pedagogy invoked by the example with which I began, when the past and present of popular culture tend to separate the teacher from the student, and where our frames of reference will be quite different.

Popular Culture and the Climate of Anti-intellectualism

If the idea that popular culture could be the subject-matter for academic inquiry is gradually gaining acceptance, there are still many who regard the whole exercise as essentially trivial. This suspicion is perhaps most regularly exhibited in Britain – where an odd combination of stuffiness and cynicism has given rise to a chorus of sneers about media and cultural studies. Whether it is dismissed for being too lightweight or too pretentious, the assumption is that popular culture – especially popular youth culture – lacks the gravitas and tedium required of an academic subject. The paradox of these dismissals, I would argue, is that the claim to promote academic standards is delivered from a profoundly anti-intellectual stance.

The gist of the argument against popular culture is that university teaching and research should be difficult and complex, while media and popular culture is so patently easy and accessible that it scarcely requires a degree to understand it. Popular culture, it is suggested, should be what students do outside their classes, not in them.

In its most virulent form, this argument presents the media or cultural studies teacher as a figure of derision or ridicule – a flaky pseudo-intellectual whose antics are the source of amusement or despair at the decline in educational standards. Those who teach media and cultural studies tend to be either defensive or dismissive about these criticisms. Nevertheless, we have, as a group, done

318

a poor job of countering them with an argument for taking popular culture seriously, and it is worth reminding ourselves and others why many of us write about and teach popular culture.

The problem with the attack on popular culture in the academy is three-fold. First, it assumes that if something is popular, there can't be much to it. Second, it entirely overlooks the importance of popular culture in shaping or defining human development. And third, it tends to assume that popular culture is the expression of public taste (and hence something that needs little explanation), rather than the product of an array of structural conditions.

The first of these problems is, as Pierre Bourdieu has pointed out, a matter of class distinction, of marking a territory of "legitimate" culture that is generally beyond the reach of popular understanding and appreciation.[2] These distinctions have traditionally been solidified by the aisles of scholarly books – on literature, art, and music – that assumed those distinctions. And yet the aesthetic differences between the popular and the refined have always been extraordinarily fragile. So fragile, indeed, that critics have expended enormous amounts of energy in explaining *why* something is worthy of scholarly scrutiny. We can read F. R. Leavis, for example, as an attempt to police the boundaries of legitimate culture: his grudging acceptance of just *one* Dickens novel into *The Great Tradition* is a way to acknowledge the author's flair – but one senses that any further embrace would have been, for Leavis, a little too accepting of the novelist's links to popular culture (see Leavis 1948).

Leavis may no longer be fashionable, but the arts and humanities are still largely premised on notions of value. Canons may shift to reflect contemporary concerns – feminism and multiculturalism being particularly important in this regard – but inclusion in course syllabi is still generally based on a series of qualitative judgments, on the notion that something is worthy of study because it is worthy. This was a notion that some of the Marxist cultural theorists of the Frankfurt School were just as committed to as the less complicated exponents of elite culture.[3] Even Roland Barthes, whose work opened many avenues into the study of popular culture, afforded considerably more attention to Racine that he did to wrestling (see Barthes 1964 and 1988).

In this context, it is not hard to imagine the jaw-dropping incredulity felt by many when university libraries start filling their shelves with books about romance novels, *Star Trek*, or rap music. When Chris Woodhead, the Chief Inspector of Schools in Britain, launched a familiar attack on media studies, reporters had no difficulty finding academics to wax sardonically. So, for example, *The Independent* quoted Professor Alan Smithers thus: "So far there are not things like Shakespeare and Chaucer on some of the media being studied. I don't think it's the same having someone watch all 57 episodes of *The Sweeney*" (March 3, 2000). The carefully constructed distinctions that elevate cultural texts and objects to the professorial gaze are not so much threatened by such attention to popular culture as resolutely flouted. In this context, any backlash against such rude intrusions is entirely predictable.

But most of those in cultural studies who read, write, and teach such books are not making an argument that popular culture is (or can be) "as good as" traditional forms of art and literature – on the contrary, it is the *attacks* on media and cultural studies that tend to speak in terms of quality. If media and cultural studies draw a great deal from the arts and humanities (where much of the work in fields such as semiotics and poststructuralism has been developed), it also has roots in the social sciences, where qualitative judgments about what is worthy of scrutiny have nothing to do with whether something is considered good or bad.[4] The reason for analyzing popular culture is not to assess its value but, in a more anthropological sense, its *significance*. In other words, a cultural object can be worthy of study regardless of whether it is considered good or bad.

As a consequence, it is important to resist the temptation to resort to qualitative judgments in defending popular culture.[5] This kind of response is all too common in cultural studies, from Richard Hoggart's *The Uses of Literacy* (1958) onwards. Once the study of popular culture is predicated on aesthetic criteria it can only become embroiled in pointless arguments about the nature of those criteria. Popular culture is important, first and foremost, because it is popular.

In these terms, popular culture is, for most people most of the time, considerably more ubiquitous than most of the literature, music, or art studied in universities. Our lives are more often occupied by the television we watch, the magazines we read, the sports teams we support, the places we shop, the music we listen to, and so on. This is not to belittle the study of more rarefied forms of culture, nor to ignore the profundity of an encounter with cultural forms, but merely to appreciate the range of cultural forms available in a given society in attempting to understand that society. This has been understood by historians for some time.[6]

Which raises the second problem with the refusal to take popular culture seriously. To imagine that we live in a cognitive universe in which we file popular forms like television, fashion, or pop music into a mental compartment labeled "trivial ephemera" is sociologically naive. In short: popular consciousness is shaped by popular culture. Part of the failure to fully appreciate this point comes from the assumption that the influence of popular culture only matters if it leads to antisocial behavior or crude forms of mimicry – a kind of robotic response to commands from the cultural industries – or that the influence of popular culture relies on some form of gullibility. Since popular culture is not usually issued in the form of overt directives – "vote this way" or "challenge/obey authority" – its influence is unlikely to be felt in these terms.

One of the ways in which I make this point to my students is by asking them what they know. I begin by asking them to name the occupations of characters – either real or fictional – who are firmly inscribed in popular culture (such as Homer Simpson or Vanna White). This is familiar ground, and most raise their hands confidently. I then ask them to tell me the occupations of people who might be regarded as important but whose presence in popular culture is minimal (such as UN general secretary Kofi Annan or John Sweeney, the head of the

AFL–CIO). Very few raise their hands (thus John Sweeney may be the head of the largest labor organization in the US while occupying a position of almost complete obscurity in the culture), and many students look sheepish as if expecting an admonition for absorbing trivia at the expense of more important information. And yet the point of the exercise is simply to demonstrate that much of what we know about the world – the people, images, stories, and associations that accumulate in our heads – comes from popular culture. Even if this knowledge had little impact on people's opinions (an epistemologically absurd proposition, in my view), its voluminous presence is part of what defines contemporary life. And this is hardly a trivial matter.

This, in turn, raises the third difficulty of ignoring popular culture as an object of study. As Stuart Hall (1986) points out, popular culture may be for the people but it not by the people. And cultural studies has long insisted that the cultural industries are far more than mere reflections of something produced elsewhere (whether popular desires or dominant ideologies). There is, in this sense, nothing "natural" or inevitable about popular culture. Why is it, for example, that soccer is largely ignored by North American adults when it is so popular in most of the places that their ancestors came from? If the question seems fairly unimportant in the scheme of things – which it may well be – the answer involves a complex understanding of the way culture works, part of which requires us to appreciate the role television plays in promoting certain sports and, as a consequence, the very particular history of commercial broadcasting in the United States. So, for example, if the United States is unusual in ignoring soccer, it is also distinctive in having a broadcasting system that has – at least since the 1930s – been conceived primarily (from an industry perspective) as a marketing tool. In such a system, a sport that requires 45 to 50 minutes of uninterrupted program time is, if not quite an impossibility, certainly less attractive than sports with frequent breaks – like boxing or baseball – or sports that could be easily molded around frequent breaks – like basketball or American Football. Similarly, if commercial media seem quintessentially "American," their evolution was not inexorable, nor was it a response to public demand – it was the highly contested victory of one set of forces against another (see e.g. McChesney 1990; Douglas 1987; Kellner 1990). And as Michael Real (1989) has argued, the consequent development of American Football (as opposed to soccer) has a range of cultural resonances.

This is by no means the only answer to this question – there are cultural histories involved here that go beyond the political economy of sport and media, while cultural expectations can become self-determining – but it is one that illustrates the way in which economic or social structures can limit or shape cultural possibilities in very specific ways. Even the pop music industry – which is, perhaps, striking for its moments of aesthetic autonomy (thus, for example, punk rock in Britain developed *before* a huge rise in youth unemployment rather than being a straightforward reaction to socioeconomic conditions) – consists of rhythms and tunes arising from a backdrop of industry structures, immigration patterns, social welfare policies, and an array of ideological struggles around gender, sex, race, family, age, authority, and power.

Understanding contemporary society is therefore central to an understanding of popular culture. And since popular culture is the terrain upon which social and ideological struggles are played out, understanding popular culture is central to an understanding of contemporary society.

In this context, to regard the study of popular culture as trivial is to deny any serious engagement with our cultural environment, whether to appreciate why it is thus, how it could be different, or what its consequences are for our social development. Indeed, even if we accepted the unlikely proposition that popular culture was a discrete realm of no significance beyond an imagined set of boundaries, to imagine life without advertising, or sport, or television – regardless of whether we view it as an absence or a freedom – is to imagine a social transformation. To refuse to imagine it is to stifle intellectual inquiry and, as a consequence, a range of cultural possibilities.

As I have suggested, it is in Britain that this stubborn anti-intellectualism is most often articulated. This is all the more notable given the intellectual history of the study of popular culture. Rather than celebrate the enormous global influence of British cultural studies, the study of media and popular culture is more often portrayed as an embarrassment – the "media studies lecturer" being regarded in many circles with much the same snickering contempt reserved for British sociologists in the sixties and seventies. The strength of this kind of British anti-intellectualism is a complex articulation whose roots might be found scattered amidst ideas of class, sexuality, and the self-regarding professionalism in some quarters of British journalism. But it is by no means an exclusively British phenomenon. Even in the Unites States – a place that is much more receptive to the study of popular culture – there are areas of lingering suspicion. When I first proposed teaching a regular course in popular culture at the University of Massachusetts in 1990, the Faculty Senate Committee charged with approving new courses expressed initial concern about its "academic" content – a response that revealed a certain unease with the presence of the popular in the academy (teaching *un*popular forms of culture, on the other hand, is assumed to have a certain scholarly worthiness).

Needless to say, negative reactions to teaching popular culture have done little to halt its growth in colleges and universities. This is, in part, because of the influence of such work on young academics and the popularity of – and demand for – such courses among students (a demand that generally exceeds supply, sometimes leading – interestingly – to more rigorous academic requirements than for less popular subjects). It would be overoptimistic to assume that its popularity with students is always a product of the same kinds of concerns that drive those of us who teach it.[7] At the same time, teaching young adults about *their* popular culture is precarious for all concerned. Enrollment may not be a problem, but provoking engagement in a serious analysis of popular youth culture is a little trickier. I want to consider two difficulties here: the problem of establishing a critical distance with a subject that may involve a high degree of emotional investment, and the gap between student and teacher in their popular cultural references.

The Politics of Pleasure

I am often asked by my students – and this will be familiar to others who teach media and cultural studies – about my *own* experience of popular culture. After all, my apparent desire to analyze everything most people do for fun does seem a little peculiar. How, they ask, do I do everyday things like watching television or going shopping? Do I exist in a permanent state of critique, in which popular culture is consumed through a relentlessly analytical lens? Since I seem, to them, inclined to deconstruct everything from sitcoms to photo albums, it is impossible for them to imagine me relaxing in front of the TV set. Or, to put it another way, I appear to have become emotionally and intellectually divested from the entire realm. While some are faintly in awe of this idea, for most people the image conjures up an alien and rather clinical existence. All work and no play must give the professor a dull life.

The question is partly a consequence of the link between investment and pleasure. If we do not have a stake in popular culture – if we are always critically disengaged – then how can we enjoy it? While the question may seem quaint or naive, it is nonetheless an important one – one that forces us to address ways in which we might deal with the various commitments people have to popular cultural forms.

A recent study by Chyng Sun (1999) examines some of the pedagogical issues that confront teachers who want to equip their students with the tools for a critical textual analysis of a piece of popular culture in which they are invested. The study involved Disney's *The Little Mermaid* – a film most of the students had seen countless times, and which was, for many, a fond (and not too distant) childhood memory. Students were asked to read Hans Andersen's original story and then to compare the two in order to consider some of the ideological moves made by the Disney version – particularly in relation to gender stereotyping. Sun's study of this process powerfully conveyed the degree to which the students' investment in the film – as part of their own cultural history – made it difficult for them to accept an analysis that in other circumstances they may have found compelling. In brief, ideological scrutiny of Disney's *The Little Mermaid* was difficult to accept because it seemed to belittle their own cultural history – to trample clumsily over a happy childhood memory. It was, in a sense, killjoy criticism.

Asking students to examine their popular culture requires them to confront their own fragile subjectivity. This can be especially uncomfortable in a culture that promotes notions of independence, individuality, and free will – especially in matters of cultural consumption. To see oneself as socially constructed and

323

popular culture as part of that process is unsettling – all the more so when the analysis throws up contradictions between politics and pleasure. So, for example, many of the students in Sun's study might have been more inclined to endorse a critique of gender stereotyping in contexts in which they were less obviously invested. This may be why Jean Kilbourne's critique of gender roles in advertising has been so extraordinarily successful in its appeal to students[8] – while they may enjoy a particularly well-crafted or witty commercial, few young people feel they have an emotional stake in advertising as a genre. Disney's *The Little Mermaid*, on the other hand, was something they wanted to feel nostalgia towards without being burdened by the need to either embrace or ignore traditional images of female passivity. Female students were put in the particularly difficult position of confronting their own hitherto unquestioning acceptance of stereotypical gender roles.

If this investment attracts students to the study of popular culture – here, after all, is subject-matter they already feel they know and perhaps enjoy – it can, by the same token, make them wary of attempts to mess with their pleasures and preconceptions. Some, like John Fiske (1989) or Henry Jenkins (1992), have partly avoided this problem by invoking their own "fandom" and by stressing the semiotic potential of popular texts. Such a position allows a degree of common ground from which critiques might be developed. So, for example, Jenkins described how gay fans of *Star Trek* were able to exploit the textual ambiguities of the show, and to then move to a more critical position in terms of representational politics. Such an approach creates a degree of solidarity, because, like much literary criticism, it comes from a generally appreciative standpoint. But regardless of whether or not this "insider" posture makes analysis more or less astute, it is not a position that can be easily sustained across a syllabus. Apart from anything else, it either limits us to those forms of popular culture we enjoy, or else requires a rather disingenuous posturing.

We need, nonetheless, to find ways to negotiate the politics of pleasure, of showing how certain popular pleasures are articulated with constraining ideologies (like patriarchy) and how they might be rearticulated with other ideological possibilities.[9] This is more straightforward in instances where the culture offers glimpses of both (say, for example, music video or rap music). There are, however, important instances where cultural forms have become naturalized, and where alternatives seem remote, difficult to imagine, or unsettling in their unfamiliarity.

In the US, perhaps the most significant example of this is the commercial model of broadcasting. It is difficult for students to understand the constraints and proclivities of this system without them appreciating how else it could be. To this end, we can take students through broadcasting history in order to demonstrate how notions of public-service broadcasting were marginalized and, after a brief resurgence in the 1960s, virtually eradicated. We can then examine the many limitations that come with corporate oligopolies using television and radio as a mechanism for selling audiences to advertisers, both in terms of ideological limits (whereby broadcasting is required to promote an ideology of individual consumerism) and the aesthetic limits of programs that must successfully deliver audiences to advertisers every 7 or 8 minutes. But while students in the US may grasp all of this in general, abstract terms, their experience of television tells them that commercial television is often entertaining while public service television (PBS) is generally drab. These powerful associations are likely to limit imaginations to such an extent that a critical history and analysis of commercial broadcasting will ultimately flounder on the suspicion that public-service television would take a popular show like *ER* and turn it into *Masterpiece Theater*. It is in this sense that one could argue that PBS in its current form – as an alternative to rather than a different kind of popular television – plays a significant role in maintaining the hegemony of the commercial system (see Ouellette 1999).

The only way to deal with these associations, I would argue, is to confront them head on, to discuss the ways in which these associations have been constructed, and whose interests they serve. This leaves the difficult task of rearticulating some of commercial television's popular pleasures – well-constructed stories, high production values, and so on – with imaginary pleasures which a public-service system might offer (such as fewer commercials or a willingness to deal with controversial material that advertiser's might be squeamish about). Although this can be a difficult and somewhat precarious task, a critical analysis of broadcasting will be merciless if it is presented as a choice between acquiescing to corporate, consumerist notions of citizenship or else submitting oneself to a diet of dreariness.

If we may stretch the analogy a little, we might say that students will see little value in divesting themselves from popular culture – in order to achieve a critical distance – if they see no opportunity of investment in other forms of pleasure. This, in turn, forces us to consider the pleasures of popular culture and how these pleasures do or do not relate to ideological positions. Thus, for example, Janice Radway (1984, 1986, 1994) recognizes the pleasure of romance novels and considers how these pleasures can be separated from patriarchal ideologies.

We may discover, of course, that what some people like about certain popular cultural forms is precisely the ideological baggage they may carry. So, for example, it may be that some people like advertising not because of its production values (which might be rearticulated with notions of citizenship rather than consumerism) but because they wish – along with the genre – to celebrate the joys of consumption. It is our job, in this instance, to point out the nature of this (or any other) ideological choice and discuss its broader social consequences.[10]

Teaching Past the Present

One of the most striking aspects of contemporary popular culture is the speed at which it changes and evolves. Many forms of popular culture therefore tend to be age-specific – particularly those linked to youth. Perhaps the most obvious example of this is the pop music industry, whose products seem to stick to us like some form of aural glue, trapping generations in a permanent taste culture. The pop music industry – particularly in the second half of the twentieth century – can thus be easily subdivided into mini-epochs, each with their distinctive sound and styles. Indeed, the simple act of naming a decade is to summon up echoes of one pop music genre or another. Bob Dylan concerts may not be exclusively the preserve of aging baby boomers, but their presence at such events is as striking as the absence of hip hop in their collections.

One can bemoan the conservatism of those who stop listening to anything genuinely new or different past the age of 30 – and teachers of popular culture often feel themselves (perhaps a little smugly) atypically transcendent in this respect – but we should not overlook why this is and what it means. To put it candidly, many will feel that there is something a little odd about someone in their forties (still fairly young for an academic, but several mini-epochs removed from most students) claiming a degree of expertise about cultural forms that are almost exclusively the preserve of those in their teens or twenties.

Despite the claims of some of the more essentialist forms of identity politics, one does not have to be of a cultural milieu to be able to speak – and speak in ways that are illuminating – about that milieu. But this is not an excuse for blundering into cultural domains in which we may be seen as outsiders without giving a certain pause. In the case of pop music culture, for example, it may be possible to know about the more recent genres and to thereby locate them within structures of ideology, aesthetics, or political economy, but this knowledge does not pre-suppose an equivalence. Pop music culture and youth culture are experientially linked in particular ways: pop music provides the sound effects for the litany of experience that defines youth and young adulthood, the freshness and excite-ment of one thereby becomes associated with the freshness and excitement of the other.

These connections are vividly evoked in Susan Douglas's (1994) cultural history *Where the Girls Are*, in which she recounts the very particular pleasure of listening to the Beatles or the Shirelles and the symbolic role they played in defining gender roles and, contradictorily, in liberating girls from those roles. Indeed, it is partly because pop music is one of the more intimate cultural forms – sex, love, pain, and rebellion, for example, are not just its subject-matter but its accompaniment – that genres tend to stick with us with the exploratory intensity of the early encounters through which we feel our way into adulthood. Growing up with hip hop is therefore quite different from encountering it in middle age. It becomes less bound up with notions of authenticity or with locales of space and place.

Equally, to return to the example with which I began, my students will experience late 1970s punk rock as part of someone else's history, something whose meaning is disconnected from the mood or a way of being that is indelibly forged in my own experience of something like *God Save the Queen*. For the students, there is no shock of the new, merely a shuffling of genealogical context.

The meaning of *God Save the Queen* is thereby slotted into a history that ends with the present.

In this context, teaching youth culture to youth is partly a matter of avoiding various pedagogical pitfalls. Adopting a posture of hip solidarity – even if one is capable of pulling it off – not only risks being regarded as an imposter, it communicates a misunderstanding of how popular music and youth culture are bound up with one another. Pop music is made up of profoundly historical texts: their meaning cannot be united from the contexts in which they appear, and from the more general intertextuality of youth culture.

Equally, the valorization of particular moments of pop music history (most notoriously the 1960s, a period some baby-boom professors are inclined to endow with an authenticity from which all subsequent periods are a falling away) as somehow more important than the present may – depending on your system of evaluation – be plausible. But for most students, the significance of the past is measured in terms of its relation to the current, and the only vibrant living youth culture available *as* youth culture is in the here and now.

Avoiding these two positions – either a hip solidarity or treatment of the present as merely an offshoot of the past – requires an attitude of measured deference: an understanding of what makes contemporary youth culture distinct rather than unique. Since we are obliged to teach the history of popular cultural forms (if we are to understand them), this involves using a teleological narrative *without* naturalizing the present. Presenting the history of popular culture as somehow leading up (or else failing to lead up) to contemporary forms or versions is more compelling for most undergraduates. This is a useful pedagogical strategy, but like most teleological narratives it can make the present *appear* to be the final chapter – the "end of history" in which the cultural industries are absorbed by a few dozen huge transnational corporations.

One way to avoid this premature ending is teach *past* the present, to ask students to use their knowledge of history to speculate about the development of the cultural industries. This can, apart from anything else, be fun. It also requires us to incorporate an understanding of *cultural policy* in teaching popular culture. For most students (especially in the US) the "invisible hand" shaping cultural policy is not the marketplace but government subsidy and regulation – "invisible" because so much cultural policy is inadvertent. So, for example, the US government's adoption of a range of policies – massive subsidy for roads rather than rapid urban transit, weak zoning regulations and tax breaks based on accelerated depreciation of property investment – led to the ubiquity of the suburban shopping mall and the decline of city centers (see Jackson 1996). But while the outcome of these policies has transformed the cultural landscape in the United States, this was not their intent. Thus although the US may have no official cultural policy, it has a vast apparatus of cultural *policies* – from the subsidizing of advertizing expenditure through tax breaks to public funding for college radio stations – which have been instrumental in shaping its cultural industries (see Dimaggio 1983; Miller 1993).

327

Once students begin to understand the relation between cultural policies and cultural forms, they can begin to imagine how things might be. The present thereby becomes a moment in a historical trajectory – privileged, but a moment nonetheless. The scope of this imagining relies upon an understanding in which history moves in zig zags, circles, and squiggles rather than straight lines. So, for example, the well-known study by Peterson and Berger (1990) demonstrates that corporate consolidation in the pop music industry has waxed and waned: the apparently ironclad control of the industry by a corporate oligopoly in the early 1950s and then again in the mid-1970s, proved, on both occasions, to be neither inexorable nor entrenched. The market power of the conglomerates was, in both instances, an insufficient basis for maintaining artistic control in an industry where the desire for novelty and innovation is purely served by the conservative corporate dynamics of minimizing risk and maximizing profit. The current state of the industry – in which the corporate sector has bought up the "independent" sector (see Miller 1997) – can therefore be seen as unstable, rather than the final triumphant return of the corporate giants.

In sum, what I am proposing here is that we use the present as our focal point, since this is the lens through which our students will understand the history of popular youth culture. But if this focal point is, in a sense, the end of the history that preceded it, the complex twists and turns of that history helps us *also* see the present as the beginning of a range of possibilities. And if students are to feel that they can have any part in shaping these possibilities, then cultural policy must be enmeshed into the pedagogy of teaching popular culture.

Notes

1   A comment with which Andrew Goodwin begins *Dancing in the Distraction Factory*, his 1992 book about MTV.
2   Outlined in Pierre Bourdieu's book *Distinction* (1984).
3   See, for example, the oft-criticized cultural elitism of Adorno and Horkheimer's famous essay on "The Culture Industry as Mass Deception" (1979).
4   An argument that has also been made by some community artists – see, for example, Kelly 1984.
5   Which is not to say that qualitative judgments are not important – on the contrary, we need to make distinctions in order to describe cultural possibilities. But to argue that we study popular culture because it is good is, in my view, to miss the point.
6   Whether it is E. P. Thompson's influential *The Making of the English Working Class* (1968) or Kenneth Jackson's discussion of shopping malls (1996), historians who want to deal with popular life rather than the history of elites have to confront popular culture, and they may do so without the obligation to make value judgments.
7   My large lecture course in popular culture is always heavily over-enrolled, but I am under no illusions that this is purely in response to a thirst for reading Antonio Gramsci or Roland Barthes.

8   Kilbourne's *Killing Us Softly* is, to my knowledge, the most successful video about media ever made. Kilbourne has, Hollywood-syle, recently made the third version of this tape *Killing Us Softly III*.

9   See Morley 1992 for a discussion of pleasure and hegemony, and Hall 1996 or Slack 1996 for a discussion of articulation.

10   See, for example, Sut Jhally's video *Advertising and the End of the World* for a rather dramatic example of spelling out the consequences of a cultural system.

References

Adorno, T. and M. Horkheimer (1979). "The Culture Industry as Mass Deception." In *The Dialectic of Enlightenment*. London: Verso.

Barthes, R. (1964). *On Racine*. New York: Hill and Wang.

Barthes, R. (1988). *Mythologies*. New York: Noonday Press.

Bourdieu, P. (1984). *Distinction: A Social Critique of the Judgment of Taste*. Cambridge, Mass.: Harvard University Press.

Dimaggio, P. (1983). "Cultural Policy Studies: What They Are and Why We Need Them." *Journal of Arts Management, Law and Society* 13(1): 241–8.

Douglas, S. (1994). *Where the Girls Are*. New York: Times Books.

Douglas, S. (1987). *Inventing American Broadcasting, 1899–1922*. Baltimore: Johns Hopkins University Press.

Fiske, J. (1989). *Understanding Popular Culture*. Boston: Unwin Hyman.

Goodwin, A. (1992). *Dancing in the Distraction Factory*. Minneapolis: University of Minnesota Press.

Gramsci, A. (1971). *Selections from the Prison Notebooks*. London: Lawrence and Wishart.

Hall, S. (1986). "Popular Culture and the State." In T. Bennett, C. Mercer, and J. Woollacott (eds.), *Popular Culture and Social Relations*. Milton Keynes: Open University Press.

Hall, S. (1996). "On Postmodernism and Articulation: An Interview." In D. Morley and K.-H. Chen (eds.), *Stuart Hall: Critical Developments in Cultural Studies*. London: Routledge.

Hoggart, R. (1958). *The Uses of Literacy*. London: Penguin.

Jackson, K. (1996). "All the World's a Mall: Reflections on the Social and Economic Consequences of the American Shopping Center." *American Historical Review* Oct. 1111–21.

Jenkins, H. (1992). *Textual Poachers: Television Fans and Participatory Culture*. New York: Routledge.

Jenkins, H. (1995). "Out of the Closet and Into the Universe." In J. Tulloch and H. Jenkins (eds.), *Science Fiction Audiences*. London: Routledge.

Kellner, D. (1990). *Television and the Crisis of Democracy*. Boulder, Colo.: Westview Press.

Kelly, O. (1984). *Community, Art and the State*. London: Comedia.

Leavis, F. R. (1948). *The Great Tradition*. London: Chatto & Windus.

McChesney, R. (1990). "The Battle for the US Airwaves, 1928–1935." *Journal of Communication* 40(4): 29–57.

Miller, M. (1997). "Who Controls the Music?" *The Nation*, Aug. 25/Sept. 1, pp. 11–16.

Miller, T. (1993). *The Well-Tempered Self: Citizenship, Culture and the Postmodern Subject*. Baltimore: Johns Hopkins University Press.

Morley, D. (1992). *Television, Audiences and Cultural Studies*. London: Routledge.

Ouellette, L. (1999). "TV Viewing as Good Citizenship?: Political Rationality, Enlightened Democracy and PBS." *Cultural Studies* 13(1): 62–90.

Peterson, Richard A. and David G. Berger (1990). "Cycles in Symbol Production: The Case of Popular Music." In S. Frith and A. Goodwin (eds.), *On Record*. New York: Pantheon.

Radway, J. (1984). *Reading the Romance*. Chapel Hill: University of North Carolina Press.

Radway, J. (1986). "Identifying Ideological Seams: Mass Culture, Analytical Method, and Political Practice." *Communication* 9.

Radway, J. (1994). "Romance and the Work of Fantasy: Struggles over Feminine Sexuality and Subjectivity at Century's End." In J. Cruz and J. Lewis, *Viewing Reading Listening*. Boulder, Colo.: Westview Press.

Real, M. (1989). "Super Bowl Versus World Cup Soccer: A Cultural Structural Comparison." In L. A. Wenner (ed.), *Media, Sports and Society*. California: Sage.

Slack, J. (1996). "The Theory and Method of Articulation in Cultural Studies." In D. Morley et al. (eds.), *Stuart Hall: Critical Dialogues in Cultural Studies*. London: Routledge.

Sun, C. (1999). "Reading Disney." Paper presented at the University Film and Video Association Conference, Aug.

Thompson, E. P. (1968). *The Making of the English Working Class*. London: Pelican Books.

Chapter 19

Looking Backwards and Forwards at Cultural Studies

Paul Smith

It's probably a completely boring thing to be doing, as we enter the twenty-first century, to be looking back over cultural studies and its history and trying to imagine its future. For one thing, the issues involved in thinking about this field, or about what could or should constitute it, have rather been done to death over the last four decades, even if there's not much sign of the activity abating. On the other hand, it seems to be the case that this perpetual undertaking of defining and redefining, looking backwards and forwards, has often been taken as a sign of the very vitality of the field, and sometimes as an essential and positive part of its nature and task; therefore, insofar as a constitutive claim of that sort keeps being made, it still needs attending to. Cultural studies, we often hear, is what it is and is valuable in part because it doesn't rest or stand still but rather continually reinvents itself to adjust to new information and new circumstances. We might argue, on the other hand, that this state of flux is rather more a symptom of confusion and uncertainty than an essential strength in the enterprise. It might be that at this juncture, as before in the history of the field, nobody really quite knows what cultural studies is, and what it will be, even where it is, where it will be.

As well as risking the boredom of yet more of such rehashing, this chapter will probably also be a somewhat foolhardy thing, since in a way it comes to try and bury cultural studies – at least, the cultural studies that I see in front of us right now, as well as some of its central claims or most frequently repeated vanities. And by that token it will also probably be a somewhat hubristic chapter in that I'll be trying to make some recommendations and even exhortations around the topic of cultural studies. It will be a somewhat difficult project to keep under control, as well, at least in part because of my own history, a history that underlines – if not exemplifies – the disjuncture in cultural studies between British and American "versions." Having been educated in the British cultural studies vein I've spent almost 20 years in the US, working in the first cultural studies undergraduate program in the country (at Carnegie Mellon) and more lately in one of the first Ph.D. programmes (at George Mason University). Now returning to the

This chapter was first published in Timothy Bewes and Jeremy Gilbert (eds.), *Cultural Capitalism*. London: Lawrence & Wishart, 2001

UK, I'm possibly out of touch and my view parochial. But all these risks seem worth taking because of what still seems to me the most important potential of cultural studies: that is, its promise to be an intellectual endeavor with an overt claim on the political shape of contemporary culture and society.

Real cultural studies junkies will no doubt have noticed that the title for my article refers to – or rather it repeats almost verbatim – the title of one of Stuart Hall's more extraordinary pieces of writing, a talk he gave first in 1989 and which was published in 1992 in *Rethinking Marxism*.[1] Hall's work is, of course, everywhere taken to be seminal for cultural studies and is consistently understood as definitive in many respects. I don't want to argue with that assessment, but rather want to use that particular article to follow up some questions which continue to provoke debate within contemporary cultural studies, namely, the relation between politics and culture. In order to approach such issues, I begin with a somewhat skeptical reading of Hall's article.

In his own looking back Hall presents one version of what is by now an almost canonical view of the history of cultural studies. But it's also a history that, for my purposes here, is rather emblematic: in a symptomatic reading it can show some of the strange maneuvers and weird leaps that cultural studies has consistently made and still makes. At its beginnings, Hall suggests, cultural studies stood in opposition to positivist social science departments which had seen cultures merely as analyzable systems composed of abstract norms and values; cultural studies was equally a corrective to the disciplines of the humanities which had chronically refused to "name let alone theorize or conceptualize culture." Then – and here's the first of several of Hall's emblematic moves that I want to point to – he goes on to precisely not offer a definition or conceptualization of culture. Or rather, he falls back on a version of those large nebulosities that cultural studies has been pleased to be able to pull down wholesale from Raymond Williams' altogether more satisfying work where culture is defined very generally as "whole ways of communicating . . . whole ways of life, where popular culture intersects with the high arts . . . where power cuts across knowledge . . . where cultural processes anticipate social change."

This is the first thing I want to point to by way of Hall's article – the propensity in cultural studies to avoid offering up any especially firm definition or methodologically suggestive view of what culture really is. This isn't the only place where Hall offers such a vagueness at the heart of the endeavor. In another well-known article, for instance, "Cultural Studies: Two Paradigms," he goes further and suggests that in the foundational work of the Centre for Contemporary Cultural Studies there had been "no single, unproblematic definition of culture" to be found. What the CCCS operated with was, rather than a logically or conceptually clarified notion of culture, a convergence of what he calls "interests."[2]

What I want to suggest here is that this determination not to define the central object of cultural studies has led to what can only be described as a pluralistic tendency at the heart of the project. This is a tendency that has authorized cultural studies to take many forms, of course, and in that sense might be considered a good thing, especially by those who think of cultural studies as precisely an opportunity to escape the perceived rigors of the usual disciplinary structures. But it seems unarguable at this point that the lack of willingness to define the central object of study has also and necessarily implied a lack of methodological and procedural consistency and denied any but the loosest cohesion to cultural studies. We might here consider John Frow's recent claim that by and large the cultural studies version of culture is in fact an embarrassment, not only in its lack of clarity and definition but also in its inability to properly engage with other disciplinary and methodological approaches to culture, such as those found in ethnographic and anthropological traditions.[3]

But as I've pointed out, it's often this very looseness and openness that many cultural studies practitioners have chronically held to be most valuable about the enterprise. Certainly, Hall has been by no means alone in talking out against the "codification" of CS and reminding us that there can be no final paradigm for the field.[4] Some of the most prominent names in cultural studies have made analogous claims on the grounds that the flexibility of cultural studies assumptions and procedures allow for a kind of analytical freedom which can flexibly react to the ever-changing complexities of cultural life. Perhaps the strongest version of these claims is made in the editors' introduction to one of the most influential anthologies in the field, *Cultural Studies*. There the editors object to the idea that the field should be policed in any way and recommend a loose and open intellectual approach, one equivalent to a kind of *bricolage* in method. The line is, in all its glory, that "cultural studies has no guarantees about what questions are important to ask within given contexts or how to answer them; hence no methodology can be privileged or even temporarily employed with total security and confidence, yet none can be eliminated out of hand."[5]

This position has been so internalized in the field by now that it's almost an article of faith to say that cultural studies does not need definition because it is antidisciplinary or nondisciplinary and that some large part of its strength lies in its capacity to offer intellectual freedom. Indeed, as the argument runs, any moves towards a "disciplined" cultural studies would constitute a policing of the project in a discourse where the notion of policing is understood as authoritarian from the start and therefore somehow antithetical to cultural studies. This championing of the openness, looseness, or unfinished character of cultural studies work thus becomes the sign of a properly liberated intellectual project.

Such a position is exactly what Hall adopts in his article – the second move he makes to which I want to draw attention. Armed first of all with the vaguest definition of culture, Hall goes on to claim that cultural studies gets its specificity from its contingent location, its flexible positions, and its self-reflexivity. There can be no argument: those features have indeed tended to establish the specific character of what we know as cultural studies, but at the not inconsiderable price of rendering cultural studies an at best eclectic, at worst unprincipled intellectual endeavor. This is a perspective that produces the kind of argument that

Lawrence Grossberg makes when he insists that cultural studies is and must always be influenced by its outside, or that the nature of work in cultural studies must somehow be dictated by existing concerns.[6] There is clearly a problem with this perspective in that cultural studies is perhaps the only current form of knowledge production that explicitly argues that the processes of knowledge production are ideologically and historically contingent; to then throw cultural studies itself at the mercy of existing concerns is to refuse to allow it any possibility of breaking through the ideological construction of knowledges into what Hall himself has called "useful knowledges."

Equally to the point, the assumptions of this somewhat reactive approach – what I'd call a wait-and-see methodology – are that the object of knowledge will automatically make evident the mode of analysis proper to it, or that method and intellection can somehow be pulled from the air in order to deal with changing circumstances and variable phenomena. Such a view mystifies the relationship between object and knowledge, and it seems to me that such a mystification is a high price to pay for what the argument intends to buy, namely, the freedom of the individual scholar or researcher to follow their track without the constraint of discipline. Obviously such methodological freedom compromises intellectual results.

From the point of view of intellectual method, this all leaves cultural studies with only one place to go. With no focused definition of the object and with what amounts to an *ad hoc* or merely opportunistic methodology, cultural studies can then justify itself only in terms of the topics it approaches. In other words, cultural studies can do no more than become a thematically organized area of study where the choice of specific topic or theme comes to be of more import than the choice of method or procedure. And this indeed is illustrated by the third emblematic move in Hall's essay, which arrives pat on cue as his discussion of procedural or methodological issues is displaced onto largely thematic concerns. Cultural studies is visibly transformed, in Hall's account, into a topical enterprise. In this particular essay, the privileged topic is race and ethnicity which emerge as the essential point of the field. My pointing out this third move on Hall's part is not, I want to emphasize, to say that race and ethnicity are not amongst the proper objects of investigation for cultural studies. It's simply to suggest that, given the history and assumptions that I'm examining, it seems inevitable that this topic, or some topic quite like it, should have emerged as a quasi-definitional element for the field at the same time as any particular or "codified" way of approaching it is eschewed.

That's not to say that the way Hall approaches the chosen topic is entirely unfamiliar, nor that he doesn't try to sketch out something like a recognizable cultural studies approach. The set of bedrock ideas to which he appeals in that regard in order to approach the question of race include a predictable tour around Fanon's phenomenological schemas and related bits of Lacanian psychoanalysis and side-trips to Freud and Lévi-Strauss. Those points of reference are, evidently, familiar from the chapbook that cultural studies has been peddling for

334

many years now, and they sit alongside the forms of semiotic analysis, deriving mostly from Saussure via Roland Barthes, which have stood unchallenged in the field for decades as tokens for a common methodology. To see how deeply those points of reference have taken root, one has only to look at the kind of work published under the rubric of cultural studies in the last few years. The heady mix of Fanon and psychoanalysis that Hall concocts, a rather *ad hoc* schema of self and other, has since been taken to its intellectual extremes by Homi Bhabha and more recently to its purest banality by Kevin Stevenson.[7] The persistence of the semiotic model for the analysis of meaning is fully evident even in the kind of work which is currently claimed to be a recasting of cultural studies, like the essays collected in Angela McRobbie's *Back to Reality*. And perhaps the strongest indication of the unreconstructed nature of the influence of the semiotic model is to be found in two recent Open University textbooks: *Representation*, edited by Stuart Hall himself, and *Doing Cultural Studies*, a primer of the field construed around an extended case-study of the Sony Walkman. In each of the three mentioned texts, a Barthesian semiotics is taken as read, as it were, with little regard for the numerous critiques of such a model of meaning production and still less regard for alternative theories.[8]

Whatever else can be said about what I'm calling the cultural studies chapbook, it's easy to see that the points of reference it contains construct a field that is simultaneously eclectic and narrow and that many of its most frequently deployed components have been pressed into service for many years now without serious renewal or reconsideration. In any case, it would be hard to dignify this set of coordinates as anything approaching a coherent methodology, even if it's a set that guides a majority of cultural studies practitioners. In the face of such a situation it becomes hard to resist the accuracy of Meaghan Morris's observations about what she calls banality in cultural studies, whereby the limited and yet eclectic range of theoretical coordinates tends to produce and reproduce a kind of template cultural studies article in which essentially the same thing can be said about any object in the cultural life.[9]

We can now leave Hall's article, having pressed it perhaps a little too hard in any case, especially considering its admittedly schematic nature. But the points I've tried to draw from it remain for me emblematic of a certain set of problems within cultural studies. If I've stressed the issue of methodology it's not that I rather simple-mindedly believe that in order to rediscover itself cultural studies needs to be able to establish protocols and procedures which would be more rigorous and more intellectually consistent. I *do* believe that, but also reckon that the kinds of analysis that remain acceptable and even applauded in contemporary cultural studies have consistently proceeded on the faulty assumption that to address a certain set of thematically construed issues is to willy-nilly be doing politics. In other words, and to generalize, cultural studies work often seems to assume that to undertake cultural analysis and commentary is tantamount to undertaking political analysis and even political intervention. In that sense politics is understood as an automatic engagement, as the necessary and inevitable outcrop of a certain kind of intellection. If we then turn to the question of what relation, if any, to existing political projects in theory or practice cultural studies can claim, we might have to understand that to discover any such relation might not be altogether welcome. For instance, what relation is there between current cultural studies in the UK and the ascendancy of New Labour, a relation going back at least to "New Times" and the critique of Thatcherism which simply admired Thatcherism too much;[10] or the relation between the policy strain of cultural studies in Australia and the erosion of labor politics in that country; or the relation between cultural studies in the United States and the forms of individualism and identity politics which resonate with a permanent strain of reactionary thought in the history of that republic. Those are questions which I won't be attempting to answer here, even though they are surely questions which cultural studies needs to be asking.[11] And this would seem especially appropriate where, in the UK particularly, cultural studies not only takes the political for granted but often claims a connection to an organic politics of resistance.

Perhaps as much to the immediate point would be to try to suggest ways in which cultural studies might reinvigorate its idea of the political, or even begin the task of drawing up a new political agenda for the field. And it might be as well to cut to the chase, at were, by saying that the way forward seems to me to be a way back. That is, somewhere in the past of cultural studies is an almost forgotten engagement with Marxism and with the analysis of capital that should, in my view, reside at the heart of any serious consideration of culture. I do realize that for many cultural studies practitioners such a suggestion can only cause a groan of weary recognition or boredom, since it would appear on the face of it that any debate about the place of Marxist analysis has given way to what is essentially an absence of Marxism in cultural studies.

The coming about of that absence has, of course, a lengthy history by now. Indeed, Colin Sparks' account of the relation between cultural studies and Marxism points first of all to the relatively weak or skeptical Marxism of the "founding fathers" of cultural studies, Richard Hoggart, Raymond Williams, and E. P. Thompson. Even though Marxism gained some prominence in cultural studies in the aftermath of 1968, particularly with the stress on ideology under the influence of Althusser's work, this was part of a much more generally eclectic searching around for theoretical tools and was in any case almost immediately eclipsed by the liberal and selective version of Gramsci adopted by Hall, and/or the almost explicitly anti-Marxist version of Gramsci promulgated by Laclau and Mouffe in their influential book *Hegemony and Socialist Strategy*.[12] The influence of Laclau's and Mouffe's work on cultural studies can hardly be underestimated, especially in the USA where its assault on the supposedly intractable essentialism of Marxism was taken up with great relief by cultural studies practitioners for whom the (more imagined than real) whiff of Marxism around cultural studies had been an embarrassment in a context where red-baiting is still a popular sport.

Inevitably, too, the eclectic tastes of cultural studies have found much to like in the well-stocked kitchen of poststructuralism, and the tendency of poststructuralism to elide Marxism has been easily adopted. The elision is almost total if one looks at recent cultural studies metacommentaries such as *Cultural Studies in Question*, a collection of essays on the current state of the field.[13] There, in the course of more than a dozen supposedly cutting-edge essays, Marxism is mentioned a handful of times, and even then only as a historical curiosity (in relation to theories of ideology, for instance). Even the contributions of Nicholas Garnham (someone whose long insistence on the importance of political economy for any study of culture has been more or less ignored within cultural studies) and Doug Kellner (writing on the use of political economy for cultural studies) seem to feel constrained not to mention the M-word, even while they argue strongly for the use of what are Marxist analytical tools.

The standard or most frequently repeated objection to Marxism in cultural studies is probably the double-headed notion that Marxism is "reductive" and "economically determinist." Those two charges still get used as a shorthand way of dismissing Marxism – though to them has been added the claim that Marxism's emphasis on class position necessarily precludes the dynamic studies of other forms of subjectivity, race and gender in particular. Such claims are mostly mere rhetoric, pointing to a kind of Marxism that I, for one, almost never see, but which in any case would be far outweighed by other kinds of Marxist theory and analysis. The charges seem in any case peculiarly problematical when made from within a discourse that has clearly been unable to even begin to think the question of determinations within the processes of culture – and this even despite promptings from one of the "founding fathers," Raymond Williams, whose work came to insist on the need to establish "the real order of determination between different kinds of activity. That there always is such an order of determination cannot be doubted . . . This is the necessary, theoretical base for the recognition of genuinely different social orders."[14]

The understanding of determinations – and, of course, of levels of over-determinations – within cultural life is really no more than a single one of the huge gaps in the knowledge produced by cultural studies, but it is an important one. I can recall no cultural studies text which has argued specifically against the "necessary theoretical base" Williams recommended; and that's perhaps because the mere possibility of thinking through issues of determination disappears once the specter of Marxism's economic determinism has been raised. More crucially even, the absence of that register of analysis from cultural studies authorizes the treatment of particular thematically selected cultural elements more or less in isolation from each other, or at least as discrete entities whose contextual relations are not importantly to do with the mode of production. Or else, in the extreme, such an absence authorizes a kind of reading operation to be done on cultural objects or events as, essentially, *texts* with no necessary reference to the place or conditions of their productions.

What I'm pointing to is what Fredric Jameson has noted in his carefully understated but ultimately quite scarifying indictment of cultural studies; that is, the tendency of cultural studies to eschew the economic and the whole question of determinations and thence land up in what he calls "a kind of forthright anarchistic stance on the thing itself" – a critique similar to what John Clarke has called, even more loudly, "the abolition of the object" itself within cultural studies.[15] A clear example of what analysis then looks like from that kind of anarchist or nihilistic stance in relation to the object might be provided by one of the books I mentioned earlier, Paul du Gay's textbook, *Doing Cultural Studies*, where all questions of the economic are turned into a mere contextualization of the object and where all questions of determinism are rejected as unthinkable. In other words, for work of this sort the role of what are clearly political-economic elements can be no more than instrumental – political-economic elements may be used to help provide "readings" of particular features of the object but must not be used to forge an explanation of the logic of the object itself. In this case the object is the highly successful commodity, the Sony Walkman, but there is no recognition that its role in the general circuits of the commodity is a crucial part of its identity as object. The notion that the representational logic of the object itself could be in the end no more than a function of a political-economic logic is always already ruled out of court.

In a more ordered and calm way than I, John Frow has recently addressed some of the kinds of problems that I'm pointing to in cultural studies. His view is that the kind of work that I'm criticizing, with its emphasis on the production of meaning rather than the production of commodities, will always be at a distance from work which stresses the political-economic elements of culture. Indeed, Frow thinks that as a field cultural studies is at an impasse with an impossible job of reconciliation on its hands. His position seems worth quoting fully:

> There is no simple way (apart from straightforward reductionism) of squaring a methodological concentration on the productive working of texts with a methodological concentration on the productive work of the [capitalist] system. They are not complementary, and the effect of this tension is a kind of necessary indeterminacy principle. Both positions are "correct," but there is no way of reconciling them in a single perspective. By the same token, to elaborate a "correct" position is therefore by definition to fail to perform the countervailing analysis.[16]

In my view Frow's point here is a little pessimistic. It doesn't seem quite or necessarily impossible to produce the kind of cultural studies analysis that would make the connections between the production of meanings and subjectivities and the production of commodities. The important point is to be able to consider and analyze the processes of determination amongst and between the different levels of production. This implies, at very least, an agreement that it is impossible to think of any kind of cultural form or any kind of cultural artifact or event as being autonomous. Rather, cultural phenomena, far from being autonomous texts, are caught in a logic of totality (a totality considered, of course, in all of its contradictions). The task of thinking any object whatsoever in that manner has traditionally fallen to Marxism, and the particular attention that Marxism has paid to all realms – the cultural, the social, the political, and the economic – still constitutes a more advanced and difficult project than the vagueness of this thing called cultural studies which, it would seem, has shied away from such difficulties, preferring instead a lack of rigor that has somehow come to think of itself as radically democratic and liberating.

In the end cultural studies has not been a radical intellectual movement that upset disciplines, reformulated knowledge, continually interrogated itself and its methods, opened out onto a thriving area of politics beyond the academy, and addressed the public sphere. It's really been none of those things, if we're honest about it. Cultural studies has never managed to fill the gaps it made in itself when it elided Marxism; no other feasible theoretical forms have come to do the job that Marxism did and that cultural studies always claimed it wanted to do. To now rehabilitate a set of ideas and methods which are associated with Marxism would not make cultural studies Marxist *per se*. But it would mean that cultural studies could no longer afford an antipathy to Marxist theory, an antipathy that has helped lead it into numerous dead ends and crises and held it back from realizing its best intellectual and political aspirations.

Notes

1 Stuart Hall, "Race, Culture, and Communications: Looking Backward and Forward at Cultural Studies," *Rethinking Marxism* 5(1) (1992): 10–21.
2 S. Hall, "Cultural Studies: Two Paradigms," *Media, Culture and Society* 2(2): 57–72.
3 J. Frow, *Cultural Studies and Cultural Value*, Oxford: Oxford University Press, 1995.
4 S. Hall, "On Postmodernism and Articulation" (an interview edited by L. Grossberg), in D. Morley and Chen Kuan-Hsing (eds.), *Stuart Hall: Critical Dialogues in Cultural Studies*, London: Routledge, 1996.
5 L. Grossberg, C. Nelson, and P. Treichler (eds.), *Cultural Studies*, New York: Routledge, 1992, p. 2.
6 See L. Grossberg, "Cultural Studies: What's in a Name?," in his *Bringing It All Back Home*, Durham, NC: Duke University Press, 1997 [1995].
7 See H. Bhabha, *The Location of Culture*, London: Routledge, 1994; K. Stevenson, *The Transformation of the Media: Globalisation, Morality and Ethics*, London: Longman, 1999 (especially the final chapter on the Rwandan genocide).
8 See A. McRobbie (ed.), *Back to Reality? Social Experience and Cultural Studies*, Manchester: Manchester University Press, 1997; S. Hall (ed.), *Representation: Cultural Representations and Signifying Practices*, London: Sage/The Open University, 1997; P. du Gay, S. Hall, L. Jones, H. Mackay, and K. Negus (eds.), *Doing Cultural Studies*, London: Sage/Open University, 1997.
9 M. Morris, "Banality in Cultural Studies," *Discourse* 10: 3–29.

10   This point is made more fully in my *Millennial Dreams: Contemporary Culture and Capital in the North*, London: Verso, 1997, pp. 152–7.

11   More along the same lines will be found in my forthcoming *Cultural Studies: A Manifesto*, Minneapolis: University of Minnesota Press, 2001.

12   C. Sparks, "Stuart Hall, Cultural Studies and Marxism," in Morley and Chen (eds.), *Stuart Hall*. Perhaps Hall's most productive use of Gramsci is in "Gramsci's Relevance for the Study of Race and Ethnicity," in Morley and Chen (eds.), pp. 411–40. See too E. Laclau and C. Mouffe, *Hegemony and Socialist Strategy: Towards a Radical Democratic Politics*, London: Verso, 1985; and my critique of it along these lines, "The Secret Agent of Laclau and Mouffe," in Miami Theory Collective (eds.), *Community at Loose Ends*, Minneapolis: University of Minnesota Press, 1991.

13   M. Ferguson and P. Golding (eds.), *Cultural Studies in Question*, London: Sage, 1997.

14   R. Williams, *Towards 2000*, London: Chatto and Windus, 1983, p.15.

15   F. Jameson, "On 'Cultural Studies,'" *Social Text* 34 (1993): 45; J. Clarke, *New Times and Old Enemies: Essays on Cultural Studies in America*, London: HarperCollins Academic, 1991, p. 25.

16   Frow, *Cultural Studies*.

Chapter 20

Close Encounters: Sport, Science, and Political Culture

C. L. Cole

Recent changes in the character of sport, its reconfigured location in the economy, and its transformed physical presence seem to be drawing the attention of an increasing number of critical scholars. For example, in *Rich Media, Poor Democracy*, Robert McChesney (1999) highlights sport's high profile and extended role in late-capitalist media expansion. In fact, McChesney contends that sport is "arguably the single most lucrative content area for the global media industry" (p. 95). Relatedly, John Hannigan (1998), author of *Fantasy City*, identifies tourism, sport, and entertainment as principal forces reshaping the new urban economy. No doubt, sport holds multiple positions in contemporary urban America's infinite growth projects. But, heightened visibility does not necessarily lead to greater academic insights or scholarly tolerance.

Indeed, the well-entrenched and popular stereotype of sport as anti-intellectual has been hard for academics to shake. To put it tersely, within a context in which respect is linked to content area, sport has been less than lucrative. Perhaps the reasons behind the skepticism about, even strong opposition to, the study of sport are familiar: the mind/body split, the related denigration of the physical, academic divisions of labor. But how do we explain the line drawn around sporting matters in a field that has otherwise successfully intervened in academe's prejudice against matters of the popular? While a cultural criticism of sport has been undertaken by scholars employed in spheres devoted to studying sport (for example, sport studies and sociology of sport), and despite converging interests, practitioners of a more mainstream cultural studies (by which I mean better known and more authoritative) have been reluctant to cross the sport studies' border. Certainly, cultural critics' routine avoidance of sporting topics needs be thought about in relation to the enormous anxieties surrounding sport.

Given the above, it is not surprising that Randy Martin and Toby Miller (1999), in their introduction to *SportCult*, suggest that "the interrogation of sport raises questions of how popular culture gets studied" (p. 9). What is unanticipated, even extraordinary, is their wager about the utility of sport-related scholarship. Martin and Miller claim that:

A close encounter with the bodies at play and at work in athletic contests promises to help us rethink not only the parameters of sport itself, but the very conception of the practical and the popular as they have been understood in cultural studies more broadly. (p. 1)

In translating sport's potential to intervene in cultural studies' conventional wisdom, Martin and Miller conceptualize sport, not as discrete, but as a proliferation of sites and a problematic that unsettles apparently neat divisions that govern ways of thinking. Sport, they argue, can connect that which have been routinely disconnected: social sciences and the humanities, eroticism and violence, justice and identity, value and recognition. They contend that sport troubles the active/passive spectator articulated in the society of the spectacle; that its complexity of movement complicates geopolitics (the coexistence and dispersion, reinforcing and challenging tendencies of the local, national, global, and the personal); and that sport's ceaseless remarkability questions what constitutes the quotidian (enlarging the field of cultural politics).

As it happens, Elspeth Probyn (2000) makes similar claims about comparable close encounters. Rather than advocating a model cultural studies, she, too, argues for the conceptually enabling aspects of sporting bodies. Confronting sporting bodies, for Probyn, potentially displaces the "taming" tendencies of the now conventional "disciplined or transgressive" divide governing body and sexuality studies. Hence, she implies that sporting bodies potentially intervene in the limiting construct of power guiding the twinned problematic. Like Martin and Miller, she views sporting bodies as a means to reopen connections, to resurrect the "promiscuous nature of the body as a sociological object."

To a great extent, Probyn's wager is motivated by the stigma of sport and more precisely its "insistence on the gritty, 'shameful' aspects of human activity" (p. 13). Building on recent scholarship that attends to the affect of shame/pride (e.g., Sally Munt, T. Scheff, and Eve Sedgwick), Probyn examines sport's implication in their everyday connections. She foregrounds the shame/embodiment relationship by addressing competition, one of sport's most public but neglected (in sociological accounts) dimensions:

If a touch of shame spurs on competitive drive, it may be that sport reaches parts of the body that analyses of embodiment have shied away from . . . Following the cue of several cultural theorists, it is clear that shame as a very bodily affect has the potential to focus attention on the body as a vehicle of connection. As a frequently shamed entity, the sporting body fundamentally connects with class and race matters in ways that may embarrass middle-class sensibilities. Sporting bodies also compete, and remind us of the visceral dynamics of pride, shame and bodily affect in ways that have been notably missing within much feminist and cultural analysis. (p. 14)

To illustrate, Probyn draws attention to the Gay Games, and, more specifically, their discursive constitution. Pride is the Games' primary interpretive device; personal best and participation their featured values; while competition is seemingly displaced. In combination, Probyn argues, the categories promote an ontology of gay life that works hard to deny shame. Accordingly, the Gay Games' ethical and supportive infrastructure facilitates their normalizing function, commercialization, and the erasure of sexuality, politics, and questions about human rights. In so doing, the Games participate in the very configurations of power they seemingly oppose. This dynamic, Probyn argues, is not exclusive to the Gay Games but central to modern sport.

To extend her point, Probyn considers an interview with Sang Ye, a Chinese national athlete, that highlights, rather than ignores, competition and shame. He "names the unspeakable" by underscoring the consequences and shame of losing. Later he illuminates the burden of sport's moral ground, arguing that performance-enhancing drugs, in fact, can be a means of leveling the playing field. Probyn uses the testimonial to provide insight into a demonizing mechanism through which the West claims "fair play" as its most cherished ideal. By asking whether "the facts of competition and shame are the province of the other," she draws attention to the complex network of connections between the modern developments of nation, sex/gender, race in which the sporting body is embedded.

Modern Sporting Bodies

Much of the cultural studies informed scholarship emanating from sport studies has addressed familiar themes associated with modern transformations: modern state formation, industrialization, urbanization, colonization, and stratification. For example, John Hargreaves (1987) examines the role of modern sport in cultivation of an English self and, in particular, shows how sport was used to legitimate social stratifications. Richard Gruneau and Hargreaves consider the relationship between nation, disciplinary activities like sport, social improvement, and workers' bodies. In their study on the formation of the nation–state in France, Jean Harvey and Robert Sparks trace the role of gymnastics and the making of the modern citizen. Harvey and Sparks contend that accounts of modern sport must address "fundamental questions about the political status of the body ... the political ends the body serves and the political means used to secure those ends" (p. 164). Yet, it is precisely the complexity of the connections that shape the body, sport, and politics relation that is missing in the sport studies scholarship, and to which Martin & Miller and Probyn call attention.

In their conceptual efforts, Martin and Miller offer a deceptively simple observation about sport's position in drawing bodies together and sorting them out. Tracing the forces behind those collectivities and distinctions, the multiple relations of power invested in both, as well as their effects, is one of the epistemological demands of cultural studies of sport. As Probyn suggests, such a study entails examining the ethical ground attributed to sport and, by exten-

343

sion, the ethical ground attributed to nation and science. Indeed, it requires considering what is mobilized in the name of the sporting contract, which itself relies on and invokes an ontology and epistemology of the "human."

Consider "the suspicion" incited by "remarkable performances," the ostensible goal of high-performance sport. Such performances are not simply declared breakthroughs but typically facilitate our imaginations of what and who are responsible for, the origin of, the accomplishment (the hidden hand of drugs? science? the state?). Rather than provoking debates about the boundaries of the natural (e.g., self/other; free will/compulsive will; human/machine; man/woman), visualizing strategies (e.g., drug testing and sex testing) manage the natural and, by extension, sport's idealized coding. While, comparatively, only a small number of people are directly subjected to biosport surveillance strategies, the scientific visual system exemplifies the everyday ways "we" are encouraged to "read" and position ourselves in relation to athletic bodies. Hence, sportsmanship, sport's ethical ground, is an interpretive device inextricably linked to modern categories, scientization, and the biological. Rather than revealing that which already exists, science, biology, and sport shape, in very specific political contexts, whether athletic bodies are met with enthusiasm and pleasure, anxiety and horror, or some combination of these.

With these connections in mind, I discuss two events that bring into relief, albeit in different ways, the effects of the modern sporting optic – the invisible powers that regulate and shape bodies and identities in what we imagine to be the isolated spaces of sport. More specifically, I seek to show how sport is bound up with biological and political claims, claims about social justice and economic injustices, and the efficacy retained by the nation form, even in a moment dominated by the transnational. Underlying the discussion of these events is the claim that political theory and science and technology studies are important for cultural studies in general and cultural studies related to sport in particular.

Close Encounters I: Defining Olympic Anatomies

In 1968, the International Olympic Committee (IOC) implemented a policy that required that all competitors seeking to compete as females pass a "sex test" before they could compete in the Olympic Games. Since then, the IOC has deployed various diagnostic technologies, ranging from external visual, probing gynecological to chromosomal-buccal smear and gene amplification, to determine an athlete's femaleness. Although the criteria for passing have been modified, the IOC appears to have settled on a chromosomal definition of sex, and, by extension, for determining the authenticity of the performance. While common sense suggests that science simply documents sex and that sex testing would be simple and straightforward, a wide range of boundary creatures appear within sex testing narratives: drug-crafted athletes, steroid men/women, intersexed, transsexed, hypermuscular females, hypernormal females, innocent victims, communist athletes, embryos and maternal bodies. Despite the overwhelming complexity and multiple knowledges mobilized through sex testing, academic criticisms of sex tests have repeatedly been concerned with whether or not the test should be continued. Curiously, the arguments for and against sex testing rely on and suggest the difficulty of thinking outside and historically situating the familiar terms that govern sport and sexual difference: biology and equality.

In an effort to make the sorts of connections imagined by Martin & Miller and Probyn, I side step the dominant for-or-against debates and, instead, concentrate on a specific visual domain through which Olympic sex testing (including the terms governing the tests) gains meaning: the Cold War of 1950s America. Introducing "America" as an analytic category intervenes in the almost complete erasure of national context in accounts of sex testing and, as I argue, illuminates the gendered production of the communist athlete as a means to manage American anxieties related to democracy.

America's visual paradigm

Even before the 1952 Olympics, Soviet sport was narrated in the US through apocalyptic language. America's seemingly ambiguous response (couched in terms of discomfort, suspicion, and accusation) was, from the moment the Soviets announced their Olympic plans, in the final instance, one of outright rejection. Prominent media accounts, which underscored Soviet boasts of athletic prowess, regularly included semi-detailed reports of systematic Soviet violations of fair play, even falsified reports of final outcomes. Soviet claims were not simply dismissed as inauthentic, they were represented as symptomatic of the Soviet's excessive competitiveness, deceptiveness, and disregard for rules through which they were advancing their expansionist strategy.

Questions generated in response to Soviet sport, inseparable from the threat of Soviet imperialism, were continually and thematically grounded in truth. Indeed, Richard B. Walsh (Office of General Manager of the International Information and Education Program) began his 1951 speech "The Soviet Athlete in International Competition" by declaring America's widespread commitment to truth:

> To meet and beat down these [Soviet] lies the US Government, assisted by private groups, has greatly stepped up its truth-telling programs. In the main, our efforts are meeting with success. Through press, radio, motion pictures, overseas information centers, and the exchange of persons, we are telling the truth on an unprecedented scale. We have done well as far as we have gone. (p. 1007)

America's truth-claims rested on two beliefs: sportsmanship and all that entailed, and the complete opposition between Soviet and American characters. Echoing what would become national sentiment, Walsh concluded: "We can expect nothing finer than American sportsmanship, for sportsmanship is *democracy at work*."

Between his opening and closing claims, Walsh systematically recounted examples of Soviets cheating, their use of sport for propaganda, and their desperation to win. Regardless of the final medal count, he assured his audience an American triumph because, "Sportsmanship is deeply rooted in our country's heritage." While naming sportsmanship as that which most mattered and a simple expression of America's avowed political commitments, he identified communism and sport as internally contradictory, guided by incommensurable logic and irreconcilable values. Curiously, Walsh never directly discussed the topic of his speech, the Soviet athlete, although he emphatically expressed the logic behind sportsmanship. The expression was symptomatic of sportsmanship's role as a technology of national fantasy: it linked embodiment and political culture, and conduct, physical performance, and moral superiority, yielding a being called the communist athlete. As a product of democracy at work, the communist athlete would play a crucial role in enchanting the imagination of America and the body of the American athlete.

Democracy at work: the communist athlete

In 1952, US newspapers and magazines, including *US News & World Report* and *Life*, offered accounts and images of Soviet athletes. The impetus, of course, was the literal (and figural) appearance of the Soviets at the Finnish Olympics, and the anticipation, generated by the earlier narratives, of visible transgressions. Under the headline, "Stalin's 'Iron Curtain' for Athletes," *US News & World Report* sketched the key characteristics informing the narratives of Soviet sport: isolation and secrecy, state-sanctioned interactions, violations of the amateur code, athlete political indoctrination, susceptibility to the pleasures offered by the Western way of life, and heavy scrutinization and regulation. Although sexual difference remains peripheral to the account, the photograph of discus thrower Nina Dumbadze, subtitled "A Russian specialty: Soviet Amazons," suggests its underlying centrality.

Life seemingly approaches the Soviet athlete from a different angle. The article's opening image (US athlete Jim Fuchs gazing admirably at Nina Dumbadze) suggests that even international politics are not powerful enough to overcome the natural order of things. While sexual difference renders visible a "common humanity," nature, humanity, and heterosexuality do not deny the state nor do they render the state invisible. Yet, American anxieties about the need to see difference are apparent as visual images repeatedly direct attention to and from sameness. *Life's* commentary similarly negotiates the complex tensions between sameness and difference as one, then the other, is asserted and erased.

Ultimately the Soviet system was depicted through twinned threats of hybridity and imitation. Photographs of Soviet athletes in which there are no visible signs of the Soviet state were narrated as state-sanctioned performances of the ideal body, translated into impersonations of the American body. In a word, American bodies were represented as registers of life itself, as the original site of vibrancy and spontaneity. In the final instance, it is a photograph of Soviet track and field athlete, Tamara Press, cropped to accentuate her female musculature (in *Life's* words, her "tank-shape"), that underscores the sort of mutants the Soviet experiment, if not controled, would continue to produce. As a sign of Soviet excesses, the image questions the body's integrity as it recalls the article's opening image (expressing America's anxieties about recognizing the natural and arguably the natural ground of heterosexuality). For at least the next 20 years, Tamara Press would be America's most prominent figure of communist femininity. That she never failed the test in fact (she quit competing prior to the sex testing requirement), only enhanced her position in America's fantasy.

American pride: sexual difference

In 1964, *Life* magazine prominently featured America's female athletes in a 10-page, celebratory photo-essay entitled "The Grace of Our Olympic Girls." The possessive pronoun positions sporting women as part of national culture and points to their bodies as signs of meanings and values entangled in community, nation, gender, and American identity. In short, the bodies are depicted as independent, autonomous, and free of constraints, devoid of mixed signifiers and boundary violations. Quintessential signifiers of masculinity, strength and muscle, are concealed through gesture, clothing, camera angle, distance, and setting. Individualism is asserted over a collective symmetry and proportion established through gestures and claims of gracefulness, pleasure, and effortlessness. A series of artistic poses, repeated fluid and rhythmic lines and forms, suggest that sameness, unity, and coherence are what matter. Arizona diver Barbara Talmage, who appears on the cover, signifies the angelic and the (suburban) girl next door.

Two years later *Life* ran an article, strikingly different in tone, explaining the need for the upcoming sex tests. Accusations of falsity, imitation, and hybridity seemingly replace the celebratory terms of the 1964 narrative. Asking if girl athletes were really girls, *Life* foregrounds tales of suspicion, imposters, and sex-change surgery. Accompanying photographs distort bodies (Russian athletes Tamara Press and her sister are two of the featured monstrosities) and offer before and after (sex reassignment) surgery images. Noticeably missing from this account is America's claim to these girls: these are *their* Olympic girls, those girls from whom American girls needs protecting. Thus, like the 1964 article, these hybrid bodies are part of a national culture industry that accomplishes solidarity and national pride through historical specific regulatory ideals of gender.

In 1976, NBC would amplify the by then familiar threat by drawing a line from security measures put in place at the Montreal Olympics (as a result of the 1972 Munich massacre) to security measures around sex. In this account, sex security is quickly translated into an issue of national security: as the camera offers glimpses of the troubling bodies of others, the American audience meets two American suburban swimmers who express their gratitude for the fairness ensured by the sex tests. This logic takes yet another form in a 1974 NBC news clip that focused on liberation, suburban girls, and track and field. In a narrative context that represents suburban lifestyle and the Women's Liberation Movement as mutually supportive, Tamara Press is introduced as the factor undermining suburban girls' desire to participate in track and field. While seemingly celebrating the liberation of girls' track and field, the narrative is complicated by race and heterosexuality, and the division between playful and serious athletics. African American teenagers are visualized as serious athletes (unaffected by Tamara Press) who continue their running careers, even after suburban girls outgrow their preheterosexual playful interests. In effect, then, this narrative shores up the ideals and future of America's community of suburbs.

Cold War America's sanctioned female athletic body fundamentally relied upon the communist athlete. The Soviet body, which served as a phantasmatic space on which anxieties, speculations, and fantasies were projected, ultimately served as a means to imagine the American body and operations of power in America. As Americans were invited to read the body that apparently violated sexual difference as un-American and undemocratic, they were also asked to imagine a nationally sanctioned femininity, entwined with suburbanization, through the nation's female athlete and that body's place in American democracy. As a sign of suburbanization, the female athletic body was traversed by a politics of place, the promises and desires linked to racially coded, gendered forms of work, consumption, and sexuality. That is, the body became a mechanism to shape identities and conduct through the ideology of the nuclear family, secure jobs, and home ownership. More insidiously, the body was embedded in and advanced an illusory innocence, autonomy, and self-sufficiency. That is to say that while the US government directly (mortgages and tax breaks) and indirectly (federally funded water and sewage facilities) financed postwar suburbia, an illusory autonomy was managed through racially codified classifications for loan eligibility and what did and did not count as government support. It was also caught up in the multiple effects of the suburban trajectory invested whiteness and that equated the good life and quality of life to consumption and distance from the inner city.

Although it is difficult to imagine that the nationally sanctioned female athlete has much in common with America's response to the NBA (the following example), the broader cultural and economic mechanisms sustaining suburbanization were creating the conditions that would give rise to the national prominence of inner-city sport, particularly basketball, during the 1980s and 1990s.

Close Encounters II: Urban Anatomies

America's reception of African American NBA stars during the 1980s was implicated in its collective fascination with "real life in urban America." The nation's literacy of urban life, acquired through scientific and government reports, news reports, advertisements (including Nike's *Just do it* and Ronald Reagan's *Just say no* campaigns), and coming of age narratives, relied on the overarching themes of drugs, family, violence, crime, and sport. The genre, which gained particular authority when circulated in the name of particular NBA players, identified what and who were "urban problems" as it provided images of America as progressive, inclusive, and multicultural. Thus, the popularity of NBA images and real life in urban America were not expressions of an innocent cultural enthusiasm, but expressions of America's imagined innocence.

America's sport/gang dyad

The apparently distinct and distant categories of inner-city sport and gangs gained prominence during the 1980s. Particularly through America's so-called war on drugs, black urban masculinity was visualized through a fundamental dividing line that distinguished two individuals: the athlete (figured through the urban basketball player) and the criminal (figured through the gang member). In this dyad, sport was depicted simultaneously as: the site of conventional values, a practice leading to a healthy, productive life, that which distinguished the previous inner-city generation from that of the 1980s, and a practice that determined the inner city's access to America's utopic promises. The gang member's deviance was imagined through the breach of the work ethic, failed discipline, pathological greed, compulsion, and inexplicable violence. In the sport/gang narrative, gangs were depicted as what and who were responsible for declining sport participation in the inner city, and, by extension, the breakdown, disorder, and forms of violence dominating urban America.

Although not immediately apparent, the figures of sport and gangs were joined by a third factor intimately bound up with nation – the nuclear family. Sport and gangs, apparent channels for the corporeal predispositions of black youth, were the imagined substitutes for the so-called failed black family (figured through the mythic welfare mother and the absent inseminating black male). While the coach represented the sanctioned father–child relationship, sport was represented as indispensable to community production and well-being. The "failed black family" and the sport/gang dyad occupied the same symbolic space: both explained inner-city poverty and violence. Stated differently, both worked to displace the complex forces (unemployment and poverty related to post-industrialization and Reagan's defunding of social programs) shaping the lives of already vulnerable populations. Through the sport/gang dyad, material conditions and their consequences were reterritorialized (classified, visualized, and essentialized) through somatic identities. Somatic reterritorializations established the plausibility of an explanation that reduced participation in sport or gangs to an expression of truth-in-being and individual choice.

In sum, the sport/gang dyad served as a relatively uncontested frame of reference in public-service announcements and public policy concerned with urban youth, crime, and violence. Coded through the commonsense and scientific epistemology of representation, the dyad governed and organized ways of looking, seeing, and recognizing urban problems – that is, it shaped what and who were and were not defined as the inner city's problems as well as its solutions. Rather than identifying discrete, corporeal identities or the truth-in-being of urban youth, the dyad was an expression of the nation's state of mind, an expression of America's collective investment in these categories.

Made in America: the prison industrial complex and Michael Jordan

In this context, Len Bias's death induced by cocaine intoxication was made to matter in the racist imaginary. An African American basketball star at the University of Maryland, Bias's death, 48 hours after he was drafted by the Boston Celtics, was made into a pivotal event in Reagan's war on drugs. That war, including harsh sentences for crack possession (100 times greater than that for powder cocaine), was justified through images of threat to law and order and atrocity tales. In a context dominated by racially coded images of gangs, drugs, violence, and inner-city decay, national calls for severe punishment appeared self-evident.

Provisions established through crime bills passed in 1984, 1986, 1988, and 1994 yielded what is now called the prison industrial complex, the substantial expansion of prison construction and prison populations. Although serious crimes actually declined during this period, at least one-third of African American males aged 18–34 who lived in a major area were under some sort of control by the criminal justice system – the result of racialized patterns of arrest, conviction, and sentencing associated with the drug war. Moreover, the declaration of war, the increasing demand for harsher punishment directed at younger offenders, suggests that what called for punishment was more complex than it appeared. Indeed, the sport/gang dyad helped manage the contradictions and anxieties created through America's self-representation as a caring and compassionate nation and its increasing calls for harsher criminal punishment directed at black youth.

It was in the midst of America's panic about urban crime that Michael Jordan was made into a national icon. Jordan was seen as an uplifting figure, a sign of excellence that extended beyond his basketball skills to his character. Surrounded by categories of authenticity, sincerity, generosity, and responsibility, Jordan was routinely glorified in terms that rendered him extraordinary and godlike. Indeed, he was made intelligible through the category of transcendence – a category that distanced him from the weight of history and marks a moral designation. Under the signs of transcendence and morality, apparently unrelated figures and spaces were brought together, coordinated, and unified – Nike (a transnational corporation) and America were given a face and a body. The Nike/Jordan hybrid was seen as an exemplary figure of America's political order and the embodiment of the abstract concepts and promises invoked by America (rights, justice, freedom, and community)

Like Michael Jordan, Nike and its advertising campaigns appear distant from the harsher policing mentality dominating America. For example, PLAY (Participate in the Lives of America's Youth) is part of a promotional network through which Nike sought a patriotic, charitable, and socially responsible profile. Through PLAY, Nike called for national solidarity around children's rights to play and encouraged individuals and corporations to help provide safe, clean recreational opportunities for kids. Through publications like "A Revolutionary Manifesto: A Kid's Bill of Rights," the campaign invoked diverse national sentiments and the authority that is America. PLAY's most compelling and recognized image appeared in a television advertisement featuring Jordan. Against the familiar codes of urban America, Jordan asked Americans to imagine what and who would he be if there were no sports. Here, we have a positive image and a call to action: if we don't provide opportunities for kids, the next Michael Jordan may not appear.

American pride and consumption

The line drawn from childhood to sport to Michael Jordan narrates "belonging" and the making of America's ideal, productive citizen. PLAY builds on and articulates America's bourgeois fantasy of innocent childhood, the precious and sacred moral center of the nation, with America's past, present, and future. A sportless and playless landscape would represent the loss of childhood and hope, as well as the absence of democratic culture as we imagine it. In this sense, Nike is part of a national culture industry that seeks to fulfill the aims of national reproduction. In a period a high cynicism and in which people struggle everyday to fulfill the need to be part of something meaningful, projects like PLAY provide feelings and opportunities which suggest that "we" (members of an imagined community) can be, or are, part of something that makes a difference. Promotional discourse like PLAY offers faith in America, the American system, and the American way of life. In so doing, they stabilize the constantly threatened personal and national identities that rely on free will and responsibility.

Yet, and ironically, the PLAY narrative also suggests that not all children are visualized through the trope of innocence. That black youth exist outside the discourse of innocence is displayed by geography as certain kids are marked as sources of danger. While sport shores up America's fantasy of childhood fun and play for white middle-class youth, sport functions to regulate, discipline, and police already deviant bodies in urban areas. Childhood, for black urban youth, is represented as a compromised category, and sport, a moral and normative imperative. Without sport (the nationally sanctioned surrogate family), inner-city youths are at once at risk from peer pressure and the source of danger. Our attention is once again directed to crime, law and order, discipline, and their correlates: gangs, drugs, sport, and Nike.

While Nike and Jordan are narrated as caring, compassionate, charitable, and virtuous, and while both are implicated in liberal-humanist themes of "self-made" and "made in America," both are products of transnational capital and its reorganization of America's urban economy. America's founding categories, the authority that is America, forge a deceptive unity only through violence. While their meanings appear certain and while they operate as absolutes in what is presumed to be a universal language of democratic ideals, their contingencies can only be masked by wasting those who threaten to disturb them. Indeed, the sport/gang narrative animating PLAY imagines sovereign agents who make choices about their fate. The violences of their conditions (produced through late-capitalist dynamics and public policies driven by the mythic family) are displaced, as the incomprehensibility of their "crimes" mobilizes desire for revenge.

The reduction of the conditions of urban America during the 1980s to individual choice functions to stabilize America's foundational categories (those categories and values that ground America's identity but whose stability requires ignoring material conditions and forces). Moreover, the sport/gang dyad, its corresponding somatic territorializations, and the naturalness of the categories inscribe a racialized criminal and threatening masculinity that produce desires for policing, punishment, and revenge directed at African American inner-city youth. Although Jordan exemplifies late-modern America's self-made man, he was "made in America," implicated in the themes guiding American pride, alongside and within an explosion of popular images of African American youth as threatening and in need of policing.

Sport Connections

Given the wide range of issues that follow sport, I have necessarily restricted my comments and examples in this chapter. I focused on two boundary figures, the communist athlete and the gang member, to illuminate the complex connections behind the pure athletic body. Although it seems otherwise, boundary creatures are regular products of sport, they suggest illicit acts and unethical creations; they are meant to disturb, to incite feelings of horror and condemnation.

Indeed, in her now classic essay, historian of science Donna Haraway explains, "[W]e are chimeras, theorized and fabricated hybrids of machine and organism; in short, we are cyborgs. The cyborg is our ontology; it gives us our politics." To live as a cyborg is to live in a condition where purportedly pure categories are always "contaminated" by the other, in which we are creatures of natural artifice as well as creators of hybrids and monsters. The opposition between nature/ artifice, the nonhuman/human, and the effort to maintain/create the purity of each, as Bruno Latour notes, tends to render the processes by which hybrids are produced unrepresentable and thus invisible. The dual yet opposed processes of hybridization and purification are the root of the awesome power and product- ivity of modern civilization. Both Haraway and Latour suggest the pursuit of pure bodies and categories tends to foster the irresponsible production of hybrids and monsters by rendering invisible their processes of production. And they do so in particular contexts – bound up with official knowledges of power, politics, and citizenship.

Perhaps the search for pure bodies seems an archaic dream, a utopian desire that signals a time before late modernism, but their continued and repeated appearance in sporting narrative suggests otherwise. Indeed, we need only consider the recent formation of WADA (the World Anti-Doping Agency charged with coordinating drug-testing programs, standardizing scientific and technical procedures, and implementing sanctions against athletes charged with using illicit performance enhancing substances) to see the ongoing effects of the sporting optic. WADA is the new millennium's transnational effort to uphold the transcendent and universal qualities of sport, forged around a utopian investment in maintaining a worldwide level playing field. In the name of a clean sport war, WADA is celebrated as part of a discourse of the globalized citizen that erases the specificity of bodies in a transnational moment. Illuminating the networks behind WADA, the various multinationals attempting to corner this market, and its production of boundary creatures requires attending to relations that are allusive, overlapping, generative, and repressive; and the personal, local, national, and global. By attending to the complex array of connections advocated by Martin & Miller and Probyn, we do more than contextualize an object of study, we necessarily challenge the parameters of sport, and the conventional cultural studies wisdom of the practical and political.

References

"Are Girl Athletes Really Girls?" *Life*, Oct. 7, 1966, pp. 63–6.

Cole, C. L. (1996). "American Jordan: P.L.A.Y., Consensus, & Punishment." *Sociology of Sport Journal* 13: 366–97.

"The Grace of our Olympic Girls." *Life*, July 31, 1964, pp. 38–47.

Gruneau, R. (1993). "The Critique of Sport in Modernity: Theorizing Power, Culture and the Politics of the Body." In E. G. Dunning, J. A. Maguire, and R. E. Pearton (eds.), *The Sports Process: A Comparative and Developmental Approach*. Champaign, Ill. Human Kinetics.

Hannigan, J. (1998). *Fantasy City: Pleasure and Profit in the Postmodern Metropolis*. New York & London: Routledge.

Haraway, D. (1991). "A Cyborg Manifesto: Science, Technology and Socialist-feminism in the Late Twentieth-century." In *Simians, Cyborgs, and Women: The Reinvention of Nature*. New York: Routledge.

Hargreaves, J. E. (1986). *Sport, Power and Culture*. New York: St. Martin's Press.

Hargreaves, J. E. (1987). "The Body, Sport and Power Relations." In J. Horne, D. Jary, and A. Tomlinson (eds.), *Sport, Leisure, and Social Relations*. London: Routledge & Kegan Paul.

Harvey, J. and R. Sparks (1991). "The Politics of the Body in the Context of Modernity." *Quest* 43: 164–89.

C. L. Cole

Latour, B. (1993). *We Have Never Been Modern*. Cambridge, Mass.: Harvard University Press.

Martin, R. and T. Miller (1999). "Fielding Sport: A Preface to Politics." In R. Martin and T. Miller (eds.), *SportCult*. Minneapolis: University of Minnesota Press.

McChesney, R. W. (1999). *Rich Media, Poor Democracy: Communication Politics in Dubious Times*. Urbana: University of Illinois Press.

Munt, S. R. (1998). "Introduction." In Munt (ed.), *Butch/ Femme: InsideLesbian Gender*. London: Cassell.

"Muscles Pop Through the Iron Curtain." *Life*, July 28, 1952, pp. 15–16.

Probyn, E. (2000). "Sporting Bodies: Dynamics of Shame and Pride." *Body & Society* 6: 13–28.

Scheff, T. (1994) "Emotions and Identity: A Theory of Ethnic Nationalism." In C. Calhoun (ed.), *Social Theory and the Politics of Identity*. Oxford: Blackwell.

Sedgwick, E. and A. Frank. (1995). "Shame in the Cybernetic Fold: Reading Silvan Tomkins." In E. Sedgwick and A. Frank (eds.), *Shame and its Sisters: A Silvan Tomkins Reader*. Durham: Duke University Press.

Smith, M. "To Win the Olympic War." *Life*, July 28, 1952, pp. 17–19.

Walsh, R. W. (Dec. 24 1951), "The Soviet Athlete in International Competition." Department of State Bulletin, Washington DC.

Further Reading

Andrews, D. L. (1993). "Desperately Seeking Michel: Foucault's Genealogy, the Body, and Critical Sport Sociology." *Sociology of Sport Journal* 10: 148–67.

Andrews, D. L. (ed.) (1996). "Deconstructing Michael Jordan: Reconstructing Post-industrial America." *Sociology of Sport Journal* 13(4).

Baker, A. and T. Boyd (eds.) (1997). *Out of Bounds: Sports, Media, and the Politics of Identity*. Bloomington and Indianapolis: University of Indiana Press.

Bolin, A. (1992a). "Vandalized Vanity: Feminine Physiques Betrayed and Portrayed." In E. Mascia-Lees and P. Sharpe (eds.), *Tattoo, Torture, Mutilation, and Adornment*. Albany: State University of New York Press.

Bolin, A. (1992b). "Flex Appeal, Food, and Fat: Competitive Bodybuilding, Gender, and Diet." *Play & Culture* 5: 378–400.

Brownell, S. (1995). *Training the Body for China: Sports in the Moral Order of the People's Republic*. Chicago: University of Chicago Press.

Butler, J. (1998). "Athletic Genders: Hyperbolic Instance and/or the Overcoming of Sexual Binarism." *Stanford Humanities Review* 6: 103–11.

Cahn, S. (1994). *Coming on Strong: Gender and Sexuality in Twentieth-Century Women's Sport*. Cambridge, Mass.: Harvard University Press.

Coakley, J. (1998). *Sport and Society: Issues and Controversies*. Chicago: Mosby.

Defrance, J. (1987). "*L'excellence corporelle: La formation des activités physiques et sportives modernes 1770–1914*" [*Excellence of the body: The emergence of modern sport and physical activities*]. Rennes, France: Presse Universitaires Rennes.

Dunning, E. and K. Sheard (1979). *Barbarians, Gentlemen and Players: A Sociological Study of the Development of Rugby Football*. Oxford: Martin Robertson.

354

Elias, N. and E. Dunning (1986). *Quest for Excitement: Sport and Leisure in the Civilizing Process*. Oxford: Blackwell.

Farred, G. (2000). "Cool as the Other Side of the Pillow: How ESPN's *Sportscenter* has Changed Television Sports Talk." *Journal of Sport & Social Issues* 24: 96–117.

Franklin, S. (1996). "Postmodern Body Techniques: Some Anthropological Considerations on Natural and Postnatural Bodies." *Journal of Sport and Exercise Psychology* 18: 95–106.

Gruneau, R and D. Whitson (1993). *Hockey Night in Canada: Sport, Identities and Cultural Politics*. Toronto: Garamond Press.

Guttman, A. (1994). *Games and Empires: Modern Sports and Cultural Imperialism*. New York: Columbia University Press.

Haber, H. (1996). "Foucault Pumped: Body Politics and the Muscled Woman." In S. Hekman (ed.), *Feminist Interpretations of Michel Foucault*. University Park: Pennsylvania State University Press.

Hargreaves, J. (1994). *Sporting Females: Critical Issues in the History and Sociology of Women's Sports*. London: Routledge.

Holmlund, C. (1989). "Visual Difference and Flex Appeal: The Body, Sex, Sexuality, and Race in the Pumping Iron films." *Cinema Journal* 28: 38–51.

Holt, R. (1981). *Sport and Society in Modern France*. London: Macmillan Press

Howell, J. (1991). "A Revolution in Motion: Advertising, and the Politics of Nostalgia." *Sociology of Sport Journal* 8: 258–71.

Jarvie, G. and J. Maguire (1994). *Sport and Leisure in Social Thought*. London: Routledge.

Kimmel, M. (1990). "Baseball and the Reconstitution of American Masculinity, 1880–1920." In M. Messner and D. Sabo (eds.), *Sport, Men, and the Gender Order: Critical Feminist Perspectives*. Champaign, Ill: Human Kinetics.

King, S. (1993). "The Politics of the Body and the Body Politic: Magic Johnson and the Ideology of AIDS." *Sociology of Sport Journal* 10: 270–85.

King, S. (2000). "Consuming Compassion: AIDS, Figure Skating, and Canadian Identity." *Journal of Sport & Social Issues* 24: 148–75.

Linder, G. (1995). "An Ethnography of Discipline: Elite Bodybuilding in Los Angeles." Unpublished doctoral dissertation, University of North Carolina at Chapel Hill.

Loy, J., D. A. Andrews, and R. Rinehart (1993). "The Body in Culture and Sport: Toward an Embodied Sociology of Sport." *Sport Science Review* 2: 69–91.

McKay, J. (1990). " 'Just Do It': Corporate Sports Slogans and the Political Economy of Enlightened Racism." *Discourse: Studies in the Cultural Politics of Education* 16: 10–13.

MacAloon, J. (1990). "Steroids and the State: Dubin, Melodrama and the Accomplishment of Innocence." *Public Culture* 2: 41–64.

Maguire, J. (1991). "Bodies, Sportscultures and Societies: A Critical Review of Some Theories in the Sociology of the Body." *International Review for the Sociology of Sport* 18: 33–51.

Miller, T. (1997). "Sport and Violence: Glue, Seed, State, or Psyche?" *Journal of Sport and Social Issues* 21: 235–8.

Miller, T. (2001). *Sportsex*. Philadelphia: Temple University Press.

Moore, P. (ed.) (1997). *Building Bodies*. New Brunswick, NJ: Rutgers University Press.

Morrison, T. and C. Lacour (eds.) (1997). *Birth of a Nation'Hood: Gaze, Script, and Spectacle in the O. J. Simpson Case*. New York: Pantheon Books.

355

Morse, M. (1983). "Sport on Television: Replay and Display." In E. A. Kaplan (ed.), *Regarding Television*. Los Angeles: American Film Institute.

Mrozek, D. (1989). "Sport in American Life: From National Health to Personal Fulfillment." In K. Grover (ed.), *Fitness in American Culture: Images of Heath, Sport, and the Body, 1830–1940*. Amherst: The University of Massachusetts Press, and the Margaret Woodbury Strong Museum, Rochester, NY.

Rail, G. and J. Harvey (1995). "Body at Work: Michel Foucault and the Sociology of Sport." *Sociology of Sport Journal* 12: 164–79.

Rowe, D., G. Lawrence, T. Miller and J. McKay (1994). "Global Sport? Core Concern and Peripheral Vision." *Media, Culture & Society* 16: 661–75.

Schulze, L. (1990). "On the Muscle." In J. Gaines and C. Herzog (eds.), *Fabrications: Costume and the Female Body*. New York: Routledge.

Sparks, R. (1990). "Social Practice, the Bodily Professions and the State." *Sociology of Sport Journal* 7: 72–82.

Theberge, N. (1991). "Reflections on the Body in the Sociology of Sport." *Quest* 43: 123–34.

Wacquant, L. (1998) "A Fleshpeddler at Work: Power, Pain and Profit in the Prizefighting Economy." *Theory and Society* 27: 1–42.

Wannell, G. (1992). *Fields in Vision: Television Sport and Cultural Transformation*. London: Routledge.

Chapter 21

Intellectuals, Culture, Policy: The Practical and the Critical

Tony Bennett

There are now ample signs that cultural policy is emerging as an increasingly important area of theoretical and practical engagement for intellectuals working in the fields of sociology and cultural studies. This has occasioned a good deal of debate concerning the roles of intellectuals and the relationships they should adopt in relation to the bureaucratic and political processes through which cultural policies are developed and put into effect. It is with these debates that I engage here with a view to distinguishing the light that might be thrown on them by different accounts of the social roles and distribution of different kinds of intellectual function. My concerns here will center on the relations between two traditions of social theory. The first derives from Jürgen Habermas's classic study of the public sphere (Habermas 1989) and theorizes the role of intellectuals in terms of the distinction between critical and technical intellectual functions which characterizes Habermas's construction of the relationships between different forms of rationality. The second comprises the tradition which, following in the wake of Michel Foucault's essay on governmentality (Foucault 1978), has concerned itself with the roles of particular forms of knowledge and expertise in organizing differentiated fields of government and social management.

My starting-point will be with the Habermasian tradition. The concept of the public sphere is, of course, one that now need no longer be constrained by its Habermasian lineage. In its post-Habermasian history, moreover, the concept has made positive contributions to both the theory and practice of cultural policy. It has supplied the language through which governments have been called on – with some success – to develop forms of media regulation that will inhibit the oligopolistic tendencies of media industries by providing for at least some semblance of democracy and diversity in the role of the media in the organization and circulation of opinion (Collins & Murroni 1996). The differentiation of Habermas's singular public sphere into plural public spheres – feminist and indigenous, for example – has also been important in legitimating claims on the public purse which have helped in winning new forms of public, and publicly educative, presence for groups excluded from the classical bourgeois public sphere. My concerns, however, are less with these adaptations of the Habermasian concept than with Habermas's initial account of the public sphere and the role it has played, in subsequent debates, when viewed in the light of the splitting of intellectual work between the differentiated functions of *critique* and *praxis* which he proposes. (I should add, to avoid possible confusion, that my attention is limited to Habermas's initial account of the public sphere. While acknowledging that Habermas has subsequently revised this in the light of the critical debates it has generated, no account is taken of these revisions here.)

My engagements with this tradition of work will be of two kinds. First, I shall argue that Habermas's polarizing procedures do not offer us a cogent basis for debating and assessing the politics of contemporary intellectual practice. Their main weakness is that of dividing reason into two without then being able to offer any means of reconnecting its severed parts except through the endlessly deferred mechanism of the dialectic. Second, I shall argue that Habermas's account of the development and subsequent deterioration of the bourgeois public sphere seriously misunderstands the role that the main institutions of public culture have played in the development of modern practices of cultural governance.

The vantage points from which I pursue these concerns are ones supplied by different branches of the post-Foucauldian literature on governmentality. In developing the first argument, I draw on work which stresses the ethical comportment which characterizes the conduct of bureaucratized intellectual functions. This aspect of my argument serves to undercut the view that the exercise of practical intellectual functions within bureaucratic contexts can serve as an "ethics–free zone" in counterpoint to the ethical purity of the critical intellectual. The second point is developed by looking again at Habermas's historical account of the public sphere through the lens of post-Foucauldian inquiries into the development of modern forms of government and culture.

The Critical and the Practical

Jim McGuigan's *Culture and the Public Sphere* offers a convenient point of entry into the first set of issues. This closes in posing two questions: How can critical intellectuals be practical? And how can practical intellectuals be critical? By critical intellectuals McGuigan has in mind intellectuals whose work is academic in the sense that the conditions in which it takes place disconnect it from any immediate practical outcomes for which those intellectuals can be held responsible. The problem for such intellectuals, then, is that the opportunity for critically reflexive work which such conditions make possible is purchased at the price of a loss of any immediate practical effectivity. The practical intellectuals McGuigan refers to are cultural workers "engaged in some form of communication and cultural management" in practical contexts where, as he defines them, "the possibilities of critical knowledge . . . have already been closed off" by the need for "recipe knowledge" (McGuigan 1996: 190). Two kinds of intellectual, then, each of whom, at least at first sight, seems to lack what the other possesses. It becomes clear on further inspection, however, that the relations between these different categories of intellectual are not, and cannot become, relations of exchange. Rather, they take the form of a one-way street in which the task enjoined on the critical intellectual is that of dislodging the forms of reasoning – the "recipe knowledge" – which govern the contexts in which practical intellectuals do their work. The most that can be asked of practical intellectuals – parties to a gift relationship in which they can only be receivers – is that they should be prepared to jettison those forms of reasoning which spontaneously characterize their work in favor of the essentially different forms of reasoning represented, and selflessly donated, by critical intellectuals.

How is it that these lowly servants of a mere "recipe knowledge" find themselves placed on the opposite side of a divide separating them from the realms in which critical intellectuals operate? This separation is the local manifestation of a more fundamental division between critical and instrumental reason which has its roots in Habermas's account of the division between system and lifeworld and their opposing principles of rationality. In the latter, where communication is relatively undistorted by uneven relationships of power and where there is a common interest in shared horizons of meaning arising out of shared conditions of life, communicative rationality is orientated to mutual understanding. By contrast, the instrumental rationality which characterizes the world of system is one which displaces questions of human value and meaning in favor of a means–end rationality whose direction is dictated by existing structures of class and bureaucratic power. This opposition between system and lifeworld is most economically represented in the terms of Habermas's distinction between *praxis* and *techne*. The first of these, as Habermas glosses it, is concerned with the reasoned assessment of the validity of norms for action, whereas *techne* is concerned solely with the rational selection of the best instruments for achieving particular outcomes once the normative goals for social action have been determined (Habermas 1974: 1–3).

When these broader aspects of the argument are taken into account, it is clear that the form of mediation that McGuigan proposes for overcoming the separation of critical and practical intellectuals would extend the sway of *praxis*, whose spokesperson is the critical intellectual, beyond the lifeworld into the world of system where it would ideally displace, or provide a superordinate context for, the application of *techne*. At the same time, however, the prospects of this actually happening are not good, to the degree that the conditions of work of intellectuals located within the world of system predispose them to focus exclusively on narrowly technical forms of reason and action. Thus lessons of *praxis*, since they do "not tell us *directly* what to do," will "always be regarded as unsatisfactory by those who prefer to act without thinking; in effect, those who want recipe knowledge but not critical thought, information but not ideas" (McGuigan 1996: 1987). McGuigan seems not to notice the paradoxical effects of a body of theory which, on the one hand, holds out the possibility of universally valid norms of communication and mutual understanding arising out of the shared conditions of the lifeworld while, on the other, dividing reason into two antinomial realms – *praxis* and *techne* – whose separation, once established, cannot be overcome except by imposing the values of one on the other. What is perhaps more harmful, however, is the mapping of this opposition between different kinds of reason onto the relations between different kinds of intellectuals working in different contexts.

The dubious value of this procedure is all the more evident when it is considered that, in most other regards, the differences between so-called critical and practical intellectuals would seem to be so slight. From everything that we know of the demographic characteristics and shared occupational cultures of academics and cultural intermediaries and policy professionals, it might have been thought that they would be able to communicate effectively with one another on matters of common practical and intellectual concern from the perspective of a shared horizon of professional, social, and cultural understandings. Indeed, I would contend that this *is* so, except in the world of Habermasian dualities where it *cannot* be so. For once critical intellectuals take it upon themselves to connect their work to the realm of system, the democratic norm that all parties to any communicative interaction should be treated as equal is abandoned as the critical intellectual assumes a discursive position – a capacity for critical independence and detachment – that is, by definition, superior to that of the purely technical competence of the administrator or manager. This superiority is invested with further normative significance in the related assumption that the "culture of dissatisfaction" that results from the restlessly self-reflexive persona of the critical intellectual is the sole source of progressive change within the administration of culture, and one that is pitched constantly against the inertia and conservatism of the agencies and personnel that are actually responsible for the development and implementation of cultural policies. As McGuigan puts it:

> The culture of dissatisfaction is the perpetual bugbear of any official cultural policy: the very officialness of governmental policy, in effect, makes it conservative, the upholder of the status quo, from the point of view of a restless dissatisfaction with the way things are presently constituted. (McGuigan 1996: 50)

It is easy to see here how the dualities constructed by the Habermasian apparatus have an element of self-fulfilling prophecy built into them. For if McGuigan's purpose really is to build bridges between critical and practical intellectuals, the Habermasian spin he gives to this task makes him a poor diplomat in his own cause. For what are the chances that the communications and cultural managers who *do* read his book might feel parties to an open and unconstrained dialogue in which the positions, perspectives, and experiences of intellectual workers situated in different contexts might be regarded as matters for genuine debate? Not strong, I'd have thought, given that they have been defined in wholly negative terms owing to their incapacity for critical or independent thought.

This is a pity, and especially so as there are no good reasons for taking the virtues of *critique* so much for granted. There is now a substantial body of work which, far from taking *critique* to be a transcendent and self-subsistent norm, historicizes and relativizes it in ways which seriously question its ethical and epistemological credentials. Indeed, it is possible to read the tradition of critical sociology, to which Habermas's work belongs, as itself a powerful form of "recipe knowledge." A significant case in point is Bruno Latour's recent questioning of emancipatory rhetorics. Contending that the prospect of revolutionary simplifications of the social has now ceded place to the challenge of "coexistence between totally heterogeneous forms of people, cultures, epochs and entities," he argues that the complexities this entails mean that the arrow of time can no longer run from "slavery to freedom" but only from "entanglement to more entanglement" (Latour 1999: 13–15). As heir to the tradition of post-Kantian philosophy, it guarantees a continuing role for *critique* by its formulaic construction of the historical process as one which establishes divisions (in this case, between *praxis* and *techne* and its various derivatives) which have then to be overcome and reconciled with the aid of the philosopher-sociologist's critical intellectual mediation. It is by means of this operation that *critique*, as a stylized intellectual practice, is substituted for more grounded forms of critical inquiry in making an entirely predictable set of intellectual routines whose form, moves, and conclusions – in setting up oppositions and projecting their reconciliation while simultaneously regretting the factors which impede the unfolding of this ideal dialectic – stand in the place of an analytical engagement with the recalcitrant positivity and dispersed diversity of social relations and forces.

I am more concerned, here, however with the other side of the Habermasian division of the sphere of reason into two. For the purely means–end rationality of bureaucratic reason can be rescued from the terms of Habermas's condemnation by recognizing that it can lay its own claims to virtue on grounds that are simultaneously ethical, critical, and historical. Ian Hunter's spirited defense of the bureaucratic vocation will serve as a good point of entry into these concerns. For in restoring an appropriate degree of virtue to the bureaucrat, Hunter also calls into question the absolutist forms of authority which those who speak in the voice of the critical intellectual spontaneously and unreflectively claim as their own.

Hunter takes his initial bearings from those ways of depicting the persona of the bureaucrat which project it "as 'one side' of a full moral personality, the other side of which is represented by the 'humanist intellectual'" who is the mirror image of the bureaucrat in espousing "a commitment to substantive values" while lacking the "technical means for realising them" (Hunter 1994: 146). While this division of the world of reason into two rests on Weber's neo-Kantian distinction between instrumentally rational and value-rational forms of social action, Weber's position differed from Kant's in refusing to make the humanist

361

intellectual the ultimate arbiter of value-rational action. Weber's stance was rather pluralistic and sociological, regarding the ends of value-rational action as being multiple and specific to particular spheres of life and giving rise to distinctive ethical dispositions and capacities. This included, Hunter is shrewd to note, an assessment of the bureaucracy's commitment to instrumentally rational action as itself constituting a distinctive ethos of office requiring particular ethical capacities rather than figuring as a sphere of moral vacuousness and critical emptiness.

This leads Hunter to suggest that what Habermas devalues as mere *techne* is the result of a specific ethical training rather than a form of ethical lack. The bureau, he says, is not something that has been separated off from critical reason as a result of some split in the lifeworld or the opening of some historical chasm in the organization of public life. Rather, it is the site for the formation of a distinctive ethical persona in the sense that "the office itself constitutes a 'vocation' (*Beruf*), a focus of ethical commitment and duty, autonomous of and superior to the holder's extra-official ties to kith, kin, class or, for that matter, conscience" (Hunter 1994: 156). From this perspective, to denounce the instrumentalism of bureaucracy for its apparently amoral indifference to qualitative ends is to fail to appreciate the historically distinctive form of morality which such an ethos of office represents:

> The ethical attributes of the good bureaucrat – strict adherence to procedure, acceptance of sub-and super-ordination, *esprit de corps*, abnegation of personal moral enthusiasms, commitment to the purposes of the office – are not an incompetent subtraction from a "complete" (self-concerned and self-realising) comportment of the person. On the contrary, they are a positive moral achievement requiring the mastery of a difficult milieu and practice. (Hunter 1994: 156–7)

Why, then, is the critical intellectual more likely, instead, to devalue the bureaucrat as a one-sided and incomplete embodiment of the function of reason? In answering this question, Hunter draws on Weber's general sociological principles, treating the post-Kantian construction of the critical intellectual as a person committed to a higher and universal sense of moral duty as itself a particular ethos requiring analysis in terms of its relations to particular kinds of social prestige and power. When considered sociologically, "the persona of the self-reflective scholar acting on the basis of inner conviction is no more ethically fundamental than that of the official, whose ethos involves subordinating his inner convictions to the duties of office" (Hunter 1994: 163). Both represent specific moral dispositions cultivated through the exercise of particular spiritual disciplines and routines. *Critique*, however, arranges these differences hierarchically by "treating its own status-persona – the self-reflective scholar, the 'complete' person . . . – as 'ultimate' for all comportments of the person, the bureaucrat and citizen included" (Hunter 1994: 163). Hunter is clear in seeing this absolutizing tendency of *critique* as part of a tactics of intellectual life through which a particular stratum of intellectuals, while disconnected from the actual administrative forms through which social life is organized, aspires to a distinctive kind of social influence. This is to be achieved by cultivating the status of moral notables who, speaking to the world at large, claim the mantle of a "secular holiness" which, as part of a practice of "world flight," allows them to "criticise the dominant organisation of social life by practising an exemplary withdrawal from it" (Hunter 1994: 167).

Said's *Representations of the Intellectual* provides a convenient example of this practice of "secular holiness" and of the forms of critical intolerance and ethical bullying it entails. For Said's strategy in elaborating his view of the intellectual as an exile and marginal, as an amateur whose true vocation is "to speak the truth to power" (Said 1994: p. xiv), depends on trapping professionals, experts, and consultants – those false intellectuals who have traded their critical independence for wealth, power, and influence – in the contaminating mire of their associations with worldly powers and the limitations, of perspective or of moral capacity, that these entail. Said's "world flight" into universality is thus sustained by the role in which the bureaucratic or managerialist intellectual is cast as the low other against whom the stellar trajectory of the true intellectual – the amateur whose activity "is fuelled by care and affection rather than by profit, and selfish, narrow specialisation" (Said 1994: 61) – can be mapped:

> In other words, the intellectual properly speaking is not a functionary or an employee completely given up to the policy goals of a government or a large corporation, or even a guild of like-minded professionals. In such situations the temptations to turn off one's moral sense, or to think entirely from within the speciality, or to curtail scepticism in favour of conformity, are far too great to be trusted. (Said 1994: 64)

But how clear-sighted is this particular universal intellectual when he has cut a moral trench between himself and other intellectual workers? In truth: not very. Said, in what he has to say about the relationships between intellectuals and government, surveys the world through the tinted lenses of a metropolitan parochialism whose belief in its universal validity is based on nothing so much as a constitutive blindness to its own forms of limiting particularity. For when Said – speaking to and for all the world – places true intellectuals outside of government and charges them to speak the truth to power, it is clear that he imagines government always and only in the form of some branch of the US science-military-industry complex that has rightly been at the center of his engagements with US Israel–Palestine policies. The possibility that, in other parts of the world, intellectuals might see themselves as speaking the truth to *and for* more local forms of power with a view to muting or qualifying the effects of other forms of power is simply not thinkable from within Said's elementary bipolar construction of the relations of truth and power. I have in mind here the role that intellectuals – whether as academics, government employees, or as public intellectuals – have played in the development of progressive nationalist cultural policies in contexts (France, Australia, Scotland, Wales, Canada) where this is seen as involving both setting limits and nourishing alternatives to the invasive influence of other dominant national cultures (American, English). The same is true of intellectuals who work within government as cultural workers of various kinds – curators, community arts workers, arts administrators – in cultural diversity, community, or art and working life programs.

This is not to suggest that any of these contexts for intellectual work are without their ambiguities and contradictions. Nor is it to suggest that it should be the *only* focus for intellectual work: there are, in the complex relations between government and civil society, many different ways (from action research linked to social movements to applied policy research) in which intellectuals can be productively practical. My point is rather that the simplified and polarized construction Said places on the politics of intellectual life does not allow an adequate recognition, let alone resolution, of those ambiguities and contradictions. More important, it eviscerates the work of the critical intellectual in sanctioning a refusal to engage with those ambiguities and contradictions. For Said, the intellectual must choose "the risks and uncertain results of the public sphere – a lecture or a book or article in wide and unrestricted circulation – over the insider space controlled by experts and professionals" (Said 1994: 64). Yet this either–orism is misleading owing to its inability to distinguish the radically different forms in which – depending on the issue and the context – the relationships between specific regions of government and specific realms of public debate might be related to one another.

There is a need, then, for those who aspire to be critical intellectuals to look more closely at their own practice and the conditions which sustain it. This, in its turn, will require a clearer differentiation of *critique*, as a highly specific practice – a moral technology, in effect – dependent on the discursive coordinates of post-Kantian philosophy, from the more general categories of criticism or critical thought. This is necessary if we are to recognize that intellectuals can both contribute critically to public debate about particular forms of social and cultural policy, assessing these in terms of their shortcomings when viewed from particular ethical and political standpoints, while at the same time contributing their expertise to particular areas of policy formation and learning from the other intellectuals, working within the policy process, with whom such work brings them into contact. To engage in critical thought in this way, however, does not require – and is not assisted by – any rigid separation of means–end from normative rationality of the kind proposed by *critique*. Nor does it require any elevation of the latter over the former. Critical thought, no matter who its agent might be, is most productive when conducted in a manner which recognizes the need to take account of the contributions of different forms of expertise without any *a priori* prejudicial ranking of the relations between them and, equally, when it takes account of the forces – social, economic, political, and moral – which circumscribe the field of the practicable.

This would be greatly assisted if questions of mediation, rather than being seen as ones concerning how to overcome the apparently irreconcilable divisions which split the realm of reason into its critical and instrumental forms, were posed as questions concerning the need for new forms of *institutional and organizational* connection capable of interrelating the work that intellectual workers of different kinds do in different contexts. For there is no cognitive or, indeed, ethical gulf separating intellectuals working in government and industry centers of cultural management from those working in universities. There are, to be sure, different pressures, exigencies, and priorities bearing on these different contexts. The very real benefits afforded by academic contexts – the latitude to canvass a broader range of issues, to bring a historical perspective to bear, to have long-term considerations in view, to take the points of view of constituencies who might otherwise be marginalized – should, of course, be valued as enabling distinctive contributions to be made to the actual, and no doubt compromised and contested, processes through which cultural life is organized and managed. However, intellectuals working in such contexts will constantly marginalize themselves and what they have to offer if they broach this task as involving haughtily hailing across a moral and cognitive divide rather than a matter of devising institutionalized mechanisms of exchange that will allow academic knowledges to connect productively with the intellectual procedures of policy bureaux.

To approach these matters productively, however, will require that we review our sense both of where public spheres are and the nature of our relations to them. This requires a cautious assessment of the value of Habermas's work on this subject. For the support it has lent the view that the public sphere or spheres comprise an institutional and discursive realm which might provide a critical exterior in relation to the power effects of both state and economy is both historically misleading and politically unhelpful.

Relocating the Public Sphere

The general contours of Habermas's account of the rise and fall of the classical bourgeois public sphere are well known. The classical bourgeois public sphere is understood in terms of its role in forming a public which, through reasoned debate, aspired to articulate a public will as a set of demands arrived at independently of the state or public authority and advanced in the expectation that they would need to be taken into account in the exercise of state power. The radical implications of this commitment to a critical rationality are then subsequently lost as a consequence of the increasing commercialization and bureaucratization of public communications from the mid-nineteenth century onwards. While I cannot engage here with the detail of this account, I want to propose a different way of reading the historical unfolding of the relations between government and culture. Rather than seeing the founding ideals of the public sphere as being subsequently overturned through bureaucratic forms of statism and new forms of commercial cultural production and distribution, this would trace the steps through which the institutions and practices of the public sphere have been translated into modern forms of cultural governance in which cultural resources are applied to varied tasks of social management. This is not, though, a matter of offering a history that is entirely at odds with Habermas's account. Rather, the view I wish to develop can be arrived at by means of, first, highlighting an aspect of his discussion of the classical bourgeois public sphere that has not always received the attention it merits, and, second, commenting on an equally little-remarked absence in the account he offers of the subsequent structural transformation of the public sphere.

The first point is most easily introduced via a commentary on Habermas's diagramatic representation of the bourgeois public sphere at the moment of its emergence in the eighteenth century. His depiction is reproduced in figure 2 (from Habermas 1989: 30).

The division that most concerns Habermas is that between the sphere of public authority and the private realm: hence the double line separating the two. He accordingly approaches the manner in which the different components of the private realm interact with one another from the point of view of their common differentiation from the sphere of public authority. From this perspective, what matters most about the public sphere in the world of letters (or, as Habermas also calls it, the literary public sphere) is its role as a set of sites for forming opinions that are to be taken heed of in the exercise of state power. Similarly, the market for cultural products plays a historical role in desanctifying cultural products with the consequence that they are able to play a role in these secular processes of opinion formation. In detaching such products from their aura, the market allows works of culture to become objects of critical discussion with the consequence, first, that they become embroiled in the critique of both the state and courtly society and, second, that they become vehicles for the enunciation of new generalized rights of public accessibility: the public for culture becomes, for the first time, theoretically universal.

Private Realm		Sphere of Public Authority
Civil society (realm of commodity exchange and social labor)	Public sphere in the political realm Public sphere in the world of letters (clubs, press)	State (realm of the "police")
Conjugal family's internal space (bourgeois intellectuals)	(markets of culture products) "Town"	Court (courtly-noble society)

Figure 2 The bourgeois public sphere
Source: Habermas 1989: 30.

It is noteworthy that Habermas sees the historical emergence of culture's autonomy as a necessary precondition for the process through which culture is then enlisted as a political instrument in the formation of a public opinion critical of, and opposed to, the realm of public authority. This instrumental view of culture – the notion, that is, that cultural forms and institutions are shaped into new instruments to serve new purposes – emerges from the language of "functional conversion" which Habermas uses to account for the detachment of the literary public sphere from its earlier tutelage to the publicity apparatus of the prince's court and its refashioning into a properly bourgeois public sphere. This bourgeois status, however, is clearly an historically acquired rather than an autochthonous attribute. The procedures and the composition of the institutions comprising the public sphere, and the role these play in allowing cultural resources to be harnessed in the cause of rational and public critique, are the results of a historical process through which earlier institutions and practices are functionally converted to new uses:

> The process in which the state-governed public sphere was appropriated by the public of private people making use of their reason and was established as a sphere of criticism of public authority was one of functionally converting the public sphere in the world of letters already equipped with institutions of the public and with forums for discussion. (Habermas 1989: 51)

The institutions of the literary public sphere, then, comprised a site in which culture, via the new forms of critical commentary and debate through which its reception was mediated, was forged into a means of acting against the sphere of public authority. It did so in a manner that was conditioned by the role those institutions played in forging a critical and public rationality out of the differentiated interests comprising the private realm. But this does not exhaust what Habermas has to say about this new realm of public culture, or about the directions in which it faced and the surfaces on which it acted. To the contrary, he is clear that, through the literary public sphere, cultural goods became involved in new spheres of action in the relationships they entered into in connection with what Habermas variously characterizes as civil society or the sphere of the social: that is, with the institutions comprising the left-hand column in figure 2. For if the public sphere mediated between the sphere of public authority and the social, it faced both ways in doing so, with the result that the use of cultural resources within the public sphere also had a dual aspect to it. It was, at one and the same time, a means for forming a public opinion in a rational critique of state power, and a means of acting on the social to regulate it. This is made clear in the terms Habermas uses to differentiate the functioning of the modern public sphere from that of the ancient public sphere:

> With the rise of a sphere of the social, over whose regulation public opinion battled with public power, the theme of the modern (in contrast to the ancient) public

sphere shifted from the properly political tasks of a citizenry acting in common (i.e., administration of law as regards internal affairs and military survival as regards external affairs) to the more properly civic tasks of a society engaged in critical public debate (i.e., the protection of a commercial economy). The political task of the bourgeois public sphere was the regulation of civil society (in contra-distinction to the *res publica*). (Habermas 1989: 52)

This dual orientation of the public sphere is reflected in the contrasting positions that the personnel of culture were obliged to adopt according to whether their activities were directed toward the sphere of public authority or that of the social. In the early stages of the public sphere's formation, the new cultural role of art critic was thus, according to Habermas, "a peculiarly dialect-ical" one in view of the requirement that he serve "at the same time as the public's mandatary and as its educator" (Habermas 1989: 41), both taking a lead from the public and directing and organizing it. The point, however, is a general one: all of the new forms of criticism (art, theatrical, musical, moral weeklies) and institutions (theaters, museums, concerts, coffee houses) Haber-mas is concerned with had, in the late eighteenth and early nineteenth centuries, this dual orientation. Nor, at this time, was this perceived as a contradiction: it was by acting on the social that the institutions of the public sphere formed a public opinion which was then able to act on the sphere of public authority.

Habermas associates these aspects of the public sphere with what he char-acterizes as "the tension-charged field between state and society" (Habermas 1989: 141). His account of the subsequent social-structural transformation of the public sphere rests mainly on his argument concerning the tendencies which, in closing down the gap between state and society, led to what he calls a "refeudal-ization of society." This resulted from two intersecting processes in which public functions were transferred to private corporate bodies (the modern firm) while, at the same time, the sway of public authority was extended over the private realm. "Only this dialectic of a progressive 'societalisation' of the state," as Habermas puts it, "simultaneously with an increasing 'statification' of society gradually destroyed the basis of the bourgeois public sphere – the separation of state and society" (1989: 142). Caught in the pincer movement comprised by these two tendencies, the public sphere, in its liberal form, ceased to exist. The contradictory space in which it had operated was no longer there: the autonomy of the social as an independent realm was no longer sustainable as a result of the new forms of private and public administration which directly repoliticized society in subjecting it to increasingly direct and extensive forms of control. At the same time, the development of new forms of mass consumption deprived culture of that hard-won historical autonomy that had earlier allowed it to function as an instrument of criticism through its connection to the public sphere. The forms in which the new mass culture was distributed – book clubs, for example – disconnected it from any public context of debate and criticism except for administered forms (Habermas's examples are the adult education class and the radio panel discussion). The commercialization of culture which had once provided for culture's autonomy now takes it away.

There are two aspects of this account which, taken separately, might occasion no particular concern but which, when looked at together, suggest a different light in which the tendencies Habermas is concerned with might be described and accounted for. The first concerns his characterization of the last quarter of the nineteenth century, the period in which the public sphere is structurally transformed, as marking the end of the liberal era. The second concerns the marked narrowing in the focus of his attention which results from his limiting his account of the transformation of the public sphere to the press and the book industry. The broader range of institutions which form a part of his account of the historical formation of the classical bourgeois public sphere – museums, concerts, art galleries – do not enter into his account of this later period any more than does the new institution which arguably ought to have been at the center of an account organized primarily in relation to the literary public sphere: the public library.

Habermas's perspectives on the first of these matters are drawn from what were, at the time he was writing, the standard Marxist accounts of the shift from liberal to monopoly capitalism. For Habermas, this transformation in the structure of the economy entailed a related move away from liberal forms of government and a consequent closure of the relations between state and society which he summarizes as a tendency toward the "refeudalization" of society. This is extremely questionable. It is, of course, true, to take the British case that he dwells on so much, that the last quarter of the nineteenth century did see the introduction of a new form of liberalism which, in comparison with the "Manchester liberalism" of the earlier period, supported a stronger role for state intervention, particularly in the moral sphere. But it is equally true that the programs of liberal government developed over this period, especially insofar as they involved using cultural resources to regulate the moral sphere, depended on – and worked to maintain – a separation between state and society. This was evident in their construction of the social as a realm which the state might intervene in only indirectly, through the mechanisms of moral reform, primarily with a view to making the members of society voluntarily self-regulating and self-directing without the need for more direct forms of state intervention. It is clear, moreover, that the programs of late nineteenth-century liberal cultural reformers and administrators were explicitly motivated by a commitment to retain the separation of state and society in opposition to the closure of the gap between the two that was involved in the panoptic and directly interventionist forms of state action implied by eugenic conceptions of the role of government.

However, I shall not pursue this line of analysis further except to suggest that, to the degree that the separation of state and society was undermined in this period, this had little to do with any "refeudalization" of state–society relations. Rather, it was an effect of the increasing racialization of relations of government as new conceptions of biopower gave rise to increasingly direct forms of state administration orientated toward the purification of the population (see Stoler 1995). My interest here, to come to my second point, concerns the role that was accorded the institutions Habermas neglects – museums, art galleries, and libraries – in the liberal programs of cultural management characterizing this period. For, although enabling legislation for the establishment of public museums, libraries, and art galleries had existed since the mid-century period, it is not until the last quarter of the century that European governments – at both the national and local levels – begin to invest significantly in the provision of such institutions which, alongside public schooling, constituted the backbone of the public cultural infrastructure until the advent of public broadcasting. While this might accurately be described as a process which resulted in the incorporation of components of the earlier liberal or bourgeois public sphere into the state, this did not result in a closure of the gap between state and society. To the contrary, the purpose of redeploying these institutions of public culture as instruments of government was, precisely, to obviate the need for the state to exercise direct forms of social control by developing a capacity for moral self-regulation in the population at large. The realm of public culture, however much it was now integrated into and directed by the state, continued to function – as in Habermas's account of its earlier phase of development – as a means for acting on the social as a realm that was still conceived as separate from government. What had changed was not the action of culture as a set of resources deemed capable of shaping the conduct and attributes of individuals through their voluntary self-activity, but the social relations within which that action was put to work. The field of "the social" to which the action of culture was to be applied now comprised not the civil society of Habermas's private realm but a set of problematic behaviors – defined mainly in class terms – that were to be managed while, just as important, this action was to be put to work in the context of institutions that were located within the sphere of government rather than in a realm outside of and opposed to it (see Bennett 1995 and 1997).

Indeed, from a global perspective, this location of the public sphere within the realm of government has more typically characterized its origins as well as its point of contemporary arrival. To read these institutional complexes in terms of their colonial histories proves instructive in this regard. For the late nineteenth century was also the period in which the public cultural institutions developed in western Europe first began to go global. They did so, however, as parts of histories which fall quite outside the terms of the story Habermas proposes for their European origins, early development, and subsequent transformation. Martin Prosler has written usefully on this subject, remarking that, in the case of museums, their initial spread up to and including the mid-nineteenth century was limited to white settler colonies in the Americas, India, Australia, and South Africa, and to British colonial territories in Asia (Madras, Lucknow, Lahore, Bangalore, Mathura, and Colombo) (Prosler 1996). It is clear, however, that the functioning of these institutions in these colonial contexts was sharply different from their European origins. In Australia, for example, museums were parts of a public sphere that was nurtured into existence by government rather than having an earlier history in a preexisting and separate realm (see Finney 1993). Their formation was, in this sense, as parts of a process through which a civil society was fashioned into being. Similar tendencies characterized their major period of growth in the late nineteenth century (see Kohlstedt 1983) which, like that of the other institutions of public culture such as libraries, art galleries, and art schools (see Candy & Laurent 1994), relied more extensively on direct forms of government support than had been true of early stages in the development of their European counterparts. There was, to put the point bluntly, no point at which these institutions had ever been developed in opposition to, or in critique of, the state in a way that would make it intelligible to view their integration into government as a structural transformation of an earlier condition. In Australia, public culture was thoroughly governmentalized from the outset.

Conclusions

My purpose, then, is to suggest that, with a little "tweaking," Habermas's account of the "'societalisation' of the state" and the "'statification' of society" can usefully be seen as addressing the same historical processes Foucault is concerned with – albeit from a different theoretical perspective; Foucault is explicit in his critique of the concept of "the *étatisation* of society" (Foucault 1978: 103) – in his account of the "governmentalization of the state." I do so not because Foucault's approach to governmentalization or the role that it plays in his account of the emergence of liberal forms of government is without problems. There are, however, some advantages in superimposing a Foucauldian optic on the historical processes Habermas is concerned with. The first is that it becomes possible to account for a transformation in the functioning of the classical bourgeois public sphere which results from the incorporation of its institutions into government in a manner which leaves open to inquiry the ways in which such institutions operate in the context of historically mutable relations between government and the social rather than attributing to them a generalized function of social control arising from some general historical closure of state/society relations. The advantages of this for a historical approach to cultural policy are evident. It makes thinkable a much greater variability in the relations between government, culture, and the social as a consequence of the ways in which cultural resources are organized to act on the social in different ways in accordance with shifting governmental conceptions and priorities.

A second advantage is that an account couched in these terms can help prevent a polarization of the relations between critical and practical intellectuals of the kind that Habermasian constructions tend to propose. I have suggested, in my discussion of Habermas's approach to the early formation of the public sphere, that the action of culture within this had a dual orientation in both acting on the social to regulate it while also functioning as means for forming an opinion in which state power was subjected to rational forms of critique. If my emphasis so far has fallen on showing how the transformation of this first orientation might be viewed from a Foucauldian perspective, there is also much to be gained from considering how the institutions of public culture have continued to perform aspects of the second function in spite of their having become branches of government. Indeed, it is, in some cases, precisely because they are branches of government that these institutions have assumed a function of criticism that is, now, more or less institutionalized. The translation of antisexist and cultural diversity policies into the exhibition practices of collecting institutions, for example, has resulted in a considerable amount of cultural effort being dedicated to depicting both past and, where they persist, present culturally discriminatory practices as unacceptable with a view to the role this might play in fashioning new norms of civic conduct. In such cases, where the institutions of public culture have comprised the cultural and intellectual spaces that have played leading roles in both developing and disseminating specific forms of social and cultural criticism, governing and criticism go hand in hand.

Notes

This chapter is a shortened version of a paper originally published under the title "Intellectuals, Culture, Policy: The Technical, the Practical and the Critical," *Pavis Papers in Social and Cultural Research*, no. 2, Milton Keynes, The Open University.

References

Bennett, T. (1995). "The Multiplication of Culture's Utility." *Critical Inquiry* 21(4).

Bennett, T. (1997). "Regulated Restlessness: Museums, Liberal Government and the Historical Sciences." *Economy and Society* 26(2).

Candy, P. and J. Laurent (eds.) (1994). *Pioneering Culture: Mechanics' Institutes and Schools of Art in Australia*. Adelaide: Auslib Press.

Collins, R. and C. Murroni (1996). *New Media, New Policies: Media and Communications Strategies for the Future*. Cambridge: Polity Press.

Finney, Colin (1993). *Paradise Revealed: Natural History in Nineteenth-century Australia*. Melbourne: Museum of Victoria.

Foucault, M. (1978). "Governmentality." In G. Burchell, C. Gordon, and P. Miller (eds.) (1991) *The Foucault Effect: Studies in Governmentality*. Hemel Hempstead: Harvester Wheatsheaf.

Habermas, J. (1974). *Theory and Practice*. London: Heinemann.

Habermas, J. (1989). *The Structural Transformation of the Public Sphere – An Inquiry into a Category of Bourgeois Society*. Cambridge: Polity Press.

Hunter, Ian (1994). *Rethinking the School: Subjectivity, Bureaucracy, Criticism*. Sydney: Allen and Unwin.

Kohlstedt, S. G. (1983). "Australian Museums of Natural History: Public Practices and Scientific Initiatives in the 19th Century." *Historical Records of Australian Science*, vol. 5.

Latour, B. (1999). "Ein ding ist ein thing: A (Philosophical) Platform for a Left (European) Party." *Soundings* 12.

McGuigan, J. (1996). *Culture and the Public Sphere*. London: Routledge.

Prosler, Martin (1996). "Museums and Globalisation." In S. MacDonald and G. Fyfe (eds.), *Theorizing Museums*. Oxford: Blackwell Publishers/The Sociological Review.

Said, E. W. (1994). *Representations of the Intellectual*. London: Vintage.

Stoler, A. L. (1995). *Race and the Education of Desire: Foucault's History of Sexuality and the Colonial Order of Things*. Durham and London: Duke University Press.

Further Reading

This bibliography provides guidance in relation to two further areas of reading: the critical literature on, in response to, and in extension of, Habermas's concept of the public sphere; and the positive revaluation of bureaucratic and other forms of technical expertise associated with post-Foucauldian scholarship.

On the first of these, see Calhoun (1992) for an excellent collection of essays on Habermas from a series of European and Anglo-American perspectives, including an essay in which Habermas revises the concept of the public sphere in the light of the various criticisms it has spawned. For feminist engagements with the concept, see Landes (1988), Riley (1988), and Ryan (1990). On the question of its relations to indigenous cultures, see Michaels (1994). For a selection of the issues raised by attempts to relate the concept to the sociocultural structures of a variety of Asian countries, see Chun (1996), Hanada (1995), and Milner (1995).

For post-Foucauldian perspectives on bureaucracy and other technical forms of expertise, see Minson (1993), Rose and Miller (1992), and, for a longer historical perspective, Saunders (1997). See also Latour (1987) for a defense of bureaucracy from the scorn of scientific forms of intellectual elitism.

Calhoun, C. (ed.) (1992). *Habermas and the Public Sphere*. Cambridge, Mass.: MIT Press.

Chun, A. (1996). "Discourses of Identity in the Changing Spaces of Public Culture in Taiwan, Hong Kong and Singapore." *Theory, Culture and Society* 14(1).

Hanada, T. (1995). "Can There Be a Public Sphere in Japan?" *ISICS Research Papers*, no. 50.

Landes, Joan B. (1988). *Women and the Public Sphere in the Age of the French Revolution*. Ithaca and London: Cornell University Press.

Latour, B. (1987). *Science in Action*. Cambridge, Mass.: Harvard University Press.

Michaels, E. (1994). *Bad Aboriginal Art: Tradition, Media and Technological Horizon*. Sydney: Allen and Unwin.

Milner, A. (1995). *The Invention of Politics in Colonial Malaya: Contesting Nationalism and the Expansion of the Public Sphere*. Cambridge: Cambridge University Press

Minson, Jeffrey (1993). *Questions of Conduct: Sexual Harassment, Citizenship, Government*. London: Macmillan.

Riley, D. (1988). *Am I That Name? Feminism and the Category of "Women" in History*. London: Macmillan.

Rose, N. and P. Miller (1992). "Political Power Beyond the State: Problematics of Government." *British Journal of Sociology* 43(2).

Ryan, M. P. (1990). *Women in Public: Between Banners and Ballots, 1825–1880*. Baltimore and London: The Johns Hopkins University Press.

Saunders, D. (1997). *Anti-lawyers: Religion and the Critics of Law and State*. London and New York: Routledge.

Chapter 22

Listening to the State: Culture, Power, and Cultural Policy in Colombia

Ana María Ochoa Gautier

The cultural studies project of textual deconstruction is partially based on a high valuation of the political importance of uncovering the power agendas in discursive formations.[1] Struggles against conditions of inequity as varied as feminism in different parts of the world or the transformation of oppressive class conditions in Latin America have often been based on the idea that a new politics of naming will bring about a transformation in the politics of identity and consequently in the practices that determine power structures. But under certain historical conditions and in specific institutional contexts the disjuncture between a politics of naming, new practices of representation and identity, and the emergence of new conditions of equity that this new naming is supposed to bring about, becomes painfully evident.

Latin American intellectuals in cultural studies (and other fields as well)[2] often have a role as mediators between critical discourse and the practice of the transformation of political structures through participation in NGOs, governmental committees or programs, involvement in development of public policy, or even assuming public office. This fluidity between a discourse on knowledge and public institutions is not new in Latin America, as founding figures of the nations have often played the role of leading figures in the history of Latin American thought (Ramos 1989; Von der Walde 1997). What is new is trying to bring together that dimension of critical discourse which opens the way for assuming "different or even divergent interpretations, escaping the need for substantive and closed definitions" (Telles 1994: 50) within an institutional framework or at an historical moment which demands the making of decisions that have historically been based on substantive definitions. It is one thing to deconstruct a text at the level of the symbolic; but applying these deconstructions to a daily praxis makes visible, as a quotidian work ethic, the complex locus of cultural policy as a matter of both institutional (administrative, legal, financial) and cultural (expressive, fluid, mobile) dimensions in the midst of societies characterized by a "contradictory and unfinished modernity" (García Canclini 1989). This confronts us with the difference between engaging with cultural politics solely at the level of the symbolic, that is as "disembodied struggles over meanings and representations" (Alvarez, Dagnino, Escobar 1998: 5) – which we often do as academics – versus engaging at the level where discourses and practices meet at a moment of profound redefinition of the public sphere in Latin America. It is the implication of this difference for the construction of critical thought regarding cultural policy in Latin America, that I want to explore in this chapter.

In 1997 I returned to Colombia from finishing my doctoral degree in the US and began working as an ethnomusicologist of the Music Archives of the Government's office of culture, Colcultura. By 1998, all of the arts archives – Music, Theater, Dance, and Visual Arts – were united under one large conglomerate as Colcultura became the Ministry of Culture. I was offered and accepted the job as the head of these archives but quit the job in January 1999 largely due to frustration with inconsistent state administrative and bureaucratic practices. At that moment the Colombian Institute of Anthropology (then part of the Ministry of Culture), with the financial support of the Office of Regional Affairs of the Ministry of Culture and an Ibero-American NGO, the Convenio Andrés Bello, offered me the job of researching the effects of the major program of multi-culturalism designed and promoted by the Ministry, a job I eventually accepted, not without hesitation. The transformation from the role of administrator to that of researcher entailed a transition in my mode of existence within the power structure of the Ministry of Culture that demanded a new form of listening to the complaints that characterize people's involvement with bureaucratic structures. And this transition made evident the difficulties of mediating between academic discourse and cultural policy even in an institution (and at a historical moment) which has invited the active participation of critical intellectuals in policy-making. The (dis)juncture between critical studies and cultural policy in Colombia is quite revealing about both the institutional and historical determinants of "cultural studies" in Latin America and about the problems of building bridges between critical perspectives and democratization processes through cultural policy. The question that emerged as research progressed was what is the role of the researcher in public institutions that are increasingly defining "culture" through policy programs – from national ministries to international forums such as UNESCO? The question demands not solely the deconstruction of the uses of culture in public arenas but also a decentering of labor relations and of our role as academics in an increasingly interinstitutional sphere of work. I will begin by contextualizing historically the emergence of culture (especially cultural diversity) as a central theme of public discourse in the past decade in Colombia.

Cultural Diversity as a National Agenda

During approximately the past 15 years in Colombia, "culture" has increasingly become an arena of political concern, inviting, on the one hand, the critical reflection of scholars and, on the other, the design and implementation of new agendas of cultural policy from different governmental sectors, creating a complex field of interaction between both.[3] This interaction became more explicit through the debates and forums that led to the process of writing the Constitution of 1991. This was done by an exceptionally participatory National Constitutional Assembly that included persons from different political parties, ex-guerrilla members recently reinserted into civilian society, leaders from the indigenous movement, Christian groups, scholars from different fields of the social sciences, among others. The new Constitution marked a radical departure in judicial, administrative, territorial, and cultural terms from the 1886 Constitution that, with numerous reforms, was in effect until 1991. The democratization process in Colombia during the past decade has involved the difficult and often contradictory implementation of legislative and administrative reforms that seek to enact the new mode of definition of the state named by the 1991 Constitution. Also, in 1997, under the auspices of the Samper government, the governmental office of cultural affairs, Colcultura, was replaced by the Ministry of Culture.

Both the rewriting of the Constitution and the creation of the Ministry of Culture generated, in their respective moments, academic events organized either by the state or jointly with universities and NGOs, as well as prolonged and heated controversies in the press concerning the relationship between culture, power, and the state.[4] Much of the governmental cultural policy developed during the 1990s is derived from these discussions as well as from the engagement of professionals (scholars and artists) that had historically been involved with other types of participatory processes (such as social movements or alternative artistic explorations) in the design and implementation of new programs of cultural policy.

The processes of public debate and writing that led to the 1991 Constitution and the General Law of Culture of 1997, whereby the Ministry of Culture was created, named a new sphere of cultural politics that has been crucial in determining state cultural policy in effect in Colombia today. The principal transformations named by these documents are:

1. Article 7 of the Constitution officially declares Colombia as a "pluriethnic and multicultural nation," radically transforming the relationship between nation and culture prevailing in the 1886 Constitution, namely that of "a mestizo nation in the process of whitening, united under one God and one race" (Wills 1999). As a consequence, the Ministry of Culture adopted in 1997, in Title I, Article 1 of the General Law of Culture, a (still) much-debated definition of culture as "the distinctive, spiritual, material, intellectual and emotional features that characterize human groups and that comprehends, beyond arts and letters, modes of life, human rights, systems of value, traditions and beliefs." The political gesture that this definition invokes is that of relativization – the usage of a definition of culture that allows ample possibilities of inclusion, leads away

from a notion of culture as a specific domain of expressions (historically in Colombia, in the form of high culture or patrimony as certain accepted forms of folklore), and thus opens the way for a transformation in the way the link between expressive culture and the construction of society is established through cultural policy by the state. This is a radical departure not only from the 1886 Constitution but from Colombia's historical relation to valid cultural expressions, which was mainly that of exclusion due to grammarian presidents that at the turn of the century obsessively sought to determine correct forms of speaking and writing (Deas 1993). Thus, even though this notion of culture is a definition much critiqued by scholars and professionals engaged in cultural policy-making, we still have to recognize the change of cultural politics it makes possible.

2. Multiculturalism is seen as the cultural dimension of a process of decentralization of the state that is principally enacted through administrative, fiscal, and territorial reforms. As stated by historian Orlando Fals Borda, who is largely responsible for the territorial and cultural dimensions of the new constitution, administrative decentralization and territorial reorganization are basic processes for the recognition of the cultures and cultural expressions of regions previously excluded by a highly centralized state structure (Fals Borda 1996). The deployment of specific projects of cultural diversity from the sphere of the state during the past decade has partially been the responsibility of the Ministry of Culture. This has involved not only the implementation of programs that seek to recognize regional Colombian culture in different ways (through community radio programs and networks, educational projects based on regional artforms, construction of stages that make local cultures visible to the nation, local awards for research and creativity, etc.), but also an administrative restructuring of specific aspects (such as decentralization of some financial resources) of the Ministry.

3. The discussions leading to constitutional and legislative reforms, in tandem with mobilizations enacted by social movements and the growth of critical discourse on cultural politics in Colombia, have generated a public forum in which the idea of culture as an essential domain for the construction of a civil society and, ultimately, of a peace process, is clearly recognized. In other words, the interaction of academic critical discourse, legislative reforms, and the effects of the growth of social movements in Colombian society, has entailed a redefinition of the domain of political culture; that is, "of the particular social construction . . . of what counts as political" (Alvarez, Dagnino, Escobar 1998: 8). Thus, not only the Ministry of Culture but the municipality of Bogotá as well, have sought to bring about the restructuring of civil society through cultural policy in a country highly fragmented by political violence and with one of the highest crime rates in the world (Franco 1999).[5] What is in evidence, at least in the design of many of the programs, is an increasing awareness in the public sector of a notion of culture as a communicative process that permits the transformation of social relations through a new politics of identity and recognition. This has

implied a transformation in a general conception of cultural policy as an instrument solely designed for *bringing services and giving access* (culture, libraries, theaters, etc.) in the regions of Colombia to cultural policy as an instrument that can also be used primarily for transforming social relations through *recognition and support* of local cultures and values.

In Latin America the redefinition of the relationship between culture and politics as a restructuring of both meanings and specific practices has often been analyzed by theorists dealing with social movements. Increasingly these theorists have called attention to the way the discourses, practices, and demands of these movements "circulate in weblike, capillary fashion . . . in larger institutional and cultural arenas" (Alvarez, Dagnino, Escobar 1998: 16). What is particularly significant about the Colombian case in relation to cultural policy has been the ways in which a new politics of culture is mobilized from within the state in articulation with discourses and practices of scholars, newspaper columnists, and professionals with different institutional or group affiliations, who are working on designing new agendas for policy-making. This points to the fact that public space is not an autonomous sphere but rather a "zone open to unanticipated forms of participation"; or at the very least to modes of articulation between different spheres (Yúdice 1994).

However, this aperture in terms of culture discourse in the Colombian state has occurred simultaneously with neoliberalization policies that have radically increased levels of poverty and unemployment and minimized the social responsibilities of the state. This at a time of drastic escalation of the armed conflict from all armed actors involved in the war, to the point that the very legitimacy of the state has been questioned. We thus have an exacerbation of extremes – implementation of democratization processes through cultural policy or other administrative and legal procedures, coupled with neoliberalization and escalation of armed conflict – that generates a complex public space "where projects and values [and forces in the case of Colombia] in dispute are set one against the other" (Telles 1994: 43). Thus the apparent (or real) conquests of social actors in redefining public spaces through a politics of recognition and identity exists in conflictive ways with economic and military practices whose ethical and political relation to society is moving in exactly the opposite direction. Moreover, all of this takes place within an administrative structure that, despite recent reforms, is still partially defined by the personalist and clientelist dimensions that have historically determined "an oligarchic conception of politics" in Latin America (Alvarez, Dagnino, Escobar 1998: 9). What we have then is an unequal and disjunctive process of democratization that is particularly revealing of the problematic ways in which a politics of culture is differentially and fragmentarily deployed in the public space through the enactment of cultural policy. A process whose more profound political implications become evident in the quotidian experiences of designing and implementing cultural policy in such a context.

Critical Discourse in the Public Sphere

When I was offered the job of researching the major multicultural program in the Ministry, I felt myself literally standing at a crossroads. *CREA: An Expedition through Colombian Culture*, was a program implemented by the government between 1992 and 1998, which sought to "rescue, value, promote, and divulge our [Colombian] cultural manifestations throughout the national territory."[6] In practice, the program consisted primarily, although not exclusively, of a series of "cultural encounters," that is, displays of local and regional Colombian culture that were successively staged at the municipal, departmental, regional, and finally "national" (which significantly stands for Bogotá, the capital) levels. The movement from the local to the national terrain involved a process of selection of cultural expressions that covered a wide variety of creative milieux – from culinary delicacies to video production – that were to represent the different regions of Colombia in the capital and, in the process, "invert the cultural flow from the center to the periphery that had historically characterized Colombia," create a "culture of dialogue and tolerance" in a country torn apart by armed conflict, and construct the scenario for the "multicultural and pluriethnic" nation defined by the recently drafted Constitution of 1991 (Jaramillo ca. 1992). By 1998, two complete cycles of CREA had taken place. The first began in 1992 and culminated in 1995 with a "national encounter" that brought 1,687 artists from the regions to Bogotá. Prior to this, there had been 102 intermunicipal encounters, 26 departmental, and 6 regional ones. The second cycle of CREA which ended in 1998, took place on August 4, 5, and 6, on the days prior to the possession of the recently elected government of Andrés Pastrana, thus marking CREA as a policy clearly associated to the Samper government which had actively promoted the creation of the Ministry of Culture as one of its vanguard policies in a government marked by scandal and corruption related to narcotraffic. The second cycle of CREA consisted of 150 intermunicipal, 26 departmental, and 4 regional encounters which culminated in Bogotá with the presence of 2,235 artists from different regions of Colombia.

The magnitude of CREA was unique in the history of Colombian cultural policy. The research involved major topics I had been interested in – the relationship between culture, power, and the state; the effects of cultural display; multiculturalism as democratization; the effects of displacement of local cultures; the relationship between culture and the peace process. What made me hesitate? Looking back a year and a half later, I realize the movement from Director of Artistic Archives of the Ministry of Culture to researcher of CREA involved a redefinition of my role within the power structure and implied a change in quotidian labor relations. That is, I went from being a competitor for attention from the high administrative offices in order to get financial resources and political space for mobilizing policy programs, to being a person who undertakes the exact same institutional field ethnographically and is being asked to come up with a proposal for addressing the problems of a polemical program. One of the major reasons why the Ministry undertook the CREA research was because they did not know what to do with it. Some people thought the program was the best in the Ministry – it involved new participatory and democratic dimensions; others, that it was the worst – a space for the spectacularization and abuse of politics. I was being asked to be a mediator in this conflict through my research. This was not the classical move from "insider" to "outsider" so often cited in anthropological literature. This was a redefinition of my labor relations *within* the same institution. As I realize today, one of the major changes that took place was a redefinition of the mode of listening to the state, or to the daily problems of working in the public sphere.

I had to learn to listen to the complaints of my colleagues (and to my own dissatisfaction in working with the state) under a new light. This "new mode of listening" did not suddenly appear. It emerged throughout the year as I progressively established new forms of communicative relations determined largely by the fact that I was no longer a competitor in the power scheme of the Ministry. Two elements were crucial for this to take place during the research. One, I had a knowledge of the quotidian practice of public policy-making. I was aware of the coexistence of illogical administrative practices and personal favoritisms as well as sincere and knowledgeable efforts, on the part of many program directors, in designing and implementing policies that aimed at the construction of new democratic spaces from within their work positions. But I had to go beyond the frustrating tautological logic that often permeates bureaucracy and its accompanying scheme of complaints (Herzfeld 1992) and listen to my colleagues and my own frustration with the state in a new way. It was not just a matter of denouncing unjust administrative practices. It was a matter of locating the contradictory relations between a "culture of politics and a politics of culture" in the quotidian interaction of practices and discourses within the specific work sphere of the Ministry. Second, my new role as a researcher made me a relative outsider, but "insiders" knew who I was and related to me as a person located within the Ministry. It was clear that even though I had the responsibility of the research, we were all in the business of trying to handle the contradictions of thinking and implementing cultural policy programs.

The research agenda was partially designed with what I already knew. The Ministry is structured as a series of areas (*Direcciones*) each of which has major divisions which carry out a variety of programs. This structure was largely inherited from Colcultura. Although new areas were created (cinematography, for example) and others changed with the creation of the Ministry, hierarchies of work remained largely the same. The most important areas through which policy programs are deployed include Arts, Communications, Youth and Infancy, Regional Development, Patrimony, Awards and Scholarships.[7] As is obvious by this list, the criteria for creating areas vary from one to the other: in one case it is population (Infancy and Youth), in another territory (Regional Office), in another expressive media (the arts), in yet another the nature of the policy (awards). This responds largely to the fact that most of the areas grew slowly out of Colcultura and became more solid as the programs within the divisions of each area developed. Due to this history of relative independent development, most areas are handled with little or no connection with others. Thus, the Ministry of Culture (initially Colcultura) has slowly been structured through the implementation of programs that became long-term projects that eventually and in articulation with other reform processes in the state (notably those of the Constitution and the creation of the Ministry) have become cultural policy agendas. The interaction between guiding abstract words of the new decade (decentralization, participation, multiculturalism, democratization) and the practice of cultural policy is determined largely by this institutional structure and history.

To be sure, the directors of specific divisions design their own policy programs according to the general state guidelines mentioned above. But how these abstract words get translated into actual practice is very much up to the directors, not even of each area, but of each division. This means that the ultimate definition of what cultural policy is, gets done at the level of division directors with loose connections to either top administrative guidelines or to other divisions and areas in terms of conceptualizing the relationship between culture and the ideas that guide the democratization process. To take an example. The Arts Area in which I worked as Director of Artistic Archives includes the arts archives, music, visual arts, theater, and dance divisions as well as the National School for Dramatic Arts. The music division has favored the implementation of programs dealing with education in and organization of (creation of networks of interaction) different types of music throughout the country: symphonic music and choirs, local wind bands, traditional musics. They thus cover both popular and elite expressions and their main mode of action is educational and organizational. The visual arts division, however, works almost exclusively with expressions associated with Western visual arts (no crafts), and its main activity is organizing the National and Regional State Exhibitions of contemporary artists. This difference responds both to the historical factors mentioned above and to the philosophical and political orientation of division directors who choose one mode of action or one sphere of culture over another. This means that the Ministry of Culture is not a monolithic institution but one with great variables in terms of conceptualization of cultural policy and the practices derived from it.

While this type of structure generates a certain flexibility in the implementation of programs (something which can be positive if used creatively and critically), it also generates problems. On the one hand, the fact that the dialogue across areas is highly fragmentary (if not non-existent) leads to cross purposes and difficult encounters when disparities regarding the design and deployment of programs becomes evident. This often happens when difficulties emerge in the coexistence of different programs in the same region of the country. At the moment of implementing programs in the regions (not inside the Ministry), directors of different divisions (or their assistants) often meet for the first time, and it is there that the differing views of how to work in the country get exposed.

This can be very conflictive when the programs involve the same population or area of influence. Moreover, the conflict is generated not only by the lack of internal dialogue and discussion about cultural policy but also because much of cultural policy design and implementation is based on tacit assumptions about the relationship between the transformation of society and culture. For example, for some division directors, educational and organizational agendas are crucial in transforming civil society, an idea very much inherited from appropriations of a Freirean discourse. For others, popular culture speaks for itself and is by its very nature a sphere of construction of civil society. For this group, the exhibition of local culture then naturally leads to creating social dialogue. The question that is never asked is how social transformation actually happens through cultural policy enactment. The frequent and informally stated idea within the Ministry, that "the Ministry of Culture does not have a clear cultural policy," speaks not so much of differences in modes of action or population objectives in the different programs, but of the unexplored assumptions underlying these agendas. Not only do we have an institutional history of fragmentary development. We also have the gradual consolidation of cultural policy programs that in the contradictions that have been generated have played a role in creating a set of questions regarding cultural policy. That is, cultural policy emerges as a critical field not only out of academic interest in the topic but also out of the contradictions that begin to be more visible as culture becomes increasingly accepted as a political arena.

Second, the decisions that determine the financial distribution of resources handed from the Ministry of Finance are taken in the upper echelons of the Ministry, and this is partially mediated through personalist and favoritist relations, thus creating an unclear and in some areas unjust distribution of finances without explanations for program directors, an issue that obviously affects internal relations. For example, CREA was designed initially in 1991–2 as one of the major programs of the Office of the First Lady, Ana Milena de Gaviria, during the Gaviria government (1992–8). By the time CREA arrived from the First Lady's office to become Colcultura in 1992 (after heated polemics) it practically became a parallel structure within the Arts Area, and later in the Regional Area to which it was moved in 1996 due to the magnitude of the program. CREA began, comparatively speaking, with a larger budget than other areas in the Ministry, one that received direct approval and/or had direct communication channels to other financial resources, due to the support of the First Lady's office. Also, the design of CREA involved a long process of consultation. But this process did not include people within Colcultura who were already implementing programs of a similar nature in the regions on a much smaller scale – notably the Jornadas de Cultura Popular led by anthropologist Gloria Triana in the previous administration.[8] A privileged place in the public sphere thus gets confounded with the unexplained lack of continuity of previous programs. This mode of insertion of CREA into Colcultura (later the Ministry) largely determined labor relations between people in CREA and people in other areas of the Ministry for a long time. By the time I was asked to do the research in 1998, the discontent inside the Ministry of Culture was due not only to very contradictory effects of the program in the region (by then highly visible both in positive and negative terms) but also to the type of labor relations established by the mode of existence of CREA within the Ministry. This is compounded by the fact that effects of programs are not evaluated democratically by external figures.[9]

As can be imagined, the tensions that are generated by differences in conceptualizing cultural policy, by the lack of communication between areas, coupled with the presence of a personalist structure in determining, at least partially, the distribution of resources, creates an unstable and often difficult and unjust work environment which program directors have to mediate constantly. The implementation of cultural policy thus involves not only establishing an agenda for cultural transformation but also the mediation of a politics of culture through institutional structures and quotidian work practices. CREA was the major program promoted as a decentralization and participatory strategy in an administration largely concerned with these issues. And undoubtedly, it had transcendent consequences in this respect, an aspect I am not dealing with in this chapter. But what I wish to point out is that the decentering of notions of culture that has led to the design of new programs and ways of implementing cultural policy is not accompanied by a decentering of quotidian work practices and of tacit political structures, and this ultimately affects the possibilites of constructing the democratization processes that the notions of decentralization, participation, and multiculturalism invoke. It is in the contradictory interaction between institutional structure and the practices that determine a quotidian work sphere, and the new modes of policy-making based on the idea that culture can transform society, that some of the disjunctures between critical theory and public policy-making are located. The problem of democratization through the implementation of new cultural policy agendas then not only involves constructing new scenarios for cultural mobilization. It also implies addressing the contradictions inherent in state structures at the level of quotidian work practices and how these influence the possibility of implementing much-desired reforms.

Bridging the Gap between Critical Theory and Quotidian State Practices

During the past two years, Maria Adelaida Jaramillo, the director of the National System of Artistic Education, an office that was created with the Ministry of Culture, has brought together the different division directors in order to try to solve the problem of extreme fragmentation and create a space of dialogue at least around the educational dimensions that the different programs have. This has been an important space where many problems began to be aired and shared. But the task has not been easy. On the one hand, the purpose of the meetings was partially to construct a shared policy for the Education Program based on bringing together the notions of education that each had. For many this involved an extra work agenda which was difficult to incorporate in the face of already excessive work schedules which were largely determined by the immediacy of production of documents demanded in public spheres. Also, since the meetings – as most public policy meetings – had specific purposes in the production of documents that showed results, there was no time to clearly deconstruct the different (and often unconscious) assumptions about public policy that often got in the way of resolving differences between people. Moreover, discussions were often mediated by the coexistence of different power hierarchies, many of which could not be explicitly addressed, or if addressed, could not be transformed.

These different problems that emerged in the process of attempting to redress the problem of fragmentation of the Ministry, point to a characteristic of communicative practices within public institutions. "There is no time to think" is a complaint commonly heard, not only in the Ministry but also beyond. Not only is there no time. The quotidian work agenda structures the communicative sphere in such a way that for program directors, critical thinking is practically impossible to do simultaneously with designing and implementing policy. In most meetings people have to mediate some sphere of recognition of their program and this makes it very difficult to assume critical thought as an integral dimension of the practice of public policy. Martín Barbero (1995) has stated that cultural policy assumes (not always explicitly) a communicative theory at its basis. But this not only pertains to the way the transformation of society is assumed to take place through a politics of culture; it also implies the way cultural policy is determined by communicative practices within the workday politics and hierarchical structures of the institutions that implement policy.

Even with these structural difficulties, getting together to talk was a major first step that two years later is bearing fruits in the way certain programs have been able to come up with shared objectives. Largely based on the obvious need to construct spaces of dialogue between Division and program directors that the experience with the Education Office had made visible, as well as in accordance with my research needs, I created – as a research methodology – a biweekly seminar where division directors could meet to discuss issues related directly to the problem of implementing cultural policy programs in different regions of Colombia. As a researcher it was important for me to have a comparative perspective based on the experiences of different policy programs. The seminar on Region, Culture, and Cultural Policy was largely designed to provide a space to talk about these problems. It revolved around issues that I knew were important for the directors largely due to my previous work within the Ministry – notions of region, implications of the transformation of local culture, effects of globalization in the regions, modes of action in cultural policy, etc. Contrary to an academic course, the idea was to keep reading to a minimum due to the lack of time that state functionaries have. Also, each person was supposed to analyze and question a problematic dimension of their own program. I had been assigned the task of shedding new light on CREA through critical theory. Why not let each director bring critical theory into her/his own program?

Initially, I designed this as a strategy for listening to the problems people were having in the regions. What was surprising for me (and the other people in the seminar as well) was that the seminar created a radically different space for listening than is generally present in the public sphere. On the one hand, I was not competing for a comparative position or for financial resources with them, which made me a comfortable, semi-outside figure; one who nevertheless could understand what was going on because of my previous administrative experience. On the other hand, program directors were personally assuming the responsibility of a critical discussion of their own programs. Not only did they bring a tremendous amount of experience and knowledge of the specific problems they had to confront but had no space to share without the pressures of public office: in directly assuming their own critique they were propitiating a communicative critical space that transformed the ambiguous and difficult nature of cross-criticism in bureaucratic spaces; especially in one institutionally structured by lack of communication between areas and by favoritist practices. This institutional structure obfuscates critical thinking. What is often disguised as the criticism of other people's programs is actually a tremendous frustration with unjust and/or ambiguous institutional practices. It soon became obvious that program directors were sharing similar problems. The effects of favoritist structures on daily relations and critical analysis were unmasked, and thus people began to distinguish between questioning the cultural dimension of a program and its internal mode of insertion within the institution. This of course did not transform the favoritist structure within the Ministry; this persists until today and takes new forms under each administration. But this was one small step in learning to listen to each other and begin sharing agendas of which we were not conscious before. Undoubtedly a small step in translating confusing practices into separate and more understandable dimensions.

Several issues about the institutional nature of Latin American "cultural studies," cultural policy, and democratization processes come up here. In the first place, it has often been argued that "much of cultural studies, particularly in the United States, continues to be heavily oriented towards the textual" (Alvarez, Dagnino, Escobar 1998: 5), while "cultural analysis in Latin America is more directly part of the study of civil and political society than in the United States" (Yúdice, this volume). This has most often been related to the intervention of scholars in social movements. As such, a theoretical division predominates between social movements, which are seen as democratizing civil society, while the democratic reform of the state is analyzed as consisting generally of the "stability of formal representative political institutions and practices" (Alvarez, Dagnino, Escobar 1998: 13). But what the Colombian case makes evident is that institutions are not monolithic structures but are rather permeated by the uneven flows that result from the effects of the interaction between the different types of groupings, associations, persons that characterize civil society, the social, and cultural transformations brought about through their influence (such as the writing of the 1991 Constitution) with historically inherited modes of authoritarian politics. The implementation of new agendas of cultural policy from within the state involves a difficult negotiation between the opening of new democratic spaces in institutional politics and the persistence of authoritarian ones. Democratizing institutions (or formal state policy) is not solely a legislative agenda. It implies reforming the nature of the day-to-day work space. And as such, tactics that are apparently small (such as creating a critical space for discussing problems in a public sphere which does not have such a possibility) can be a step in creating more democratic working ethics within institutions and eventually may aid in destructuring undemocratic practices within them.

What we see, in the midst of this contradictory working sphere is "an emerging form of institutionality that opens up spaces of representation, interlocution and negotiation" (Telles 1994: 49) that were not formerly there. Undoubtedly, many programs in the Ministry emerged through the new sphere of cultural policy validated by the Constitution and the General Law of Culture. But one cannot be blind to the coexistence within the Ministry of authoritarian political and democratizing cultural practices. This means that not only the nature of politics or culture have been decentered in the past decades. We also need to address the way work itself has been decentered "due to the strong presence of conflict in the new forms that work is adopting" (Hopenhayn 2000). What one finds in the contradictory effects of many cultural policy programs in the Ministry is a difficult and unequal process of democratization that involves the inclusion of a highly conflictive agenda as a daily work ethic.

Here lies one of the crucial aspects of the interaction between critical theory and public policy. When deconstruction solely addresses the level of meanings, critical theory assumes a radically different form than when it is inserted in practical political spaces. Paul Bromberg, a philosopher-mathematician turned mayor of Bogotá, stated it by saying that when he assumed public office he realized that every time he took a decision, he created a problem. That is, the practice of critical theory is immersed in the contradictory dimensions that characterize public space. His statement points to a philosophical problem that underlies much of the relationship between critical theory and public policy: how does one translate the abstract principles which guide not only critical thinking but the ideological bases of public policy or democratization processes (decentralization, multiculturalism, etc.) into quotidian practices? As stated by anthropologist Michael Jackson, "Fieldwork experience has taught me that notions of shared humanity, human equality and human rights always come up against the micropolitical exigencies of ethnic, familial, and personal identity, and the dialectic between particular and universal frames of reference often dissolves into a troubled dialogue between the privileged microcosm of anthropologists and the peoples of the Third world whose voices, struggles and claims define with far more urgency the conditions that define our global future" (Jackson 1998: 5). One can easily extend this to the field of cultural studies and cultural policy. The interaction between critical theory and policy-making is crucial but not solely at the level of deconstructing meanings but of getting involved in the contradictory dimensions of daily practice. This does not necessarily mean that researchers have to hold public office. It rather leads to the need for trying to bridge the gap between the theory and practice of cultural policy from both sides: people who implement cultural policy should have the opportunity for open spaces for discussion of their problems within the structure of their working agendas, and scholars need to interact more closely in the day-to-day workings of transformation of the public sphere and not only in the construction of abstract, guiding principles in policy-making, crucial as they are. This would not only "pluralize the frontiers of academic authority" (Richard 1999) but also perhaps address some of the gaps in theorizing cultural policy, especially those related to establishing a link between the daily practice of bureaucracy and cultural deconstruction.

The democratizing practices made possible by the new space for cultural politics opened in formal institutions in the decade of the nineties in Colombia have been crucial in generating new participatory spaces that are having concrete effects in the regions despite the problems and contradictions involved, a topic I do not deal with in this chapter. However, these democratic spaces are fragile, fragmentary, and uncertain. In Colombia, as persons working within the spheres of cultural policy, we often feel trapped between the sense of hope, creativity, and democratization that some of the cultural policy programs seem to generate, and the very real and drastic limitations imposed by the extreme fragmentation of a society increasingly trapped by neoliberal policies and armed conflict. Maybe that is why in Colombia today many of the people involved in the daily routine of cultural policy-making constantly move between the different sides of that precarious balance between hope and disenchantment.

Notes

1 This chapter was written while I was a Rockefeller fellow at the Privatization of Culture Project in the American Studies Program, New York University. I would like to thank the Rockefeller Foundation, George Yúdice, and Toby Miller for their support. Evelina Dagnino provided valuable bibliography. Financial support for research leading to this chapter was provided by the Ministry of Culture of Colombia, The Instituto Colombiano de Antropología and the Convenio Andrés Bello. This chapter is dedicated to the participants in the seminar "Region and Culture" of the Ministry of Culture of Colombia.

2 The notion of cultural studies as a field in Latin America is constructed quite differently than in the US and is currently being questioned. See Néstor García Canclini, *La Globalización Imaginada*, Barcelona, México: Paidós, 1999; Daniel Mato, *Investigaciones sobre Cultura y Política en América Latina y Dilemas de su Institucionalización*. Paper presented at the Seminario de Estudios Culturales; George Yúdice, this volume.

3   From other sectors such as NGOs as well. However, in this chapter I will only be dealing with the interaction between government and culture.
4   The debates concerning the creation of the Ministry of Culture are gathered in: *Crear es Vivir, Gran Foro Cultural*, Barranquilla, abril 29 de 1994, Bogotá: Presidencia de la República, 1994. *Debate Cultural*, Coordinación Juan Gustavo Cobo Borda, Bogotá: Presidencia de la República, 1995. *El Trabajo Cultural en Colombia*, Juan Gustavo Cobo Borda, coordinador, Bogotá: Presidencia de la República, 1996. *Ministerio de Cultura, Ministerio de la Paz*, coordinador: Juan Gustavo Cobo Borda, Bogotá: Presidencia de la República, 1997.
5   For documentation and interpretation of statistics on violence in Colombia see Saúl Franco, *El Quinto: No Matar: Contextos Explicativos de la Violencia en Colombia*. Bogotá: TM Editores, IEPRI, Universidad Nacional, 1999.
6   *CREA: Una Expedición por la Cultura Colombiana*. Bogotá: Colcultura, 1997, p. 1.
7   The Ministry also includes the National Museum, the National Library, and, until recently, the Colombian Institute of Antrhopology, among other units. These are not viewed as areas but as independent administrative units.
8   For a discussion of the effects of the Jornadas as cultural policy see Gloria Triana, compiladora, *Aluna: Imagen y Memoria de las Jornadas Regionales de Cultura Popular*. Colcultura, Universidad Nacional de Colombia, Bogotá, 1990.
9   A series of evaluations of CREA were done by the people of CREA in interaction with outsiders. But these evaluations are characterized by a notable absence of theoretical critique. All the problems are reduced to operational problems, a characteristic which in itself is quite telling of modes of questioning within public spaces.

References

Alvarez, Sonia E., Evelina Dagnino, and Arturo Escobar (1998). "Introduction: The Cultural and the Political in Latin American Social Movements." In eds. Alvarez, Dagnino, and Escobar, *Cultures of Politics, Politics of Cultures: Re-visioning Latin American Social Movements*. Boulder: Westview Press.

Deas, Malcolm (1993). "Miguel Antonio Caro y amigos: gramática y poder en Colombia." In *Del Poder y la Gramática y otros ensayos sobre historia, política y literatura colombianas*. Bogotá: TM Editores.

Deas, Malcolm (1999). "La Paz: Entre los principios y la práctica." In ed. Francisco Leal Buitrago, *Los laberintos de la guerra: Utopías e intertudumbres sobre la paz*. Bogotá: TM Editores, Universidad de los Andes.

Fals Borda, Orlando (1996). *Región e Historia. Elementos sobre ordenamiento y equilibrio regional en Colombia*. Bogotá: TM Editores, IEPRI, Universidad Nacional.

Franco, Saúl (1999). *El Quinto: No Matar. Contextos Explicativos de la Violencia en Colombia*. Bogotá: TM Editores, IEPRI, Universidad Nacional.

García Canclini, Néstor (1989). *Culturas Híbridas: estrategias para entrar y salir de la modernidad*. México: Grijalbo.

Gómez Sierra, Francisco (compilador) (1998). *Constitución Política de Colombia*. Bogotá: Grupo Editorial Leyer.

Herzfeld, Michael (1992). *The Social Production of Indifference: Exploring the Symbolic Routes of Western Bureaucracy*. Chicago and London: University of Chicago Press.

Hopenhayn, Martin (enero 2000). "Nueva Secularización, Nueva Subjetividad: el descentramiento del trabajo y de la política." *Revista de Estudios Sociales* 5: 85–92.

Jackson, Michael (1998). *Minima Ethnographica: Intersubjectivity and the Anthropological Project*. Chicago: University of Chicago Press.

Jaramillo, Rosita (ca. 1992). Crea: Una Expedición por la Cultura Colombiana. Unpublished government document.

Martín Barbero, Jesús (1994). "Por unas políticas de communicación en la cultura. In Pre-textos." *Conversaciones sobre la comunicación y sus contextos*. Cali: Universidad del Valle.

Presidencia de la República de Colombia (1997). "Ley General de Cultura." In *Ministerio de Cultura, Ministerio de la Paz*. Bogotá: Presidencia de la República.

Ramos, Julio (1989). *Desencuentros de la modernidad en América Latina: literatura y política en el siglo XIX*. México: Fondo de Cultura Económica.

Richard, Nelly (1999). *Algunas notas en borrador sobre el impacto en América Latina de la creciente institucionalización de los cultural studies en países de habla inglesa*. Manuscrito.

Telles, Vera (1994). "Sociedade civil, Direitos e Espaços Públicos." In ed. Evelina Dagnino, *Os Anos 90: Política e Sociedade no brasil*. Sao Paulo: Brasiliense.

Von der Walde, Erna (Jan.–June 1997). "Limpia, fija y da esplendor: El letrado y la letra en Colombia a fines del siglo XIX." *Revista Iberoamericana* 63 (178–9): 71–83.

Wills, Maria Emma (Dec. 1999). "Continuidades y cambios en la Constitución del 91." Paper presented at the symposium *Museum, Memory and Nation*. National Museum of Bogotá. Unpublished typescript.

Yúdice, George (May 1994). "Estudios culturales y sociedad civil." *Revista de Crítica Cultural* 8: 44–53.

Chapter 23

Museum Highlights: A Gallery Talk

Andrea Fraser

Posters, placards, signs, symbols must be distributed, so that everyone may learn their significations. The publicity of punishment must not have the physical effect of terror; it must be an open book to be read. Le Peletier suggested that, once a month, the people should be allowed to visit convicts, "in their mournful cells: they will read, written in bold letters above the door, the name of the convict, his crime and his sentence..." Let us conceive of places of punishment as a Garden of the Laws that families would visit on Sundays... a living lesson in the museum of order.

Michel Foucault, Discipline and Punish, 1977

In every home in Philadelphia, youth will be taught to revere the things that are housed here.

Mayor Harry A. Mackey, at the opening of the new Pennsylvania Museum building,
March 27, 1928

The West Entrance Hall of the Philadelphia Museum of Art, February 5, or 11 or 12 or 18 or 19, 1989. Two or three dozen museum visitors are waiting in the southeast corner of the visitor reception area; some are waiting for a Contemporary Viewpoints Artist Lecture by Andrea Fraser; some are waiting for one of the Museum's many guided tours; some are just waiting for friends.

At three o'clock, Jane Castleton enters the West Entrance Hall and begins to address whoever appears to be listening. She is dressed in a silver and brown hounds tooth check double-breasted suit with a skirt just below the knee in length, an off-white silk button-down blouse, white stockings and black pumps. Her brown hair is gathered into a small bun held in place with a black bow:

Good afternoon, uh ... Everyone? Good afternoon. My name is Jane Castleton, and I'd like to welcome all of you to the Philadelphia Museum of Art. I'll be your guide today as we explore the museum, uh, it history, and its collection.

Our tour today is a collection tour – it's called Museum Highlights – and we'll be focusing on some of rooms in the Museum today, uh, the Museum's famed Period Rooms; Dining Rooms, Coat Rooms, etcetera, Rest Rooms, uh – can everyone hear me? If you can't hear me, don't feel shy, just tell me to speak up.

That's right. As I was saying, we'll also be talking about the visitor reception areas, and various service and support spaces, as well as this building, uh, this building, in which they are housed. And the Museum itself, the Museum itself, the "itself " itself being so compelling.[1]

Of course, we'll only be able to visit a small portion of the Museum on our tour today; its over 200 galleries contain hundreds of thousands of art objects spanning the globe and centuries. But, just to give you a general idea, uh, to help you orient yourself, this may be your first visit, your very first visit to the museum today – welcome again.

This is the West Entrance Hall. Uh. Opposite, of course, is the East Entrance, where we'll be going shortly. This is really the center of the Museum which – as you can see on these maps here – consists of a long central building with wings extending back at each end. It's four stories high including a basement.

This West Entrance Hall provides access to the ground floor of the South Wing which houses some of the Museum's public facilities that we'll be visiting uh, later on today . . .

Jane walks to the information desk in the center of the West Entrance Hall.

It also houses the Museum's brand new combination information desk, admissions desk – I hope that all of you have paid your admission fee – and, uh, membership desk. If you're a Museum Member, of course, you don't have to pay an admissions fee.

Membership, you know, "plays a vitally important role in the life of the Museum. Many Members indicate that they joined the Museum because they perceive it to be an institution of the highest quality, one of the world's great repositories of civilization. They see it as a place apart from the mundane demands of reality where an individual can fortify his or her linkage with the creative forces of the world, old and new."[2]

And, uh, if you're a Museum Member, you'll also be able to use the Members Only Lounge located on the balcony directly above my head and to the right as you see . . .

I myself did not pay an admission fee. Uh. I'm not a Museum Member, nor am I a Museum employee. I'm a visiting lecturer, a guest of the Division of Education. Uh, I am also, like the Board of Trustees and the Museum Guides, a volunteer.[3] It is thus my privilege, my privilege, as a guest, as a volunteer – and, shall I say, as an artist – to be able to express myself here today simply as a unique individual, an individual with unique qualities.

And I sincerely hope that I express my best qualities – as do we all, if I may say so. That's why we're here.[4]

Let's move on to the East Entrance shall we. Follow me if you will. To the elevator . . .

Jane leads the group to the elevators.

Uh, here we are. We're going to the second floor.

When the group reassembles on the second floor in the Great Stair Hall, Jane continues.

Is everyone here? All right, let's continue.

This is the Great Stair Hall, and, as you can see, we're on the second floor, just inside the East Entrance. As I said earlier, this is really the center of the Museum, and it provides access to the Museum's collections. To my right is the South Wing where the American art is generally kept to itself on the first floor, with the South Asian, Near and Far Eastern, and Medieval art on the second floor. To my left is the North Wing where you'll find European and Twentieth-century Art on the first floor and, on the second floor, more European art and the Period Rooms that we'll be talking about later today.

Uh. The Philadelphia Museum of Art is one of the oldest art museums in the United States. It was originally the Pennsylvania Museum and School of Industrial Art and it was established in 1877, 1877. Uh, that was in Memorial Hall, not this building.[5] This building opened to the public in 1928. It wasn't originally supposed to be the new home of the Pennsylvania Museum. It was first envisioned about 1907 as, uh, just as a, as "a great building [to be the] terminal feature of the [Benjamin Franklin] Parkway. The purpose of the building was secondary."[6]

But an art museum is not just a building, not just a collection of objects. An art museum – particularly a municipal art museum like our own – is a public institution with a mission, with a mandate. And the Philadelphia Museum of Art, uh, like all public institutions, was the product of a public policy.

What was that policy?

Well, writing about *The New Museum and Its Service to Philadelphia* in 1922, the Museum wrote that, uh, they wrote: "We have come to understand that to rob . . . people of the things of the spirit and to supply them with higher wages as a substitute is not good economics, good patriotism, or good policy."[7]

Like the other municipal institutions of the day – uh, the Zoological Garden and the Aquarium also of course in Fairmount Park; the new free library on the Parkway; the new municipal stadium; Camp Happy, "for undernourished children"; Brown's Farm, for "dependent and abandoned children"; the new House of Correction; the new Hospital for Mental Diseases at Byberry; the new General Hospital at Blockly; the Hospital for Contagious Diseases at Blockly; the Hospital for the Feeble-Minded at Blockly; the Home for the Indigent at Blockly;[8] the Commercial Museum next to Blockly, where homeless men were sometimes housed "dedicated to economic education" – now the Philadelphia Civic Center; the poorhouses of Germantown, Roxborough, and Lower Dublin . . .[9]

Called living tombs and social cemeteries, vile catchalls for all those in need, squalid warehouses for the failures and cast-offs of society,[10] no one would enter the poorhouse voluntarily. The receipt of public assistance was made into a ritual of public degradation so abhorrent that even the meanest work for the meanest wages was preferable.[11]

Jane walks to a window and leans against the grand piano standing in front it.[12]

The Municipal Art Gallery "that really serves its purpose gives an opportunity for enjoying the highest privileges of wealth and leisure to all those people who have cultivated tastes but not the means of gratifying them." And for those who have not yet cultivated taste, the Museum will provide "a training in taste."[13] But, above all, the Municipal Art Gallery should be "generous enough to fitly symbolize the function of art as the expression of all that is noblest in either the achievements or the aspirations of humanity... 'where there is no vision the people perish...' "[14]

Jane throws open the curtains covering the window and reveals a perfect vista of the Benjamin Franklin Parkway.

And just look at this view! Magnificent!

"If we do not possess art in a city, or beautiful spots in the city, we cannot expect to attract visitors to our home town."[15]

Jane gestures toward group.

"Because young people in particular are drawn to the area, Philadelphia attracts a huge labor pool of college-educated and trained technical people. And, due to its old manufacturing traditions, skilled laborers are also plentiful."[16]

Jane leaves the window and walks through and past the group. She gestures generally as she walks.

"The climate is healthy. Quality space is available and affordable...The systems for success are in place and working well. But even more important, Philadelphia is livable."

"You can choose from 5 professional sports teams, a world-class symphony, 100 Museums, the largest municipal park system in the country, and a restaurant renaissance the whole world is talking about."[17]

Plus: "8 million square feet of new commercial office space...High-tech, Healthcare, Medical Publishing and Printing, General Business Services, Financial Services, Heavy Manufacturing [and] Fashion..."[18]

I'd like to move on now to the galleries where we'll be talking about some of the Museum's period rooms, uh, as I mentioned earlier, the Museum's famed period rooms. If you'll just follow me please.

Jane leads the group through the European Art galleries to one of the Museum's period rooms.

And here we are.

This is the Grand Salon from the Chateau de Draveil. It's French, uh, eighteenth century...

Few eras in history were more preoccupied with "living in style" than eighteenth-century France...

Notice "the chaste style, characteristic of the later years of Louis XVI's reign...revealed here in the simplicity of the broad surfaces, in the slender proportions of their frames, and in the classical ornaments...carved with the most extreme crispness and brilliance...of great beauty and refinement... unusual interest...of the utmost delicacy..."[19]

Next, I'd like to talk about another period room. It's just across the gallery. If you'll follow me please...

Jane walks across the gallery to another period room, entered through a short, narrow corridor that also contains the door to the Men's Room.

Uh, this is a Paneled Room from England, dating from 1625. It contains seventeenth-century Dutch paintings, and was installed in the Museum in 1952, uh...

And in here, this is the Men's Room.

"What a difference there may be on opposite sides of a thin partition-wall! On this side of the wall is a family inclined to dirt and disorder because of its unperfect social education... Cleanliness of persons or rooms is wholly forgotten. The floors become littered with filth, for no one feels the desire or obligation to have it otherwise. The rights of property are disregarded or are only respected through fear and personal force.

"On the other side of the wall only a few inches away, the floor, neatly carpeted, is spotless. The center-table holds a... lamp, [and] a vase with fresh grasses... There are pictures on the walls, of... landscapes [and] the family...

"One may find a bureau turned into a shrine.

"It stands to reason that slovenly and destructive occupants are not accorded the same attention that is given to... those who are clean and careful and prompt in their payments.[20]

Jane leaves the Paneled Room.

"The public, who buy clothes and table china and wall paper and inexpensive jewelry, must be forced to raise their standards of taste by seeing the masterpieces of other civilizations and other centuries."[21]

Here for example...

Jane gestures around the gallery.

"Imposing architectural installations provide noble settings within the Museum's... galleries."[22]

Jane walks north into the next gallery. Then, addressing "The Birth of Venus" by Nicolas Poussin:

"Resplendently... amazingly flawless... sumptuous... This figure is among the finest and most beautiful creations... An image of exceptional rhythm and fluidity..."[23]

Jane walks across the room to address "Saint Luke" by Simon Vouet.

"This is the most spectacular... prized for their clear bold patterns and relatively few yet strong and harmonious... of the more than one thousand works collected by celebrated Philadelphia Lawyer... monumental, sculptural ... in an austere setting..."

Jane walks north into a gallery containing "The Four Seasons" attributed to Augustin Pajou. As she walks:

["Steady, thrifty, forehanded and domestic in their habits... independent and self-helpful... quietly self-assured."[24]]

Addressing "The Sacrifice of the Arrows of Love on the Altar of Friendship" by Jean Pierre Antoine Tassaert:

"One of the most jarring and emotionally effective interpretations... The writhing, enchained, muscular... majestic, frenzied... vast and vigorous... perfectly complimented Europe's opulent palaces and churches..."

[Let's move on to the next gallery shall we...]

Jane walks north into the next gallery. Gesturing generally:

"One of the most complex and graceful compositions of the seventeenth century..."

Addressing "Cabinet" attributed to Adam Weisweiler:

"This charming group of dancing maidens... graceful, life-size, mythological... a creation of almost visionary splendor. The sweeping and surging... exaggerated, lunging... at once so splendidly theatrical and so obviously individualized..."

Jane walks back into the gallery containing "The Four Seasons." She addresses the group:

["Though she was from 'out of town' her background was similar to theirs, and she fit in to the routine of afternoons 'at home,' the Tuesday box at the Academy of Music, the opening night of the Oil Painting Show..."[25]]

Speaking generally:

"...where the best qualities of taste were sustained until late in the century..."

Addressing a guard's stool in the corner of the gallery:

"In scale and complexity... the most ambitious undertaking... in the great European tradition... abundance and grace... free from time and change..."

Addressing "The Four Seasons: Autumn as Bacchus":

And here...

"American, mother, three brothers distinctly subnormal, herself mentally deficient, violent, undisciplined and lacking in every qualification of motherhood, shiftless, irresponsible..."

"Her second husband is one of the most degraded, of a low and vicious family... extremely backward and incorrigible... father being of less than average intelligence... generally... regarded by all who have dealt with her as weak... and a dangerous character on account of her immoral propensities... grossly low condition... unable to learn... of no service in the home, and constantly... given to self abuse... almost entirely nude... stretched out on floor with a dirty, blackened pan..."[26]

Addressing the group:

I want to be graceful.

Rituals of family and love and orderliness...

Jane walks back to gallery with "The Birth of Venus." Speaking generally:

"Gentle, private... charm and originality... Total restraint... utilitarian... rectilinear..."[27]

Addressing "The Birth of Venus":

"Lower class culture: there is a substantial segment of present-day American society whose way of life, values, and characteristic patterns of behavior are the product of a distinctive cultural system which may be termed 'lower class.' "[28]

Jane walks back into the gallery between the Grand Salon and the Paneled Room. Speaking generally as she walks across the gallery:

"Plain grace ... harmony and perfection ... impressive ... severely formal, yet tender ... vigorous ... humble ... joyful ..."[29]

"Shiftless, lazy, unambitious ...; chronic poor ...

Addressing "Rape of the Sabines" by Luca Giorgano:

"Unable to 'make a go of it' because of character deficiencies or lack of skill ...; [If you'll just follow me ...] 'the new poor'; 'multi-problem families'; 'the culture of poverty'; 'disreputable poor,' 'paupers,' 'cannot cope,' 'make noise,' cause trouble and generally 'create problems' ... 'lower-lowers' "[30]

Addressing an exit sign above door at the far end of the gallery:

"Firm in painting, delicate in color and texture, this picture is a brilliant example of a brilliant form."[31]

"Or over here ..."

Jane exits the gallery leaving most of the group some distance behind her. She continues into the Medieval art galleries, walking back toward the Great Stair Hall. Speaking generally:

"Unstable and superficial interpersonal relationships ... low levels of participation ... little interest in, or knowledge of, larger society ... sense of helplessness and low sense of personal efficiency ... Low 'need achievement' and low levels of aspirations for the self."

Turning to address the group:

["The love of beauty is one of the finer things that makes life worth living."[32]]

Again speaking generally:

"Jobs at the lowest level of skills ... unskilled ... and menial jobs ..."

Gesturing toward various parts of the gallery:

"in hotels, laundries, kitchens, furnace rooms, nonunionized factories and hospitals ..."[33]

"Scattered brick houses ... dreary warehouses ... blank walls and junk yards ... drab, enclosing ... sometimes blue ..."[34]

Jane walks through the doors to the Great Stair Hall. She stops and turns to address group:

Really! I mean ... Here for example ...

Jane moves in the direction of the stairs as she speaks, gesturing generally at benches, the stone railing, tapestries, etcetera.

"You take your ordinary, barnyard room, so to speak, the familiar room that you have lived in, that you never thought of as a work of art, and somehow, insensibly, you pull it about, you put a chair in a different place, you arrange the mantelpiece, get rid of half the impedimenta of the mantelpiece – you know how most people load up the mantelpieces – you simply strip it and you put one or two things there and you put them in the right place ... an artist will do that ... Well, that's what a museum does, I think, for all of us."[35]

I'd like to continue on now to the first floor . . .

Jane descends the Great Stair with the group. At the second landing she begins speaking, gesturing in various directions around the Great Stair Hall as she walks. When she reaches the bottom of the stair she walks around it to the left.

As I mentioned earlier, it "consists of a center building, with wings at each end extending back . . . It is four stories high, including the basement . . .

"The inmates are lodged in rooms of about 22 feet by 45 feet (of which there are 42) from 20 to 24 persons in each room, and are classed according to their general character and habits, separating the more deserving from the abandoned and worthless, and thus removing the most obnoxious feature consequent to such establishments. The Americans are generally by themselves; so are the Irish; and the Blacks also have their separate apartments.

"[It] also contains a penitentiary, a hospital for the sick and insane, several large buildings for workshops, schoolrooms, lodging rooms for children, and the various outhouses of a large and well regulated establishment . . ."[36]

She stops in front of Diego Rivera's "Liberation of the Peon," which is hung outside the door to the coat room underneath the stair.

And isn't this a handsome drinking fountain!

Jane walks into the Coat Room, gesturing toward the drinking fountain at the far end. Addressing the drinking fountain:

Hmm " . . . a work of astonishing economy and monumentality," " . . . it boldly contrasts with the severe and highly stylized productions of this form . . ." [Uh, notice, uh . . .] "The massiveness . . . the vast [uh] . . . most ambitious and resolved. . . .!"[37]

Graceful, mythological, life-size . . .

I want to be graceful.

Jane leaves the coat room, gesturing for the group to follow her.

You know – come along. You know "each individual, no matter how untutored, [can find] a thousand objects (or better still, just one . . .) so obviously perfect and so directly in the line of [her] own half-understood striving for perfection that . . ."[38]

Here for example . . .

Jane walks to a David Smith sculpture. Standing next to it, she holds her arm outstretched.

Notice how the light catches the fabric, the tiny hounds tooth checks of the suit, and silvers the fabric a little more brightly, as it falls about the arms, the legs, uh, just below the knee, and creases slightly at the waist, double-breasted . . .

But look at the face. The skin is broken. She turns her head away slightly . . .

Jane begins walking to the stairs leading to the West Entrance Hall, still speaking.

While her dress and bearing may suggest an upper-class, uh, lady, the discriminating, uh, the discriminating, viewer, will notice that her hands are scarred and poorly manicured, and her teeth have not been straightened.

I'd like to move on to the West Entrance now . . .

Half way down stairs to the West Entrance Hall, Jane turns to address the group.

"The museum's task could be described as the continuous, conscientious and resolute distinction of quality from mediocrity."[39]

"Hunger is the best sauce, and everything that is eatable is relished by people with a healthy appetite. [But]...a satisfaction of this sort shows no choice directed by taste. It is only when the want is appeased that we can distinguish which of many men has or has not taste."[40]

In the West Entrance Hall:

"Still, it takes very little to produce a perfect plate of fruit and cheese." Here for example...

Addressing one of the "Dancing Nymphs" by Claude Michel (known as Clodion):

"...hunks of sharp white Vermont cheddar served in rough hewn blocks, and a single perfect apple are elegant in their simplicity and preferable..."

Turning to address the second of the "Dancing Nymphs":

"...to such daunting combinations as chicken medallions with avocado."[41]

Jane walks away from "The Dancing Nymphs." She walks past the coat room and into a corridor with rest rooms, telephones, the Art Sales and Rental Gallery, and some contemporary art. She speaks while walking, turning occasionally to address the group.

"I heard at a Sunday Brunch not long ago...Everybody, it seems, now has horror stories:

"A man with a magnificent house on Delancy Place says he can't keep flowers outside, because every morning he finds the pots overturned and his sidewalks covered with filth and litter.

"Another man tells of seeing a street bum [who seem to have taken every available nook, cranny and stairwell] sprawled in front of Nan Duskin on Walnut Street, in our prime retail location. Nobody could move this bum, not even the police.

"A woman who has always been a patron of the Art Museum can't believe what a shambles the landscaping there has become...

"...there is no longer any place to escape [no civilized oasis]"[42]

Jane stops at the end of the corridor and turns to address the group.

This corridor houses some of the Museum's public facilities: the coat room, rest rooms, telephones, uh...it doesn't really have a name, but uh...

Down the hall here...

Jane walks down an adjoining corridor toward the Drawing and Print Galleries opposite the Museum Shop.

Down the hall here we have the Muriel and Philip Berman Drawing and Print Galleries. They were named as part of the Museum's Donor Recognition Program. The Museum you know provides prospective donors with a veritable cornucopia of Named Space Opportunities.

Here for example...

Jane walks across the corridor to address the Museum Shop.

...for $750,000 you could name the Museum Shop.

You know, I'd like to name a space, why, if I had $750,000 I would name this Shop um...Andrea. Andrea is such a nice name.

399

Jane walks a few feet further down the corridor and stops again to address the group.

This is our Museum Shop, Andrea, named in 1989 by Mrs. John P. Castleton, a onetime Museum guide and eternal art appreciator. Jane, as she was called, always liked to say that "patronage creates a personal sense of ownership in a beautiful home of the arts and unites the most enlightened spirits of the community in a high devotion to the public good."[43]

"Did you know her? To know her was to love her. She was special . . . with her long stride and tailored profile, a [blond] of medium height dressed in understated refinement, incredibly 'finished.' She often carried a briefcase . . . apologizing . . . Her voice surprised, deep and husky and resonant with emotion, drawing out and lingering over the vowels . . . a serious student, humble, hungry, analytic . . . She read . . . and would look and invite us to look . . . there was time to see more clearly."[44]

Jane is silent for a moment and then continues speaking as she walks past the Museum Shop and on through the series of harshly lit and empty corridors that lead to the Museum's cafeteria.

"The Museum wants and needs an informed, enthusiastic audience whose . . . knowledge of the collections and programing continue to grow."[45]

The Museum says: here you will find "satisfaction," you will find "contentment," you will find "pleasure," here you will find "the finer things that make life worth living," here you will be liberated "from the struggle imposed by material needs," here you will find your "ideal beauty," you will find "inspiration," here you will find "a place apart," you will find "standards," here you will find "civilization . . . "[46]

Jane stops just outside the cafeteria.

Oh, I've known happiness; intense happiness, exquisite happiness, here in the museum, beside these tiles, or across the room from those or, or over here, between these two.

It's nice to feel alive.

I'd like to live like an art object. Wouldn't it be nice to live like an art object.

"A sophisticated composition of austere dignity, vitality, and immediate quality; a strict formality softened by an exquisitely luminous atmosphere . . . "[47]

How could anyone ask for more.

Graceful, mythological, life size . . .

Jane enters the cafeteria.

"This room represents the heyday of colonial art in Philadelphia on the eve of the Revolution, and must be regarded as one of the very finest of all American rooms."[48]

Jane moves through the room as she speaks, gesturing at tables, chairs, trash bins, cafeteria patrons, etcetera.

Notice "the architectural decoration . . . [It] combines the classical vocabulary of broken pediments and fluted pilasters familiar in English house design, with the flamboyant, asymmetrical plaster ornamentations derived from the French Rococo style. The beautiful upholstered sofa, Chippendale style chairs, and marble-top table show the variety of form for which Philadelphia furniture makers were justly famous."[49]

And ... "This room was much frequented by Washington while Commander-in-Chief and President."[50]

Jane leaves the cafeteria and walks back the way she came.

"Stately men and women – above all things stately – measured, ordered, with a certain quiet elegance about them ... sober color, dignified composition, the arrangement ... that is simple, fine, and sympathetic to us all [certain habits of good drawing ... things which I like to call the 'good manners of painting'] ... a little more measure, a little more calm, a little more serenity ... dignity and a certain technical rectitude ... taste, the sense of measure and decorum ...

"Well, frequent this museum of yours and get in contact with tradition. You drink in the tradition that exists [here] and that is ... piled up [here], all the epochs, all the great ages. You will feel with me that these touchstones, these standards, after all, are not pedantic things [but] standards for a cultivated, governed, discriminating instinct."[51]

Let's not just talk about art. Because finally, the Museum's purpose is not just to develop an appreciation of art, but to develop an appreciation of values ...

"By appreciation of values we have in mind the ability to distinguish between the worthy and the unworthy, the true and the false, the beautiful and the ugly, between refinement and crudity, sincerity and cant, between the elevating and the degrading, the decent and indecent in dress and conduct, between values that are enduring and those that are temporary,"[52] between ...

Here ... Over here, between ...

Jane walks quickly back into the corridor with the telephones, coat room, rest rooms, Art Sales and Rental Gallery, etcetera. She moves around the corridor, gesturing to these things as she refers to them.

... here, the ability to distinguish between a coat room and a rest room, between a painting and a telephone, a guard and a guide; the ability to distinguish between yourself and a drinking fountain, between what is different and what is better and objects that are inside and those that are outside; the ability to distinguish between your rights and your wants, between what is good for you and what is good for society.

Well. That's the end of our tour for today.

Thank you for joining me and have a nice day.

Notes

1 "Museums Highlights: A Gallery Talk" was developed as part of the Contemporary Viewpoints Artist Lecture Series, which was organized by the Tyler School of Art of Temple University, and funded by the Pew Charitable Trusts. The performance owed its existence to Hester Stinnett, the director of Contemporary Viewpoints, who invited me to Philadelphia, and to Danielle Rice, the Philadelphia Museum of Art's

Curator of Education, who supported the performance from within the Museum. I would also like to thank Donald Moss for his comments on various drafts of this script; Allan McCollum, for first calling the activities of docents to my attention; and Douglas Crimp, at whose request the script was first prepared for publication in *October* magazine.

2 Robert Montgomery Scott and Ann d'Harnoncourt, "From the President and the Director." *Philadelphia Museum of Art Magazine* (Spring 1988).

3 This is partly true. For the first performance, I received an honorarium from Contemporary Viewpoints. The following four performances were "voluntary." Providing the services of a guide in the galleries and at the information desk, a volunteer docent is not just someone who gives tours for a small percentage of the museum's visitors; she is the Museum's representative. Unlike the members of the museum's nonprofessional maintenance, security, and gift shop staff that visitors come in contact with, the docent is a figure of identification for a primarily white, middle-class audience. And unlike the museum's professional staff, the docent is the representative of the museum's voluntary sector. The Philadelphia Museum of Art, like many municipal or civic museums in the United States, is a hybrid of public and private nonprofit, volunteer and professional. The city owns the building and provides municipal employees for its security and maintenance; volunteer trustees own everything in the building and govern a private nonprofit corporation which engages other volunteers and hires a professional staff. While docents are usually trained by the professional staff, I would say that they aspire less to professional competence than to what Pierre Bourdieu calls the "precocious," "status-induced familiarity" with legitimate culture that marks those to whom the objects within the museum belong(ed); an "Imperceptible learning" that can only be "acquired with time and applied by those who can take their time" (Bourdieu, *Distinction: A Social Critique of the Judgment of Taste*, trans. Richard Nice (Cambridge, Mass.: Harvard University Press, 1984), pp. 71–2).

4 While Jane is a fictional docent, I would like to consider her less as an individual "character" with autonomous traits than as a site of speech constructed within various relations constitutive of the museum. As such, Jane is determined above all by the status of the docent as a non-expert volunteer. As a volunteer, she expresses the possession of a quantity of the leisure and the economic and cultural capital that defines a museum's patron class. It is only a small quantity – indicating rather than bridging the class gap that compels her to volunteer her services in the absence of capital; to give, perhaps, her body in the absence of art objects. Yet it is enough to position her in identification with the museum's board of trustees, and to make her the museum's exemplary viewer.

5 The Pennsylvania Museum and School of Industrial Art was a product of the Centennial Exposition held in Philadelphia in 1876. In 1893 the School of Industrial Art moved to a "property formerly belonging to the Institution for the Deaf and Dumb." The Pennsylvania Museum maintained a large study collection of decorative arts. By 1910 it began to be derided as a "mixed up collection of industrial exhibits and curiosities, as well as art, in . . . the cluttered gloom of Memorial Hall" (Nathaniel Burt, *Perennial Philadelphians* (Boston: Little Brown, 1963), p. 344). "Occupied by specimens of Industrial Art," Memorial Hall was considered

unsuitable "for the exhibition of paintings and fine art" (*Report of the Commissioners of Fairmount Park for the Year 1912*, p. 9).

6   George and Mary Roberts, *Triumph on Fairmount* (Philadelphia: J. B. Lippincott Co., 1959), p. 24.

7   Anonymous, *The New Museum and Its Service to Philadelphia* (Philadelphia: The Pennsylvania Museum and School of Industrial Art, 1922), p. 19. Art museums began to be established in large numbers in the United States in the last quarter of the nineteenth century. At that time there was a general movement, spearheaded by bankers and industrialists, to tighten public relief and reorganize public policy. The primary aim of this movement was to eliminate all direct outdoor or extra-institutional public relief which, Frances Fox Piven and Richard Cloward write, "was making it possible for some of the poor to evade the new industrial assault" by providing a choice between work under any conditions and starvation (Fox Piven and Cloward, *The New Class War* (New York: Pantheon, 1982), p. 64). Direct material relief would be limited to the poorhouse, where "discipline and education 'should be inseparably associated with any system of relief'" (Michael B. Katz, quoting Josephine Shaw Lowell, *In the Shadow of the Poorhouse* (New York: Basic Books, 1986), p. 71).

8   According to the *Report of the Committee on Municipal Charities of Philadelphia* (1913), Blockly was "a reproduction on a large scale of conditions often found in country almshouses," an overcrowded and "unscientific massing of several types of dependents" (p. 11). In 1928, the year that the new Pennsylvania Museum on the Parkway opened to the public, Philadelphia's Home for the Indigent was described in municipal reports as follows: "In this division of the bureau is the City's poor of both sexes; some who have served their apprenticeship in crime and shady transactions, as lax in caring for their bodies as their morals, acquainted with the usages and customs of reformatories and prisons, graduates from the House of Correction and similar institutions, having 'sold their birthright for a mess of pottage,' and when unable to continue the customary mode of existence owing to age or infirmities, have drifted into the home and become a public charge..." (*The Fourth Annual Message of W. Freeland Kendrick, Mayor of Philadelphia, Containing the Reports of the Various Departments of the City of Philadelphia for the Year Ending December 31, 1927*, p. 244).

9   This list was compiled from *The First Annual Message of Harry A. Mackey, Mayor of Philadelphia, Containing the Reports of the Various Departments of the City of Philadelphia for the Year Ending December 31, 1928*.

10 Nineteenth-century descriptions of nineteenth-century poorhouses quoted in Walter I. Trattner, *From Poor Law to Welfare State* (New York: Free Press, 1984), p. 59.

11 The establishment of public institutions, particularly poorhouses, as deterrents to their use and goads to work at menial jobs at below subsistence wages is an idea that was perhaps first codified in England in the 1834 Report from His Majesty's Commissioners for Inquiring into the Administration and Practical Operation of the Poor Laws: "Into such a house no one will enter voluntarily; work, confinement, and discipline, will deter the indolent and vicious; and nothing but extreme necessity will induce any to accept... the sacrifice of their accustomed habits and gratifications." (Quoted in Frances Fox Piven and Richard Cloward, *Regulating the Poor* (New York: Random House, 1971), p. 35.)

12   Where Mrs. Robert Montgomery Scott is wont to give impromptu recitals.

13   The Museum Fund, *A Living Museum: Philadelphia's Opportunity for Leadership in the Field of Art* (Philadelphia: Pennsylvania Museum and School of Industrial Art, 1928), pp. 2, 17.

14   Fairmount Park Art Association, *Forty-Second Annual Report of the Board of Trustees* (1913), p. 18. I would like to consider the art museum, then, as one term in an organization of public institutions, and of publicity, into a system of incentives and disincentives, goads and deterrences. As coupled ideas, paired and opposing representations, this system might function similarly to what Foucault described in *Discipline and Punish* as the tactics of nineteenth-century penal reform: "Where exactly did the penalty apply its pressure, gain control of the individual? Representations: the representations of his interests, the representation of his advantages and disadvantages, pleasures and displeasures... By what instruments did one act on the representations? Other representations, or rather couplings of ideas (crime–punishment, the imagined advantages of crime–disadvantages perceived in the punishments); these pairings could function only in the element of publicity: punitive scenes that established them or reinforced them in the eyes of all" (Foucault, *Discipline and Punish: The Birth of the Prison*, trans. Alan Sheridan (New York: Vintage Books, 1979), pp. 127–8).

15   Joseph Widener, "Address." In *Fairmount Park Art Association, Fifty-Sixth Annual Report of the Board of Trustees* (1928), p. 44.

16   Philadelphia Industrial Development Corporation, "How a Unique Combination of Location, Lifestyle and Low Costs Is Sparking a Regional Economic Boom in the Nation's Birthplace." *Business Week*, April 18, 1986, p. 27.

17   Philadelphia Industrial Development Corporation, "Philadelphia Is a Decision You Can Live With." *Business Week*, April 18, 1986, p. 13.

18   Philadelphia Industrial Development Corporation, "Unique Combination of Location, Lifestyle and Low Costs," p. 27.

19   Fiske Kimball, "Six Antique Rooms From the Continent." *The Pennsylvania Museum Bulletin* 24 (Oct. /Nov. 1928), p. 7. (Kimball was the Parkway Museum's founding director.)

20   Octavia Hill Association of Philadelphia, *Good Housing that Pays* (Philadelphia, 1917), p. 83.

21   Anonymous, *The New Museum and Its Service to Philadelphia*, p. 5.

22   The following descriptions (except those otherwise footnoted) were taken in the order that they appear from *Introduction to the Philadelphia Museum of Art* (Philadelphia: Philadelphia Museum of Art, 1985).

23   I would like to consider the following descriptions as representations not of paintings, but of the museum's ideal visitor – representations of her interests, representations of her advantages and disadvantages, pleasures and displeasures. They are representations less addressed to than constructing the museum's audience – constructing out of a heterogeneous field of different, conflicting interests, a homogeneous public. They would do so by taking hold of those interests, wants, needs, desires; taking hold of them and representing them, reforming them, directing them, and determining the space, the language, and the logic in which they can be articulated.

24   Descriptions of Philadelphians from Burt, *Perennial Philadelphians*, p. 108, and John Lukacs, *Philadelphia: Patricians and Philistines 1900–1950* (New York: Farrar, Straus & Giroux, 1981), p. 72.

25   A description of Mrs. Eli Kirk Price. Price, according to George and Mary Roberts, was responsible for getting the new Fairmount Museum building on the city plan. See Roberts and Roberts, *Triumph on Fairmount*, p. 21.

26   Department of Public Health and Charities of Philadelphia, *The Degenerate Children of Feeble-Minded Women* (1910), pp. 2–8: "THE HISTORIES OF THESE FEEBLE-MINDED WOMEN AND THEIR FEEBLE-MINDED CHILDREN ARE PRACTICALLY THE SAME. THEIR UNFORTUNATE BIRTH, HELPLESSNESS, PAUPERISM AND RUIN IS PART OF A CONTINUOUS SERIES WHEREBY THE COMMUNITY IS CONSTANTLY SUPPLIED WITH THE ELEMENTS OF DEGENERACY" (p. 8).

27   *Introduction to the Philadelphia Museum of Art.*

28   Walter B. Miller, quoted in Chaim I. Waxman, *The Stigma of Poverty: A Critique of Poverty Theories and Policies* (New York: Pergamon Press, 1977), p. 26.

29   *Introduction to the Philadelphia Museum of Art.*

30   Z. D. Blum and P. H. Rosi, "Social Class Research and Images of the Poor: A Biographical Review." In *On Understanding Poverty*, ed. Patrick Moynihan (New York: Basic Books, 1969), p. 350.

31   This sentence is the complete description of a painting in "The Display Collections: European and American Art." *Pennsylvania Museum of Art Handbook* (1931), p. 65.

32   Museum Fund, *A Living Museum*, p. 27.

33   Blum and Rosi, "Social Class Research," p. 351.

34   Description of approach to Philadelphia Twentieth Street Station on a train. From Roberts and Roberts, *Triumph on Fairmount*, p. 17.

35   Royal Cortissoz, "Life and the Museum." In Fairmount Park Art Association, *Fifty-Seventh Annual Report of the Board of Trustees* (1929), p. 55.

36   Philadelphia Board of Guardians, "Report of the Committee Appointed by the Board of Guardians of the Poor of the City and Districts of Philadelphia to Visit the Cities of Baltimore, New York, Providence, Boston, and Salem (1827)." In *The Almshouse Experience: Collected Reports*, ed. David Rothman (New York: Arno Press, 1971), p. 8.

37   *Introduction to the Philadelphia Museum of Art.*

38   *The New Museum and Its Service to Philadelphia*, p. 20.

39   Alfred H. Barr, Jr., quoted from a plaque in the Museum of Modern Art.

40   Immanuel Kant, *Critique of Judgment*, trans. J. H. Bernard (New York: Hasner Press, 1951), p. 44.

41   Fran R. Schumer, "Salad and Seurat: Sampling the Fare at the Museums." *The New York Times*, April 22, 1987, p. C1.

42   D. Herbert Lipson, "Off the Cuff." *Philadelphia Magazine*, Dec. 1988, p. 2.

43   Museum Fund, *A Living Museum*, p. 19.

44   *The Weekday Museum Guides' Twenty-Fifth Anniversary 1960–1985*, p. 2.

45   "From the President and the Director." *Philadelphia Museum of Art Magazine* (Spring 1988).

46   From "From the President and the Director," *Philadelphia Museum of Art Magazine*; Museum Fund, *A Living Museum*; and anonymous, *The New Museum and Its Service to Philadelphia*.

47   Descriptions of art in *The Metropolitan Museum of Art Guide* (New York: Metropolitan Museum of Art, 1983).

48   "The Display Collections: European and American Art."

49   *Guide* (Philadelphia: Philadelphia Museum of Art, 1977).

50   *Pennsylvania Museum of Art Handbook* (1931).

51   Cortissoz, "Life and the Museum," p. 53.

52   Edwin C. Broome, "Report of the Superintendent of Schools." In *One Hundred and Tenth Report of the Board of Public Education for the Year Ending December 31, 1928*, pp. 275–6.

Chapter 24

The Scandalous Fall of Feminism and the "First Black President"

Melissa Deem

Feminism is always on trial. The most recent indictments occurred during the popular coverage of the Clinton/Lewinsky affair. Ironically, this time feminism was called forth to defend itself against the charge of silence. One commentator argued that this latest indictment "signifies the end of feminism as we know it." He continues, "the once shrill voice of feminist outrage is suddenly, deafeningly still" (Horowitz 1998). These comments represent a new trend within the popular discourses concerning feminism in the United States. This may be the first moment in history when feminists have been castigated for too little speech. The "fall" of Bill Clinton (which never came to completion but saturated the political public sphere for two long years) was accompanied by another antici-pated fall: the demise of feminism. Public discourse across the political spectrum heralded the "death of feminism" when commenting on the relative silence of feminists in regard to the Clinton/Lewinsky scandal. Feminism's "silence" has been found especially noteworthy when contrasted to the loud anti-Republican pedagogy concerning sex and power with which feminists trumped patriarchy during the earlier Clarence Thomas and Bob Packwood scandals.

Feminism may be the most visibly culpable post-1960s political movement called into question by the discourses of the Clinton/Lewinsky scandal, but it is certainly not alone. Clinton has come to embody a set of complaints against feminism and post-1960s racial and class politics more generally. His embodi-ment of minoritarian politics has been striking. Attached to Clinton's body are all the anxieties engendered by post-1960s US racial and sexual politics. In the 1990s, Clinton became the cultural icon of the 1960s, the body traumatized by a decade that transformed and, by some accounts, destroyed and degraded Amer-ican politics and civic life (Shalit 1997; Lears 1998; Rosen 1998; Beinart 1999; Ponnuru 1999; Shapiro 1999). From the discourses of addiction and abuse to redemption and healing through shared pain, Clinton is encumbered by history as the post-civil-rights president who bears the trauma of a degraded America. Women and African Americans are represented as the two major categories of citizens who support Bill Clinton without question. Not incidently, it is the transformations in the positioning of African Americans (male) and women (white) which undergird post-1960s political change.

This chapter addresses the way in which the fate of post-1960s leftist political movements was tightly bound to that of Bill Clinton as the emergent mainstream narrative demonized both Clinton and feminism, while simultaneously reducing African Americans to "dupes." Feminism and racial politics are left compromised by the scandal. Clinton ultimately regained his "zone of privacy" (Berlant 1997), allowing for the reconstitution of the majoritarian body. The purpose of this analysis of the popular trials of feminism and the racializing rhetorics of Clinton is to call for an expanded field of reference, and hence a more challenging representational space, for minoritarian politics in the United States. The field of reference for these discourses must be expanded in order to create possibilities for multiplying the painfully constricted speaking positions which are currently possible. Readings of the discourses positioning feminists and African Americans are necessary for identifying the different strategies of reference which work to produce certain descriptions. I examine the production of speaking positions within these discourses which situate feminism as hypocritical and African Americans as dupes. Thematizing these structures may open spaces for the creation of effective strategies for minoritarian politics within US public culture.

By telling a story of Clinton/feminism in the intimate public sphere, I want to change the conditions of possibility for feminism by enabling a space of internal difference. In order to multiply the political possibilities for feminism, I argue for the necessity of radically recontextualizing feminism in the public sphere such that it can be viewed as a contextual practice. The field of reference for feminism within the popular must be expanded in order to disarticulate feminism from its representation as a moral dogma. The production of new histories that allow for the complexity of feminism's contextual political practices is crucial.

The struggle in the contemporary public sphere over the space of feminism is instructive as a struggle over the space of history. In this case, "the personal is political" is blamed for the problem of compromising leftist and feminist positions, the nation, and civility since the 1960s. Feminism and other minoritarian politics and practices are reduced to complaints within the public sphere partly through "paramnesiac" morality mongering. In order to best understand these positions and the place of the "personal" it is necessary to engage public discourses. At particular moments, political politics becomes public/popular culture through the site of scandal. This intermingling can be seen as producing key moments for understanding the strategies of reference involved in producing particular descriptions, descriptions that have everything to do with what is possible within a particular context. The becoming popular of political politics demonstrates that something is at stake, in this case, beyond the fate of the president – specifically feminism, race and leftist politics. Morris (1988) interrogates the relationship of leftist intellectual work to the popular and argues for the need to learn from the theories that circulate in and as the popular. It is important to pay attention to moments of optimism as well as moments of failure

(Morris 1990). However, within the critical practice of Cultural Studies, political politics and cultural politics are often at odds, with often little engagement of their intersections (Morris 1990; Berube 1994) and hence opportunities for political effectiveness are missed.

Cultural Studies, like feminism, has been accused by the right and the left of being caught up in identity politics. Cultural Studies, often regardless of the multiple practices which circulate under its sign, is attacked for partaking in the politics of identity. Identity politics and political correctness become the signs under which Cultural Studies and leftist political practices more generally are disciplined within the public sphere (Grossberg 1992; Berube 1994; Brown 1995; Roiphe 1993; Gubar 2000). Any position which advances a politics concerned with race, gender, sexuality, and class is too easily conflated with regressive politics and hence easily dismissed. Contrary to this position, I want to take seriously Berlant's (1988) claim that identity is being deployed by the right through a rhetoric and affect of intimacy within the public sphere. The struggle within public culture over the categories of identity is fierce and most often employed to contain and limit the authority of those on the cultural left. The strategies of delegitimation of feminism, race politics, and Cultural Studies work to contain the radical possibilities of these political projects. It is important that those working within Cultural Studies read these discourses and examine their rhetorical practices in order to develop multiple and provisional political strategies that do not simply accept the terms of the debate as they are given.

I want to embed this analysis within a discussion of the critical practice of Cultural Studies in the hope that lessons can be learned from the rhetorical machinations involved in compromising feminism and racial politics. Cultural Studies can learn from feminism the necessity of a self-awareness of the political discourses which circulate around its name. Feminism has never had the "luxury" of being an academic discourse disarticulated from the political activism and practices of women within public and everyday life. Cultural Studies, on the other hand, has no such direct connection to public political activities. In this sense, Cultural Studies has not been forced by necessity into the self-awareness that feminism has developed. Hence feminism is not only an intellectual/political project, but an object of study. Feminism is continually studying its own circulation. Cultural Studies, while engaged in debates around its status as a discipline, has not often engaged itself as an object of study within public life. Cultural Studies must develop more of an awareness of its own circulation. The popular debates over political correctness and identity politics have done much to represent Cultural Studies within public discourses as a morally dogmatic and inconsistent intellectual practice. This representation is foisted upon Cultural Studies, allowing the latter no power in its representational politics. Following Morris (1990) these moments of failure are also important sites of study and can prove instructive for future practice. In this sense, it is important for feminism, minoritarian politics, and Cultural Studies to be objects of study at particular moments, and as I argue in this paper, the site of scandal becomes one such moment. Feminism, racial politics, and Cultural Studies are scandalous, and importantly it is at this site of scandal that political politics and cultural politics come together.

Feminism may be most culpable for the national trauma and the concomitant degradation of civic life; however, it is not alone among 1960s political movements to be vilified by the discourses on Clinton. This nostalgia yearns for a time when public discourse was clean, and the iconic masculine body retained the prophylaxis of the nation to shield his physicality. In many ways, the discourses on Clinton can be read as overt and insidious attacks against the transformations in US public culture – the publicness of minoritarian politics and bodies. These corporeal inscriptions demonstrate yet again the interrelatedness of the transformations in US culture wrought by minoritarian politics. Simply put, this is just the latest narrative of heteronormative majoritarian culture, the story of humiliation, degradation, trauma, and desire for the national body.

Scandal, Civility, and Post-1960s Nostalgia

It might be commonplace to say that public discourse often proceeds from scandal to scandal. In relation to feminism in the public sphere, however, the logic of scandal seems to take on specific characteristics. The feminist discourses circulating in and through the Clinton sex scandal demonstrate, yet again, that the primary manner in which feminism gains access to majoritarian political space is through anxiety over the bodies of men (see also Deem 1996). In this instance, the hypermasculinized iconic figure of the "most powerful" man in the world, the US President, provides the grounds for feminism's prominence. The "failure" of feminists to condemn Clinton outright and take a stand for an unmitigated sisterhood has served as a rallying cry for a virulent attack against feminism. Thus, the Clinton sex scandal serves as an object lesson for feminism in the national public sphere regarding the mechanisms of containment and discipline that operate to contain, reduce, and obfuscate feminism within the political. Feminism has variously been charged with hypocrisy for failing to take a stand on the scandal and also for supporting only certain women as sisters (Kathleen Willey but not Paula Jones or Monica Lewinsky). At the same time, feminism is held responsible for the intimate turn within the political by changing that which is appropriate for public discourse. Feminism and Clinton are both charged with bringing into public discourse the intimate aspects of peoples' lives (Taylor 1998). Thus, feminism stands accused of hypocrisy and the degradation of public discourse – which is to say, it stands accused of the degradation of morals.

Feminists might rather discuss the implications of the 1996 Personal Responsibility Act or the effects of NAFTA, but they are called forth to testify most often when the issue is one of sexual conduct. Within the contemporary political climate, sexual harassment has become the sign of feminism. Feminism is reduced to a molar politics aligned with the state and juridical apparatus. Yet even within these discourses, it is not masculinist conduct held up for scrutiny but the fracturing and splintering of women and the "sisterhood" as feminism loses its moral undergirding by doing anything other than conform to a particular dogma. The "cramped space" of feminism within the national political imaginary severely constricts the possibilities of feminist positions.

While the discourses surrounding President Clinton's sexual exploits may be seen by many as trivial, sensational, and most of all not properly the "public's" concern, the discourses mark an important moment in the multiple mechanisms of containment for female and feminist speech within majoritarian political space. Discourses concerning feminism have yet again entered the political imaginary. Not, however, to herald the positive transformations of US public culture wrought by feminism, or over the commemorations of feminism's past (the 150th anniversary of the Seneca Falls Declaration of Rights and Sentiments and the Woman's Movement in 1998), but instead over the indecorous "Malthusian" erotic proclivities of President Bill Clinton. This is not the first time that Clinton and feminism have been linked in the national political imaginary, or the first time that the vagaries of the majoritarian male body have propeled feminism onto center stage. And it is not the first time that feminists' relationship to Clinton has resulted in the disciplining and indictment of feminism.

This move to the majoritarian body and the policing of previously "personal" practices requires a complex reexamination of the place of intimacy and the "personal" within public sphere politics. Lauren Berlant (1997) argues that "intimacy has been transformed from a private relation to a structuring aspect and affect of citizenship in the contemporary US public sphere" (p. 131). The point is not so much that the intimate aspects of people's lives are media fodder but that their nonfamilial sexual practices are at odds with the familial intimacy which structures US public culture – hence the rebuke of any engaged in sexual practices not in line with familial intimacy. Importantly, it is not the influence of identity politics or feminist discourse that has wrought such change to public discourse, but rather the conservative Right which has brought about the intimate transformation of public discourse in order to preserve majoritarian identity (Berlant 1997). Of course, the assaults on the body of the president, the iconic figure of masculinity, bring about a palpable anxiety over the vulnerability of the majoritarian body. Placing feminism in such a powerful position in this transformation works to shield Reaganite politics at the expense of feminism.

Familial politics have collapsed the personal and the political into a world of "public intimacy" (Berlant 1997: 1). The Clinton scandal has precipitated a mass experience of sexual unease. Clinton is a stunning example of an icon losing the protections and accoutrements of national iconicity. He is a politician who has been seen to have lost and then regained his "zone of privacy." The zone of trauma around the body of the masculinist icon turns to a form of political therapy and redemption to end the suffering and trauma of the national body.

411

Rather than see the political as a space of struggle over racial, sexual, and economic inequality, "the dominant idea marketed by patriotic traditionalists is a core nation whose survival depends on personal acts and identities performed in the intimate domain of the quotidian" (Berlant 1997: 4). Clinton is decried as unfit to be a citizen-president, not because of his civic acts, but because of personal acts of nonfamilial sex. This is clearly demonstrated by the continuing irrelevance of his possible financial malfeasance to his standing in polls. Scandal is the site within US public culture for the policing of nonfamilial forms of intimacy through the trauma of the national body. The therapeutic discourses of addiction dominate as an explanation of nonfamilial forms of intimacy (Clemetson & Wingert 1998; Handy 1998; Steinem 1998; Franks 1999; Rich 1999). A nostalgia permeates public discourses for a time when the zone of privacy was intact and feminists had not yet destroyed the political. Feminists are blamed for the national trauma, the crisis in the regime. Feminism stands in as the cause of national suffering.

Familial intimacy joins comfortably with the contemporary interest in civility in public life. One of the features of traditional male privilege that is most glaringly violated or transformed in this scandal is the privileged position of male lockerroom talk. In fact, one could argue that the nation has been transformed into a lockerroom. Speculations run rampant about Clinton and Vernon Jordan bonding over "pussy jokes" as late night comedians have produced an extensive repertoire on the scandal. The nation's newspaper publishers have been forced to publish "a document that fused civic, legal and sexual issues into one seamless, X-rated package" (Barringer 1998: 27). Daytime television has been forced to run explicit sexual language warnings before presidential testimony. Newt Gingrich has lectured members of the House about decorum, saying, "Freedom of speech in debate does not mean license to indulge in personal abuses or ridicule" (quoted in Berke 1998: 1). Even Ken Starr's report can be classified as government-produced pornography. Clinton has been charged with lowering the standards of public discourse; representatives of the antifeminist "Concerned Women for America," for example, have claimed that he brought this low culture to the nation. This lack of "erotic decorum" is exhibited by the national fascination with the stained dress of Monica Lewinsky and the specificity of the sexual practices that constitute sex. The president is blamed for having brought to new lows this kind of intimate talk, while feminists are blamed for having started it all. A veritable industry has sprung up around speculations over the details of Clinton's sexual exploits as well as his sexual taste. It is not incidental that Clinton is charged with lowering cultural standards of civil discourse. After all, he is the "white trash president" from Hope who has a taste for women with "big hair and bad pumps" (Feirstein & Peretz 1998). Clinton is most certainly not the first president to have indulged in extramarital sex; however, he is the most closely linked to sexual politics in recent history with his "defense" of gay and lesbian rights, gender equity, and reproductive freedom, as well as his own sexual exploits which have earned him such nicknames as the "Viagra Kid" (Rich 1998; Dowd 1998; Grann 1998). Bob Dole, the spokesperson for Viagra, may have become the butt of jokes, but he did not lose his "zone of privacy" through admissions of erectile dysfunction and the use and promotion of Viagra to treat this condition. Dole ingests Viagra in the service of national familial intimacy. Thus his consumption becomes an act of citizenship as it enables him to perform the very quotidian acts that situate him within a certain patriotic traditionalism.

The National Body Minoritized

The relatively recent attention paid to the previously shielded masculine body has led the online magazine *Suck* (1998) to name the 1990s the "decade of the penis." Even as white masculinity is the privileged site of political agency, so also has it become commodified and hyperembodied. The majoritarian body has been rendered visible, vulnerable, and traumatized with the prophylaxes of the nation no longer functioning to shield its visibility (Warner 1993; Berlant 1997). When white heterosexual masculinity has lost many of the protections of abstraction – when political figures have lost their privacy – Clinton stands as exemplar of the national body minoritized. It is precisely the site of masculine sameness (the decade of the penis, whereby the racial, class, and sexual differences which break the homogeneity of the masculine are elided), which betrays the cultural panic underwriting the move to gender and racial equity (Wiegman 1995).

Ironically, it is through this minoritization that class, race, and sexual politics are brought into public discourse. The minoritizing of the white heterosexual male body is situated precisely in the contradiction of citizenship. The recalcitrance of the privilege of corporeal abstraction for white masculinity functions within a "visual culture predicated on a commodification of those very identities minoritized by the discourses and social organizations of enlightened democracy" (Wiegman 1995: 49). In tension are the visual's increasing demand for difference and citizenship's "philosophic dis-incorporation" as embedded within privileged bodies. Wiegman has demonstrated how the disciplinary regime of visibility, working through an anatomical logic, commodifies minoritarian bodies. However, in this case, it is the majoritarian body *par excellence* which is minoritized by this regime. Within this visual terrain of the mass-mediated public, the specificities and positivities of all bodies do not signify equally (Warner 1993; Wiegman 1995). In the case of Clinton, the process of minoritizing the national body becomes a ruse for undermining post-1960s political transformations around race, sexuality, class, and gender. It is not Clinton who is damaged, but minoritarian politics.

Hyperembodiment functions through the denial of any "private" bodily space as "Clinton" is consumed by minor excesses. For Clinton, the loss of masculine privilege through intimate publicity is complicated by the complex discourses articulated through his body: Democrat, hypersexual, hyperconsumptive,

413

Southern, feminized affect, rapacious appetites, woman, and "black." Clinton's body has been traumatized by the movements for social justice and reform that he has been seen to represent and that have been "compromised" by his "fall."

The intersections of the body of the president, minoritarian politics, and the crisis of the regime are revealing. The crisis of the regime is explicitly linked to the sexual proclivities, or more accurately the sexual prowess of the president. Toby Miller (1998) has argued that the ubiquitous "First Penis" and the health of the regime connect over anxieties of governance. Clinton, through his hyper-sexuality, has been transformed from a masculine body of governance into a sexual body which cannot govern itself, let alone govern others. The ability of the "Comeback Kid" (Brookhiser 1998) to reconstitute the masculine body of the president has media pundits acting as if the future of the national regime is at stake (Goldstein 1998). Goldstein claims that media coverage has put "male hysteria on the map" (p. 67). In fact, this male hysteria concerns the transformation of iconic masculinity within the national imaginary.

According to Goldstein, Clinton draws so much fire because he represents a far more fundamental shift in masculinity than John F. Kennedy ever did. JFK functioned as a traditional icon of masculinity, while Clinton's iconic masculinity is saturated with affect: "I feel your pain." Specifically, he feels the pain of women. This "feminization" of masculine power produces in Clinton an ability to "project affect" (Goldstein 1998). However, this "feminization" does more as it is clearly coupled with a transformation in class politics. What Goldstein has neglected is the crucial role of the Kennedy women – specifically Jackie Kennedy – in shoring up this heteronormative fantasy of masculinity. The decorous aristocratic woman who always knows her place, both in public and in relation to her husband, is what undergirds the masculinist regime. Hillary Clinton, on the other hand, doesn't seem to know her place and continually transgresses the proper role of women and the first lady (Campbell 1998). Hillary is referred to as a "ball breaker," "a lesbian," and "a congenital liar"; the "nightmare image of potent woman" (Goldstein 1998: 67). So, even while Clinton's sexual exploits are well known, the image of the strong wife and the "bimbo" flings undermine the shoring up of traditional masculinity.

Feminism has been placed in an impossible position: to challenge Starr equals hypocrisy, and to question Clinton is prudery. Robust attacks on feminists have flourished in the media accounts of the scandal. Female supporters of Clinton are assumed to bear any humiliation rather than "abandon their guy." Feminism is depicted as selling out for political goals (O'Beirne 1998; Podhoretz 1998). Morality and purity of principle is the domain of feminism. In this way, when feminists act strategically in a given situation they are defiled by the world of politics, a world they should be above inhabiting. When feminists exhibit any political acumen they are hypocrites, and each individual woman who doesn't fall in line invalidates feminism. Borger (1998a) exemplifies this approach impeccably as she argues, "Sisters, we have a problem" (p. 33). She claims that the "personal is political" is not even needed to show feminists the contradictions of their position on Clinton because, more importantly, feminists used to personify the virtue of an insistence on principle. Instead of feminists leading the cry for virtue, they are being politically expedient. Thereby, a feminist history of purity of purpose which constrains possibilities and serves as a moral yardstick with which to measure feminism is constructed. In fact, the discovery that feminism is political has revealed it to be the "Democratic Party in drag" (Podhoretz 1998: 26). Feminism is caught within discursive traps that restrict the possibilities of women and feminists to articulate positions within the political. Consequently, feminism is in a bind: either it must refuse to speak or it must speak but not fulfil stereotypes.

The argument from the left merely repeats that from the right as it both exhibits an anxiety about transformations in masculinity and shores up traditional masculinity, again at the expense of feminists. Christopher Hitchens (1998), in an article entitled "Viagra Falls," indicts feminism for lowering the bar on what constitutes consensual sex by putting feminism into a context of hypermasculine heteronormativity. Feminism has been "cowed" by the "hydraulic of patriarchy" (p. 8). The "cowing" of feminism by the powers of patriarchy and its reinvigoration from a pharmocological fix is reiterated by Bob Guccione (1998), the publisher of *Penthouse*, who claimed that, "Feminism has emasculated the American male, and that emasculation has led to physical problems. This pill [Viagra] will take the pressure off men. It will lead to new relationships between men and women and undercut the feminist agenda" (p. 56). The transformations of gender relations in US public culture are stymied by the political performance of a newly reinvigorated masculinity. The reconstituted majoritarian body invests Clinton with renewed masculine vigor.

Clinton's power over feminists reconstitutes the masculine sexuality lost by the "ball-breaking" wife, whose image is now mediated by her victimage and loyalty as she stands by her man and thereby compromises not only herself, but feminism as well. Hillary as both feminist icon (though Hillary Clinton herself has carefully avoided identifying herself as feminist) and betrayer of feminism saturates the media discourses. Margaret Talbot (1998) in "Wife Story" not only inscribes Hillary as feminist icon, but as with Hitchens, levels all of feminism through an indictment of Hillary. Hillary has not only damaged her own image, but ironically enough, the gender politics of the Clinton administration. Talbot supports this last accusation by charging Hillary with colluding with the administration on its "bashing" of the women who have accused Bill Clinton of misconduct. As if this were not enough, Talbot also claims that by staying with Bill Clinton, she has compromised the "internal consistency of contemporary feminism" (p. 19). All feminism, embodied in Hillary, becomes the accomplice of Clinton. What enables Talbot to perform such a rhetorical maneuver is her indictment of feminism for popularizing the slogan "the personal is political." Feminists are caught in a bind. They are accused of producing the problem by violating the domain of the personal, while all of feminist politics are reduced to the personal. Hence, the relationship of feminism to Bill Clinton becomes analogous to Hillary's relationship with Bill, thereby further metonymically reducing feminisms' complex relations to the state and masculine authority. Talbot further condemns feminism for not meeting the demands of sisterhood, which for her and others is the unequivocal, univocal support of *all* women.

The scandal surrounding President Clinton's sexual exploits has much to say about the containment of feminism, the proliferation of intimacy, and the concomitant crisis in the national body. Feminism is captured by a double movement of majoritarian discursive containment. First, heteronormative logics cast feminists as women desirous of their oppressor (in this case Clinton). These very logics conflate women and feminism, before reducing all women/feminists to the same through the homogenizing trope of sisterhood. In this way, any woman is presupposed to speak in the name of feminism, regardless of her political positioning, on the assumption that her "sex" gives her privileged access to the inside story of the feminist establishment. Any feminist who does not support all women all the time (at stake is what constitutes support) is then held up as a hypocrite and a traitor to the sisterhood. The conflation of the female body and feminism has proven disastrous for feminism, producing a regime in which bodily and linguistic deportment are highly surveilled and disciplined. This hyperpoliticization demands of all feminists/women complete consistency between deportment, speech, politics, and the body. Second, feminism's containment functions through reductive and paramnesiac historical representations. Feminisms and feminists are cast within a narrative of moral purity and consistency between "public" politics and "private" life which prevents feminism from either being grounded within a complex history or from being a contextual practice.

Lynching the President

Just as the fate of feminism has been read onto Clinton's body, so has his relationship with African Americans and civil rights politics. As his fall has been embodied in feminism's own fall, so has he come to embody "blackness." The articulation of hypervirility (he is the Viagra kid) and tropes of blackness are not incidental given the historical depictions of black hypersexuality in US public culture. The predatory hypersexuality of the African American male articulated through rape narratives and the publicly available sexuality of the African American female have never been afforded the zone of privacy attached to the majoritarian body (Davis 1981; Giddings 1984; Collins 1991; Carby 1992; Morrison 1992; Wiegman 1995).

Clinton's relationship to civil rights as well as his relationship to individual African Americans has been called into question. He has been vilified for his friendship with Vernon Jordan, his spiritual relationship with Jesse Jackson, his legal relationship to Deputy White House Council Cheryl Mills, and his trip to Africa (Bates 1998; Jackson 1998; Lavelle 1998; French 1999). Wiegman (1995) argues that depictions of interracial fraternity come to signify the post-civil-rights era. The cultural panic over race and gender transformations can be read through Clinton's "fraternity" with African Americans. *Primary Colors*, which can be read as indicative of the popular discourses on Clinton, calls into question his relationships with African Americans, inscribes Clinton within a discourse of corporeal excess, and situates Clinton within a narrative of betrayal of the political ideals and constituencies of 1960s radicalism (Anonymous 1996).

Not only is Clinton questioned for his "use" of race, African Americans have been questioned for their support of Clinton. The arguments on race in some ways mirror those on feminism, with a critical difference. While it has been argued that race politics have been damaged by African American supporters of Clinton such as John Lewis, civil rights is not compromised as completely as feminism. Instead of being represented as hypocritical, African Americans are merely "dupes." The political platform of raced-based politics is damaged while feminism is simply destroyed. Culpability for the damage to racial politics, however, does not rest with those involved. Instead, Clinton's diabolical use of race through his racially galvanizing rhetoric is indicted.

Toni Morrison (1998), writing in the *New Yorker*, offered what has become a highly controversial reading of black male support for Clinton. She turns not only to the history of racial prejudice and violence but to the inscriptions of Clinton's body to explain why the majority of African American men do not condemn Clinton and in fact understand the dynamics of the scandal. Morrison simply states, "white skin not withstanding, this is our first black president. Blacker than any actual black person who could ever be elected in our children's lifetime" (p. 32). Morrison dislodges the dominant practice of reading race as visible anatomical markers and resituates race within a complex field of racializing cultural practices. It is, in fact, Clinton's embodiment of almost every trope of blackness that leads Morrison to her conclusion: he's the iconic "single-parent household, born poor, working-class, saxophone-playing, McDonald's and junk-food loving boy from Arkansas" (p. 32). Morrison reads the "disappearance" of virtually all of Clinton's African American appointees coupled with the focus on the president's body, his privacy, and his sexuality, as metaphoric seizure and body search. So, rather than support the charge that Clinton "sells out" women and minorities, Morrison is able to rearticulate these discourses as part and parcel of the anti-Clinton/black fervor within US public culture. Black men know what is being said: "No matter how smart you are, how hard you work, how much coin you earn for us, we will put you in your place or put you out of the place you have, albeit with our permission, achieved" (p. 32). The targeting of Clinton and the criminalization of his life not only tramples crucial freedoms, but becomes part of a rhetorical chain proceeding from "targeting" through "lynching," and "crucifiction," which joins Clinton with the history of black oppression in this country. For Morrison, the "*coup d'état*," which is a danger to the nation, is not the president's conduct, but the history of racial violence within US public culture which now adheres to the president's body.

In an interview on election eve (Nov. 1998), Tavis Smiley asks Bill Clinton to discuss this racial inscription by reflecting on the politics of hate that are directed at Hillary Rodham Clinton and himself. Smiley suggests that many African Americans feel that it is not just his support of "African American political issues," but his very comfort with "black folk and other people of color, and women" (p. 2235) that have led to his vilification. In questioning Clinton, Smiley turns to Morrison's *New Yorker* piece and says that "a lot of black folk feel" that Clinton is indeed the first black president (p. 2235). He then asks if the attacks against Clinton have in fact been motivated by Clinton's openness to diversity. Clinton gives a noncommittal response that emphasizes his abiding love of diversity, which was instilled in him by his mother and grandparents.

Even Congressional leaders such as Cynthia McKinney (1998, *Jet*) have argued that, while she deplores Clinton's conduct, opponents of Clinton's policies "are trying to lynch him during a congressional trial" (p. 8). By embedding Clinton into a history of African American torture and spectacle through lynching, McKinney inscribes Clinton as raced. Ida Lewis called forth this corporealized cultural memory even more vividly in an open letter published in *Crisis*, "To those who fail to understand why the majority of African-Americans do not support the removal of President Clinton" (p. 5). Lewis argues that it is precisely Clinton's antiracism and his "American Rainbow Administration" that has brought forth the right-wing attacks against him. In fact, Lewis terms these attacks a "bloodless" *coup d'état* that is televised and "inked in black." Not only does Lewis depict the scandal as part of the strategies of "media lynchings" and "electronic assassination" of the right wing, she depicts the current scandal as the "Niggerization of Bill Clinton" (p. 5). Lewis is quite powerful in her claim that the conservative Right is indeed putting the nation in peril through their attacks: "The result is that they are decapitating the office he holds, and the constituencies whose will he embodies, as surely as the good ole boys of Jasper, Texas, last June reduced decency, humanity, and compassion to bloody clumps of torn flesh littering a country road" (p. 5). Lewis concludes that as far as the Right is concerned, Clinton made the unforgivable error; he betrayed their trust by "giving access to people of color and women based on merit" (p. 5).

Clinton as the "first black president" was not ignored by conservative commentators. Walter Shapiro (1999) leads the virulent attacks against Clinton as both black and female. In the article "Blind Faith," Shapiro finds the mystery to be "the collective decision by the leading lights of American liberalism to serve as Clinton's enablers" (p. 12). Shapiro links Clinton's body with that of "another lustily oversized Democratic president (Grover Cleveland)" in a revealing move before proceeding to an anti-impeachment rally at NYU (p. 13). What Shapiro found most memorable at the rally was "novelist Mary Gordon gushing over Clinton without a tinge of irony: 'Toni Morrison said that he may be our first black president. He may also be our first female president'" (p. 13). Shapiro finds the claim so ludicrous as to be transparent. It is a short slide from collapsing the "self-centered values of the American left" (p. 13) to the expedient politics of race and gender. For Shapiro, as for so many of the conservative pundits, Clinton embodies the post-1960s cultural revolution, the politics of which are discredited through his fall. The attack therefore is not focused on Clinton, but the entire Left.

Jay Nordlinger (1999), writing in the *National Review*, moves from an indictment of Clinton to an indictment of the way white liberals used race during the Clinton scandal. He argues that if you were tempted to forget that the house managers in charge of the case against Clinton were white, Democrats and their "cheerleaders in the media" reminded you every two seconds (p. 20). Nordlinger sarcastically asks, "So, you hadn't realized the Clinton scandal was about race?" (p. 20). Even though to the "tranquil" mind it seems far afield, this scandal is actually about race. For Nordlinger, a complex history of racial discrimination is not the reason. Instead, race has become an issue because, "black political leaders made it that way. So, to an extent did white demagogues on the Democratic left. But Bill Clinton, more than anyone else, is responsible. He plays race as shrewdly as any southern governor" and, contrary to his "healer image," Clinton has aggravated the nation's "racial sores." Nordlinger further argues that when Clinton is in trouble, he reaches for black people "as if for a shield" (pp. 20–2). In effect, Clinton serves as a shield for racist politics. Of course, as I argued earlier it is through attacking Clinton that this rhetorical strategy functions to discredit African Americans. They may not be dangerous, but they are certainly gullible in Nordlinger's reading. Further, African Americans who are either in close proximity with Clinton and/or who have achieved national prominence are simply used. As Nordlinger argues, "for a liberal of his type, there is no higher validation of goodness than the approval of black people. It washes away every complaint" (p. 22). Clinton was able to link his political survival to the cause of black progress. In this manner, the "moral capital of a beloved movement [was] spent on Clinton." Clinton, by this logic, played race in an event that had nothing whatsoever to do with race. Casting himself as the defender of African Americans, Nordlinger concludes with the patronizing assertion that there is enough to hurt African Americans without reading race where it isn't. Whereas feminists are culpable, African Americans are exploitable.

What is most striking in the contrast between depictions of African American Clinton supporters and the detractors is the ability to discuss race as an historically situated and complex category. The history of racism in the United States has figured within the political imaginary of Black America in quite graphic ways. Alexander (1994) argues that "Black bodies in pain have been an American national spectacle for centuries" (p. 78). The archive of collective pain has traveled from public rapes, lynchings, and beatings to the 1990s display of African American bodies on video tapes exhibiting national trauma. The spectacle of the consumption of black bodies for a largely white audience has dominated black experience in the United States (Alexander 1994). Minoritarian historical memory produces a different reading of the Clinton spectacle, one attuned to histories of racialized spectacles for the national body. In this manner, the history of "lynching" as a disciplinary apparatus comes to bear during the virulent attacks and technologies of surveillance cohering around Clinton's body. Lynching is an historically raced practice that punishes transgression and polices borders that have become too permeable. These practices break the "rhetorical homogeneity" of masculinity along racial lines (Wiegman 1995). In this context, the minoritization of Clinton's body can be articulated to African American masculinity.

African American masculinity, with its predatory sexuality, has never been afforded the zone of privacy of the majoritarian body. However, as Wiegman (1995) argues, black masculinity's threat of hypersexuality is nonetheless feminized through lynching and its often attending practices and mythologies of castration – the symbolic removal of black male potential for citizenship. Similarly, the racializing discourses policing Clinton's personal behavior are used as a warrant for Clinton's lack of fitness for citizenship and presidency.

A remarkable feature of the discourse on Clinton as black is Clinton's own metacommentary. In the interview with Smiley, Clinton would only laugh and admit that he loved the depiction of himself as the first black president (1998). However, by late September in a speech before the Congressional Black Caucus, Clinton (1999) more closely addressed the discourses heralding him as such. He recognized that this status had been conferred from both the right and the left, admittedly for different ends. After acknowledging these inscriptions, Clinton shared an anecdote about a black actor who came to the White House to research a role he was about to play as the first black president. Clinton revealed to his audience, "I didn't have the heart to tell him that I already had the job." Clinton does not say, "I am the first black president," but instead "I already have the job." The rhetorical maneuvering, which like Morrison dislodges race from the strictly anatomical, posits that a set of structuring discourses and practices within racist US culture can indeed position a white man into the "job." However, as Wiegman (1995) notes, race signifies differently when worn by certain bodies. Soon after this speech, Clinton resigned from this particular job.

Going Down on Feminism

Along with articulating minoritarian excess onto the body of Clinton, the discourses surrounding the Clinton scandal depict feminism as both part of a complex debate and as the epitome of inappropriate levels of female speech. The mainstream is never so fascinated with feminism as during a sexual harassment case. And no such forum has been available since the Hill/Thomas hearings. Benedict (1998) sees all of this discussion as healthy because it has allowed a multitude of feminists' voices to circulate and hence performatively contest the dominant conception that feminism is monolithic, antimale, and antisex. But as seductive as the idea of a heterogeneous feminist discourse in the public sphere might be, it proves little more than a feminist fantasy. The discourses that circulate as and about feminism through the Clinton scandal demonstrate all too clearly the multiple mechanisms of containment for feminist and female speech in US public culture. This containment calls into questions the very politics of visibility.

Feminists who speak are held responsible for loose morals and a crisis in the body politic, while those who don't are deemed hypocritical and lacking in judgment. Katha Pollitt (1998) argued that immediately following Kathleen Willey's appearance on the TV news program *60 Minutes*, any feminist who didn't join Patricia Ireland in condemning Clinton's alleged conduct received a scarlet H for hypocrisy. Of course, by later that week, any who did was branded "a dupe of the right-wing conspiracy, a Victorian maiden with the vapors, a female chauvinist who thought all women were angels, [or] a sergeant in the sex police" (p. 9). Ironically, conservative women's groups which previously fought sexual harassment legislation were galvanizing arguments based on this legislation and were hence deemed the protectors of morals (Beinart 1998, Rosin 1998, Young 1998). Of course, the ultimate irony may have been President Clinton's own part in promoting laws governing sexual harassment.

Podhoretz (1998) argues that the Clinton scandal has discredited feminism, and to prove this he both deploys the homogenizing trope of sisterhood and constructs a history for feminism. His history begins with the Hill/Thomas hearings. In fact, he claims that feminists' instant support of Anita Hill infected the body politic with the disease of "sexual harassment." He holds Anita Hill singly responsible for transforming sexual harassment from the "arcane lucubrations of marginal academics into the very center of our mainstream culture." Sexual harassment has "metastasized its way through the body politic," with no indication that its growth can be abated (p. 24). Its very codification and enforcement parallels the Salem Witch Trials.

No feminist received more attention than Gloria Steinem. From the initial moments of the controversy, feminists have been indicted and even vilified for their lack of support for the women that have accused Clinton of sexual harassment. Steinem (1998) wrote a rebuttal to charges against feminists by invoking a history of feminism, which included a critique of the standards to which feminists are held. Steinem also defended Clinton by comparing the charges against him to those leveled against Bob Packwood and Clarence Thomas. First, Steinem argued that forcing feminists to take a stand on Clinton exemplifies a double standard. No other Clinton supporters are expected to repudiate him over the Lewinsky scandal except feminists. For instance, no one is questioning environmentalists' support of Clinton, at least not in relation to his sexual practices. This double standard functions by collapsing identity and political practice in a manner that punishes feminists and delineates in advance the political and discursive possibilities that feminists are allowed to occupy.

The other claim Steinem critiques – feminist hypocrisy – compares feminist charges against Thomas and Packwood to the lack of feminist support for accusations against Clinton. In this way, feminists are charged with a "deadly" inconsistency. According to Steinem, Clinton (unlike Thomas or Packwood) adhered to precisely what the feminists had been arguing all these years; "no means no and yes means yes." For Steinem, Willey illustrates no, while Lewinsky illustrates yes (p. 15). Steinem thus preserves the female agency for which feminism has fought. However, virulent attacks took place against Steinem precisely because her position was not intelligible in the discursive terrain of public sphere feminism. My point is not necessarily to support Steinem's position, but rather to examine the discursive logics which disallow and render inarticulate certain forms of feminist speech. The scandal of feminist failure (to be feminist enough or in the right way) engenders conventional responses as any animating event justifies a rehearsal of the usual ambivalence.

Gwedolyn Mink (1998) takes "some feminists" to task for painting "the rest of us in a corner" by arguing that what Clinton is doing is not sexual harassment (p. A17). Mink claims that this argument trivializes women's experiences and distorts the law. While it might be productive for Mink to initiate a discussion concerning sexual harassment, she goes further by participating in the same discursive machinations which have disciplined feminism. She particularly takes Gloria Steinem to task for her *New York Times* piece. Rather than take women's experiences seriously, which is "what feminism is supposed to be about," Steinem is protecting a man and "in effect compromising 20 years of sexual harassment jurisprudence" (p. A17). Again, the speech of one feminist can be seen as compromising a complex historical movement.

The New York Times ran an editorial in response to Steinem's OpEd piece just two days after it was published. According to Faludi (1998), this was the only time in her memory that the *New York Times* ran a piece repudiating an earlier editorial. In "A Feminist Dilemma" the *Times* rebukes Steinem, not for her interpretation of legal doctrine, but for the "danger involved" in her position (1998: A22). As a feminist, Steinem's attention to "technicalities" such as the law are likened to "philosophical sellout" (A22). A movement such as feminism cannot afford such strategic thinking. The editorial warns that allowing the president to "get away with it," raises the possibility that any boss will be "free to behave abominably" (A22). Any erosion of women's hard-won progress in the workplace must be prevented. Abe Rosenthal (1998) goes even further than the *Times* editorial when warning of the dangers for women involved in a position such as Steinem's. Rosenthal claims that, "for a feminist leader, this is an act of grievous intellectual self-mutilation" (A19). In fact, the danger for women from men's sexual advances cannot be underestimated; "we are talking about acts that could terrorize some women, and lead them to horrified flight, even to death."

Faludi (1998) argued that what is most striking in the responses to Steinem is the display of male hysteria. Rather than asking what is the danger to women of a feminist taking a complex position on sexual harassment, Faludi refigures the discussion to interrogate the threat to men. The male writers depict women as "maiden underlings" who are in danger from all men at all times (p. 5). Faludi points out that this is just the flipside of seeing women as available to harass at all times. What these discourses can't allow for are feminists to step outside of the confines of the rigid sex police perpetuating a PC orthodoxy.

When feminists exhibit a more complex understanding of female sexual agency, they not only jeopardize women, they compromise feminism. A recent edition of CNN/Time "NewsStand" asked the question, "has feminism sold out or just grown up?" (1998). This question is not unique; feminism is always being prematurely autopsied in order to understand and render impotent its remains. Not only is the Clinton scandal used as an alibi for the special on feminism, "NewsStand" also refers to the recent issue of *Time* entitled, "Is Feminism Dead?" (1998). *Salon*, the on line magazine, issued a special called "Is *Time* Brain Dead?" which criticized the contemporary and barely pubescent representatives that *Time* chose for feminism (Brown 1998). For instance, Bellafante (1998), writing for *Time*, chose the Spice Girls and Ally McBeal to represent contemporary feminism and measured them against earlier, and what they clearly saw as more serious women's groups and political practices, such as the creation of *Ms.* magazine and Vietnam War protests. "NewsStand" is interesting both for the women called forth to speak on and against feminism as well as for the rhetorical strategies it exemplifies. After displaying pictures of feminist marches and protests from the television archives, CNN/Time trots out a parade of racially homogenous feminist talking heads. Tellingly, even though Steinem had been the most "newsworthy" feminist and did appear on the cover of *Time*, she is absent from the field of feminists interviewed.

Camille Paglia, the first person interviewed, collapses the complexity of feminism through her usual charges against the "feminist establishment," its state of disarray, and its inability to articulate a collective position. Paglia is billed as a dissident feminist, thereby occupying that most respected of positions, the political outsider who is more credible than any other because of her dissident status; she speaks the truth. Next Katie Roiphe, the author of the attack on feminism *The Morning After* (1993), blames feminists for creating hysteria over rape on college campuses. Roiphe makes the outrageous claim that feminism is in a profound identity crisis and has nothing to do with sexuality, for it was a mistake to ever argue that the "personal is political." Feminism is yet again to blame for bringing the personal into public life. Roiphe fails to recognize feminism as a contextual practice situated within historical milieux which might allow for strategic response. Naomi Wolf, alone among the feminists, evades the constraints of the question and sticks to workplace harassment and argues that it affects all in the workplace, rather than indicting women for masculinist behavior. However, this discussion of the workplace can't be heard within the parameters that feminism has been placed.

Patricia Ireland and Betty Friedan are the two remaining feminists on this edition of "NewsStand." Along with defending feminism's ability not to be morally pure in their politics, both women make a dangerous and troubling conflation between heterosexual women's relationships with their husbands

423

and all women's relationships to male politicians and employers; a rhetorical move similar to those employed by conservatives celebrating feminism's collapse. Ireland argues that women's acceptance of their husbands' behavior as the best they can get is the same acceptance that women give to Clinton. It is not so much that women are fans of Clinton, just that they understand their relation to him in a familial logic which tolerates male indiscretion. Friedan, who is cast not only as the matriarch of modern feminism but as a friend of the Clintons, is shown holding the issue of *Time* which proclaims feminism's death. After pointing out the performative contradiction between the question of feminism's death and the interview of prominent feminists, Friedan turns to the wall with photos of herself with various celebrities, most notably with Bill Clinton, and with Hillary Rodham Clinton. Friedan gestures to the photo of Bill Clinton and comments on his sexiness, as if that serves as an explanation for Clinton's power, before further establishing the intimacy of her relations with the first couple. Friedan is at her most disturbing as she moves from the particulars of Clinton's sexual exploits to all workplace harassment. Workplace harassment is reduced to sexual passes made by a male superior to a female subordinate. Just as Clinton's indiscretions should be dealt with by Hillary slapping Bill in the face each morning before breakfast, the female subordinate should slap her male boss when he makes inappropriate sexual advances. Thus, the complexities of the workplace and the political sphere are reduced to the intimate confines of the heterosexual and hence private marriage.

The deployment of Friedan, as an historical figure from the "early days" of feminism, provides a paramnesiac function by reducing the complex history of feminism to the maternal figure of Friedan as she marched for the rights of women in an earlier era, an era when feminism was "clear" about its goals and principles. This form of cultural amnesia has ruptured feminism from its recent past and homogenizes the multiplicity of feminist practices. Even though it has been little more than 25 years since the prominence of second-wave discourses in the public sphere, the discourses produced in this historical milieu are usually seen as distinct from and largely irrelevant to both contemporary feminist theoretical debates and public sphere politics.

Popular feminisms, often under the rubrics of "Third Wave" or "Postfeminism," distance themselves from this recent past through homogenizing and essentializing narratives of the political practices of this earlier generation of women. Popular standards of effectivity or "success" for feminist politics most often look for clear identifiable effects within institutional, legal, and everyday life. Unfortunately, for a politics such as feminism or the radical movement of women in the late twentieth century, change or success cannot so easily be measured. This set of criteria works to either elide women's political practices, dismiss them as ineffectual, or on the other hand, is used to discipline feminists. Popular discourses often blame feminists for any "undesirable" restructuring of women's cultural/economic conditions and everyday lives. Feminism is only given credit for "positive" change in women's lives as the grounds of an argument about the obsolescence of feminism (hence, postfeminism). As Bonnie Dow (1996) has argued, feminism becomes the problem in postfeminism.

Mapping contemporary feminism is a daunting yet necessary task. Since the late 1960s in the United States, there has been something of a boom in feminist discourse and discourses concerning feminism. Not only in the academy but within the popular media as well, feminism is at moments symptomatic of cultural anxieties concerning nation, masculinity, femininity, and boundaries. Neoconservative cultural commentators such as Rush Limbaugh, Christina Hoff Sommers, and Katie Roiphe have captured the ability to tell feminism's public story and history. Serious attention must be paid to the popular stories of feminism, not so much to debunk, but because the lack of feminist history in the public sphere limits the possibilities for contemporary feminist politics. The restricted field of reference for feminism not only limits or contains the possibility for complex feminist discourses by reducing feminism to questions of representation and definitional disputes, it has produced a pluralism which allows any discourse to circulate as feminist within the political.

The "identity crisis" or amnesia of contemporary feminism, coupled with the lack of context and history for feminist practices, must be recognized as precisely the crisis which, as a matter of displacement, has been articulated to a new conservatism. Without adroit reading practices the "moments of juxtaposition, flirtatious encounter, or even embrace" between these discourses will appear unintelligible (Morris 1984: 55). This caution is particularly pertinent at a time when feminism is on trial over its refusal to take a position on the scandals surrounding Clinton's sexual activities. Being able to tell which positions belong to the "conservatives" or the "liberals" and which, if any, further the interest of women is an unintelligible task. It is for this reason that an insistence on the necessity of reading practices which refuse the tried route is crucial for developing histories of feminism which can interrupt contemporary narratives and politics that discipline feminism and strain women's everyday lives.

Conclusion

Expanding the field of reference for contemporary minoritarian politics is crucial. In the case of feminism expanding the field of reference requires the possibility of speech which does not fall in line with dominant conceptions of feminism's perceived dogmas to register as other than compromise, betrayal, and hypocrisy. Internal inconsistency within feminism must not only be intelligible, but a hallmark of the multiplicity of feminists and feminisms. Within the discursive terrain of the scandal it seems that no matter how sophisticated, no matter how articulate, African Americans are condemned to the position of "dupes" whenever race is a factor. Ultimately, unless race is unproblematically "visible," it cannot be argued. As demonstrated throughout the discourses of the

Clinton/Lewinsky scandal, post-1960s minoritarian politics converge in ways which shield and reconstitute majoritarian masculinity.

The necessity of radical contextualization turns on the ephemerality of the object of cultural studies (Grossberg 1992, Morris 1998). This contextualization for Morris (1998) not only prolongs the life of the ephemeral, but as it saturates "with detail an articulated place and point in time, a critical reading can extract from its objects a parable of practice that converts them into *models* with a past and a potential for reuse, thus aspiring to invest them with a future" (p. 3). The creation of context becomes both the method and object of cultural studies research. As such, the move to examine the sites, such as scandal where the political and cultural converge in revealing and important ways, is crucial to further the project of Cultural Studies. The job for Cultural Studies, feminism, and leftist politics more generally is to capture the representational power, or to at least strategize to do so. What is at stake is the ability to foster contextuality, internal inconsistency and the ability to tell histories that do not conform to dogmas and pieties; the ability to be minor.

Ultimately, the lesson of this chapter is not about Clinton and Lewinsky, but about black men and feminism. They are the subjects who "fell" and paid the price for the minoritization of the national body. It wasn't and never could be a story of the fall of Clinton.

Notes

For giving me the opportunity to think about the fate of feminism in the Clinton/Lewinsky scandal in a forum piece for *Critical Studies in Mass Communication* (Deem 1999), I want to thank Bonnie Dow. I am grateful for insightful readings offered by Christopher Kamrath, Toby Miller, Lauren Berlant, Kyra Pearson, Max Thomas, and Mary Coffey. Further, I thank the members of the English Department Faculty Colloquium and the Project on the Rhetoric of Inquiry at the University of Iowa for their responses to an earlier version of this chapter. Valuable research assistance was provided by Kathryn Cady and Jessica James.

References

(1998). A feminist dilemma. *The New York Times*, March 24, A22.

(1998). Larry Flynt and *Hustler* magazine announce a cash offer of up to $1,000,000. 8 Oct. online, http://www.hustler.com/preview/million.html.

(1998). Larry Flynt offers Ken Starr position at *Hustler*. Reprinted from *LA Weekly*, Sept. 18–24, online, http://www.hustler.com/preview/starrjob.html.

(1998). McKinney blasts white Democrat for comments about black support of President Clinton. *Jet*, Oct. 26, 8.

(1998). *Suck. com.* Oct. 9, online, http://suck.com/daily/98/10/09/daily.html.

Alexander, E. (1994). "Can you be black and look at this?": reading the Rodney King video(s). *Public Culture* 7: 77–94.

Anonymous (1996). *Primary Colors: A Novel of Politics*. New York: Warner Books, Inc.

Bates, B. L. (1998). Clinton's African triumph. *Ebony*, June: 54–60.

Barringer, F. (1998). Many editors decide to publish details of the report. *The New York Times*, Sept. 13, 27.

Beinart, P. (1998). Hypocritics. *The New Republic*, March 30, 9–10.

Beinart, P. (1999). Private matters. *The New Republic*, Feb. 15, 21–5.

Bellafante, G. (1998). Feminism: it's all about me. *Time*, June 29, 54–60.

Benedict, H. (1998). Fear of feminism. *The Nation*, May 11, 10.

Berke, R. (1998). Playing it safe, the Republicans try silence. *The New York Times*, Sept. 13, 1.

Berlant, L. (1988). The female complaint. *Social Text*, Fall: 237–57.

Berlant, L. (1997). *The Queen of America goes to Washington City: Essays on Sex and Citizenship*. Durham: Duke University Press.

Berube, M. (1994). *Public Access: Literary Theory and American Cultural Politics*. New York: Verso.

Blount, M. and Cunningham, G. P. (eds.) (1996). *Representing Black Men*. New York: Routledge.

Borger, G. (1998a). Sisters, we have a problem. *US News and World Report*, May 11, 33.

Borger, G. (1998b). Her Bill and their enemies. *US News and World Report*, Aug. 17–24, 26.

Brookhiser, R. (1998). Clinton and Nixon. *National Review*, Feb. 23, 41–3.

Brookhiser, R. (1999). Daddy dearest. *National Review*, Feb. 22, 16–17.

Brown, J. (1998). Is *Time* brain dead? *Salon*, June 25, online, http://www.salon.com.

Brown, W. (1995). *States of Injury: Power and Freedom in Late Modernity*. Princeton: Princeton University Press.

Campbell, K. K. (1998). Hating Hillary. *Rhetoric and Public Affairs* 1: 1–25.

Carby, H. V. (1992). Policing the black woman's body in an urban context. *Critical Inquiry* (Summer): 738–55.

Clemetson, L. and Wingert, P. (1998). Clinton on the couch. *Newsweek*, Sept. 28, 46.

Clinton, B. (1999). Speech, Congressional Black Caucus Awards Dinner, Sept. 18.

CNN/Time. (1998). NewsStand. Sept. 20.

Collins, P. H. (1991). *Black Feminist Thought*. New York: Routledge.

Davis, A. Y. (1981). *Women, Race and Class*. New York: Vintage Books.

Deem, M. (1996). From Bobbitt to SCUM: re-memberment, scatological rhetorics, and feminist strategies in the contemporary United States. *Public Culture* 8: 511–37.

Deem, M. (1999). Scandal, heteronormative culture, and the disciplining of feminism. *Critical Studies in Mass Communication* 46: 83–93.

de Lauretis, T. (1987). *Technologies of Gender: Essays on Theory, Film, and Fiction*. Bloomington: Indiana University Press.

Deleuze, G. and Guattari, F. (1987). *A Thousand Plateaus: Capitalism and Schizophrenia*. Minneapolis: University of Minnesota Press.

Denby, D. (1996). *Great Books*. New York: Simon and Schuster.

Dooling, R. (1998). The end of harassment. *National Review*, May 4, 26–7.

Dow, B. (1996). *Prime Time Feminism: Television, Media Culture, and the Women's Movement since 1970*. Philadelphia: University of Pennsylvania Press.

Dowd, M. (1998). Father's little helper. *The New York Times*, April 26, sec. 4, 15.

Echols, A. (1989). *Daring to be Bad: Radical Feminism in America 1967–1975*. Minneapolis: University of Minnesota Press.

Faludi, S. (1998). Sex and the *Times*. *The Nation*, April 20, 5–6.

Feirstein, B. and Peretz, E. (1998). A tale of two scandals. *Vanity Fair*, May, 170 .

Flynt, L. (1998). Letter to Kenneth Starr. Oct. 8, online, http://www.hustler.com/preview/starrjob.html.

Franks, L. (1999). The intimate Hillary. *Talk*, Sept., 166–74 .

French, M. A. (1999). Cheryl Mills. *Essence*, May, 78.

Giddings, P. (1984). *When and Where I Enter: The Impact of Black Women on Race and Sex in America*. New York: Bantam Books.

Goldstein, R. (1998). The Zippergate gap. *Ms.*, May/June, 66–7.

Grann, David. (1998). Saint Lewis. *The New Republic*, Oct. 5, 12–14.

Grossberg, L. (1992). *We Gotta Get Out of This Place: Popular Conservatism and Postmodern Culture*. New York: Routledge.

Gubar, S. (2000). *Critical Condition: Feminism at the Turn of the Century*. New York: Columbia University Press.

Guccione, B. (1998). What's being said about Viagra by the famous . . . and the not so famous. *Time*, May 4, 56–7.

Hall, S. (1981). Notes on deconstructing "The Popular." In R. Samuels (ed.), *People's History and Socialist Theory*. Boston: Routledge and Kegan Paul.

Handy, B. (1998). Oh, behave! *Time*, Feb. 2, 55.

Hitchens, C. (1998). Viagra Falls. *The Nation*, May 25, 8.

Horowitz, D. (1998). We believe you, scumbag. *Salon*, Nov. 11, online, http://www.salon1999.com/col/horo/1998/01/26horo.html.

Jackson, J. (1998). Keeping faith in a storm. *Newsweek*, Aug. 31, 43.

Lavelle, M. (1998). A race factor? *US News and World Report*, July 6, 22–8.

Lears, J. (1998). Comments and opinions: the president and the prosecutor. *Dissent*, Spring, 5–6.

Levitt, L. (1973). She: the awesome power of Gloria Steinem. *Esquire*, Oct., 87–9 .

Lewis, I. E. (1998). Bill Clinton as honorary black. *Crisis*, Sept./Oct., 5.

Miller, T. (1998). *Technologies of Truth: Cultural Citizenship and the Popular Media*. Minneapolis: University of Minnesota Press.

Mink, G. (1998). Misreading sexual harassment law. *The New York Times*, March 30, A17.

Mitchell, A. (1996). Clinton signs bill denying gay couples US benefits. *The New York Times*, Sept. 21, 8.

Morris, M. (1988). *The Pirate's Fiancee: Feminism, Reading Postmodernism*. London: Verso.

Morris, M. (1990). Banality in cultural studies. In P. Mellencamp (ed.), *Logics of Television*. Bloomington: Indiana University Press.

Morris, M. (1994). "Too soon, too late": reading Claire Johnston, 1970–1981. In C. Morrie (ed.), *Dissonance: Feminism and the Arts, 1970–1990*. St. Leonard's, New South Wales: Allen and Unwin.

Morris, M. (1998). *Too Soon Too Late: History in Popular Culture*. Bloomington: Indiana University Press.

Morrison, T. (ed.) (1992). *Race-ing Justice, En-gendering Power: Essays on Anita Hill, Clarence Thomas, and the Construction of Social Reality*. New York: Pantheon Books.

Morrison, T. (1998). Talk of the town. *The New Yorker*, Oct. 5, 31–2.

Nordlinger, J. (1999). The race ace. *National Review*, March 8, 20–4.

O'Beirne, K. (1998a). Year of the intern. *National Review*, Feb. 23, 26.

O'Beirne, K. (1998b). Paula Jones, for the defense. *National Review*, April 20, 28.

Podhoretz, N. (1991). Rape in feminist eyes. *Commentary*, Oct., 29–35.

Podhoretz, N. (1998). "Sexgate," the sisterhood, and Mr. Bumble. *Commentary*, June, 23–36.

Pollitt, K. (1998a). Did someone say "hypocrites?" *The Nation*, April 13, 9.

Pollitt, K. (1998b). September thong. *The Nation*, Oct. 5, 10.

Ponnuru, R. (1999). Sexual hangup. *National Review*, Feb. 8, 42–4.

Purdum, T. S. (1996). Gay rights groups attack Clinton on midnight signing. *The New York Times*, Sept. 22, sec. 1, 22.

Rich, F. (1998). The Viagra kid. *The New York Times*, April 4, A13.

Rich, F. (1999). What Tony Soprano could teach Bill Clinton. *The New York Times*, Aug. 14, A27.

Roiphe, K. (1993). *The Morning After: Sex, Fear, and Feminism on Campus*. Boston: Little, Brown.

Rosen, J. (1998). Jurisprurience. *The New Yorker*, Sept. 28, 34–8.

Rosenthal, A. M. (1998). Murdered in the park. *The New York Times*, March 27, A19.

Rosin, H. (1997). Radical chicks. *The New Republic*, Oct. 13, 16–18.

Rosin, H. (1998a). NOW gets the Willeys. *New York*, March 30, 18–19.

Rosin, H. (1998b). People of gender. *The New Republic*, May 25, 15–17.

Sanchez-Eppler, K. (1992). Bodily bonds: the intersecting rhetorics of feminism and abolition." In S. Samuels (ed.), *The Culture of Sentiment: Race, Gender, and Sentimentality in 19th Century America*. New York: Oxford University Press.

Shalit, W. (1997). Daughters of the (sexual) revolution. *Commentary*, Dec., 42–5.

Shapiro, W. (1999). Blind faith. *The New Republic*, Feb. 1, 12–13.

Slater, J. (1998). Talk of the town. *The New Yorker*, Oct. 5, 33.

Smiley, T. (1998). Interview with Tavis Smiley of Black Entertainment Television. *Weekly Compilation of Presidential Documents*, Nov. 2, 2232–8.

Stacey, J. (1983). The new conservative feminism. *Feminist Studies* 9 (Fall): 559–83.

Steinem, G. (1998). Feminists and the Clinton question. *The New York Times*, March 22, 15.

Steinem, G. (1998). Yes means yes, no means no: why sex scandals don't mean harassment. *Ms.*, May/June, 62–3.

Talbot, M. (1998). Wife story. *The New Republic*, Feb. 16, 19–20.

Taylor, S. (1998). National journal. *MSNBC*, Aug. 2.

Warner, M. (1993). The mass public and the mass subject. In B. Robbins (ed.), *The Phantom Public Sphere*. Minneapolis: University of Minnesota Press.

Wiegman, R. (1995). *American Anatomies: Theorizing Race and Gender*. Durham: Duke University Press.

Young, C. (1998). Harassment hypocrites. *National Review*, Nov. 9, 24–8.

Chapter 25

Rap and Feng Shui: On Ass Politics, Cultural Studies, and the Timbaland Sound

Jason King

? (body and soul – a beginning . . .

Buttocks date from remotest antiquity . . . They appeared when men conceived the idea of standing up on their hind legs and remaining there – a crucial moment in our evolution since the buttock muscles then underwent considerable development . . . At the same time their hands were freed and the engagement of the skull on the spinal column was modified, which allowed the brain to develop. Let us remember this interesting idea: man's buttocks were possibly, in some way, responsible for the early emergence of his brain.

Jean-Luc Hennig

the starting point for this essay is the black ass. (buttocks, behind, rump, arse, derriere – what you will)
like my mother would tell me – *get your black ass in here*!
The vulgar ass, the sanctified ass. The black ass – whipped, chained, beaten, punished, set free. territorialized, stolen, sexualized, exercised. the ass – a marker of racial identity, a stereotype, property, possession. pleasure/terror. liberation/ entrapment.[1]
the ass – entrance, exit. revolving door. hottentot venus. abner louima. jiggly, scrawny. protrusion/orifice.[2] penetrable/impenetrable. masculine/feminine. waste, shit, excess. the sublime, beautiful. round, circular, (w)hole. The ass (w)hole) – wholeness, hol(e)y-ness. the seat of the soul. the funky black ass.[3] the black ass (is a) (as a) drum.

The ass is a highly contested and deeply ambivalent site/sight . . . It may be a nexus, even, for the unfolding of contemporary culture and politics. It becomes useful to think about the ass in terms of metaphor – the ass, and the asshole, as the "dirty" (open) secret, the entrance and the exit, the back door of cultural and sexual politics. The ass as a site (sight) of accrued ambivalence offers us the chance to dance out of the constrictions of binaries like ugly–beauty and static–kinetic toward a politics of hybridity and (w)holeness[4] . . .

If we attend to the (w)hole message, a discourse on the ass provides a means for monitoring the flow of spirit in the space–time of late modernity. The ass is an integral phenomenon to contemporary black dance-oriented music, especially at that crossroads where, at any given moment, funk, disco, boogie, jazz, classical, R&B, and various forms of electronica might be enveloped under the banner of rap. We might refer to this hybrid sound in terms of its corporeal effect: "ass music."[5]

This chapter zeroes in on the compositional practice of one of the hottest contemporary rap producers, Timbaland. His bold percussive ventures in popularizing "ass music" on the landscape of contemporary urban radio have set new standards for artistic achievement in black popular culture as a (w)hole. When considered in tandem with his videos and celebrity discourse, Timbaland's synthesized and excessively groovy songs provide a forum in which we might imagine how the pursuit of metaphysical freedom has evolved in the age of techno-modernity.

Timbaland's adventures in the programing of ass music invite discussions of *breath*, *space*, and *flow*, and, as such, find companionship in Feng Shui, the Chinese cultural practice of siting, placement, and architectural composition. Perhaps the only form of spiritual architectural practice that has become popularized in Western cosmopolitan circles, contemporary Feng Shui provides a model for (re) thinking the relation between the spatial-physical environment and the body/soul. Unlike other forms of popular urban design, Feng Shui is chiefly interested in the spiritual valence of how place and space *feels*.

Rap music and contemporary Westernized Feng Shui may be complementary diasporized cultural practices. In rap, the reconstructed and phenomenal hip hop is cultivated through the drum machine: it jumps up to hit the body at the level of the ass in order to impact the soul. In Feng Shui, manipulation of the built environment which surrounds and envelops the body brings good ch'i.

In both rap and Feng Shui, the soul – the life source – maintains a direct and immediate relationship to the external environment and its physical culture. Rap and Feng Shui might therefore be considered *technologies of soul*: through these practices, the soul might come to be cultivated and holistically treated by way of the vibrational lightwaves of the chakras.

Rap and Feng Shui come together at the charged representational form of the music video. Here the performance of the black "good life" – that modern lifestyle in which bodily "flow" is imagined to be optimized – is announced. In these texts, the power of ass music to cultivate ch'i is homologized with the beautiful design of the physical spaces in which the black celebrity's cultivation of spirit is made possible. The style in motion of these videos cross-references the musical architecture, composed around the fantastic beat, which in turn wants to jump up and hit the body at the level of the ass in order to inspire the soul.

With respect to the experimental suggestions for sonic-funky revolution put forth by Timbaland, the ass becomes not only a way to think more deeply about the place of soul in cultural studies, but it becomes the way we might imagine the body itself to think . . .

The Timbaland Sound

What the fuck was [Timbaland's] "Are You That Somebody?" doing in the [pop] top 10? It was the most aggressively experimental hit single since, I don't know, "I Am the Walrus." The only way Timbaland could top it would be to cover John Cage's "433" on a drum machine.

David Krasnow, in a letter to *The Village Voice*

This entire country is completely full of shit and always has been – from the Declaration of Independence to the Constitution and the Star Spangled Banner, it's still nothing more than one steaming pile of red, white and blue All American bullshit. Because think of how we started. Think of that. This country was founded by a group of slave owners who told us all men are created equal. Oh yeah, all men – except for Indians, niggers and women, right?

George Carlin

Born Tim Mosley, Timbaland appeared in the latter half of the 1990s as a rap and R&B producer on his label Blackground Enterprises (Atlantic Records). The visionary twentysomething-year-old songwriter and engineer has served behind a stable of successful artists from Aaliyah ("One in a Million"); SWV ("Can We"); Ginuwine ("Pony," "What's So Different"); to his co-writing partner Missy "Misdemeanor" Elliot ("The Rain (Supa Dupa Fly)" and "She's a Bitch").

In early 1997, Timbaland emerged from behind the producer's velvet curtain to launch his own project as a rapper. "Welcome to Our World" features Timbaland alongside his other partner-in-rhyme Magoo, while the 1998 release "Tim's Bio: Life From 'Da Basement" features the producer/rapper in his first solo effort, supported by artists from Kelly Price to Jay-Z to Nas. Voted by *Rolling Stone* as 1998's Producer of the Year, Timbaland also produced and performed on the soundtrack to the film *Dr. Doolittle* starring Eddie Murphy, and he has remixed songs for a number of successful groups including the UK's All Saints.

What's most striking about Timbaland's work is the dense, polyrhythmic layering of his drum track.[6] Since the drum has always been the central feature of African and Afro-Diasporic music and dance (Chernoff 1979), part of Timbaland's contribution has been to test the relationship of this traditional form of communication to modern musical technologies. Urban music producers have been playing with the sonic valence of percussion with an increased fervor since the industrialization of synthesizer equipment and drum machines in the 1970s. How the beat might not only bang against the eardrum, but seductively take hold of the body through sonic inspiration in various spaces of/for listening – the club, the jeep, the home – has become a major issue in black popular compositional practices.

Since his debut on the popular music scene in 1997, Timbaland's peculiar flair for percussive deep pocket funk has reconstructed and monopolized the sound of black urban radio.[7] The sound he introduced to radio has cut and augmented black popular music in such a way that the bridge back is no longer traversable. Because lesser producers have rushed to copycat the magic of his sound, Timbaland has, for some, become the latest scapegoat for the supposed death of soul in funk music.

Urban music (which is a marketing term to describe a hybrid sound that incorporates rap and R&B among other styles) has flattened itself out horizontally since the early 1990s. Simple, lock-pattern grooves have taken precedence over dramatic chord changes. Except for the mainstream alternative R&B scene, live instrumentation has been somewhat devalued in urban music. These changes have been mobilized as evidence for the shrinking or reduction of the musicality if not the soul of the urban sound. The reason for these changes has something to do with the lack of traditional musical training available to many of the hot contemporary young urban music producers.[8]

At the same time, this new horizontalism has placed a greater emphasis on formal qualities of texture and density, the feeling of the music. In a different context, Steven Feld has referred to processing multidimensionality in sound as "textural denisification" (1988: 82). The rich acoustic guitar work on Usher's "You Make Me Wanna," Blaque's "808," and TLC's "No Scrubs" – all songs which borrow heavily from the trademark Timbaland sound – is but one demonstration of this tactile, expanding dimensionality of sound. This is a vertical, layered sound you can really *feel*.

Indeed, Timbaland has played with the spatiotemporal properties of urban music in unique ways that deserve close scrutiny. Unlike many peer producers, Timbaland doesn't just use machinery to approximate live instrumentation. Rather, he's equally prone to using computerized instrumentation that sounds deliberately robotic, machinistic. As a consequence, his body of work is often described in terms of space–time metaphors, like "space age funk" and "futuristic funk." In a recent article, a journalist calls the Timbaland sound "back to the future" music (Rogers 1997: 23), while Sasha Frere-Jones deems his sound "ancient modernism." Both these descriptions become useful for thinking about Timbaland's contribution as a warped and possibly radical reconception-reconstruction of linear time and frontier space logic.

Echoing some of the work of Mantronix and C&C Music Factory's David Cole and their respective adventures in percussion, the Timbaland sound offers up a spare, arid landscape highlighted by the drum track, a dark, funky thumping bass and electronic keyboards. Because keyboards are traditionally a form of percussion, his music is very much focused around the power of the beat (always in relation to groove). His collection of beats and grooves is staccato, hypertense, and caffeinated.

Music critic Barry Walters has previously described Timbaland's drum orchestrations in the following manner: "brittle, nervous, simultaneously small and loud, as if someone had held a mike to a ticking clock prone to sudden spasms of syncopation. His emphatically mechanical drum programming recalls the rattle of Miami bass, but downplays the jeep-bumping boom, and often suggests an American cousin of English drum 'n' bass" (1997). The particularly attentive might also notice flavors of jungle, East Coast hip hop, disco, reggae, soca, calypso, alternative rock, and electronica as also overt influences in the Timbaland sound.

Alongside this vista of global influences, Southern-bred Timbaland produces a sound that necessarily emerges in the localized setting of the American South. Along with his peer performers and producers in rap from Jermaine Dupri to OutKast and Goodie Mob (all from Atlanta), to New Orleans' Master P and his No Limit crew, Timbaland has ushered in the so-called "Dirty South" beat to late 1990s black urban radio. Dupri has previously defined this Dirty South beat in relation to (auto)mobility: it is essentially "music for the broken cars . . . like an Impala that ain't really hooked up. Real heavy on the bass. A lot of live keyboards. And we ain't scared of the 808 [drum machine] down here. Niggas get in that car and pound somethin' all the way to the strip club." The writer of the article in which Dupri's quote appears follows suit in his description: "when those twanged out rappers of the South Coast get goin', you feel that laid-back bass in your *rump*" (Conroy et al., my italics).

The 1990s emergence of the Dirty South beat, this funky beat that engages and animates the rump, is reflective of the institutionalization of the South as a discrete production center for urban music. What is precisely "dirty" about the beat is that it's sullied with the turbulent racial-political history of American South.[9] The beat contains that violent and bloody history, it *illuminates* it – even if it cannot signify or determine it as such.

If, as George Carlin muses, the founding American narrative of exclusion turns the nation into a steaming pile of shit, then the beat, produced in the American South, can only be shitty. The dirty ass, really at the center of bodily geography but often imagined to be at the bottom or south slope, naturally produces a dirty, smelly beat.[10]

Dirt is nothing more than loose matter, substance which is always already out of place, matter which must be *moved* (out of sight!). Dirt becomes an illuminating metaphor not only for the historical content of this Southern beat that is spun into motion, but for the kinetic-corporeal impulse at the heart of this new, reconstructed beat. This beat wants to move the body, and the body must learn to (re)move to the beat.

Thinking the Body

How can the Negro Past be used?
James Baldwin

The kinetic, tactile body is more than a problem for cultural studies. This body is (like) the question-mark that punctuates and marks the limit of cultural studies. And, in its ambivalence, its refusal to close, and its desire to mark a continual beginning, the sensate body in motion performs the very accretion and mobilization of the cultural studies project that it questions.

In general, cultural scholars have tended to skirt rather than confront the "phenomenal" difficulty of reading and writing the tactile body in performance.[11] Perhaps with the exception of progressive dance scholars and some cultural geographers, few connections have been made between the body in motion and forms of sociopolitical mobilization. Even fewer connections are made between the tactile body and its phenomenal faculties in cognition. The question becomes not only whether we could (re) think the body, but whether we could think *through* the body[12] . . .

Cultural studies must first be credited with the strides it continues to make in opening up space to consider the political agency of the body. Two of the more important texts of British (sub) cultural studies from the 1970s, the edited volume *Resistance Through Rituals* (Hall and Jefferson) and Dick Hebdige's *Subculture: The Meaning of Style*, claim this micropolitics of the body that is reflected ambivalently through style. Cultural studies must also be recognized for its power to envision the body as a social construct, to address the mapping of the social and political onto the contours of the body over time. In this way, cultural studies continues to derail the physical sciences' monopoly of the *truth* of the body and the way the sciences render the body (as if) knowable in its totality through the rationality of *proof*.

But the epistemological anchor of cultural studies – in spite/despite/perhaps because of its internal differentiation as a discipline – remains rooted in semiotic theory. In its exclusive emphasis on the determinability of acts and interpretations and the causality of referential chains, semiotic theory has traditionally made it difficult to claim the representational abstractions engendered by the body in motion, labor, and performance.[13] The motion of body, its tactile life in performance and labor, is frequently rendered inconsequential in the writing of culture.

Feeling, emotion, and sensate experience refer to the phenomenality of the living body. Related metaphysical terms like soul, spirit, and aura exceed both the (il) logic of determination and critical reading/writing practices based in self-referential linguistic systems (see Jackson 1998; Moten 1994). The kinetic body reconstructs the very grammar of legibility (if not the logic of grammar itself).

435

The body in motion/performance/labor is the question-mark for cultural studies since it cannot be determinative except that it might determine its own indeterminability. It also calls into question the tendency to theorize the "flow" of history in disregard for the agential bodies which mobilize that same history (Martin 1998).

In its attention to "liveness," the newer interdiscplinary field of performance studies might amend these problems of the cultural studies approach to the body. Yet institutionally, performance studies becomes disempowered in its longing to focus exclusively on speech acts. This focus, in its own desire to reduce the phonic substance, functions to demobilize and desensualize the body before it can be thought, read, or written (Jackson 1998). Especially where musical performance is concerned, the Saussurean reduction of the phonic substance is also an immobilization if we remember that sound moves not only in time but in space.

This cryogenically frozen body, whose truth in abstraction is obscured in favor of its potential to signify, also freezes the productive study of culture and performance. In any system that prizes determinate meaning in the effort to eclipse the abstracted content of the illumination, it becomes difficult to assess the sensual impact of (industrial) modernization on corporeity, and near impossible to claim the sensual agency of the body on the forward momentum of modernization itself. In such a closed system, the sensual body is always rendered primitive and agentially weak.[14]

If the body is the question-mark of cultural studies, perhaps blackness is the question-mark of scholarship on the body.[15] Soul is institutionalized as black vernacular practice. The phenomenon of soul, that substance which gives life to the body, punctuates and simultaneously mobilizes the cultural studies project.[16] As that which always already bears a relation to the corporeal, soul is irreducible to the market, even though it can quite easily be accommodated within the marketplace and travel as a fetish within its circuitous routes. In part because of traditional African cosmologies that predate slavery, as well as the brutal conditions of the middle passage, and the long, arduous, and religiously inflected relationship of unfree blacks to property and material, the metaphysical remains the accursed blessing of black performance traditions.

So the question-mark for cultural studies that is *body and soul* must in some way go through blackness, not around, above, below, or on top of it, but *through* it. It must particularly go through black music, a massive global resource where soul is more actively cultivated than anywhere else and where the spirit is most frequently called down. Cultural studies must also recognize, rather than annul, the marriage between diasporized black musical forms and co-constitutive vernacular dance moves. Screams, shouts, jerks, and twists are coded illuminations, willfully indeterminate, rich in content, the very hallmarks of a sensual avant-garde black modernity, erotic specters of a critical, *counter* public culture.

Black bodies in motion further trouble the cultural studies distinction between labor and leisure (work and pleasure) toward a more generative notion of bodywork (see Joseph 2000). Bodywork disrupts the related distinction between labor and rationality, where the white body comes to symbolize rationality while the black body exists to perform the physical labor which that abstracted rationality produces and requires manifest. This racialized divide, which is also a conflation of the human laborer with property, is tragically transconstituted in terms of gender. It is a divide that can only be enacted through terror and spectacle, in the space where these terms come to pass (Hartman 1997).

What remains to be learned from the black body, treated as primitive and dangerous, eliminated, exiled, bloodied, brutalized, exoticized; and yet in its motion/labor/performance offers us not only new claims to history but new ways to produce history, and to imagine – above and beyond and through representation and identification – the vision of a social totality emancipated from mental slavery? To respond to James Baldwin's query, the Negro past, which is always and only embodied, can not only be used, it can be performed and thus mobilized.[17] The black body thus remains a question-mark in and of itself, a threat to the foundations of Western philosophy because it has already witnessed and puts into performative motion a practice of freedom that it has not yet been officially granted and from which it has been historically excluded . . .

Black Ass Politics

Sasha Frere-Jones' review of Timbaland's "Welcome to Our World" album brings us to the heart of these questions of metaphysics and the body. Describing the hit first single, "Up Jumps da Boogie," she says,

> Ask my downstairs neighbor about this song. Every hour I get a *limbic urge* to play it very loud and do the Cabbage Patch or Elastic Cornflake (write for details) . . . when the chorus drop in, it sounds like Labelle, a Masai drum circle, and a Survival Research Laboratories contraption all jamming together. *This orgasmic moment typifies the beauty of a very movement-oriented party album*, which is not a song cycle, threat, or deeply felt impression of America: *it's high powered ass music*. And if you're asking for anything more from today's pop music, you're going to get lonely. (my italics, 1997)

Frere-Jones's hourly desire to hear Timbaland's song played at a loud volume is limbic, or corporealized. As captivating as a drug habit or masturbatory addiction, the dangerous and infectious rhythm has seduced her. It comes to her hourly: Timbaland's scientific-erotic funk is on time and in time and out of time and past time.[18]

All at once, the music allows Frere-Jones to recall transtemporalized sounds: Labelle (a black female R&B vocal trio who by 1975 found themselves clothed in futuristic styles); traditional African ritual (Masai drum circle), and American pseudo-scientific performance art (Survival Research Laboratories). The orgasmic coming together of these elements toward the (w)hole produces, at last, a "very movement-oriented party album" which is also beautiful, a word not often applied to rap aesthetics. Frere-Jones has no problem reconciling the fact that she has described the music in relation to the "ass" – so often conceived as the site of shameful vulgarity which cannot be spoken about in public places – and also as a work of beauty. I would argue that the music itself provides an impetus for amending this traditional ugly–beauty binary toward a vision of (w)hole-ness.

Although the Timbaland sound can be enjoyed individually or communally, in private space or in public space or both, the thread between the public and private is the kinetic impetus. The Timbaland sound is movement oriented, it "inspires" you to move.[19] In this sense his trademark sound is holistic (especially in relation to the relationship of the sum and parts to which holism – or (w)holism, if you will – refers) and something like a cure.[20] As George Clinton has proclaimed, "funk can not only move, it can re-move, you dig?"

The danger of the beat is wrapped up not only in its ability to pollute, to contaminate, and seduce others into its ensemble, but to heal through its insistence on rhythm as a cure for various ills (see Browning 1998). You don't play the beat so much as the beat plays you. Timbaland's rapid takeover of the sound of urban popular radio, virus-like in speed and effect, might be related to the power of his trademark sound to offer its listeners (w)holistic bodywork, an aural (rather than hands on) manipulation of the physical body that inspires the soul.

I want to break, however, with Frere-Jones' dismissal of the threatening and impressionistic elements contained in Timbaland's work. I would challenge her argument that Timbaland's dissident sound is not a "deeply felt impression of America" since it does lay out an unequivocal politics of (w)holeness in motion that emerges locally from the dirty American South (but exceeds that locale in its ability to circulate globally). Her refusal to feel the danger of the music must suppress her own erotic identificatory relation to the sound, the conscious trance of distracted contemplation her body succumbs to every hour in its desire to consume the song.

Cribbed from the well-known hook of the first mainstream rap hit "Rappers' Delight," the title of "Up Jumps da Boogie" viscerally describes the kinetic power of the beat in its groove. (The orgasmic chant in the song fully describes the motion of the beat: "up jumps da boogie, boogie jumps me, up jumps da boogie, boogie jumps me.") The sound spontaneously compels Frere-Jones to rehearse perennial black vernacular dance styles like the Elastic Cornflake and the Cabbage Patch. The erotic boogie beat jumps up and hits her body at the level of the ass. Hence she calls the Timbaland sound "high powered ass music."

If, as Baraka reminds us, the word "fuck" is loosely translated as "hit," then the power of the beat to jump up and hit the body at the level of the ass could be envisioned as a kind of sonic sodomy. If we can also imagine the body to think, then we could imagine the power of the beat as a kind of *mindfuck* – a kind of erotic cognitive anarchy.

Timbaland's compositional impulses help bring together the ass with the sound which is always already corporeally designed to get the ass in motion. He's prone to using unusual tempos and time signatures that seductively inspire the body into rethinking how it must move (or re-move) to stay on time. "One in a Million," the single Timbaland co-wrote and produced for Aaliyah, crawls along at a snail's pace only to turbo boost into double-time during the bridge. Unlike traditional dance-oriented music that plays around 120 beats per minute or more, Timbaland's most successful tunes flow at about 60 beats per minute. To count them in double time would be to falsely accentuate their tempos. At the same time, he's prone to doubling the speed of his hi-hats and related background percussion. His music, as a result, feels extremely fast and achingly slow at the same time.

This sound requires and produces new listening and movement skills, new ways to think through feeling. The alligator pace of the beat instructs the body to slow down, maybe it even arrests the feet. Instead, the beat animates various other parts of the body and it becomes easy, if not pleasurable, to loosen the hips, pelvis, and shake the ass. The influence of Timbaland's sound, and the urban sounds it has spawned, has contributed (along with Caribbean music styles) to the ubiquity of "bounce music" in black vernacular dance. Bounce music is closely related to "ass music," and the term itself might partially describe the effect of the music on the movement of the (jiggly) ass and breasts – they bounce.[21]

I have always found Timbaland's irregular beats extremely difficult to dance to at first: one cannot very easily apply to the music the kind of expansive or extended motility that was more prevalent in vernacular dance styles prior to the introduction of the Timbaland sound (think of the movements of Michael Jackson in the early 1980s or John Travolta in *Saturday Night Fever*).[22] To maximize pleasure from the Timbaland sound in bounce movement, the feet should remain more contained spatially. This containment of movement might be related to what Paul Gilroy's addresses as the "shrinking orbits of freedom" around the black body in postmodern cultural practice (1998). But there is still freedom to be found despite/in spite/because of this containment of the feet because it only opens up a different stylistic form of corporeal mobility that focuses on the hips and groin, and finally on the controversial and contested ass. The Timbaland sound inspires the body to recognize what it does not already know of itself. In place, the body must relearn its own relation to the process of self-mobilization. Newly gravitationally centered around the ass, the body becomes its own intimate dance floor, an ever more knowledgeable site where new "steps" are rehearsed and practiced. This beat wants to move the body, and the body must learn to re-move to the beat.

The rise of ass music, this pursuit of percussive tactility, might be a continuation of the subaltern longing for corporeal freedom from and against the "shitty" history (and therefore the "shitty" present and future) of Western imperial civilization. Here is how the Negro past might be used. Invert George

439

Clinton/Dr. Funkenstein's classic principle "free your mind and your ass will follow." Instead, the new dance styles implore "free your ass and your mind will follow" (or, hopefully, they begin to amend the (culturally specific) binary that separates "ass" and "mind" into a discourse of waste versus use-value). The architecture of the Timbaland beat implores us to free our asses – lest we not only look but *feel* unfunky and obsolete.

At once, this inversion returns us to an ass politics in which the most controversial body part next to the gendered genitals and breasts becomes the locus point for the pursuit of enlightenment. Freeing up the ass is a movement toward a sensual new rationality. The ass thinks. Amiri Baraka may provide some direction here: "We seek Wholeness. Atonement. Not Nietzsche saying feeling made it hard for him to think. For us what cannot feel cannot think. They say Dr. J, Magic, Michael Air are 'instinctive.' Boston Larry B, etc., intelligent. The highest intelligence is dancing, not the Arthur Murray footsteps advertising! The highest thought is a doing, a being, not an abstraction" (p. 107). Baraka's revisionist epistemology is complemented by a recent trend in urban slang, which is the substitution of "You understanding me?" for "You feelin' me?" The implied tactility in the latter expression demonstrates the need for revised corporeal epistemologies in Afro-diasporic cultures.

If we are attuned to its power to mobilize the cognitive faculties of the body at the level of the ass, the Timbaland sound may indeed be a dissident threat. Colored folk have traditionally been imagined as the cultural bottom, the Southern "ass" of the world (Africa, Asia, Caribbean) in relation to the rational "mind" of the Euro-Northwest (Europe, America), according to the economic (re)enactment of the Cartesian mind–body dialectic on geographical space. Then we might imagine that Euro-Western freedom and humanity depends in a big way on containing the corporeal freedom of the black ass, both metaphorically and literally. The historic white repression (and periodic engagement with and hybridization of) black vernacular dance (and music that inspires and/or is inspired by such dance) has to be linked, therefore, to the historic subjugation of the black body, and by extension, its fugitive claims to rationality.

The body in motion may also pose a threat to the social order because the freedom of cognitive corporeality organizationally corresponds to forms of political activity that value the social and communal over practiced individualism. Ntozake Shange has written that

> i mean / in habana / everybody knows fidel can mambo a revolutionary rhumba / if fidel can do it / it cant be so hard to love yr people n keep in step/ at the same time/everybody in the ford assembly line cd do it / the folks in soweto cd do it / *i mean think n dance at the same time* / but i've never heard tell of the ny times takin notice of that moment when "CASTRO LEADS HABANA IN NATIONAL RHUMBA" just like they make no mention of the fact that jimmy carter cant dance to any rhythm known to man. (p. 124, my italics)

Here, Shange locates a revolutionary communist politics in the rhythmic aesthetics of the vernacular dances of Cuba and South Africa. (These are in turn transnationally linked to the proletarian rhythms of industrial labor at Ford.) In the process she illuminates new discourses on subaltern corporeal rationality that fundamentally engage rather than displace the erotic power of the body in motion toward an improvisational practice of freedom.[23]

The Motion of Wind and Water

When there is dancing the buttocks are no longer depressed, bored or seeing no future in life. For dancing creates something miraculous within the buttocks: they shake. This shaking is a sudden movement which makes the buttocks jerk, twitch, even register seismic shocks. Shaking in a way is a storm within the buttocks.

Jean-Luc Hennig

Feng Shui provides a referential model for thinking about the Timbaland sound in and its relation to the space–time of the built environment. A traditional Chinese art of placement, siting, and architecture, Feng Shui can be more or less summarized as the "feel" of a place, good or bad (Walters 1998: 9). A rigorously interdisciplinary practice, it straddles site planning, dealings in the built and natural environment, as well as the redistribution of material objects within the interiors of a building, among many other traditions.

Feng Shui meets formal properties of composition (lighting, ventilation, color, shade) with practices of science and religion: some of its concerns include ch'i (energy) and the magnetism of the earth, and the symbolism of shapes with reference to the Five Elements. We might say that the ultimate aims for practitioners are harmony, happiness, tranquillity, peaceful co-existence with nature (Walters 1998).

Emerging out of the intense religio-mathematics of geomancy, Feng Shui has become increasingly popular in Western bourgeois urban culture at least since the late 1960s. Brought to international visibility by traveling writers like Derek Walters and Sarah Rossbach, Feng Shui's new cosmopolitan identity in and outside of Asian Diasporic cultural practice has naturally altered the traditions of the form. I have often grimaced in dismay as my friends claim to practice Feng Shui as they do nothing more than reposition Pottery Barn tables and nail mirrors purchased at Ikea to the wall of a room to make the reconstructed space more "happy."

Contemporary Feng Shui was ushered into modernity through its circulation in a transcontinental marketplace of asymmetrical exchange. It has thus had to respond to pressures of technological modernization and improvisational routines of diasporization. In fact, as both black music and Chinese spiritual architecture have been circulated to ever larger audiences, the flow of these

441

exoticized practices is tested against the appeal of hard machine technologies and the monotonous rhythms of (post)Fordist industry . . .

I would say the popularity of Feng Shui has only gained in relation to certain bourgeois crises over the death of the spirit in late global capitalism.[24] The cultural practice in its popular diasporized format carries only the trace elements of traditional geomancy. For instance, the book *Feng Shui Tips for the Home* limits its discussion to an anorexic 100 pages, providing hand tips for *instant* Feng Shui in the home. A recent article in *House Beautiful* magazine similarly reduces the practice to its lowest common denominator: "With references to 'the 24 Terms of the Solar Calendar,' the eight trigrams, and the five energies, some of the new books add up to a lot of confusion. Still, you don't have to be a China scholar to understand the basics of Feng Shui" (Picker 1996).

Always shadowed by the ancient interrelations between Ifa divination systems and Chinese cosmology, popular African-and Asian-diasporic composition practices bear a deep relationship. Especially since the cultural studies movement has tended to neglect metaphysics, the powerful resonance between I-Ching and Yoruba ache is worthy of a longer discussion than is possible here. But it is useful to note that these terms have no interpretative equivalents in Western contexts. Although they are two culturally specific practices, at some basic level rap and Feng Shui share concerns with flow. Derek Walters notes that: "There can be no exact translation of Feng Shui . . . since it has not true equivalent in Western terms. The words themselves mean 'wind' and 'water': both wind and water 'flow,' and this gives some clue to the nature of Feng Shui."

Flow is a term that illuminates motion in space and time, the phantasmal style of trace and ephemera, wind rustling the leaves on the branch of a tree, or water brilliantly illuminated by the light which seems to dance on its surface.[25] Flow (energy in motion) is also a key element in black oral vernacular practices and is interrelated to both the "breath" of the performance, its inspiration, as well as to the drumbeat, whose simplest rhythm might be said to mirror the beat of the heart.[26] Walters also notes that ch'i translates directly as "breath" or "blowing into" while yun (as in chi-yun) might be said to translate as the resonance of the spirit.

Like Feng Shui, Timbaland's music bears a relation to the (w)holistic in that it works to energize the body, to organize the flow between the concentrated vibrations of the chakras. The music wants to optimize soul, to augment the freedom of embodied spirit. So if current popular Feng Shui is at times reduced to a pseudo-contemplative practice of reorganizing beds, tables, and adding mirrors to a room, it is still about the organization of hard materials in the external environment toward the progressive flow of internal energies. In the same way, we can look at Timbaland's practice of reconstructing that which bears a relation to the hard materiality of the built environment (not only his use of the synthesizer but its ability to generate robotic sounds that mimic factory and machinery rhythms) in its relation to (w)holistic bodywork that links flow to the politics of the ass.

In Aaliyah's "Are You That Somebody," written and co-performed by Timbaland, the infectious melody is tied to the stress of the drumbeat. It starts and stops in a regular rhythmic pattern, leaving open gaps and (w)holes of space. I liken these gaps to gasps of air that regulate the flow of the track itself. Timbaland also received accolades for sampling a baby's joyous gurgle that becomes the recurring motif of the song. A baby's laugh is nothing if not an exercise of the lungs, an effect of respiration.

This "inspired" sample of spirited breath, a uniquely "live" found object that is always already inspiration in and of itself, is the source of the song's flow. Its inclusion in the track begins to counteract the possibility that the sound might become hopelessly dehumanized by its use of "hard" synthesizers and computer musical technology.[27] The aesthetic binary between hardness and the liquidity of flow is being effortlessly reconstructed or warped toward the (w)hole by Timbaland's compositional choices.

Beside the drum, the central ingredient in the Timbaland sound is its groove, which aims to lock and seduce you into its steady flow. Steven Feld defines the groove in relation to the drumbeat in kinetic terms: "one's intuitive feelingful sense of a 'groove' or 'beat' is a recognition of *style in motion*" (my italics, 1988: 76). This style in motion is orchestrated into the flow of the music itself. What really anchors the quirky rim shots and the dancing hi-hats of the Timbaland sound is a rhythmic groove that illuminates the conditions of labor in the techno-industrial age. In the tight, interlocking funk groove of his hit single "Luv 2 Luv Ya," the repetitive clanging, steely instrumentation recalls, for me, the intense and monotonous rhythms of the assembly line, of mechanized industrial labor and proletarian work practices . . .

In "Clock Strikes," Timbaland samples the theme from the 1980s television show "Knight Rider," referencing that show's main gimmick, a high-tech sleek black sports car named Kit, which travels at intense speeds, speaks in a robotic tone, and has a mind of its own. The echo of the Kit car in "Clock Strikes," style in (auto)motion, brings to mind a phallic image of technologized black speed as flow.[28] Timbaland's conjoining of diasporized African drumming practices with techno-machinery works to amend the traditional binary of technology as acceleration–speed (modern) with the sensuality of ritual (the "primitive" African drumming).

This is not only an acoustic reconstruction of the traditional spatial-geographic configuration of these discourses (North and West as technologized-rational, the South and East as sensual-primitive) but also a temporal reconstruction that syncretizes categories of past, present, future toward a nonlinear, newly cyclical model of human existence. The meaning of life is/as the circle, and the opposite of being funky is what? Square.

Groove by its nature is cyclical, and so it becomes useful to address the motif of circularity that characterizes the Timbaland sound. This circularity is not only literalized by the repetitiveness of the groove but it's never less than guaranteed by the politics of (w)holeness that Timbaland's brand of ass music makes

443

possible.[29] Ultimately, the circularity of the Timbaland sound has much to do with the way it formats a postmodern drum circle (again, see the quote by Frere-Jones) which bridges the song and spectator(s) at the level of sensual bodywork.

I have already referred to how the Timbaland sound might work to syncretize socially constructed binaries like local/global and ugly/beauty toward the (w)hole. The Timbaland sound also reimagines the presence of the kinetic within the static toward the (w)hole in ways that might reinvigorate the possibilities for mobilization within the sociopolitical. Although it might be possible to make this argument exclusively considering Timbaland's musical output, video – in its relation to his trademark sound – provides the clearest example of the relationship between politics and flow.

The hip hop video has become a privileged site in which the cultivation of soul is explicitly visualized and therefore managed. In the late 1990s, the trend in hip hop music videos was to depict rap stars living the "good life," partying, socializing, and residing in expensively decorated and lavish homes.[30] Stars are called stars in part because they are imagined to be filled with intense forms of vibrational light that suggests their internal flow of energies is optimized or unblocked. Stars' homes are imagined to illuminate the energetic faculties of the people who reside in them. Where beautiful homes are not displayed in music videos, exceptional leisure spaces are often substituted, such as the millennial streamlined silver rooms that appear in TLC's "No Scrubs" video, directed by Hype Williams.

While critics have celebrated the avant-garde aesthetics of these videos, others have criticized their depiction of materialism gone rampant, conspicuous consumption, and bourgeois upward mobility.[31] Are these spectacular videos nothing more than what Manthia Diawara envisions as a black "metropolitan modernity" which promises the realization of a new Aquarian age in which "black people do not divorce ethics from the material conditions that reproduce the good life" (1992; 1995 [1994]: 52)?

To rescue these videos from both their uncritical celebration of class and privilege and from the academic critique and/or lack of critique of that original lack of critique, we must begin to question how these videos look and what that tells us about how they feel. Beautiful million-dollar homes and futuristic architectural design may signify ostentatious wealth, celebrity privilege, the accumulation of individual profit, the lifestyles of the rich and famous. But the representational spaces may also be attempting to illuminate the abstracted power of funk to (re)move the body from material pursuits and to optimize inner flow. To move beyond the materialist critique of the videos, we must claim the synergy of at least three elements in these videos: 1. the beat that inspires the ass to elevate the soul; 2. the illuminated body of the celebrity which makes the video possible; and 3. the expansive, avant-garde design and direction of these productions.

The financial expense of some of these videos has much to do with their attempt to capture in visual form the warped spatio-temporality within the aural itself. Color saturation as well as state-of-the art lighting is especially important in their artistic design. Special care has been taken to highlight properties of symmetry and balance in the built environments of the sets in these videos. The visual design attempts to approximate not only the mood of the music and its emphasis on textural densification, but its *feeling*. So many of the spaces and places in these hip hop videos not only look beautiful but they feel good: these videos have texture. They could only have been produced at the turn of the century and the turn of the Millennium, as they "flow futuristic" (to coin Jay-Z) not unlike the music itself.

From this temporal lens of style in motion, Feng Shui provides an analogy for (re)thinking the relationships between the body and soul, flow and the built environment. The video for Timbaland and Jay-Z's "Lobster and Scrimp," with its jittery staccato screen, canted frames, midnight imagery, and neon-lighted green floor captures the manic, robotic quirkiness of the trademark Timbaland percussive sound.[32] Busta Rhymes and Janet Jackson's video for "What's It Gonna Be," which borrows heavily from the Timbaland sound but is not written by Timbaland himself, imagines the two celebrities in an environment of silver, mercurial walls, illuminating through special effects Busta's rap skills, his ability to flow, the stylistic motion of his performance self and his inner essence.

Malik Hassan Sayeed's video for Timbaland, Jay-Z, and Amil's "Nigga Wha, Nigga Who" features several scenes in which the performers walk toward the camera in graceful slow-mo, battered from behind with bursts of light in motion jutting out like electricity in sharp angles against the dark backgrounds. (Sayeed repeats this same affect of the flow of light, only bathed in deep blue, for the video for Lauryn Hill's melancholy "X-Factor.") The sloth-like attitude of the video for "Nigga Wha, Nigga Who" works (as if) in counterpoint to the pungent percussive track of the song, which sounds to me like a jar of jellybeans or coins shaken intermittently, rhythmically, and hard. The breaks and pauses in the percussion echo (for me) the rhythms of hard breathing, like the way the body sounds and sluggishly heaves, up and down, as it recovers from exercise.

As the illuminated bodies of Jay-Z and Amil approach the television screen in the video, moving so magically slow that time seems to nearly freeze, we become aware of the motion of silence, how silence looks and feels, the ghosted evidence of style in motion, or groove. The divided temporalities of the song (fast) and the video (slow) are not divided at all – they're actually synchronous and asynchronous at the same time. It is on time in time out of time and past time. Sayeed brilliantly captures in visual form the *molasses frenzy* of the Timbaland sound, the slowsugarsweet coming together of staticitykinesthesia which is already being worked out in the sonic architecture, so dirty it's funky, and in the effect of his brand of Southern fried liveness on the stylized ass in motion . . .

body and soul (more . . .

What is funky is history, what comes goes.
Amiri Baraka

This is just a beginning . . .

The gendered and slick video for Aaliyah's funkfest "Are You That Somebody" (written by Timbaland for the *Doctor Doolittle* soundtrack[33]) presents a group of black men on motorcycles magically bursting through the outer (vaginal) "walls" of a cave in which Aaliyah and her female dancers await. Once inside the cave with its streamlined, silver walls, the men and women perform a quixotic urban courtship dance that is not only choreographed to the triplet stress beat of the music but also to the lyric itself that features syllables which largely rest on the beat as well. The video performs how the dirty South sound, its emphasis on loosening up the motion of the ass, should look and feel as it hits the body. It is nothing if not an instructional text on how to dance to the new dirty South beat.

In 1999 the choreographer of the video, Fatima, released her own video in stores, entitled *Go Fatima!* During the course of the one-hour instructional video she breaks down step by step some of the best moments from the popular videos she helped design, and the first video on the tape is "Are You that Somebody." Fatima informs us that to start preparing for this choreography, one must begin with the bounce. I would consider this instructional video as a kind of notation or transcription. But it is almost akin to "thrice behaved behavior" – it not only transcribes the choreography from Aaliyah's video, but the original choreography in video could be seen *by itself* as a transcription of the movement already contained and inspired by the music but not yet corporealized.

When the song was released into New York clubs in the summer of 1998, I remember watching awestruck as couples would reenact moves from the video itself on the dancefloor. This kind of mimetic bodywork, which requires skill, practice, and desire, declares the power of funk to call the body into mobilization, to maximize flow and mix the interpersonal vibrations of the chakras. Aaliyah's video is an added feature in the relationship between music and the body, something like a bridge between the individual and the social.

Whether by watching it on TV or by watching Fatima's instructional tape, the practitioner-listener rearranges and mimetically reconstructs Aalyiah's video and/in its choreography to move his body to inspire his soul. A non-essential but useful item, the video brings us that much closer to the reconstructive corporeal impulses that are always already housed within the Timbaland sound from the get go.

The labor spent by the video in reconstructing the feel of the Timbaland sound is matched by the bodywork returned by the audiences whose souls do much better once their asses shake to the music.[34] Although enacted in a public club, this revisionist primal scene is not entirely different than Frere-Jones' "limbic urge" to move in time on time out of time and past time to the Timbaland sound in her private space . . .

So the mindfuck of the Timbaland sound is that it forces you or me not only to rethink our body[35] in terms of the rhythmic motion of our hips and ass, but to think through our dancing body in order to be funky – to stay in time and on time and ultimately to move through time, to avoid *feeling* square, to avoid stepping outside of the percussive circle.

The Timbaland sound formats this new circular politics of freedom that supports dirty beautiful cognitive feeling. It becomes ever more necessary to think through the agency of the funky ass in motion to consider how the sensate, kinetic body always already mobilizes and produces history rather than remains oppressed by its *flow*.

We always knew "Dancin' in the Streets" had a progressive subtext, but who knew "Shake Your Groove Thing" was prophecy?

Notes

1 See James Earl Hardy's B-Boy Blues on this point: "The next 'characteristic' that caught my eye was what Gene calls their 'tail waggin'.' As mentioned before, B-boys wear their pants hanging off their asses. Most of them have juicy behinds to begin with, so when they bebop down the street, it just jingles and jangles – and *that* is a sight to see. I am convinced that most B-boys, whatever their orientation, really enjoy the attention that their asses attract; I mean, why advertise like that if you don't want it to be seen and salivated over? When you think about it, this is very homoerotic. Homosexuals are often accused of 'flaunting' their sexuality (a tired charge, since straight folks bombard us every day with images that glorify their sexuality), but B-boys, who are supposedly a heterosexual lot, seem to do it more, especially in this area" (p. 29).

2 I am not attempting here to conflate the buttocks and the anus, merely to open up a more sophisticated conversation about the interrelationship between the part and the (w)hole.

3 For more on the "ass" as a subject of critical inquiry, see Hennig (1995), Madonna (1992), Hardy (1994), Bersani (1995), Sadownick (1996, esp. 101–3). This writing will surely be criticized for attempting to locate a sacred politics of transcendence in the metaphor of the ass. But like the old spiritual song says "my soul's so hot I can't sit down." Here is a traditional phrase that already posits a direct relationship between the soul, spiritual frenzy (the motion of anarchy), and the ass.

4 My influence here is Geeta Patel's meaningful complication of hybridity (1997), as well as the work of Amiri Baraka (1991).

5 I borrow this term from Sasha Frere-Jones (1997). More on this later.

6   I have chosen not to focus on lyrics for two reasons. One: the logistics of space. I would not want to focus on his lyrics unless I could also be guaranteed enough room to focus on the sound of his lyrics in performance. Two: despite Timbaland's immense contributions to new black popular music aesthetics, the producer has not attained the level of success or visibility of his peer rapping producers in part because of what many perceive as his weak skills as both a lyricist and performer. Word on the street is, he can't write lyrics and he can't rap. The banality of many of his lyrics, taken in tandem with his tendency toward "unsophisticated" rhyme scheme, has alienated any number of rap purists, who instead look toward 'visionary' and more hardcore artists like Jay-Z and Nas for inspiration. Yet I would argue that the tendency to label Timbaland's musical contributions as 'nonsense' is a useful gesture. Nonsense is meaninglessness, rubbish, trash, waste, excess – and already this takes us back to a discourse on (black) ass politics. As George Clinton states, "nonsense is a positive force." Thinking of Timbaland's work as nonsense also allows us to think more deeply about the politics of abstraction and content. If much (but not all) the power of Timbaland's funk is located in the nonrepresentational possibilities of his music and its performative effects on the body, then we might move away from a discourse on what his music is saying, or even how it sounds, and towards a revolutionary discourse on how his music *feels*.

7   Of the 1999 Grammy-nominated TLC release *Fan Mail*, Ann Powers notes that "the sound is sharper, more aggressive; clearly, Austin and his musical partners, L. A. Reid and Babyface, have been feeling the heat generated by their Virginia neighbor" (1999).

8   Or whether they would want such training at all if it were hypothetically offered to them. I'm not convinced by this line of argumentation in the first place, since anyone who believes composing music on computer programs like ProTools or CuBase requires reduced (or no) skills has probably never actually spent time using such complicated programs. In some ways, it is more difficult, not only musically, but in the sense that one must have a developed skill for mathematics to perform cut and mix programing. Timbaland nonetheless displays an extra-special musical sensitivity: "Timbaland says he builds his mixes around the harmonics of the speaking voices of his male and female rappers. He notices the 'key' a rapper performs in, then places all his melodic and percussive effects in complementary keys. The technique proves that working up the musicality in rap does not have to result in transforming it into R&B" (Cooper 1998: 134).

9   My use of "dirty" here is influenced by Douglas (1966).

10 We can therefore imagine that the beat only gets dirty when man stands up to walk, when he starts using his brain (Hennig). Cleaning up, laundering or containing this black beat, its messiness and its smell – while pleasurably engaging its magic – has been a perpetual project in the Western ethical pursuit of freedom. But as George Clinton, my funk guru, has said: "Because funk by any other name would still be funky – still make a motherfucker say shit, it damn near smell. 'Cause it's that primal thing, and that funny kind of nasty humor. Cats can't be cool when they hear that music. And you either love it 'cause it will make you twitch, or you hate it. But if you stay with it, you will dance" (quoted in an interview with Chip Stern 1979 [1994]: 15).

11 There are of course many within and outside cultural studies who have made excellent strides toward this goal. Among them see Foster (1996), Polhemus (1978), Nast and Pile (1998), Eshun (1998), Jackson (1998).

12 Randy Martin is useful here (1998). To think about thinking through the body would necessarily involve the continued study-practice of corporeal epistemologies, such as muscle memory and gut feeling, that might exceed the limits of the foundational Descartesian logic of Western thought. On a different tip, Kodwo Eshun (1998) has made great strides in rethinking the digital sensorium.

13 Motion, performance, and labor are three terms each with their own weight and history. I do believe that in relation to corporeality they can be productively theorized in concert. We might think of the motion of labor in relation to the labor of motion in relation to the performance of labor in relation to the labor of performance, and so on.

14 The frozen body of cultural studies and performance studies can only, therefore, signal the foreclosure of the postcolonial movement.

15 Blackness in this context has a relation to but always exceeds epidermal proof (melanin), proof of hair and voice, as well as the genes or any other aspect related to the physical. It could be thought of more generatively as a subordinate class positioning (in relation to the dominant class) within the social (Hall 1990: 226). If I am in danger of reconstituting racist logic by linking blackness not only to the body, but to emotion, sensuality, essence, and spirit, let it be recalled that blacks in the Diaspora do not monopolize nor own soul. See Green and Guillory (1998).

16 We could distinguish soul from spirit here in that the spirit may enter and leave the body, and as such is not bound by the corporeal. Soul, however, must be embodied although it is not reducible to the body. The soul that leaves the physical body causes it to die. Therefore, we cannot talk about the health of the body outside of its relation to the soul. The soul of the body cannot be exclusively conflated with the term "soul" that is used to market records, books, hair products, and so on. At the same time, the interrelations of the terms are crucially important.

17 For Baldwin, the use-value of black history is complicated by the truth that everyone is "carrying one's history on one's brow, whether one likes it or not" (1971: 167). The body cites the history from which it is produced; the body can, as such, never be free of its own history. This "burden" of history is thus embodied. History is then complicated by the admission that subordinated peoples under oppressive regimes do not necessarily "own" their bodies: skin, hair, lips, genitals, and ass are contested properties along asymmetries of race and gender. If oppressive history is corporealized, Baldwin remains utopic in his belief that bodies do not only move through history – bodies move history itself (1971). Despite the oppressive faculty of history, the agency rests with people to imagine a better future. And if the body can never be outside of history it can certainly be emancipated from its totalizing power. Then we could also think about the body in performance as an articulation or mobilization of the terms of that history.

18 George Clinton sizes up the link between funk, temporality, and utopia in "Unfunky UFO" when he claims: "We're unfunky and we're obsolete (and out of time)."

19 I use the term "inspire" here rather than "discipline" or "force" for the sake of the breath which inspire implies, which is in turn related to flow. I use it to break from

the concept of the beat as an exclusively disciplinary force (Hughes 1994). There seems to be some way in which Frere-Jones' ascetic practice of moving to the Timbaland sound has to do with inspiration in the context of flow that would contest any easy notion of the recalcitrance of the master–slave relationship in beat culture. If the beat enslaves the body, turns us into slaves to the rhythm, we also imply that the body, like the subaltern slave, has no life in consciousness, no cognitive scream or voice of/or rationality that would contest the brutality.

20   A useful analogy here for thinking about (w)holism is the tossed salad. A food item which literalizes what Dick Hebdige has defined as the "cut 'n' mix" practices of Caribbean Diasporic cultures (1987), the tossed salad holds particular value in its tactile apprehension (in this case, eating, but we might also use the term consumption) as a whole, not in individual elements of the preparation (tomatoes, lettuce, carrots). Tossed salad is also a useful metaphor here because it is used in US slang for oral–anal contact, and its equivalent, "rimming," is the active verb, the kinetic manifestation, of the noun "rim" which is the term used to describe the outer perimeters of the circular drum.

21   The dance style inspired by the Timbaland sound is related to, but probably exceeds, the Black Bottom, an "underground" but hugely popular dance style – popular among whites as well – of the earlier half of the twentieth century.

22   I am immensely grateful to Kobena Mercer for pointing this out to me.

23   Also see Randy Martin (1998) for his work on nationhood and hip hop dance aesthetics.

24   I am particularly thinking of the mantra of television's *The Oprah Winfrey Show* at the turn of this century and Millennium: "remember your spirit." This mantra is for me a bourgeois proposition in that it assumes that to remember the spirit one must have already temporally moved past it in linear terms or lost it altogether. I would argue that to lose the spirit in order to (re-)remember it is itself a luxury. Do the dispossessed and disenfranchised have the luxury to *not* remember their spirit?

25   With much reservation, I would suggest here Csikszentmihalyi (1990).

26   Baraka writes that "Spirit is literally breath as in in/spire or ex. Where you aspire is where you (go be at) headed, like the church spire. No breath. No life. But the drum replicating the first human instrument keeps life, the sun replicating itself inside us. Its beat. Night and Day. In and out, the breath. Coming and going, the everything. The Pulse, the flow, the rhythm carrier" (p. 104).

27   We might now contest R&B legend Charles Wright's statement: "I've dealt with the electric drum, for five years now I've tried. There's absolutely no spirit in it. You can't put spirit into a machine" (quoted from an interview with Charles Wright at www. RandB.com). It is not necessarily that one must look for spirit in the machine (although there it may well be) but that one must reconsider one's relationship to the machine itself in order to play it with spirit. Feng Shui again provides a referential model: it is not necessarily the built environment that contains ch'i but the way in which the built environment can be arranged and reconstructed that cultivates ch'i in the practitioner of Feng Shui. This same line of reasoning might apply to Gilroy's public mourning for the dormancy or death of soul in contemporary rap. "I'm always wary about this argument because I feel it has a kind of generational specificity to it, and I would not want to turn around and be seen to be

saying, well, this particular quality has completely disappeared from the musical culture. It may still be there, but I know that *I can't hear it*" (p. 254, my italics).

In the 1970s, R&B singer and instrumentalist Billy Preston adapts his gospel-trained keyboard skills to the synthesizer (an instrument which he first makes use of in his song "Space Race"). Here he describes performing on the synthesizer: "It's the spirit of it, the feeling of it, the heart of it, and the love that's put into it, the touch and the sensitivity of it, that's what makes the difference, cause everybody [plays] the same notes... There's only so many notes you can play... It's how it's played, how it's touched and the emphasis and the approach, you know, the attack, the release, the sustain... I never play the song the same way twice" (quoted from an interview with Billy Preston at www.RandB.com).

28   In his song "Here We Come," the producer samples the sing-song theme from the Saturday morning cartoon show *Spiderman*, echoing the title superhero's ability to defy gravity, to scale buildings with grace and speed in defiance of the grammar of space–time.

29   Dyer calls the repetitive groove and long format structure of disco music "whole body eroticism," a phrase which again brings us back to this notion of (w)holeness in relation to the rhythmic flow in dance music (1990 [1979]).

30   R. Kelly's 1999 video for the urban pop song "Home Alone" is perhaps the most explicit example (next to the Notorious B.I.G.'s "One More Chance"). The plot is as follows: R. Kelly is relaxing in his dazzling, stylishly decorated mansion when his doorbell rings. He walks in a stylized motion to the door, grumbling to himself since the doorbell has distracted him from his activities. Meanwhile, the camera shoots him from below and behind, focusing and bringing attention to the motion of his ass in his gym pants. Kelly opens the door and is bum-rushed by crowds of people who have come to have nothing but a good time in his home. The video wants to say; one should never be "home alone" in such a beautiful space, and by extension, R. Kelly, the star, should never be "home alone" when he has so many fans. I would argue the shot of his ass in the beginning of the video, before his friends enter the house, frames what we will see for the rest of the video, which is the performance of the social, of the collective, of the pleasure principle, the orgy which is always already sexual even when no clothes are removed. No matter that the video is crass in its depiction of materialism. From the beginning of the video, with the ass shot, we know that this clean spacious house has to get funky and dirty. With the ass shot, we know that something has to shake.

31   I, for one, have previously argued that the avant-garde aesthetics of the contemporary black music video are inseparable from the performance of celebrity privilege (1999).

32   It also prominently features the celebrities cruising in a car, suggesting the auto-mobility that is at the heart of the Dirty South beat.

33   The 1998 film remake starring Eddie Murphy had more bathroom humor ass jokes per scene than any I can remember in recent history. Coincidence?

34   George Clinton: "Funk is a non-profit organization." That which funk spends it returns in equal measure. Organizationally, funk is probably anticapitalist.

35   I purposefully use body here, rather than its plural equivalent.

References

Baldwin, James and Margaret Mead (1971). *A Rap on Race*. New York: Laurel Books.
Baraka, Amiri (1991). "The 'Blues Aesthetic' and the 'Black Aesthetic': Aesthetics as the Continuing Political History of a Culture." *Black Music Research Journal*, Fall: 101–10.
Bersani, Leo (1995). *Homos*. Cambridge, Mass.: Harvard University Press.
Browning, Barbara (1998). *Infectious Rhythms: Metaphors of Contagion and the Spread of African Culture*. New York: Routledge.
Chernoff, John Miller (1979). *African Rhythm and African Sensibility: Aesthetics and Social Action in African Musical Idioms*. Chicago: University of Chicago Press.
Conroy, Tom, Rob Sheffield, et al. (1998). "Hot Region: The South Coast." *Rolling Stone*, Aug. 20: 68.
Cooper, Carol (1998). "Tim's Bio." *Village Voice*, Dec. 15: 134.
Csikszentmihalyi, Mihaly (1990). *Flow: The Psychology of Optimal Experience*. New York: Harper & Row.
Diawara, Manthia (1992). "Afro-Kitsch." In *Black Popular Culture*, ed. Gina Dent. Seattle: Seattle Bay Press.
Diawara, Manthia (1994). "Malcolm X and the Black Public Sphere: Conversionists versus Culturalists." *Public Culture* 7: 35–48. Reprinted in *The Black Public Sphere* (1995), ed. Black Public Sphere Collective. Chicago: University of Chicago Press.
Douglas, Mary (1966). *Purity and Danger: An Analysis of Concepts of Pollution and Taboo*. New York: Praeger.
Dyer, Richard (1990 [1979]). "In Defense of Disco." In *On Record: Rock, Pop and the Written Word*, ed. Simon Frith and Andrew Goodwin. New York: Pantheon.
Eshun, Kodwo (1998). *More Brilliant than the Sun: Adventures in Sonic Fiction*. London: Quartet Books.
Feld, Steven (1988). "Aesthetics as Iconicity of Style, or 'Lift-up-over Sounding': Getting into the Kaluli Groove." *Yearbook for Traditional Music*, XX: 74–113.
Frere-Jones, Sasha (1997). "Welcome to Our World." *Spin*, Jan.: 111.
Foster, Susan (ed.) (1996). *Corporealities: Dancing, Knowledge, Culture, and Power*. New York: Routledge.
Gilroy, Paul (1998). "Questions of a Soulful Style: An Interview with Paul Gilroy." In *Soul: Black Power, Politics, Pleasure*, eds. Richard C. Green and Monique Guillory. New York: New York University Press.
Green, Richard C. and Monique Guillory (eds.) (1998). *Soul: Black Power, Politics, Pleasure*. New York: New York University Press.
Hall, Stuart and Tony Jefferson, (eds.) (1976). *Resistance Through Rituals: Youth Subcultures in Post-war Britain*. London: Hutchinson.
Hall, Stuart (1990). "Cultural Identity and Diaspora." In *Identity: Community, Culture, Difference*, ed. Jonathan Rutherford. London: Lawrence and Wishart.
Hartman, Saidiya (1997). *Scenes of Subjection: Terror, Slavery, and Self-Making in Nineteenth-Century America*. New York: Oxford University Press.
Hardy, James Earl (1994). *B-Boy Blues*. New York: Alyson Books.
Hebdige, Dick (1979). *Subculture: The Meaning of Style*. London: Methuen.

452

Hebdige, Dick (1987). *Cut 'n' Mix: Culture, Identity and Caribbean Music*. London, New York: Methuen.

Hennig, Jean-Luc (1995). *The Rear View: A Brief and Elegant History of Bottoms Through the Ages*, trans. Margaret Crosland and Elfreda Powell. New York: Crown Publishers, Inc.

Hughes, Walter (1994). "In the Empire of the Beat: Discipline and Disco." In *Microphone Fiends: Youth Music and Youth Culture*, eds. Andrew Ross and Tricia Rose. New York: Routledge.

Jackson, John L. (1998). "Ethnophysicality, or An Ethnography of Some Body." In *Soul: Black Power, Politics, Pleasure*, eds. Richard C. Green and Monique Guillory. New York: New York University Press.

Joseph, May (2000). "Introduction" to Bodywork Issue, *Women and Performance: A Journal of Feminist Theory* 21, Winter.

King, Jason (1999). "Form and Function: Superstardom and Aesthetics in Black Music Videos." In *Velvet Light Trap: A Journal of Film, Radio and Television*, Fall.

Krasnow, David (1999). Letter to the *Village Voice*, "Cracking the Code," March 2.

Lip, Evelyn (1997). *What is Feng Shui?* London: Academy Group Ltd.

Madonna (1992). *Sex*. New York: Warner Books.

Martin, Randy (1998). *Critical Moves: Dance Studies in Theory and Politics*. Durham: Duke University Press.

McClary, Susan and Robert Walser (1994). "Theorizing the Body in African-American Music." *Black Music Research Journal*, Spring: 75–84.

Moten, Frederick C. (1994). *Ensemble: The Improvisation of the Whole in Baraka, Wittgenstein, Heidegger and Derrida*. Ph.D. dissertation, University Of California, Berkeley.

Nast, Heidi J. and Steve Pile (eds.) (1998). *Places Through The Body*. London: Routledge.

Patel, Geeta (1997). "Home, Homo, Hybrid." *College Literature*, Feb.: 133–50.

Picker, Lauren (1996). "Well Placed." *House Beautiful*, March.

Polhemus, Ted (ed.) (1978). *The Body Reader: Social Aspects of the Human Body*. New York: Pantheon Books.

Powers, Ann (1999). "Fan Mail" review, *Rolling Stone*, March 18: 61–2.

Rogers, Charles E. (1997). " 'Boogie' Breaks Big for Magoo and Timbaland." *Amsterdam News* 10/23: vol. 88, issue 43: 23.

Sadownick, Douglas (1996). *Sex Between Men: An Intimate History of the Sex Lives of Gay Men Postwar to Present*. Harper Collins: San Francisco.

Stern, Chip (1979 [1994]). "The Serious Metafoolishness of Father Funkadelic, George Clinton." Reprinted in *The Rock Musician*, ed. by Tony Scherman. New York: St. Martin's Press.

Shange, Ntozake (1981). "boogie woogie landscapes." In *Three Pieces*. New York: St Martin's Press.

Walters, Barry (1997). "Even Better: The Surreal Thing." *Village Voice*, Nov. 18: 97.

Walters, Derek (1998). *Feng Shui: The Chinese Art of Designing a Harmonious Environment*. New York: Fireside.

Chapter 26

Fashion

Sarah Berry

Fashion is a tangential concern to most academic disciplines; outside of historical costume studies there has been little sustained attention to the topic. When approached within a traditional discipline, fashion is usually slotted into a broader theoretical framework rather than addressed with any conceptual specificity. The relative paucity of research on fashion can be easily attributed to its association with femininity and trivial consumerism, but it is also a tremendously difficult object to define and analyze. Cultural studies of fashion have brought new life to the topic by looking beyond familiar notions that fashion is a manifestation of the marketplace, social stratification, erotic drives, or cultural zeitgeists. Cultural studies have begun to articulate the variety of questions one can ask about fashion: is it a set of social protocols, aesthetic discourses, or a nexus of culture industries? Is it a distinctively modern phenomenon or similar to traditionial uses of dress? I would argue that it is all of the above, but that each of these areas needs exploring in order to understand the complexity of the topic. This chapter offers a brief overview of some disciplinary approaches to fashion and an introduction to new insights offered by interdisciplinary cultural studies.

Is Fashion Modern?

Cultural studies of fashion have their roots in the 1970s work of the Birmingham Centre for Cultural Studies on youth subcultures, which sought to understand the resistive potential of marginalized cultural production with the help of theorists like Raymond Williams and Antonio Gramsci. More recently, cultural approaches to fashion have drawn on two primary theoretical influences: performance theory and social practice theory. Performance theory in its current form is indebted to Judith Butler's linguistics-derived model of the "citational" nature of social identity, as well as the work of Michel Foucault and the dramaturgical sociology of Erving Goffman. Social practice theory is drawn primarily from the work of Pierre Bourdieu and has its roots in the anthropology of Marcel Mauss and Marshall Sahlins, among others. While I would argue that these two approaches to fashion are not incompatible, they focus on different aspects of fashion and are often used to define the topic very differently. Performance theory focuses on the link between fashion and modernity, and in particular the "self-fashioning" implied by each individual's participation in social role playing and identity construction (Finkelstein 1991). Social practice theory, on the other hand, sees less individual agency in the enactment of such roles, while recognizing that they exist because they are habitually readopted due to cultural constraints rather than determined or unchanging. Social practice theory is thus less concerned with the way modern (or postmodern) fashion is different from earlier forms of dress than with the ways that dress continues to function as an aspect of socialization.

The majority of fashion studies, however, have begun from the premise that fashion is a distinctively modern phenomenon that is fundamentally different from earlier uses of dress. Central to this argument is the idea that modern fashion is about novelty – the production of endless objects of minute differentiation and planned obsolescence. Early fashion theory contrasted the modern emphasis on change with the perceived stability of dress in premodern societies. In 1890, Gabriel de Tarde argued in his book *The Laws of Imitation* that in traditional societies dress serves to promote continuity with the past and the imitation of ancestors, while modern fashion promotes novelty and the imitation of contemporary innovators and exotic foreigners. Fashion historians have supported Tarde's notion that fashion represents a significant break with earlier uses of dress, noting that Europe in the fourteenth century saw clothing styles begin to change more frequently and reflect a wider range of influences than in earlier periods. These changes are attributed to the rise of modern states and a mobile bourgeoisie, and are seen to have produced a form of "aesthetic individualism" within court society. Fashion quickly became a sociopolitical tool for trend-setting aristocrats, rather than just a means of representing traditional status divisions (Lipovetsky 1994, Campbell 1987, Mukerji 1983, Breward, 1995). Social theorist Giles Lipovetsky concludes from these events that fourteenth-century Europe initiated a paradigm shift away from the traditional meaning of dress: "Clothing no longer belonged to collective memory; it became the singular reflection of the predilections of sovereigns and other powerful people" (Lipovetsky 1994: 34).

Anthropologist Arjun Appadurai has supported this argument, observing that "In general, all socially organized forms of consumption seem to revolve around some combination of the following three patterns: interdiction, sumptuary law, and fashion" (Appadurai 1996: 71). He points out that in small, "ritually oriented societies," rules about dress tend to be based on the culture's cosmology and are thus fairly static. Long-distance trade provokes changes in material culture, but new commodities appear relatively infrequently and are thus incorporated into existing value structures (Appadurai 1996: 71). Similarly, Lipovetsky argues that

455

while depictions of clothing in ancient Greece, Rome, Egypt, or Asia show variations of detail and arrangement, the basic elements of premodern dress changed very infrequently and variations were "predetermined by a closed set of possible combinations" rather than individual innovation (Lipovetsky 1994: 35). In 1930, J. C. Flügel described the difference between modern and pre-modern dress by arguing that non-Western dress tended to be more locally variable (as in tribal costume) but also more "permanent," while Western fashion was more uniform throughout its sphere of influence but changed far more rapidly than non-Western dress (Flügel 1950: 129–30).

From this perspective, fashion is defined as a system of conventions that requires both constant innovation and individual decision-making, and is thus specific to modern societies. Appadurai cautions, however, that while Europe may have experienced a shift in the mid-fourteenth century from sumptuary law to fashion, "what we need to avoid is the search for pre-established sequences of institutional change, axiomatically defined as constitutive of the consumer revolution . . . [so that] the rest of the world will not simply be seen as repeating, or imitating, the conjunctural precedents of England or France" (Appadurai 1996: 72–3). In other words, if fashion is specific to modern consumer culture, it may be so in a wide variety of culturally and historically distinct ways.

This definition of fashion sees the shift from imitating the past to imitating contemporaries of high status as a step towards increasing autonomy and individualism in dress: "the beginning of the right of personalization" (Lipovetsky 1994: 37). The association of fashion with relative individual autonomy is supported by the failure of the sumptuary laws of the middle ages to prevent the European bourgeoisie from wearing the fabrics, colors, and style of the aristocracy (Hunt 1996). Fashion has thus come to be seen as a tool of capitalist social mobility, inscribing group affiliation on a more voluntary level than previously possible. Paradoxically, however, fashion reinforces the role of dress to signify status and social distinction while also making those signs more appropriable. For this reason, sociological studies of fashion have focused almost exclusively on the role of fashion in displaying social status and facilitating upward mobility through the imitation of elites.

But recent theories of comsumer culture have looked at fashion and seen more than the functionalism of Thorstein Veblen's "conspicuous consumption." Appadurai agues, along with Colin Campbell and Chris Rojek, that the key to modern forms of consumerism is pleasure (Appadurai 1996: 83, Campbell 1987, Rojek 1987). This argument takes up where Max Weber leaves off, suggesting that what moderns crave is not hard-earned leisure but rather the ephemerality of fashion and its rejection of utility. In particular, fashion offers the pleasure of seeing the social self as malleable and open to constant reinvention. The argument that fashion is exclusively modern thus emphasizes the performative aspect of modern subjectivity and the "ambiguity and indeterminacy" it allows (Morris 1995: 567). It sees fashion as a corollary to the instability of modern social identity and its "logic of indetermination," which allows for a historically unprecedented degree of individual agency in communicating social and personal characteristics (Lipovetsky 1994: 77–9).

There are, however, a number of arguments against making a category distinction between premodern dress and modern fashion. Without diminishing the importance of modern identity and consumerism to the meaning of fashion, one can point to some significant continuities between the traditional and modern meanings of dress. For example, anthropologists draw attention to the traditional use of clothing to indicate gender, age, group identity, and rank, as well as to modify behavior. Each of these functions still applies in modern fashion culture, in spite of increased choice in group affiliation and the relative indetermination of social castes. In other words, there is continuity in the most basic meanings of dress even though the social constraints associated with them have changed significantly. For example, Jennifer Craik draws on the concepts of anthropologist Marcel Mauss to argue that although modern fashion is peculiar in its emphasis on planned obsolescence and arbitrary design innovations, in everyday life it is still a "body technique" – a term coined by Mauss in the context of premodern societies. According to Mauss, body techniques are forms of self-presentation that individuals copy from members of their social group who are deemed behavioral models (Craik 1994: 9; Mauss 1973: 73–5). This reiteration of norms (which Mauss called "prestigious imitation") helps define the basic rules or "habitus" of a particular community and the way it circumscribes individuality.

This definition downplays the importance of fashion's shift away from traditional sources, arguing that regardless of its trendiness, modern "self-fashioning" still takes place within and is structured by a social habitus. Craik's position draws on social practice theory, seeing the fashion system as simply "custom in the guise of departure from custom" (Sapir 1931: 140; Bourdieu 1990, de Certeau 1984, Sahlins 1976). Accordingly, modern fashion in everyday life has much in common with premodern uses of dress, since it is both diverse (across social groups) and restrictive (based on the reiteration of social norms). Craik concludes that "in this sense, fashion is a technology of civility, that is, sanctioned codes of conduct in the practices of self-formation and self-presentation" (Craik 1994: 5). She acknowledges, however, that in modern cultures "there is a tension between unstructured and untrained impulses (license and freedom) and structured and disciplined codes of conduct (rule-bound, deliberate) in the dynamic creation of declarations of the limits of the habitus of the body" (Craik 1994: 5).

The challenge for cultural studies of fashion is to address this tension between fashion as a normative set of rules *and* as a tool of individuation and selective group-identification. For some time this tension was addressed primarily in terms of fashion's relationship to ideology and questions of structure versus agency. The legacy of the Frankfurt School has led most Marxist scholars to align fashion with other culture industries in a top-down model of commodity aesthetics. Within the Frankfurt model, dominant culture was seen to determine both fashion norms and the pseudo-individuation of fashion iconoclasts (Haug 1987, Ewen 1976). With the influence of poststructuralism, however, resistance to dominant culture in the form of subcultual style gained legitimacy as a form of political resistance and social formation (Hebdidge 1979, McRobbie 1988). More recently, ethnographic research methods have informed such user-centered approaches, demonstrating how complex and negotiated people's relationships to fashion can be (Craig 1997).

In addition, recent work on consumerism and material culture has questioned the foundations of Marx's theory of commodity fetishism, arguing that the social value of goods is not only tied to labor value, but to the broader "social life of things" (Appadurai 1996, Miller 1987; Frow 1997: 102–217). This means that marketplace exchange does not simply mystify the value of commodities, but instead places them in a complex arena of resocialization. This focus on the reception and use of objects does not negate the importance of the political economy of their production; it would be impossible, for example, to adequately describe contemporary fashion without an account of the labor conditions, corporate structure, and marketing apparatus that make it possible. Nevertheless, the dual nature of fashion makes it, as Don Slater has described consumerism more generally, "a privileged site of autonomy, meaning, subjectivity, privacy and freedom" and simultaneously a site of "strategic action by dominating institutions" (Slater 1997: 31).

Fashion and Anthropology

Anthropologists were for years almost alone in acknowledging the wide range of social meanings attached to dress. Initially, however, it was fitted into a universalist concept of human development and "psychic unity," marked by stages of development from "savagery to barbarism to civilization" (El Guindi 1999: 50). This evolutionary model described a trajectory from simple body ornamentation, protection, and concealment to more "civilized" forms of dress, and sought to identify each stage of development (Crawley 1931: 77, 22; cited in El Guindi). This universal evolution model was abandoned, but some anthropologists have maintained a tendency to describe the relationship between traditional dress and introduced commodity fashions as one of "contamination" rather than as a constitutive dynamic of culture (Miller 1995: 265).

Among the most significant anthropological contributions to fashion studies was Mary Douglas and Baron Isherwood's 1996 study *The World of Goods*. Though not concerned with fashion *per se*, the book challenged a basic premise of mainstream theories of consumerism: that consumption decisions are about the individual selection and purchase of goods. Douglas and Isherwood argued that consumption is tied to collective values and the social "use of material possessions that is beyond commerce" (Douglas & Isherwood 1996: 37). In doing so they both legitimized the study of consumer goods as material culture and made that project more coherent by erasing the division between cultures with and without commerce (Miller 1995: 266–7). Subsequently, research on dress by anthropologists like Joanne Eicher and others has given "coherence to the data scattered throughout the literature and order to the various attempts to include dress in conceptualizations of culture and society" (EI Guindi 1999: 55; Barnes & Eicher 1992, Eicher 1995). Recent work, such as Fadwa EI Guindi's book on the complex meaning of the veil in contemporary Islamic cultures, combines the methodological rigor of anthropology with the political and theoretical reflexivity of cultural studies.

Fashion and Sociology

Clothes for climbing, or what to wear on your way up the ladder; to build that graciousness which leads first to charm and eventually to financial advancement, proper, attractive clothes are a sound investment. (Clothing advertisement cited in Barber and Lobel 1961: 326)

The field of sociology has made a primary contribution to fashion studies, beginning with the seminal work of Gabriel de Tarde (1890), Thorstein Veblen (1899), and Georg Simmel (1904). As noted above, Tarde's work emphasized the break between traditional dress and modern fashion, arguing that fashion arises from a fluid social system in which tradition has less importance than the present behavior of highly regarded individuals or groups. Most early sociological studies thus assumed that fashion trends originated in the upper classes and were then copied by others in a competitive form of economic status display. It's worth nothing that Veblen wrote his well-known critique of "conspicuous consumption" at a moment in the rise of an American consumer economy when social theorists were searching for "some means of organizing and controlling the chaotic potential of the proliferating meanings attached to commodities" (Lears 1989: 85). Jackson Lears argues that Veblen's work was informed by factors like the sudden increase of wealth among American elites, immigration from non-Protestant traditions of "ritual and carnivalesque display," and the new "commercial theatricality" of department stores (Lears 1989: 85).

Simmel, on the other hand, was less anxious about the wasteful and competitive nature of fashion than Veblen and more interested in its role in adapting individuals to the demands of modernity. Simmel echoed Veblen in his chase-and-flight account of fashion innovation by elites and emulation by plebeians:

the latest fashion . . . affects only the upper classes. Just as soon as the lower classes begin to copy their style, thereby crossing the line of demarcation the upper classes have drawn and destroying the uniformity of their coherence, the upper classes turn away from this style and adopt a new one, which in its turn differentiates them from the masses; and thus the game goes merrily on. (Simmel 1971: 299)

But Simmel was as interested in the way that fashion bound people together in groups as he was in its role in reinforcing class hierarchies. He saw fashion as dependent on "the need of union on the one hand and the need of isolation on the other," and argued that only modern, class-based societies produced this conflicting need, since traditional cultures were structured more by collective "union" than the desire for individual differentiation (Simmel 1971: 301). Simmel's "top-down" model of fashion diffusion has been turned on its head (and occasionally its side) by later research showing the complexity of fashion innovation and diffusion (Blumer 1969), but his idea that fashion both binds individuals within groups while allowing them a sense of individual taste has become a truism of fashion theory. In addition, Simmel's argument that the transitory nature of fashion acculturates modern subjects to the constant change required by modern (and postmodern) civilization continues to be influential (Simmel 1904: 303; Lipovetsky 1994; Wilson 1987).

Early sociology's emphasis on fashion and class differentiation has been replaced by interest in the way it conveys a wide range of social meanings, including age, gender, ethnicity, personality, occupation, religion, and politics. A number of approaches have addressed these issues, including symbolic interactionism, social group theory, and the dramaturgical analyses of Erving Goffman. The school of symbolic interactionism, which was founded by Herbert Blumer and drew on the social psychology of George Herbert Mead, posits that individual identity is the product of ongoing self evaluation in relation to external conditions and interaction with other people (Blumer 1969; Mead 1934). Blumer attributed the sociological neglect of fashion in the early twentieth century to a blanket acceptance of Simmel's theories, along with a distaste for fashion as both trivial and nonrational:

> fashion seem[ed] to represent a kind of anxious effort of elite groups to set themselves apart by introducing trivial and ephemeral demarcating insignia, with a corresponding strained effort by non-elite classes to make a spurious identification of themselves with upper classes by adopting these insignia. (Blumer 1969: 276)

Blumer's alternative to top-down fashion diffusion became one of the most influential, introducing the concept of "collective selection." He argued that "design has to correspond to the direction of incipient taste of the fashion consuming public," and that in the competitive process of attempting to articulate this taste, "fashion readily ignores persons with the highest prestige and, indeed, by-passes acknowledged 'leaders' time after time." Blumer does not define the mechanism at work in the "collective selection" of designers, buyers, and consumers, but characterizes it in terms of a consensus model rather than a simple taste hierarchy determined by economic prestige (Blumer 1969: 281). Economic status continues to be emphasized by some classical economists to generalize about consumer behavior in terms of "Veblen effects." This term describes consumer activity in terms of "bandwagon" or "snob" behavior. Both are a reaction to the behavior of other consumers, but in very limited terms:

Either an individual's demand for goods or services is increased by the fact that others are seen to be consuming them (bandwagon), or decreased by the fact that others are consuming them (snob). (Campbell 1987: 50)

The inadequacy of this binary model is indicated by Blumer's work as well as sociological reference-group theory, which examines the complex varieties of imitation and emulation that characterize fashion consumption. Such analyses indicate that "any one person may make use of a variety of positive, negative, comparative and normative reference groups (or role models) when deciding what course of action to take" (Campbell 1987: 51).

Social Psychology and Aesthetics

The social psychology of fashion has tended to focus on questions of influence and change, reflecting a market-driven research agenda aimed at making fashion trends more predictable (Belk 1995). Along with consumer behavior research, this kind of analysis looks for patterns and ways to anticipate the dynamics of fashion or account for its history. One of the most widely-debated issues in the social psychology of fashion is the nature and meaning of gendered clothing, with an emphasis on women's fashion. The best-known of these is James Laver's theory of the "shifting erogenous zone." According to Laver, women's fashion change is driven by men's interest in the parts of the female body they cannot easily see. As soon as one such part is fashionably exposed, male desire shifts restlessly to another, more hidden part, necessitating a stylistic change in order to keep men interested in women:

This erogenous zone is always shifting, and it is the business of fashion to pursue it, without ever actually catching it up. It is obvious that if you really catch it up you are immediately arrested for indecent exposure. If you almost catch it up you are celebrated as a leader of fashion. (Laver 1937: 254)

In the case of the Victorian woman, concealed legs and a prominent bust were replaced by more visible legs and deemphasized *décolletage*. But as Valerie Steele has pointed out, Laver's theory essentially disregards social and historical factors in fashion change. For example, Laver explains the rise of the backless dress in the 1930s as result of men's boredom with women's exposed legs, but Steele notes that the trend followed swimsuit designs that were cut to expose the back for sun-tanning, as well as stricter film censorship in Hollywood, where low-cut necklines were replaced by backless dresses (Steele 1989: 42).

Rene König modified Laver's notion of the elusive "erogenous zone" into a more Freudian theory of clothing-as-erotic-concealment whereby clothing hides "hidden parts" (the genitals) in order to sublimate and intensify curiosity about them (König 1973: 91). But clothing can exaggerate, as well as conceal, body parts that signify gender, accentuating sexual difference by featuring secondary

461

sexual characteristics (breasts, hips, shoulders, etc.). In this sense, clothing's concealment evokes not only an inquisitive eroticism focused, as König suggests, on hidden – but clearly gendered – genitals, but also on the eroticism of making gender itself ambiguous. Marjorie Garber has suggested that this dynamic of sexual exaggeration and concealment is part of the impact of cross-dressing, which functions not simply to appropriate or displace one gender onto another, but as "a sign of the provocative destabilization of gender that is the very signature of the erotic" (Garber 1992: 25).

While it is difficult to avoid seeing clothes as an expression of interiority, social psychologies of fashion are almost always theoretically unsustainable from a cultural constructionist viewpoint. They are often based on unifying concepts of human psychology; they downplay the variety of social reference-groups within which clothing takes on context-dependent meanings, and – perhaps most important – they overestimate clothing's ability to communicate via a coherent master-code of psychic meanings. Sociologist Fred Davis points out that if fashion is a communicative code, it is one with very "low semanticity." He argues that although fashion "must necessarily draw on the conventional and tactile symbols of a culture, [it] does so allusively, ambiguously, and inchoately, so that the meanings evoked by the combinations and permutations of the code's key terms (fabric, texture, color, pattern, volume, silhouette, and occasion) are forever shifting or "in process" (Davis 1992: 5). Thus, even within a particular social group the way that clothing is interpreted will depend on a nexus of other discourses and interactions.

Fashion and Visual Culture

The indeterminacy of fashion's social meanings is linked to the enigma of fashion change, not only from a social standpoint, but in relation to the visual arts and other forms of cultural production. How autonomous and influential are fashion designers? Is their work determined by artistic trends, personal inspiration, or internal industry dynamics? A wide range of factors are at play in the design process, including production technology, new fabric innovation (such as synthetic fibers), and labor practices (Fine & Leopold 1993: 87–147; Watkins 1995, Phizacklea 1990). Within that context, Valerie Steele sees fashion innovation as being "rather like the legal profession: once a precedent has been set, a host of later decisions can be based on that first case" (Steele 1989: 59). Other fashion theorists argue that design decisions are essentially arbitrary, and that most fashion trends are "the almost haphazard outcome of going as far as one can go in a direction which circumstances may have rendered inevitable" (Langley Moore 1949: 13, cited in Steele 1985: 35; Davis 1992: 200–6). This "internalist" position highlights the self-referential nature of fashion design, but it ignores the "trickle-up" effect that occurs when the fashion industry appropriates vernacular styles such as denim jeans, leather jackets, and countless other components of "street style" (Fiske 1989, Polhemus 1994). Internalist arguments ignore the relationship between popular and designer fashion, and promote an aesthetically isolated reading of *la mode pour la mode*.

At their best, aesthetic analyses of fashion trace the complex interrelationship between fashion, industry, and history. For example, John Harvey begins his book *Men in Black* with the proposal that "fashions change, and so do meanings; and the color black, naturally emphatic, has been used at different times to mark off individuals or groups in quite different ways ... the meaning of a color is to a great extent the history of the color" (Harvey 1995: 13). This approach sees fashion as part of visual culture, linked closely to other aesthetic discourses. In *Seeing Through Clothes* Ann Hollander argues that within a particular culture, fashion works to "contribute to the making of a self-conscious individual image, an image linked to all other imaginative and idealized visualisations of the human body" within that culture (Hollander 1975: xiv). Her work sees Western figurative art as a collective projection of the body, with fashion as the link between those ideals and individual bodies.

The primary danger of aesthetic analyses is that the world of art and design is arbitrarily separated from the industries and discourses that support it. As Paul Hirsch notes, "In modern, industrial societies, the production and distribution of both fine art and popular culture entail relationships among a complex network of organizations which both facilitate and regulate the innovation process" (Hirsch 1991: 314). In addition to the separation of aesthetics from the context of cultural production, Hollander tends to limit fashion's frame of reference to the world of high art (with the inclusion of film and photography). This puts fashion in a traditional art-historical limbo, an approach Hollander suports in her book *Sex and Suits*:

> I have therefore continued in the old custom of speaking as if fashion in dress were a force with its own will, something that the collective desire of Western people brought into existence so that it might have an independent life ... Clothes show that visual form has its own capacity, independent of practical forces in the world, to satisfy people, perpetuate itself, and make its own truth apart from linguistic reference and topical allusion. (Hollander 1994: 12–13)

While art and fashion do not simply mirror their cultural or industrial contexts, those contexts require more attention than Hollander allows. Separating fashion from the social specificity of its production and reception simplifies its definition as an object of study, but at the cost of its cultural richness.

Fashion and Cultural Studies

Cultural studies of fashion have been, for the most part, less concerned with formulating broad theories of fashion than with observing its social uses in relation to broader issues of social power. Two early influences on this work were the semiotics of Roland Barthes and the youth-subculture studies of the Birmingham Centre for Contemporary Cultural Studies (Barthes 1972, Hall & Jefferson 1976, Hebdidge 1979). Malcolm Barnard also sees the work of Raymond Williams as a powerful factor in cultural studies of fashion, because Williams' view of cultural production saw "both the designing and wearing of fashions and clothing as versions of forms of creativity... As such, fashion and clothing are productive of the world in which we live" (Barnard 1996: 44; Williams 1958 and 1961). This view broke away from the dismissal of fashion as either trivial or simply reflective of the status quo, and drew attention to the ways in which subcultural groups use clothing to articulate identities and values.

Cultural studies of fashion thus tend to focus on the vernacular use of clothing and body ornamentation to represent a constellation of values and social practices rather than looking for general rules of fashion change and meaning. This has been called a "populist" approach by Fred Davis, who makes a counterargument for the continuing validity of a "center-to-periphery fashion system model" of innovation and diffusion. He complains that "populist critics are given to detect a veritable babble of dress 'discourses' in the postmodern society... [which are] engaged in symbolic identity construction exchanges of one kind and another" (Davis 1992: 202–3). He argues that, regardless of the proliferation of popular style cultures, the industry and its design dictates remain the primary engine of fashion adoption.

But a reception-oriented reading of fashion does not imply that large-scale production has no impact on popular clothing. It suggests that the significance attached to that clothing is contextual and has as much to do with its circulation in local style cultures as with its commercial production and marketing. It does not assume, in other words, that the widespread popularity of a particular style means that it carries a uniform set of meanings. Davis's argument that today's international fashion conglomerates represent the continued presence of a unidirectional design elite also overlooks the fact that many contemporary fashion conglomerates are profitable primarily due to licensed products like jeans and perfume rather than innovative design. As a retail industry economist notes, "the focus has shifted away from designing, [but]... if you have enough money and are good at marketing, you can create a strong brand" (Agins 1995: A1). It can be argued that fashion conglomerates increasingly capitalize on and repackage the stylistic innovations of "peripheral" social groups.

Angela Partington has taken up this issue in relation to the popularity of Dior's postwar New Look among working-class British women. Referring to a 1951 snapshot of a woman in a modified New Look gown, Partington notes that in terms of a "trickle-down" model, this dress would be considered a "watered down" version of the Dior design. This model implies two things, according to Partington: that non-elite fashion consumers are "less innovatory or adventurous in their preferences," and that class difference is, to some extent, masked by working-class emulation of the fashions associated with higher social status. She argues, however, that "the mass-market systems on which consumer culture depends provide specific conditions...under which class differences are re-articulated, rather than eroded or disguised," and that "the popular version of the New Look in the photograph is a deliberately different appropriation of it, not a poor copy" (Partington 1993: 145–6). Partington argues that,

> In a mass-market system, adoption of new styles is a process which depends on the flow of information within social strata rather than between them...there is no "emulation" of privileged groups by subordinate groups in such a system. Difference exists in the ways in which fashions are adopted, rather than in any time lag. (Partington 1993: 150–1)

As with the "Dior" dress she analyzes, even widely-diffused styles can be differently inflected within particular style cultures; in the post-war Britain she describes, the conflicting modes of femininity attached to the New Look (considered decorative and extravagant) versus the "Utility" dress (which signified restraint and practicality) were often "sampled and mixed together by the consumer to create fashions which depended on class-specific consumer skills for their meaning" (Partington 1993: 157).

This negotiation of fashion trends according to specific cultural values is also demonstrated in ethnographic research such as Maxine Craig's work on African-American men and women's complex relationship to hair straightening. For years many women saw "the process" of hair straightening as a requirement for respectability, while men's lye-straightened "conk" was associated with street style, hoodlums, and musicians. Rather than simply representing "identification with a white hair aesthetic," straight hair signified a variety of meanings related to class and gender. Craig concludes that African-Americans "created meanings that defined hair straightening in terms of status within their own communities rather than in terms of racial identification" (Craig 1997: 402–3). Similarly, Elizabeth Wilson has pointed out that such style cultures can easily turn against dominant culture, as in the case of "black hairstyles for both sexes which cannot successfully be imitated by whites." Like Partington, Wilson concludes that there is far more to fashion than the imitation of dominant culture, since style frequently serves to "reinforce class barriers and other forms of difference" (Wilson 1987: 9).

Conclusion

The proliferation of style cultures stimulated by consumerism has made the dynamics of fashion increasingly relevant to the study of social relations (Featherstone 1991). To the extent that fashion functions as a set of internalized social norms and disciplines, it also has the power to generate and express resistance to those norms. Cultural studies has been part of a significant shift in attitudes toward such phenomena and a growing recognition that fashion, like other forms of material culture, can be a powerful medium of collective identity and cultural expression. Like consumerism, it may also be seen as "the very arena in which culture is fought over" (Douglas & Isherwood 1996: 37), and cultural studies of fashion must continue to articulate those struggles.

References

Agins, T. (1995). "Not So Haute: French Fashion Loses Its Primacy as Women Leave Couture Behind." *The Wall Street Journal* 226.41, 29 Aug., A1.

Appadurai, A. (ed.) (1996). *The Social Life of Things*. Cambridge: Cambridge University Press.

Ash, J. and Wilson, E. (1993). *Chic Thrills: A Fashion Reader*. Berkeley: University of California Press.

Barber, B. and Lobel, L. (1961). "'Fashion' in Women's Clothes and the American Social System." In Bendix, R. and Lipset S. M. (eds.), *Class, Status and Power*. Glencoe, Ill.: The Free Press of Glencoe. (Original work published 1957.)

Barnard, M. (1996). *Fashion as Communication*. London: Routledge.

Barnes, R. and Eicher, J. (eds.) (1992). *Dress and Gender: Making and Meaning*. Providence, RI and Oxford: Berg.

Barthes, R. (1972). *Mythologies*, trans. J. Cape. New York: Hill and Wang. (Original work published 1957.)

Belk, R. (1995). "Studies in the New Consumer Behavior." In Miller, D. (ed.) *Acknowledging Consumption: A Review of New Studies*. London and New York: Routledge.

Blumer, H. (1969). "Fashion: From Class Differentiation to Collective Selection." *Sociology Quarterly* 10: 275–91.

Bourdieu, P. (1990). *The Logic of Practice*, trans. R. Nice. Stanford: Stanford University Press.

Breward, C. (1995). *The Culture of Fashion: A New History of Fashionable Dress*. Manchester: Manchester University Press.

Campbell, C. (1987). *The Romantic Ethic and the Spirit of Modern Consumerism*. Oxford: Blackwell.

Craig, M. (1997). "The Decline and Fall of the Conk; or, How to Read a Process." *Fashion Theory* 1(4): 399–420.

Craik, J. (1994). *The Face of Fashion: Cultural Studies in Fashion*. London: Routledge.

Crawley, E. (1931). *Dress, Drinks, and Drums: Further Studies of Savages and Sex*. ed. T. Besterman. London: Methuen.

Davis, F. (1992). *Fashion, Culture and Identity*. Chicago: University of Chicago Press.

De Certeau, M. (1984). *The Practice of Everyday Life* trans. S. Rendall. Berkeley: University of California Press.

Douglas, M. and Isherwood, B. (1996). *The world of Goods: Towards an Anthropology of Consumption*. New York: Routledge. First published 1979.

Eicher, J. (ed.) (1995). *Dress and Ethnicity: Change Across Space and Time*. Washington, DC and Oxford: Berg.

El Guindi, F. (1999). *Veil: Modesty, Privacy and Resistance*. Oxford and New York: Berg.

Ewen, S. (1976). *Captains of Consciousness: Advertising and the Roots of the Consumer Culture*. New York: McGraw Hill.

Featherstone, M. (1991). *Consumer Culture and Postmodernism*. London: Sage.

Fine, B. and Leopold, E. (1993). *The World of Consumption*. London: Routledge.

Finkelstein, J. (1991). *The Fashioned Self*. Cambridge Polity Press.

Fiske, J. (1989). *Understanding Popular Culture*. Boston: Unwin Hyman.

Flügel, J. C. (1950). *The Psychology of Clothes*. London: Hogarth Press. (Original work published 1930.)

Frow, J. (1997). *Time and Commodity Culture: Essays in Cultural Theory and Postmodernity*. Oxford and New York: Oxford University Press.

Garber, Marjorie (1992). "Strike a Pose." *Sight and Sound* 2(5): 25.

Goffman, E. (1959). *The Presentation of Self in Everyday Life*. New York: Doubleday.

Hall, S. and Jefferson, T. (eds.) (1976). *Resistance Through Rituals: Youth Subcultures in Post-war Britain*. London: Hutchinson.

Harvey, J. (1995). *Men in Black*. Chicago: University of Chicago Press.

Haug, W. F. (1987). *Commodity Aesthetics, Ideology and Culture*. New York: International General.

Hebdidge, D. (1979). *Subculture: The Meaning of Style*. New York: Methuen.

Hirsch, P. M. (1991). "Processing Fads and Fashions: An Organization-Set Analysis of Cultural Industry Systems". In Mukerji, C. and Schudson, M. (eds.), *Rethinking Popular Culture: Contemporary Perspectives in Cultural Studies*. Berkeley: University of California Press.

Hollander, A. (1975). *Seeing Through Clothes*. New York: Viking.

Hollander, A. (1994). *Sex and Suits: The Evolution of Modern Dress*. New York: Alfred A. Knopf.

Hunt, Alan. (1996). *Governance of the Consuming Passions: A History of Sumptuary Law*. New York: St. Martin's Press.

Kidwell, C. B. and Steele, V. (eds.) (1989). *Men and Women: Dressing the Part*. Washington, DC: Smithsonian Institution Press.

König, R. (1973). *A La Mode: On the Social Psychology of Fashion*. New York: Seabury Press.

Laver, J. (1937). *Taste and Fashion from the French Revolution Until To-Day*. London: George G. Harrap & Co.

Lears, T. J. J. (1989). "Beyond Veblen." In Bronner, S. (ed.), *Consuming Visions: Accumulation and Display of Goods in America, 1880–1920*. New York: Norton.

Lipovetsky, G. (1994). *The Empire of Fashion: Dressing Modern Democracy*, trans. Catherine Porter. Princeton: Princeton University Press.

Mauss, M. (1973). "Techniques of the Body." *Economy and Society* 2(1): 70–88.

McRobbie, A. (ed.) (1988). *Zoot Suits and Second-Hand Dresses: An Anthology of Fashion and Music*. Boston: Unwin Hyman.

Mead, G. H. (1934). *Mind, Self, and Society*, ed. C. W. Morris. Chicago: University of Chicago Press.

Miller, D. (1987). *Material Culture and Mass Consumption*. Oxford: Blackwell.

Miller, D. (1995). "Consumption as the Vanguard of History." In Miller, D. (ed.), *Acknowledging Consumption: A Review of New Studies*. London and New York: Routledge.

Morris, R. (1995). "All Made Up: Performance Theory and the New Anthropology of Sex and Gender." *Annual Review of Anthropology* 24: 567–92.

Mukerji, C. (1983). *From Graven Images: Patterns of Modern Materialism*. New York: Columbia University Press.

Partington, A. (1993). "Popular Fashion and Working-Class Affluence." In Ash, J. and Wilson, E. (eds.), *Chic Thrills: A Fashion Reader*. Berkeley: University of California Press.

Phizacklea. A. (1990). *Unpacking the Fashion Industry: Gender, Racism, and Class in Production*. London: Routledge.

Polhemus, T. (1994). *Streetstyle: From Sidewalk to Catwalk*. London: Thames and Hudson.

Roach, M. E. and Eicher, J. B. (eds.) (1962). *Dress Adornment and the Social Order*. New York: John Wiley and Sons.

Rojek, C. (1987). *Capitalism and Leisure Theory*. London: Tavistok.

Sahlins, M. (1976). *Culture and Practical Reason*. Chicago: University of Chicago Press.

Sapir, E. (1931). "Fashion." *Encyclopedia of the Social Sciences*, Vol. 6. New York: Macmillan.

Simmel, G. (1971). "Fashion." In Levine, D. (ed.), *On Individuality and Social Forms*. Chicago and London: The University of Chicago Press. (Original work published 1904.)

Slater, D. (1997). *Consumer Culture and Modernity*. Cambridge: Polity Press.

Steele, V. (1985). *Fashion and Eroticism: Ideals of Feminine Beauty from the Victorian Era to the Jazz Age*. New York and London: Oxford University Press.

Steele, V. (1989). "Clothing and Sexuality." In Kidwell, C. B. and Steele, V. (eds.), *Men and Women: Dressing the Part*. Washington, DC: Smithsonian Institution Press.

Tarde, G. de (1962). *The Laws of Imitation*, trans. E. C. Parsons. Boston: Peter Smith. (Original work published 1890.)

Veblen, T. (1953). *The Theory of the Leisure Class*. New York: Mentor Books. (Original work published 1899.)

Watkins, S. (1995). *Clothing: The Portable Environment*, 2nd edn. Ames: Iowa State University Press.

Williams, R. (1958). *Culture and Society 1780–1950*. London: Chatto & Windus.

Williams, R. (1961). *The Long Revolution*. London: Chatto & Windus.

Wilson, E. (1987). *Adorned in Dreams: Fashion and Modernity*. London: Virago.

Further Reading

Babuscio, J. (1993). *Camp Grounds: Style and Homosexuality*. Amherst: University of Massachusetts Press.

Baines, B. B. (1981). *Fashion Revivals from the Elizabethan Age to the Present Day*. London: B. T. Batsford.

Barthes, R. (1983). *The Fashion System*, trans. W. Ward and R. Howard. New York: Hill and Wang.

Benstock, S. and Ferriss, S. (eds.) (1994). *On Fashion*. New Brunswick, NJ: Rutgers University Press.

Berry, S. (2000). *Screen Style: Fashion and Femininity in 1930s Hollywood*. Minneapolis: University of Minnesota Press.

Blau, Herbert. (1999). *Nothing in Itself: Complexions of Fashion*. Bloomington: Indiana University Press.

Blumer, H. (1968). "Fashion." *International Encyclopedia of the Social Sciences*. New York: Macmillan.

Bocock, R. (1993). *Consumption*. London: Routledge.

Bourdieu, P. (1984). "Haute couture et haute culture." In *Questions de Sociologie*. Paris: Editions de Minuit.

Brain, R. (1979). *The Decorated Body*. New York: Harper & Row.

Breward, C. (1995). *The Culture of Fashion: A New History of Fashionable Dress*. Manchester: Manchester University Press.

Butler, J. (1993). *Bodies That Matter: On the Discursive Limits of "Sex."* New York: Routledge.

Butler, J. (1990). *Gender Trouble*. New York: Routledge.

Damhorst, M. L., Miller, K. A., Michelman, S. (eds.) (1999). *The Meanings of Dress*. New York: Fairchild Publications.

Davis, K. (1995). *Reshaping the Female Body: The Dilemma of Cosmetic Surgery*. New York: Routledge.

De Grazia, V. and Furlough, E. (eds.) (1996). *The Sex of Things: Gender and Consumption in Historical Perspective*. Berkeley: University of California Press.

Faurschou, G. (1987). "Fashion and the Cultural Logic of Postmodernity." *Canadian Journal of Political and Social Theory* 11(1–2): 68–82.

Featherstone, M. (1982). "The Body in Consumer Culture." *Theory, Culture and Society* 1(2): 18–33.

Finkelstein, J. (1996). *Fashion: An Introduction*. New York University Press.

Garber, M. (1992). *Vested Interests: Cross-Dressing and Cultural Anxiety*. New York: Routledge.

Goffman, E. (1962). "Attitudes and Rationalizations Regarding Body Exposure." In Roach, M. E. and Eicher, J. B. (eds.), *Dress Adornment and the Social Order*. New York: John Wiley and Sons.

Green, N. (1997). *Ready-To-Wear and Ready-To-Work: A Century of Industry and Immigrants in Paris and New York*. Durham: Duke University Press.

Hall, L. (1992). *Common Threads: A Parade of American Clothing*. Boston: Little, Brown and Company.

Horn, M. J. and Gurel L. M. (1981). *The Second Skin: An Interdisciplinary Study of Clothing*, 3rd edn. Boston: Houghton Mifflin.

Joseph, N. (1986). *Uniforms and Nonuniforms: Communication Through Clothing*. Westport, Conn.: Greenwood Press.

Kaiser, S. B. (1985). *The Social Psychology of Clothing*. New York: Macmillan.

Kidwell, C. (1974). *Suiting Everyone: The Democratization of Clothing in America*. Washington, DC: Smithsonion Institution Press.

Kunzle, D. (1982). *Fashion and Fetishism: A Social History of the Corset, Tight-Lacing, and Other Forms of Body-Sculpture in the West*. Totowa, NJ: Rowman and Littlefield.

Kuriyama, S. (1999). *The Expressiveness of the Body and the Divergence of Greek and Chinese Medicine*. New York: Zone Books.

Laquener, T. (1990). *Making Sex: Body and Gender from the Greeks to Freud*. Cambridge, Mass.: Harvard University Press.

Lunt, P. and Livingstone, S. (1992). *Mass Consumption and Personal Identity: Everyday Economic Experience*. Buckingham: Open University Press.

McCracken, G. (1990). *Culture and Consumption: New Approaches to the Symbolic Character of Consumer Goods and Activities*. Bloomington: Indiana University Press.

Miles, S. (1998). *Consumerism as a Way of Life*. London: Sage.

Nava, M. (1991). "Consumerism Reconsidered: Buying and Power." *Cultural Studies* 5(2): 157–73.

Peiss, Kathy. (1999). *Hope in a Jar: The Making of America's Beauty Culture*. New York: Owl Books.

Polhemus, T. and Proctor, L. (1978). *Fashion and Anti-Fashion: An Anthropology of Clothing and Adornment*. London: Thames and Hudson.

Roche, D. (1994). *The Culture of Clothing: Dress and Fashion in the Ancien Regime*, trans. J. Birrell. Cambridge: Cambridge University Press.

Rouse, E. (1989). *Understanding Fashion*. Oxford: Blackwell Scientific.

Sennett, R. (1978). *The Fall of Public Man: On the Social Psychology of Capitalism*. New York: Vintage.

Turner, B. (1984). *The Body and Society*. Oxford Blackwell.

Weiner, A. and Schneider, J. (eds.) (1989). *Cloth and Human Experience*. Washington: Smithsonian Institution Press.

Wollen, P. (1993). "Fashion/Orientalism/The Body." In *Raiding the Icebox*. London: Verso.

Woolson, A. (ed.) (1974). *Dress Reform*. New York: Arno Press.

Chapter 27

Cultural Studies and Race

Robert Stam

Issues revolving "race" impact cultural studies in myriad ways, not all of them obvious. An examination of the relation between cultural studies and race might begin with the narrativization of the history of cultural studies itself. In the conventional narrative, "cultural studies" traces its roots to the 1960s work of such British leftists as Richard Hoggart (*The Uses of Literacy*), Raymond Williams (*Culture and Society*), E. P. Thompson (*The Making of the English Working Class*), and Stuart Hall, associated with the Centre for Contemporary Cultural Studies, founded in 1964 at the University of Birmingham. Conscious of the oppressive aspects of the British class system, the members of the Birmingham Centre, many of whom were associated with adult education projects, deployed Gramscian categories to illuminate issues of class, looking both for aspects of ideological domination and for new agents of social change.

Some Precursors of Cultural Studies

With all due respect for the extraordinary achievements of the Birmingham School, it is also possible to see a more diffuse and international genealogy for cultural studies. Although the by-now-ubiquitous catch-all term "cultural studies" must be credited to Birmingham, one can also posit a more international lineage for the movement in the work of figures such as Roland Barthes and Henri Lefebvre in France, Leslie Fiedler in the United States, Frantz Fanon in Martinique, France, and North Africa, and C. L. R. James in the Caribbean. Indeed, their writing casts suspicion on the Anglo-diffusionist narrative that cultural studies "began" in England and then spread elsewhere. In our perspective, when James Baldwin spoke about black preaching and the differentiated reception of films like *The Defiant Ones*, when Roland Barthes spoke of the "mythologies" of toys, detergents, and *Le Guide Michelin*, when Leslie Fiedler anatomized the myth of the "vanishing Indian" and found homoeroticism in *Huckleberry Finn*, when Henri Lefebvre analyzed the politics of urban space and

471

everyday life, and when C. L. R. James analyzed cricket and *Moby Dick*, they were all doing "cultural studies" *avant la lettre*.

Indeed, one could carry this archaeological project even further, going back to the 1920s and Bakhtin in the Soviet Union and Kracauer (e.g. *The Mass Ornament*) in Germany. One could even call attention to some completely unsung heroes of cultural studies. My personal candidate for most neglected precursor would be the brilliant Brazilian essayist/poet/novelist/anthropologist/musicologist Mario de Andrade. A man of African, indigenous, and European ancestry, de Andrade was a key participant in the Brazilian modernist movement in the 1920s. In his writing, he mingled a wide spectrum of references – the surrealists, Brazilian indianism, popular music, Afro-Brazilian religion, nursery rhymes, Amazonian legends – in a splendid tapestry of analysis and creation. In my opinion the equal of his contemporary James Joyce, his major "mistake" was to write in a nonhegemonic language: Brazilian Portuguese.

Before speaking more generally of cultural studies and race, I would like to highlight just one "proto-cultural-studies" figure: Frantz Fanon. A contemporary rereading of Fanon reveals him to be an important precursor for a number of currents within contemporary cultural studies. Although Fanon never spoke of "Orientalist discourse," for example, his critiques of colonialist imagery provide proleptic examples of anti-orientalist and postcolonial critique. Although often caricatured as a racial hardliner, in *Black Skin, White Masks* Fanon anticipated the anti-essentialist critique of race. In Fanon's relational view, the black man is obliged to be black "in relation to" the white man. The black man, as Fanon put it, *is* comparison." Nor was colonialism essentially a racial matter; colonialism, he argued, "was only *accidentally* white." (Ireland, as the first British colony, was subjected to the same processes of otherization that other, later, epidermically darker colonies also suffered.) For Fanon, racialized perception was inflected even by language; "the black will be the proportionately whiter . . . in direct relation to his mastery of the French language." Fanon thus saw race as languaged, situated, constructed. As someone who was seen as black by white Frenchmen, but as culturally European (i.e. white) by Algerians, Fanon had a clear sense of the conjunctural, constructed nature not only of racial categorizations but also of communitarian self-definition. Fanon thus anticipated the "constructivist" current within cultural studies, yet for Fanon the fact that race was on some level constructed did not mean that antiracism was not worth fighting for. His was a mobilizing sense of construction, one which embraced fluidity and ambivalence but without abandoning the struggle for such "constructs" as black solidarity, the Algerian nation, and Third World Unity.

Fanon worked at the point of convergence of anti-imperial politics and psychoanalytic theory, as Diana Fuss (1995) points out, finding a link between the two in the concept of "identification."[1] For Fanon, identification was at once a psychological, cultural, historical, and political issue. One of the symptoms of colonial neurosis, for example, was an incapacity on the part of the colonizer to identify with colonialism's victims. Fanon was also a critic of the media.

"Objectivity" in the news, Fanon pointed out in *The Wretched of the Earth*, always works against the native. The issue of identification also had a cinematic dimension, one closely linked to later debates in film theory, which also came to speak of identification and projection, of narcissism and regression, of "spectatorial positioning" and "suture" and point-of-view, as basic mechanisms constituting the cinematic subject.

Fanon was also one of the first thinkers to bring Lacanian psychoanalysis into cultural theory, including film theory. Fanon saw racist films, for example, as a "release for collective aggressions." In *Black Skin, White Masks* (1952), Fanon used the example of Tarzan to point to a certain instability within cinematic identification:

> Attend showings of a Tarzan film in the Antilles and in Europe. In the Antilles, the young negro identifies himself de facto with Tarzan against the Negroes. This is much more difficult for him in a European theatre, for the rest of the audience, which is white, automatically identifies him with the savages on the screen.

Anticipating many of the concerns of cultural studies, Fanon here points to the shifting, situational nature of colonized spectatorship: the colonial context of reception alters the processes of identification. The awareness of the possible negative projections of other spectators triggers an anxious withdrawal from the film's programed pleasures. The conventional self-denying identification with the white hero's gaze, the vicarious acting out of a European selfhood, is short-circuited through the awareness of being "screened" or "allegorized" by a colonial gaze within the movie theater itself. While feminist film theory later spoke of the "to-be-looked-at-ness" (Laura Mulvey) of female screen performance, Fanon called attention to the "to-be-looked-at-ness" of spectators themselves, who become slaves, as Fanon puts it, of their own appearance: "Look, a Negro! . . . . I am being dissected under white eyes. I am fixed." Although Fanon never used the talismanic phrase "cultural studies," in sum, he can still be seen as its proleptic practitioner. Already in the 1950s, he examined a wide variety of cultural forms – the veil, trance, language, radio, film – as sites of social and cultural contestation. Although never part of an explicit cultural studies project, he certainly practiced what now goes by that name. It is also no surprise, therefore, that some key figures in cultural theory – Henry Louis Gates, Jr., Diana Fuss, E. Sam Juan Jr., Isaac Julien, Kobena Mercer – have turned again to Fanon.

The Racing of Structuralism

Another way in which race impacts cultural studies has to do with the always already raced nature of its theoretical influences and antecedents. For example, two major influences on cultural studies were the related movements of struc-

473

turalism and semiotics. But these movements too were also "raced," in a double way. Although the practitioners were constructed as "white" and first world, third worldist thinking was a strong influence within these currents. Both structuralism and third-worldism had their long-term historical origins in a series of events that undermined the confidence of European modernity: the Holocaust (and in France the Vichy collaboration with the Nazis), and the postwar disintegration of the last European empires. Although the exalted term "theory" was rarely linked to anticolonial theorizing, structuralist thinking in some ways merely codified what anticolonial thinkers had been saying for some time. The subversive work of "denaturalization" performed by what one might call the left wing of semiotics – for example Roland Barthes' famous dissection of the colonialist implications of the *Paris Match* cover showing a black soldier saluting the French flag – had everything to do with the external critique of European master-narratives performed by Third World Francophone decolonizers like Aimé Césaire (*Discourse on Colonialism*, 1955) and Frantz Fanon (*The Wretched of the Earth*, 1961). In the wake of the Holocaust, decolonization, and Third World revolution, Europe started to lose its privileged position as model for the world. Lévi-Strauss's crucial turn from biological to linguistic models for a new anthropology, for example, was motivated by his visceral aversion to a biological anthropology deeply tainted by antisemitic and colonialist racism. Indeed, it was in the context of decolonization that UNESCO asked Lévi-Strauss to do the research which culminated in his *Race and History* (1952), where the French anthropologist rejected any essentialist hierarchy of civilizations.

Poststructuralism as well is indebted to anticolonialist and antiracist thinking. Césaire's and Fanon's anticolonialist decentering of Europe can now be seen as having both provoked and foreshadowed Derrida's claim (in "Structure, Sign and Play in the Discourse of the Human Sciences," 1966) that European culture has been "dislocated," forced to stop casting itself as "the culture of reference." Both the structuralist and the poststructuralist moments, in this sense, coincide with the moment of self-criticism, a veritable legitimation crisis, within Europe itself. Many of the source thinkers of structuralism and poststructuralism, and thus of cultural studies, furthermore, as Robert Young (1995) points out, were biographically linked to what came to be called the Third World: Lévi-Strauss did anthropology in Brazil; Foucault taught in Tunisia; Althusser, Cixous, and Derrida were all born in Algeria, where Bourdieu also did his anthropological fieldwork.

In England, cultural studies began by being more oriented toward issues of class; it came to engage issues of gender and race relatively "late." In 1978 the Women's Study Group lamented the "absence from CCCS of a visible concern with feminist issues." And in the 1980s cultural studies was challenged to pay more attention to race, under the pressure both of internal critique and of US cultural studies, which had always focussed more on gender and race while too often downplaying class. But all these issues must be seen within a much larger historical, geopolitical, and discursive frame. What all these currents have in common is their democratizing, egalitarian, and antihierarchical thrust. British cultural sudies, in this sense, subverted the high-art elitism of literature departments by extending sophisticated methods of analysis to "low" popular arts and practices. At the same time, British cultural studies in its early incarnations was somewhat less attentive to other forms of hierarchical oppression. "There was no black," to paraphrase Paul Gilroy, "in Raymond Williams-style cultural studies."

Multiculturalism and Eurocentrism

In racial terms, cultural studies can be seen as a surface manifestation of a larger seismological shift – the decolonization of global culture. In the 1980s, "multiculturalism" became one of the buzzwords to evoke this decolonizing attack on white supremacist institutions and modes of thinking. Although Neoconservatives caricature multiculturalism as calling for the violent jettisoning of European classics and of "western civilization as an area of study,"[2] multiculturalism is actually an assault not on Europe (in the broad sense of Europe and its affiliates spread around the world) but on Eurocentrism – on the procrustean forcing of cultural heterogeneity into a single paradigmatic perspective in which Europe is seen as the unique source of progress, as the world's center of gravity, as ontological "reality" to the rest of the world's shadow. As an ideological substratum or discursive residue common to colonialist, imperialist, and racist discourse, Eurocentrism is a form of vestigial thinking which permeates and structures *contemporary* practices and representations even after the formal end of colonialism. Eurocentric discourse is complex, contradictory, historically unstable. But in a kind of composite portrait, Eurocentrism as a mode of thought might be seen as engaging in a number of mutually reinforcing intellectual tendencies or operations. Eurocentric thinking attributes to the "West" an almost Providential sense of historical destiny. Like Renaissance perspective in painting, it envisions the world from a single privileged point. It bifurcates the world into the "West and the Rest"[3] and organizes everyday language into binaristic hierarchies implicitly flattering to Europe: *our* "nations," *their* "tribes"; *our* "religions," *their* "superstitions"; *our* "culture," *their* "folklore." A "plato-to-Nato" teleology sees history as moving North-by-Northwest, projecting a linear historical trajectory leading from the Middle East and Mesopotamia to classical Greece (constructed as "pure," "western," and "democratic") to imperial Rome and then to the metropolitan capitals of Europe and the US. In all cases, Europe, alone and unaided, is seen as the "motor" for progressive historical change: democracy, class society, feudalism, capitalism, the industrial revolution. Eurocentrism appropriates the cultural and material production of non-Europeans while denying both their achievements and its own appropriation, thus consolidating its sense of self and glorifying its own cultural anthropophagy.

For Cornel West (1993), Eurocentrism superimposes three white-supremacist logics: Judeo-Christian racist logic; scientific racist logic; and psychosexual racist logic. A multicultural view critiques the universalization of Eurocentric norms, the idea that any race, in Aimé Césaire's words, "holds a monopoly on beauty, intelligence, and strength." Needless to say, the critique of Eurocentrism is addressed not to Europeans as individuals but rather to dominant Europe's historically oppressive relation to its external and internal "others" (Jews, Irish, Gypsies, Huguenots, peasants, women). It does not suggest, obviously, that non-European people are somehow "better" than Europeans, or that Third World and minoritarian cultures are inherently superior.

On one level, the multicultural idea is very simple and transparent; it refers to the multiple cultures of the world and the historical relations between them, including relations of subordination and domination. The multiculturalist *project* (as opposed to the multicultural *fact*) proposes an analysis of world history and contemporary social life from the perspective of the radical equality of peoples in status, intelligence, and rights. In its more co-opted version, it can easily degenerate into a state or corporate-managed United-Colors-of-Benetton pluralism whereby established power promotes ethnic "flavors of the month" for commercial or ideological purposes, but in its more radical variants it strives to decolonize representation not only in terms of cultural artifacts but also in terms of power relations between communities. It is the need to ward off co-optation that generates all the qualifiers on the potentially innocuous word "multiculturalism": *critical* multiculturalism, *radical* multiculturalism, *subversive* multiculturalism, *polycentric* multiculturalism.

A radical or polycentric multiculturalism calls for a profound restructuring and reconceptualization of the power relations between cultural communities. It sees issues of multiculturalism, colonialism, and race not in a ghettoized way, but "in relation." Communities, societies, nations, and even entire continents exist not autonomously but rather in a densely woven web of relationality. As Ella Shohat and I argue in *Unthinking Eurocentrism*, it is possible to distinguish between a co-optive liberal pluralism, tainted at birth by its historical roots in the systematic inequities of conquest, slavery, and exploitation, and a more radical *polycentric multiculturalism*. The notion of polycentrism has implications for cultural studies because it globalizes multiculturalism. It envisions a restructuring of intercommunal relations within and beyond the nation-state according to the internal imperatives of diverse communities. Within a polycentric vision, the world has many dynamic cultural locations, many possible vantage points. The "poly" in "polycentrism" does not refer to a finite list of centers of power but rather introduces a systematic principle of differentiation, relationality, and linkage. No single community or part of the world, whatever its economic or political power, should be epistemologically privileged.

Race and Racism

But to further talk about the relation between "race" and "cultural studies" requires us to sketch out what we mean by such notions as "race" and "racism." An emerging consensus within various fields suggests that although "race" does not exist – since "race" is a pseudo-scientific concept – racism as a set of social practices most definitely *does* exist. There is no race, then, but only racism. By analogy, there is no "other," but only processes of otherization; no exotics – no one is exotic to *themselves* – but only exoticization.

Racism, although hardly unique to the West, and while not limited to the colonial situation (antisemitism being a case in point), has historically been both an ally and the partial product of colonialism. The most obvious victims of racism are those whose identity was forged within the colonial cauldron: Africans, Asians, and the indigenous peoples of the Americas as well as those displaced by colonialism, such as Asians and West Indians in Great Britain, Arabs in France. Colonialist culture constructed a sense of ontological European superiority to "lesser breeds without the law." Albert Memmi (1968: 186) defines racism as "the generalized and final assigning of values to real or imaginary differences, to the accuser's benefit and at his victim's expense, in order to justify the former's own privilege or aggression."

Racism is above all a social relation – "systematized hierarchization implacably pursued," in Fanon's pithy formula[4] – anchored in material structures and embedded in historical relations of power. In fact Memmi's definition, premised on a kind of one-on-one encounter between racist and victim, does not fully account for more abstract, indirect, submerged, even "democratic" forms of racism. Since racism is a complex hierarchical system, a structured ensemble of social and institutional practices and discourses, individuals do not have to actively express or practice racism to be its beneficiaries. Racism cannot be reduced, as it is in the anti-"hate" discourse of public-service announcements, to the ravings of pathological maniacs. In a systemically racist society, racism is the "normal" pathology, from which virtually no one is completely exempt, including even its victims. Racism traces its deep psychic roots to fear of the "other" (associated with a suppressed, animalic, "shadowy" self) and to phobic attitudes toward nature and the body. As Ralph Ellison (another proleptic practitioner of cultural studies) put it, it was the "negro misfortune" to be caught up associatively:

> on the negative side of [the] basic dualism of the white folk mind and to be shackled to almost everything it would repress from conscience and consciousness.[5]

The paired terms "black" and "white" easily lend themselves to the Manicheanisms of good/evil; matter/spirit; devil/angel. And since everyday speech posits blackness as negative ("black sheep," "black day"), and posits black and white as

477

opposites ("it's not a black and white issue") rather than as nuances on a spectrum, blacks have almost always been cast on the side of evil. It is resistance to this Manichean temptation that has led many – from Franz Boaz in the 1920s to Jesse Jackson in the 1980s – to call for a move from a terminology based on color and race to one based on culture, to speak not of blacks and whites, for example, but rather of African-Americans and European-Americans. (Paul Gilroy's latest book, revealingly, is entitled *Against Race*.)

Individuals are traversed by social forcefields, and specifically by relations of social domination and subordination. Cultural producers and receivers are not just individuals in the abstract; they are of a specific nationality, class, gender, and sexuality. Much of cultural studies work has focused on these axes of social identity and oppression, the diverse forms of stratification summed up in the "mantra" of race, gender, class, and sexuality. Which brings up the issue of the relation between all these distinct axes of social representation. We have to ask whether one of the axes of oppression is primordial, the root of all the others? Is class the foundation of all oppressions, as canonical Marxism had suggested? Or is patriarchy ultimately more fundamental to social oppression than classism and racism, as some versions of feminism might suggest? Or is race the overarching determinant? Are there "analogical structures of feeling" which would lead one oppressed group to identify with another? What are the analogies between antisemitism, antiblack racism, sexism, and homophobia? Both homophobia and antisemitism have in common a penchant for projecting enormous power onto their targeted victims: "they" control everything, or "they" are trying to take over. But what is unique and specific to each of these forms of oppression? A person can be the victim of homophobia within his/her own family, for example, something far less likely in the case of antisemitism or antiblack racism. To what extent can one "ism" hang out, as it were, with other isms? Sexism, racism, and classism can all tinge themselves with homophobia, for example. What is most important, perhaps, is not to ghettoize these axes of representation, to see the operations of what critical race theorists call "intersectionality," that race is classed, gender raced, class sexualized, and so forth.

Stereotype and the Burden of Representation

For our purposes, racism in popular culture refers to all the contextual and textual practices whereby racialized difference is transformed into "otherness" and exploited or penalized by and for those with institutionalized power. The hair-trigger sensitivity about racial stereotypes partially derives from what James Baldwin called the "burden of representation." On the symbolic battlegrounds of the mass media, the struggle over representation in the simulacral realm homologizes that of the political sphere, where questions of imitation and representation easily slide into issues of delegation and voice. Any negative behavior by any member from the oppressed community, for example that of O. J. Simpson, is instantly encoded as pointing to a perpetual backsliding toward some presumed negative essence. Representations thus become allegorical; within hegemonic discourse every subaltern performer/role is seen as synecdochically summing up a vast but putatively homogenous community. Socially empowered groups need not be unduly concerned about "distortions and stereotypes," since even occasionally negative images form part of a wide spectrum of representations. Each negative image of an underrepresented group, in contrast, becomes sorely overcharged with allegorical meaning.

The sensitivity around stereotypes and distortions largely arises then, from the powerlessness of historically marginalized groups to control their own representation. A full understanding of filmic representation therefore requires a comprehensive analysis of the institutions that generate and distribute mass-mediated texts as well as of the audience that receives them. Whose stories are being told? By whom? How are they manufactured, disseminated, received? Cultural studies, in this sense, needs to engage not only consumption but also production. Despite the success of celebrities like Oprah Winfrey and Bill Cosby, for example, only a handful of blacks hold executive positions with film studios and television networks.[6]

Film and television casting, as an immediate form of representation, constitutes a kind of delegation of voice with political overtones. Here too Europeans and Euro-Americans have played the preponderant role, relegating non-Europeans to supporting roles and the status of extras. Within Hollywood cinema, Euro-Americans have historically enjoyed the unilateral prerogative of acting in "blackface," "redface," "brownface," and "yellowface." This asymmetry in representational power has generated intense resentment among minoritarian communities, for whom the casting of a nonmember of the minority group is a triple insult, implying (*a*) you are unworthy of self-representation; (*b*) no one from your group is capable of representing you; and (*c*) we, the producers of the film, care little about your offended sensibilities, for we have the power and there is nothing to be done about it.

Important work has already been done on the ethnic/racial representation and stereotypes in the media. (See Miller 1980; Pettit 1980; Woll & Miller 1987; Churchill 1992; Guerrero 1993; Shohat & Stam 1994; Wiegman 1995.) Critics such as Vine Deloria (1969), Ralph and Natasha Friar (1972), Ward Churchill (1992), Jacqueline Kilpatrick (1999), and many others have discussed the binaristic splitting that has turned Native Americans into bloodthirsty beasts or noble savages. A number of other scholars, notably Donald Bogle (1988, 1989), Daniel Leab (1976), James Snead (1994), Ed Guerrero (1993), Jim Pines (1992), Clyde Taylor (1998), Thomas Cripps (1977, 1979, 1993), Gray (1995), have explored how preexisting stereotypes – for example the jiving sharpster and shuffling stage sambo – were transferred from antecedent media to film and television. Important work has also been done on the stereotypes of other ethnic groups such as Latinos. (See Noriega 1992; Fregoso 1993, Ramirez Berg 1992.)

479

There is no point in summarizing the work on stereotypes here; rather, I would like both to defend the importance of such work and raise some methodological questions about the underlying premises of character or stereotype-centered approaches. To begin, stereotype analysis has made an indispensible contribution by (1) revealing oppressive *patterns* of prejudice in what might at first glance have seemed random and inchoate phenomena; by (2) highlighting the psychic devastation inflicted by systematically negative portrayals on those groups assaulted by them, whether through internalization of the stereotypes themselves or through the negative effects of their dissemination; by (3) signaling the social *functionality* of stereotypes, demonstrating that stereotypes are not an error of perception but rather a form of social control. The call for "positive images," in the same way, corresponds to a profound logic which only the representationally privileged can fail to understand. Given a dominant cinema that trades in heros and heroines, minority communities rightly ask for their fair share of the representational pie as a simple matter of representational parity.

At the same time, the stereotype approach entails a number of pitfalls from a theoretical-methodological standpoint. First, the exclusive preoccupation with images, whether positive or negative, can lead to a kind of *essentialism*, as less subtle critics reduce a complex variety of portrayals to a limited set of reified formulae. Such reductionist simplifications run the risk of reproducing the very racism they were designed to combat. This essentialism generates in its wake a certain *ahistoricism*; the analysis tends to be static, not allowing for mutations, metamorphoses, changes of valence, altered function; it ignores the historical instability of the stereotype and even of language. Stereotypic analysis is likewise covertly premised on *individualism*, in that the individual character, rather than larger social categories (race, class, gender, nation, sexual orientation), remains the point of reference. The focus on individual character also misses the ways in which whole cultures, as opposed to individuals, can be caricatured or misrepresented without a single character being stereotyped. Countless films and TV programs reproduce Eurocentric prejudices against African spirit religions, for example, by regarding them as superstitious cults rather than as legitimate belief-systems, prejudices enshrined in the patronizing vocabulary ("animism," "ancestor worship," "magic") used to discuss the religions. In sum, a vast cultural complex can be defamed without recourse to a character sterotype.

A moralistic approach also sidesteps the issue of the relative nature of "morality," eliding the question: positive for whom? It ignores the fact that oppressed people might not only have a *different* vision of morality, but even an *opposite* vision. What is seen as "positive" by the dominant group, e.g. the acts of those "Indians" in westerns who spy for the whites, might be seen as treason by the dominated group. The taboo in classical Hollywood was not on "positive images" but rather on images of racial equality, images of anger and revolt. The privileging of positive images also elides the patent differences, the social and moral heteroglossia, characteristic of any social group. A cinema of contrivedly positive image betrays a lack of confidence in the group portrayed, which usually itself has no illusions concerning its own perfection. It is often assumed, furthermore, that control over representation leads automatically to the production of "positive images." But African films like *Laafi* (1991) and *Finzan* (1990) do not offer positive images of African society; rather, they offer *African* perspectives on African society. "Positive images," in this sense, can be a sign of insecurity. Hollywood, after all, has never worried about sending films around the world which depicted the US as a land of gangsters, rapists, and murderers. More important than turning characters into heroes is that they be treated as subjects (not objects). More important than image is the question of agency.

While on one level film is mimesis, representation, it is also utterance, an act of contextualized interlocution between socially situated producers and receivers. It is not enough to say that art is constructed. We have to ask "constructed for whom?" and in conjunction with which ideologies and discourses? In this sense, art is a representation in not so much a mimetic as a political sense, as a delegation of voice.[7] One methodological alternative to the mimetic "stereotypes and distortions" approach is to speak less of "images" than of "voices" and "discourses." The very term "image studies" symptomatically elides the oral and the "voiced." A more nuanced discussion of race in the cinema would emphasize less a one-to-one mimetic adequacy to historical truth than the interplay of voices, discourses, perspectives, including those operative within the image itself. The task of the critic would be to call attention to the cultural voices at play, not only those heard in aural "close-up" but also those distorted or drowned out by the text. The question is not of pluralism but of multivocality, an approach that would strive to cultivate and even heighten cultural difference while abolishing socially-generated inequalities.

Culture in the Multination State

Strangely, the practitioners of "multicultural media studies," on the one hand, and of "cultural studies," on the other, often seem to go about their business without fully taking cognizance of one other. But what are the implications of multiculturalism for cultural studies? One implication is that in the present postcolonial, globalized yet still racist present day, all cultures are in a sense "multicultures." Speaking of the Americas, Canadian political theorist Will Kymlicka argues that countries like Brazil and the United states are not "nation states" but rather "multi-nation states," in that their cultural/racial diversity derives from the presence of three major constellations of groups: (1) those who were already in the Americas (i.e. indigenous peoples in all their tremendous variety); (2) those who were forced to come to the Americas (i.e. enslaved

Africans in all *their* variety); and (3) those who *chose* to come to the Americas (immigrants in all *their* variety). But the other sites of cultural studies, such as England, Australia, and France, are also multicultural. Thanks to colonial karma, England is now also Indian, Pakistani, and Caribbean. British films like *Sammy and Rosie Get Laid* (1987), *London Kills Me* (1991), *Young Soul Rebels* (1991), and *Bhaji at the Beach* (1989) bear witness to the tense postcolonial hybridity of former colonials growing up in what was once the "motherland": In the multi-cultural neighborhood of *Sammy and Rosie Get Laid*, the inhabitants have "lines out," as it were, to the formerly colonized regions of the globe. France, similarly, is now Asian, Maghrebian, African, and Caribbean. The New Wave has given way to *beur* ("Arab" spelled backwards) cinema, the production of North Africans in France, while African-American hiphop culture pervades the Parisian *banlieux*.

The popular culture which "cultural studies" examines, in sum, is now constitutively, irrevocably multicultural, mixed, mestizo. Music especially has been the privileged site of syncretism. The falsely open rubric "World music," in this sense, is just another name for "international music produced by people of color," just as the falsely closed rubric "best foreign film," in the Oscar Cere-monies, is really another name for "World film." The "dangerous crossroads" (Lipsitz) of musical traditions offer mutually enriching collaborations between the diverse currents of Afro-diasporic music, yielding such hybrids as "samba reggae," "samba rap," "jazz tango," "rap reggae," and "roforenge" (a blend of rock, forro, and merengue). Diasporic musical cultures mingle with one another, while simultaneously also playing off the dominant media-disseminated tradition of First world, especially American, popular music, itself energized by Afro-diasporic traditions. An endlessly creative multidirectional flow of musical ideas thus moves back and forth around the "Black Atlantic" (Thompson, Gilroy), Afro-diasporic music displays an anthropophagic capacity to absorb influences, including Western influences, while still being driven by a culturally African bass-note. In the Americas, musicians such as Stevie Wonder, Taj Mahal, Ruben Blades, Gilberto Gil, Caetano Veloso, Marisa Monte, and Carlinhos Brown not only practice syncretic forms of music but also thematize syncretism within their lyrics. The new fluidities of cultural exchange enabled by cable and satellite TV, meanwhile, amplify these exchanges. Rap music has by now become the world-wide *lingua franca* of musical protest. If Martians were to come to earth and listen to the radio, as Robert Farris Thompson once put it, they would conclude that there had been an African takeover of the planet.

Cultural studies approaches to popular media almost inevitably engage issues of race, whether in the negative sense of race as stereotype or as structuring absence, or in the positive sense of media productions which call attention to the raced nature of culture. Since race is a constitutive rather than a secondary feature of American national identity, for example, we should not be surprised to find racial undertones and overtones haunting countless Hollywood films, just as the repressed stories, the sublimated agonies, and the buried labor of minorities "haunt" everyday social life. In Hollywood musicals, African Americans constituted not only a suppressed historical voice but also a literally suppressed ethnic voice, since Black musical idioms became more associated on the screen with "white" stars, authorizing a Euro-American signature on what were basically African American cultural products. In a power-inflected form of ambivalence, the same dominant society that "loves" ornamental snippets of black culture excludes the black performers who might best incarnate it. These politics of racial representation were not "unconscious," they were the object of explicit debate and negotiation within the Hollywood production system, a question of the competing influences of Southern (and Northern) racists, liberals, black public advocacy groups, censors, nervous producers and so forth. Thomas Cripps describes the processes by which blackness in films was edited out: the way the African-American music that inspired George Gershwin was gradually elided from the biopic *Rhapsody in Blue* (1945), for example, leaving Paul Whiteman to "make a lady out of jazz"; or the way *Lydia Bailey* (1952) turned from a story about Toussaint l'Ouverture and the Haitian revolution into a white-focalized romance.

Another way that "race" impacts cultural studies has to do with the fact that the Anglo-American popular culture that cultural studies tends to analyze is projected around the world. For cultural studies to focus narcissistically only on Anglo-American popular culture, while ignoring the effects of that culture in the world and while also ignoring the popular culture of what is dsmissively called the "rest of the world," is to reinscribe the existing asymmetries of knowledge, rooted in neocolonial structures of power, whereby the peoples of Africa, Asia, and Latin America invariably know first-world languages and culture better than first worlders know theirs.

In a more positive sense, American popular culture bears constant witness to the "dialogue" not only between different marginal groups but also between Euro-American culture and its "others." Literary analysts point to the (admittedly assymetrical) dialogue of Crusoe and Friday in *Robinson Crusoe*, Huck and Jim in *Huckleberry Finn*, Ishmael and Queequeeg in *Moby Dick*. Many literary scholars have tried to "desegregate" American literary history. What happens, Eric Sundquist asks in *To Wake the Nations*, when we regard works like Melville's novella about a slave revolt (*Benito Cereno*) as part of a *black* literary tradition? In film, this dialogue has often taken the alienated form of hero-and-sidekick (the Lone Ranger and Tonto, latter-day avatars of Crusoe and Friday), or of hero and valet (Jack Benny and Rochester), or of hero and entertainer (Rick and Sam in *Casablanca*, 1942). In *The Defiant Ones* (1958) Tony Curtis and Sidney Poitier carry a chain-heavy allegory of racial interdependency. The 1980s and 1990s offer more upbeat versions of the biracial "buddy film": Richard Pryor and Gene Wilder in *Stir Crazy* (1980) and *See No Evil* (1989), Eddie Murphy and Nick Nolte in *48 Hours* (1982), Billy Crystal and Gregory Hines in *Running Scared* (1986), and Mel Gibson and Danny Glover in the various *Lethal Weapons*. Films like *Driving Miss Daisy* (1991), *Grand Canyon* (1992), *Passion Fish* (1992), *White*

Men Can't Jump (1992), *Ghost Dog* (1999), and *Black and White* (2000) similarly place black–white dialogue at the center of their concerns. The appeal, including the box-office appeal, of such films suggests that they touch something deep within the national Unconscious, a historically-conditioned longing for inter-racial harmony. And indeed images of ethnic utopia percolate all through American popular culture, from the perennial Thanksgiving celebrations through the latest multiethnic music videos. One finds echoes of the same utopian trope, at a more advanced stage of development, in contemporary TV talkshows (*Oprah*, *Politically Incorrect*), MTV, soft-drink commercials, TV sports, public service announcements, and in the amiable multiethnic camarad-erie of *Eyewitness News*, with its consolatory performance of ethnic harmony (contrasting brutally with the reports of innocent black men slain by white policemen).

In a multiracial society, the self is inevitably syncretic, especially when a preexisting cultural polyphony is amplified by the media. It is no accident that any number of American films stage the processes of ethnic syncretism: white men learning native American ways in films like *Hombre* (1967) and *A Man Called Horse*; Richard Pryor showing Gene Wilder how to "walk black" in *Silver Streak* (1976); young (white) boy David learning Jamaican patois from Clara in *Clara's Heart* (1988); Chinese immigrants learning street slang from Chicanos in *Born in East LA* (1987); Charlie Parker in a yarmulka jazzing up a Hassidic wedding in *Bird* (1988); Whoopie Goldberg teaching white nuns Motown dance routines in *Sister Act* (1992); and a host of black wannabes learning blackhand-shakes in *Black and White* (2000).

It is therefore also no accident that many films – *Watermelon Man* (1970), *Soul Man* (1986), *True Identity* (1987), *Zelig* (1983), *Whiteboy* (1999) – play on the trope of racial transformation. Sandra Bernhardt, in the opening sequence of *Without You I am Nothing*, sings "My skin is black" and is lit, and dressed, so as to appear black. But the trope is hardly limited to film. The all-white rap group "Young Black Teenagers" speak of being "Proud to be Black," arguing that "Blackness is a state of mind." Standup comics, finally, constantly cross racial boundaries through a kind of racial ventriloquism. Whoopi Goldberg imperson-ates (presumably white) "valley girls," while Billy Crystal impersonates (pre-sumably black) jazz musicians. These racial metamorphoses reach their apotheosis in Michael Jackson's "Black or White" music video, where morphing scrambles a succession of multiracial faces into an infinity of hybridized combin-ations. And more and more, American popular culture is a mestizo, dominated by "cultural mulattoes" such as Prince, Madonna, Maria Carey, Michael Jack-son, and Michael Boulton, symptomatic of a situation where people transcultur-ally metamorphize into their neighbors. Indeed, any binary grid which pits anglo whiteness against black/red/yellow others inevitably misses the complex contra-dictory gradations of syncretized culture, in a world where many young Germans fantasize about becoming Native Americans, and where Euro-American youth wear dreads and thicken their lips.

Whiteness Studies

Cultural studies has both been an infradisciplinary ferment *within* disciplines *and* an inclusive transdisciplinary umbrella *over* disciplines. Cultural studies is sufficiently "hot" that many disciplines are eager to claim, often speciously, that they had been doing cultural studies all along. At this point, it is hard to draw clear and distinct boundaries between such disciplinary fields as media studies, visual culture/studies, postcolonial studies, queer studies, diaspora studies, border studies, performance studies, Latino studies, Jewish studies, and whiteness studies, many of which engage, albeit differentially, with the same basic texts and issues. The 1990s have witnessed an attempt to move beyond ghettoized studies of isolated groups – native Americans, African Americans, Latinos – in favor of a relational and contrapuntal approach. The period has also witnessed the emergence of "whiteness studies." This movement responds to the call by scholars of color for an analysis of the impact of racism not only on its victims but also on its perpetrators. The "whiteness" scholars questioned the quiet yet overpowering normativity of whiteness, the process by which "race" was attributed to others while whites were tacitly positioned as unmarked norm, leaving whiteness as an uninterrogated space. Although whiteness (like blackness) was on one level merely a cultural fiction without any scientific basis, it was also a social fact with all-too-real consequences for the distribution of wealth, prestige, and opportunity (Lipsitz 1994: vii). In the wake of historical studies by Theodor Allen and Noel Ignatiev of how diverse "ethnics" (for example the Irish) became "white," whiteness studies "outed" whiteness as just another ethnicity, although one historically granted inordinate privilege. This movement hopefully signals the end of "the innocent white subject," and an end to the venerable practice of unilaterally racializing the Third World or minority "others," while casting whites as somehow "raceless."

Toni Morrison, bell hooks, Coco Fusco, George Lipsitz, Ruth Frankenberg, George Yúdice, Nelson Rodriguez, Noel Ignatiev, and Richard Dyer are among the many who have problematized normative notions of "whiteness." Dyer's book *White* (1997) focuses on the representation of white people in Western culture. The term "people of color" as a designation for "nonwhites," Dyer points out, implies that whites are "colorless" and thus normative: "Other people are raced, we are just people" (Dyer 1997: 1) Even lighting technologies, and the specific mode of movie lighting, Dyer points out, have racial implications, and the assumption that the "normal" face is the white face runs through most of the manuals on cinematography.

"Whiteness" studies at its best denaturalizes whiteness as unmarked norm, calling attention to the taken-for-granted privileges (e.g. not to be the object of media stereotypes) that go with whiteness. At its most radical, it calls for "race treason" and "abolitionism" in the John Brown tradition, for an opting out of white privilege. At the same time, "whiteness studies" runs the risk of once again recentering white Narcissism, of changing the subject back to the assumed center – a racial version of the Show Business dictum: "speak ill of me but speak." Whites, it has been pointed out, cannot divest themselves of privilege even when they want to. Whiteness studies also needs to be seen in a global context where black and white are not always the operative categories of difference but rather caste (in India) or religion (in the Middle East). The important thing is to maintain a sense of the hybrid relationality and social co-implication of communities, without falling into a facile discourse of easy synthesis.

From Cultural Studies to Multicultural Studies

Given the fact that all cultures are multicultures, it makes more sense to me to speak not of "cultural studies" but rather of "multicultural studies," as a way of normalizing the syncretic, mixed nature of all popular culture. Various subcurrents mingle in the larger stream of what might be called "multicultural studies": the analysis of "minority" discourse and representation; the critique of imperialist and orientalist media; the work on colonial and postcolonial discourse, the theorization of "minority," "diasporic," and "exilic" art; reflexive and dialogical anthropology, critical race theory; "whiteness" studies; the work on antiracist and multicultural media pedagogy.

And in a globalized world, it is perhaps time to think in terms of *comparative* multicultural studies, of relational studies which do not always pass through the putative "center." The global nature of the colonizing process, and the global reach of contemporary media, virtually oblige the cultural critic to move beyond the restrictive framework of the nation-state. What are the relationalities between Indian and Egyptian popular culture, for example? At times, even multiculturalists glimpse the issues through a narrowly nationalist and exceptionalist grid, speaking of the "contributions" of the world's diverse cultures to "the development of American society," unaware of the nationalist teleology underlying such a formulation. "Multiculturedness" is not a US monopoly, nor is multiculturalism the handmaiden of US identity politics. One of the consequences of Eurocentrism, for example, is that both North Americans and South Americans tend to look to Europe for self-definition and self-understanding, rather than to the other multiracial societies of the Americas. Yet the question of racial representation in North American cinema might be profitably studied within the relational context of the cinematic representations offered by the other racially plural societies of the Americas, with their shared history of colonialism, slavery, and immigration. A cross-cultural "mutually illuminating" dialogical approach would stress the analogies not only *within* specific national film traditions – e.g. the analogies and disanalogies in the representation of indigenous peoples, Africans, and immigrants, but also *between* them, the kind of comparative study which George Yúdice calls for in this volume and which I have attempted in relation to Brazil in my *Tropical Multiculturalism: A Comparative*

History of Race in Brazilian Cinema and Culture. How are issues of race and caste formulated in other national contexts? What discourses are deployed? What are the operative terms? How do positive and negative images of blacks vary from culture to culture? How has slavery been depicted in the cinemas of the Black Atlantic? Such studies would constitute a first step in deprovincializing a discussion that has too often focused only on Anglo–American issues and representations.

Notes

1 See Diana Fuss, *Identity Papers* (1995).
2 For Roger Kimball, multiculturalism implies "an attack on the . . . idea that, despite our many differences, we hold in common an intellectual, artistic, and moral legacy, descending largely from the Greeks and the Bible [which] preserves us from chaos and barbarism. And it is precisely this legacy that the multiculturalist wishes to dispense with." See Roger Kimball, *Tenured Radicals: How Politics has Corrupted Higher Education* (New York: Harper Collins, 1990), postscript.
3 The phrase "the West and the Rest," to the best of our knowledge, goes back to Chinweizu's *The West and the Rest of Us: White Predators, Black Slaves and the African Elite* (New York: Random House, 1975). It is also used in Stuart Hall and Bram Gieben (eds.), *Formations of Modernity* (Cambridge: Polity Press, 1992).
4 Frantz Fanon, "Racism and Culture," in *Présence Africaine* 8/9/10 (1956).
5 Ralph Ellison, *Shadow and Act* (New York: Vintage, 1972), p. 48.
6 See *The New York Times* (Sept. 24, 1991).
7 Kobena Mercer and Isaac Julien, in a similar spirit, distinguish between "representation as a practice of depicting" and "representation as a practice of delegation." See their "Introduction: De Margin and De Centre," *Screen* 29(4) (1988): 2–10.

References

Baker, Houston A. Jr., Manthia Diawara, and Ruth H. Lindeborg (eds.) (1996). *Black British Cultural Studies*. Chicago: University of Chicago Press.
Berg, Charles Ramirez (1992). *Cinema of Solitude: A Critical Study of Mexican Film, 1967–1983*. Austin: University of Texas Press.
Bogle, Donald (1988). *Blacks in American Films and Television: An Illustrated Encyclopedia*. New York: Simon and Schuster.
Bogle, Donald (1989). *Toms, Coons, Mulattoes, Mammies, and Bucks: An Interpretative History of Blacks in American Films*. New York: Continuum.
Bowser, Pearl (2000). *Writing Himself into History: Oscar Micheaux, His Silent Films, and His Audiences*. New Brunswick, NJ: Rutgers University Press.
Césaire, Aimé (1972). *Discourse on Colonialism*. New York: Monthly Review Press.
Churchill, Ward (1992). *Fantasies of the Master Race*. Maine: Common Courage Press.
Cripps, Thomas (1977). *Slow Fade to Black*. New York: Oxford University Press.
Cripps, Thomas (1979). *Black Film as Genre*. Bloomington: Indiana University Press.

Cripps, Thomas (1993). *Making Movies Black: The Hollywood Message Movie From World War II to the Civil Right Era*. New York: Oxford University Press.

Deloria, Vine, Jr. (1969). *Custer Died for Your Sins*. New York: Avon Books.

Derrida, Jacques (1978). "Structure, Sign and Play in the Discourse of the Human Sciences." In *Writing and Difference*. Chicago: University of Chicago Press.

Dyer, Richard (1997). *White*. London, New York: Routledge.

Fanon, Frantz (1964). *The Wretched of the Earth*. New York: Grove Press.

Fanon, Frantz (1967). *Black Skin, White Masks*. New York: Grove Press.

Fregoso, Rosa Linda (1993). *The Bronze Screen: Chicana and Chicano Film Culture*. Minneapolis: University of Minnesota Press.

Friar, Ralph and Natasha Friar (1972). *The Only Good Indian: The Hollywood Gospel*. New York: Drama Book Specialists.

Gilroy, Paul (1987). *There Ain't No Black in The Union Jack*. London: Hutchinson.

Gilroy, Paul (2000). *Against Race: Imagining Political Culture Beyond the Color Line*. Cambridge, Mass.: Belknap Press.

Gray, Herman (1995). *Watching Race: Television and the Struggle for "Blackness."* Minneapolis: University of Minnesota Press.

Guerrero, E. (ed.) (1993). *Framing Blackness: The African American Image in Film*. Philadelphia: Temple University Press.

Hoggart, Richard (1958). *The Uses of Literacy*. New York: Oxford University Press.

Jones, Jackie (1998). *Contemporary Feminist Theories*. New York: New York University Press.

Kilpatrick, J. (1999). *Celluloid Indians*. Lincoln: University of Nebraska Press.

Kracauer, Sigrified (1995). *The Mass Ornament*, trans. and ed. Thomas Y. Levin. Cambridge, Mass.: Harvard University Press.

Leab, Daniel J. (1976). *From Sambo to Superspade: The Black Experience in Motion Pictures*. Boston: Houghton-Mifflin.

Lévi-Strauss, Claude (1952). *Race and History*. Paris: UNESCO.

Lipsitz, George (1994). *Dangerous Crossroads: Popular Music, Postmodernism, and the Poetics of Place*. New York: Verso.

Memmi, Albert (1968). *Dominated Man*. Bosont: Beacon Press.

Miller, Randall M. (ed.) (1980). *The Kaleidoscopic Lens: How Hollywood Views Ethnic Groups*. Englewood, NJ: Jerome S. Ozer.

Noriega, Chon (1992). *Chicanos and Film: Essays on Chicano Representation and Resistance*. New York: Garland, 1991, rpt. University of Minnesota, 1992.

Pettit, Arthur (1980). *Images of the Mexican American in Fiction and Film*. College Station: Texas A&M University Press.

Pines, Jim (1992). *Black and White in Colour: Black People in British Television since 1936*. London: BFI.

Shohat, Ella and Robert Stam (eds.) (1994). *Unthinking Eurocentrism: Multiculturalism and the Media*. New York: Routledge.

Snead, James (1994). *White Screens, Black Images*. New York and London: Routledge.

Sundquist, Eric (1993). *To Wake the Nations: Race in the Making of American Literature*. Cambridge, Mass.: Harvard University Press.

Taylor, Clyde (1998). *The Mask of Art: Breaking the Aesthetic Contract – Film and Literature*. Bloomington and Indianapolis: Indiana University Press.

Thompson, E. P. (1963). *The Making of the English Working Class*. New York: Vintage.

West, Cornel (1993). *Beyond Eurocentrism and Multiculturalism*, vols. I and II. Monroe, Me.: Common Courage Press.

Wiegman, Robyn (1995). *American Anatomies: Theorizing Race and Gender*. Durham: Duke University Press.

Williams, Raymond (1958). *Culture and Society, 1780–1950*. London: Chatto and Windus.

Woll, Allen and Randall M. Miller (1987). *Ethnic and Racial Images in American Film and Television*. New York: Garland.

Young, Robert (1995). *Colonial Desire: Hybridity in Theory, Culture and Race*. New York: Routledge.

Chapter 28

Globalization and Culture

Toby Miller and Geoffrey Lawrence

We live in a moment popularly understood as "the global triumph of the United States and its way of life" (Hobsbawm 1998: 1). Henry Kissinger goes so far as to say that "globalization is really another name for the dominant role of the United States" (1999). The *Wall Street Journal* trumpets this loudly: "the US enters the 21st century in a position of unrivaled dominance that surpasses anything it experienced in the 20th.... America's free-market ideology is now the world's ideology; and the nation's Internet and biotechnology businesses are pioneering the technologies of tomorrow" (Murray 1999). For all the misery internal to that country (in 2000, even as 74 percent of college students expected to become millionaires, 44 million people had no medical cover), the US has international influence beyond the reach of other régimes. Consider a mundane expectation of sovereignty – that the modern state make its own stamps, featuring national images. Today, 70 countries, mostly in the Third World, have their stamps produced by the New York-based Inter-Governmental Philatelic Corporation. The dominant images are recycled icons from US popular culture (Mingo 1997). This US cultural imperialism is often understood as the apex of a wider phenomenon – globalization – that sees North American corporations wiping out the state system and obliterating the cultures of the world.

If that is so, it is the outcome of what is known as the "Washington Consensus." Dominant since the late 1970s, the "Consensus" favors open trade, comparative advantage, deregulation of financial markets, and low inflation. It has, of course, presided over slower worldwide growth and greater worldwide inequality than any time since the Depression, with job security and real wages down and working hours up in the industrialized market economies (IMECS). At the same time, the world's richest 20 percent of people earned 74 times the amount of the world's poorest in 1997, up from 60 times in 1990 and 30 times in 1960, as inequalities between North and South increase. The manifold catastrophes of the "Consensus" across the late 1990s – Mexico, southeast Asia, Russia, and Brazil – were explained away as aberrations by its apologists (Palley 1999: 49; Levinson 1999: 21; Galbraith 1999: 13).

The "Consensus" is animated by neoliberalism's mantra of individual free-dom, the marketplace, and minimal government involvement in economic mat-ters. This provides the intellectual alibi for a comparatively unimpeded flow of capital across national boundaries, and the rejection of labor, capital, and the state managing the economy together. On behalf of capital, the state undermines the union movement through policies designed to "free" labor from employment laws. (The Keynesian welfare system, which helped to redistribute funds to the working class, is dismantled in the process.) Ralph Nader refers to this as "a slow motion *coup d'état*," with the historic gains to representative discussion and social welfare made by working people and subaltern groups comprehensively proble-matized and rejected by corporate power (1999: 7).

Where does culture fit here? In an increasingly global division of labor, how cultural citizenship is theorized and actualized matters enormously for working people. Can their participatory rights be asserted in terms of: (i) where they live, were born, or work; (ii) the temporary or permanent domicile of their employer; or (iii) the cultural impact of a foreign multinational on daily life? These concerns form the backdrop to our investigation, and they should transform cultural studies. Why?

Montréal hosted the fourteenth quadrennial World Congress of Sociology in the late Northern summer of 1998. The conference marked the end of post-modernity – in a sense. The postmodern is often taken to include: an aesthetic style that tropes or quotes other forms in a *mélange* of cultural features; an economic turn by the IMECS towards trade and the service industries and away from self-sufficiency and manufacturing; a philosophical discourse that deconstructs existing forms of knowledge by using their own precepts to under-mine them; a priority on identity politics that transcends constitutional and class bases for defining political agency; the decline of the major forms of social reasoning of the past century (liberalism, Marxism, psychoanalysis, and Chris-tianity); and cultural theories derived from and informing the above (Collins 1992: 327).

This trope, ever-present four years earlier at the thirteenth Congress, was gone by 1998, erased (or at least rendered palimpsestic) by globalization: "and the postmodern/the postmodern and" saw their status as suffix and prefix written all over. Globalization had arisen from 1960s origins in French and US discussions of the future to a position of great prominence (Held et al. 1999: 1). So polysemous was the term that it included sameness, difference, unity, and disunity – in short, globalization, like postmodernity before it, had come to stand for nothing less than *life itself*. Something similar has gone on in cultural studies. The postmodern was "our" trope, signifying the end of grand narrative, rational expectation, and unitary power. But that very textual, impressionistic term, opposed to common sense in its very formulation, has become, in its own ahistorical way, *passé*. There is a huge array of cultural studies writings on the global, which again offers distinctive features of interest to the humanities left: mobility, hybridity, transnationalism, and chaos (Sinclair et al. 1996;

491

Mohammadi 1997; Mowlana 1996; Sussman & Lent 1998; Allen et al. 1996; Braman & Sreberny-Mohammadi 1996).

What *The Financial Times* (1997) calls "the G-word" is not the exclusive property of sociologists or cultural studies folks. The concept has great currency in the logics of businesses, unions, and governments – *Forbes* magazine launched *Forbes Global* in 1998 via a full-page social-realist-like advertisement, complete with red flags (which included currency signs), Castro- and Mao-garbed workers, and the slogan "Capitalists of the World Unite!" The avowed intent was to acknowledge and sell "the final victory of capitalism" as embodied in the new 'zine.

Globalization is a knowledge-effect with definite impacts on intellectual, economic, social, and governmental practice. Most accounts of it veer between three tendencies: celebration or lamentation in the face of the supposed universal triumph of the market and decline of the state; skepticism about the degree of change and the reality of a nonstate system; and caution that the fallout from transformations in the relation of private and public is not yet clear (Held et al. 1999: 2). In this chapter, we adumbrate relevant discourses about global economics, the nation-state, and the New International Division of Cultural Labor (NICL), concluding with a case-study from screen culture to exemplify issues confronting cultural studies.

Our analysis takes as its touchstone Bruno Latour's observation that "the words 'local' and 'global' offer points of view on networks that are by nature neither local nor global, but are more or less long and more or less connected" (1993: 122). Such terms are often binarized (and hence all-encompassing) in the globalization literature, where the plenitude of one becomes the lack of the other, and *vice versa*: a graceless zero-sum game between national and international, public and commercial. In place of this logic, we follow the dictum that "if one wants the great systems finally to be open to certain real problems, it is necessary to look for the data and the questions in which they are hidden" (Foucault 1991: 151).

Global Economics

The notion that space and time are routinely compressed under globalization draws on two key events: the Treaty of Tordesillas in 1494 and the Washington Conference of 1884. The first of these acknowledged the emergence of empire, as the Pope mediated rivalries between Portugal and Spain through a bifurcation of the world – the first recorded conceptualization of the globe as a site of conquest and exploitation. The second event, taking place the same year as the imperial division of Africa at the Conference of Berlin, standardized Greenwich as the axis of time and cartography. This development effectively marked the world as a site of interconnected government and commerce (Schaeffer 1997: 2, 7, 10–11).

Capitalism's uneven and unequal development paralleled the trends of Tordesillas and Washington, as mercantilist accumulation and imperialism between 1500 and 1800 were followed by the classical era of capital and its Industrial Revolution, founded on the use of natural resources for manufacturing copper, steel, and fuel. A period of Northern industrial development and agrarian change was partnered by European emigration to the Americas to deal with population overflow, while colonial possessions offered raw materials and enslaved labor (Amin 1997: 1, x; Reich 1999). A key shift occurred between 1870 and 1914 (not surprizingly, Bahá'u'lláh coined the phrase "New World Order" in 1873 [quoted in Calkins and Vézina 1996: 311]). During this period, global output and exchange increased by upwards of 3 percent annually – an unprecedented figure (Hirst 1997: 411). In response to these developments, socialists, syndicalists, and anarchists formed large international associations of working people (Herod 1997: 167).

Up to the Second World War, trade focused on national capitals, controled by nation-states. The period from 1945 to 1973 represented an "interregnum between the age of competing imperial powers and the coming of the global economy" (Teeple 1995: 57), while the international régime following the Second World War was based on US hegemony articulated with the expansionary needs of its corporations. As other economies grew, so did the interdependence between nations, and between companies within nations. After 1950, world trade was dominated by the triad of Europe, Japan, and the US, "each with their immense hinterland of satellite states" (Jameson 1996: 2). Between 1950 and 1973, total trade increased by almost 10 percent annually, and output by more than 5 percent, most of it between the triad (Hirst 1997: 411). Whereas modern manufacturing techniques were restricted in the nineteenth century to Europe and the northeastern US, they proliferated across the world, as applied intellect and science deterritorialized (Hindley 1999; Reich 1999). The Cold War constructed a polarized world of two totalizing ideologies, struggling just as empires had done over the previous century. This totality, which obscured other differences, encouraged the view that the future would see the triumph of one pole (Bauman 1998: 58) – hence today's mavens of *laissez-faire* and the supposed demise of the state.

Under the "Washington Consensus," at issue is the extent to which the historic promises made by established and emergent governments after 1945, to secure (*a*) the economic welfare of citizens and (*b*) their political sovereignty, can still be kept. Neoliberalism is the latest lever for these guarantees, and the one that has gone furthest towards breaking them. Governments want to deliver voters ongoing sovereignty and controled financial markets, along with international capital markets – what *The Economist* calls an "[i]mpossible trinity" ("Global Finance" 1999: 4, Survey Global Finance).

The promise of economic welfare initially seemed locally workable, via state-based management of supply and demand and the creation of industries to substitute imports with domestically produced items. The second promise,

493

sovereignty, required concerted international action to convince the colonial powers (principally Britain, the Netherlands, Belgium, France, and Portugal) that the peoples whom they had enslaved should be given the right of self-determination via nationalism. The latter became a powerful ideology of political mobilization as a supposed precursor to liberation. When this second promise was made good, the resulting postcolonial governments undertook to deliver the first promise. Most followed import-substitution industrialization, frequently via multinational corporations (MNCs) that established local presences. But Third World states suffered dependent underdevelopment and were unable to grow economically. Their formal *political* postcoloniality rarely became *economic*, apart from some Asian states that pursued export-oriented industrialization and service-based expansion. With the crises of the 1970s, even those states which had bourgeoisies with sufficient capital formation to permit a welfare system found that stagflation had undermined their capacity to hedge employment against inflation. We know the consequences: "the space of economic management of capital accumulation [no longer] coincided with that of its political and social dimensions" (Amin 1997: xi).

Import substitution of the 1950s and 1960s was progressively problematized and dismantled from the 1970s to today, a tendency that grew in velocity and scope with the erosion of state socialism. We have reached a point where it is said that "the state remains a pre-eminent political actor on the global stage," but "the aggregation of states . . . is no longer in control of the global policy process," a fundamentally non-normative system that is run by banks, corporations, and finance traders (Falk 1997: 124–5, 129–30). In the new system, core and periphery are blurred, the spatial mobility of capital is enhanced, unions are disciplined, the strategic strength of labor is undermined, and the power of the state is circumscribed by the ability of capital to move across borders – a fundamental shift in the bargaining and power relations between capital and labor, facilitated by transportation and information technologies, but still displaying the traces of specific national modes of integration into the NICL (Ross & Trachte 1990: 63; Thompson & Smith 1999: 197).

Because of their mobility, MNCs can discipline both labor and the state, such that the latter is reluctant to impose new taxes, constraints, or pro-worker policies in the face of possible declining investment. Post-state-socialist labor movements are advised on "appropriate" forms of life by the American Federation of Labor–Council of Industrial Organizations, in keeping with the latter's strong opposition to Marxism–Leninism over many decades (Herod 1997: 172, 175). The "uncompetitive" countries of the Arab world and Africa have their labor forces bracketed by MNCs as a reserve army of low-cost potential workers who will be imported to the North if required (Amin 1997: ix), while throughout the world, "household and informal sector activities" increase "to sustain global reproduction" (Peterson 1996: 10).

The global economic system that evolved from the mid-1970s saw Northern class factions support a transnational capital that displaced noncapitalist systems elsewhere (Robinson 1996: 14–15). Regulatory and other mechanisms were set in place to liberalize world trade, contain socialism, promote legislation favorable to capitalist expansion, and aggregate world markets. The latter, which included the formation of the European Union (EU) and other trade groupings, was crucial for the promotion of free trade régimes in the 1980s and beyond (though trade since then has not exceeded that of the postwar quarter century [Hirst 1997: 412]). The growth of corporate power had provided enough strength for corporations to demand the removal of national barriers to trade. The spread of foreign capital and currency markets has meant that economic decisions were taken outside the context of the nation-state, in ways that favored the market. And by 1994, half of the hundred biggest economies in the world "belonged" not to nation-states, but to MNCs (Donnelly 1996: 239). Four hundred of the latter accounted for two-thirds of fixed assets and 70 percent of trade (Robinson 1996: 20). Viewing the market as a deterritorializing movement does not imply a borderless world, but it is transforming the state. Through structural adjustment and liberalization, states adopt policies to manage global, rather than national, economic relations. These policies, with considerable variation, typically facilitate global circuits of money and commodities at the expense of social stability and environmental security within the nation-state (McMichael, forthcoming; McMichael & Lawrence, forthcoming).

Certain critics argue that the promiscuous nature of capital has been overstated, that the nation-state, far from being a series of "glorified local authorities" (Hirst 1997: 409) is in fact crucial to the regulation of MNCs, with regional blocs strengthening, rather than weakening, the ability of the state to govern. Most people continue to look to the latter for both economic sanction and return (Smith 1996: 580). In addition, the US, western Europe, and Japan are really the only key sites of MNC activity, housing more than two-thirds of MNC sales and assets. Direct foreign investment elsewhere is limited (Hirst 1997: 418; Kozul-Wright & Rowthorn 1998). Perhaps one in twenty MNCs actually function globally (Gibson-Graham 1996–7: 7–8). Multinationals look around for marginal utility and then retreat to what is known and controlable – so the explosion of foreign investment in the three years from 1994 saw an increase of 40 percent in MNC money poured into the US, while investment the other way was primarily in Britain, the Netherlands, Canada, France, and Australia ("Trade Barriers," 1997).

The "relationship between capitalism and territoriality" shifted (Robinson 1996: 18) but was still governed by interstate bodies as much as ever, albeit dominated by the G7 (Hirst 1997: 413; McMichael 2000: 177). Capital markets, for example, operated internationally but with national supervision and regulation; all conceivable plans for dealing with their transnational reach still involved formal governance ("Global Finance," 1999). Workers have dealt with these changing conditions via international trade secretariats, with many US unions following the very logic of Manifest Geo-Destiny that animates their bosses.

Transnational worker solidarity has tended to apply only at the grassroots rather than the peak level, and today is severely compromised by an isolationist labor stance that romanticizes national glories in opposition to a globalizing managerialism, while the latter is a gruesome business-leach discourse that has displaced international working-class solidarity as the prevailing international utopianism (Herod 1997: 168, 171, 185; Amsden & Hikino 1999: 7).

Clearly, the capitalist goal of worldwide liberalization has been supported by the institutionalization of market rules, involving the explicit reorganization of states to facilitate the circulation of money and commodities. John Wiseman (1998), for example, has reminded us that nation-states are not "blameless victims" of globalization, but colluders in the creation of policies which have facilitated global integration. Michael Porter's (1990) updated theory of comparative advantage has led many states to adopt policies which favor state-led, quasi-official, voluntaristic, and institutional structures that anchor economic activities for the benefit of transnational capital. The nation-state has embarked upon regulatory policies which have favored an enterprise-focused local state and new systems of local governance (Le Heron et al. 1997; Pritchard 1999) at the same time as they have justified and promoted global integration. Public institutions, many of them international but many also domestic, still provide the framework and in fact much of the investment for the world economy (Atkinson 1997; Gibson-Graham 1996–7: 8).

Nation-states, Past and Present (With a Future)

After the First World War, as national self-determination was proving to be panacea, placebo, and disorder all at once, Ernest Barker outlined three material bases to the nation: race, as a source of human identification; environment, as both a physical border and internal geography; and population, as a set of statistical forms. Now while the first and second terms were conceived as natural divisions (although never encountered as such, given struggles over race and resources) the population was deliberately brought into discourse as an object of care to be quantified, qualified, modeled, and bettered, a concept derived from sociology, biology, and ethnology that then became "real" in the eyes of public policy. Barker almost celebrates the fact that this last category, already muddied, is the only one really applicable to the architectonics of nations (Barker 1927: 2–3, 12). As May Joseph says, "[t]here has never been a pure space within the nation-state" (1995: 3).

The demise of the nation-state and the emergence of international sovereignty have been routinely – and mistakenly – predicted over the past century. More and more such entities appear, even as the discourse announcing their departure becomes increasingly insistent (Miller 1981: 16–18). The internationalism of new communications technologies and patterns of ownership and control, and increases in the variety and extent of global diasporas, *extend* the significance of the state as a regulatory and stimulatory entity. The corollary has been a developing need for each state to create a national subjectivity from disparate identities. Internationalization is perhaps nowhere better exemplified than in the work done by states to build belonging amongst their polyethnic populations, and the labor performed by those populations to seek new forms of state representation. It is our contention that, while the nation-state is beset with problems caused by the pressure of ethnicity from below and supranationalism from above, pronouncements that nationhood is dead – the signal achievement of globalization – are seriously premature (Hirst & Thompson 1996). Popular managerialist tracts like *The End of the Nation-State* (Ohmae 1995) can be viewed in this context as capitalist conceits, appearing as they have during the era of a supposedly exemplary open-market specimen, the North American Free Trade Agreement/Trato de Libro Comercio Norte Americano, that needs a mere thousand pages of governmental rules to "work" (Palley 1999: 50)!

Forming nation-states requires the establishment of both order and authenticity. The order may be new in its type and operation, but it invokes an older connection to essences as part of its claim to be. The nation becomes a base for this claim. It is "authentic," cannot be superseded, and represents a one, true culture (Smith 1990: 1, 9). Yet the manifestation of fealty to culture is of course in the apparatus of the state. Any sense of the nation-state as a discrete entity selected by persons with a common ethnic and political heritage can be applied to half a dozen cases at most. The rest of us are testimony to massive migration and/or the cartographic fancies of colonial powers. And when groups claim a national identity that is not expressed in existing political arrangements, this is necessarily phrased in terms of the desire to form governments.

As Tom Nairn (1993) paradoxically remarks of the break-up of states and their multiple splits, "[s]mall is not only beautiful but has teeth too (speaking both technically and politically)." This is the difference between the apparently outmoded "medieval particularism" of small nationalism that Lenin derided and the really rather modish "nonlogical, untidy, refractory, disintegrative, particularistic truth of nation-states"; the revolutions of 1989 made medieval particularism the future (Nairn 1993: 157–8). Our contemporary moment equally references intra- and transnationalism, with diasporic subjects and First Peoples gathering political momentum. Most studies of cultural nationalism have seen it as an alibi for state activity, a *raison d'être* for state-building. But the intensity of feeling generated amongst diasporas and nonstate actors has drawn this into question (Hutchinson 1999). Threats to secular modernity through the state come not only from economic change, but from religious opposition to representative government, as recent events in Turkey and India have underscored (Benhabib 1999: 709). Most national communities of common interest have been formed inside the nation-state (Miller 1984: 285n1). Is that, however, sustainable given a global division of labor?

The New International Division of Cultural Labor

Philip McMichael (2000) views globalization as a project driven by transnational capital that produces uncertainty and a crisis of legitimacy for the nation-state, creating a worldwide labor surplus and provoking global migrations. Such processes do not happen automatically or evenly. Differentiation and polarization are as much an outcome as similarity between communities throughout the world. Findings from contemporary studies of social changes have indicated that globalization:

- includes transnational practices which are largely independent of any nation-state via flows of money, ideas, people, and information;
- heralds, via labor market deregulation, the disciplining of the working class, as union strength is weakened by the unregulated movement of capital;
- is catalyzed by the North and finds expression, but also produces resistance, in sites throughout the world;
- has begun to produce global citizens whose identity is based not upon the nation and its history, but upon their status within wider networks of interaction;
- has called into question rights, obligations, and traditional laws in relation to trade, bilateral negotiations, and local social engagement. This has encouraged the development of societies which are no longer coterminous with the nation-state and which form new sociospatial groupings throughout the world (for example, the green movement) (see Lawrence 2000).

This follows a longstanding pattern. In the fourteenth and fifteenth centuries, a mercantile system arose from business-driven calculations and manipulations of climate, geography, flora, and fauna. The exchange of goods came to be matched by an exchange of labor. As food commodities made their way around the globe, so did people, often as slaves. When machinery was developed, work split into an industrial mode. Cities grew into manufacturing sites and populations urbanized as wages displaced subsistence across the sixteenth, seventeenth, and eighteenth centuries. The latter is the moment of Adam Smith's famous text on pinmaking:

> One man draws out the wire, another straightens it, a third cuts it, a fourth points it, a fifth grinds it at the top for receiving the head; to make the head requires three distinct operations; to put it on is a peculiar business, to whiten the pins is another; it is even a trade by itself to put them into the paper.... The division of labor ... occasions, in every art, a proportionable increase of the productive powers of labor. (1970: 110)

As developed countries moved onto the global stage, new forms of labor were institutionalized in empire. In the eighteenth and nineteenth centuries, manufacturing went on at the center, with food and raw materials imported from the periphery. Today, divisions of labor occur via sectoral differences in a national economy, the occupations and skills of a labor force, and the organization of tasks within a firm. Life-cycle models of international products suggest that they are first made and consumed in the center, in an IMEC, then exported to the periphery, and finally produced "out there," once technology has become standardized and savings can be made on the labor front. Goods and services owned and vended by the periphery rarely make their way into the center as imports (Lang & Hines 1993: 15; Strange 1995: 293; Keynes 1957: 333–4; Cohen 1991: 129, 133–9; Evans 1979: 27–8).

The idea of the NICL (Miller, 1990, 1996, 1998a,b) derives from retheorizations of economic dependency theory that followed the inflationary chaos of the 1970s. Developing markets for labor and sales, and the shift from the spatial *sensitivities* of electrics to the spatial *insensitivities* of electronics, pushed businesses beyond treating Third World countries as suppliers of raw materials, to look on them as shadow-setters of the price of work, competing amongst themselves and with the First and Second Worlds for employment. This development broke up the prior division of the world into a small number of industrialized nations and a majority of underdeveloped ones, as production was split across continents. Folke Fröbel et al. (1980) christened this the New International Division of Labor.

What might this analysis do for those working in cultural studies? We turn now to instances from film and TV that embody a crisis of labor, the state, the nation, transnational agencies, and the border-riding rituals that seek to separate culture from commerce and nation from nation. They show the importance of (*a*) the global as discourse; (*b*) the complex specificities of the cultural and the economic; and (*c*) the need for a blend of political economy and cultural studies.

We suggest that just as manufacturing fled the First World, cultural production has also relocated, though largely within the IMECs. This is happening at the level of popular textual production, marketing, and information and high-culture, limited-edition work, as factors of production, including state assistance, lure cultural producers. Obviously, the US film industry has always imported cultural producers, such as the German Expressionists. But this was one-way traffic during the classical Hollywood era. Postwar antitrust decisions and the advent of television compelled changes to the vertically integrated studio system. The decade from 1946 saw production go overseas. Location shooting became a means of differentiating stories, and studios purchased facilities around the world to utilize cheap labor. Between 1950 and 1973, just 60 percent of Hollywood films' in-production began their lives in the US. American financial institutions grew practiced at buying foreign theaters and distribution companies, thus sharing risk and profit with local businesses. This was in keeping with the close historic relationship between the film industry and finance capital: as American banks looked overseas for sources of profit through the 1960s, so they endorsed and assisted efforts by Hollywood to spread risk and investment as widely as possible. By the end of the 1980s, overseas firms were crucial suppliers of funds invested in American film or loans against distribution rights in their countries of origin. Joint production arrangements are now well-established between US firms and French, British, Swedish, and Italian companies, with connections to theme parks, cabling, and home video. Co-production sees host governments working together or with US companies, as when the film *JFK* was funded by a Hollywood studio, a French cable network, a German production house, and a Dutch financier, while *The Full Monty* is of course owned by Fox. Toronto has doubled as New York City in over a hundred films, thanks to the appeal of government subsidies. Labor market slackness, increased profits, and developments in global transportation and communications technology have diminished the need for colocation of these factors, which depresses labor costs and deskills workers. Animation is frequently undertaken in southeast Asia and Europe by employees at lower rates of pay than US workers. The trend towards offshore work is gathering pace: between 1990 and 1998, 31 national film commissions were set up across the globe to secure such business. Many of them are solely concerned with attracting foreign capital. For some critics, this represents a restructuring from the vertically integrated production-line studios of the 1930s and 1940s to a flexible system where finance, management, and production are physically and industrially splintered. To others, the fact that US management prevails is the relevant fact (Christopherson & Storper 1986; Wasser 1995: 424, 431; Buck 1992: 119, 123; Briller 1990: 75–8; Wasko 1994: 33; Miège 1989: 46; Wasko 1982: 206–7; Marvasti 1994; Kessler 1995; "The PolyGram Test," 1998; Wasko 1998: 180–1; McCann 1998; Lent 1998; "Culture Wars," 1998).

Any decision by a multinational firm to invest in a particular nation-state carries the seeds of insecurity, because companies move on when tax incentives or other factors of production beckon (Allan 1988: 325–6; Browett & Leaver 1989: 38; Welch & Luostarinen 1988; Fröbel et al. 1980: 2–8, 13–15, 45–8). The hold on international capital is always tenuous and depends heavily on foreign exchange rates. This too relates to state activity – the UK government's decision to float the pound and free the Bank of England from democratic consultation contributed to a situation in 1998 where a strengthening currency raised costs for overseas investors and encouraged locals to spend elsewhere, with severe implications for offshore film funds. So the late 1990s offshore-production boom in Australia and Canada, driven in part by scenery, infrastructure, language, and lower pay levels than the US, combined with equivalent skill levels, still depended on weak currencies (Woods 1999; Pendakur 1998: 229).

The cultural domination of the US is both facilitated and compromised by the NICL. Localization occurs at the level of the consumer, as international audience targeting becomes increasingly specific: Sean Connery is cast as a Hollywood lead because European audiences love him, while each US film is allotted a hundred generic descriptions for use in specific markets (*Dances with Wolves* was promoted in France as a documentary-style dramatization of Native American life, and *Malcolm X* with posters of the Stars and Stripes aflame) (Danan 1995: 131–2, 137; Wasser 1995: 433).

The American Film Institute is anxious about any loss of cultural heritage to internationalism, critics question what is happening when US drama is scripted with special attention to foreign audiences, and political economists argue that a newly transnational Hollywood no longer addresses its nominal audience. George Quester laments that British costume history crowds out the space for indigenous "quality" television, claiming there is more Australian high-end drama on US TV than locally produced material (1990: 57). But the trend remains for North America to attract talent developed by national cinemas to compete with it. Peter Weir's post production for *The Truman Show* or *Witness* might take place in Australia, satisfying off-screen indices of localism in order to obtain state financing there, but does that make for a real alternative to the US? And what does it mean that Michael Apted, James Bond and *7 Up* series director, can speak with optimism of a "European-izing of Hollywood" when Gaumont points out that "a co-production with the Americans... usually turns out to be just another US film shot on location" ("Top," 1994; Apted quoted in Dawtrey 1994: 75; Gaumont quoted in Kessler 1995: n. 143)? Attempts by the French film industry in the 1980s to attract US filmmakers may have the ultimate effect of US studio takeovers, while diplomatic efforts to maintain local screen subsidies continue even as Hollywood producers and networks purchase satellite and broadcast space across Europe (Hayward 1993: 385). AOL–Time Warner, Disney–ABC, Viacom, NBC, and others are jostling their way into the center of the vast and growing western European industry as sites of production as much as dumping-grounds for old material. The new stations throughout the Continent invest in local programing with cost savings from scheduling American filler (Stevenson 1994: 6).

Britain has been a major participant in the NICL recently, as both a foreign investor and a recipient of offshore film and TV production funds. The long-term strategy of successive UK governments since 1979 has been to break up unions within the media in order to become a Euro-Hollywood by default: the skills generated in a regulated domain of the screen would be retained without the "inefficiency" of the so-called "X-factor" – labor. In short, "flexibility" signifies the aim of supplanting wage stability and orienting texts towards export. As a consequence, the UK now has a negative balance of screen trade for the first time in history. Associated deregulation produced a proliferation of networks and the inevitable search for cheap overseas content (Cornford & Robins 1998: 207–9). From the 1980s, it became impossible to recoup the cost of most British feature films domestically. The necessity of finding jobs for skilled workers and their employers made the industry a true welcome mat. In 1991 a British Film Commission (BFC) was formed to market UK production expertise and locations by providing overseas producers with a free service articulating talent, sites, and subsidies and generating a national network of urban and regional film commissions. In 1997, seven Hollywood movies accounted for 54 percent of expenditure of feature-film production in the UK, but Britain faces increasing competition to capture Hollywood production finance. The government opened a British Film Office in Los Angeles in an attempt to normalize traffic with Hollywood by offering liaison services to the industry and promoting British locations and crews, and the BFC announced the Blair government's outlook on cinema: "set firmly at the top of the agenda is the desire to attract more overseas film-makers" (Guttridge 1996; Hiscock 1998; British Film Commission, n.d.).

One key agency, the London Film Commission, was formed in 1995 with a grant from the Department of National Heritage to attract offshore film production (you work out the connection to the portfolio). The Commission promotes the capital to overseas filmmakers, arranges police permits, and negotiates with local residents and businesses. Its defining moment was *Mission: Impossible*, when the Commissioner proudly said of that film's Hollywood producers: "They came up with all these demands and I just went on insisting that, as long as they gave us notice, we could schedule it" (Jury 1996).

In order to keep British studios going, regulations were promulgated in the early 1990s that meant films entirely made in Britain counted as British, regardless of theme, setting, or stars. So *Judge Dredd* with Sylvester Stallone was "British," but *The English Patient* did too much of its postproduction work abroad to qualify. Until 1998, 92 percent of a film had to be created in the UK. At the end of that year, the government reduced this requirement to 75 percent to encourage American companies to make their films in Britain (Woolf).

What do film industry mavens make of this? Michael Kuhn (1998), managing director of Polygram Filmed Entertainment (PEE), the company which dominated the British film industry in the 1990s, considers that "Europe (when you talk about mainstream movies) is almost a vassal state to that Hollywood business." Only "supra-national government institutions" can turn this around, because of the lack of a firm financial base to compete with Hollywood's mix of production and distribution and the United States' cartel-like discrimination against European producers. Ironically, PFE has now been taken over by Seagram, and its interests will merge in some form with another of Seagram's subsidiaries, the Hollywood major, Universal.

In contrast to Kuhn, Rupert Murdoch (1998) welcomes "new joint ventures between the Hollywood majors and both public and private broadcasting" in Europe, citing the numbers of European workers invisibly employed in the making of *Titanic*: "this cross-border cultural co-operation is not the result of regulation, but market forces. It's the freedom to move capital, technology and talent around the world that adds value, invigorates ailing markets, creates new ones." This view finds support in the upper echelons of the EU, which has offered US film marketers unhindered access to the European marketplace.

There are other models of the NICL. Consider the Grundy Organisation. It produced Australian TV drama and game shows from the 1950s that were bought on license from the US. The company expanded to sell such texts across the world, operating with a strategy called "parochial internationalism" that meant leaving Australia rather than exporting in isolation from relevant industrial, taste, and regulatory frameworks. Following patterns established in the advertising industry, it bought production houses around the world, making programs in local languages, based on formats imported from Australia that themselves drew on US models. From a base in Bermuda, the Organisation produced about 50 hours of TV a week in 70 countries across Europe, Oceania, Asia, and North America until its sale in the mid-1990s to Pearson. This is the NICL offshore, utilizing experience in the Australian commercial reproduction industry to manufacture American palimpsests in countries relatively new to profit-centered TV. The benefits to Australia, where a regulatory framework birthed this expertise by requiring the networks to support such productions as part of cultural protection, are unclear (Cunningham & Jacka 1996: 81–7; Moran 1998: 41–71; Stevenson 1994: 1).

In an era when US network television is desperately cutting costs, there are opportunities for outsiders, but only major players. The trend seems to be towards smaller investments in a larger number of programs for television, in the simultaneously splintered and concentrated media domain of North America. Put another way, a huge increase in the number of channels and systems of supply and payment is also producing unprecedented concentration of TV ownership. Some examples of the NICL represent a form of vertical investment, with production processes fragmented across the world. Horizontal licensing and joint ventures that mirror domestic retailing systems may be the wave of the future. The ability to make locally accented infotainment is one way of nations using the NICL (Schwab 1994: 14; Roddick 1994: 30).

To summarize, the screen is back where primary and secondary extractive and value-adding industries were in the 1960s, needing to make decisions not just about export, but about the site of production. Advances in communications technology permit electronic off-line editing across the world, but also enable special effects problematizing the very need for location shooting. The trend is clearly towards horizontal connections to other media, global economy and administration, and a break-up of public–private distinctions in ownership, control, and programing philosophy (Wedell 1994: 325; Marvasti 1994). Screen texts are fast developing as truly global trading forms: the costs of a global market in cultural labor must be monitored across a broad matrix of factors, as must the nationalist or culturalist claims mounted against it.

Conclusion

Globalization stands for something real, a sense from across time, space, and nation, that those very categories are in peril. Our sense of the temporal is questioned – think of the panic generated by the thought of computers dealing with the difference between 1900 and 2000. Space is problematized by the NICL, as jobs are undertaken by folks on the basis of price and docility rather than locale. And nations are threatened by corporate control, as unelected, far-distant elites displace locally accountable politicians. In each category, the cultural corollary is clear. Time is manipulated in concert with the interests of global capital, and space is torn asunder, as traditional social bonds are compromised by ownership based on profit rather than township. At the political, economic, and class level, this can lead to "a sense of social and economic fatalism and chronic insecurity." Democracies seem unable to deal with economic forces (Held et al. 1999: 1).

But counterpower is always at work. The 1999 Seattle and Washington 2000 actions in opposition to "Washington Consensus" hacks illustrated as much. Environmentalists, trade unions, and consumer groups have problematized globalization as defined by neoliberal *nostra*. Textiles, shipping, and agriculture remain massively subsidized across the world. The US, supposedly a poster-child for free trade and true competition, has hundreds of anti-dumping measures aimed at blocking imports where prices have been "unfairly" set, maintains a semi-secret deal with Japan to restrict steel sales, and is serviced by no fewer than 196 public film commissions in generating its putatively *laissez-faire* screen industries, while the EU remains firm on refusing to import bananas and genetically modified beef. All of this leads *The Economist*, a key neoliberal business advocacy voice, to admit "Globalization is not irreversible" ("Storm Over Globalization," 1999).

Pierre Bourdieu postulates a model of world culture that continues the bipolarity of the Cold War, if without its political ramifications, military corollaries, and economic isolations. His vision of the struggle for world culture pits the United States *contra* France – *laissez-faire* dogma juxtaposed against cultural nationalism. This Enlightenment conflict, between anomic monads and collective identities, sets bourgeois individualism and collaborative unity against each other, with reincarnations of the Depression and Sovietism hanging over each model. Bourdieu calls for a pre-Marxist, Hegelian way through the debate, a democratic mode that favors the state not as totalitarian or an aid to capital accumulation, but as the expression of a popular will that contemplates itself collectively, rather than atomistically, and acts under the sign of a general interest rather than singular egotism (1999: 20). That struggle of structure and agency, of capital and the state intricated in the production and symbolism of culture, requires analysis via political economy mixed with cultural studies.

References

"Culture Wars." (1998). *The Economist*, 12 Sept.: n.p.
"Global Finance: Time for a Redesign?" (1999). *The Economist*, 30 Jan.: 4–8, Survey Global Finance.
"The G-Word." (1997). *The Financial Times*, 30 July: 15.
"The PolyGram Test." (1998). *The Economist*, 15 Aug.: n.p.

"Storm Over Globalisation." (1999). *The Economist*, 27 Nov.: 15–16.

"Top 100 All-Time Domestic Grossers." (1994). *The Variety*, 17–23 Oct.: M60.

"Trade Barriers, Erected in Fear, Hurt US Workers." (1997). *USA Today*, 16 Oct. 10A.

Allan, Blaine. (1988). "The State of the State of the Art on TV." *Queen's Quarterly* 95, no. 2: 318–29.

Allen, Donna, Ramona R. Rush, and Susan J. Kaufman, eds. (1996). *Women Transforming Communications: Global Intersections*. Thousand Oaks: Sage.

Amin, Samir. (1997). *Capitalism in the Age of Globalization*. London: Zed.

Amsden, Alice H. and Takashi Hikino. (1999). "The Left and Globalization." *Dissent* 46, no. 2: 7–9.

Anderson, Benedict. (1983). *Imagined Communities: Reflections on the Origin and Spread of Nationalism*. London: Verso.

Atkinson, G. (1997). "Capital and Labor in the Emerging Global Economy." *Journal of Economic Issues* 31, no. 2: 385–91.

Barker, Ernest. (1927). *National Character and the Factors in its Formation*. London: Methuen.

Bauman, Zygmunt. (1998). *Globalization: The Human Consequences*. New York: Columbia University Press.

Benhabib, Seyla. (1999). "Citizens, Residents, and Aliens in a Changing World: Political Membership in the Global Era." *Social Research* 66, no. 3: 709–44.

Bourdieu, Pierre. (1999). "The State, Economics and Sport." Trans. Hugh Dauncey and Geoff Hare. In *France and the 1998 World Cup: The National Impact of a World Sporting Event*, ed. Hugh Dauncey and Geoff Hare. London: Frank Cass.

Braman, Sandra and Annabelle Sreberny-Mohammadi, eds. (1996). *Globalization, Communication and Transnational Civil Society*. Cresskill: Hampton Press.

Briller, B. R. (1990). "The Globalization of American TV." *Television Quarterly* 24, no. 3: 71–9.

British Film Commission (n.d.) <http://www.britfilmcom.co.uk/content/filming/site.asp.

Browett, John and Richard Leaver. (1989). "Shifts in the Global Capitalist Economy and the National Economic Domain." *Australian Geographical Studies* 27, no. 1: 31–46.

Buck, Elizabeth B. (1992). "Asia and the Global Film Industry." *East-West Film Journal* 6, no. 2: 116–33.

Calkins, P. and M. Vézina. (1996). "Transitional Paradigms to a New World Economic Order." *International Journal of Social Economics* 23, nos. 10–11: 311–28.

Christopherson, Susan and Michael Storper. (1986). "The City as Studio; the World as Back Lot: The Impact of Vertical Disintegration on the Location of the Motion Picture Industry." *Environment and Planning D: Society and Space* 4, no. 3: 305–20.

Cohen, Robin. (1991). *Contested Domains: Debates in International Labor Studies*. London: Zed Books.

Collins, Jim. (1992). "Television and Postmodernism." *Channels of Discourse, Reassembled: Television and Contemporary Criticism*, 2nd edn. Ed. Robert C. Allen. Chapel Hill: University of North Carolina Press.

Cornford, James and Kevin Robins. (1998). "Beyond the Last Bastion: Industrial Restructuring and the Labor Force in the British Television Industry." In *Global Productions: Labor in the Making of the "Information Society,"* eds. Gerald Sussman and John A. Lent. Cresskill: Hampton Press.

Cunningham, Stuart and Jacka, Elizabeth. (1996). *Australian Television and International Mediascapes*. Melbourne: Cambridge University Press.

Danan, Martine. (1995). "Marketing the Hollywood Blockbuster in France." *Journal of Popular Film and Television* 23, no. 3: 131–40.

Dawtrey, Adam. (1994). "Playing Hollywood's Game: Eurobucks Back Megabiz." *Variety* 7–13 March: 1, 75.

Donnelly, Peter. (1996). "The Local and the Global: Globalization in the Sociology of Sport." *Journal of Sport & Social Issues* 20, no. 3: 239–57.

Evans, Peter. (1979). *Dependent Development: The Alliance of Local Capital in Brazil*. Princeton: Princeton University Press.

Falk, Richard. (1997). "State of Siege: Will Globalization Win Out?" *International Affairs* 73, no. 1: 123–36.

Foucault, Michel. (1991). *Remarks on Marx: Conversations with Duccio Trombadori*, trans. J. R. Goldstein and J. Cascaito. New York: Semiotext(e).

Fröbel, Folke, Jürgen Heinrichs, and Otto Kreye. (1980). *The New International Division of Labor: Structural Unemployment in Industrialised Countries and Industrialisation in Developing Countries*, trans. P. Burgess. Cambridge: Cambridge University Press; Paris: Éditions de la Maison des Sciences de l'Homme.

Galbraith, James K. (1999). "The Crisis of Globalization." *Dissent* 46, no. 3: 13–16.

Gibson-Graham, J. K. (1996–7). "Querying Globalization." *Rethinking Marxism* 9, no. 1: 1–27.

Guttridge, Peter. (1996). "Our Green and Profitable Land." *Independent* 11 July: 8–9.

Hayward, Susan. (1993). "State, Culture and the Cinema: Jack Lang's Strategies for the French Film Industry." *Screen* 34, no. 4: 382–91.

Held, David, Anthony McGrew, David Goldblatt, and Jonathan Perraton. (1999). *Global Transformations: Politics, Economics and Culture*. Stanford: Stanford University Press.

Herod, A. (1997). "Labor as an Agent of Globalization and as a Global Agent." *Globalization: Reasserting the Power of the Local*, ed. K. R. Cox. New York: Guilford Press.

Hindley, B. (1999). "A Bogey and its Myths." *Times Literary Supplement* 22 Jan.: 28.

Hirst, Paul. (1997). "The Global Economy – Myths and Realities." *International Affairs* 73, no. 3: 409–25.

Hirst, Paul and G. Thompson. (1996). *Globalization in Question: The International Economy and the Possibilities of Governance*. Cambridge: Polity Press.

Hiscock, John. (1998). "Hollywood Backs British Film Drive." *Daily Telegraph* 24 July: 19.

Hobsbawm, Eric. (1998). "The Nation and Globalization." *Constellations* 5, no. 1: 1–9.

Hutchinson, John. (1999). "Re-Interpreting Cultural Nationalism." *Australian Journal of Politics and History* 45, no. 3: 392–407.

Jameson, Fredric. (1996). "Five Theses on Actually Existing Marxism." *Monthly Review* 47, no. 11: 1–10.

Joseph, May. (1995). "Diaspora, New Hybrid Identities, and the Performance of Citizenship." *Women and Performance* 7, no. 1: 3–13.

Jury, Louise. (1996). "Mission Possible: Red Tape Cut to Boost Film Industry." *Independent* 4 July: 3.

Kessler, Kirsten L. (1995). "Protecting Free Trade in Audiovisual Entertainment: A Proposal for Counteracting the European Union's Trade Barriers to the US Entertainment Industry's Exports." *Law and Policy in International Business* 26, no. 2: 563–611.

Keynes, John Maynard. (1957). *The General Theory of Employment Interest and Money*. London: Macmillan; New York: St. Martin's Press.

Kissinger, Henry. (1999). "Globalization and World Order." Independent Newspapers Annual Lecture, Trinity College Dublin, 12 Oct.

Kozul-Wright, R. and R. Rowthorn. (1998). "Spoilt for Choice? Transnational Corporations and the Geography of International Production." *Oxford Review of Economic Policy* 14, no. 2: 74–92.

Kuhn, Michael. (1998). "How Can Europe Benefit from the Digital Revolution?" Presentation to the European Audiovisual Conference, Birmingham, 6–8 April.

Lang, T. and C. Hines. (1993). *The New Protectionism: Protecting the Future Against Free Trade*. New York: New Press.

Latour, Bruno. (1993). *We Have Never Been Modern*, trans. C. Porter. Cambridge, Mass.: Harvard University Press.

Lawrence, Geoffrey. (2000). "Global Perspectives on Rural Communities – Trends and Patterns." *Changing Landscapes – Changing Futures: Proceedings of the First International Landcare Conference*, ed. D. Beckingsale. Melbourne: Melbourne Convention Centre.

Le Heron, Richard, Ian Cooper, Martine Perry, and David Hayward. (1997). "Commodity System Governance: A New Zealand Discourse." In *Uneven Development: Global and Local Processes*, eds. M. Taylor and S. Conti. Aldershot: Avebury.

Lent, John A. (1998). "The Animation Industry and its Offshore Factories." *Global Productions: Labor in the Making of the "Information Society,"* eds. Gerald Sussman and John A. Lent. Cresskill: Hampton Press.

Levinson, Mark. (1999). "Who's in Charge Here?" *Dissent* 46, no. 4: 21–3.

McCann, Paul. (1998). "Hollywood Film-makers Desert UK." *Independent* 14 Aug.: 7.

McMichael, Philip. (2000). *Development and Social Change: A Global Perspective*, 2nd edn. Thousand Oaks: Pine Forge.

McMichael, Philip. (forthcoming) "Globalisation: Trend or Project?" In *Global Political Economy: Contemporary Theories*, ed. R. Palan. London: Routledge.

McMichael, Philip and Geoffrey Lawrence. (forthcoming) "Globalising Agriculture: Structures of Constraint for Rural Australia." In *Sustaining Rural Australia*, ed. S. Lockie and L. Bourke. Rockhampton: Central Queensland University Press.

Marvasti, A. (1994). "International Trade in Cultural Goods: A Cross-sectional Analysis." *Journal of Cultural Economics* 18, no. 2: 135–48.

Miège, Bernard. (1989). *The Capitalization of Cultural Production*, trans. J. Hay, N. Garnham, and UNESCO. New York: International General.

Miller, J. D. B. (1981). *The World of States: Connected Essays*. London: Croom Helm.

Miller, J. D. B. (1984). "The Sovereign State and its Future." *International Journal* 39, no. 2: 284–301.

Miller, Toby. (1990). "Mission Impossible and the New International Division of Labour." *Metro* 82: 21–8.

Miller, Toby. (1996). "The Crime of Monsieur Lang: GATT, the Screen and the New International Division of Cultural Labour." In *Film Policy: International, National and Regional Perspectives*, ed. Albert Moran. London: Routledge.

Miller, Toby. (1998a). *Technologies of Truth: Cultural Citizenship and the Popular Media*. Minneapolis: University of Minnesota Press.

Miller, Toby. (1998b). "Hollywood and the World." In *The Oxford Guide to Film Studies*, eds. John Hill and Pamela Church Gibson. Oxford: Oxford University Press.

Mingo, J. (1997). "Postal Imperialism." *New York Times Magazine* 16 Feb.: 36–7.

Mohammadi, Ali, ed. (1997). *International Communication and Globalization*. London: Sage.

Moran, Albert. (1998). *Copycat TV: Globalisation, Program Formats and Cultural Identity*. Luton: University of Luton Press.

Mowlana, Hamid. (1996). *Global Communication in Transition: End of Diversity?* Newbury Park: Sage.

Murdoch, Rupert. (1998). Presentation Prepared for the European Audiovisual Conference, Birmingham, 6–8 April.

Murray, Alan. (1999). "The American Century: Is it Going or Coming?" *Wall Street Journal* 27 Dec.: 1.

Nader, Ralph. (1999). "Introduction." In *The WTO: Five Years of Reasons to Resist Corporate Globalization*, eds. Lori Wallach and Michelle Sforza. New York: Seven Stories Press.

Nairn, Tom. (1993). "Internationalism and the Second Coming." *Daedalus* 122, no. 3: 155–70.

Ohmae, K. (1995). *The End of the Nation-State: The Rise of Regional Economies*. New York: Free Press.

Palley, Thomas I. (1999). "Toward a New International Economic Order." *Dissent* 46, no. 2: 48–52.

Pendakur, Manjunath. (1998). "Hollywood North: Film and TV Production in Canada." In *Global Productions: Labor in the Making of the "Information Society"*, eds. Gerald Sussman and John A. Lent. Cresskill: Hampton Press.

Peterson, V. S. (1996). "The Politics of Identification in the Context of Globalization." *Women's Studies International Forum* 19, nos. 1–2: 5–15.

Porter, Michael (1990). *The Competitive Advantage of Nations*. New York: The Free Press.

Pritchard, Bill (1999). "Australia as a Supermarket to Asia? Government, Territory, and Political Economy in the Australian Agri-Food System." *Rural Sociology* 64, no. 2: 284–301.

Quester, George H. (1990). *The International Politics of Television*. Lexington, Mass.: Lexington.

Reich, Robert. (1999). "Brain Trusts." *New York Times Book Review* 19 Dec. 10.

Robinson, W. I. (1996). "Globalization: Nine These of our Epoch." *Race & Class* 38, no. 2: 13–31.

Roddick, Nick. (1994). "A Hard Sell: The State of Documentary Film Marketing." *Dox* 2: 30–2.

Ross, Robert and Kent Trachte. (1990). *Global Capitalism: The New Leviathan*. Albany: State University of New York Press.

Schaeffer, R. K. (1997). *Understanding Globalization: The Social Consequences of Political, Economic, and Environmental Change*. Lanham: Rowman & Littlefield.

Schwab, S. (1994). "Television in the 90's: Revolution or Confusion?" *Tenth Joseph I. Lubin Memorial Lecture*. New York University, 1 March.

Sinclair, John, Elizabeth Jacka, and Stuart Cunningham, eds. (1996). *New Patterns in Global Television: Peripheral Vision*. Oxford: Oxford University Press.

Smith, Adam. (1970). *The Wealth of Nations Books I–III*, ed. A. Skinner. Harmondsworth: Penguin.

Smith, Anthony D. (1990). "The Supersession of Nationalism?" *International Journal of Comparative Sociology* 31, nos. 1–2: 1–31.

Smith, Anthony D. (1996). "LSE Centennial Lecture: The Resurgence of Nationalism? Myth and Memory in the Renewal of Nations." *British Journal of Sociology* 47, no. 4: 575–98.

Stevenson, Richard W. (1994). "Lights! Camera! Europe!" *New York Times* 6 Feb.: 1, 6.

Strange, Susan. (1995). "The Defective State." *Daedalus* 124, no. 2: 55–74.

Sussman, Gerald and John A. Lent, eds. (1998). *Global Productions: Labor in the Making of the "Information Society."* Cresskill: Hampton Press.

Teeple, G. (1995). *Globalization and the Decline of Social Reform*. New Jersey: Humanities Press.

Thompson, Paul and Chris Smith. (1999). "Beyond the Capitalist Labor Process: Workplace Change, the State and Globalisation." *Critical Sociology* 24, no. 3: 193–215.

Wasko, Janet. (1982). *Movies and Money: Financing the American Film Industry*. Norwood: Ablex.

Wasko, Janet. (1994). *Hollywood in the Information Age: Beyond the Silver Screen*. Cambridge: Polity Press.

Wasko, Janet. (1998). "Challenges to Hollywood's Labor Force in the 1990s." In *Global Productions: Labor in the Making of the "Information Society,"* eds. Gerald Sussman and John A. Lent. Cresskill: Hampton Press.

Wasser, Frederick. (1995). "Is Hollywood America? The Trans-nationalization of the American Film Industry." *Critical Studies in Mass Communication* 12, no. 4: 423–37.

Wedell, George. (1994). "Prospects for Television in Europe." *Government and Opposition* 29, no. 3: 315–31.

Welch, L. S. and R. Luostarinen. (1988). "Internationalization: Evolution of a Concept." *Journal of General Management* 14, no. 2: 34–55.

Wiseman, John. (1998). *Global Nation? Australia and the Politics of Globalization*. Cambridge: Cambridge University Press.

Woods, Mark. (1999). "Foreign Pix Bring Life to Biz." *Variety* 3–9 May: 37, 44, 46, 59.

Woolf, Marie. (1998). "Why the Next English Patient Will be British." *Independent on Sunday* 20 Dec.: 9.

Chapter 29

"Cricket, with a Plot": Nationalism, Cricket, and Diasporic Identities

Suvendrini Perera

The Sri Lankan–Australian dramatist Ernest MacIntyre recently outlined a new play for the Sri Lankan theater, a national epic staged in the form of "cricket, with a plot". His model was Bertolt Brecht's call for a new epic theater "like a circus, with a plot." In the revival of post-Independence Sinhala theater in Sri Lanka Brechtian models have played a germinative role, as traditional forms of verse storytelling, song, and mime were combined with techniques of Brechtian antirealism to produce a distinctive form. In the climate of chauvinist Sinhala nationalism that led to the current civil war, this renewed Sinhala drama is represented as a unique "national" form, expressive of a brave post-independence Sri Lanka.

MacIntyre's proposal recognizes that both theater and cricket have been mobilized in the service of the Sri Lankan state's Sinhala nationalism. He seeks a dramatist "fearless in making visible the historical and social material thick in the air or stored under the turf" to produce a new Sri Lankan epic reminiscent of the Brechtian circus, but performed in the form of "slowed down stylized cricket action" to enact a *different* national story. The story will be told, in the style of a Brechtian narrator, by a series of cricket commentators, including the Australian Tony Greig. Instead of Brecht's acrobats and dancers, MacIntyre proposes "somersaulting fieldsmen, striking and running batsmen . . . bowlers with pace, bowlers with spin, and a solitary bowler with an action as fascinating as it is strange to the eyes of some white men (called umpires)."

This is of course a reference to the "throwing" or "chucking" charges leveled at the Sri Lankan bowler Muthiah Muralitharan (the only Tamil on the team) during two successive tours to Australia. MacIntyre merges the spectacle of theater and the spectacle of sport in the performance of a "national" story that also exceeds the plot of the nation: a story that necessarily includes other relations and histories, the interplay between the various peoples of Sri Lanka, and between white and nonwhite, colonial and postcolonial. By turning cricket into epic MacIntyre cannily brings onstage the implicit relationship between sport (and especially cricket) and nation, between performance and identity, and the

510

ways in which spectators of this performance are themselves interpellated as national subjects.

Although it refers to recent cricketing contests between the Australian and Sri Lankan cricket teams, this is not an essay about cricket, but about cricket as a site where questions of nation, identity, desire, and agency are played out. It shuttles between there and here, then and now, defeating my attempts to produce a seamless, sequential narrative out of its various parts. As such the chapter is also about the positionalities, locations, and politics of this diasporic subject. It examines some problems of the performance of identity, and of nation, migration, and difference in the context of cricket.

The chapter engages three intersecting discussions: first, a distinguished tradition of writing on cricket and decolonization by cultural critics including Manthia Diawara, Ashis Nandy, Arjun Appadurai, and, most crucially, C. L. R. James. James's *Beyond a Boundary* is a classic autobiography of the decolonization of consciousness and also one of the earliest works to focus, through cricket, on the predicament of the diasporic intellectual (Farred 1996: 177–8). As a text that enabled questions of race, identity, and sport to be asked in other colonial contexts, *Beyond a Boundary* also informs the second set of writings to which I refer, discussions of Australian cricket, racism, and orientalism by Michael Roberts, Subash Jaireth, Colin Tatz, Peter Kell, and others.

In his recent book *Good Sports: Australian Sport and the Myth of the Fair Go*, Kell writes,

> Australians have a powerful belief that sport is one of the few social institutions where everyone still gets "a fair go" . . . Far from being a source of unity . . . sport in Australia has always been a source of divisiveness and a site of exclusion. Sport has reinforced anxieties and fears about outsiders . . . heightening irrational fears about Australia's Asian neighbours, China in particular. Some sports have been utilised as a tool of established elites, with imperial and anglocentric linkages. (2000: 10–11)

This chapter examines the spectatorship of non–Anglo Australians in this climate of anglocentrism and divisiveness.

Thirdly, I hope to contribute to a conversation begun by Michael Roberts and Qadri Ismail about Sri Lankan spectatorship, nationalism, and cricket. I address in particular a question posed by Ismail about the possibility of making a theoretical "*space for the spectator unmarred by nationalism, for the spectator who would cheer the team but not the nation*" (1997: 16, original emphasis). Currently, Ismail argues, this space does not exist in South Asian cricket discourse, as "inspired by C. L. R. James. In this reading cricket is nationalism; its spectators nationalist" (p. 16). Taking Ismail's fine essay as a point of departure, I want to complicate his representation of James's writings on cricket as "cricket as nationalism." Rather, I want to propose, James was ahead of contemporary theorists of nationalism in showing how factors such as diaspora and migration destabilize and challenge the idea of the nation. In theorizing a space for a

Figure 3 Cartoon by Jon Kudelka, first published in *Weekend Australian*, Nov. 6–7, 1999. Reprinted with permission.

spectator who does not reenact the exclusionary practices of nationalism, I focus on the spectator who is *both* inside and outside the space of "the nation," the spectator produced through migration, diaspora, and dislocation.

I

Ismail characterizes his essay as written both contra and "with the Jamesian: with a love for, and intellectual and aesthetic pleasure in observing, the game" (1997: 16). The critics cited above all write, implicitly or explicitly, as loving and knowing observers of cricket; not entirely uncoincidentally, perhaps, these writings are also by male authors. My piece, on the other hand, needs to be subtitled

"Meditations of a reluctant cricket watcher." It makes no pretensions to cricketing expertise.

As the youngest girl in a family of four boys, a good part of my energy during my growing up was expended in NOT knowing about cricket. Appadurai's comments on female cricket spectatorship in India are also applicable to Sri Lanka, where the game as both spectacle and embodied activity addresses a public gendered as male. "The Indian female gaze . . . is twice removed: watching males watching other males play" (1995: 44). I got on fine not knowing about cricket in Sri Lanka and during the years I spent in the US – until I came to Australia. In retrospect I can point to the exact moment when I understood that from now on my identity in Australia would have to include learning and caring about cricket. Soon after I started teaching at La Trobe in the mid-1990s the subaltern historian Dipesh Chakrabarty, then an academic at Melbourne University, asked me a question about the Sri Lankan cricket team touring Australia at the time. I replied, blithely and unashamedly, that I didn't know, marking my ignorance as a gendered one. (I think my response sank me irretrievably in Dipesh's estimation.) When I think about this conversation now I understand that what was being opened up and negotiated here, and what I had failed to respond to at the time, was something about the codes and shared practices of being a South Asian in Australia.

Soon after, during the 1995 Sri Lankan tour of Australia, I found out that there was no way I could be, especially, a Sri Lankan in Australia and have the luxury of remaining ignorant about the cricket. During this tour I was interpellated constantly everywhere *as a Sri Lankan* on the basis of cricket, not just in the context of cultural criticism – of reading newspapers and watching TV – but also at the level of the everyday, at the Victoria market or on Lygon Street. Here I was addressed primarily as a raced subject, since ethnicity marks my salient point of difference as "an *Asian* woman" in Australia (Perera 1999: 195–6).

Simultaneously, I found that the passionate conversations about cricket begun by, say, southern European-or East Asian-Australians who mostly occupy these spaces, people who often had their heritage in countries that historically didn't play cricket, were really about negotiations of cultural and racial difference in Australia: about the significance of embodied and behavioral practices (for instance, the imperative of shaking hands at the end of a game) and about cultural values (e.g., loyalty versus correctness). During these weeks and months I found out that I had no choice but to know about the cricket – and also that there was no way I could not take sides about the cricket. My discovery is an inversion of James's, when he declares in *Beyond a Boundary*, "cricket had plunged me into politics long before I was aware of it" (1963: 70). Living in Australia, everyday politics had plunged me into cricket long before I was aware of it.

But cricket's politics are no uncomplicated matter when taking sides in the cricket, by a series of slippages, is collapsed with taking sides with the state in a climate where sporting wins, both in Sri Lanka and Australia, are constructed largely as victories for a national identity and a national way of life, and appropriated into the project of the state. When Australia replaced Sri Lanka as champions in the 1999 World Cup the winning team was met with ticker-tape parades and a state reception; its captain, Mark Taylor, was described by Prime Minister Howard as having achieved "almost" the "pinnacle of human achievement" (Booth & Tatz 2000: 228) and appointed Australian of the Year. Rumors surfaced soon after that at Howard's request Taylor would publicly support the monarchist cause in the republic referendum.

On its return home the Sri Lankan team which beat Australia in the 1996 World Cup had a coin struck in its honor, with the players given the title of "Desha Bandu" or national defenders, and thus placed symbolically on a par with the government's army. As the cricket team was officially elevated to the status of champions of the state in Sri Lanka, continual attempts were also made to produce the team's *spectators* as a unified community through the practices of state-controled media. As Yolanda Foster writes, domestically, in the 1990s "cricket becomes a convenient narrative to write over failed aspiration, instability and atrocities," acting as both a buffer and a decoy from the war, and from state practices of repression. It is in this context that Ismail, who locates himself "as a Sri Lankan passport holder" living abroad (1997: 22) seeks to locate a space for the spectator who supports the Sri Lankan *team*, but not the project of Sinhala nationalism to which it is appropriated. In sympathy with Ismail's search, I want to pursue a different set of questions about the politics of viewing and location.

Within the plot of the nationalism, only two opposed positions are made available to the viewer: inside or outside, either as a subject of the nation or as a depoliticized "lover of the game." In what follows I want to examine the possibilities of a viewing position constituted by wider relations of power, and by forces of diaspora, history, and identity. This is my own version of "cricket, with a plot," or with several intersecting plots, of places, nationalisms, and histories.

II

In 1995, following the bitterness of the Sri Lankan team's visit to Australia and the "chucking" allegations against Muralitharan, the Australian team canceled a scheduled return tour in Sri Lanka, citing fears about security. The importance the Sri Lankan government attached to the visit was demonstrated by its increasingly extravagant offers of protection, including a proposal to lodge the entire team in India and fly them to and from each game with full military escort. To no avail. Even an undiplomatic taunt of "sissies" by the Sri Lankan Foreign Minister (and, more significantly, a charge of being "lily-livered" by the British tabloids) failed to move the Australians. The team, which had no qualms about playing in England despite IRA bombings, remained determined to give Sri Lanka a wide berth. In mid-1996, however, following their loss to Sri Lanka in the World Cup, an Australian tour did eventuate. Before the first match, sports writer Malcolm Knox produced this version of what his team could look forward to:

> When Ian Healy leads his team into Colombo's R. Premadasa stadium tomorrow night he will face a crowd whose exuberance makes those pockets of Sri Lankan madness we saw in Australia last summer seem like genteel expatriate chess clubs.
>
> In scenes of utter bedlam, Sri Lanka overran India's total on Monday night... The constant drums, trumpets, dancing, cymbals, hand-clapping and other musical instruments that have no equivalent or name in English, all played with remarkable cohesion, make cricket here more like a fertility feast than a sporting event.
>
> The air will be filled with the smell of rotting garbage... Feral dogs, cats and goats will be roaming under the stands... A man with... an aerosol bazooka will come on at drinks and wicket breaks to shoot the insects down... Australia will also be facing two opening batsmen for whom... business as usual involves using the cricket bat in ways not previously known.

Mercifully, not too much needs to be said about this exercise in orientalist delirium. Here cricket is transported from the comparatively contained and chaste theater of the "sporting event," to a wildly carnivalesque performance which collapses the boundaries between players and spectators.[1] Not only bedlamite humans, but also "feral dogs, cats and goats" get in on the action, and the anticipated violence of the location is displaced onto ferocious midges requiring extermination with aerosol bazookas. The stadium becomes a veritable "fertility feast" of licentiousness where the senses swoon in an assault of sights, sounds, and smells, and the proprieties of cricket in more civilized climes – even when these are now contaminated by "pockets of [migrant] madness" – are violently swept away. Worse, there is a method in all this madness: the clamorous "musical instruments that have no equivalent or name in English" are still "all played with remarkable cohesion," and the two opening batsmen "for whom... business as usual involves using the cricket bat in ways not previously known" are following a systematic game plan that, while not infallible, is capable of producing extraordinary upsets and victories and, more significantly, has changed styles of one-day cricket among the established cricketing nations (Bouts, Roebuck).

Knox contemplates the frightening transformation of cricket into something Other. In this fevered vision an implicit body of Australian national virtues is pitted against an onslaught of orientalist terrors, and fears to be found lacking. Appadurai's discussion of the significance of national styles in cricket is pertinent here. In *Beyond a Boundary*, Appadurai points out, James's description places cricket in the category of a "hard" cultural form, "in which rigid adherence to external codes is part of a discipline of internal moral development" (Appadurai 1995: 24). Although it may seem to follow from this that cricket resists change in its practice, as James himself demonstrates, cricket as *performance* in different parts of the world became "profoundly indigenized and decolonized" (ibid.).

515

It is of course at this level of embodied practice, of performance, that the "meaning" of cricket is perceived as a site of conflict, not just between opposing national "styles," but even as representative of a clash between national ideologies and cultures. For the imperial order, as Alan Clarke and John Clarke discuss, to teach cricket was to teach a whole world of values associated with the "sporting English"; teaching colonial and working-class men to "play the game" was to teach "respect for the rules and authority," to instill a sense of discipline, "to substitute the constructive and healthy use of free time for uncivilised, irrational or undisciplined time" (1982: 81) – the last a point adds resonance to Knox's remarks about the "fertility feast" of Sri Lankan cricket. But as English self-representations of a sporting people upheld notions such as "fairplay, respect for authority and self discipline," they also "silenced divergent experiences and expressions... [since] authority, the rule of Law, the sense of order, are not experienced as the universal natural and inevitable good that the mythology of Englishness proclaims them to be" (ibid., 81–2).

Taking this further, Grant Farred argues that on colonial cricket grounds, despite what Appadurai refers to as its "Victorian civilities" (p. 42), "the game constituted the metaphor *par excellence* for the colonizer–colonized relations Britain desired":

> The discrepancy in authority between player and umpire is an unerringly accurate reflection of colonizer–colonized relations... [T]he game of cricket and how it is played demonstrates the most subtle interpellation of the colonized into the social arrangement. (Farred 1996: 170)

While a number of intervening elements mediated the teaching of cricket at the level of performance (Appadurai 1995: 29–30), part of what Farred calls the "subtle interpellation... into the social arrangement" of empire was the implicit assumption that, along with the embodied practice of cricket, the colonized imbibed the practice of a particular style of English masculinity, one that also underwrote assumptions of future self-government and "national" status.

Anglo-Australia, as a colonizing *and* a colonial society, mobilizes these ideologies of the "sporting nation" in complex ways. According to the government television commercials broadcast in the lead-up to the centenary of Federation in 2001, this is "a country that had a national cricket team before it had a national parliament." Certainly, a team of indigenous cricketers from Victoria, captained by a white man, did tour England and play at Lords in 1868 – with the indigenous players also performing, in the customary role of colonized-as-exhibit, displays of spear- and boomerang-throwing following each game.[2] But to represent the players of 1868 as a "national team," and the team as the natural precursor to the achievement of self-government, is a wild travesty of the power relations that characterize Australian history. None of the indigenous team members, nor their descendants, would play any role as national subjects, *except by their exclusion*, in the process that culminated in the making of a

Federated state, "Australia," in 1901. In that process the function of the dubious category of "the Aborigine" was to guarantee and consolidate the national status and civic identity of its defining other, "the (white) Australian." The year after the England tour the establishment of the "Aborigine's Protection Board" marked a new era of systematized control over indigenous peoples, and a series of legislative moves between 1877 and 1905 effectively excluded them from the rights and privileges of citizenship in the newly constituted state (Booth & Tatz 2000: 40–2).

The federated state of Australia performs multiple roles in the imperial hierarchy. As a "settler" society it unambiguously operates as the colonizer of indigenous peoples, part of the "master race" of empire. The cultivation of selected racial/cultural affinities with Britain also enable it to occupy a superior position among other, especially nonwhite, colonies. Sport played a key role here in proving that despite transportation and migration "the 'manhood and muscle of their English sires ... flourished' ... and that the English 'race' had not physically degenerated in the bright Australian climate" (Booth & Tatz 2000: 4–5). At the same time, in the process of moving from colonial to independent status, nationalist energies were continuingly harnessed through sport to assert a distinctly "Australian" (that is, non-British) identity. In episodes such as the Bodyline tour of 1934 Anglo–Australia represented itself as the true inheritor of "the spirit of the game" that had degenerated in the "mother country." These representations continue today, complicated by anxieties of Asianization, globalization, and fears for the dissolution of Anglo–Australian identity.

Self-representations of Anglo–Australia as the true custodian of cricket's laws and values were very much in evidence during the 1995 and 1998 Sri Lankan tours, when a number of umpires and cricket writers found the Sri Lankan team guilty of "not playing the game" at the level of embodied practice – most obviously in the allegedly "unlawful action" of their main bowler, but also in their "unorthodox" and "swashbuckling" style (words like "violence," "plunder," and "loot" were routinely used to describe the Sri Lankan batting). The gesture, performance, and body language of the visitors were frequently under attack, as in the notorious hand-shaking incident when the Sri Lankan team refused to end the game with the traditional show of bonhomie. Also seen as not quite cricket was the visiting team's use of "expert" testimony, since cricket is enduringly imagined as a "gentleman's game," clinging, in spite of its thorough-going professionalization, to a romantic image of the "amateur." The Sri Lankan management's use of video technology and expert medical opinion to support their case that Muralitharan's bowling performance could not be judged "unlawful" contradicted common-sense tenets of "calling 'em as you see 'em," or "seeing is believing." In 1998 the use of lawyers in the disciplinary tribunal against the then Sri Lankan captain was again seen as a breach of the game's gentlemanly spirit, not taking into account that a lack of fluency in English might have necessitated professional representation. Also at stake throughout the tour, implicitly or explicitly, were styles of racialized masculinity – images of the "stiff upper lip" and "taking it on the chin," as against allusions to the hysterical oriental, or an emotionally uncontrolled, feminized, excess.

The extent to which each team's cricketing practice was understood as both embodying and performing a drama of national identity was most tellingly manifested in a comment made by the then Sri Lankan Captain, Arjuna Rana-tunga, to the British media: "We come from 2,500 years of culture, and we all know where they come from" (Blake 1996). Here Ranatunga drew on a founda-tional narrative of Sinhala nationalism, used domestically to delegitimize the role of other ethnicities in Sri Lankan history, combining it with a classic colonial snub about Anglo-Australians' "convict origins" (it is significant that the com-ment was made in Britain). Ranatunga's slur made indignant headlines all over Australia, but no one pointed out the commonalities in the official histories of the two groups. Turning one of Sinhala nationalism's cherished myths on itself, one could say that the Sinhala nation also has criminal origins insofar as it founds its national claims on the dissolute Prince Vijaya, whose father banished him to sail away with his thuggish companions, never to return. The arrival of a convict ship on an island, the violent dispossession of its indigenous inhabitants: a shared foundational moment that in each national story underwrites contemporary repressions of racial/cultural difference.

"Decolonization," as Appadurai says, "is a dialogue with the colonial past," and "nowhere are the complexities and ambiguities of this dialogue more evident than in the vicissitudes of cricket" in the former colonies (1995: 23). In the contest of "culture," "nation," and "sportsmanship" played out between Sri Lanka and Australia, both parties drew, in selective ways, on colonial representa-tions and ideologies of cricket. It is to the continuing afterlife of these colonial ideologies and representations, undead phantoms and hoary old ghosts, I now want to turn, in an attempt to illuminate the mobilization of cricket in very contemporary nationalisms.

III

In colonial discourse cricket works in contradictory and complex, even protean, ways as a practice that both substitutes for war *and* transcends it. The classic expression of cricket as the great allegory for war is Henry Newbolt's "Vitae Lampada," where a British rout on some imperial battleground is transformed into a victory by the memory of a school cricket match. At the sametime, cricket, as a memory of childhood, safety, and innocence, is also imagined as an interlude or respite from conflict and "politics," a space that should be kept decently apart from war.

On the eve of the 1996 World Cup final between Sri Lanka and Australia the newsagency Reuters interviewed Lawrence Thilakar, the Paris spokesperson of the Liberation Tigers of Tamil Eelam (LTTE), the army fighting a war of separation against the Sri Lankan state. Thilakar is quoted as saying, "All Tamils in the North and East love cricket... All the schoolchildren love cricket and football... I cannot wish Australia to win. At the same time, it's difficult to wish Sri Lanka to win" (quoted in Ismail, p. 20). Ismail comments on this:

> Though perhaps "spontaneous" this is not a *careless* response. Even the ranks of the LTTE it would seem, could scarce forbear to cheer the Sri Lankan team. The nuance... must be noted: while Thilakar "cannot"... desire an Australian victory, he merely found it "difficult" – not impossible... – to desire a Sri Lankan one. There is a pathos here too. For this statement could be read as expressing a yearning to take politics, the politics of nationalism, out of cricket; so that the LTTE – still *citizens* of Sri Lanka, could cheer the Sri Lankan *team* without embarrassment or treachery, without being complicitous with Sinhala nationalism. (p. 20, original emphasis)

Ismail's use of the term "citizen" here is interesting, both in contrast to his earlier use of "passport holder," and given that it is against the very notion of being subjects of the Sri Lankan state that LTTE is waging a war of separation. The submerged allusion in the passage is to a famous line from "Horatius" by Thomas Babbington Macaulay. Macaulay is no accidental presence to materialize at this moment. Generations of school children all over the former British empire have him to thank, not only for the tiresome "Lays of Ancient Rome" from which "Horatius" is taken, but for an even more influential document of imperialism, the infamous "Minute" on Indian education. Macaulay's ghost summons into this thoroughly postcolonial discussion the meretricious romance of the British public school and its comprehensive mystification of cricket, war, and nation.

While Ismail finds a kind of "pathos" in Thilakar's remarks, there is another story I want to tell against the "yearning" attributed to the LTTE spokesperson "to take politics, the politics of nationalism, out of cricket". A succinct way to tell it is by quoting from M. R. Narayan Swamy's history, *Tigers of Lanka: From Boys to Guerrillas*:

> On June 26, Chelliah Anandarajah, principal of St. John's College in Jaffna, was shot dead by the LTTE. Anandarajah was also a leading member of the Jaffna citizen's committee... [His] crime was he had organised a cricket match in Jaffna between Jaffna schools and the Sri Lankan army to mark the [1985] ceasefire. A second match was due when he was killed. (1996: 177)

One understanding of this story is that Chelliah Anandarajah was a casualty of the colonial mystification of cricket, or precisely of the same yearning attributed to Thilakar, "a yearning to take politics, the politics of nationalism, out of cricket." But before continuing I need to declare an investment here, for this is the withheld cricket story of my life before Australia. Chelliah Anadarajah was my father's brother's son, my first-cousin, though in generational terms I thought of him as my uncle, a large, laughing, strikingly handsome man, well into his twenties when I was born. For years I could read his death only as a cautionary lesson about the dangers of a neocolonial schooling. The Anglican school where he and the older men in my family studied, and which he later headed, the counterpart of the CMS girls' school I attended, traded in just these constructs. Through poems like Macaulay's "Horatius" and Newbolt's "Vitae Lampada," war, cricket, and patriotism were thoroughly confounded. Confusingly, cricket was both a stand-in for war (as in "Vitae Lampada") and something above war ("it matters not whether you win or lose ... "). Though as members of a colonized society, we all shared the unspoken understanding that winning or losing did matter a great deal, and that what was at stake was far more than a game.

A scene in Shyam Selvadurai's *Funny Boy*, where the central character Arjie is asked to memorize two Newbolt poems for Prize Day, articulates the mystifications associated with cricket even in 1980s Sri Lanka:

> the precise meaning of the poems eluded me. They spoke of a reality I did not understand. "Vitae Lampada" was about cricket, but not the way I understood it. It said that through playing cricket one learned to be honest and brave and patriotic. This was not true ... Cricket, here, consisted of trying to make it on the first eleven by any means ... Cricket was anything but honest. "The Best School of All" was no better. (1994: 233)

Arjie, a "funny boy" alienated from the homophobic, elitist, and sports-crazy world of the school, can barely bring himself to memorize the poems. But, as a Tamil, he is told that to recite the poems well would strike a blow for the "old" values in the face of increasing Sinhala nationalism. Arjie's triumph is his realization that to pose the problem in this way is to succumb to a false dilemma: the thuggish violence of Sinhala nationalism represents a *continuity*, not a rupture, from the brutality of the colonial school system:

> Sundaralingam had said Black Tie was strict, not cruel, but he was wrong. Black Tie was cruel. If not ... how could he have slapped Shehan for having long hair and then cut off his hair in such a terrible way? ... I thought of ... the way Salgado and his friends had assaulted that Tamil boy. I thought of the way Black Tie had beaten both Shehan and me. Was one better than the other? I didn't think so. (1994: 247)

Between the murderous nationalism of the LTTE and the murderous nationalism of the Sinhala state, is one much better than the other? These days when I try to think about Chelliah Anandarajah's attempt to organize a cricket match between the Sri Lankan army and the Jaffna schools, I know he was not caught up in any public school glamorizations of cricket. Rather than yearning to take politics, the politics of nationalism, out of cricket, I think he was acknowledging the inescapable implication of politics in cricket. His action, as the LTTE well understood when they killed him on the streets of Jaffna, was a political one, rather than any wistful gesture to transcend politics through cricket.

IV

Contrary to imperial mythologies, cricket in the colonies, as in the colonizing country, has been a source not of unity and cohesion, but of division and antagonism. Gyan Pandey and other historians have demonstrated that the ethnic and sectarian division that operate in contemporary India were often produced and reinforced in the colonial period. What is perhaps less well known is the role of sport in solidifying and marking such distinctions in India (Appadurai 1995: 3) and elsewhere. In Sri Lanka, the most prestigious cricket clubs in Colombo still have names like "Sinhalese Sports Club" and "Tamil Union." Similarly, as James reveals in *Beyond a Boundary*, West Indian clubs were divided according to minute gradations of race, color, class, or "caste." In *Beyond a Boundary* James describes as a "personal Calvary" (p. 72) the pressure to choose between Trinidad's two middle-class clubs, Maple and Shannon, representing lighter and darker skinned players:

> The British tradition soaked into me was that when you entered the sporting arena you left behind the sordid compromises of everyday existence. Yet for us to do that we would have had to divest ourselves of our skins ... Nor could the local population see it otherwise. The class and racial rivalries were too intense ... Thus the cricket field was a stage on which selected individuals played representative roles which were charged with social significance. (p. 72)

The idea of the *national team* continues to rest on the impossible demand that its players "divest ourselves of our skins," casting aside the layers of social division and antagonism that are, especially, a legacy of most former colonies. This implied demand also continues to underlie representations of the sporting arena as a forge for a unified national identity, where petty rivalries of ethnicity, class, and region can be at least temporarily cast aside or transcended. As Toby Miller has shown, this assumption also underlies the move to de-ethnicize soccer in Australia through the proscription of ethnic names and logos in local clubs (Miller 1992: 109–11; Booth & Tatz 2000: 165–9).

The idea of the team as a unit in which social divisions are submerged in the service of the national cause continues to have a strong purchase across a range of political positions. The respected British critic Chris Searle, recently writing in the journal *Race and Class*, described Ranatunga's action in the 1999 Adelaide test (where Ranatunga led the team off the field when Muralitharan was "called" for an "unlawful" delivery) as a gesture that moved "Beyond the Boundary of communalism" (Searle 1999: 115). Here Searle discards other possible readings of Ranatunga's act – say, as a case of different sorts of loyalties between the

521

players, or as a response to the treatment the Sri Lankans had received in Australia, the constant taunting of Muralitharan by the public (Booth & Tatz 2000: 225), or the mounting climate of media condemnation (Roberts & James 1998: 112–24). For Searle, the Sri Lankan Captain's is primarily an act of *national* solidarity with Muralitharan as the sole Tamil member of the team. Rather than understanding the team as a site of unresolvable contradictions, Searle's reading seeks to place members of the team in the realm "beyond." Such a reading of course coincides with the co-optation of cricket by the Sri Lankan government, where the presence of a Tamil on the team is supposed to guarantee the nondiscriminatory and nonracist nature of the state.

In order for Searle to produce his reading of the Sri Lankan Captain's breach of the rules of cricket as in accordance with a higher priority, to act "Beyond the Boundary of communalism," the team has to be isolated from other Sri Lankan institutions with which inextricably bound up, and by which it is constituted: most obviously, the army, the education system, and structures of state control and patronage. To see the cricket team as acting out a script of ethnic solidarity is also to ignore the ways in which the team is fundamentally shaped by ethnic discrimination: the processes by which the team is selected in an ethnically unequal society, the material conditions of the war which limit opportunities for Tamils to focus on sport, the *de facto* segregation in key cricket-playing schools, and so on.[3] None of these factors can be eliminated from the field of play – in fact they constitute that field.

The more interesting, and more difficult, question, then, is not whether or how the team transcends the constraints and inequalities of the state, but how, *in spite of these constraints*, it becomes a site of pleasure and desire for a range of unequally positioned spectators. This is the question I begin to address, in the context of different forms of diasporic spectatorship, in the final section of this chapter.

V

As mentioned above, within Sri Lanka, cricket is a key site through which institutions of the state, and especially state media, attempt to produce a unified national community, or a sense of what Roberts describes as an overarching, "transcendent . . . and composite" Sri Lankanness (Roberts & James 1998: 100). According to Foster, the national telecasting of the cricket by state TV is seized on as a useful means of creating a unified viewing community. Even prior to the cricket team's success, a narrative of television's unifying effects was much favored by optimistic social commentators in a society where television sets are luxury items. In the early days of television in the 1970s for example, domestic workers in affluent households were allowed to complete their labors early in order to watch primetime television in their employers' living rooms (though social distinctions would not be overridden – usually the workers would stand, sit on the floor, or in some more self-consciously "enlightened" households, be provided with special chairs). Since linguistic distinctions remain a clear indicator of class, some social negotiation did take place: English-speaking households would sometimes tune in to popular Sinhala – or more rarely Tamil – soap operas "because of the servants." The unifying function attributed to cricket needs to be placed in the context of these preexisting narratives of a collective viewing public produced by television, where distinctions of class, ethnicity, gender, language, and religion were imagined to be submerged. However, as Foster points out, to read a collective viewing situation as producing a unified spectatorship or community is to ignore the differentiated gaze of particular viewers. The elderly Ammes (female domestics) who are often cited in these discussions for example, may read in the spectacle of Australia or England vs. Sri Lanka cricket match not a struggle between East and West or a conflict of postcolonial virilities, but the aspirations of rural, working-class young men (like the current captain Sanath Jayasuriya), who have in recent years supplanted private-school educated, English-speaking young men from upper-and middle-class families on the national team.

While such differentiated positions of class, gender, and language characterize an internal viewing audience, the community of diasporic viewers is constituted by a range of additional factors. In order to discuss this point I want to shift, briefly, to two key moments in Australian sporting history. The first is a meditation on the great Anglo-Australian cricketing hero, Sir Donald Bradman, but via James. James tells us, "it took an Australian . . . in a little book on Bradman . . . to make me fully conscious of what I had always known about our cricket heroes and their worshippers in the West Indies of my day" (p. 97). He then quotes a passage by a starving Australian journalist in London, Philip Lindsay, who keeps himself alive by reading newspaper reports of Bradman's successful 1930 tour. "Perhaps," James remarks at the end of this passage,

> it is only we on the periphery who feel this way . . . I do not know of any West Indian in the West Indies to whom the success of a cricketer means so much in a personal way. There may be some among the emigrants . . . Jimmy Durante, the famous American comedian has popularised a phrase in the U S: "that's my boy." I am told that its popularity originates in the heart of the immigrant struggling with the new language, baffled by the new customs . . . Wilton St Hill was our boy. (p. 99)

Here James moves between a number of vastly different *diasporic* scenes: from an Anglo-Australian in 1930s London, to Chinese migrants in the West Indies and West Indian migrants in Britain, to the non-Anglo migrants of Durante's USA, to suggest the forms of desire and identification that constitute the gaze of a diasporic spectatorship. Migration, colonization, and assimilation are the key factors in each scene, modifying and mediating the viewers' relationship to an originary country, whether Australia, the West Indies, or China.

I want to juxtapose with James's catalogue one more diasporic group, as represented in a letter to the editor that recently appeared in Melbourne's *Age* newspaper. The letter comments on a famous 'mark' at the 1970 Australian Football League Grand Final:

> the significance of the impact on Australian culture of that mark, and Jesaulenko cannot be underestimated. At the age of 14, and with my dark Mediterranean complexion and black curly hair, I was sitting on the top deck of the northern stand when Jezza on his ascent pierced a hole in the sacred canopy of Anglo-Celtic Australia's prejudices; and, as he grabbed the ball out of the hands of an angel, the messenger whispered what Jezza heard as a tremendous roar from the crowd: "wogs are ok."
>
> Jesaulenko made the "ethnic" supporters feel as if they belonged . . . He couldn't be put down by the Anglo-Celts. Carlton supporters of ethnic background don't just admire Jezza; they adore him. He made them feel lovable in a rejecting society. (John Bacash)

The power of this decades-old memory, one experienced, indeed, as a revalatory moment, in which a whisper from the heavens is echoed in a roar from crowd, is the consolidation and confirmation of a new identity: "wogs are ok." The affirmation of 'wog' (a word whose problematic aspects I am bracketing in today's discussion) has little to do with Turkish, Macedonian, Italian, Bosnian, Greek, or Lebanese nationalism on the part of the audience. Rather it is a response that affirms an identity produced in, and referring to, the viewer's Australian context.[4]

Whereas much of the writing on migrant and diasporic communities tends to see them as focused nostalgically on the past, on "imagined *home* lands," less attention is paid to diaspora as dynamically producing or *creating* identities, identities that, as in this instance, exceed the nationalist reach of an originary state or nation through the claiming or formation of new categories of identification (Gilroy). These identifications, like 'wog,' are conscious responses to the inhospitality of the viewer's location: here the writer significantly refers to a 14-year-old self who at this moment for once felt "lovable in a rejecting society." Against the institutionalized and everyday racism of seventies Australia, a reactive identity, "wog," is announced from the heavens, splintering open the notion of a unified Australian team or nation.

It is worth pursuing the connections between this scene of annunciation and the one cited by James, Jimmy Durante's famous line, "That's my boy." In both scenes, a child – a "boy" – is conferred an identity from on high, an identity constituted in response to pressures of racism and assimilation. In his discussion of this passage Farred unpacks the "provocative" implications of James's transposition of a scene of assimilationist anxiety from Durante's United States to Afro-Caribbeans in London. As the migrant child masters the language and lessons of the dominant culture,

A fissure, drawn mostly among lines of generation and class, opens up between the "boy" and his, it is seldom her, community. There is an anxiety contained in the enthusiasm with which the immigrant community claims the "boy" as "ours." Having learned the new language and customs, he could easily become someone else's boy .... More disturbing is the possibility that the cultural remove could translate into an economic dependence upon the dominant community, literally reducing the immigrant boy to the diminutive ... The public embracing of their "boy" by the immigrants represents both an effort to secure links with the primary community and a ... recognition that ... the immigrant community has to create a new understanding and functioning of community. (Farred 1996: 184)

What occurs in all three scenes is a renegotiation, or changed understanding of the space of "home" and belonging as new identifications and oppositions are articulated. Throughout *Beyond a Boundary*, Farred argues, James is engaged in an "ongoing negotiation with the concept of home" (Farred 1996: 179), a negotiation constituted by diaspora and removal. To characterize James's position as simply "nationalist" is to miss *Beyond a Boundary's* location as a text of the Afro-Caribbean diaspora, and the complexities of his reimagining of "home" for the diasporic spectator. As Paul Gilroy puts it (via Rakim) in another context, "*it ain't where you're from, it's where you're at*" (Gilroy 1991: 3–6). The defiant and creative identifications produced by migration are not necessarily the result of a subject's interpellation by an unproblematized nationalism of the "homeland," but a response to the realities of the present: "where you're at."

To return to the questions with which I began, a Sri Lankan, Tamil, woman suddenly called on to 'take sides' in the cricket: my viewing position can be explained neither by my assent to the nationalist appeal of a unitary Sri Lanka, nor by a position "outside" politics, as a knowing connoisseur of the game. It is constituted, rather, by my constant interpellation as foreign to the country whose *passport* I now hold, but whose privileges of *citizenship* I can never fully assume. A discussion that does not take account of these dialectics of diasporic identity will remain unable to comprehend the forms of agency available to an oppositional spectatorship. Such a gaze, moreover, exceeds the narrow identifications of "country of origin": as I said at the outset, anti-Australian, pro-Sri Lankan sympathies during the tour extended to include many categories of minoritized "wogs" and "ethnics" in Australia.

But the question remains open: can this minoritized, oppositional spectatorship coincide with, or be recuperated by, that of Sinhala nationalism? I have tried to suggest that the mobilizations of "culture," "nation," and "sportsmanship" by Australian and Sinhala nationalisms are in fact complicitous and complementary. To the spectator located between nationalisms, the two work together to open up the historical and ongoing frameworks, the "plots," within which such contests are played out.

Notes

First published in *Diaspora: Asian Australian Cultural Negotiations*, eds. Helen Gilbert, Tseen Khoo, and Jacqueline Lo: *Journal of Australian Studies* 65, 2000, University of Queensland Press. My warm appreciation to Mahinda Perera, Rodney Noonan, and Rajiva Wijesinghe for giving me the benefit of their formidable cricketing knowledge; any solecisms that remain are entirely my own doing. A version of this chapter was originally given as a keynote address at the Performing Asian-Australian Identities Conference at the Australian National University, and in the South Asia Seminar series at Monash University.

1   On the role of the boundary between players and spectators see Burton 1991: 9–10.
2   For more on indigenous cricketers in the years leading up to Federation, see Martin Flanagan's remarkable novel, The Call.
3   An editorial in the *Daily News* of March 10, 1998, laments the "shaming ethnic divide" that turns cricket into an "apartheid regime" in some city schools. In this context I find a little disingenuous Ismail's remark that "whereas the nationalist would support the team no matter what, the kind of spectator I have constructed here wouldn't – for instance if the selection of the team was 'ethnically discriminatory' " (1997: 26).
4   For a discussion of the complexities of the word 'wog' see Perera and Pugliese 1998, and Perera 1999.

References

Appadurai, Arjun. "Playing with Modernity," in Carol Breckenridge (ed.), *Consuming Modernity: Public Culture in a South Asian World* (Minneapolis: University of Minnesota Press, 1995).

Bacash, John. "Marking Time," Letter to the Editor, *Age*, Sept. 5, 1999.

Blake, Martin. "Warne Cops Fine for Ranatunga Attack," *Age*, May 16, 1996, p. 4.

Booth, Douglas and Colin Tatz. *One-Eyed: A View of Australian Sport* (St. Leonards: Allen & Unwin, 2000).

Bouts, Trent "Going Over the Top Only Solution to Overcoming Sri Lankans," *Australian*, Sept. 9, 1996, p. 30.

Burton, Richard. "Cricket, Carnival and Street Culture in the Caribbean," in *Sport Racism and Ethnicity*, ed. Grant Jarvie (London: The Falmer Press, 1991).

Clarke, Alan and John Clarke, "Highlights and Action Replays – Ideology, Sport and the Media," in Jennifer Hargreaves (ed.), *Sport, Culture and Ideology* (London: Routledge, 1982).

Farred, Grant. "The Maple Man: How Cricket made a Postcolonial Intellectual," in Grant Farred (ed.) *Rethinking C. L. R. James* (Cambridge, Mass.: Blackwell, 1996).

Flanagan, Martin, *The Call* (St Leonards: Allen & Unwin, 1998).

Foster, Yolanda. "Battening on Cricket?" *Island*, Sept. 28, 1997.

Gilroy, Paul. "The Dialectics of Diasporic Identification," *Third Text* 13 (1991): 3–16.

Ismail, Qadri. "Batting Against the Break: On Cricket, Nationalism and the Swashbuckling Sri Lankans," *Pravada* 5.1 (1997): 16–26.

Jaireth, Subash. "Tracing Orientalism in Cricket: A Reading of Some Recent Australian Cricket Writing on Pakistani Cricket," *Sporting Traditions* 12.1 (1995): 103–20.

James, C. L. R. *Beyond a Boundary* (London: Stanley Paul, 1963).

Kell, Peter. *Good Sports: Australian Sport and the Myth of the Fair Go* (Annandale: Pluto Press, 2000).

Knox, Malcolm. "Utter Chaos the Order On and Off the Pitch," *Age*, Aug. 30, 1996.

MacIntyre, Ernest. "Hora, Hora, Umpire Hora!" *Sunday Times,* May 16, 1999.

Miller, Toby. "The Unmarking of Soccer: Making a Brand New Subject," in *Celebrating the Nation,* eds. Tony Bennett et al. (St Leonards: Allen & Unwin 1992).

Narayan Swamy, M. R. *Tigers of Lanka: From Boys to Guerillas* (Colombo: Vijitha Yapa, 1996).

Perera, Suvendrini. "Whiteness and its Discontents," *Journal of Intercultural Studies* 20.2 (1999): 183–98.

Perera, Suvendrini and Joseph Pugliese, "Wogface, Anglo-Drag, Contested Aboriginalities: Making and Unmaking Identities in Australia," *Social Identities* 4.1 (1998): 39–72.

Roberts, Michael and Alfred James. *Crosscurrents: Sri Lanka and Australia at Cricket* (Petersham: Walla Walla Press, 1998).

Roebuck, Peter. "Magnificent Cup Mayhem," *Age*, March 11, 1996.

Searle, Chris. "Teacher and Interrupter," *Race & Class* 41.1/2 (1999): 109–21.

Selvadurai, Shyam. *Funny Boy* (New Delhi: Penguin, 1994).

PART IV

Sources

Chapter 30

Bibliographical Resources for Cultural Studies

Toby Miller

Journals

Journal of Communication, Critical Studies in Mass Communication, Journal of Broadcasting & Electronic Media, Journalism & Mass Communication Quarterly, Gazette, Cultural Studies, Journal of Radio Studies, Journal of Communication Inquiry, Journal of Popular Film and Television, Media, Culture & Society, European Journal of Communication, camera obscura, Canadian Journal of Communication, Feminist Media Studies, differences, Convergence, Continuum, International Journal of Cultural Studies, Historical Journal of Film, Radio, and Television, European Journal of Cultural Studies, Asian Journal of Communication, Quarterly Journal of Film, Television, and Video, New Media & Society, Mass Communication Review, Feminist Media Studies, Media International Australia, Visual Anthropology, Visual Anthropology Review, Media Studies Journal, Resaux: The French Journal of Communication, Media History, Howard Journal of Communication, Women's Studies in Communication, Quarterly Journal of Speech, Communication Theory, M/C – A Journal of Media and Culture, Journalism History, Electronic Journal of Communication, International Journal of Communication, Visual Sociology, Social Text, Socialist Review, Public Culture, European Journal of Cultural Studies, Hong Kong Cultural Studies Bulletin, South Atlantic Quarterly, Third Text, Social Identities.

General Texts

"Asia/Pacific as Space of Cultural Production." *boundary 2* 21, no. 1 (1994).

"Cultural Studies." *Critical Studies in Mass Communication* 6, no. 4 (1989).

"Cultural Studies/Cultural Politics: Articulating the Global and the Local." *Politics & Culture* 6 (1994).

"Cultural Studies: Crossing Boundaries." *Critical Studies* 3, no. 1 (1991).

"Cultural Studies in the Asia Pacific." *Southeast Asian Journal of Social Science* 22 (1994).

"Cultural Studies/Les études culturelles." *Canadian Review of Comparative Literature/ Revue Canadienne de Littérature Comparée* 22, no. 1 (1995).

"The Future of the Field – Between Fragmentation and Cohesion." *Journal of Communication* 43, no. 3 (1993).

"Rethinking Black (Cultural) Studies." *Callaloo* 19, no. 1 (1996).

"Review Forum on Cultural Studies." *Victorian Studies* 36, no. 4: 455–72 (1993).

Abelove, Henry, Michèle Aina Barale, and David M. Halperin, eds. *The Lesbian and Gay Studies Reader*. New York: Routledge, 1993.

Agger, Ben *Cultural Studies*. London: Falmer Press, 1992.

Alexander, Jeffrey C. and Philip Smith. "The Discourse of American Civil Society: A New Proposal for Cultural Studies." *Theory and Society* 22, no. 2 (1993): 151–207.

Althusser, Louis. *Lenin and Philosophy and Other Essays*. Trans. Ben Brewster. London: New Left Books, 1977.

Anderson, Talmadge. *Black Studies: Theory, Method, and Cultural Perspectives*. Pullman: Washington State University Press, 1990.

Ang, Ien. "Dismantling 'Cultural Studies'?". *Cultural Studies* 6, no. 3 (1992): 311–21.

Angus, Ian and Sut Jhally, eds. *Cultural Politics in Contemporary America*. New York: Routledge, 1989.

Appadurai, Arjun, ed. *The Social Life of Things: Commodities in Cultural Perspective*. Cambridge: Cambridge University Press, 1986.

Baker, Houston A., Jr., Manthia Diawara, and Ruth H. Lindeborg, eds. *Black British Cultural Studies: A Reader*. Chicago: University of Chicago Press, 1996.

Barker, Martin and Anne Beezer, eds. *Reading into Cultural Studies*. London: Routledge, 1992.

Barthes, Roland. *Mythologies*. Trans. Annette Lavers. London: Paladin, 1973.

Becker, Howard S. and Michael M. McCall, eds. *Symbolic Interaction and Cultural Studies*. Chicago: University of Chicago Press, 1990.

Bennett, Tony, Colin Mercer, and Janet Woollacott, eds. *Popular Culture and Social Relations*. Milton Keynes: Open University Press, 1986.

Bennett, Tony, ed. *Popular Fiction: Technology, Ideology, Production, Reading*. London: Routledge, 1990.

Berry, Sarah and Toby Miller. (2000). *Blackwell Cultural Theory Resource Centre*. <*http://www.blackwellpublishers.co.uk/cultural/*>.

Blundell, Valda, John Shepherd, and Ian Taylor, eds. *Relocating Cultural Studies: Developments in Theory and Research*. London: Routledge, 1993.

Bourdieu, Pierre. *Distinction: A Social Critique of the Judgment of Taste*. Trans. Richard Nice. Cambridge, Mass.: Harvard University Press, 1984.

Brantlinger, Patrick. *Crusoe's Footsteps: Cultural Studies in Britain and America*. New York: Routledge, 1990.

Bronner, S. and D. Kellner, eds. *Critical Theory and Society: A Reader*. London: Routledge, 1989.

Buckingham, D., ed. *Teaching Popular Culture: Beyond Radical Pedagogy*. London: University College London Press, 1998.

Budd, Mike, Robert M. Entman, and Clay Steinman. "The Affirmative Character of US Cultural Studies." *Critical Studies in Mass Communication* 7, no. 2 (1990): 169–84.

Carey, James W. "Overcoming Resistance to Cultural Studies." In M. Gurevitch and M. Levy (eds.), *Mass Communication Review Yearbook*, Vol. 5. London: Sage, 1985.

Chaney, David. *The Cultural Turn: Scene Setting Essays on Contemporary Cultural Theory*. London: Routledge, 1994.

Chatterjee, Partha. *The Nation and its Fragments: Colonial and Postcolonial Histories*. Princeton: Princeton University Press, 1993.

Chen, Kuan-Hsing and David Morley, eds. *Stuart Hall: Critical Dialogues in Cultural Studies*. London: Routledge, 1996.

Chen, Kuan-Hsing, ed. *Trajectories: Inter-Asia Cultural Studies*. London: Routledge, 1998.

Chow, Rey. *Writing Diaspora: Tactics of Intervention in Contemporary Cultural Studies*. Bloomington: Indiana University Press, 1993.

Collins, Jim. *Uncommon Cultures: Popular Culture and Post-Modernism*. New York: Routledge, 1989.

Conley, Verena Andermatt, ed. *Rethinking Technologies*. Minneapolis: University of Minnesota Press, 1993.

Cross, Gary. *Time and Money: The Making of Consumer Culture*. New York: Routledge, 1993.

Cunningham, Stuart. *Framing Culture: Criticism and Policy in Australia*. Sydney: Allen and Unwin, 1992.

Curran, J., D. Morley, and V. Walkerdine, eds. *Cultural Studies and Communication*. London: Arnold, 1996.

Czaplicka, John, Andreas Huyssen, and Anson Rabinach. Introduction: Cultural History and Cultural Studies: Reflections on a Symposium." *New German Critique* 22, no. 2 (1995): 3–17.

Davies, I. *Cultural Studies and Beyond: Fragments of Empire*. London: Routledge, 1995.

de Certeau, Michel. *The Practice of Everyday Life*. Trans. Steven F. Rendall. Berkeley and Los Angeles: University of California Press, 1984.

de Lauretis, Teresa, ed. *Feminist Studies/Critical Studies*. Bloomington: Indiana University Press, 1986.

Debord, Guy. *Society of the Spectacle*. Detroit: Black and Red Press, 1983.

Denning, Michael. "The Academic Left and the Rise of Cultural Studies." *Radical History Review* 54 (1992), 21–47.

Diawara, Manthia. "Black Studies, Cultural Studies, Performative Acts." In *Race, Identity and Representation in Education* eds. Cameron McCarthy and Warren Crichlow. New York: Routledge, 1994.

Dirks, Nicholas B., Geoff Eley, and Sherry B. Ortner, eds. *Culture/Power/History: A Reader in Contemporary Social Theory*. Princeton: Princeton University Press, 1994.

Docherty, Thomas, ed. *Postmodernism: A Reader*. New York: Harvester Wheatsheaf, 1993.

Donald, James, ed. *Psychoanalysis and Cultural Theory: Thresholds*. New York: St. Martin's Press, 1991.

During, Simon, ed. *The Cultural Studies Reader*. London: Routledge, 1993.

Dworkin, Dennis. *Cultural Marxism in Postwar Britain: History, the New Left, and the Origins of Cultural Studies*. Durham: Duke University Press, 1997.

Easthope, Antony and Kate McGowan, eds. *A Critical and Cultural Theory Reader*. Toronto: University of Toronto Press, 1992.

Eco, Umberto. *Travels in Hyperreality*. Trans. William Weaver. London: Picador, 1987.

Ferguson, M. and P. Golding eds. *Cultural Studies in Question*. London: Sage, 1997.

Ferguson, Russell, Martha Gever, Trinh T. Minh-ha, and Cornel West, eds. *Out There: Marginalization and Contemporary Culture*. New York: The New Museum of Contemporary Art; Cambridge, Mass.: MIT Press, 1990.

Fiske, John. *Reading the Popular*. Boston: Unwin Hyman, 1989.

Fiske, John. *Understanding Popular Culture*. Boston: Unwin Hyman, 1989.

Fiske, John. *Power Plays Power Works*. London: Verso, 1993.

Forbes, Jill and Michael Kelly, eds. *French Cultural Studies: An Introduction*. Oxford: Oxford University Press, 1996.

Forgacs, David and Robert Lumley, eds. *Italian Cultural Studies: An Introduction*. Oxford: Oxford University Press, 1996.

Foster, Hal, ed. *The Anti-Aesthetic: Essays on Postmodern Culture*. Port Townsend: Bay Press, 1983.

Franklin, Sarah, Celia Lury, and Jackie Stacey, eds. *Off-Centre: Feminism and Cultural Studies*. London: Routledge, 1991.

Frith, Simon. "The Good, the Bad and the Indifferent: Defending Popular Culture from the Populists." *Diacritics* 21, no. 4 (1991): 102–15.

Frow, J. *Cultural Studies and Cultural Value*. Oxford: Oxford University Press, 1995.

Frow, John and Meaghan Morris, eds. (1993a). *Australian Cultural Studies: A Reader*, eds. Frow and Morris. Sydney: Allen and Unwin.

Frow, John and Meaghan Morris. "Introduction." *Australian Cultural Studies: A Reader*, eds. Frow and Morris. Sydney: Allen and Unwin, 1993.

Gans, Herbert. *Popular Culture and High Culture*. New York: Basic Books, 1974.

Gever, Martha, John Greyson, and Pratibha Parmar, eds. *Queer Looks: Perspectives on Lesbian and Gay Film and Video*. New York: Routledge, 1993.

Gibson, Mark and John Hartley. "Forty Years of Cultural Studies: An Interview with Richard Hoggart, October 1997." *International Journal of Cultural Studies* 1, no. 1 (1998): 11–23.

Giroux, Henry. *Disturbing Pleasures: Learning Popular Culture*. London and New York: Routledge, 1994.

Giroux, Henry and Peter McLaren, eds. *Between Borders: Pedagogy and the Politics of Cultural Studies*. New York: Routledge, 1994.

Gordon, D. "Feminism and Cultural Studies: Review Essay," *Feminist Studies* 21(2) (1995): 363–77.

Graham, Helen and Jo Labanyi, eds. *Spanish Cultural Studies: An Introduction: The Struggle for Modernity*. Oxford: Oxford University Press, 1996.

Gramsci, Antonio. *Selections from the Prison Notebooks*. Trans. Quentin Hoare and Geoffrey Nowell-Smith. New York: International Publishers, 1971.

Gray, Ann and Jim McGuigan, eds. *Studying Culture: An Introductory Reader*. London: Edward Arnold, 1993.

Greenblatt, Stephen J. *Learning to Curse: Essays in Early Modern Culture*. New York: Routledge, 1990.

Grossberg, Lawrence and Della Pollock. "Editorial Statement." *Cultural Studies* 12, no. 3 (1998): 2.

Grossberg, Lawrence, Cary Nelson, and Paula Treichler, eds. *Cultural Studies*. New York: Routledge, 1992.

Grossberg, Lawrence. "Cultural Studies and/in New Worlds." *Critical Studies in Mass Communication* 10, no. 1 (1993): 1–22.

Grossberg, Lawrence. "The Formations of Cultural Studies: An American in Birmingham." In *Relocating Cultural Studies: Developments in Theory and Research*, eds. Valda Blundell, John Shepherd, and Ian Taylor. London: Routledge, 1993.

Grossberg, Lawrence. *Bringing it all Back Home: Essays on Cultural Studies*. Durham: Duke University Press, 1997.

Guha, Ranajit, ed. *Subaltern Studies*. Delhi: Oxford University Press, 1982–.

Hall, Stuart. "Introduction." *Representation: Cultural Representations and Signifying Practices*, ed. Stuart Hall. London: Sage, 1997.

Hall, Stuart. "Culture and Power." *Radical Philosophy* 86 (1997): 24–41.

Hall, Stuart and Bram Gieben, eds. *Formations of Modernity*. Cambridge: Polity Press, 1992.

Hall, Stuart and Paddy Whannel. *The Popular Arts*. New York: Pantheon, 1965.

Harper, Phillip Brain. *Framing the Margins: The Social Logic of Postmodern Culture*. New York: Oxford University Press, 1993.

Harris, David. *From Class Struggle to the Politics of Pleasure: The Effects of Gramscianism on Cultural Studies*. London: Routledge, 1992.

Hartley, John. "Editorial (with Goanna)." *International Journal of Cultural Studies* 1, no. 1 (1998): 5–10.

Hartley, John. *The Politics of Pictures: The Creation of the Public in the Age of Popular Media*. New York: Routledge, 1992.

Harvey, David. *The Condition of Postmodernity: An Enquiry into the Origins of Cultural Change*. Oxford Blackwell, 1989.

Hawkes, Terence. *Structuralism and Semiotics*. London: Methuen, 1977.

Hebdige, Dick. *Hiding in the Light: On Images and Things*. London: Comedia/Routledge, 1988.

Heim, Michael. *The Metaphysics of Virtual Reality*. New York: Oxford Unviersity Press, 1993.

Henriques, J., W. Hollway, C. Urwin, C. Venn, and V. Walkerdine. *Changing the Subject*. New York: Methuen, 1984.

Hirschkop, K. and D. Shepherd, eds. *Bakhtin and Cultural Theory*. Manchester: Manchester University Press, 1989.

Hodge, Robert and Gunther Kress. *Social Semiotics*. Oxford: Polity Press, 1988.

Hoggart, Richard. *The Uses of Literacy: Aspects of Working-Class Life with Special Reference to Publications and Entertainments*. Harmondsworth: Penguin, 1957.

Hunter, Ian. "Setting Limits to Culture." *New Formations* 4 (1988): 103–23.

Huyssen, Andreas. *After the Great Divide: Modernism, Mass Culture, Postmodernism*. Bloomington: Indiana University Press, 1986.

Inglis, Fred. *Cultural Studies*. Oxford: Blackwell, 1993.

Jameson, Fredric. *Postmodernism, or, the Cultural Logic of Late Capitalism*. Durham: Duke University Press, 1991.

Jameson, Fredric. "On 'Cultural Studies'." *Social Text* 11, no. 1 (1993): 17–52.

Jenks, Chris, ed. *Cultural Reproduction*. London: Routledge, 1993.

Kaplan, E. Ann, ed. *Postmodernism and its Discontents: Theories and Practices*. New York: Verso, 1989.

Kellner, Douglas. "Toward a Multiperspectival Cultural Studies." *Centennial Review* 36, no. 1 (1992): 5–42.

Kellner, Douglas. *Media Culture: Cultural Studies, Identity, and Politics Between the Modern and the Postmodern*. London and New York: Routledge, 1995.

Kelly, C. and D. Shepherd, eds. *Russian Cultural Studies: An Introduction*. Oxford: Oxford University Press, 1998.

King, Anthony, ed. *Culture, Globalization and the World-System: Contemporary Conditions for the Representation of Identity*. London: Macmillan, 1991.

Kuan-Hsing, Chen. "Post-Marxism: Between/Beyond Critical Postmodernism and Cultural Studies." *Media, Culture and Society* 13, no. 1 (1991): 35–51.

Lash, Scott, *Sociology of Postmodernism*. London: Routledge, 1990.

Leavis, F. R. and Denys Thompson. *Culture and Environment: The Training of Critical Awareness*. London: Chatto and Windus, 1933.

Lee, Martyn J. *Consumer Culture Reborn: The Cultural Politics of Consumption*. London: Routledge, 1992.

Lefebvre, Henri. *Everyday Life in the Modern World*. Trans. S. Rabinovitch. New Brunswick: Transaction Books, 1984.

Lembo, Ronald and Kenneth H. Tucker, Jr. "Culture, Television, and Opposition: Rethinking Cultural Studies." *Critical Studies in Mass Communication* 7, no. 2 (1990): 97–116.

Leonard, Jerry D., ed. *Legal Studies as Cultural Studies: A Reader in (Post) Modern Critical Theory*. Albany: State University of New York Press, 1995.

Leong, Laurence Wei-Teng. "Cultural Resistance: The Cultural Terrorism of British Male Working-Class Youth." *Current Perspectives in Social Theory* 12 (1992): 29–58.

Levine, Lawrence W. *Highbrow/Lowbrow: The Emergence of Cultural Hierarchy in America*. Cambridge, Mass.: Harvard University Press, 1988.

Long, E., ed. *From Sociology to Cultural Studies: New Perspectives*. Oxford: Blackwell, 1997.

Lovell, Terry, ed. *Feminist Cultural Studies Volumes I and II*. Aldershot: Elgar, 1995.

Lury, Celia. *Cultural Rights: Technology, Legality and Personality*. London: Routledge, 1993.

Lyotard, Jean-François. *The Postmodern Condition: A Report on Knowledge*. Trans. Geoffrey Bennington and Brian Massumi. Minneapolis: University of Minnesota Press, 1984.

MacCabe, Colin. "Cultural Studies and English." *Critical Quarterly* 34, no. 3 (1992): 25–34.

Martin, Randy, ed. *Chalk Lines: The Politics of Work in the Managed University*. Durham: Duke University Press, 1998.

Mattelart, Armand and Michèle Mattelart. *Rethinking Media Theory: Signposts and New Directions*. Trans. James A. Cohen and Marina Urquidi. Minneapolis: University of Minnesota Press, 1992.

Mattelart, Michèle. *Women, Media and Crisis: Femininity and Disorder*. London: Comedia, 1986.

Maxwell, Richard. "Cultural Studies." In *Understanding Contemporary Society: Theories of the Present* eds. Gary Browning, Abigail Halci, and Frank Webster. London: Sage, 2000.

McGuigan, Jim. *Cultural Populism*. New York: Routledge, 1992.

McGuigan, J., ed. *Cultural Methodologies* London: Sage, 1997.

McHoul, Alec and Tom O'Regan. "Towards a Paralogics of Textual Technologies: Batman, Glasnost and Relativism in Cultural Studies." *Southern Review* 25, no. 1 (1992): 5–26.

McRobbie, Angela. *Postmodernism and Popular Culture*. London: Routledge, 1994.

Miller, D. *Material Culture and Mass Consumption*. Oxford: Blackwell, 1987.

Miller, Toby. "Beyond the Ur-Text of Radicalism." *Australian Journal of Communication* 17, no. 1 (1990): 174–84.

Miller, Toby and Alec McHoul. *Popular Culture and Everyday Life*. London: Sage, 1998.

Miller, Toby. *Technologies of Truth: Cultural Citizenship and the Popular Media*. Minneapolis: University of Minnesota Press, 1998.

Modleski, Tania, ed. *Studies in Entertainment: Critical Approaches to Mass Culture*. Bloomington: Indianapolis University Press, 1986.

Modleski, Tania. *Feminism Without Women: Culture and Criticism in a "Postfeminist"Age*. New York: Routledge, 1991.

Morley, David. "So-called Cultural Studies: Dead Ends and Reinvented Wheels". *Cultural Studies* 12, no. 4 (1998): 476–97.

Morris, Meaghan. "Banality in Cultural Studies." In *Logics of Television: Essays in Cultural Criticism*, ed. Patricia Mellencamp. Bloomington: Indiana University Press, 1990.

Morris, Meaghan. *Ecstasy and Economics: American Essays for John Forbes*. Sydney: EM Press, 1992.

Morrow, Raymond A. "The Challenge of Cultural Studies." *Canadian Review of Comparative Literature/ Revue Canadienne de Littérature Comparée* 22, no. 1 (1995): 1–20.

Muecke, Stephen. *Textual Spaces: Aboriginality and Cultural Studies*. Sydney: University of New South Wales Press, 1992.

Mukerji, Chandra and Michael Schudson. "Popular Culture". *Annual Review of Sociology* 12 (1986): 47–66.

Murdock, Graham. "Across the Great Divide: Cultural Analysis and the Condition of Democracy." *Critical Studies in Mass Communication* 12, no. 1 (1995): 89–95.

Naremore, James and Patrick Brantlinger, eds. *Modernity and Mass Culture*. Bloomington: Indiana University Press, 1991.

Nederveen Pieterse, Jan. *White on Black: Images of Africa and Blacks in Western Popular Culture*. New Heaven: Yale University Press, 1992.

Nelson, Cary, ed. *Will Teach for Food: Academic Labor in Crisis*. Minneapolis: University of Minnesota Press, 1997.

Penley, Constance and Andrew Ross, eds. *Technoculture*. Minneapolis: University of Minnesota Press, 1991.

Probyn, Elspeth. *Sexing the Self: Gendered Positions in Cultural Studies*. New York: Routledge, 1993.

Punter, David, ed. *Introduction to Contemporary Cultural Studies*. London: Longman, 1986.

Redhead, Steve. *Unpopular Cultures: The Birth of Law and Popular Culture*. Manchester: Manchester University Press, 1995.

Regan, Stephen and Elaine Treharn, eds. *The Year's Work in Critical and Cultural Theory Volume 1*. Oxford: Blackwell, 1994.

Regan, Stephen, ed. *The Politics of Pleasure: Aesthetics and Cultural Theory*. Milton Keynes: Open University Press, 1992.

537

Ringer, R. Jeffrey, ed. *Queer Words, Queer Images: Communication and the Construction of Homosexuality*. New York: New York University Press, 1993.

Roseneil, S. and J. Seymour eds. *Practising Identities: Power and Resistance*, London: Macmillan, 1999.

Ross, Andrew. *No Respect: Intellectuals and Popular Culture*. New York: Routledge, 1989.

Rosteck, Thomas. "Cultural Studies and Rhetorical Studies." *Quarterly Journal of Speech* 81, no. 3 (1995): 386–403.

Said, Edward. *Orientalism*. London: Routledge and Kegan Paul, 1978.

Salzman, Jack. "Editor's Note." *Prospects: An Annual Journal of American Cultural Studies* 1 (1975): iii.

Schwichtenberg, Cathy. "Feminist Cultural Studies." *Critical Studies in Mass Communication* 6, no. 2 (1989): 202–8.

Sedgwick, Eve Kosofsky. *The Epistemology of the Closet*. Berkeley and Los Angeles: University of California Press, 1990.

Shannon, Patrick and Henry A. Giroux. "Editor's Comments." *Review of Education/Pedagogy/Cultural Studies* 16, no. 1 (1994): v.

Shiach, Morag. *Discourse on Popular Culture*. London: Polity Press, 1989.

Shiach, Morag, ed. *Feminism & Cultural Studies*. Oxford: Oxford University Press, 1999.

Silverstone, Roger and Eric Hirsch, eds. *Consuming Technologies: Media and Information in Domestic Spaces*. New York: Routledge, 1992.

Smith, Barbara Herrnstein. *Contingencies of Value: Alternative Perspectives for Critical Theory*. Cambridge, Mass.: Harvard University Press, 1988.

Soja, Edward. *Postmodern Geographies: The Reassertion of Space in Critical Social Theory*. New York: Verso, 1989.

Stallybrass, Peter and Allon White. *The Politics and Poetics of Transgression*. London: Methuen, 1986.

Stam, Robert. *Subversive Pleasures: Bakhtin, Cultural Criticism, and Film*. Baltimore and London: The Johns Hopkins University Press, 1989.

Steele, T. *The Emergence of Cultural Studies, 1945–65: Cultural Politics, Adult Education and the English Question*. London: Lawrence and Wishart, 1997.

Storey, John. *An Introductory Guide to Cultural Theory and Popular Culture*. Athens: University of Georgia Press, 1993.

Tagg, John, ed. *The Cultural Politics of "Postmodernism."* Binghamton: SUNY at Binghamton, 1989.

Thompson, Denys, ed. *Discrimination and Popular Culture*, 2nd edn. London: Penguin, 1973.

Thompson, E. P. *The Making of the English Working Class*. Harmondsworth: Penguin, 1968.

Thompson, E. P. *The Poverty of Theory*. London: Merlin, 1978.

Tudor, Andrew. *Decoding Culture: Theory and Method in Cultural Studies*. London: Sage, 1999.

Turner, Graeme, ed. *Nation, Culture, Text: Australian Cultural and Media Studies*. London: Routledge, 1993.

Turner, Graeme. *British Cultural Studies: An Introduction*. Boston: Unwin Hyman, 1990.

Valdivia, Angharad ed. *Feminism, Multiculturalism, and the Media*. London: Sage, 1995.

Vattimo, Gianni. *The End of Modernity: Nihilism and Hermeneutics in Post-Modern Culture*. Trans. Jon R. Snyder. Oxford: Polity Press, 1988.

Veeser, H. Aram, ed. *The New Historicism Reader*. New York: Routledge, 1994.

Virilio, Paul and Sylvère Lotringer. *Pure War*. New York: Semiotext(e), 1983.

Waites, Bernard, Tony Bennett, and Graham Martin, eds. *Popular Culture: Past and Present*. London: Croom Helm, 1982.

Weedon, Chris and Glenn Jordan. *Cultural Politics*. Oxford: Blackwell, 1994.

Williams, Patrick and Laura Chrisman, eds. *Colonial Discourse/Post-Colonial Theory*. New York: Columbia University Press, 1993.

Williams, Raymond. *Culture and Society: 1780–1850*. Harmondsworth: Penguin, 1961.

Williams, Raymond. *The Long Revolution*. Harmondsworth: Pelican, 1975.

Williams, Raymond. *Marxism and Literature*. Oxford: Oxford University Press, 1977.

Williams, Raymond. *Culture*. London: Fontana, 1981.

Williams, Raymond. *Keywords: A Vocabulary of Culture and Society*. London: Fontana, 1983.

Williams, Raymond. *The Politics of Modernism: Against the New Conformists*. Ed. Tony Pinkney. London: Verso, 1989.

Williamson, Judith. *Consuming Passions: The Dynamics of Popular Culture*. London: Marion Boyars, 1986.

Willis, Paul. *Common Culture*. Milton Keynes: Open University Press, 1990.

Willis, Susan. *A Primer for Daily Life*. New York: Routledge, 1991.

Wollen, Peter. *Raiding the Icebox: Reflections on Twentieth-Century Culture*. London: Verso, 1993.

Women's Studies Group of the Centre for Contemporary Cultural Studies. *Women Take Issue: Aspects of Women's Subordination*. London: Hutchinson, 1978.

Workplace. 2, no.2 (1999). http://www.louisville.edu/journal/workplace/ issue4/contents22.html.

Wright, Handel Kashope. "Take Birmingham to the Curb, Here Comes African Cultural Studies: An Exercise in Revisionist Historiography." *University of Toronto Quarterly* 65, no. 2 (1996): 355–65.

Centre for Contemporary Cultural Studies/Open University

Brunt, Rosalind and Caroline Rowan, eds. *Feminism, Culture and Politics*. London: Lawrence and Wishart, 1982.

Centre for Contemporary Cultural Studies. *The Empire Strikes Back: Race and Racism in 70s Britain*. London: Hutchinson, 1982.

Centre for Contemporary Cultural Studies. *On Ideology*. London: Hutchinson, 1978.

Chambers, Iain, John Clarke, Ian Connell, Lidia Curti, Stuart Hall, and Tony Jefferson. "Marxism and Culture [Reply to Rosalind Coward "Class"]." *Screen* 18, no. 1 (1977): 109–19.

Chambers, Iain. *Popular Culture: The Metropolitan Experience*. London: Methuen, 1986.

Clarke, John. *New Times and Old Enemies: Essays on Cultural Studies and America*. London: Harper Collins Academic, 1991.

Clarke, John, Chas Critcher, and Richard Johnson, eds. *Working Class Culture: Studies in History and Theory*. London: Hutchinson, 1979.

Coward, Rosalind. "Class, 'Culture' and the Social Formation." *Screen* 18, no. 1 (1977): 75–105.

Hall, Stuart. "Cultural Studies: Two Paradigms." In *Culture, Ideology and Social Process: A Reader*, eds. Tony Bennett, Graham Martin, Colin Mercer, and Janet Woollacott. London: Open University Press, 1981.

Hall, Stuart. "Notes on Deconstructing 'The Popular.'" in *People's History and Socialist Theory*, ed. Raphael Samuel. London: Routledge, 1981.

Hall, Stuart. "Cultural Identity and Cinematic Representation." *Framework* 36 (1989): 68–81.

Hall, Stuart. "The Emergence of Cultural Studies and the Crisis of the Humanities." *October* 53 (1990): 11–23.

Hall, Stuart and Tony Jefferson, eds. *Resistance Through Rituals: Youth Subcultures in Post-war Britain*. London: Hutchinson, 1976.

Hall, Stuart, Chas Critcher, Tony Jefferson, John Clarke, and Brian Roberts. *Policing the Crisis: Mugging, the State, and Law and Order*. London: Macmillan, 1978.

Hall, Stuart, Dorothy Hobson, Andrew Lowe, and Paul Willis, eds. *Culture, Media, Language*. London: Hutchinson, 1980.

Hebdige, Dick. *Subculture: The Meaning of Style*. London: Methuen, 1979.

Hebdige, Dick. "Postmodernism and 'The Other Side.'" *Journal of Communication Inquiry* 10, no. 2 (1986): 78–98.

Hoggart, Richard. *Speaking for Each Other. Volume 1: About Society. Volume 2: About Literature*. Harmondsworth: Penguin, 1973.

Johnson, Richard. "The Story So Far: And Further Transformations?" *Introduction to Contemporary Cultural Studies*, ed. David Punter. New York: Longman, 1986.

Johnson, Richard. "What is Cultural Studies Anyway?" *Social Text* 16 (1986–7): 38–80.

Morley, David. *Television, Audiences and Cultural Studies*. New York: Routledge, 1992.

Walkerdine, Valerie. *Schoolgirl Fictions*. London: Verso, 1990.

Willis, Paul. *Profane Culture*. London: Routledge and Kegan Paul, 1978.

Race

"Critical Multiculturalism." *Continuum* 8, no. 2 (1994).

Anderson, Benedict. *Imagined Communities: Reflections on the Origin and Spread of Nationalism*, 2nd edn. London: Verso, 1991.

Anthias, Floya and Nira Yuval-Davis. *Racialized Boundaries: Race, Nation, Gender, Colour and Class and the Anti-Racist Struggle*. London: Routledge, 1992.

Bhabha, Homi. *The Location of Culture*. New York: Routledge, 1993.

Churchill, Ward. *Fantasies of the Master Race: Literature, Cinema and the Colonization of American Indians*, ed. M. Annette Jaimes. Monroe: Common Courage Press, 1992.

Collins, Patricia Hill. *Black Feminist Thought: Knowledge, Consciousness, and the Politics of Empowerment*. London: Harper Collins Academic, 1990.

Dent, Gina, ed. *Black Popular Culture: A Project by Michele Wallace*. Seattle: Bay Press, 1992.

Donald, James and Ali Rattansi, eds. *"Race," Culture and Difference*. London: Sage, 1992.

Fabre, Genevieve, Melvin Dixon, and Robert O'Meally, eds. *History and Memory in Afro-American Culture*. Cambridge, Mass: Memory and History Group of the Dubois Institute, Harvard University.

Fanon, Frantz. *The Wretched of the Earth*. New York: Grove Press, 1965.

Fanon, Frantz. *Black Skin, White Masks*. New York: Grove Press, 1967.

Frankenberg, Ruth. *White Women, Race Matters: The Social Construction of Whiteness*. Minneapolis: University of Minnesota Press, 1993.

Fregoso, Rosa Linda. *The Bronze Screen: Chicana and Chicano Film Culture*. Minneapolis: University of Minnesota Press, 1993.

Gay, Geneva and Willie L. Baber. *Expressively Black: The Cultural Basis of Ethnic Identity*. New York: Praeger, 1987.

Gilroy, Paul. *The Black Atlantic: Modernity and Double Consciousness*. Cambridge, Mass.: Harvard University Press, 1993.

Giroux, Henry. *Living Dangerously: Multiculturalism and the Politics of Difference*. New York: Peter Lang, 1993.

Goldberg, David Theo, ed. *Multiculturalism: A Critical Reader*. Oxford: Blackwell, 1994.

Gooding-Williams, Robert, ed. *Reading Rodney King/Reading Urban Uprising*. New York: Routledge, 1993.

Gray, H. (1997). *Watching Race: Television and the Struggle for the Sign of Blackness*. Minneapolis: University of Minnesota Press.

Hall, Stuart. "Gramsci's Relevance for the Study of Race and Ethnicity." *Journal of Communication Inquiry* 10, no. 2 (1986): 5–27.

Hamamoto, Darrell Y. *Asian Americans and the Politics of TV Representation*. Minneapolis: University of Minnesota Press, 1994.

Holloway, Joseph, ed. *Africanisms in American Culture*. Bloomington: Indiana University Press, 1990.

hooks, bell. *Black Looks: Race and Representation*. Boston: South End Press, 1992.

Joseph, May and Jennifer Natalya Fink, eds. *Performing Hybridity*. Minneapolis and London: University of Minnesota Press, 1999.

LaCapra, Dominick, ed. *The Bounds of Race: Perspectives on Hegemony and Resistance*. Ithaca: Cornell University Press, 1991.

MacDonald, J. Fred. *Blacks and White TV: African Americans in Television Since 1948*, 2nd edn. Chicago: Nelson-Hall, 1992.

McCarthy, Cameron and Warren Crichlow, eds. *Race Identity and Representation in Education*. New York: Routledge, 1993.

Mercer, Kobena. *Welcome to the Jungle: New Positions in Black Cultural Studies*. New York: Routledge, 1994.

Muñoz, C., Jr. *Youth, Identity, Power: The Chicano Movement*. New York: Verso, 1989.

Nederveen Pieterse, Jan. *White on Black: Images of Africa and Blacks in Western Popular Culture*. New Haven: Yale University Press, 1992.

Rattansi, Ali and Sallie Westwood, eds. *On the Western Front: Racism, Modernity and Identity*. Cambridge: Polity Press, 1994.

Said, Edward. *Orientalism*. London: Routledge and Kegan Paul, 1978.

Shohat, Ella and Robert Stam. *Unthinking Eurocentrism: Multiculturalism and the Media*. New York: Routledge, 1994.

541

Spillers, Hortense J. *Comparative American Identities: Race, Sex, and Nationality in the Modern Text*. New York: Routledge, 1992.

Spivak, Gayatri Chakravorty. *In Other Worlds: Essays in Cultural Politics*. New York: Methuen, 1987.

Spivak, Gayatri Chakravorty. *The Post-Colonial Critic: Interviews, Strategies, Dialogues*, ed. Sarah Harasym. New York: Routledge, 1990.

Trinh, T. Minh-ha. *Woman, Native, Other: Writing Postcoloniality and Feminism*. Bloomington: Indiana University Press, 1989.

Trinh, T. Minh-ha. *Framer Framed*. New York: Routledge, 1992.

UNESCO. *Final Report of World Conference on Cultural Policies*. Mexico City and Paris: UNESCO, 1982.

Wallace, Michele. *Black Macho and the Myth of the Superwoman*. London: Verso, 1990.

Wallace, Michele. *Invisibility Blues: From Pop to Theory*. London: Verso, 1990.

West, Cornel. "The New Cultural Politics of Difference." *October* 53 (1990): 93–109.

Gender and Sexuality

"Critically Queer." *Critical Quarterly* 36, no. 1 (1994).

"Imaging Technologies, Inscribing Science." *camera obscura* 28 (1992).

"The Male Body (Part One)." *Michigan Quarterly Review* 32, no. 4 (1993).

"The Male Body (Part Two)." *Michigan Quarterly Review* 33, no. 1 (1994).

"The Politics of AIDS." *Minnesota Review* 40 (1993).

"Symposium: Queer Theory/Sociology: A Dialogue." *Sociological Theory* 12, no. 2 (1994): 178–248.

Adams, Parveen and Elizabeth Cowie, eds. *The Woman in Question*. Cambridge, Mass.: MIT Press, 1990.

Bad Object-Choices, ed. *How Do I Look? Queer Film and Video*. Seattle: Bay Press, 1991.

Ballaster, R., M. Beetham, E. Frazer, and S. Hebron, eds. *Women's Worlds: Ideology, Femininity and the Woman's Magazine*. Basingstoke: Macmillan, 1991.

Bennett, Tony and Janet Woollacott. *Bond and Beyond: The Political Career of a Popular Hero*. London: Macmillan, 1987.

Bergman, David, ed. *Camp Grounds: Style and Homosexuality*. Amherst: University of Massachusetts Press, 1993.

Boffin, Tessa and Jean Fraser, eds. *Stolen Glances: Lesbians Take Photographs*. London: Pandora, 1991.

Bordo, Susan. *Unbearable Weight: Feminism, Western Culture, and the Body*. Berkeley and Los Angeles: University of California Press, 1993.

Brown, Peter. *The Body and Society*. London: Faber and Faber, 1990.

Burroughs, Catherine B. and Jeffrey David Ehrenreich, eds. *Reading the Social Body*. Iowa City: University of Iowa Press, 1993.

Butler, Judith. *Gender Trouble: Feminism and the Subversion of Identity*. New York: Routledge, 1990.

Butler, Judith. *Bodies That Matter: On the Discursive Limits of "Sex"*. New York: Routledge, 1993.

Caplan, P., ed. *The Cultural Construction of Sexuality*. London: Tavistock, 1987.

Carter, Erica and Simon Watney, eds. *Taking Liberties: The Cultural Politics of AIDS*. London: Serpent's Tail, 1989.

Castle, Terry. *The Apparitional Lesbian: Female Homosexuality and Modern Culture*. New York: Columbia University Press, 1993.

Chapman, Rowena and Jonathan Rutherford, eds. *Male Order: Unwrapping Masculinity*. London: Lawrence and Wishart, 1988.

Chartier, Roger, ed. *A History of Private Life: Passions of the Renaissance*. Cambridge, Mass.: Harvard University Press, 1993.

Christian-Smith, Linda K. *Becoming a Woman Through Romance*. London: Routledge, 1991.

Coward, Ros. *Female Desire: Women's Sexuality Today*. London: Paladin, 1984.

Craig, Steve, ed. *Men, Masculinity, and the Media*. Newbury Park: Sage, 1992.

Crimp, Douglas, ed. *AIDS: Cultural Analysis/ Cultural Activism*. Cambridge, Mass.: MIT Press, 1988.

de Lauretis, Teresa. *The Practice of Love: Lesbian Sexuality and Perverse Desire*. Bloomington: Indiana University Press, 1994.

Devor, Holly. *Gender Bending: Confronting the Limits of Duality*. Bloomington: Indiana University Press, 1989.

Donzelot, Jacques. *The Policing of Families*. Trans. Robert Hurley. London: Hutchinson, 1979.

Doty, Alexander. *Making Things Perfectly Queer: Interpreting Mass Culture*. Minneapolis: University of Minnesota Press, 1993.

Easthope, Antony. *What A Man's Gotta Do: The Masculine Myth in Popular Culture*. London: Paladin, 1986.

Erni, John Nguyet (1994) *Unstable Frontiers: Technomedicine and the Cultural Politics of "Curing" AIDS*. Minneapolis: University of Minneasota Press.

Evans, David. *Sexual Citizenship: The Material Construction of Sexualities*. London: Routledge, 1993.

Fee, Elizabeth and Daniel M. Fox, eds. *AIDS: The Burdens of History*. Berkeley and Los Angeles: University of California Press, 1988.

Foucault, Michel. *The History of Sexuality*. Trans. Robert Hurley. Harmondsworth: Penguin, 1984.

Fuss, Diana, ed. *Inside/ Out: Lesbian Theories, Gay Theories*. London: Routledge, 1992.

Gallop, Jane. *Thinking Through the Body*. New York: Columbia University Press, 1988.

Gamman, Lorraine and Margaret Marshment, eds. *The Female Gaze: Women as Viewers of Popular Culture*. London: Verso, 1988.

Gibson, Pamela Church and Roma Gibson, eds. *Dirty Looks: Women, Pornography, Power*. London: BFI, 1993.

Goldstein, Laurence, ed. *The Female Body: Figures, Style, Speculations*. Ann Arbor: University of Michigan Press, 1994.

Gray, Ann. *Video Playtime: The Gendering of a Leisure Technology*. London: Routledge, 1992.

Gross, Larry. *Contested Closets: The Politics and Ethics of Outing*. Minneapolis: University of Minnesota Press, 1993.

Haraway, Donna. *Simians, Cyborgs, and Women*. New York: Routledge, 1991.

Hart, Lynda and Peggy Phelan, eds. *Acting Out: Feminist Performances*. Ann Arbor: University of Michigan Press, 1993.

Hearn, Jeff, ed. *Men in the Public Eye: The Construction and Deconstruction of Public Men and Public Patriarchies*. London: Routledge, 1992.

Heath, Stephen. *The Sexual Fix*. London: Macmillan, 1982.

Hirsch, Marianne and Evelyn Fox Keller, eds. *Conflicts in Feminism*. New York: Routledge, 1990.

Hubbard, Ruth. *The Politics of Biology*. New Brunswick: Rutgers University Press, 1990.

Hunter, Ian, David Saunders, and Dugald Williamson. *On Pornography: Literature, Sexuality and Obscenity Law*. London: Macmillan, 1993.

Jacobus, Mary, Evelyn Fox Keller, and Sally Shuttleworth, eds. *Body/Politics: Women and the Discourses of Science*. New York: Routledge, 1990.

Jagose, Annamarie. "Way Out: The Category 'Lesbian' and the Fantasy of the Utopic Space." *Journal of the History of Sexuality* 4, no. 2 (1993): 264–87.

Jardine, Alice and Paul Smith, eds. *Men in Feminism*. New York: Methuen, 1987.

Jeffords, Susan. *Hard Bodies: Hollywood Masculinity in the Reagan Era*. New Brunswick: Rutgers University Press, 1993.

Johnson, Lesley. *The Modern Girl: Girlhood and Growing Up*. Milton Keynes: Open University Press, 1992.

Kaplan, E. Ann. *Motherhood and Representation: The Mother in Popular Culture and Melodrama*. New York: Routledge, 1992.

Keller, Evelyn Fox. *Reflections on Gender and Science*. New Haven: Yale University Press, 1985.

Kipnis, Laura. *Ecstasy Unlimited: On Sex, Capital, Gender, and Aesthetics*. Minneapolis: University of Minnesota Press, 1993.

Luke, Carmen and Jennifer Gore, eds. *Feminisms and Critical Pedalogy*. London: Routledge, 1992.

McRobbie, Angela. *Feminism and Youth Culture*. London: Macmillan, 1991.

McRobbie, Angela and Mica Nava, eds. *Gender and Generation*. London: Macmillan, 1984.

Modleski, Tania. *Loving with a Vengeance: Mass-Produced Fantasies for Women*. New York: Methuen, 1982.

Morris, Meaghan. *The Pirate's Fiancée: Feminism, Reading, Postmodernism*. London: Verso, 1988.

Munt, S. (1998) *Heroic Desire: Lesbian Identity and Cultural Space*. London: Cassell.

Nicholson, Linda J., ed. *Feminism/Postmodernism*. New York: Routledge, 1990.

Owens, Craig. *Beyond Recognition: Representation, Power and Culture*, eds. Scott Bryson, Barbara Kruger, Lynne Tillman, and Jane Weinstock. Berkeley and Los Angeles: University of California Press, 1992.

Patton, Cindy. *Inventing AIDS*. London: Routledge, 1991.

Penley, Constance and Sharon Willis, eds. *Male Trouble*. Minneapolis: University of Minnesota Press, 1993.

Phelan, Peggy. *Unmarked: The Politics of Performance*. New York: Routledge, 1993.

Radway, Janice. *Reading the Romance: Feminism and the Representation of Women in Popular Culture*. Chapel Hill: University of North Carolina Press, 1984.

Rajan, Rajeswari Sunder. *Real and Imagined Women: Gender, Culture and Postcolonialism*. London: Routledge, 1993.

Riley, Denise. *"Am I That Name?" Feminism and the Category of "Women" in History*. Minneapolis: University of Minnesota Press, 1988.

Roman, L., L. Christian-Smith, and E. Ellsworth, eds. *Becoming Feminine: The Politics of Popular Culture*. London: Falmer Press, 1988.

Ronell, Avital. *Crack Wars: Literature, Addiction, Mania*. Lincoln: University of Nebraska Press, 1992.

Rose, Jacqueline. *Sexuality in the Field of Vision*. London: Verso, 1986.

Ruiz, V. and E. Dubois, eds. *Unequal Sisters*. London: Routledge, 1991.

Sawicki, Jana. *Disciplining Foucault: Feminism, Power, and the Body*. New York: Routledge, 1991.

Smith, Paul. *Clint Eastwood: A Cultural Production*. Minneapolis: University of Minnesota Press, 1993.

Snitow, Ann, Christine Sansell, and Sharon Thompson, eds. *Desire: The Politics of Sexuality*. London: Virago, 1984.

Stanton, Domna C., ed. *Discourses of Sexuality: From Aristotle to AIDS*. Ann Arbor: University of Michigan Press, 1993.

Steedman, Carolyn. *Landscape for a Good Woman: A Story of Two Lives*. London: Virago, 1986.

Stein, Arlene, ed. *Sisters, Sexperts, Queers: Beyond the Lesbian Nation*. New York: Penguin, 1993.

Stein, Edward, ed. *Forms of Desire: Sexual Orientation and the Social Constructionist Controversy*. New York: Routledge, 1993.

Suleiman, Susan Rubin, ed. *The Female Body in Western Culture*. Cambridge, Mass.: Harvard University Press, 1986.

Treichler, Paula. 1999. *How to Have Theory in an Epidemic: Cultural Chronicles of AIDS*. Durham: Duke University Press.

Vance, Carol, ed. *Pleasure and Danger: Exploring Female Sexuality*. London: Routledge and Kegan Paul, 1984.

Walters, Suzanna Danuta. "Material Girls: Feminism and Cultural Studies." *Current Perspectives in Social Theory* 12 (1992): 59–96.

Warner, Michael, ed. *Fear of a Queer Planet: Queer Politics and Social Theory*. Minneapolis: University of Minnesota Press, 1993.

Watney, Simon. "Missionary Positions: AIDS, 'Africa,' and Race." *differences* 1, no. 1 (1988): 83–100.

Watney, Simon. *Policing Desire: Pornography, AIDS and the Media*, 2nd edn. Minneapolis: University of Minnesota Press, 1989.

Weeks, Jeffrey. *Against Nature: Essays on History, Sexuality and Identity*. London: Orams River Press, 1991.

Winship, J. *Inside Women's Magazines*. London: Pandora Press, 1987.

Class and Ideology

"The Legacy of Althusser." *Studies in 20th Century Literature* 18, no. 1 (1994).

Althusser, Louis. *Lenin and Philosophy and Other Essays*. Trans. Ben Brewster. London: New Left Books, 1977.

Anderson, Perry. *Arguments Within English Marxism*. London: Verso, 1980.

Barker, Martin. *Comics: Ideology, Power and the Critics*. Manchester: Manchester University Press, 1989.

Barrett, Michèle, Philip Corrigan, Annette Kuhn, and Janet Wolff, eds. *Ideology and Cultural Production*. New York: St. Martin's Press, 1979,

Caudwell, Christopher. *Studies and Further Studies in a Dying Culture*. New York: Monthly Review Press, 1971.

Coward, Ros and John Ellis. *Language and Materialism*. London: Routledge and Kegan Paul, 1977.

Eagleton, Terry. *The Ideology of the Aesthetic*. Oxford: Blackwell, 1990.

Frow, John. "Knowledge and Class." *Cultural Studies* 7, no. 2 (1993): 240–81.

Hall, Stuart. "The Problem of Ideology – Marxism Without Guarantees." *In Marx 100 Years On*, ed. B. Matthews. London: Lawrence and Wishart, 1983. 57–86.

Hall, Stuart. "Signification, Representation, Ideology: Althusser and the Post-Structuralists." *Critical Studies in Mass Communication* 2, no. 2 (1985): 91–114.

Harris, David. *From Class Struggle to the Politics of Pleasure: The Effects of Gramscianism on Cultural Studies*. London: Routledge, 1992.

Haug, Wolfgang Fritz. *Commodity Aesthetics, Ideology and Culture*. New York: International General, 1987.

Laclau, Ernesto and Chantal Mouffe. *Hegemony and Socialist Strategy: Towards a Radical Democratic Politics*. London: Verso, 1985.

Laing, S. *Representations of Working-Class Life, 1957–1964*. London: Macmillan, 1986.

Larrain, Jorge. "The Postmodern Critique of Ideology." *Sociological Review* 42, no. 2 (1994): 289–314.

Lott, E. *Love and Theft: Black Face Minstrelsy and the American Working Class*. New York: Oxford University Press, 1993.

Munt, S. (ed.) *Cultural Studies and the Working Class: Subject to Change*. London Cassell.

Sinclair, John. *Images Incorporated: Advertising as Industry and Ideology*. London: Croom Helm, 1987.

Sparks, Colin. "Experience, Ideology, and Articulation: Stuart Hall and the Development of Culture." *Journal of Communication Inquiry* 13, no. 2 (1989): 79–87.

Thompson, J. B. *Ideology and Modern Culture; Critical Social Theory in the Era of Mass Communication*. Cambridge: Polity Press, 1990.

Wolff, Janet. *The Social Production of Art*. London: Macmillan, 1981.

Žižek, Slavoj. *The Sublime Object of Ideology*. London: Verso, 1989.

Cultural Policy

"From Cultural Studies to Cultural Policy." *Culture and Policy* 6, no. 2 (1994).

Bennett, Tony. *Outside Literature*. London: Routledge, 1990.

Bennett, Tony. *The Birth of the Museum: History, Theory, and Politics*. London: Routledge, 1995.

Bennett, Tony. *Culture: A Reformer's Science*. Sydney: Allen and Unwin, 1998.

Berland, Jody and S. Hornstein, eds. *Capital Culture: A Reader on Modernist Legacies, State Institutions and the Value(s) of Art*. Montréal: McGill-Queens University Press, 1996.

Bianchini, Franco and Michael Parkinson, eds. *Cultural Policy and Urban Regeneration*: The West European Experience. Manchester: Manchester University Press, 1993.

Bolton, Richard, ed. *Culture Wars: Documents from the Recent Controversies in the Arts*. New York: The New Press, 1992.

Crimp, Douglas. *On the Museum's Ruins*. Cambridge, Mass.: MIT Press, 1993.

Cunningham, Stuart. *Framing Culture: Criticism and Policy in Australia*. Sydney: Allen and Unwin, 1992.

Dávila, Arlene M. *Sponsored Identities: Cultural Politics in Puerto Rico*. Philadelphia: Temple University Press, 1997.

Duncan, Carol. *Civilizing Rituals: Inside Public Art Museums*. London: Routledge, 1995.

Foucault, Michel. "On Governmentality." Trans. Colin Gordon. *Ideology and Consciousness* no. 6 (1979): 5–21.

Fox, Claire F. *The Fence and the River: Culture and Politics at the US–Mexican Border*. Minneapolis: University of Minnesota Press, 1999.

Frith, Simon. "Knowing One's Place: The Culture of Cultural Industries." *Cultural Studies Birmingham* no. 1 (1991): 134–55.

Lewis, Justin. *Art, Culture and Enterprise*. London: Routledge, 1990.

Looseley, David L. *The Politics of Fun: Cultural Policy and Debate in Contemporary France*. Oxford: Berg, 1997.

McGuigan, Jim. *Culture and the Public Sphere*. London: Routledge, 1996.

McWilliams, Wilson Carey. "The Arts and the American Popular Tradition." In *Art, Ideology, and Politics*, eds. Judith H. Balfe and Margaret Jane Wyszomirski. New York: Praeger, 1985.

Martin, Randy. *Socialist Ensembles: Theater and State in Cuba and Nicaragua*. Minneapolis: University of Minnesota Press, 1994.

Miller, Toby. *The Well-Tempered Self: Citizenship, Culture, and the Postmodern Subject*. Baltimore and London: The Johns Hopkins University Press, 1993.

Ouellette, Laurie. "TV Viewing as Good Citizenship? Political Rationality, Enlightened Democracy and PBS." *Cultural Studies* 13, no. 1 (1999): 62–90.

Price, Clement Alexander. *Many Voices Many Opportunities: Cultural Pluralism and American Arts Policy*. New York: American Council for the Arts; Allworth Press, 1994.

Sellars, Richard West. *Preserving Nature in the National Parks: A History*. New Haven: Yale University Press, 1997.

Streeter, Thomas. *Selling the Air: A Critique of the Policy of Commercial Broadcasting in the United States*. Chicago: University of Chicago Press, 1996.

Throsby, C. D. and G. A. Withers. *The Economics of the Performing Arts*. New York: St. Martin's Press, 1979.

Fashion/Consumption

"The Sociology of Consumption." *Sociology* 24, no. 1 (1990).

Ash, Juliet and Elizabeth Wilson, eds. *Chic Thrills: A Fashion Reader*. Berkeley and Los Angeles: University of California Press, 1993.

Ash, Juliet and L. Wright, eds. *Components of Dress*. London: Routledge, 1988.

Attfield, J. and P. Kirkham, eds. *A View from the Interior: Feminism, Women and Design*. London: Women's Press, 1989.

Barber, B. and L. Lobel. "'Fashion' in Women's Clothes and the American Social System." *Social Forces* 31 (1952): 124–31.

Barthes, Roland. *The Fashion System*. Trans. Matthew Ward and Richard Howard. New York: Hill and Wang, 1983.

Benstock, Shari and Suzanne Ferriss, eds. *On Fashion*. New Brunswick: Rutgers University Press, 1994.

Berry, Sarah. (2000). *Screen Style: Fashion and Femininity in 1930s Hollywood*. Minneapolis: University of Minnesota Press.

Blumer, Herbert. "Fashion." *Encyclopedia of the Social Sciences*. Glencoe: Free Press, 1968.

Bocock, Robert. *Consumption*. London: Routledge, 1994.

Bowlby, Rachel. *Shopping with Freud*. London: Routledge, 1993.

Breward, C. *The Culture of Fashion: A New History of Fashionable Dress*. Manchester: Manchester University Press, 1995.

Campbell, Colin. *The Romantic Ethic and the Spirit of Modern Consumerism*. Oxford: Blackwell, 1989.

Chibnall, Steve. "Whistle and Zoot: The Changing Meaning of a Suit of Clothes." *History Workshop Journal* 20 (1985): 56–81.

Craik, Jennifer. *The Face of Fashion: Cultural Studies in Fashion*. London: Routledge, 1994.

Davis, Fred. *Fashion, Culture, and Identity*. Chicago: University of Chicago Press, 1992.

Eckert, Charles. "The Carole Lombard in Macy's Window." *Quarterly Review of Film Studies* 3, no. 1 (1978): 1–21.

Emberley, J. "The Fashion Apparatus and the Deconstruction of Postmodern Subjectivity." In *Body Invaders: Panic Sex in America*, eds. A. and M. Kroker. New York: St. Martin's Press, 1987.

Ewing, E. *History of Twentieth Century Fashion*. London: Batsford, 1986.

Falk, Pasi. *The Consuming Body*. London: Sage, 1994.

Featherstone, Mike. *Consumer Culture and Postmodernism*. London: Sage, 1991.

Ferris, Lesley, ed. *Crossing the Stage: Controversies on Cross-Dressing*. New York: Routledge, 1993.

Fine, Ben and Ellen Leopold. *The World of Consumption*, London: Routledge, 1993.

Finkelstein, J. *The Fashioned Self*. Cambridge: Polity Press, 1991.

Fregoso, Rosa Linda. "The Representation of Cultural Identity in Zoot Suit." *Theory and Society* 22, no. 5 (1993): 659–74.

Garber, Marjorie. *Vested Interests: Cross-Dressing and Cultural Anxiety*. London: Routledge, 1992.

Gardner, C. and J. Sheppard. *Consuming Fashion: The Rise of Retail Culture*. London: Unwin Hyman, 1989.

Gronow, Jukka. "Taste and Fashion: The Social Function of Fashion and Style." *Acta Sociologica* 36, no. 2 (1993): 89–100.

Herzog, Charlotte and Jane Gaines, eds. *Fabrications: Costume and the Female Body*. New York: Routledge, 1991.

Hollander, Anne. *Seeing Through Clothes*. Berkeley and Los Angeles: University of California Press, 1993.

Keat, Russell, Nicholas Abercombie, and Nigel Whiteley. *The Authority of the Consumer*. London: Routledge, 1994.

Kidwell, C. and V. Steele, eds. *Men and Women: Dressing the Part*. Washington: Smithsonian Institute Press, 1989.

Lurie, Alison. *The Language of Clothes*. New York: Random House, 1981.

Mazón, Mauricio. *The Zoot-Suit Riots: The Psychology of Symbolic Annihilation*. Austin: University of Texas Press, 1984.

McCracken, Grant. *Culture and Consumption: New Approaches to the Symbolic Character of Consumer Goods and Activities*. Bloomington: Indiana University Press, 1988.

McRobbie, Angela, ed. *Zoot Suits and Second-Hand Dresses: An Anthology of Fashion and Music*. Boston: Unwin Hyman, 1989.

Otnes, P., ed. *The Sociology of Consumption: An Anthology*. New Jersey: Humanities Press International, 1988.

Packard, S. *The Fashion Business*. New York: Holt, Rinehart and Winston, 1983.

Reekie, Gail. *Temptations: Sex, Selling and the Department Store*. Sydney: Allen and Unwin, 1993.

Schneider, J. "In and Out of Polyester: Desire, Disdain and Global Fibre Competitions." *Anthropology Today* 10, no. 4 (1994): 2–10.

Shields, Rob, ed. *Lifestyle Shopping: The Subject of Consumption*. London: Routledge, 1992.

Simmel, Georg. "Fashion." *International Quarterly* 10, no. 1 (1904): 130–55.

Tait, Gordon. "Youth, Personhood and 'Practices of the Self': Some New Directions for Youth Research." *Australian and New Zealand Journal of Sociology* 29, no. 1 (1993): 40–54.

Wilson, Elizabeth. *Adorned in Dreams: Fashion and Modernity*. London: Virago, 1985.

Frankfurt School

Adorno, Theodor. *The Culture Industry: Selected Essays on Mass Culture*. London: Routledge, 1991.

Adorno, Theodor and Max Horkheimer. *Dialectic of the Enlightenment*. Trans. J. Cumming. New York: Continuum, 1982.

Arato, Andrew, ed. *The Essential Frankfurt School Reader*. New York: Continuum, 1987.

Benhabib, Seyla. *Situating the Self: Gender, Community and Postmodernism in Contemporary Ethics*. Cambridge: Polity Press, 1992.

Benjamin, A., ed. *The Problems of Modernity: Adorno and Benjamin*. London: Routledge, 1991.

Benjamin, Walter. *Illuminations*. Trans. Harry Zohn; ed. Hannah Arendt. New York: Schocken, 1968.

Bloch, Ernst, ed. *Aesthetics and Politics*. London: New Left Books, 1977.

Bronner, S. and D. Kellner, eds. *Critical Theory and Society: A Reader*. London: Routledge, 1989.

Habermas, Jürgen. *The Philosophical Discourse of Modernity: Twelve Lectures*. Trans. Frederick Lawrence. Cambridge: Polity Press, 1990.

Hoy, David and Thomas McCarthy. *Critical Theory*. Oxford: Blackwell, 1994.

Marcuse, Herbert. *One Dimensional Man*. London: Routledge, 1964.

Rasmussen, David, ed. *The Handbook of Critical Theory*. Oxford: Blackwell, 1994.

Wellmer, Albrecht. *The Persistence of Modernity*. Trans. David Midgley. Cambridge: Polity Press, 1991.

Sport

Baker, Aaron and Todd Boyd, eds. *Out of Bounds: Sports, Media, and the Politics of Identity*. Bloomington: Indiana University Press, 1997.

Buscombe, Edward, ed. *Football on Television*. London: BFI, 1975.

Elias, Norbert. "An Essay on Sport and Violence." *In Quest for Excitement: Sport and Leisure in the Civilizing Process*, eds. Norbert Elias and Eric Dunning. Oxford: Blackwell, 1986.

Goldlust, John. *Playing for Keeps: Sport, the Media and Society*. Melbourne: Longman Cheshire, 1987.

Hargreaves, Jennifer. *Sporting Females: Critical Issues in the History and Sociology of Women's Sports*. London: Routledge, 1994.

Hargreaves, John. *Sport, Power and Culture: A Social and Historical Analysis of Popular Sports in Britain*. Cambridge: Polity Press, 1986.

Jenkins, C. and M. Green, eds. *Sporting Fictions*. Birmingham: Centre for Contemporary Cultural Studies, 1982.

Lawrence, Geoffrey and David Rowe, eds. *Power Play: The Commercialisation of Australian Sport*. Sydney: Hale and Ironmonger, 1986.

Maguire, Joseph. "Bodies, Sportscultures and Societies: A Critical Review of Some Theories in the Sociology of the Body." *International Review for the Sociology of Sport* 28, no. 1 (1993): 33–52.

Martin, Randy and Toby Miller, eds. 1999. *SportCult*. Minneapolis: University of Minnesota Press.

Morse, Margaret. "Sport on Television: Replay and Display." *Regarding Television: Critical Approaches – An Anthology*, ed. E. Ann Kaplan. Los Angeles: AFI, 1983.

Peters, Roy. *Television Coverage of Sport*. Birmingham: Centre for Contemporary Cultural Studies Stencilled Paper 1, 1976.

Pronger, Brian. *The Arena of Masculinity: Sports, Homosexuality, and the Meaning of Sex*. New York: St. Martin's Press, 1990.

Rose, Ava and James Friedman. "Television Sport as Mas(s)culine Cult of Distraction." *Screen* 35, no. 1 (1994): 22–35.

Rowe, David and Geoff Lawrence, eds. *Sport and Leisure: Trends in Australian Popular Culture*. Sydney: Harcourt Brace Jovanovich, 1990.

Rowe, David and Geoffrey Lawrence, eds. *Tourism, Leisure, Sport: Critical Perspectives*. Melbourne: Cambridge University Press, 1998.

Tomlinson, Alan. 1999. *The Game's Up: Essays in the Cultural Analysis of Sport, Leisure and Popular Culture*. Arena: Avebury.

Wenner, Lawrence A., ed. *Media, Sports and Society*. London: Sage, 1989.

Wenner, Lawrence A., ed. *MediaSport*. New York and London: Routledge, 1998.

Whannel, Garry. *Fields in Vision: Television Sport and Cultural Transformation*. New York: Routledge, 1992.

Music and Dance

Attali, Jacques. *Noise: The Political Economy of Music*. Trans. Brian Massumi. Minneapolis: University of Minnesota Press, 1985.

Bennett, A. *Popular Music and Youth Culture: Music, Identity and Place*. Basingstoke: Macmillan, 2000.

Bennett, Tony, Simon Frith, Lawrence Grossberg, John Shepherd, and Graeme Turner, eds. *Rock and Popular Music: Politics, Policies, Institutions*. London: Routledge, 1993.

Brett, Philip, Gary C. Thomas, and Elizabeth Wood, eds. *Queering the Pitch: The New Gay and Lesbian Musicology*. New York: Routledge, 1994.

Browning, Barbara. *Infectious Rhythms: Metaphors of Contagion and the Spread of African Culture*. New York: Routledge, 1998.

Burnett, Robert. 1996 *The Global Jukebox: The International Music Industry*. London and New York: Routledge.

Chambers, Iain. *Urban Rhythms: Pop Music and Popular Culture*. London: Macmillan, 1985.

Chernoff, John Miller. *African Rhythm and African Sensibility: Aesthetics and Social Action in African Musical Idioms*. Chicago: University of Chicago Press, 1979.

Cohen, Stanley. *Folk Devils and Moral Panics: The Creation of Mods and Rockers*. London: MacCribbon and Kee, 1972.

Cross, Brian. *It's Not About a Salary. . . . Hip Hop in Los Angeles from the Watts Prophets to the Freestyle Fellowship*. London: Verso, 1993.

Foster, Susan, ed. *Corporealities: Dancing, Knowledge, Culture, and Power*. London; New York: Routledge, 1996.

Frank, Lisa and Paul Smith, eds. *Madonnarama: Essays on Sex and Popular Culture*. Pittsburgh: Cleis Press, 1993.

Frith, Simon, ed. *Facing the Music*. New York: Pantheon, Books, 1988.

Frith, Simon, ed. *World Music, Politics and Social Change*. Manchester: Manchester University Press, 1989.

Frith, Simon and Andrew Goodwin, eds. *On Record*. New York: Pantheon, 1990.

Frith, Simon, Andrew Goodwin, and Lawrence Grossberg, eds. *Sound and Vision: The Music Video Reader*. London: Routledge, 1993.

Garafalo, Reebee. "How Autonomous is Relative: Popular Music, the Social Formation and Cultural Formation." *Popular Music* 6, no. 1 (1987): 77–92.

Goodwin, Andrew. *Dancing in the Distraction Factory*. Minneapolis: University of Minnesota Press, 1992.

Green, Richard C. and Monique Guillory, eds. *Soul: Black Power, Politics, Pleasure*. New York: New York University Press, 1998.

Hebdige, Dick. *Cut 'n' Mix: Culture, Identity and Caribbean Music*. London: Comedia, 1987.

Kaplan, E. Ann. *Rocking Around the Clock: Music Television, Postmodernism and Consumer Culture*. London: Methuen, 1987.

Laing, Dave. *One Chord Wonders: Power and Meaning in Punk Rock*. Milton Keynes: Open University Press, 1985.

Lewis, Lisa A. *Gender Politics and MTV: Voicing the Difference*. Philadelphia: Temple University Press, 1990.

Lull, James, ed. *Popular Music and Communication*, 2nd edn. Newbury Park: Sage, 1992.

Martin, Randy. *Critical Moves: Dance Studies in Theory and Politics*. Durham: Duke University Press, 1998.

McClary, Susan. *Feminine Endings: Music, Gender and Sexuality*. Minneapolis: University of Minneasota Press, 1991.

McClary, Susan and Robert Walser. "Theorizing the Body in African-American Music." *Black Music Research Journal*, Spring (1994): 75–84.

Middleton, R. *Studying Popular Music*. Milton Keynes: Open University Press, 1990.

Moore, Allan F. Rock: *The Primary Text: Developing a Musicology of Rock*. Milton Keynes: Open University Press, 1992.

Negus, Keith. *Producing Pop: Culture and Conflict in the Popular Music Industry*. London: Edward Arnold, 1992.

Pickering, M. and T. Green, eds. *Everyday Culture: Popular Song and the Vernacular Milieu*. Milton Keynes: Open University Press, 1987.

Ramet, Sabrina Petra, ed. *Rocking the State: Rock Music and Politics in Eastern Europe and Russia*. Boulder: Westview Press, 1994.

Robinson, D., E. Buck, and M. Cuthbert. *Music at the Margins: Popular Music and Global Cultural Diversity*. Newbury Park: Sage, 1991.

Robinson, Deanna. "Youth and Popular Music: A Theoretical Rationale for an International Study." *Gazette* 37 (1986): 33–50.

Rose, Tricia. *Black Noise*. Wesleyan State University Press, 1994.

Ross, Andrew and Tricia Rose, eds. *Microphone Fiends: Youth Music and Youth Culture*. London and New York: Routledge, 1994.

Schwichtenberg, Cathy, ed. *The Madonna Connection: Representational Politics, Subcultural Identities, and Cultural Theory*. Sydney: Allen and Unwin, 1993.

Solie, Ruth, ed. *Musicology and Difference: Gender and Sexuality in Music Scholarship*. Berkeley and Los Angeles: University of California Press, 1993.

Subotnik, Rose Rosengard. *Developing Variations: Style and Ideology in Western Music*. Minneapolis: University of Minnesota Press, 1991.

Toop, David. *Rap Attack 2: African Rap to Global Hip Hop*. London: Serpent's Tail, 1991.

Wallis, Roger and Krister Malm. *Media Policy and Music Activity*. London: Routledge, 1993.

Whiteley, Sheila. *The Space Between the Notes: Rock and the Counter-Culture*. New York: Routledge, 1992.

Index

Note: Abbreviations used in the index are: CS   cultural studies; NAFTA   North American Free Trade Agreement; PE   theoretical political economy; STS   science and technology studies.

Abbas, A., 269, 271
Acland, C. R., 197, 202
Adorno, T. W., 66, 150, 189–90, 328
adult education
    British CS, 277–9, 289, 292
    disciplinarity, 25–9
aesthetics
    British CS, 143, 147–8
    fashion, 462–3
    interdisciplinarity, 32–4
    Latin American/US CS, 227–30
    teaching youth culture, 320
Africa, 4, 6
    electronic printer narrative, 109–12
    political economy in CS, 118–19
African Americans
    Clinton/Lewinsky discourse, 407–8,
        416–20, 425–6
    hair straightening, 465
    raced nature of culture, 483
Afro-diasporic cultures, 482
    ass music, 432–4, 437–47
Agins, T., 464
Agnew, V., 40
Alexander, E., 419
Alexander, J. C., 10
Allan, B., 500
Allen, D., 491

Allen, R., 196
Allen, T., 485
Allor, M., 188, 198
almshouses, 398, 403
Alpers, S., 106
Althusser, L., 3, 67
Alvarez, S. E., 376, 378–9, 386
Amawi, A., 123–6
Americanization, 301–2, 306
Amin, S., 233, 493–4
Amsden, A. H., 495
Anderson, B., 160, 177, 300
Anderson, P., 83–4
Andrade, M. de, 472
Ang, I., 198–9, 234, 254–5, 301–3, 305–6,
        312–13
anthropology
    and archaeology, 156–7
    and CS, 169–71
        boundaries, 171–3, 180–4
        channels from CS, 178–84, 185
        definitions, 171–3
        in Hong Kong, 261–2
        Latin America, 224
        Public Culture project, 173–4,
            176–8
        "Writing Culture" critique, 173–6
    and fashion, 458–9

553

anthropology (*cont.*)
  legal, 36, 42–3
  and STS, 106
antiessentialism, and a CS of law, 39–40
Antipodean CS, 202, 246–56
antireductionism, dangers of, 90–1
Aoki, K., 40, 48
Appadurai, A., 27–30, 174, 194, 307, 455–6,
    458, 513, 515–6, 518, 521
archaeology, 154–5
  and cultural studies, 159–60
    the future, 165–6
    gender, 162–4
    nationalism, 160–2
    picture of archaeology, 164–5
  and culture, 158–9
  key terms, 155–6
  postprocessual, 157–9, 165
  processual, 157, 165
  US–European differences, 156–7
architecture, Feng Shui, 441–2
Arendt, H., 190
Arnold, M., 29
Aronowitz, S., 63
art
  British CS, 142–3, 147–8
  cultural turn in sociology, 69
  racial stereotyping, 481
art critics, cultural role, 368
art museums and galleries
  governmentalization, 369–70
  Philadelphia, 391–405
Arteaga, A., 235
Asad, T., 173
Ashmore, M., 103, 105
Asia, 6
  cricket and Sri Lanka, 513–15, 517–21
    diasporic identities, 522–5
    nationalism, 510–11, 514, 518–22, 525
    television's role, 522–3
  CS in, 270–1
    Hong Kong, 259–72
    mainland China, 260–1, 270
  globalization, 493, 495, 504
  political economy in CS, 118–19
ass politics, 430–1
  thinking the body, 435–7
  Timbaland, 431–4
    body–soul bridge, 446–7
    dissident threat of, 437–41

and Feng Shui, 442–5
  videos, 444–7
Atkinson, G., 496
Attali, J., 69
audience reception
  and critique in CS, 144–5
  in the cultural circuit, 91
  media studies, 198
  metatheory of CS, 140, 143–4
Australasian CS, 202, 246–56
Australia
  contribution of CS, 254–6
  cricket, 510–11
    colonialism, 516–18
    diasporic spectatorship, 523–4
    nationalism, 513–18, 524
    orientalism, 511, 514–15
    racism, 511, 517–18, 524–5
  film industry, 249–50, 253, 255, 500–1,
    502–3
  institutions of public culture, 371
  and New Zealand CS, 246–8
  origins of CS, 248–54
  Sydney CS, 202
authoritarianism, Latin America, 222
avant garde movements, British CS,
    142–3, 147

Babe, R., 124
Bacash, J., 524
Back, L., 281
Bahn, P., 158
Baker, H. A. Jr., 9, 283
Bakhtin, M., 67
Baldwin, J., 435, 437, 449, 471
Baraka, A., 438, 440, 446, 450
Barber, B., 459
Barker, C., 278–9
Barker, E., 496
Barnard, M., 464
Barnes, R., 459
Barrett, M., 67, 84–5
Barringer, F., 412
Barthes, R., 68, 192, 319, 464, 471, 474
Bates, B. L., 416
Baudrillard, J., 69
Bauman, Z., 493
Beck, U., 106, 109
Becker, H. S., 11, 65, 69
Behar, R., 174

Beinart, P., 407, 421
Belk, R., 461
Bell, C., 253
Bell, D., 66, 300
Bell, S., 52
Bellafante, G., 423
Belleau, M. C., 41
Bello, A., 221
Benavidez, M., 239
Benedict, H., 420
Benhabib, S., 497
Benjamin, W., 143
Benn Michaels, W., 44
Bennett, A., 285
Bennett, T., 30–3, 63, 150, 195–6, 226, 255, 370
Bennett, W. L., 46
Berelson, B., 189
Berger, D. G., 328
Berke, R., 412
Berlant, L., 71, 408–9, 411–13
Bernbeck, R., 164
Berry, S., 10, 63
Bersani, L., 447
Berube, M., 409
Bhabha, H., 335
Biagoli, M., 106
Binford, L. R., 157, 163
Binford, S. R., 157
Bird, J., 307
Birmingham School see Centre for Contemporary Cultural Studies (CCCS)
black ass politics, 439–47
Black Legend discourses, 232–4
Blake, M., 517
Blau, J., 67
Blum, A., 65
Blum, Z. D., 405
Blumer, H., 460–1
Blumler, J. G., 189
Blundell, V., 255
body, the
    ass politics, 430–2, 435–7
        and Feng Shui, 442
        and Timbaland sound, 437–47
    Clinton/Lewinsky discourse, 407, 410–11, 413–20
    contemporary British CS, 285–6
    female

and feminism, 416
    legal narrative, 50–1
sport studies, 343
    ethical ground, 344
    purification, 352–3
    sex testing, 344–8
    shame/pride relationship, 342–3
body piercing, 285–6
body techniques, and fashion, 457
bodywork, 437
Bogle, D., 479
Bonfill, G., 224
Bonnell, V., 73
book publishing, 9–10
    Latin American/US CS, 225–6
Booth, D., 513, 516, 520–1
border crossings, European CS, 303
Bordwell, D., 218
Borger, G., 414–15
Bourdieu, P., 67, 241, 319, 402, 457, 503
Bouts, T., 514
Bower, L., 56–7
Bowker, G., 109
Bowser, P., 479
Brabazon, T., 248, 252
Braman, S., 492
Braudel, F., 132
Breward, C., 455
Briller, B. R., 500
Britain, 3–6
    anthropology, 169, 171–2, 184–5
    anti-intellectualism, 318, 322
    archaeology, postprocessual, 157–8
    and Australasian CS, 249, 251–2, 254–6
    and Chinese CS in Hong Kong, 260–3, 269
    contemporary CS in, 275–6
        accounts of origins of, 276–9
        Britishness of, 279–85
        empowerment through, 291
        objectives, 291–3
        relation to politics, 336
        role of texts, 277–9, 286–7
        trends, 285–7
        versus sociology, 287–90
    cricket and colonialism, 515–16, 518
    and critique in CS, 145–8
    CS of race, 474–5
    Englishness, 232–4, 304, 515
    film industry, 500–2
    institutions of public culture, 370

Britain (*cont.*)
    interdisciplinarity
        and adult education, 25–7
        and class, 23–5
        and government, 31
        in sociology, 90–1, 93–5
    and Ireland, 310
    metatheory of CS, 140–3
    multiculturalism, 482
    Northern Ireland, 310–12
    political CS, 149–50
    political economy in CS, 117–19
    poorhouses, 403
    sociology
        and contemporary CS, 285–91
        disciplinary boundaries, 91–7
        and emergence of CS, 89–91
        Hoggart's role, 25, 79–82
        of literature, 83–5
        recent history of, 86–9, 275–6
    and Spanishness, 232–4
    teaching youth culture in, 318, 322
    and US media studies, 190–3
Britishness of CS, 234, 279–85
Britton, A., 254
broadcasting
    Australasian CS, 253–4
    Ireland, 310
    and politics of pleasure, 324–5
    and popular consciousness, 321
    see also television
Bromberg, P., 387
Bronner, S., 143
Brookhiser, R., 414
Brooks, P., 47, 49
Browett, J., 500
Brown, J., 409, 423
Brown, M. E., 64, 66, 69
Browning, B., 438
Brundson, C., 279
Brunner, J. J., 224
Bryson, L., 189
Buck, E. R., 500
Buckingham, D., 291
Bumiller, K., 50
bureaucrats, 361–3, 365, 371–2
    Colombia, 375–88
    ethics, 358, 362–5
Bürger, P., 143
Burgess, E., 64

Burke, K., 189
Burnett, R., 199
Burns, R., 298–9, 301
Burt, N., 402
Butler, D., 311
Butler, J., 39–40, 291
Butsch, R., 70
buttocks, 430
    see also ass politics
Buxton, W., 202

Cabral, Amilcar, 119
Calhoun, C., 70
Calkins, P., 492
Callon, M., 109
Campbell, C., 455–6, 461
Campbell, K. K., 414
Canada, CS, 254
Candy, P., 371
capitalism
    Chinese CS, 260
    empirical political economy, 117–21
    Feng Shui, 442
    global media studies, 201–6
    globalization, 492–6, 504
        film industry, 499–503
        Washington Consensus, 490–1, 493, 504
    Latin American/US CS, 220–1
    Marxism in CS, 336–9
    metatheory of CS, 140–2
    politics of representation, 220
    refeudalization of society, 369
    theoretical political economy, 122–36
    US Spanish-language studies, 240–3
Carby, H. V., 416
Carey, J. W., 118, 160, 187–8, 192–3
Carlin, G., 432, 434
case-oriented research, 256
Castells, M., 67, 91, 93–4, 240
Castillo, A., 242
Centre for Contemporary Cultural Studies
    (CCCS), 6
    Australasian CS, 251–2
    Britishness of CS, 234, 281–2
    contemporary trends in CS, 285
    cultural turn in sociology, 89–90
    definitions of CS, 332
    Hoggart's proposal for, 81–2
    identity constitution, 227

media studies, 191–2
metatheory of CS, 140–2
precursors of CS, 471
Césaire, A., 474, 476
chain gangs, 55
Chambers, I., 195, 304
Chan, H. M., 262
Chan, S. C. K., 263–5
Chang, R., 40, 43–4, 48–50
Chatterjee, P., 6
Cheah, P., 51
Chen, K.-H., 63, 235, 278, 287
Chernoff, J. M., 432
Cheung, S. C. K., 262
Chicano studies, 233–4, 236–9, 242–3
Chinese cultural studies
   in Hong Kong, 259–72
   in mainland China, 260–1, 270
Chinweizu, 487
Chiu, F. Y. L., 260
Choi, P. K., 270
Christopherson, S., 500
Chunn, D., 39–40, 44
Churchill, W., 479
cinema *see* film
citizenship
   Clinton/Lewinsky discourse, 413
   Latin America, 224–5, 227
civil rights
   Clinton/Lewinsky discourse, 416–20
   identity politics, 227–8
civility in public life, 412–13
Clarke, A., 515
Clarke, D. L., 166
Clarke, J., 338, 516
Clarke, S., 125
class
   analysis in British sociology, 87–9
   British CS, 277–82
      contemporary trends, 285–6
      Hoggart's writings, 24–5, 80–1
      and sociology, 289–90
   Chinese CS, 260
   cricket, 520–2
   cultural turn in sociology, 66–7
   fashion, 456, 459–60, 464–5
   interdisciplinarity, 24–5, 28, 30
   metatheory of CS, 140–2
   museums, 393–403
   political economy in CS, 117–20, 124

digital divide, 120
   Marxist property relations, 128–9
popular culture, 195
race in Latin America, 222
racism, 478
Clemens, E.S., 9
Clemetson, L., 412
Clifford, J., 173–6, 239
Clinton, B.
   Kennewick Man, 161–2
   Lewinsky discourses, 407–8
      feminism, 407–8, 410–17, 420–5, 426
      minoritization, 413–16, 425–6
      public culture structures, 411–13
      racial politics, 407–8, 416–20, 425–6
Clough, P., 63
Cloward, R., 403
Cohen, J., 55
Cohen, R., 499
Cold War
   globalization, 493
   Olympic sex testing, 345–8
Colker, R., 38
collective selection, fashion, 460–1
Collins, J., 491
Collins, P. H., 416
Collins, R., 357
Colombia, cultural policy, 375–6
   critical discourse, 380–4
   diversity as national agenda, 376–9
   theory–practice gap, 384–8
colonialism
   British CS, 280, 282
   Chinese CS in Hong Kong, 260, 267–9
   cricket, 511, 515–22
   critique by US anthropology, 173
   global economics, 493–4
   governmentality, 42
   political economy in CS, 118–19
   race, 472–5
      multiculturalism, 476, 482
      polycentrism, 476
      racism, 477, 511, 517–18, 521–2
   Spanish-language cultures, 233–5
colonies, public culture institutions, 370–1
colonization, global media studies, 202
commodification, through culture, 308
commodity fetishism, 131–2, 458
communication, cultural policy in Colombia,
      378–9, 381–6

communication studies, 187–8
  global, 201–6
  identity-based, 198–9
  ideological criticism, 196–8
  path to media studies, 188–93
  political economy, 199–201
  politics of popular culture, 194–6, 200
communication technology
  critical sociology of culture, 150–1
  European CS, 304–5
  global media studies, 202–3
  Marxist PE, 132
communicative codes, fashion, 462
communism, Olympic sex testing, 345–8
comparative advantage, 123–4
competition, sport studies, 342–8
Conkey, M. W., 157
Conroy, T., 434
conscientización, 223
consciousness
  cultural turn in sociology, 66
  legal, 43, 52–3, 55–6
  popular, 320–2
  social repression, 52–3
  teaching youth culture, 320–2
  Veblen's socialism, 124–5
Constable, M., 46, 51, 52
construction, cultural production, 70
constructionism
  of the body, 50–1
  Latin American/US CS, 227–9
  legal, 36–44, 49
  race, 472
consumerism, fashion, 455–61, 465–6
consumption
  British sociology, 88
  Chinese CS, 260
  cultural turn in sociology, 69–70
  digital divide, 120
  fashion, 455–9
  Latin American/US CS, 220, 223
  politics of representation, 220
  theoretical political economy, 124, 127
    Fordism, 133–5
    value, 129–32, 135–6
  US sport/gang dyad, 351–2
  and what CS is, 11–12
Cooley, C. H., 64
Coombe, R., 39, 44, 46, 55–7
Cooper, C., 448

Cornell, D., 52
Cornford, J., 501
corporeality *see* body, the
counterhegemonic narratives, 49
counterhegemonic practices, 66
Couture, J., 52
Craib, I., 288
Craig, M., 458, 465
Craik, J., 457
Crane, G. T., 123–6
Crawley, E., 458
Crenshaw, K., 40
cricket
  nationalism, 510–11
    colonial discourses, 511, 515–22
    diasporic spectatorship, 511–14, 522–5
    identifications, 524–5
    Sinhala, 510–11, 514, 518–22, 525
    social divisiveness, 521–2
    television's role, 522–3
  orientalism, 514–15
  racism, 511, 517–18, 521–2, 524–5
crime
  Colombian cultural policy, 378–9
  sport/gang dyad, 349–52
Cripps, T., 479, 483
critical intellectuals, 358–65, 371–2
  Colombia, 375–88
critical pedagogy, 148–9
critical political economy *see* Marxism,
    political economy
critical theory
  and critique in CS, 144–8
  and cultural policy, 387–8
    see also critical intellectuals
  Frankfurt School–British CS compared,
    140–3, 149–50
  and media studies, 188, 190–1, 192–3
  metatheory of CS, 143–4
critics, cultural role, 368
critique, and *praxis*, 358–65, 371–2
  Colombia, 375–88
cultural anthropology *see* anthropology
cultural circuit, 91
cultural identity, European CS, 310–12
cultural imperialism, 490
  European CS, 301–2
  Latin America, 222
  political economy in CS, 119, 127–8
cultural materialism, 5–6

cultural policy, 357
  Australasia, 253–6
  institutions of public culture, 365–72
    Philadelphia Museum of Art, 391–405
  Latin America, 226–7
    Colombia, 375–88
  role of intellectuals, 357–8
    Colombia, 375–88
    critical/practical split, 358–65, 371–2
  teaching youth culture, 327–8
  USA, 327
cultural populism
  in British CS, 142, 144–5
  Latin America, 222
cultural production, 67, 70
  contemporary British CS, 286–7
  division of labor, 499–504
  fashion, 462–5
  global media studies, 202–3
  Latin American/US CS, 220
  US Spanish-language cultures, 236–7
cultural protectionism, 127–8
cultural sociology, 69–73
cultural studies' introduction, 1–14
cultural studies' origins, 3–6
  Australasia, 248–54
  precursors, 471–3
  problems with account of, 276–9
  US tradition, 193
  see also Hall, S.; Hoggart, R.; Thompson,
    E. P.; Williams, R.
culture
  anthropology, 170–1, 261–2
  archaeology, 157–9
  common, 309
  critical pedagogy, 148–9
  critical sociology of, 150–1
  critique in CS, 146–8
  dialectics of, 147–8
  evaluation, 86, 96–7
    teaching youth culture, 319–20
  history of British sociology, 87–9, 92
  inflections in sociology, 64–74
  institutions of public, 365–72
    Colombia, 375–88
    Philadelphia, 391–405
  lack of definitions of, 332–3
  media studies, 191–3
  metatheory of CS, 140–4
  NAFTA effects, 225–6
  politics of, media studies, 194–6, 200
  Public Culture project, 176–8
  race in Latin America, 221–2
  relation to politics, 332–9
  STS, 101–5, 107–9, 111
culture industry
  Australasia, 247, 249–50, 253–5,
    500–3
  commodification, 308
  division of labor, 499–504
  and European CS, 303–4, 308, 310
  Fordism, 134–5
  political CS, 150–1
  political economic analyses, 200
  and popular consciousness, 320–2
  racial stereotypes, 479–81
  regulation, public sphere and, 357
  sport
    Nike's PLAY narrative, 351–2
    Olympic sex testing, 346–8
  teaching youth culture, 320–1, 328
"cultures", and British sociology, 88
Cunningham, S., 248, 255, 502
Curran, J., 192, 196
Curtin, M., 199
Czaplicka, J., 1

Dagnino, E., 376, 378–9, 386
Dai, J., 270
Daley, P., 199
Dalton, H., 48
Danan, M., 501
dance, ass music, 437–47
Danielson, D., 44
Darian-Smith, E., 36
Davies, I., 278
Davies, N., 95
Davis, A. Y., 416
Davis, F., 462, 464
Dawtrey, A., 501
Dayan, J., 55
de Certeau, M., 457
De Laet, M., 109
Deas, M., 378
decolonization, and cricket, 510, 514–20
deconstructionism, and justice, 52
Deem, M., 410
Delgado, R., 40, 48
Delia, J., 187
Deloria, V., 479

democracy
  citizenship, 224–5, 227
  Colombian cultural policy, 378–9, 384,
    386–7
  cultural turn in sociology, 72–4
  globalization, 504
  Olympic sex testing, 345–8
Dermody, S., 250
Derrida, J., 52, 68, 474
Dershowitz, A., 47
desire, identity politics, 228–9
determinations, Marxism in CS, 337–9
developmentalism
  European CS, 306
  Latin America, 223
Dewey, J., 189
di Leonardo, M., 174
Diawara, M., 6, 283, 444, 479
digital divide, 120
Dimaggio, P., 327
disciplines, intersections with CS, 1, 11–12
  anthropology, 169–85
  archaeology, 154–66
  in Hong Kong, 263–8, 271–2
  interdisciplinarity, 23–34, 90–1
  law, 36–57
  media studies, 187–207, 268
  in New Zealand, 253
  philosophy, 139–51
  see also political economy; sociology
diversity
  and interdisciplinarity, 27–30
  US faculties, 241
docents, 402
Donnelly, P., 495
Dosse, F., 67
Douglas, M., 458–9, 466
Douglas, S., 321, 326
Dow, B., 425
Dowd, M., 413
Downey, G., 106
Downey, R., 161
Downing, J., 201
dress, fashion in see fashion
drugs
  performance-enhancing, 343, 353
  and US sport/gang dyad, 343, 350–1
du Gay, P., 338
Duby, G., 159
Dumit, J., 106

Dunn, T., 278
Durant, A., 308
During, S., 159–60, 162
Dworkin, D., 278
Dyer, R., 451, 485

Eagleton, T., 230, 291
economic dependency theory, 499
economic determinism, Marxism in CS,
  337–8
economics see political economy
education
  anthropology, 178–85
  British CS, 277–8, 291–2
    and a European CS, 308–9
  critical pedagogy, 148–9
  NAFTA effects, 225–6
  political economy in CS, 120–1
  postmodern pedagogy, 149
  teaching youth culture, 317–28
  see also universities
Eicher, J., 459
El Guindi, F., 458–59
elite culture
  Chinese CS, 260–1
  European CS, 299–301, 312
  Latin American/US CS, 221
  metatheory of CS, 142–3
  teaching youth culture, 319
elites
  antihierarchical CS, 474–5
  archaeological discourse, 157–8
  threats to, 11–12
elitism, US cultural studies, 242–3
Ellison, R., 477
Engel, D., 43
England see Britain
Engle, K., 44
English literature
  Chinese CS in Hong Kong, 263–4
  Hoggart's move from, 23, 25, 79–82
  interdisciplinarity, 23, 25, 27–8
  New Zealand CS, 252
Englishness
  construction, 232–3
  cricket, 516
  European CS, 304
  hegemony in CS, 234
Enzensberger, H. M., 189
Erni, J. N., 197, 198, 202, 263

Escobar, A., 376, 378, 379, 386
Eshun, K., 449
Espeland, W., 43
ethical ground, sport, 343–4
ethical incompleteness, disciplinarity, 32–3
ethics, and critique, 145–7, 358, 362–5
ethnic studies, capitalism, 243
ethnicity, CS methodology, 334–5
ethnography, 169, 175, 178–184
   contemporary British CS, 285–6
   writing function, 182–3
ethnoscapes, 307, 308
Eurocentrism, 302, 312–13, 475–6, 480, 486
Europe, 4
   archaeology, 156–7
   culture industry, 500–2
   global media studies, 202–4
   globalization, 493, 495
   institutions of public culture, 370
   need for sociology in, 95
   postwar reconstruction, 307–8
   racing of structuralism, 474
   see also Britain; European cultural studies
European cultural studies, 298–9
   Americanization, 301–2, 306
   border crossings, 303–4
   common culture, 309
   concept of place, 306–8
   Eurocentrism, 302, 312–13
   everyday lived experience, 308–9
   globalization, 306–8
   high and low culture, 299, 300–1, 308–9, 312
   homogenization, 306–7
   hybridity, 302–6, 312
   identity, 300, 303–4, 306, 309–12
   the Internet, 304–5
   Irish example, 309–12
   reasons for absence of, 299–302
   recognising the "other", 305–6
European Union, significance, 203–4
evaluation *see* quality evaluation
Evans, P., 498
Ewen, S., 134–5, 458
Ewick, P., 49
exchange-value, 129–32
experience, Latin American/US CS, 227–9

Fabbri, P., 106

Fajer, M. A., 48
Falk, R., 494
Fals Borda, O., 378
Faludi, S., 422–3
Fanon, F., 472–4, 477
fantasy, identity politics, 228–30
Farred, G., 511, 516, 525
fashion, 454
   aesthetic analyses, 462–3
   anthropology, 458–9
   cultural studies, 463–5
   modernity of, 454–8
   social psychology, 461–2
   sociology, 459–61
Fawcett, C., 160
Featherstone, M., 306–7, 465
Feirstein, B., 412
Feld, S., 433, 443
Feldman, M., 46
Felman, S., 53–4
female body
   and feminism, 416
   legal narrative, 50–1
feminism
   anthropology, 173–4
   British CS, 279
   Clinton/Lewinsky discourse, 407–8, 410–13, 417, 420–5
   as contextual practice, 408–9
   a CS of law, 38–41, 50–1
   fantasy, 229
   Latin American/US CS compared, 219, 229
   metatheory of CS, 142
   minoritization, 413–16, 425–26
   as object of study, 409
   racism, 478
   sexual harassment, 420–5
feminization
   of masculine power, 414
   of workforce, 88
Feng Shui, 431, 441–2
   and rap, 431, 442–5
Ferguson, M., 122, 194, 198, 293
Ferguson, R. A., 46, 52–3
Fiedler, L., 471
film
   and debate about Europe, 204
   depictions of archaeology, 154, 164–5
   European cinema, 303–4, 310

film (*cont.*)
   multiculturalism, 483–5
   politics of pleasure, 323
   raced nature of culture, 482–3
   racial stereotypes, 479–81
film industry
   Australasia, 247, 249–50, 253, 255,
      500–3
   division of labor, 499–503
   political economic analyses, 200
film makers, identity-based media studies,
   199
film studies, Australasia, 247, 250–1,
   253
film theory, race, 473
financescapes, 307–8
Fine, B., 462
Finkelstein, J., 455
Finney, C., 371
Fischer, M., 174
Fiske, J., 142, 324, 463
Fitzpatrick, P., 43, 52
Flügel, J. C., 456
Forbes, J., 63, 299
Fordism, 133–5
Forgacs, D., 63, 281
Foster, S., 449
Foster, Y., 513
Foucauldian approaches
   cultural turn in sociology, 67
   legal constructionism, 39, 41
Foucault, M., 30, 33, 67, 108, 357, 371,
   391, 404
Fox Piven, F., 403
France, 4
   French CS, 251, 298–99
   global culture, 500–1, 504
   multiculturalism, 482
Franco, S., 378
Frankfurt School
   British CS compared, 140–3, 149–50
   fashion, 457–8
   German CS, 298–9, 301
   media studies, 190
Franklin, S., 9, 279
Franks, L., 412
Fraser, N., 225
free trade
   global economy, 490–1, 492–6, 504
   Latin American/US CS, 224–6

theoretical political economy, 123–4,
   129–30
Fregoso, R., 480
Freire, P., 149, 240
French, M. A., 416
French, P., 303
French Regulation School of PE, 133–5
Frere-Jones, S., 433, 437–8
Freyre, G., 221–2
Friar, N., 479
Friar, R., 479
Friedan, B., 423–4
Fröbel, F., 499, 500
Frow, J., 6, 7, 69, 252, 255, 333, 338, 458
Fujimura, J., 105
Fuss, D., 70, 472
future of cultural studies, 331–9

Galbraith, J. K., 125, 490
gang narrative, and sport, 349–52
Gaonkar, D. P., 63, 194
Garafalo, R., 196
Garber, M., 462
Garcia Canclini, N., 6, 219, 223, 225–6, 375
Garfinkel, H., 65
Garnham, N., 337
Gay Games, 342–3
gay sexuality *see* sexuality
Geertz, C., 37
Gehlen, A., 158
Gellner, D., 185
gender
   archaeology, 162–4
   British CS, 279
   Clinton/Lewinsky discourses, 413–16
   a CS of law, 38–41
   identity parallelism, 228
   Latin American/US CS, 219–21
   sport, sex testing, 344–8
gender roles, killjoy critiquing, 323–4
gendered clothing, 461–2
Gerbner, G., 189
Germany
   archaeology, 157
   cultural studies, 298–9, 301
Gero, J. M., 157
Geuens, J.-P., 199
Gewirtz, P., 37, 45–9
Gibson, C., 232
Gibson-Graham, J. K., 494–5

Giddens, A., 65, 91, 289–90, 294, 307
Giddings, P., 416
Gilroy, P., 232, 281–5, 293–4, 300, 439, 450–1, 482, 524–5
Giroux, H., 148, 291, 304
Gitlin, T., 199
global media studies, 201–6
globalization, 490–2
   comparative multicultural studies, 486–7
   democracy, 504
   division of labor, 498–504
   economics, 490–6, 504
   European CS, 306–8
   media event analysis, 204–6
   of multiculturalism, 476
   nation-states, 493–7, 504
   postmodernity, 491–2
   Public Culture project, 177
   "scapes" as pattern for, 307–8
   Spanish-language cultures, 235
Goffman, E., 65, 460
Goldberg-Ambrose, C., 43
Golding, P., 122, 194, 198, 293
Goldstein, R., 414
Gomery, D., 200
Gooding, S. S., 43
Goodwin, A., 328
Gopnik, A., 11
Gordon, D., 174, 279
Gouldner, A. W., 66, 287, 290, 294
governance
   Clinton/Lewinsky discourse, 414
   and what CS is, 13
government, 357
   Colombia, 375–88
   critique and *praxis*, 361–5, 371–2, 375–88
   a CS of law, 41–3
   ethics, 358, 362–5
   institutions of culture, 365–72, 375–88
   interdisciplinarity, 31
Graham, C., 312
Graham, H., 63, 299–300
Gramsci, A., 5, 66, 145, 222
Grann, D., 413
Gray, A., 279
Gray, H., 63, 150, 479
Green, M., 90
Green, R. C., 449
Greverus, I.-M., 158
Gripsrud, J., 196, 199

Grossberg, L., 3, 7, 9–10, 12, 63, 67, 118, 122, 148, 172, 191–3, 198, 254, 334, 409, 426
Grosz, E., 51
Gruneau, R., 343
Gubar, S., 409
Guccione, B., 415
Guerrero, E., 479
Guha, R., 6
guided tour, Philadelphia Museum of Art, 391–405
Guillory, M., 449
Gulbenkian Commission, 93–4
Gurevitch, M., 187, 192
Guttridge, P., 502

Habermas, J., 66, 190, 357–61, 365–72
Hainsworth, P., 308
hair straightening, 465
Hall, S., 3, 5, 13, 66, 81, 89–91, 96, 140, 145, 191–2, 195–8, 275, 277–8, 280–1, 284, 286–7, 289, 293–4, 321, 332–6, 435, 449, 464, 471
Hamelink, C., 127
Hammer, R., 149
Handy, B., 412
Hannerz, U., 199
Hannigan, J., 341
Haraway, D., 102, 106–7, 109, 352–3
Hardt, H., 187, 189
Hardy, J. E., 447
Hargreaves, J. E., 343
Härke, H., 157
Harris, A., 44
Hartley, J., 9, 254
Hartman, S., 437
Hartouni, V., 106
Harvey, D., 120, 134–5, 202, 300
Harvey, J., 343, 463
Haug, W. F., 458
Hayes, J., 262
Hayward, S., 501
Hebdige, D., 66, 142, 195, 435, 450, 458, 464
hegemonic narratives, 49
hegemony
   CS, 6–13
      identity politics, 227–8
      inflections in sociology, 66–7, 71–3
      languages, 234–5, 472
      of law, 44–50

hegemony (*cont.*)
  liberal political economy, 128–9
  media studies
    global, 202–3
    ideological critique, 196–7
Held, D., 491–2, 504
Helmreich, S., 106
Hennig, J.-L., 430, 441, 447
Henry, J., 162
Herman, 57
Herod, A., 493–4, 496
Herzfeld, M., 381
Hess, D., 106
heteroglossia, 67
Heyer, P., 187
high culture
  Chinese CS, 260–1
  European CS, 299–301, 308–9, 312
  Latin American/US CS, 221
  media studies, 194–5
  metatheory of CS, 142–3
  teaching youth culture, 319
Hikino, T., 496
Hilger, 479
Hill, J., 303–4
Hindley, B., 493
Hines, C., 499
hip hop
  teaching youth culture, 326
  US Latino, 234, 237
  videos, 444–7
Hirsch, P., 463
Hirst, P., 493, 495, 497
Hiscock, J., 502
"Hispanic", Anglophone thought, 233–4
historical cultural narratives, 48
history
  and archaeology, 156–7
  Australian, 249
  homogenization, 306
Hitchens, C., 415
Hobsbawm, E., 124, 126, 490
Hodder, I., 157
Hoffman, S., 304
Hoggart, R., 3, 23–5, 30, 79–82, 85, 96, 117,
    128, 146, 227, 276–8, 283–5, 320, 471
Hollander, A., 463
homogenization, European CS, 306–7
homophobia
  cultural turn in sociology, 71

metatheory of CS, 142
racism, 478
Hong Kong, Chinese CS in, 259
  boundary transgression, 267–8, 271–2
  camouflaged, 266–7
  class analysis, 260
  high culture, 260–1
  indigenization, 261–3
  institutionalization, 263–5
  international–local tensions, 269–71
  languages of, 269–70
  locality–totality narrative, 271–2
  national narrative, 260
Hopenhayn, M., 387
Horak, R., 301
Horkheimer, M., 66, 150, 190, 328
Horowitz, D., 407
Horrocks, R., 255
Hovland, C., 189
Hudson, B., 42
Hughes, W., 450
human rights, citizenship, 224–5, 227
Hunt, A., 456
Hunt, L., 73, 158
Hunter, I., 31–3, 255, 361–3
Hutchinson, J., 497
hybridity
  European CS, 302–6, 312
  Latin America, 224
  postcolonial identities, 40–1
Hyde, A., 38, 50
Hymes, D., 173

identification, race, 472–3
identity
  Chinese CS in Hong Kong, 260–1, 263
  contemporary British CS, 285–6
  cricket, 518, 521, 524–5
  a CS of law, 38–44, 48–9
  cultural turn in sociology, 67, 72–3
  effects of CS' concerns with, 10–11
  European CS, 300, 303–6, 309–12
  fashion, 456–7, 460
  French CS, 299
  global media, 201–4
  Ireland, 309–12
  Latin American/US CS, 220–1, 224–5,
    227–30
  left–right politics, 409
  needs interpretations, 225, 227

raced nature, 482–3
US Spanish-language cultures, 239–43
identity-based media studies, 198–9
identity parallellism, 228
ideology critique
  media studies, 192–3
  metatheory of CS, 141
ideoscapes, 307–8
Ignatiev, N., 485
imperialism
  ass music, 439–40
  British CS, 282
  cricket, 511, 516–22
  European CS, 301–2
  global economics, 492–3, 498–9
  Latin American/US CS, 221–2
  political economy in CS, 118–19, 127–8
  race, 475
  Spanish-language cultures, 233–4
incompleteness, and disciplinarity, 24–34
Indiana Jones trilogy, 154, 164–5
indigenization, Chinese CS in Hong Kong, 261–3
indigenous peoples
  cricket, 516–7
  Latin American/US CS, 219–22
  New Zealand CS, 252–3
information technology, digital divide, 120
Inglis, F., 69
inner city youth, sport/gang dyad, 349–52
Innis, H., 202
institutional political economy, 124–7, 135
institutions of public culture, 365–72
  Colombia, 375–88
  Philadelphia, 391–405
  US presidency *see* Clinton, B., Lewinsky discourse
intellectual work, 357–8
  critical and practical, 358–65, 371–2
    Colombia, 375–88
interdisciplinarity
  anthropology, 169–85
  Appadurai's view, 27–30
  archaeology, 154–66
  Bennett–Hunter position, 32–4
  Bennett's view, 30–2
  Chinese CS in Hong Kong, 268
  Hoggart's work, 23–5
  law, 36–57
  media studies, 187–207, 268

philosophy, 139–51
sociology, 90–1, 93–5
US–Latin American comparisons, 218–19
Williams' account, 25–7
see also political economy; sociology
international relations, political economy, 126–7
Internet, European CS, 304–5
interpellation, cultural turn in sociology, 67
intersectionality, a CS of law, 40–1
Ip, I. C., 260
Ireland, 309–12
Ireland, P., 423–4
Isherwood, B., 458–9, 466
Ismail, Q., 511–512, 519
Italy, 4
Ivison, D., 42

Jacka, E., 248, 250, 502
Jackson, J., 416
Jackson, J. L., 435–6, 449
Jackson, K., 327–8
Jackson, M., 387
James, A., 522
James, B., 199
James, C. L. R., 471–2, 511–13, 515, 521, 523–5
Jameson, F., 69, 148, 150, 308, 338, 493
Janowitz, M., 189
Japan, globalization, 493, 495, 502
Jaramillo, R., 380
Jarvie, G., 307
Jefferson, T., 142, 195, 435, 464
Jelin, E., 224–5
Jenkins, H., 199, 256, 324
Jhally, S., 199
Johnson, A. M., 48
Johnson, L., 256
Johnson, R., 67, 191
Jones, J., 479
Jordan, M., sport/gang dyad, 350–2
Joseph, M., 437, 496
journal publishing, 7–9, 11
judgment-making *see* quality evaluation
Julien, I., 487
juries, legal narratives, 46–7
Jury, L., 502
justice, a CS of law, 51–5

Kahn, P., 37

Kant, I., 33, 405
Kapur, R., 40–1
Karst, K., 44
Katz, E., 189
Katz, M. B., 403
Kearney, R., 301–2, 305–6
Kearns, T., 53
Kell, P., 511
Kellner, D., 140, 142–3, 148–9, 151, 160,
     293, 321, 337
Kelly, C., 63
Kelly, M., 63, 299
Kelman, M., 37
Kennewick Man, 161–2
Kessler, K. L., 500–1
Keynes, J. M., 126, 498
Kilbourne, J., 324
Kilpatrick, J., 479
Kimball, R., 10, 487
Kissinger, H., 490
Klapper, J., 189
Knorr Cetina, K., 104–6
knowledge production in CS, 334
Knox, M., 515
Kohl, P. L., 160
Kohlstedt, S. G., 371
König, R., 461–2
Kossinna, G., 157
Kowk, J. Y. C., 270
Kozul-Wright, R., 495
Krasnow, D., 432
Kuhn, M., 502
Kymlicka, W., 481–2

Labanyi, J., 63, 299–300
labor
   ass politics, 436–7
   film industry, 200, 497–502
   globalization, 491, 494, 495–6, 498–504
labor-invested value, 129, 130–1, 135–6
labor relations, Colombia, 380–4
Laclau, E., 73, 200, 222, 336
Lacombe, D., 39–40, 44
Laing, S., 278
Lam, O. W., 260
Lang, T., 499
language
   Chinese CS in Hong Kong, 263–4,
      269–70
   cultural turn in sociology, 67–8

English hegemony in CS, 234–5, 472
   interdisciplinarity, 26–7
   linguistic ability, 94
   power in legal process, 44–52
   Spanish-language cultures, 232–5
Laplanche, L., 229
Lardreau, G., 159
Lash, S., 290
Lasswell, H., 189
LatCrit Symposium, 40
Latin America, 4
   in Anglophone thought, 233–4
   cultural feedback, 236–9
   cultural policy in Colombia, 375–6
      critical discourse, 380–4
      diversity as national agenda, 376–9
      theory–practice gap, 384–8
   political economy in CS, 118–19
   and the US, comparative CS, 217–18
      aesthetics, 227–30
      citizenship, 224–5, 227
      cultural flows, 222–3
      identity politics, 227–30
      interdisciplinarity, 218–19
      knowledge flows, 218–19
      NAFTA, 224–6
      national identity, 221
      non-academic settings, 219
      policy influence, 226–7
      politics of representation, 220–2, 227
      power relations, 223–7
      race, 221–2
      reception of texts, 218–19
      social movements, 223–5
      value, 223–7
Latin American literary studies, 233–4
Latino studies, 233–9, 242–3
Latour, B., 101, 104, 108–9, 352–3,
     361, 492
Laurent, J., 371
Lave, J., 106
Lavelle, M., 416
Lavenda, R. H., 158
Laver, J., 461
law, CS of, 36–8, 55–7
   identity, 38–44, 48–9
   justice, 51–5
   narrative, 44–51
Law, J., 109
Law, W. S., 260, 263–4

Lawrence, G., 495, 498
Lazarsfeld, P., 189–90
Le Bon, G., 65
Le Heron, R., 496
Leab, D., 479
Lealand, G., 248, 252, 253
Lears, J., 407, 459
Leaver, R., 500
Leavis, F. R., 82–4, 319
Leavis, Q., 82
Lefebvre, H., 202, 471–2
leisure
    ass politics, 436–7
    British sociology, 88
    museum guides, 402
leisure class, 124
Lent, J., 128, 492, 500
Leone, M. P., 162
Leong, L. W.-T., 2
Leopold, E., 462
Leung, B. K. P., 260, 270
Leung, P.-K., 263, 271
Lévi-Strauss, C., 71, 474
Levinas, E., 190
Levine, D., 294
Levinson, M., 490
Levy, M. R., 187
Lewinsky scandal *see* Clinton, B., Lewinsky
    discourse
Lewis, I., 418
Lewis, J., 13, 199
liberal political economy, 117, 122, 123–30,
    135
    refeudalization of society, 369
libraries, governmentalization, 369–70
Lindeborg, R., 283
Lipovetsky, 455–6, 460
Lipsitz, G., 482, 485
literary public sphere, 366
    institutions, 367–9
literary studies
    anthropology influencing CS, 173–6,
        184–5
    Australia, 249
    Chicano, 234
    Chinese CS in Hong Kong, 263–4
    Hoggart's move from, 23, 25, 79–82
    interdisciplinarity, 23, 25, 27–8
    Latin American, 233–4
    New Zealand CS, 252

literature
    Latin American/US CS, 221
    sociology of, 83–5
Lobel, L., 459
local cultural behavior, European CS, 300,
    306–7
local–global binary, 492
local–global media complex, 206
local–global tensions, Hong Kong, 269–71
locality–totality narrative, Chinese CS,
    271–2
Long, E., 63, 293
Lott, E., 71
Lovatt, A., 285
Lovell, T., 9
Lowe, L., 241
Lowenthal, L., 190
ludic textualism, CS, 144–5
Luk, B. H. K., 261
Lukes, S., 192
Lumley, R., 63
Luostarinen, R., 499
Lutter, C., 159
lynching, Clinton/Lewinsky discourse,
    419–20

Ma, E. K., 259–61
MacCabe, C., 195
McCall, M. M., 11, 65
McCann, P., 500
McChesney, R., 122, 321, 341
McClintock, A., 74
McGuigan, J., 63, 116, 142, 150, 292, 308,
    358–61
McHoul, A., 196
McHugh, P., 65
MacIntyre, E., 510–11
McKenna, F., 81
McKinney, C., 418
McLaughlin, L., 116
McLennan, G., 289, 293
McLoone, M., 309–11
McLuhan, M., 189
McMichael, P., 495, 498
McNamee, S. J., 9
McPherson, T., 256
McRobbie, A., 150, 195, 279, 286, 293,
    335, 458
Maddox, J., 9
Madonna, 447

magazines, Olympic sex testing,
  346–7
Maguire, J., 307
Maltby, W. S., 232
Man, S. W., 270
Mannheim, K., 289–90
Marcum, D., 239
Marcus, G. E., 173–6, 183
Marcuse, H., 66
marginalist economics, 125
Mariátegui, J. C., 221–2
Marti, J., 222
Martin, R., 11, 341–3, 436, 449
Martín-Barbero, J., 6, 223, 385
Martinez, E., 242
Marvasti, A., 500, 502
Marxism
  British sociology, 86–7
  in contemporary CS, 336–9
  fashion, 457–8
  legal constructionism, 39
  media studies, 192, 200
  political economy, 117, 121–2, 126–33,
    135–6
  popular culture, 66–7
  US anthropology, 172–3
  US universities, 240–2
masculinity
  Clinton/Lewinsky discourses,
    413–16, 420
  racialized, in cricket, 516–17
mass communication research,
  187–92
mass culture
  metatheory of CS, 140–1
  the public sphere, 368–9
mass-market systems, fashion, 464–5
Massey, D., 202, 300, 302–3
material culture
  archaeology, 158
  fashion, 458–9
materiality, STS, 109, 112–13
Matsuda, M. J., 48
Mattelart, A., 6, 119
Mattelart, M., 6, 119
Maurer, B., 36
Mauss, M., 457
Maxwell, R., 3, 4, 13, 131, 135
Maynard, D., 46
Mazower, M., 95

Mead, 189
Mead, G. H., 64, 460
media culture
  critical pedagogy, 148
  metatheory of CS, 140–3
  political CS, 149
media explosion, British sociology,
  88
media industry
  Australasia, 247, 249–50, 253, 255,
    500–3
  division of labor, 499–503
  political economic analyses, 200
  racial stereotypes, 479–81
  regulation, public sphere and, 357
media studies, 187–8
  Australasia, 247–51, 253
  and CS, 194
    in Hong Kong, 268
    identity-based, 198–9
    ideological criticism, 196–8
    political economy, 199–201
    popular culture, 194–6, 200
  global, 201–6
  intellectual legacy, 188–94
  sociology's cultural turn, 69–70
  teaching, 318–19
mediascapes, 307, 308
Melody, W., 125
Memmi, A., 477
memory, law as site of, 53–5
men, archaeology, 162–4
mercantilist political economy, 117, 122–4,
  126–7
Mercer, K., 71, 487
metatheory of CS, 139–44
methodology in CS, 332–5, 339
Mexico
  in Anglophone thought, 233–4
  anthropology, 225
  cultural feedback, 236–9
  NAFTA, 224–6, 233
Meyrowitz, J., 189
Miège, B., 500
Miles, S., 285
Miliband, R., 87
Miller, D., 157, 458–9
Miller, J. D. B., 496–7
Miller, M., 328
Miller, R. M., 479

Miller, T., 10, 24, 32, 63, 127, 133, 196, 199, 201, 327, 341–2, 343, 414, 499, 521
Mills, C. W., 66
Mingo, J., 490
Mink, G., 422
Minogue, K., 10
minoritarian politics, Clinton/Lewinsky discourse, 407–8, 410
    feminism, 410–17, 420–6
    race, 416–20, 425–6
minorities
    cultural turn in sociology, 70–1
    diasporic identities, 511–14, 522–5
    disciplinarity, 28–30
    legal narratives, 48–9
    US Spanish-language cultures, 239
Minow, M., 45
modernist art, British CS, 143, 147
modernity, Latin American/US CS, 223–4
Mohammadi, A., 491–2
Mol, A., 103, 106, 109
Monsiváis, C., 236–8
Montoya, M., 40, 41, 48–9, 235
Moore, B., 93
morality
    critique, 145–7, 362–5
    feminist hypocrisy, 408–11, 414–16, 421–2
    racial stereotyping, 480–1
Moran, A., 503
Morgan, M., 189
Morley, D., 10, 63, 118, 145, 194, 198, 199, 202–4, 206, 278, 287, 291–3, 306, 329
Morris, M., 6–7, 250, 252, 255–6, 335, 408–9, 425–6
Morris, R., 456
Morrison, T., 416–7
Morrow, R. A., 1
Mosco, V., 121, 124–5, 201
Moten, F. C., 435
Mouffe, C., 73, 200, 222, 336
Mouzelis, N., 288
movies see film
Mowlana, H., 492
Muggleton, D., 285
Mukerji, C., 455
Mulhern, F., 277
multicultural studies, 486–7
multiculturalism, 475–6
    British CS, 283–4

cultural policy in Colombia, 376–8, 380
    implications for CS, 481–4
multicultures
    British sociology, 88
    US Spanish-language, 239–43
multinational corporations (MNCs), 494–5, 500–4
Munger, F., 47
Muñoz, C. Jr., 242
Munt, S. R., 280, 286, 342
Murdoch, R., 502
Murdock, G., 2
Murray, A., 500
Murroni, C., 357
museums
    archaeological collections, 164–5
    governmentalization, 369–371
    Philadelphia Museum of Art tour, 391–405
music
    ass discourses, 431–2
        Timbaland, 431–4, 437–47
    contemporary British CS, 285
    cultural identity in Ireland, 310–11
    cultural turn in sociology, 69
    multiculturalism, 482
    production studies, 195
    teaching youth culture, 317, 321–2, 326–8

Nader, R., 491
Nairn, T., 497
Narayan Swamy, M. R., 519
narrative, in legal process, 44–51
Nast, H. J., 449
nation, the
    Australian CS, 251–2, 255
    cricket, 516–7
    and the law, 48
    Olympic sex testing, 344–8
nation-state, globalization, 493–7, 504
national identity
    British CS, 280–5
    cricket, 518, 521, 524–5
    European CS, 300, 303–4, 306, 309–10
    Ireland, 309–10
    Latin American/US CS, 221
    raced nature, 482–3
    US Spanish-language cultures, 239
national-popular, British CS, 281, 284

nationalism
  archaeology, 160–2
  Australian, 255, 513–18, 524
  cricket, 510–11
    colonial discourses, 511, 515–22
    diasporic spectatorship, 511–14, 522–5
    identifications, 524–5
    Sinhala, 510–11, 514, 518–22, 525
    social divisiveness, 521–2
    television's role, 522–3
  globalization, 494, 497, 504
  theoretical political economy, 123–4,
    127–8
Nava, N., 279
Neale, 479
Nelson, C., 11, 63, 172, 194, 254
neoclassical economics, 125–6
neoliberalism, globalization, 493–4, 504
neo-mercantilism, 127, 135
new international division of cultural labor
  (NICL), 498–504
New Women Association, 270
New Zealand CS, 246–8, 252–4, 256
newspapers, Olympic sex testing, 346–7
Ng, C. H., 262
Nike, sport/gang dyad, 350–2
Nkrumah, K., 119
Nordlinger, J., 419
Noriega, C., 480
North American Free Trade Agreement
  (NAFTA)
  Latin American/US CS, 224–6
  the nation-state, 497
  Spanish-language studies, 233
Northern Ireland, cultural identity, 310–12
Nugent, S., 198

O'Beirne, K., 414
O'Neill, J., 65
O'Regan, T., 250
occupational structure, Britain, 87–8
Ohmae, K., 497
Olsen, F., 50
Olson, M., 72
Olson, S., 127
Olympic Games, sex testing, 344–8
Omi, M., 227
orientalism, cricket, 511, 514–15
Ortega y Gasset, J., 65
Ortiz, F., 221–2

"other", the, European CS, 305–6
Ouellette, L., 325
outsider scholarship, legal narrative, 48–50
overviews, caution with, 103
Owusu, K., 281

Paglia, C., 423
Pahl, R., 87
Palley, T. I., 490, 497
Parenti, M., 69
Park, R., 64
Parker, D., 92
Parkin, F., 87
Parsons, T., 65
Partington, A., 464–5
Patel, G., 447
patriarchy, British CS, 279
Payne, M., 298
Paz, O., 224
pedagogy
  anthropology, 178–85
  British CS, 277–8, 291–2, 308–9
  critical, 148–9
  European CS, 308–9
  postmodern, 149
  teaching youth culture, 317–28
Peller, G., 37
Pendakur, M., 500
Perea, J. F., 235
Perera, S., 513
Peretz, E., 412
performance art
  museum tour, 391–405
  Spanish-language cultures, 237–8
performance theory, fashion, 454–5
performances of experience, 227–9
Perron, P., 106
Perry, N., 253
Peters, J. D., 189
Peterson, R. A., 67, 328
Peterson, V. S., 494
Pettit, A., 479
Phelan, P., 70
Philadelphia Museum of Art tour, 391–405
philosophy, and CS, 139
  critical pedagogy, 148–9
  metatheory, 139–44
  political, 149–51
  standpoint of critique, 144–8
Phizacklea, A., 462

Piaget, J., 290
Picker, L., 442
Pickering, A., 102, 104
Pickering, M., 27
Pines, J., 479
place, and European CS, 306–8
pleasure
  cricket as site for, 522–5
  politics of, youth culture, 318, 323–5
Podhoretz, N., 414–5, 421
Polhemus, T., 449, 463
political critique
  British CS, 145
  US anthropology, 172–3
political cultural studies, 149–51
political economy
  and CS, 2–3, 116, 336–9
    contemporary British, 291–2
    and media studies, 199–201
  in CS, 116–17
    as empirical problem, 117–21
    French Regulation School, 133–5
    institutionalism, 124–7, 135
    liberal PE, 117, 122–30, 135
    marginalism, 125
    Marxist PE, 117, 121–2, 126–33, 135–6
    mercantilist PE, 117, 122–4, 126–7
  fashion, 458
  globalization, 490–6, 504
  metatheory of CS, 143–4
  refeudalization of society, 369
  Washington Consensus, 490–1, 493, 504
politics
  ass, 430–1
    Timbaland, 437–41
  Australian CS, 251–2, 255
  Clinton/Lewinsky discourses, 407–8
    feminism, 407–8, 410–17, 420–5
    race, 407–8, 416–20, 425–6
  contemporary British CS, 278–9, 280–2,
    291–2, 336
  and cricket, 518–21
  and a CS of law, 44, 45
  cultural policy, 357–72
    Colombia, 375–88
  cultural turn in sociology, 72–3, 74, 291–2
  Latin American/US CS, 220–4, 226–7
  metatheory of CS, 141–2
  of pleasure, 318, 323–5
  political and cultural, 408–10

of popular culture, media studies, 194–6,
    200
  relation to culture, 332–9
  sport studies, 343
    and Olympic sex testing, 345–8
    sport/gang dyad, 349–52
  and STS, 105
  US anthropology, 172–3
  US universities, 240–3
  US–Mexican cultural feedback, 238–9
  and what CS is, 2–3, 6–7, 10–13
politics of representation
  cultural studies, 409–10, 426
  Latin American/US CS, 220–2, 227
Pollitt, K., 421
Pollock, D., 9
polycentric multiculturalism, 476
polyphony, 67
Ponnuru, R., 407
Pontalis, J.-B., 229
poorhouses, 393, 398, 403
popular culture
  ass discourses, 431–2
    Timbaland, 431–4, 437–47
  British CS, 279–80, 282–3
    contemporary trends, 285–6
  Chinese CS in Hong Kong, 261, 269
  and critique in CS, 146
  European CS, 300–2
  evaluation, 86, 96–7
    teaching youth culture, 319–20
  inflections in sociology, 65–70
  Latin American/US CS, 221–2
  media studies and politics of, 194–6, 200
  metatheory of CS, 142–3
  multiculturalism, 482–4
  and political politics, 408–9
  political significance, 2
  sport, 341–53
  teaching youth culture, 317–18
    age-specificity problem, 325–8
    anti-intellectual climate, 318–23
    politics of pleasure, 318, 323–5
population, and globalization, 496
populism
  Australasia, 256
  in CS, 142, 144–5, 256
  Latin America, 222
Porter, M., 496
postcolonial economics, 494

postcolonial identities, hybridity, 40–1
postcolonial media studies, 202
postcolonial nations, Australasian CS, 253–5
   see also Australia; Sri Lanka
postmodern drift, British CS, 285–6
postmodern pedagogy, 149
postmodern theory, metatheory of CS, 142
postmodernity
   anthropology critiques, 173–5
   and globalization, 491–2
postprocessual archaeology, 157–9, 165
Postrel, V., 10
poststructuralism
   cultural turn in sociology, 67–8, 71–2
   Marxism in CS, 337
   racing of, 474
   US Spanish-language cultures, 240–1
poststructuralist antiessentialism, law, 39–40
poverty, cultural policy, 393–401, 403, 405
power and power relations
   archaeology, 157–8, 161–2
   Chinese CS, 260
   cricket and colonialism, 516–7
   critique in CS, 145
   and CS, 6–12, 13
      contemporary British, 286–7
      inflections in sociology, 66–7, 71–3
      Latin American and US, 220, 222–8
      of law, 44–52, 54–6
      Spanish-languages cultures, 234–9
   global economics, 494–5
   identity parallellism, 228
   Kennewick Man, 161–2
   liberal political economy, 123, 128–9
   Marxist political economy, 133
   media studies, 192, 196–7, 202–3, 205
   mercantilist political economy, 123
   racial stereotyping, 479
   sport studies, 342–4
Powers, A., 448
Pratt, M., 219
praxis, and critique, 358–65
   Colombia, 375–88
pride, sport studies, 342–3, 351–2
printing device, Zimbabwe, 109–12
prison industrial complex, 350–1
Pritchard, B., 496
Probyn, E., 342–4

processual archaeology, 157, 165
production
   cultural see cultural production
   in the cultural circuit, 91
   theoretical political economy, 123–4, 133–6
property relations, Marxist, 128–33, 135–6
Prosler, M., 370
protectionism
   cultural, 127–8
   theoretical political economy, 123–4, 127–8
public culture, institutions of, 365–72
   Colombia, 375–88
   Philadelphia Museum of Art, 391–405
   US presidency see Clinton, B., Lewinsky discourse
Public Culture project, 173–4, 176–8
public service broadcasting, 324–5
public sphere(s)
   citizenship, 225
   Clinton/Lewinsky discourse, 407–8, 410–13
   cultural turn in sociology, 66
   feminism, 408–9
   Habermas's account, 357–8, 365–72
   identity politics, 228
   institutions of culture, 365–72
      Colombia, 375–6, 380–4
   and rival needs claims, 225
publishing
   book, 9–10
   journal, 7–9, 11
   Latin American/US CS, 225–6
punk
   teaching youth culture, 317, 321, 326–7
   US–Mexican dependency, 238
Purkis, J., 285

quality evaluation
   cultural policy, 401
   in sociology and CS, 84–6, 96–7
   teaching youth culture, 319–20
queer theory
   cultural turn in sociology, 70–1
   identity parallelism, 228
Quester, G., 501

race, 471
   centrality in British CS, 280–5

a CS of law, 40, 43–4, 53–4
CS methodology, 334–5
Eurocentrism, 475–6, 480, 486
globalization, 496
identity parallelism, 228
Latin American/US CS, 219–22, 227–8
media studies, 196–7
multicultural studies, 486–7
multiculturalism, 475–6, 481–4
New Zealand CS, 252–3
Olympic sex testing, 348
precursors of CS, 471–3
sport/gang dyad, 349–52
stereotypes, 478–83
structuralism, 473–5
US Spanish-language cultures, 236–7
whiteness studies, 485–6
see also racism
racial politics
    ass music, 434
        the body, 436–7
    Clinton/Lewinsky discourse, 407–8,
        416–20, 425–6
racial representations
    media studies, 199
    stereotypes, 478–83
racism, 477–8
    cricket, 511, 517–8, 521–2, 524–5
    cultural turn in sociology, 71
    metatheory of CS, 142
    US cultural studies, 242–3
radical multiculturalism, 476
Radway, J., 198, 325
Rama, A., 221
Ramirez Berg, 480
Ramos, J., 375
Rao, P., 71
rap music
    ass discourses, 431–4, 437–47
    and Feng Shui, 431, 442–5
    multiculturalism, 482
rape, and a CS of law, 37, 51
rationality, critical/practical, 357–65
Real, M., 321
reception see audience reception
recipe knowledge, 359, 361
refeudalization of society, 368–69
Regulation School of PE, 133–5
Reich, R., 493
Reisenleitner, M., 159

Renfrew, C., 158
representation(s)
    art museums, 404
    in the cultural circuit, 91
    cultural critique, 145–6
    cultural turn in sociology, 67
    in ethnographic research, 182–3
    Latin American/US CS, 220–2, 227
    legal, 37–8, 55–6
        of bodies, 50–1
        justice, 51
        narratives, 44–51
    media studies, 199
    politics of, 220–2, 227, 409–10, 426
    racial stereotypes, 478–83
    racism, 478
    STS, 101–3, 106, 110–11, 113
Ricardo, D., 123
Rich, F., 412–13
Richard, N., 388
rights
    citizenship, 224–5, 227
    Clinton/Lewinsky discourse, 416–20
    identity politics, 227–8
Riles, A., 36
Ritzer, G., 70
Robbins, K., 199
Roberts, D., 44
Roberts, M., 511, 522
Robins, K., 133–4, 202–4, 206, 306, 501
Robinson, D., 195
Robinson, W. I., 495
Roddick, N., 503
Roebuck, P., 514
Rogers, C. E., 433
Roiphe, K., 409, 423
Rojek, C., 456
romantic aesthetics, 32–4
Rose, J., 229
Rose, N., 41
Rose, T., 195
Rosen, 46
Rosen, J., 407
Rosenthal, A., 422
Rosi, P. H., 405
Rosin, H., 421
Ross, A., 11, 104–5, 195
Ross, D., 124–5
Ross, R., 494
Rowthorn, R., 495

Sacks, H., 65
Sadownick, D., 447
Sahlins, M., 457
Said, E. W., 94, 202, 305, 363–4
Salzman, J., 11
Sanders, J., 47
Sapir, E., 457
Sarat, A., 53, 56
Saussure, F. de, 67
scandal *see* Clinton, B., Lewinsky discourse
"scapes", globalization, 307–8
Schaeffer, R. K., 492
Scheff, T., 342
Scheppele, K. L., 37
Schiller, D., 121
Schiller, H. I., 69, 116, 127–8, 135, 190
Schlag, P., 37
Schneider, W., 162–3
Scholarship Boy, 24–5
Schramm, W., 189
Schultz, E. A., 158
Schumer, F. R., 405
Schutz, A., 64
Schwab, S., 502
Schwarz, B., 293
science and technology studies (STS), 104–5
    CS, 105–9, 112–13
    culture, 101–5, 107–9, 111
    materiality, 109, 112–3
    overviews, 103
    printer in Zimbabwe story, 109–12
    representation, 101–3, 106, 110–11, 113
    universals, 101–4, 106, 109–10, 113
Searle, C., 521–2
secular holiness, 363
Sedgwick, E., 70, 342
Seidman, S., 288
Seiter, E., 198
self
    contemporary British CS, 285–6
    cultural turn in sociology, 67, 72–3
    discipline, 29–30, 32
    fashion, 456–7
Selvadurai, S., 520
semiotics
    CS methodology, 335
    cultural turn in sociology, 67
    racing of, 474
    STS, 106
sex (gender) *see* gender

sex scandal *see* Clinton, B, Lewinsky discourse
sex testing, Olympic Games, 344–8
sexism, metatheory of CS, 142
sexual harassment, 420–5
sexual identity, legal constructionism, 38–41, 43–4
sexual representations, media studies, 199
sexuality
    British CS, 279
    cultural turn in sociology, 70–1
    identity parallelism, 228
    Latin American/US CS compared, 219
    metatheory of CS, 142
    Olympic sex testing, 348
    racism, 478
    sport studies, 342–3
Shalit, W., 407
shame, sport studies, 342–3
Shange, N., 440–1
Shanks, M., 157
Shapiro, W., 407, 418–19
Shattuc, J., 256
Shepherd, D., 63
Shepherd, J., 255
Shiach, M., 9
Shohat, E., 201, 476, 479
Shore, C., 198
Shore, L., 195
Shuker, R., 253
Siegel, L., 199
Siegel, R., 53
Silberman, N. A., 160
Silbey, S., 49
Simmel, G., 276, 294, 459–60
Simpson, O. J., trial, 53–4, 479
Sinclair, J., 201, 491
Sinhala nationalism, 510–11, 514, 518–22, 525
Sinn, E., 262
Slack, J. D., 188, 329
Slater, D., 458
slavery
    archaeology, 162
    legal memory, 53, 55
Smart, C., 39
Smiley, T., 418
Smith, Adam, 123, 498
Smith, Anthony D., 495, 497
Smith, C., 494

Smith, M., 282, 294
Smith, N., 73, 202
Smith, P., 10
Smithers, A., 319
Smythe, D., 127–8, 188, 190
Snead, J., 479
soap operas, 195–6
soccer, US ignorance of, 321
social anthropology see anthropology
social change
    Colombian cultural policy, 378–9
    cultural turn in sociology, 66, 72–3, 291–2
    globalization, 498
    teaching for, 240–3
social class see class
social constructionism see constructionism
social mobility, fashion, 456
social movements
    British sociology, 88
    contemporary British CS, 291–2
    cultural turn in sociology, 72–3, 291–2
    Latin America, 223–5
social order, body in motion threatens, 440–1
social practice theory, fashion, 454–5, 457
social psychology, fashion, 461–2
social studies of science and technology see
        science and technology studies
socialism
    cultural turn in sociology, 74
    Olympic sex testing, 345–8
    state, globalization, 494
    US universities, 240–2
    of Veblen, 124–5
sociolegal studies, 36
    identity-based scholarship, 42–3
    justice, 51–2
    narrative, 45
    "new penology", 42
sociology
    class analysis, 87–9
    critical
        moral duty, 362–3
        as recipe knowledge, 361
    and CS, 10–11
        in Britain, 89–97, 275–6, 285–91
        Hoggart's role, 25, 79–82
        in Hong Kong, 268
        judgment-making, 84–6, 96–7
        moves from literature, 79–85
        in New Zealand, 252–3

    as theoretical intervention in, 63–74
    cultural turn in, 66, 72–3, 291–2
    of culture, 150–1
    discipline of, 91–5
    end of postmodernity, 491
    fashion, 459–61
    recent history, 86–9
Soja, E., 202
Solomos, J., 280–1
soul, the, ass music, 436–7
    dance, 446–7
    and Feng Shui, 431–2, 442–5
sovereignty, globalization, 493–4, 496–7
Soviet Union, Olympic sex testing, 345–8
Spanish cultural studies, 298–9
    high and low culture, 300–1
Spanish-language cultures, 233–5
    cultural feedback, 236–9
    England/Spain opposition, 233
    "outlawed", 235
    teaching for social change, 240–3
Spanishness, construction, 232–3
Sparks, C., 336
Sparks, R., 343
spectatorship, diasporic, 511–14, 522–5
spiritual, the, and Feng Shui, 431, 441–5
Spivak, G. C., 71
sport, 341
    competition, 342–3
    cricket, 510–25
    ethical ground, 343–4
    gang narrative, 349–52
    performance-enhancing drugs, 343, 353
    pride, 342–3, 351–2
    reasons for studying, 341–4
    search for purification, 352–3
    sex testing, 344–8
    shame, 342–3
    transformation themes, 343–4
    US ignorance of soccer, 321
sportsmanship, 344–6
    cricket, 516–21
Sreberny-Mohammadi, A., 492
Sri Lanka, cricket, 513–15, 517–21
    diasporic spectatorship, 522–5
    Sinhala nationalism, 510–11, 514, 518–22, 525
    television's role, 522–3
Stallybrass, P., 196
Stam, R., 201, 479

Stanton, F., 189
Star, L., 109
state *see* government; nation–state; power and
    power relations
Staudenmaier, J. M., Sj., 108
Steele, T., 278–9, 290
Steele, V., 461–2
Steinem, G., 412, 421–2
Steiner, G., 301–2, 306
stereotypes, racial, 478–83
Stern, C., 448
Stevenson, N., 335
Stevenson, R. W., 501, 503
Stoler, A. L., 370
Storey, J., 277, 293
Storper, M., 500
storytelling, in legal process, 44–51
Strange, S., 499
Stratton, J., 234, 255, 304
Striphas, T., 63
structuralism
    cultural turn in sociology, 67–8
    racing of, 473–5
structures of feeling, 6
    interdisciplinarity, 27
subcultures, 2
    Chicano, 236–9
    contemporary British CS, 285–6
    metatheory of CS, 141–2
Sumner, W. G., 64
Sun, C., 323
Sundquist, E., 483
Sussman, G., 199, 491
Sweetman, P., 285–6
symbolic interactionism, fashion,
    460
symbols, British sociology, 88

Talbot, M., 415
Tam, M. S. M., 262
Tan, S., 260
Tarde, G. de, 455, 459
taste, cultural policy, 394–96, 401
tattooing, 285–6
Tatz, C., 514, 517, 521–2
Taussig, M., 70
Taylor, Clyde, 479
Taylor, I., 255
Taylor, S., 410
techne, 359–62

technology, communication
    critical sociology of culture, 150–1
    European CS, 304–5
    global media studies, 202–3
    Marxist PE, 132
technology studies *see* science and technology
    studies
technoscapes, 307–8
technoscience, 105–7, 109
Teeple, G., 493
telecommunications, global media studies,
    202–3
television
    Australasian CS, 247–8, 253–4
    division of labor, 501–3
    media studies, 195–6
    Olympic sex testing, 347–8
    politics of pleasure, 324–5
    popular consciousness, 321
    racial stereotypes, 479–80
    unifying effects, 522–3
Telles, V., 375, 379, 387
Tester, K., 288
testimonio, 223
textual analysis
    Chinese CS in Hong Kong, 268
    contemporary British CS, 277–9, 286–7
    critical pedagogy, 148–9
    CS methodology, 335
    cultural policy in Colombia, 375–88
    metatheory of CS, 143–4
    politics of pleasure, 323–4
    standpoints of critique, 144–8
textualization, cultural turn in sociology, 67
theater, and cricket, 510–11, 515
theory
    conceptualizing CS, 141
    in contemporary British CS, 288
    cultural turn in sociology, 70–2
    invasion in CS, 91
    political CS, 150
    sociology of literature, 83–5
Thomas, D. H., 161
Thompson, E. P., 3, 93, 118, 128, 242, 276,
    278, 328, 471, 482
Thompson, G., 497
Thompson, P., 494
Ticknor, G., 232–3
Tilley, C., 157
Timbaland, 431–4, 437–47

Tomlinson, A., 290
Tomlinson, J., 127, 301
Torres, 479
Touraine, A., 73
tours, Philadelphia Museum of Art, 391–405
Trachte, K., 494
trade
  global economy, 490–96, 504
  Latin American/US CS, 224–6
  theoretical political economy, 123–4,
    129–30
transcultural spheres, 177
transculturation, Latin America, 221–2,
  238–9
transnational cultural production, 202–3
  division of labor, 499–504
transnationalization
  Chinese CS in Hong Kong, 269
  drug-testing programs, 353
  European CS, 306–7, 310–12
Trattner, W. I., 403
trauma, legal memory, 53–4
Traweek, S., 104, 106
Treichler, P., 172, 254
Trent, B., 201
Trigger, B. G., 156
Trouillot, M.-R., 71
Tudor, A., 91, 283
Tulloch, J., 199
Turner, B., 288, 290
Turner, G., 63, 202, 252, 255–6, 277, 282–3,
  292–3

UK see Britain
United Nations Development Program, 120
universals, STS, 101–3, 104, 106, 109–10, 113
universities
  anthropology, 178–84, 185
  archaeology, 156–7
  Australasian CS, 246–7, 249, 250–3
  Chicano studies, 234
  Chinese CS in Hong Kong, 262, 263–7,
    269–70
  contemporary British CS, 277–9, 289
  Hoggart's view, 24–5, 81
  interdisciplinarity
    adult education, 25–9
    Bennett's view, 30–2
    class, 24–5, 28, 30
    diversity, 27–30

US–Latin American comparisons,
  218–19
judgment-making, 86
market values, 241–3
sociology
  contemporary British CS, 289
  of literature, 84–5
Spanish-language cultures, 232–5, 240–3
teaching youth culture in, 317–18
  age-specificity problem, 325–8
  anti-intellectual climate, 318–23
  politics of pleasure, 318, 323–5
urban music, 433–4, 439
urban youth, sport/gang dyad, 349–52
Urry, J., 96
USA, 4, 6
  Americanization, 301–2, 306
  anthropology, 169–70
    boundaries of CS, 171–3
    channels from CS, 178–85
    Public Culture project, 173–4, 176–8
    "Writing Culture" critique, 173–6
  archaeology, 156–7, 161–2
  ass music, 430–47
  Australasian CS, 254–6
  Clinton/Lewinsky discourses, 407–8
    feminism, 407–8, 410–17, 420–5, 426
    racial politics, 407–8, 416–20, 425–6
  Cold War, 345–8
  cultural imperialism, 489
  cultural policy, 327
    Philadelphia Museum of Art, 391–405
  discipline of sociology, 94–5
  film industry, 499–503
  gang/sport narrative, 349–52
  globalization, 490, 493, 495, 499–504
  inner city life, 349–52
  institutional political economy, 124–5
  Kennewick Man, 161–2
  and Latin America, 217–18
    aesthetics, 227–30
    citizenship, 224–5, 227
    cultural feedback, 236–9
    cultural flows, 222–3
    identity politics, 227–30
    interdisciplinarity, 218–19
    knowledge flows, 218–19
    NAFTA, 224–6
    national identity, 221
    non-academic settings, 219

USA (*cont.*)
  and Latin America (*cont.*)
    policy influence, 226–7
    politics of representation, 220–2, 227
    power relations, 223–7
    race, 221–2
    reception of texts, 218–19
    social movements, 223–5
    value, 223–7
  Latino studies, 233–9, 242–3
  Marxism in CS, 336
  media studies, 187–8
    and CS, 194–201
    intellectual legacy, 188–94
  multiculturalism, 481–4, 486
  Olympic sex testing, 345–8
  political economy in CS, 119
  prison industrial complex, 350–1
  race relations, 236–7
  racial politics, 407–8, 416–20, 425–6
  slavery, 162
  soccer, 321
  Spanish-language cultures in, 232–43
  sport/gang narrative, 349–52
  teaching youth culture in, 322
    commercial broadcasting, 324–5
    cultural policy, 327
  tradition of CS, 193
  university interdisciplinarity, 27–30
  urban life, 348–52
use-value, 129–31, 135–6
USSR, Olympic sex testing, 345–8

Valdes, F., 44, 48
Valenzuela, J. M., 238
value-neutrality, sociology and CS, 84–6,
    96–7
value(s)
  cultural critique, 146–7
  cultural policy, 401
  Latin American/US CS, 223–7
  Marxist property relations, 129–32, 135–6
  teaching youth culture, 319–20
Valverde, M., 41
Van Dinh, T., 188
Vasconcelos, J., 240, 242
Veblen, T., 124–5, 459
vectoral movements, global media events, 205
Vézina, M., 493
videos, hip hop, 444–7

Vincent, J., 159
violence
  Clinton/Lewinsky discourses, 417–20
  Colombian cultural policy, 378–81
  sport/gang dyad, 349–52
Voloshinov, V. N., 67
volunteers, 402
Von der Walde, E., 375

Wallerstein, I., 93–4
Walsh, R. B., 345–6
Walters, B., 434
Walters, D., 441–2
Wang, J., 260, 270
Ward, B., 261–2
Wark, M., 202–6, 248
Warner, M., 228, 413
Washington Consensus, 490–1, 493, 504
Wasko, J., 500
Wasser, F., 500–1
Watkins, S., 462
Watson, S., 42
Waxman, C. I., 405
Weber, M., 64–5, 85
Weberian approaches, sociology, 86–7
Webster, D., 302
Webster, F., 133–4
Wedell, G., 502
Weisberg, R., 46, 48
Welch, L. S., 500
welfare, globalization, 493–4
West, C., 476
Whannel, P., 195
White, A., 196
whiteness studies, 485–6
Wiegman, R., 413, 416–17, 420, 479
Will, G., 241
Williams, 414
Williams, P., 48
Williams, R., 5–6, 25–9, 66, 118, 132, 141,
    146, 170, 242, 276, 278, 284, 290,
    300, 332, 337, 464, 471
Williamson, J., 132, 196
Willis, 195
Willis, C. L., 9
Willis, P., 66, 290, 309
Wills, M. E., 377
Wilson, E., 460, 465
Winant, H., 227
Wing, B., 242

Wingert, P., 412
"wired identity" theory, 202
Wiseman, J., 496
Wolf, N., 423
Wolfe, A., 10
Wolff, J., 69, 287, 293
Woll, 479
women
    archaeology, 162–4
    Clinton/Lewinsky discourse, 407–8, 416,
        420–5
    a CS of law, 37, 38–41, 50–1
    feminist politics *see* feminism
    feminization of UK workforce, 88
    Latin American/US CS, 219, 221
    Olympic sex testing, 344–8
Women's Studies Group, CCCS, 6
Wong, K.-Y., 265
Wong, W. C., 261
Woods, M., 500
Woolf, M., 502
Woolgar, S., 104, 109
workers, labor economics *see* labor
workers' education, British CS, 277–9, 289,
        292
working class
    British CS, 277–82
        Hoggart's writings, 24–5, 80–1
        sociology, 289–90
    British sociology, 87–8
    Chinese CS, 260
    cricket, 522–3

cultural turn in sociology, 66–7
interdisciplinarity, 24–5, 28, 30
metatheory of CS, 140–2
political economy, 117–20, 124, 128–9
popular culture, 195
race in Latin America, 222
world system model, 307
Wright, C. R., 189
Wright, E. O., 68
Wright, H. K., 6
"Writing Culture" critique, 173–6
writing function, ethnography, 182–3

Yates, T., 157
Young, C., 421
Young, R., 474
youth, sport/gang dyad, 349–52
youth culture
    teaching, 317–18
        age-specificity problem, 325–8
        anti-intellectual climate, 318–23
        politics of pleasure, 318, 323–5
youth subcultures, metatheory of CS,
        141–2
Yúdice, G., 379, 386

Ziegert, H., 155
Ziff, B., 71
Zimbabwe, electronic printer in,
        109–12
Znaniecki, F., 64
Zolberg, V., 69